CHRONICLES OF TIME

A World History

CHRONICLES OF TIME
A World History

June R. Chapin
Randall G. Felton
Rodney F. Allen
David C. King

Webster Division McGraw-Hill Book Company

New York   St. Louis   San Francisco   Auckland
Bogotá   Düsseldorf   London   Madrid
Mexico   Montreal   New Delhi   Panama
Paris   São Paulo   Singapore   Sydney
Tokyo   Toronto

Authors

June R. Chapin teaches at the College of Notre Dame in Belmont, California. She has also taught at the elementary and secondary levels. She has published social studies texts for elementary, secondary, and college students. She has also written professional books and articles.

Randall G. Felton is Social Studies Consultant for the Florida State Department of Education. Earlier, he was a high school social studies teacher in Jacksonville, Florida.

Rodney F. Allen teaches at Florida State University, Tallahassee, Florida. He has also taught at the junior high and high school levels. He has published instructional materials for elementary, secondary, and college students. He has also written professional books and articles.

David C. King is Director of Curriculum Development for Global Perspectives in Education, Inc., New York City, New York. He has been a high school teacher. He is the author or co-author of social studies texts at the elementary and secondary level.

Consultants

William Leslie Blackwell
New York University
New York, New York

Rosalind M. Bronsen
Washington University
St. Louis, Missouri

David Chalmers
University of Florida
Gainesville, Florida

Joshua Fogel
Harvard University
Cambridge, Massachusetts

Lyle N. McAlister
University of Florida
Gainesville, Florida

John Ruedy
Georgetown University
Washington, D.C.

Classroom Consultants

Richard A. Dryer
San Diego Unified Schools
San Diego, California

Donald S. Fuller
Kempsville Junior High School
Virginia Beach, Virginia

Frederic Pottinger
Waukegan West High School
Waukegan, Illinois

Michael Roessler
Portland Middle School
Portland, Michigan

Project Director: Neysa Chouteau
Editing and Styling: Marnie Hauff
Designer: Virginia Copeland
Photo Editor: Suzanne V. Skloot
Photo Research: Eleanore B. Goodman, C. Buff Rosenthal, Randy Matusow
Production Supervisor: Carol Barry

The Acknowledgments on pages 749-752 are a continuation of this page.

Library of Congress Cataloging in Publication Data
Chapin, June R., et al
   Chronicles of Time
Includes Index
Summary: Presents a history of the world from prehistoric times to today, focusing on the geography and culture of various regions.
Includes a glossary and atlas.
1. World history—Juvenile literature. [1. World history]
  I. Chapin, June R., date.
    D20.C53   1983   909   82-10076

Copyright © 1983 by McGraw-Hill, Inc. All rights reserved. Printed in the United States of America. Except as permitted under the United States Copyright Act of 1976, no part of this publication may be reproduced or distributed in any form or by any means, or stored in a data base or retrieval system, without the prior written permission of the publisher.

ISBN 0-07-001112-5

Contents

About This Book   xiv
Map List   xvi
Prologue: Exploring the Past   1

Unit 1: Ancient Civilizations 1,000,000-3000 B.C.   6

Chapter 1   Prehistoric People   1,000,000-8000 B.C.   8
1. People Were Hunters and Gatherers for a Long Time   9
   Did You Know? New Ideas about Prehistoric People   12
2. People Settled Down   17

Chapter 2   Ancient Egypt   7000-30 B.C.   20
1. Egypt's Geography Offered Many Advantages   21
2. The Pharaohs Held Supreme Authority   25
3. Ancient Egypt Had a Long History   28
   Did You Know? Iknaton-Religious Reformer   29
4. Egyptians Contributed to Other Civilizations   30
   Did You Know? Treasures of a Boy King   32

Chapter 3   Mesopotamia   3500-330 B.C.   36
1. A City-State Civilization Began Between Two Rivers   37
2. Desert People Took Over   41
3. The Assyrians and Persians Gained Great Empires   45
   Did You Know? The Story of the Hebrews   46

Chapter 4   Ancient India   3000-1500 B.C.   52
1. A Complex Civilization Developed in Ancient India   53

2. Invaders and Native Peoples Created a Lasting Culture — 57
3. Two Great Religions Were Born in Ancient India — 60
   Did You Know? How the Cow Came to be Sacred — 61

Chapter 5 Ancient China 50,000-202 B.C. — 66
1. Unity Was Achieved in China — 67
2. The Chinese Produced Three Great Philosophies — 72
3. China Created Lasting Patterns of Living — 74
   Did You Know? Chinese Pictographs — 75

Contemporary Parallel: Who Is Civilized? — 81

Unit 2: The Classical World 800 B.C.-A.D. 600 — 82

Chapter 6 Ancient Greece 3000-300 B.C. — 84
1. The Greeks Developed Democratic City-States — 86
   Did You Know? Minoan Civilization — 87
2. The Greek City-States Failed — 93
3. The Greeks Developed New Ways of Thinking — 98

Chapter 7 Ancient Rome 509 B.C.-A.D. 180 — 104
1. A Republic Was Established — 106
   Did You Know? About Roman Women — 110
2. Rome Dominated the Mediterranean — 112
   Did You Know? The Celts — 115
3. The Republic Failed — 116
4. Rome Brought Peace and Unity to the Mediterranean — 121

Chapter 8 India and China 200 B.C.-A.D. 600 — 130
1. Strong Rulers United Most of India — 131
2. The Arts, Learning, and Hinduism Flourished in India — 136
   Did You Know? The Reformer King — 140
3. The Han Dynasty Ruled China for 400 Years — 141

Chapter 9 The Rise of Christianity 4 B.C.-A.D. 395   148
  1. Christianity Developed in Judea   150
  2. Christianity Grew as Rome Decayed   154
  3. Christianity Became the Religion of the Roman Empire   159
      Did You Know? In Praise of Constantine and Kingship   160
Contemporary Parallel: Cultural Diffusion   165

Unit 3: The Medieval World
A.D. 370-1500   166

Chapter 10 The Collapse of the West 370-900   168
  1. The Western Roman Empire Fell to the Germans   170
      Did You Know? A Fascinating Question   176
  2. The East Turned Away from the West   177
  3. Franks Ruled Much of Western Europe   181

Chapter 11 Islam 570-1258   188
  1. Muhammad Offered Arabs a New Religion   189
  2. Islam Spread Rapidly   194
  3. The Golden Age of Islamic Civilization   198
      Did You Know? Sindbad the Sailor   200

Chapter 12 Feudalism and Faith 800-1233   206
  1. Europe Developed Feudalism   208
      Did You Know? Of Knights and Chivalry   210
  2. Manorial Agriculture Became Common   212
  3. The Roman Catholic Church Held Great Power
     in Feudal Society   217

Chapter 13   The Revival of Europe   1000-1291   222
    1. **Western Europe's Influence Widened**   224
       Did You Know? Cathedrals: Symbols of Their Times   225
    2. **Town Life Grew in Europe**   230
       Did You Know? Come to the Fair!   232

Chapter 14   The Late Middle Ages   1138-1485   238
    1. **Western Europe Faced a Time of Crisis**   239
       Did You Know? The Mechanical Clock   241
    2. **Kings Expanded Their Power**   244
       Did You Know? Clothing in the Middle Ages   252
    3. **The Roman Catholic Church Grew Weaker**   253

Contemporary Parallel: Power   257

Unit 4: Africa, Asia, and the Americas   258
40,000 B.C.-A.D. 1550

Chapter 15   Africa   900 B.C.-A.D. 1550   260
    1. **African Geography Was an Important Influence**   261
       Did You Know? Can Deserts Move?   264
    2. **African States Developed Under Muslim Rule**   266
    3. **Peoples in the Interior Developed Differently**   270
       Did You Know? African Steel Mills   272
    4. **African People Developed Unique Cultures**   275

Chapter 16   Asia   A.D. 500-1368   282
    1. **Muslims and Hindus Influenced Each Other**   284
    2. **Mongols Ruled an Enormous Empire**   287

3. China Prospered During the Tang and Song Dynasties — 293
4. Japanese Culture Was Influenced by China — 298
   Did You Know? Japanese Literature — 301

Chapter 17   The Americas   40,000 B.C.-A.D. 1532 — 306
1. Wandering Hunters Settled the Americas — 308
2. The Maya Created a Great Civilization — 312
3. The Aztecs Built an Empire in Mexico — 316
   Did You Know? The Pyramid of the Sun — 318
4. The Incas Governed in the Andes Mountains — 320

Contemporary Parallel: The Search for Roots — 327

Unit 5: Changes and Discoveries 1300-1725 — 328

Chapter 18   Renaissance and Reformation   1307-1632 — 330
1. The Renaissance Began in Italy — 332
   Did You Know? Michelangelo — 336
2. The Renaissance Moved to Northern Europe — 338
3. Martin Luther Started the Reformation — 342
   Did You Know? The Anabaptists and Other Sects — 345
4. The Roman Catholic Church Fought Back — 347

Chapter 19   Modern States   1237-1725 — 354
1. England and France Challenged the Hapsburgs — 356
2. Russia Arose as a New Nation State — 359
   Did You Know? The Ottoman Turks — 361
3. India and China Had Strong Leaders — 366

Chapter 20 Exploration and Commercial Expansion 1451-1664   374

  1. The Portuguese and Spanish Made Discoveries   376
     Did You Know? Sister Juana   380
  2. Other Nations Wanted Trade and Colonies   382
  3. The Slave Trade Affected Africa and the World   386

Contemporary Parallel: Change and the Media   393

Unit 6: Quest for Liberty 1603-1824   394

Chapter 21 Revolutions and Rights 1603-1824   396

  1. The English Revolted Against Their King   398
  2. The North American Colonists Rebelled   405
     Did You Know? Guerrilla Warfare   410
  3. Latin America Fought for Independence   412
     Did You Know? General Touissant L'Ouverture   416

Chapter 22 The Age of Reason 1543-1789   422

  1. Science Uncovered New Ideas   423
     Did You Know? Conquering Smallpox   430
  2. New Ideas About Society Became Popular   433
     Did You Know? An Early Feminist   437

Chapter 23 The French Revolution and Empire 1789-1815   440

  1. The French Revolution Began   442
  2. The Radicals Gained Control of the Revolution   446

3. Napoleon Became a Dictator — 452
    Did You Know? Madame de Staël — 454
4. Europe Fought Back — 455
    Did You Know? Preserved Food — 457
Contemporary Parallel: The Rights of Women — 463

Unit 7: Industrialism and Imperialism 1728-1914 — 464

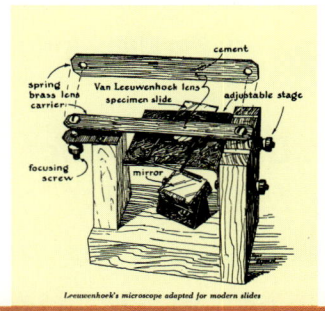

Chapter 24 Nationalism After Napoleon 1814-1890 — 466
1. Metternich Tried to Hold Back Change — 467
2. Nationalism Began to Spread — 474
    Did You Know? England's Royal Family — 478
3. New Latin American Nations Faced Many Problems — 479
4. Nationalism Grew in the United States and Canada — 483

Chapter 25 The Age of Industrialization 1760-1900 — 490
1. The Industrial Revolution Caused Many Changes — 492
    Did You Know? Travel and Holidays — 497
2. People Responded to the Industrial Revolution — 498
    Did You Know? Karl Marx — 501
3. Industrialism Soon Grew into Imperialism — 503

Chapter 26 The Exploitation of Africa 1811-1910 — 508
1. Western Influence Expanded in Africa — 510
2. The British Took Over from the Cape to Cairo — 513
3. The French and Belgians Occupied Much of Africa — 519
    Did You Know? The French Foreign Legion — 520
4. The Exploitation of Africa Was Completed — 523

xi

Chapter 27 The Exploitation of the East 1728-1914   530
   1. The Russians Moved into Siberia and Central Asia   531
      Did You Know? Russia's Search for an Outlet to the Sea   534
   2. Japan Became an Imperialistic Power   535
   3. The Great Powers Exploited Much of Asia   538
   4. Imperialism Extended Across the Pacific   545
Contemporary Parallel: Industry and Interdependence   553

Unit 8: Global Conflict 1914-1945   554

Chapter 28 The First World War 1914-1919   556
   1. Many Causes Led to the Great War   558
   2. War Led to Stalemate and Then to Allied Victory   562
      Did You Know? Ataturk   567
   3. The Allies Imposed a Peace   570

Chapter 29 The Impact of War 1914-1919   576
   1. World War I Caused Major Changes in Most Lands   578
   2. Many Nations Tried to Make Changes   583
   3. The Bolsheviks Created the Soviet State   588
   4. The Threat of Communism Grew   594
      Did You Know? The Long March   599

Chapter 30 Dictators and the Great Depression 1919-1939   602
   1. A New Age of Dictators Began   604
   2. Hitler Gained Control of Germany   609
   3. The Dictators Turned to Aggression   614
      Did You Know? The Outcast Nations   618

Chapter 31 The Second World War 1939-1945   622
   1. The Dictators Tried to Conquer the World   623
      Did You Know? Winston Churchill: Democracy's Soldier   626

2. The Allies Turned the Tide	630
3. The War Helped Shape a New World	636
Contemporary Parallel: Sparks of War	643

Unit 9: The Postwar World 1945-1982

644

Chapter 32   Postwar Europe and the Americas   1945-1982   646

  1. The Cold War Began   648
  2. The Cold War Thawed   651
     Did You Know? The Space Age   655
  3. Latin America Faced Economic and Political Problems   656
  4. Europe Became Powerful and Independent   661

Chapter 33   Postwar Asia   1945-1979   666

  1. China and Japan Became Powerful   667
  2. The Indian Subcontinent Achieved Independence   670
     Did You Know? Rich vs. Poor Nations   672
  3. Southeast Asians Revolted   674

Chapter 34   The Middle East and Africa   1945-1981   680

  1. Israel and the Arab World Clashed in the Middle East   681
  2. Political Changes Came to the Middle East   685
     Did You Know? Refugees   688
  3. African Nations Gained Independence   689
     Did You Know? Different Paths: Kenya and Tanzania   691
  4. New African Nations Faced Many Problems   693

Contemporary Parallel: The Dilemma of Disarmament   701

Epilogue: What Kind of Future for Planet Earth?   702

Atlas   706

Glossary   718

Index   723

Acknowledgments   749

About This Book

Objectives

The objectives of *Chronicles of Time* are to help you

    learn the major events and ways of life of the past;

    recognize similarities and differences among nations, governments, and people;

    recognize patterns in the rise and fall of civilizations, groups, or nations;

    relate the past to the present;

    develop study skills.

Organization

Chronicles of Time is divided into nine units and thirty-four chapters. It also includes a Prologue, an Epilogue, an Atlas, a Glossary, and an Index.

Unit Organization The units are organized chronologically by era. They vary in length from three to five chapters. Each unit begins with a Time Line and overview of what you will study in the unit. It closes with a Unit Review and a Contemporary Parallel.

Unit Reviews always follow the same format. The "Words to Know" section extends the chapter vocabulary work. "Time and Place" asks you to make connections between chronology and geography in the different chapters in the unit. "Putting It Together" requires you to do just that—put together some of the concepts you have learned.

The Contemporary Parallels will help you relate the past to the present.

Chapter Organization Each chapter begins with an introduction and a list of important dates.

Each chapter consists of from two to four sections. Section titles are written in sentences to help you in surveying each section before you read it. The Section Questions at the end of each section help you decide whether or not you have mastered the material.

Each chapter has one or more features called Did You Know? These include topics such as daily life, biographies, and little known aspects of history.

Each chapter ends with a brief section-by-section chapter summary and a thorough Chapter Review. The chapter summaries help you test and extend your understanding of the text. There are five sections to each Chapter Review. "Check Your Facts" helps you find out how well you remember basic facts. "Words to Know" checks your understanding of vocabulary introduced in the chapter. "Developing Your Skills" helps strengthen your grasp of time and place. In the "Thinking It Over" section, you will be challenged to compare, contrast, evaluate, and analyze material.

"Special Activities" suggest ideas to help you explore further the concepts and information presented.

Front and Back Sections The Prologue helps you learn just how people study the past. You will read about the methods used by archaeologists, historians, and others.

The Epilogue discusses the work of futurists, people who study possible future trends. It asks some key questions for your own speculation.

The Atlas provides maps and the Glossary provides definitions of words and phrases.

Maps, Charts, and Illustrations Every map has a "Thinking Geographically" caption which asks for an active response.

The illustrations emphasize not only major events, but also daily life and the arts. The captions help you "read" the illustrations.

The charts summarize and highlight ideas.

Study Aids The chart shows how the study aids will help you master your learning objectives.

Goals	Study Aids	Examples
Learning about Major Events	Unit Time Lines	pp. 82, 328
	Chapter List of Events	pp. 189, 355
	Chapter Summary	pp. 18, 34
	Chapter Review: Check Your Facts	pp. 205, 489
	Unit Review: Time and Place	pp. 326, 552
	Illustrations	pp. 394, 554
Learning about Ways of Life	Illustrations	pp. 339, 490
	Did You Know?	pp. 110, 252
	Charts	pp. 102, 502
Similarities and Differences Among People	Unit Opener	pp. 329, 645
	Contemporary Parallel	pp. 81, 463
	Chapter Review: Thinking It Over	pp. 439, 601
	Unit Review: Putting It Together	pp. 80, 326
Recognizing Patterns	Unit Opener	pp. 167, 395
	Contemporary Parallel	pp. 553, 663
	Unit Review: Putting It Together	pp. 164, 256
Relating the Past to the Present	Prologue	pp. 1-5
	Chapter Review: Thinking It Over	pp. 421, 621
	Contemporary Parallel	pp. 165, 393
	Epilogue	pp. 702-705
Developing Study Skills	Vocabulary	
	Words defined in text	pp. 282, 657
	Chapter Review: Words to Know	pp. 103, 129
	Unit Review: Words to Know	pp. 256, 552
	Glossary	pp. 718-722
	Map Skills	
	Thinking Geographically captions	pp. 185, 458
	Chapter Review: Developing Your Skills	p. 221
	Unit Review: Time and Place	pp. 326, 552
	Atlas	pp. 706-717
	Reasoning	
	Chapter Review: Thinking It Over	pp. 19, 51
	Unit Review: Putting It Together	pp. 80, 700
	Reference Skills	
	Table of Contents	pp. v-xiv
	Atlas	pp. 706-717
	Glossary	pp. 718-722
	Index	pp. 723-749
	Research Skills	
	Chapter Review: Special Activities	pp. 79-187

Map List

	Page
Skeletal Remains of Prehistoric People	10
Domestication of Plants and Animals	13
Ancient Egypt	22
Ancient Mesopotamia	38
Trade in the Ancient Middle East	43
Cradles of Civilization	48
Ancient India	54
Ancient China	68
Greek and Phoenician Colonies	92
Alexander's Empire	96
Ancient Italy	106
The Roman Empire at Its Greatest Extent	121
India	134
Han Dynasty	143
The Spread of Christianity	155
The Divided Roman Empire	174
Byzantine Empire at Its Height	180
The German Kingdoms *c.* A.D. 400	182
Charlemagne's Empire	185
Expansion of Muslim Territories	196
Peoples of Europe, 800-1000	208
The Crusades	228
Trade Routes in Medieval Europe	230
Europe and the Middle East in the 14th Century	244
Climates of Africa	263
Early Africa	267
West Africa	269
South Africa	271
Mongol Empire in 1294	292
China's Trade Routes in the Middle Ages	294
Early Japan	299
The Americas	311
Major Religious Groups in Europe about 1560	344
Growth of the Ottoman Empire	365
Portugal Sails to the Orient	376

	Page
Early Voyages to the New World	385
Africa, 1400-1600	386
Napoleon's Empire	458
Europe After the Congress of Vienna	469
Unification of Italy	474
The Unification of Germany	476
Crimean War	479
Independence in Latin America	480
England Before and After the Industrial Revolution	495
The British Empire in 1900	504
Africa in 1914	525
The Growth of Russia	532
The United States in the Pacific 1784-1917	547
Balkans Before and After the Congress of Berlin	559
World War I	565
The United States and Latin America	585
Japan's Expansion to 1939	615
World War II in Europe	634
World War II in the Pacific	635
Europe in 1970	650
The Korean War	668
Asia in 1970	674
The Vietnam War	676
Israel	682
Atlas	706-715
Political Map of Earth	706-707
Climates of Earth	708-709
North America	710
Nations of South America and Central America	711
Nations of Europe	712
Nations of Africa	713
Asia	714-715

Archaeologists at an excavation.

Prologue: Exploring the Past

An understanding of where we are today and of what we can do about the future rests largely on our ability to learn from history. But, how do we know what really happened back there? How do we understand what happened in the past in terms of our lives now? To understand the past and how it influences our lives today, we depend largely on scientists and historians.

Scientists The scientific study of human beings—their origins and cultural development—is called *anthropology*.

Cultural anthropologists study present-day cultures. Typically, anthropologists live for a time with a group of people and make careful records of what they observe.

Margaret Mead, a famous American anthropologist, talking to a group of Balinese people.

A fossil palm leaf.

Anthropologists study aspects of a group's culture—its family life, its religious beliefs, its economy. Then they try to see the culture as a whole.

When cultural anthropologists study such groups as the Australian Aborigines (AB uh RIHJ un neez), the original inhabitants of Australia, they also learn about how people lived on Earth 10,000 or 50,000 years ago.

For more specific information on how people lived in the past, we depend on *archaeologists* and historians. Archaeologists study how people lived long ago. They do this by examining the physical remains of people and their culture. It is often said that archaeologists study *prehistory*. Prehistory is the time before writing. However, archaeologists have also studied societies which had a written language.

Typically, archaeologists *excavate*, or dig up, *artifacts*, objects made by people. An artifact may be large or small. It may be a work of art or a simple everyday tool.

Archaeologists also work with other scientists, such as *geologists*. Geologists study the Earth. They try to learn about its history. Some geologists are *paleontologists*. They study *fossils*, the remains of plants and animals that are buried in rock. Fossils are also important clues in archaeological studies.

Archaeologists ask questions as they work with the physical remains. What is this artifact made of? What was its purpose? How was it made? Generally, archaeologists find it easiest to arrive at the purpose and usefulness of tools—at how people made a living. However, it is more difficult to answer questions about social and political institutions. Who had the most power in society? What rules were made? How were they enforced? What were the people's values?

In spite of the continuing and useful work of scientists, much of the past still remains a mystery.

Historians History is generally considered to be a record of past events. Not every deed of every person is included. Historians choose only important events—events that they believe help explain how and why things happen.

How does one decide which events are important? Historians often disagree. Further, even when historians agree on which events to include, they may interpret these same events in different ways.

Historians are something like detectives. They search for clues to help them figure out what happened. They find these clues in three main kinds of sources. One source is written records. Among these are documents, letters, diaries, memoirs, and *genealogies*, or records of descent of a family or group.

Another source is oral. This includes ballads, tales, and sagas that have been told by one generation to the next. Personal interviews are also considered to be an oral source.

A third source of evidence for historians is artifacts. Typically, historians look at paintings of wars and everyday life, portraits, sculpture, and coins. Even films are a source of evidence in modern history.

These three sources—written records,

An Ivory Coast elder tells young people tribal legends.

oral tradition, and artifacts—are called *primary sources*. Historians also use *secondary sources*. A secondary source is an account of an event or period that was written at a later time. Most secondary sources are analyses and histories.

When you examine historical material, you have to keep certain questions in mind. For example, what point of view did the source of the material have? Who else reported this event? Do the facts agree? If not, why not?

The historian searches both primary and secondary sources for *facts* and *evidence*. Facts are any pieces of information. Evidence is anything that offers proof. The historian may gather facts and develop a theory or start with a theory and try to find factual evidence to support it.

Once a considerable amount of evidence is gathered, the historian relates the evidence to the theory. Usually, the original theory of the historian changes during the process. Once the theory is explained and the evidence to support it is produced, the process of interpreting history does not end. New evidence may be found. Other historians may interpret the evidence differently.

Thus, the history that most of us read is what historians select as being most important. Then this information has to be interpreted. Historians bring personal attitudes to their study. History, as we commonly know it, therefore, is our understanding of what historians think happened in the past.

Culture and Environment There are two important factors to keep in mind as you study history. One of these factors is *culture*, which refers to the traditional body of acceptable customs that a group has.

A group's culture includes its *technology*, the use of complex tools and ideas. Culture also embraces the group's language, literature, art, and music.

A group's culture provides a set of

The culture of the Evenki of Siberia enables them to survive in a harsh physical environment.

directions for the people. It tells them what is right and wrong. It explains why things should be done in a certain way. It also includes the *institutions* of the group. Institutions are the long-lasting customs or rules in society. The family, the system of education, religion, economic practices, and government are among the most important institutions of any group.

As you read history, ask yourself questions such as these about the group's culture: What was the economy like? How did people make a living? How did they share knowledge? What inventions were important? How did their religion affect their lives? What do their arts show about them?

A culture does not exist in isolation from the *physical environment*. The air, land formations, water, climate, and natural resources are part of the physical envi-

Indians living in the high mountains of Peru use special techniques to grow and store potatoes at high altitudes.

ronment. The environment shapes and limits a group.

Even with advanced technology, the physical environment can have a big effect on people's lives. Weather such as snowstorms, hurricanes, volcanoes, earthquakes, heat waves, and droughts can cost millions of dollars in damage and cause death to thousands of people.

Climate and other natural resources also restrict what people can do. For example, certain crops are best grown in certain environments.

Remember that mountains, rivers, and deserts are not just scenery. They affect people's lives. As you study, ask yourself how the geography, the climate, and other aspects of the physical environment affected people's lives.

Why Study the Past? One of the reasons most often given for studying history is that it is fun. The story of history is a rewarding hobby for many people. The study of our past can give us pleasure. But it also gives us much, much more.

We study the past to understand what we are today and what we can do about our future. What major social, economic, or political issue can be thoroughly discussed without referring to the past?

Studying the past gives us courage. It reminds us that we are not the first generation to face overwhelming problems.

History provides great companions. It enables us to draw inspiration from the most imaginative, the most courageous, and the most influential individuals of all times.

1,000,000 B.C.	Homo habilis uses chipped tools
500,000	Humans use fire, language; cooperative hunts
150,000	"Modern" humans improve tools; art, religion
3100	King Menes unites Egypt
2500	Indus Valley civilization begins
1500	Aryans invade India
1400	Shang dynasty rules China
550	First books of Bible
500 B.C.	

Unit 1
Ancient Civilizations

Small groups search an open grassland for wild game. Their weapons are stonetipped spears. The hunt is unsuccessful, and the group decides they must move on.

A revolutionary change took place beginning about 10,000 years ago. People began to settle in one place. And they began to farm.

The great river valleys of the Middle East, India, and China were good places in which to live for ancient people. As people settled there and learned to control the river waters, they developed a new way of living: civilization.

Gradually, cities developed. And the greater numbers of people in the cities needed water-supply projects, proper sanitation, and housing. Officials were needed to enforce the rules, collect taxes, keep records, and write laws.

History—a written record—begins with civilization. Civilization was a great step forward for human beings. It meant that people had achieved a high level of organization. They had developed a means of recording information—a writing system. They had an efficient government. Art and architecture flourished.

Around 3500 B.C., civilization began in Mesopotamia (MES uh puh TA mee uh), and then in Egypt's Nile Valley. About 2500 B.C., civilization also started along the Indus (IHN dus) River in India. Later, about 1500 B.C., the Huang He (Hwang Ho) Valley saw the birth of Chinese civilization. These ancient, or first, civilizations are the focus of this unit.

A Bushmen rock painting of antelope.

The axe in the picture is not much different from axes that were used in the Stone Age.

Chapter 1 Prehistoric People

The early history of human beings is still a mystery. Scientists have to use the few remains—bones, tools, and campsites—to piece together how people lived. From these remains, scientists have put together theories about the ancestors of modern humans. The rest of this chapter presents the latest scientific theories.

Scientists usually divide prehistoric times into two parts, based on the tools that were used. The two parts are the Old Stone Age and the New Stone Age. The earliest known shaped tools were made by *Homo habilis* (HO mo huh BIH lis), Latin for "Able Human Beings." Homo habilis appears to have roamed Earth over a mil-

(early dates approximate)

OLD STONE AGE—1,000,000-8,000 B.C.

1,000,000	Homo habilis
500,000-150,000	Homo erectus
200,000-125,000	Third glacial period
150,000	Homo sapiens (e.g., Neanderthal)
40,000-25,000	Cro-Magnons
12,000	Domesticated dogs

NEW STONE AGE—8000-3500 B.C.

8000	End of Ice Age
6000-3000	Beginnings of agriculture, villages

BRONZE AGE—3000-1000 B.C.

3000	Earliest cities begin

Hunting cave bear.

lion years ago. They were scavengers and gatherers. Their brains were half the size of ours. Their crudely chipped stones mark the beginning of the Old Stone Age.

Because only a meager number of fossils and tools have been found, scientists disagree on which fossils are from humans and which are from humanlike creatures. There seems to be firm evidence, however, that human beings did live at least 500,000 years ago. So our history begins with these prehistoric people, the *Homo erectus* (HO mo ee REK tus).

1. People Were Hunters and Gatherers for a Long Time

From studying the 500,000-year-old remains of Homo erectus in Java and near Peking, scientists believe that Homo erectus were *nomads*, people who moved about from place to place.

Early Tools and Skills Homo erectus apparently gathered wild fruits and vegetables, including roots. They developed simple tools, such as sharpened sticks for digging and chipped stones for hacking.

To hunt the large game of the period, they made weapons. They also made tools for skinning and cutting and for dressing hides. They also had to hunt cooperatively. It seems, then, that these early people had good thinking skills. They knew how to speak. They could learn from experience. They could predict future events, such as the coming of autumn and the herd movements that autumn brought. They could also pass their knowledge on to their young.

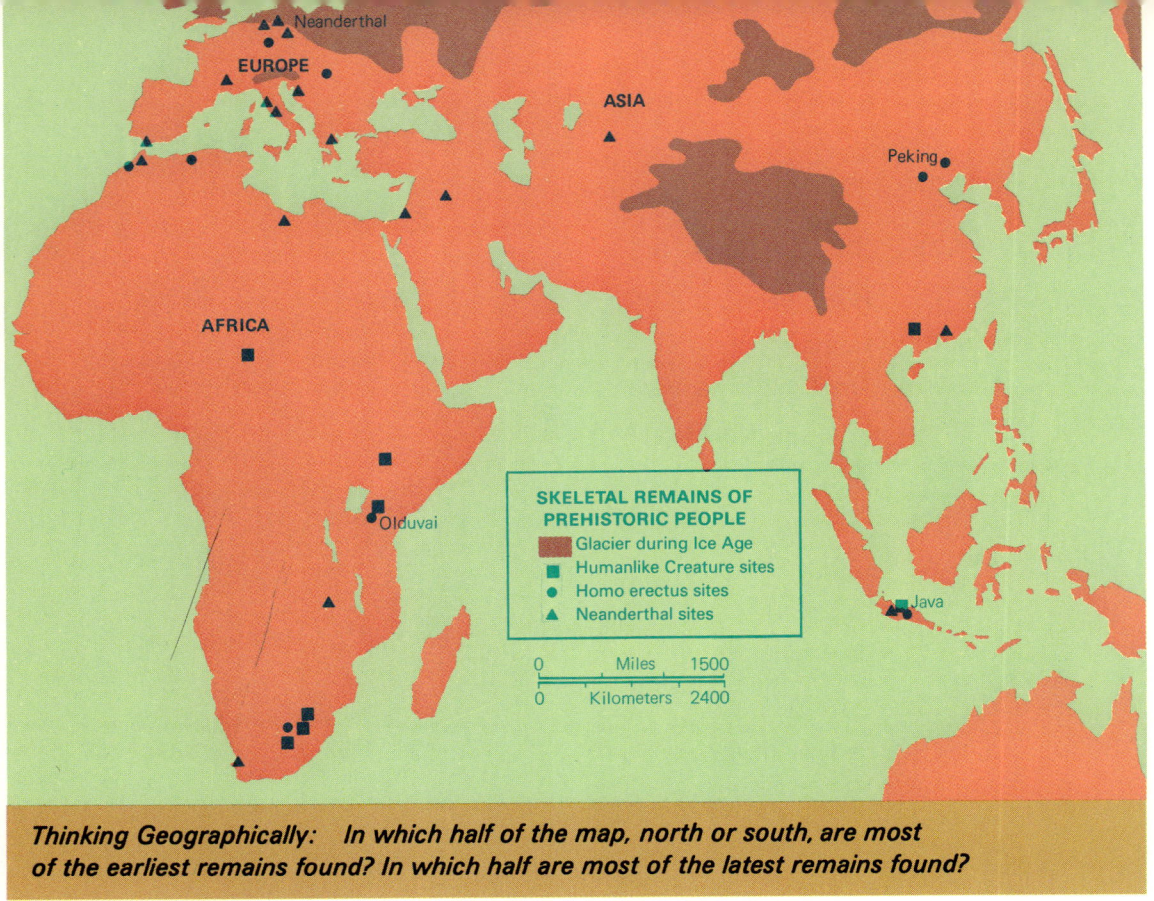

Thinking Geographically: In which half of the map, north or south, are most of the earliest remains found? In which half are most of the latest remains found?

Along with their erect stance, superior brain, and strong, agile hands, they knew how to control fire. That meant that Homo erectus could live in colder areas, eat cooked meat, and be protected from animals even while sleeping. Fire was also used during the hunt to drive animals into natural traps.

In time, people of the Old Stone Age changed. They grew taller. Their faces became more delicate. Their brains became larger. *Neanderthal* (nee AN der thall) people, who may have lived as long as 150,000 years ago, were of the species *Homo sapiens* (HO mo SAY pee enz), or "modern man." Homo sapiens means "wise, or thinking, human being." This is the species to which most scientists believe modern humans belong.

Homo sapiens were able to develop new and better tools, such as the fishhook and the needle. These humans also devoted more time to art and religion. It appears that they believed in life after death. It was for this next life that they supplied their carefully buried dead with such things as beads and weapons. The cave art found in Europe was probably also part of an early religion.

Evidence indicates that Neanderthal people disappeared around 40,000 years ago. At about this time, a group of people who looked like modern humans were living in what is now southern France. *Cro-Magnon* (kro MAG nun) people, as they are called, did not have the receding chin and skull of earlier humans. Paintings made by Cro-Magnon people are beautiful and accurate drawings of animals. They most likely believed their drawings would make the hunt successful.

The Ice Age Geological studies indicate that during much of the Old Stone Age, the Earth was a great deal colder than it is today. There were four long periods, each lasting from 70,000 to 150,000 years, when large parts of the Earth were covered with *glaciers*. Glaciers are large ice sheets. For the first half of each glacial period, the ice expanded, covering more and more of the land. The ice of the glaciers locked up huge amounts of water. As a result, the oceans shrank, exposing vast plains. These became rich grasslands.

The first glacial period lasted from 900,000 to 1,050,000 years ago. During the second glacial period, from 400,000 to 500,000 years ago, Homo erectus first learned to control fire. Without fire, people could not have lived far from the equator. Instead, they spread over great areas.

It may have been during this period or during the third glacial periods, between 125,000 and 200,000 years ago, that people first crossed a great northern plain, over 1,600 kilometers (1,000 miles) wide, between Asia and North America. This land bridge was created when the oceans receded near what today is the Bering (BEH ring) Strait. There is stronger evidence that people came that way during the last glacial period, between 10,000 and 75,000 years ago, and began populating the Americas. When the last glacial period ended, the oceans once again covered the vast grasslands. With milder weather and greater rainfall, much of the remaining grasslands became forests. So the herds of large animals, upon which the hunters depended, disappeared.

New Stone Age The end of the Ice Age also marks the end of the Old Stone Age. During the Old Stone Age, change had come slowly. But to survive in their new environment, people had to adjust quickly. And they did so because they had hundreds of thousands of years of Old Stone Age knowledge to fall back on.

In the thick forests, people could no longer hunt by trapping herds in bogs and other natural traps. So they hunted single animals by using bows and arrows and spears with barbed heads. This provided less food, so people learned to depend more on fish. They began to make barbed harpoons, sharp fishhooks, and delicate needles for sewing fishnets and clothing. To make these tools, the New Stone Age people used a new tool-making method. They used special stones to grind away small bits and get a fine edge or point—instead of chipping and flaking at a stone.

In one way, the new climate was easier on these prehistoric people. It provided more plant foods for them—vegetables, fruits, and nuts. With time, this food source became more important. In fact, it became so important that some people began to plant and harvest the plants themselves. That way, they could be more certain of the supply. So people began to farm. And farming led to a dramatically different way of life.

Why Become Farmers? The oldest known crop is grains of barley found in Egypt. These grains appear to date back to 15,000 B.C. Agriculture became widespread in Africa, Europe, and Asia from 13,000 to 8000 B.C. and in the Americas from about 7000 B.C. Within a period of only a few thousand years, great numbers of people became farmers.

There is one great advantage to farming compared with hunting and gathering. Per hectare (2.47 acres), farmers can produce more calories than any hunter or food gatherer can. Hunters and gatherers need a large territory to get the basic requirements of food.

Hunters and gatherers did take steps to prevent too many people from living in a given area. Part of the group would break off and go to a less populated area. This process appears to have occurred frequently.

Did You Know?
New Ideas about Prehistoric People

It appears that for at least half a million years, people were hunters and gatherers. Then about 10,000 years ago, they began to change. They started to domesticate plants and animals on a large scale. Why did this happen?

Scientists are revising their ideas. They once thought hunters and gatherers led very harsh, insecure lives. They thought that almost every waking moment was spent getting food. So even though these people had large enough brains, they did not have enough free time to invent more tools or develop new ideas.

Recently, however, scientists have been working with people who are still hunters and gatherers. Richard Lee, an anthropologist, studied a group of Bushmen in the Kalahari (KAH luh HAHR ee) Desert in southern Africa. He kept detailed records. Lee found that Bushmen ate more calories and protein each day than is recommended today for people of their size and activity. Furthermore, about 10 percent of the people were over sixty. This compares well with most populations in nonindustrialized nations today.

The Bushmen also did not work as long as most farm families do—even today. The average Bushman spent only about two or three days a week working. The men hunted big game. Some days they got meat, sometimes not. The women's work was more productive. They made snares to catch smaller animals. They also found lizards, grubs, turtles, and giant ostrich eggs. Women supplied about two-thirds of the group's calories.

When there was enough food for a few days, everyone rested. At camp, the adults told stories and scratched designs on ostrich eggs or pots. In the evening

A Bushman making a fire in the desert.

they might dance. The children played games.

Studies of similar groups show that they average four hours a day working. So they have more leisure time than farmers. Thus, people did not change to agriculture because it was more productive.

Many anthropologists have also noted the attitude of male hunters in various cultures. They do not want to change their way of life. To them, hunting is a game—a match of wits—and farming is work. Hunting groups all over the world resist attempts to make them farmers.

It seems, then, that the hunters and gatherers were not just "dumb" people who could not invent agriculture. Instead, they led pretty good lives.

The whole of North and South America was settled in a relatively short period of time, perhaps 25,000 years, as Indians moved from Alaska down to the southern tip of South America.

The Need for Change Many scientists believe that population pressure was the most important reason for the change to agriculture. The need to feed more mouths forced more and more people to change their way of life. They ceased to be primarily nomads and settled down to farm. But hunters and gatherers probably did not become farmers willingly. They had been used to a diet of meat, fruits, and nuts. Only compelling reasons would force human beings to make major changes in their diet. However, between 13,000 and 7000 B.C., the shrinking of the space they needed for foraging forced people to concentrate more on plants.

Women were probably the first farmers. For thousands of years, women harvested wild grains and vegetables. They were likely the ones who recognized the cycle of various

Thinking Geographically: Are any domestic animals shown on the map that are not in use today? Are any plants shown on the map not in use today?

DOMESTICATION OF PLANTS AND ANIMALS

1. maize, tomato, bean, cotton, avocado, cacao
2. potato, peanut, bean, cotton
3. yam, pineapple, sweet potato, cotton
4. oats, sugarbeet, rye, cabbage, grapes, olive
5. rice, grains, yam, watermelon, coffee, cotton
6. wheat, barley, onion, peas, lentil, fruits
7. peas, eggplant, cucumber, cotton
8. grains, alfalfa, grapes
9. soybean, cabbage, grains, onion, peach
10. rice, banana, citrus fruits, yam, sugarcane, taro, tea
11. sugarcane, coconut, breadfruit

A. turkey
B. duck, turkey
C. llama, alpaca, guinea pig
D. cattle, pig, duck, goose
E. reindeer
F. donkey, guinea fowl, duck, geese
G. sheep, goat, dromedary, cattle, pig
H. horse, camel, yak
I. cattle, buffalo, chicken
J. cattle, pig, duck
K. chicken, buffalo, pig

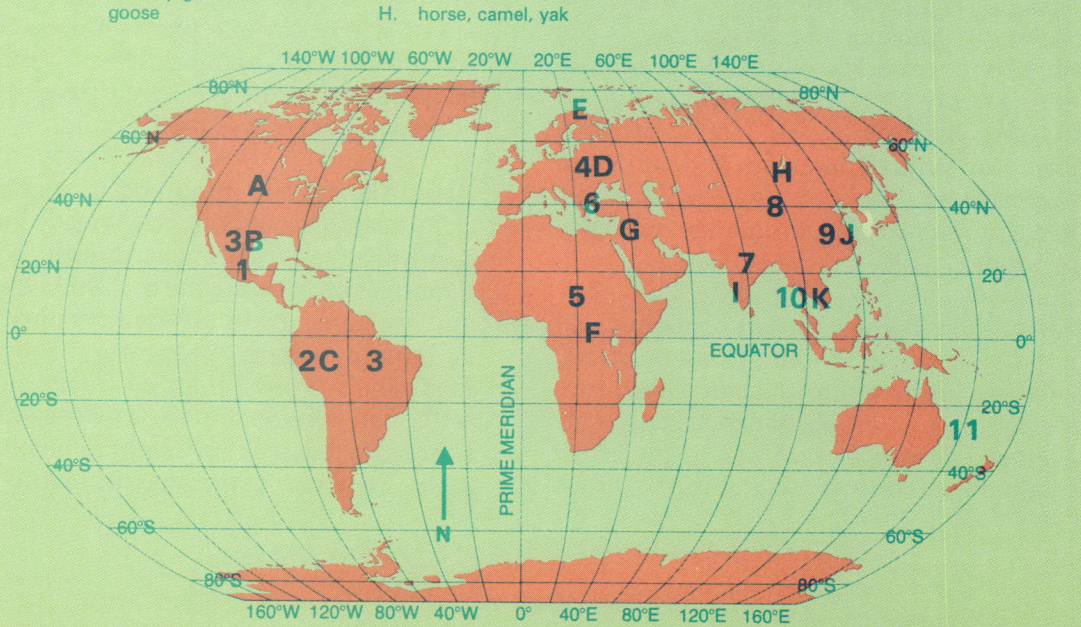

plants and who planted seeds for crops. They might sow a crop and then come back to it months later. Thus, the group depended upon some farming as well as hunting and fishing.

As farming became more important, people began to stay in one place, and more people could stay in the same place. Villages were established, often near bodies of water which provided fish. Many river valleys also had rich soil for crops.

Some groups learned to tame and breed animals such as goats and sheep. These people began to depend upon these animals for their food and clothing. They moved from place to place to find good grazing land for the animals. As they traveled, they often traded cheeses or hides to farm families in the villages. Slowly new foods and animals were spread around a given area.

Agriculture refers to two things: the cultivating of soil to produce crops and the raising of animals. In talking about how agriculture started, we should remember that plants and animals today have changed from what they once were. Many of these changes took place through *domestication*, or the taming and control of animals and plants for human advantage. Grains today are very different from what they were thousands of years ago. An ear of corn was once no bigger than your finger. By continually picking the largest seeds for replanting, American Indians gradually developed plants with large cobs. Animals have also changed in size. Horses are now taller. But animals like pigs and cattle are smaller than they are in a wild state. These animals are easier to manage if they are small.

Plants The domestication of plants and animals began at about the same time. Scientists used to think that agriculture was so new and revolutionary that it only developed in one or two places on Earth and then spread to the rest of the world. It was felt that when hunters and gatherers saw farming, they would at once adopt this way of life with its marvelous advantages. However, as you learned earlier, hunters and gatherers adopted agriculture slowly and probably because of population pressure.

It is now believed that agriculture did not just start in one part of the world. The process of raising plants in large quantities probably started in various parts of the world at about the same time, with the Americas a little behind. This was around 8000 B.C., at the end of the Ice Age.

Thus, Middle East sites show that grains, lentils, peas, and flax were grown around 7000 B.C. In Southeast Asia, rice was grown, and in China, grains and cabbage were being cultivated around 4000 B.C. In the Americas, by 7000 B.C., Indians were growing beans. Maize and squash were started about 5000 B.C. There is very little data about Africa, although grains of barley have recently been found at a 17,000-year-old campsite in Egypt.

It is difficult to identify exactly where certain plants were first grown. Different kinds of cotton appear to have been raised in India, Africa, and in different parts of South America. Yams were independently grown both in South America and in Africa. The map on page 13 gives educated guesses about where various plants were started. As you can see, many different groups of people have contributed to the development of the plants we use today.

Animals Of the hundreds of thousands of animals throughout the world, human beings have domesticated only a few. Examples of these are the bee, the silkworm, and the horse. Animals are very important to human beings. They are a source of food. Their meat or their products, such as milk, can be consumed. Their wool and skins may be used for clothing, shelter, or tools. They can carry weights, plow land,

These tomb figures from Egypt show that cattle were important to early people.

or pull vehicles. This is very important when there are no labor-saving machines. Animals are also used in hunting and in warfare. Lastly, animals can give pleasure. They can be friends and companions or serve to amuse people. Peacocks, for example, have been bred simply for their beauty.

How were animals domesticated? There are many theories. A young animal or a pregnant one may have been brought back to camp. Children may have played with the young offspring and tamed it. Or humans may have consciously watched certain animals such as reindeer. They may have begun to follow these animals and eventually control the movements and activities of these herds. Animals may also have been attracted to the fields of growing grain and penned in by the farmer. The dog is believed to have been the first animal domesticated. There are remains of domesticated dogs in Iraq from around 12,000 B.C. and in the United States (in Idaho) from around 11,000 B.C. Thus, the dog was domesticated even before large-scale farming began. The dog, related to the wolf, may have willingly joined a band of hunters. It probably stayed near the hunters in the hope of getting some food. It was then adopted and became the guardian of the group. It protected the group at night and was used in hunting. In some cultures, dogs were used as beasts of burden and as a source of food. Later, they were important in herding, since they could round up other animals.

It was relatively easy to tame a dog. But some animals were large and strong and wild. The gentle animals were kept alive to produce offspring, and the wilder ones were eaten. Cattle and pigs were domesticated around 6500 B.C. Sheep and goats were domesticated earlier. The donkey was domesticated in Egypt by 3000 B.C. and the horse was tamed in central Asia at about the same time. In the Americas, guinea pigs, the llama, and the alpaca were domesticated by 2500 B.C. An important group of birds—poultry—was domesticated in many parts of the world.

In the process of domesticating animals, human beings became dependent upon them. A few animals today—pigs, cattle, sheep, and poultry—are a major source of our food supply. Some of the domesticated animals can survive today if turned loose. But others cannot survive without human care and protection.

Section Questions

1. What superior traits did Stone Age humans have over the animals of the time? How did these qualities give humans an advantage?
2. Who were the Homo sapiens? When did they appear? How were they different from Homo erectus?
3. For approximately how long were people mainly hunters and gatherers? For how long have they been farmers?
4. What single factor probably forced hunters and gatherers to settle down and become farmers?
5. When and where does agriculture appear to have started on a large scale?
6. How are domesticated animals important to humans?

The slash-and-burn method is still used in some parts of the world.

2. People Settled Down

With a steady source of food, people started to settle rapidly into villages. These settlements were usually located in areas that were rich in some natural resource, such as fertile land for farming. Communities were small, seldom with more than a few hundred people. Settled in one place, people could build more permanent structures. They could also make plans for a longer period of time. They had to think ahead to what might happen in the years to come. For example, it took years for some domesticated animals to mature enough to be useful.

Farming Skills Farming families face a basic problem. They must have a continuous food supply. This is fairly easy to do with the animal source because animals reproduce themselves. However, planting crops year after year in the same soil wears out the soil. Farmers must do something to ensure the fertility of the land. They may abandon their old fields for a few years and use them again later. This is the typical pattern in villages that use *slash-and-burn* agriculture. They cut the trees and then burn the area. Others may use *crop rotation*. That is, they grow different crops at different times of the year so that the same minerals are not taken from the soil. Others use manure or allow silt from nearby rivers to fertilize the land.

It appears that by 4000 B.C. farming families in many places had overcome these problems. But farming was not easy. Men, women, and children put in long hours at certain times of the year. To make their work easier, people invented several new tools. These included plows, hoes, sickles, and the wheel. Some authorities think that the plow is a major invention. Oxen were used to draw the plow on land that had before been too hard to work. Women are usually given credit for the invention of

This bull from Arabia is one of many beautiful articles that early artisans made of bronze after they discovered how to create that metal.

basket weaving, pottery making, and cloth weaving. Now that people were settled, they could spend more time spinning and weaving. Pottery and baskets, which could be used to store the growing agricultural surplus, became more widespread.

The Bronze Age Around 3000 B.C., people in the Middle East began to make the first metal tools—of bronze. Bronze at that time was made from copper and tin. It was much harder than stone or wood. It was used for cutting tools, such as knives, and in weapons such as swords, shields, and battle-axes. Bronze was also used to make cups, vases, and ornaments.

With all these improvements, the farmers produced a sizable *surplus* of food. They produced more than what they needed to survive. This meant that not everyone had to farm. A *division of labor* gradually developed in the villages. Good toolmakers, for example, did not devote all their time to farm work. Instead, they traded the goods they made for food. Other workers, such as merchants, and musicians, could now be supported. This was an important change in the way people lived.

Village life also brought about other changes. Among farmers, there developed the idea of land as *private property*. Among hunters and gatherers, only personal items, like ornaments, were thought of as belonging to individuals. Now, each farming family considered the land they worked as their own. They measured their wealth by animals and land.

Private ownership meant that there was a need for more rules to settle disputes. Who was responsible if one family's cattle went into another family's wheat fields? What would be fair? To settle these kinds of conflicts, authority in the village was usually placed in the hands of a few elders.

Religious beliefs also changed as people settled down. Hunters and gatherers had wanted to be in harmony with nature. Now in the villages, the farmers wanted fine crops. Nature seemed to give or withhold rain and good weather. People set up new religions to please the gods of nature.

Village life was quite different from that of hunting and gathering. Still, villages tended to be isolated and unchanging. People did not hear about many new ideas or different ways of doing things. Life in the villages, however, was to serve as the basis for a new way of life—the life of cities.

Section Questions

1. Name two ways in which farmers had to plan for the future.
2. What inventions helped the farmers do their work?
3. Name several ways in which village life was different from the life of nomadic people.
4. Why did feelings about land ownership change? How did this affect other aspects of the culture?

Chapter Summary

1. The early history of human beings is still a mystery. Probably by 500,000 years ago there were erect human beings who were hunters and gatherers. Humans were primarily hunters and gatherers for hundreds of thousands of years, which we call the Old Stone Age. Then, about 8000 B.C., the Ice Age ended, and many changes took place. The most significant change was the gradual move from hunting and gathering to agriculture. It is believed that population pressure forced people to depend more upon grains and vegetables. People domesticated plants and animals. Agriculture probably developed at about the same time in many areas of the world.
2. As people settled down to farm, they formed villages. And, as they did, many changes took place. People invented new tools to help work the land. These improvements helped farmers produce more food than the amount they needed to survive, and a division of labor gradually developed. Ideas about private property, government, and religion changed.

Chapter 1 Review

Check Your Facts
1. Identify the following:
    a. Old Stone Age   d. Bronze Age
    b. New Stone Age   e. Neanderthal
    c. Ice Age   f. Cro-Magnon
2. Why might hunters not want to become farmers?
3. What was the single greatest advantage of agriculture over a life of hunting and gathering?
4. Which domesticated animals provide most of the meat consumed throughout the world?
5. Describe one or two theories on how animals were domesticated.

Words to Know
Match each of these terms with its definition below: *surplus, domestication, division of labor, private property, crop rotation, agriculture*.
1. Legal ownership of land and possessions
2. A systematic way of producing crops and raising animals
3. More than what is needed or required
4. The occupational structure in which workers become specialists
5. Taming and control of animals and plants
6. Growing different crops in succession on the same land

Developing Your Skills
1. Using the Atlas and the map on page 10, locate the Kalahari Desert and the places where Java and Peking remains were found.
2. Look at your map on page 13. Select three regions (an example is central Asia) and compare the plants and animals domesticated in those areas. Can you guess why some of these plants and animals were able to thrive in these environments?

Thinking It Over
1. Why was the development of agriculture revolutionary in the history of mankind?
2. Women's roles as well as those of men changed as people settled down on farms. Do you think women had a role more equal to men in hunting and gathering societies or as members of farm families? Give reasons for your answer.
3. Do you think that people, in the light of the food crisis, should have large pets? What kinds of foods do pets consume? Could this food be used by other animals or by humans? What are some benefits of having a pet?

Special Activities
1. Collect articles and news clippings about the American diet. Why do you think Americans eat some of the foods that they do?
2. The agribusiness, or food industry of the United States, is interwoven with many sectors of the economy. Find out what job opportunities are available in the following areas: pesticides, agricultural and experimental farms, fertilizer plants, food processing, slaughterhouses, refrigerator trucks and other transportation, retail food stores, and mills for processing grain. One useful source of information is *Career World* magazine.

A wall painting from Luxor's Valley of the Kings, showing a pharaoh with the gods Horus, Isis, and Hator.

Chapter 2 Ancient Egypt

Foreign observers commented that the Egyptians were probably the most religious people on Earth. If religious feelings are to be counted by the number of temples and priests, the ancient Egyptians were indeed religious.

The Egyptians worshiped hundreds of gods. At first, the gods were represented as animals and, later, with human bodies and animal heads. There were many gods of nature. There were Amon-Re (AHmun ray), the god of the sun, the gods of the wind, water, and grain, and the goddess of fertile land.

The gods had living quarters in temples and shrines. There, statues of the gods, or *idols*, were taken care of daily by many

7000-4000 B.C.	Farmers settle Nile Valley
OLD KINGDOM—3100-2200 B.C.	
2800-2400	Pyramid Age
2200-2050	Disunity, power struggles
MIDDLE KINGDOM—2050-1750 B.C.	
1750-1565	Hyksos invaders rule
NEW KINGDOM—1565-1090 B.C.	
1400-1150	Egyptians fight Hittites
1095-945	Internal power struggles
670-332	Assyrians, Persians, Greeks conquer Egypt
30	Romans take control

A statue of Queen Hatshepsut, the first female pharaoh, from her mortuary temple in Thebes.

priests. Songs, incense, flowers, food, and animal offerings were presented to the gods.

The Egyptians also believed in life after death. They believed that the body had to be preserved so that the spirit of the person could return to it. Thus, the Egyptians *mummified* the body of the dead person. They embalmed the body so that it would dry and keep through the journey to the afterworld. Egyptians also felt that the spirit needed a suitable tomb. In the tomb, the spirit would need all the things necessary for a good life—food, clothing, furniture, games, and the like. Wealthy people were buried with many expensive possessions such as furniture, statues, bowls, and cosmetics. The poor were buried with simple kitchen utensils and their personal possessions.

Moral goodness was important. Osiris (O SI rus), the powerful god of the underworld, had the authority to grant life after death. He weighed a person's good deeds against the evil deeds. The person either received life after death or was devoured by fierce dogs.

Thus, religion was a central theme of Egyptian life. Through rituals and good deeds, Egyptians tried to secure the blessings of the gods and a life after death.

1. Egypt's Geography Offered Many Advantages

Egypt's geography has two main natural features. These are the Nile River and the desert. The Nile is the longest river in the world. It is well over 6,400 kilometers (4,000 miles) long. It rises in the mountainous area of equatorial Africa and flows north toward the Mediterranean Sea. Egyptian civilization was concentrated along

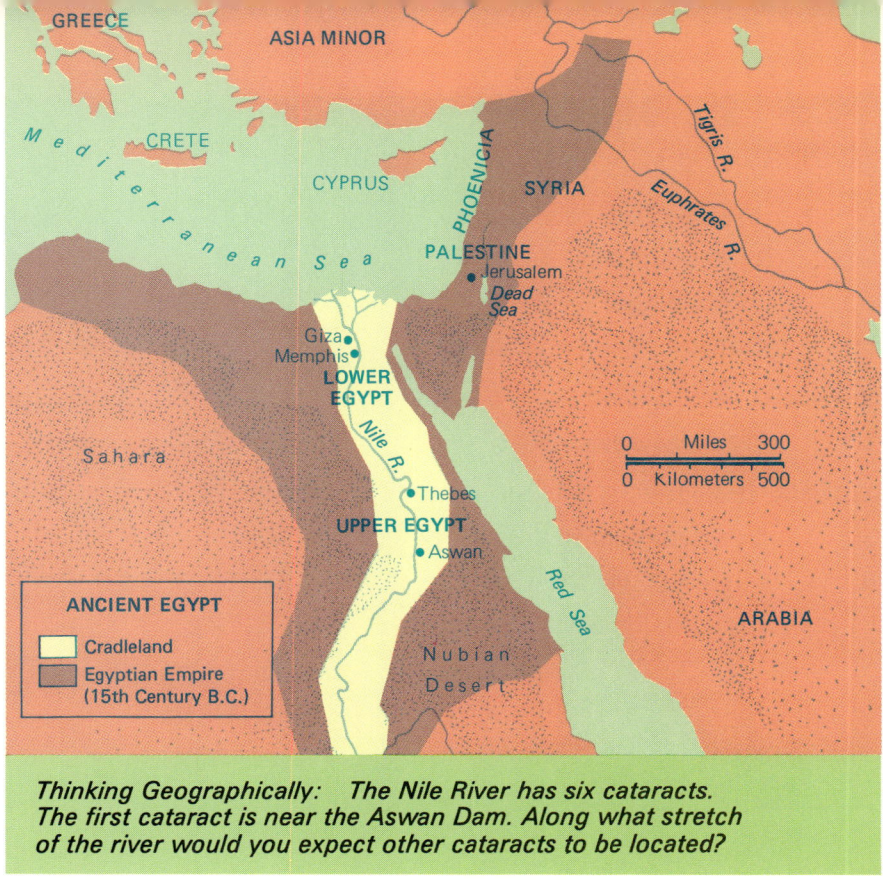

Thinking Geographically: The Nile River has six cataracts. The first cataract is near the Aswan Dam. Along what stretch of the river would you expect other cataracts to be located?

the long, narrow area of the Nile Valley. The Nile gave a unity to the whole of Egypt. It was the main transportation and communication system for the Egyptians. The Nile was also a source of fresh and saltwater fish.

The Nile Valley Within ancient Egypt, the Nile Valley was about 1,200 kilometers (750 miles) long. It included the area from the first *cataract* (rapids) to the *delta*. The delta in Egypt is the fertile triangular area at the mouth of the Nile. It is filled with marshes, shallow lakes, and canals. In the delta grew the papyrus plant, best known for its use in paper. The delta was also the home of many birds and animals.

Until a dam was built in the 1950s, the Nile flooded every year. The floodwaters came from the heavy rains of east central Africa. From about June to the end of September, the Nile gently overflowed its banks. It flooded the land on both sides and left behind a rich black soil, which was good for farming. This rich soil deposited by rivers is also called *silt*. In ancient times, the extent of flooding by the Nile was about 21 kilometers (13 miles) on each side.

After the waters of the Nile receded, the farmers sowed seeds in the mudflats left behind. The farmers grew cereals—*emmer* (a coarse wheat) and barley—and flax. These were the main crops. There was also an abundance of vegetables such as beans, lentils, onions, and lettuce. Beans and lentils were the staple food in the diet of many farm families. Fruits included grapes, figs, dates, and melons. Crops normally could only be grown in land near the Nile River or in areas that were irrigated by the Nile.

The entire community depended on the Nile. Yet this very dependence was also a problem. There might be a year or years in which the Nile would not overflow as much as normal. On the opposite extreme, too much uncontrolled water would wash away the fertile soil and people's homes.

A system of *dikes* (banks of built-up soil) and canals was built to direct the water into channels. There the water was lifted to higher areas by means of buckets on long poles. The dikes and canals had to be constantly repaired. New ones had to be built. Land had to be leveled after flood waters receded. Vegetation had to be cleared away.

In ancient times, two or three plantings were made each year. Egypt normally produced a surplus of food. Some of this was traded with foreigners. In the ancient world, Egypt was regarded as a rich area.

The Desert The ancient Egyptians called the area flooded by the Nile the black land. They named the dry desert that flanked both sides of the Nile the red land. The desert, Egypt's second major natural feature, received little rainfall. An *oasis*, or water hole, was rare. The hot sun was always present. There were swampy areas, too, with some vegetation. As in most other desert areas, a wide variety of animals lived in the Egyptian desert. These included lions, rabbits, ostriches, foxes, antelopes, and cobras.

Some people also lived in the desert. Seminomadic shepherds grazed cattle, goats, sheep, and pigs in the areas that received some rainfall. These shepherds were regarded by other Egyptians as being crude and less civilized. The shepherds, however, were freer. They escaped the forced labor that was the lot of the *peasants*, or farmers.

Other Resources The winds also helped the early Egyptians. Using sailboats, the Egyptians could go upstream with the

An agricultural scene from a tomb of a noble in Thebes.

A wooden boat from King Tut's tomb.

winds. They could use the current of the Nile to float downstream. The Egyptians built many types of sailboats and barges. Boats were used extensively and were the principal means of transportation within Egypt. Egyptian boats also hugged the shore of the Mediterranean to travel to foreign lands. Boats were used so widely that pictures showing individuals traveling to the world after death portray them as going by boat. In a few cases, boats were actually buried in a king's tomb.

The Egyptians had other natural resources besides the great Nile. Copper was mined and used in making strong tools and weapons. Limestone and granite were used in the huge pyramids and temples.

There were gold mines on the eastern desert. Gold was the product prized above all others throughout the ancient world. The Egyptians excelled in making objects—statues, knives, and jewelry—of gold. Gold and gold products were traded for goods that the Egyptians did not have, such as good, strong wood.

Geographical Protection Compared with other river-valley civilizations, the Egyptians were better protected from invaders. In the north, the Mediterranean coast would not be threatened until invaders became more sea daring. In the south, the rapids on the Nile made navigation into Egypt from the south most difficult. The deserts on both sides of the Nile also provided protection. Only on the narrow eastern area of the Sinai was it possible for invading troops to come. To do so, the invaders would have to cross 144 kilometers (90 miles) of waterless land.

Even with these physical barriers, Egypt was invaded more than once. But it was better protected than other civilizations of the time. Egypt therefore had a more stable history. There was peace for periods of hundreds of years, and ancient Egyptian civilization lasted for approximately 3,000 years. Because of this stability, the Egyptians were a confident people. They believed that they were in a land of abundance and were blessed by the gods.

Section Questions

1. What are the two main geographic features of Egypt?
2. What were the black land and red land? Name some features of each.
3. Name several of Egypt's other natural resources.
4. List several advantages that Egypt's geography offered the ancient Egyptians.

2. The Pharaohs Held Supreme Authority

The Nile influenced the whole way of life in Egypt. Strong central government was needed to organize the large irrigation system. This leadership was provided by the *pharaoh*, the ruler of Egypt. The pharaoh was considered by the Egyptians to be a god. And being a god, the pharaoh had supreme authority in all matters, great and small. Pharaohs owned all the land in Egypt and could direct how the resources would be used. They controlled trade and owned the mines. Yet the pharaohs were approachable. They heard complaints and received notices about injustice. Their duty was to protect and care for their people. In time of need, the pharaoh released grain to feed the people.

In the special conditions of ancient Egypt, when the pharaoh was strong, Egypt was strong. When the authority of the pharaoh was weakened—due to outside invaders or the internal power struggles of the priests and nobles—hard times followed.

The Pharaoh and the Nobles Egyptian society was like a *pyramid*, the famous triangular burial places of the pharoahs. At the top was the pharaoh, with absolute power. But the pharaoh could not rule all of Egypt alone. Trusted relatives and friends were needed to help. These assistants had to know mathematics and writing. They had to know when the Nile would flood and how much water should be given to various areas. They had to keep records on the amount of taxes due to the pharaoh. Taxes varied from year to year depending upon the harvest. Skilled government officials were needed to calculate the taxes due.

The second most important person, just below the pharaoh, was the *vizier* (VIH zee ur). This high official saw the pharaoh almost daily and discussed what should be done. The vizier was like a prime minister who relayed the pharaoh's wishes to other officials. The pharaoh and the few high government officials and priests ruled the whole country. Below the pharaoh in prestige were members of the pharaoh's family. Most Egyptians had only one wife, but male pharaohs were allowed to have more than one. Those wives and their many children lived at the palace. The boys attended school at the palace. The pharaoh's family, the high officials and

A gold fan, typical of the many objects Egyptians made from gold.

A relief of a young Egyptian couple, from the tomb of Ramose in the Valley of the Nobles.

high priests, and their families were the ruling class, or *nobles*, in Egyptian society.

Typically, high government officials were granted large estates. The peasants who worked the land paid taxes to the official for its use. The pharaoh, in theory, still owned the land. On these estates, the rich had a pleasant life, with many servants. One servant might be a chef who would cook only the meat. A woman might be responsible for baking the bread. Skilled *artisans* also lived on these estates. They worked on luxury items destined for the tombs, the local temple, or the house of the wealthy official.

One problem with the rule of the pharaoh was that too much depended on the ability and personality of one person. Good pharaohs were energetic and concerned. They traveled up and down the Nile supervising various projects. Such pharaohs were then available to hear complaints about injustices of the officials toward the people. The weaker and unenergetic pharaohs were not able to control their officials.

In times of weak pharaohs, the nobles made their own positions hereditary. In effect, they said that they owned the land and were due taxes from the people. As the nobles became more powerful, they became less likely to obey the pharaoh. The nobles could raise armies of their own from the men who worked on their estates. When they did, wars broke out against the pharaoh.

Merchants, Farmers, and Slaves Below the pharoah and government officials was a small group of middle-class merchants and artisans. The merchants in Egypt were not very independent or powerful. In effect, they secured materials for the elite and were servants of the nobility. There was, however, some social mobility for the talented. The middle class tried to get their sons to become *scribes*, people whose job was to read and write. Scribes were an essential group of government officials.

Most people in Egypt were farmers or peasants. They lived in mud or sundried brick huts in small villages. They had many animals—chickens, ducks, a donkey, and maybe oxen. These farm families either worked on the large estates or on land for which they paid heavy taxes and rent. The farm families lived a simple life without luxuries.

Each year the pharaoh's unpopular tax collector appeared in the village. The collector took a certain proportion of the crops that were grown or the animals that were raised. In addition, the farmers had to pay taxes to their local landlords and to the priests. The pharaoh's representatives could also ask for the farmers' services. This might include repairing the irrigation dikes. There was little choice but to do the work. Not helping might mean no irrigation water.

Demands for the labor of farmers were often made during the three months when the Nile was flooding. The farmers could not work in their fields at that time. This three-month period was a good time for the construction of large projects such as the pyramids. Thousands of workers worked on these projects, year after year. Farmers might also be asked to serve in the army in times of war.

Below the farmers were the slaves. These were usually people captured in war. Outstanding slaves might serve in the homes of the nobles. Here they were often treated like free servants. The worst lot was that of slaves who worked in the mines. They lived short lives, deprived of adequate food and rest. These slaves, being foreigners, were not considered equal to the pharaoh's people. Thus, the Jews in the Bible, being a foreign people in Egypt, complained about the lash and the toil that the pharaoh imposed upon them.

Women Throughout Egyptian society, the position of women was high. Under Egyptian inheritance customs, property descended from mother to daughter. A husband enjoyed his wife's property. But on her death, it went to the daughter and the daughter's husband. This practice helps explain why male pharaohs often married women related to them—even their own sisters. This kept the property in the family.

The economic power of inheritance strengthened the social position of women. They could serve on juries. Women could also move freely throughout the village. However, women were allowed in only a few professions. They could be lesser priests, dancers, singers, and musicians. Their main tasks were in the home. Farming women worked in the fields, baked, and went to the market to sell their surplus food.

The family was important, and family ties were considered essential for happiness. Husbands were told to be respectful toward their wives and children. Children were told to honor their parents and to help them in their old age. All members of the family felt an obligation to help one another in times of need.

A sculpture of Nefertiti, the beautiful young wife of the pharaoh Ikhnaton.

Section Questions

1. Why was the pharaoh powerful in Egypt?
2. Who were the members of the nobility? What was their source of power?
3. What groups were in the middle class in ancient Egypt? What were their roles?
4. What services did the peasants owe to the pharaoh and government officials?
5. What are the disadvantages of a system of government in which power is concentrated in the hands of one person or a few people?

3. Ancient Egypt Had a Long History

The history of ancient Egypt can be divided into three main periods. These are the Old Kingdom (3100-2200 B.C.), the Middle Kingdom (2050-1750 B.C.), and the New Kingdom (1565-1090 B.C.). These are only approximate dates, based in part on written accounts and lists of pharaohs during these periods.

The Old Kingdom The Old Kingdom began around 3100 B.C. when Pharaoh Menes (MEE neez) unified all of Egypt under one kingdom. Previously there had been a division between the northern delta and the southern area.

Many think that the Old Kingdom was the best period, or "golden age," of Egyptian civilization. It was during this time that the pharaohs, living at Memphis (MEM fus), ordered the great pyramids built. These burial places of the pharaohs show the immense wealth and power the pharaohs had. Sometimes the period is called the Pyramid Age. But this period did not just benefit the pharaohs. The Old Kingdom was also a time of peace and prosperity for most Egyptians. The basic character of Egyptian civilization was shaped during the Old Kingdom period.

The Middle Kingdom Around 2200 B.C., civil war broke out. This war lasted for about 200 years. After this long period of unrest, Theban (THEE bun) princes seized power. One became the pharaoh and started a new *dynasty*, a ruling family that maintains its position for a considerable time.

This new ruling family began the Middle Kingdom period, 2050-1750 B.C. The new pharaoh and his descendants could depend on the loyalty and support of the Theban nobility. From Thebes (THEEBZ), they could also secure men for their army. Therefore, the pharaoh made Thebes the capital city for Egypt. But Memphis, the old capital, always remained in the hearts of the ancient Egyptians as the true capital. The great pyramids were located around Memphis.

Around 1750 B.C., the Hyksos (HICK sohs), an Asian warlike people, quickly defeated the Egyptians. One reason for the Hyksos' success was their new weapons, the horse and the chariot. When the Hyksos became the pharaohs, they treated the Egyptians very harshly. After living under their rule for over 100 years, the Egyptians drove the Hyksos out of their land in 1565 B.C.

The New Kingdom A new pharaoh took charge. This was the start of the New Kingdom, which lasted for about 500 years. During this period, the Egyptians were more warlike. They wanted Egypt to be strong and never to be conquered again. To protect their frontiers, the Egyptians conquered many nearby parts of the Middle East and North Africa.

One of the most able rulers of this time was Queen Hatshepsut (HAT SHEP sut). She was the first female pharaoh. Her father was a pharaoh, and her husband, Thutmose (thut MO suh) II, became the pharaoh when he married her. Upon his death in 1500 B.C., she gradually assumed control. After a few years, she used the dress and royal titles of a pharaoh.

Hatshepsut promoted trade and peace. We know of her rule from the huge monuments that she ordered built during her reign. The most famous is the majestic temple near Luxor (LUK sawr). At this temple, Hatshepsut had carvings made of the major achievements of her rule. This included scenes of trade with Africa. She also had built two huge granite *obelisks* —tall, pointed stone columns.

Hatshepsut was a pharaoh for over twenty years. Yet we would not know of her rule if it were not for the great temple. After her death, almost all records of her rule were wiped out by Thutmose III, her stepson and a later pharaoh.

Thutmose III, unlike Hatshepsut, was warlike. His military victories made Egypt

Did You Know?

Ikhnaton—Religious Reformer

In 1375 B.C., during the New Kingdom period, Amenhotep (AM un HO tep) IV, or Ikhnaton (ik NAH tun), became pharaoh. At this time in Egypt, Amon-Re, the sun god of Thebes, was the most important of the many Egyptian gods. However, Ikhnaton wanted to make all Egyptians worship the sun god Aten (AH tun), or "solar disk." Aten was an abstract idea, not a stone idol like the other gods. Ikhnaton outlawed the worship of other gods and ordered that the taxes due all other gods be given to the sun god. These actions angered the priests, who depended on taxes to support themselves and their temples. Many of the common people, deprived of their familiar and loved gods, were also upset.

Ikhnaton promoted his new religion. At Thebes, during his first years of rule, he ordered new structures built. Relief carvings show the king and his beautiful wife, Nefertiti (NEF ur TEE tee), offering gifts to the new sun god. Ikhnaton also began the construction of many temples and buildings at a new city, Ikhnaton, to the north of Thebes. After his death, however, his temples and palaces were completely torn down.

Ikhnaton and Nefertiti.

The traditional priests, again gaining influence, gave orders that all signs of this new religion be erased.

To many, Ikhnaton is an attractive reformer. He appears to be one of the first to stress *monotheism*, a belief in one god.

the wealthiest and most powerful nation of the time. But a large kingdom eventually proved to be Egypt's downfall. Egypt was forced to worry about rebellion in the conquered lands and its expansion aroused the fears of other peoples. The later pharaohs and the nobility became greedier and more oppressive. They lost contact with their own people. By 1200 B.C., the days of Egypt's greatness were ending as the country lost its empire. No longer strong, Egypt was then invaded by many people. But the achievements of the Egyptians continued to have an impact on all people they came into contact with.

Section Questions

1. Why did the Old Kingdom end?
2. Why were the Hyksos able to defeat the Egyptians?
3. What was the basic difference between the rule of Hatshepsut and Thutmose III?

4. Egyptians Contributed to Other Civilizations

Ancient Egypt was mainly an agricultural nation, yet it had all the characteristics of a civilization—a writing system, a well-organized government, specialization of labor, trade, art and literature, and technology. In contrast with other early civilizations, Egypt did not have many cities. Yet the royal city, where the pharaoh lived, was the center of power. The royal city and the nearby area were also the center of many architectural achievements.

Architecture During the days of the Old Kingdom, the royal city of the pharaohs was at Memphis. Memphis was in a good location; it was a trade center for the Mediterranean and delta areas. The most outstanding of the Egyptian pyramids were built outside the city. The pyramids were

Sphinx and Pyramid at Giza.

designed to last for centuries. In fact, a tomb was called a house of eternity. A temple was a house of a million years. Three of the most gigantic pyramids were built at Giza (GEE zuh), north of Memphis. These are the Great Pyramid of Khufu (KOO foo), the Pyramid of Khafre (KAH fruh), and the Pyramid of Menkaure (men KOO ruh). Hidden deep down within the pyramids was the final resting place of the pharaohs who had them built.

It was not an easy task to build a pyramid. Some pyramids included over two million blocks of stone. Each block usually weighed about 2.5 metric tons and some were even heavier. These materials were usually dragged on sleds to the river's edge. Then they could be transported to the proper place on large barges.

Guarding the pyramids at Giza is the Great Sphinx (SFINGKS). Egyptian sphinxes often had the head of the pharaoh of the time and the body of a lion. They represented the god Horus (HO ruhs), who guarded temples and tombs against evil. At Giza, the head and body of the sphinx were carved out of natural rock. The paws and legs were built of stone blocks. It is only one of the many sphinxes in this area that still remain.

The remains at Giza give an idea of the greatness of Memphis during the high period of the Old Kingdom. However, there are actually few remains of the capital city at Memphis. Remaining are only a 70-metric-ton alabaster sphinx, a pharaoh's statue, and some cemeteries.

During the Middle Kingdom period, Thebes became one of the greatest cities in the ancient world. Its reputation, based upon its massive monuments, spread far and wide. The royal capital of Thebes consisted of two main religious centers on the east bank of the Nile. These were Luxor in the south and Karnak (KAHR nak) about 2.4 kilometers (1.5 miles) to the north of Luxor. The Temple of Luxor was the most outstanding building in Luxor. It was later joined by an avenue to the Temple of Amon-Re at Karnak.

The Temple of Amon-Re, the sun god, was built by many, many pharaohs. Each added another structure to it. Therefore, it was not a planned, unified whole. Probably the most impressive parts of this temple are the huge columns, which support the roof. There are 134 columns in 16 rows. Each column is about 25 meters (80 feet) in height. In and around the temple were ram-head sphinxes and towering statues of the pharaohs, queens, and gods. There were also tall obelisks and massive *pylons*, the ceremonial walls of the temple courtyards. Carved and painted scenes showing the glory of the pharaohs covered the obelisks and pylons. The ancient Egyptians are most remembered for their architecture and sculpture. Their pyramids, temples, and sphinxes were impressive both for their size and their pleasing proportions.

The Egyptian Language The ancient Egyptians also developed a written language. The Egyptians probably borrowed writing from Mesopotamia. But the Egyptians made their own writing unique. Egyptian writing is called *hieroglyphics*. It is a way of using pictures and symbols for words, ideas, and sounds. At first the Egyptians used pictures. For example, a picture of a house stood for the word "house." Later, they added twenty-four signs that stood for single spoken sounds—the consonants. This allowed them to write words that are hard to show with pictures. The Egyptians did not use vowels. This was not quite as difficult as it may seem. Y cn lrn t rd wtht vwls.

A papyrus illustration from Thebes, probably about 3000-3500 years old.

Did You Know?

Treasures of a Boy King

After the Old Kingdom days, the pharaohs stopped building pyramids as burial places. They knew that the pyramids were being robbed of their treasures, even though there were harsh penalties against such crimes. The pharaohs began to build royal tombs into the hillsides on the west bank of Thebes. These tombs had secret hiding places.

In 1922 the whole world was electrified when Howard Carter discovered the almost intact tomb of the boy king, Tutankhamen (TOO tan KAH mun). This king acquired the affectionate nickname of King Tut. His tomb with all its treasures had remained hidden for over 3,000 years. Only once had robbers entered the tomb. They did not do too much damage, only grabbing some gold.

King Tut was officially the ruler for about ten years, from 1334 to 1325 B.C. He died in 1325 B.C. at the young age of eighteen.

King Tut's early death caused burial problems. His royal tomb was not ready for him. The Egyptians probably used a structure that had been originally carved for someone else. In fact, King Tut's tomb is the smallest in the Valley of the Kings. The tomb consists of four small rooms. In these rooms were about 3,000 valuable objects--gold artwork, furniture, jewelry, games, and religious items.

Many people wonder if there are other rich tombs to be discovered in Egypt. Others believe that the important sites of the royal families have already been found. These experts want more archaeological work done on sites in everyday villages. They also want further work at the royal sites at Giza and the east bank of Thebes (Luxor and Karnak). Even after 100 years of work, these areas have not been properly excavated and recorded. These sites should give us more evidence on how the ancient Egyptians lived.

The gold funeral mask of King Tut, with the royal burial headdress and a decorative beard, symbol for Osiris, lord of the dead.

An Egyptian doctor and his assistant treat a patient.

The Egyptians were the first to use paper, made from the papyrus plant. The Egyptians also developed an extensive written literature. Religion was the most important topic, but they also wrote love songs, dramatic stories, and poems.

Egyptian writing—on both paper and as inscriptions on monuments—puzzled scholars for many years until they learned how to translate it. Understanding their writing helps us to appreciate even more the Egyptian way of life and their many achievements.

Sciences, Mathematics, and Medicine

The Egyptians of ancient times made many scientific advances. They invented a 365-day calendar. The calendar had twelve months of thirty days. At the end of the year, they added on five more days. Through careful observation they learned much about plant and animal life. They used many plants in medicine.

In mathematics, the ancient Egyptians could write numbers up to one million. They could add, subtract, multiply, and divide. They had some knowledge of fractions. The ancient Egyptians had to measure fields and buildings. Through trial and error, they learned to find the areas of triangles and rectangles and the volumes of pyramids and cylinders, as well as other aspects of geometry. In general, the ancient Egyptians were a practical people. They were not interested in theoretical, or nonpractical, problems of science and mathematics.

Egypt was said to have the best doctors in the ancient world. They influenced the Greeks and other peoples. The strength of Egyptian medicine was in the study of anatomy and the diagnosis of disease. Egyptian doctors examined patients. They checked the eyes, mouth, color, and so on to tell what was wrong. The Egyptians were the first to assign medical terms to diseases. Probably the finest contribution of Egyptian medicine was in bone setting. Egyptian doctors made splints of wood padded with linen. They also pulled and filled teeth. However, sound medical treatment was mixed with magic. A doctor's prescription was often that the patient wear an amulet for protection. The doctors found and used valuable drugs, but they also used many worthless ones.

The accomplishments of Egyptian civilization spread to many other people. These achievements encompassed architecture, sculpture, writing, and knowledge of the calendar, plant and animal life,

LEGACY OF ANCIENT EGYPT

Government: Pharaoh considered a god

Writing and Literature: First to use paper. Created hieroglyphic system. Wrote about religion, love songs, dramatic stories, poems

Science and Mathematics: Invented calendar. Could write numbers to 1,000,000, add, subtract, multiply, divide, calculate area and volume

Medicine: anatomy, diagnosis, medical terms, bone setting

Architecture: pyramids, temples, sculpture

Belief Systems: Hundreds of gods, belief in life after death

---

mathematics, and medicine. The great architectural achievements reflect the Egyptian belief in life after death. The Egyptians were proud and confident about their civilization. They were certain that Egypt would continue to exist. They felt that the gods were kind to the Egyptian people. This attitude of optimism or hope was especially true of the Old Kingdom before periods of invasion or disorder.

Section Questions

1. What was the function of a pyramid? Where are the largest pyramids?
2. What kinds of literature were developed in ancient Egypt?
3. What were Egypt's contributions in the field of medicine?
4. What attitudes did the ancient Egyptians have about life and the gods? Why?

Chapter Summary

1. Religion was very important to ancient Egyptians. They believed in many gods and in life after death. The Nile River and the desert were the two most important natural features of Egypt. The ancient Egyptians lived along the Nile, where they farmed by using irrigation techniques. They produced an abundance of food. Egypt was also rich in such resources as gold, copper, limestone, and granite. The cataracts on the Nile and the immense desert surrounding the settlements also helped protect the Egyptians against invasions.
2. The pharaoh, the king, was believed to be a god. The pharaoh ruled all of Egypt. Just below the pharaoh were the nobles. There was a small middle class of merchants and artisans. The mass of the people were farmers. They worked hard and contributed labor to the pharaoh's projects. Below the farmers were the slaves, the very lowest class. Women were respected, and the family was important.
3. Egypt's Old Kingdom period (3100-2200 B.C.) was peaceful and prosperous. After a long period of civil war, a Theban became pharaoh. This started the Middle Kingdom, 2050-1750 B.C. The Hyksos defeated the Egyptians about 1750 B.C. and ruled harshly for over 100 years before the Egyptians drove them out. The New Kingdom (1565-1090 B.C.) then began. The Egyptians were more warlike during this time. Queen Hatshepsut, the first female pharaoh, ruled during the New Kingdom Period.
4. The Egyptians made many contributions in architecture, sculpture, and writing, and to knowledge of the calendar, plant and animal life, mathematics, and medicine. Some of these achievements were spurred by the importance of religion in the lives of the ancient Egyptians. The Egyptians were a confident people, who believed Egypt would endure forever.

Chapter 2 Review

Check Your Facts

1. What are the main features of a civilization?
2. What kinds of knowledge were needed in ancient Egypt? Why?
3. What were the main crops of the Egyptians? How did Egypt's climate affect crop yields?
4. What was the most important means of transportation? Why?
5. Why was Egypt better protected from invasion than other civilizations?
6. Why, at certain times, was Egypt either conquered or in a state of disorder?
7. How are the royal cities evidence of the power of the pharaohs?

Words to Know

Complete the following statements with the most appropriate word from this list: scribes, dikes, obelisks, dynasty, hieroglyphics.

1. The irrigation system included ____ and canals that had to be repaired constantly.
2. A ____ is a family that rules for many years or generations.
3. ____ were people whose job was to read and write.
4. The Egyptian writing system used ____.
5. Tall ____ were sometimes built near temples, where statues of the gods were housed.

Developing Your Skills

1. Locate the following on the map on page 22.
   a. Nile River
   b. Nile Delta
   c. Thebes
   d. Memphis
   e. Mediterranean Sea

2. Egyptian history is usually divided into three main periods: the Old Kingdom, the Middle Kingdom, and the New Kingdom. In which of these periods did the following occur:
   a. Egypt was most warlike.
   b. Menes unified all of Egypt.
   c. King Tut was buried.
   d. Most pyramids were built.
   e. Ended with internal disorder.
   f. Ikhnaton tried to introduce a new religion.
   g. Hatshepsut ruled Egypt.

Thinking It Over

1. In what ways were the Egyptians a practical people?
2. Why were the slaves in Egypt often treated badly?
3. What brought about Egypt's downfall?
4. Look at pictures of the monuments and sculptures found in this chapter. Which ones are the most pleasing to you? Why?
5. If you followed Egyptian beliefs of ancient times, what would you put in your tomb to be buried with you? Why?

Special Activities

1. In small groups, discuss the advantages and disadvantages of rule by one person.
2. Dramatize a scene in an Egyptian village when the tax collector arrives.
3. Using recent articles from newspapers and magazines, learn about Egypt today.
   a. Find out if Egypt can feed itself.
   b. Learn about the Aswan (AS WAHN) High Dam.

A glazed brick mosaic of a lion from a gate in Babylonia, about 2600 B.C.

Chapter 3 Mesopotamia

For a long time, modern people thought that Egypt, with its great pyramids and other impressive ruins, was the oldest civilization.

What had happened to the ancient cities, such as Babylon (BAB uh lun) that were mentioned in the Bible? Only mounds, called *tells*, gave any physical indication that long ago some structures had existed. There were several other clues as well. There were the references in the Bible. Also, in 1625, European scholars were shown clay tablets with a form of writing that they had never seen before. At the time, however, they could not translate the language.

Archaeologists began digging in the Mesopotamian area around 1830. The ruins of the Assyrians (uh SIER ee unz), a later civilization, were found first. By the 1850s, Europeans learned how to translate the clay tablets. Their findings proved that an earlier people had, indeed, lived in the area.

3500-330 B.C. (early dates approximate)

3500	Cities begin in Sumer
2800	Sumerian number system
2400	Sargon conquers Sumer
1900	First Babylonian empire
1750	Code of Hammurabi
1600	Hittites rule Mesopotamia
1300	Phoenicians develop an alphabet
670	Height of Assyrian empire
550	Persian empire established
330	Persian empire falls

A bronze statue of a woman, about 2100 B.C.

In the 1900s, most of the earliest cities, those of Sumer (SOO mur), were discovered in southern Iraq. The cities of Sumer were recognized as the first civilization in the world. Even today, excavations continue.

1. A City-State Civilization Began Between Two Rivers

About 3500 B.C., long before the pharaohs gained control of all Egypt, the first civilization in the world was developing in Mesopotamia. Mesopotamia is the Greek name for the relatively flat land between two rivers, the Tigris (TI grus) and the Euphrates (yoo FRA teez). It is located in the Middle East in what is now the nation of Iraq. Civilization first began with the growth of a dozen or so cities of Sumer— Kish, Ur, Nippur (nih PUR), Lagash (LAY gash), Uruk (EE rek), Umma.

The Land Sumer was located in the delta at the southern end of the Tigris and Euphrates rivers. In ancient times, the Sumerian cities were actually on the fringe of the Persian Gulf. However, for thousands of years, silt has accumulated at the delta and has extended the shoreline. The remains of these ancient cities are now much farther from the gulf.

At first glance, Sumer does not seem like a promising place for a civilization to start. With temperatures up to 38° Celsius (100° Fahrenheit) in the summer, plants can grow rapidly. But it often rains less than 10 inches a year, and it does not rain at all in the summer. Without water, vegetation can dry up during a hot summer. Every spring, however, the Tigris and Euphrates rivers flooded the valleys. They brought water from the melting snows of the northern mountains. Sumerians, the people of Sumer, noticed that the rich soil left from the flooding often left a bank or a built-up area of soil. The Sumerians realized that they could build up the banks to protect them from severe floods.

The banks, or dikes, built by the Sumerians protected their small mud huts and their growing crops from the floods. In the summer, a hole in the dike could release water for the crops. Long, extensive canals were dug on the flat land. In this way, water was carried to what otherwise would have been barren land.

With the help of irrigation, the Sumerians grew wheat, barley, vegetables like onions and leeks, and dates. The water also was used by the farm animals—donkeys, cows, goats, pigs, and sheep. With good soil and water from the rivers and the use of an ox-drawn plow, the people of Sumer were able to produce a surplus of grain. Grain was then transported on wagons with wheels—a great technological improvement. This surplus of grain was the foundation of the cities of Sumer.

From 3500 to 3100 B.C., the population increased dramatically in the cities of Sumer. With the surplus food, more people were able to turn to occupations other than farming. Specialists began to produce items such as bricks. The potter's wheel was invented; this in turn started the mass production of pottery in the cities. The period after 3000 B.C. is also called the Bronze Age because workers began to produce stronger metals.

The cities of Sumer faced two serious problems. One was to control the rivers and keep up an irrigation system. The other was to keep their enemies from conquering them. The land of Sumer had no natural physical barriers, like mountain ranges or the vast deserts of Egypt, to protect them.

The Priests Each Sumerian city was really an independent *city-state*. A city-state consisted of the city and the surrounding lands. Each city-state had its own ruler. The city-states were rivals for land, power, and trade. Conflicts on rights to water and land frequently arose.

In the early history of Sumer, the highest priests, the priest-kings, had supreme power over the city residents and the people living

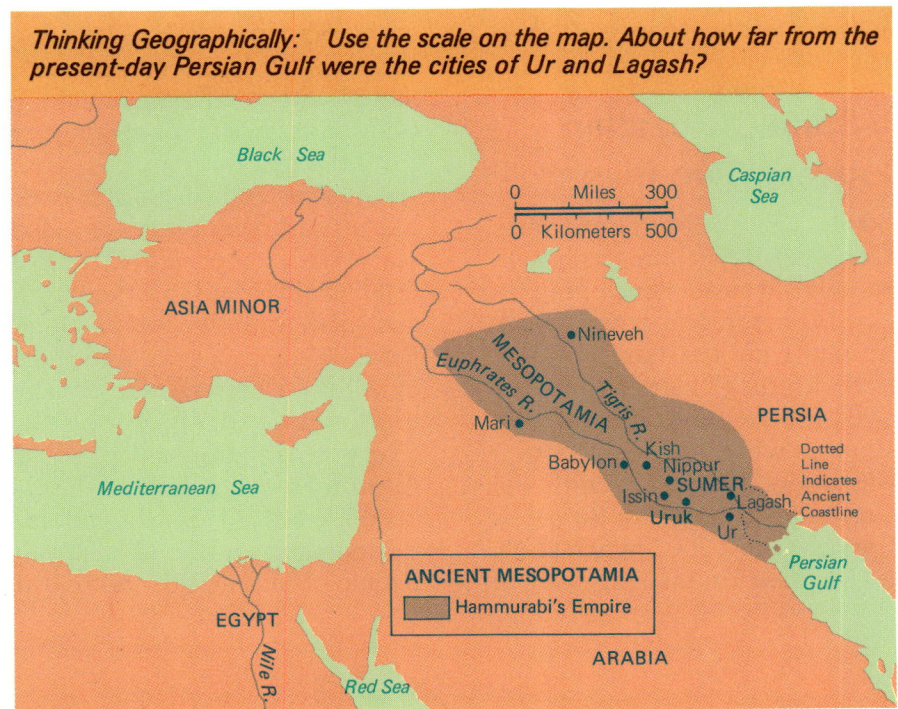

Thinking Geographically: Use the scale on the map. About how far from the present-day Persian Gulf were the cities of Ur and Lagash?

Ziggurat of Ur, Nippur, Iraq.

in the nearby countryside. The priests had power because the Sumerians believed that the land of the city-state was owned by the gods. The priests, therefore, ruled on behalf of the gods. This kind of government, where the ruler is considered a god (like the Egyptian pharaoh) or the ruler represents the gods, is called a *theocracy*. In the theocracy of Sumer, the priests owned the temples and part of the land of both the city and the rural area. They collected rents and taxes from the people for the use of the land.

The priests were the keepers of learning. They and their assistants knew how to measure land, use a calendar, and tell time. More importantly, they knew how to control the irrigation system. They made sure that the canals and dikes were kept in good repair.

The Sumerians also relied on the priests because of the uncertain times in which they lived. The Sumerians, like many agricultural people, believed in many gods.

A belief in many gods is called *polytheism*. There were the gods of the sun, the moon, and the waters, and the violent and life-giving god of the air. The Sumerians believed that these and other gods could do both good and evil things to human beings. Good people sometimes seemed to suffer through no fault of their own. A flood or an invasion could come at any moment.

Besides the priests, many people consulted experts in astrology. These experts used a *zodiac*, or map of the heavens, to predict the future. Interpretations of dreams, omens, and magic were also used as ways to know the uncertain future.

Temples of the Gods Besides the many gods, each city-state had a chief god that protected the city. Under the leadership of the priests, a large temple was built in the central part of the city to honor the chief god. This type of temple is called a *ziggurat*. A ziggurat was built of baked mud bricks

39

and decorated with patterns and color. It was usually the largest building in the crowded city. The Sumerians built the temple tall so that it would not be flooded. The temple was a terraced pyramid. Each story was a little smaller than the one below. On the top was a small, high shrine where only the priests could enter. Later, as some cities grew richer, the ziggurat was decorated with precious emeralds and other jewels. At times of religious festivals, processions of people marched up ramps to the top of the temple.

Inside a Sumerian temple was a statue of the chief god. The Sumerians believed that their gods were like human beings and would enjoy good food and other pleasures of life. So twice a day, the best of food was served to them. The statues were clothed and taken care of by the priests. Music was played before the gods. The gods in turn told the high priests what should be done in the cities. These messages were communicated through dreams, *oracles* (who are people whose voices gods use to speak), and *omens* (which are events that priests know how to interpret).

But the temple was not just a religious center. On the lower levels were libraries, storage places, residences for the male and female priests, and workshops. There might be a school nearby. People came to the temple to take oaths to prove they were telling the truth. To the temple also came engineers, surveyors, overseers, and many unskilled workers employed by the priests.

At the temple, the priests made loans, regulated the interest rates, and invested the profit. In effect, the priests controlled the economic life of the community.

Writing The Sumerians were the first people to develop a writing system. Writing systems were also developed independently by the Chinese and by the Maya in North America. But the writing system of the Sumerians spread widely throughout the Middle East. It became the basis of most of the writing systems used today.

Sumerian writing did not develop suddenly. Before the Sumerians invented writing, some records in the ancient world were kept with clay tokens. Archaeologists have found thousands of these clay tokens from as far as the Caspian (KAS pee un) border of Iran down to Khartoum (Kahr TOOM) in Africa and eastward to the Indus Valley.

One side of a 4000-year-old Sumerian clay tablet from which the world's oldest known medical text has been translated.

Some of these clay tokens were used as long ago as 8500 B.C. They had various shapes such as spheres, disks, and cones. They were often marked with *incisions*, or impressions. These incisions were of numbers, such as 1, 10, 60, 600, and symbols of things such as wool, sheep, ewe, garment, granary, dog, cow, bed, and metal. These symbols have been matched with the characters that appear in the earliest Sumerian writings. From these tokens came the valuable writing system of the Sumerians.

The Sumerians used symbols to record numbers and words. The words were cut with the pointed end of a *stylus*, or stick, on moist clay tablets. The tablet with the marks was then baked or dried. The Sumerian system of writing is called *cuneiform*. This name means "wedge" because the cuneiform strokes are broad at one end and pointed at the other. The Sumerians used cuneiform writing mainly for business purposes. They also created literature, including poems.

Frequent Invasions Each city-state feared invasion from neighboring city-states. The Sumerians were also afraid of the nomadic people who lived around them. The rich cities of Sumer were an attractive prize for the poorer, less civilized people living near them. At various times, the less civilized people invaded the cities of Sumer. Gradually, the newcomers became part of the civilization of the Sumerians.

With recurring invasions, the power of the priest-kings weakened. People began to depend on strong military leaders to protect them. Now the highest military leader became king with absolute control of the government. The king's most important task was to keep the wall of the city in good repair. He was also in charge of a professional army. With this army, some kings tried to conquer other cities of Sumer. Some achieved this but only briefly.

By 2000 B.C., the cities of Sumer had been permanently weakened. They then served as a base for a much larger political state called Babylonia. Still later, Babylonia was conquered by the Assyrians. The Assyrians used Babylonia as a base and acquired an even larger empire. Finally, by 550 B.C., the Persians had conquered this area.

Thus, depending upon the time period, Sumer, Babylonia, and the Assyrian and Persian empires all refer, at least partially, to the area of Mesopotamia. And Mesopotamia changed as it incorporated new people and ideas into its civilization.

Section Questions

1. Why were modern people not aware of the ancient cities of Sumer for a long time?
2. Where was Sumer? What advantages and disadvantages did this location offer?
3. What was the belief system of the Sumerians? How did this give power to the priests?
4. What kinds of activities were held at the temple? How do these activities show the power of the priests?
5. Why did military kings begin ruling Sumerian city-states?

2. Desert People Took Over

Time after time in the history of the world, desert nomads conquered the more civilized lands. The leader of the nomads would then become king of the conquered territory. This happened many times in Mesopotamia.

One such desert group was a Semitic (suh MIH tik) people who had settled on the fringes of Sumer. They spoke a language related to Hebrew and Arabic. Sargon (SAHR gan) I became their ruler and established the city of Akkad (AH kad) to the north. About 2400 B.C., Sargon conquered all of Sumer. He also gained control of the Persian Gulf, all of Mesopotamia, and lands to the west as far as the Mediterranean. Sargon ruled from Akkad over a loose and large *empire*, the first in the history of the world. An empire is a large area ruled by one leader or government. It often consists of a number of territories populated by different cultural groups.

Under Sargon, the conquered peoples were allowed to maintain their religions and local customs. Sargon sent his army and civil servants to the various parts of his empire. He demanded *tribute*—a form of tax—from all places he conquered. His army protected important trade routes and encouraged trade.

A relief showing Hammurabi receiving the laws from the sun god.

Sargon's successors were not able to hold the empire together. The Amorites (AH muh ritz), who lived in the Syrian Desert, took over the land of the Sumerians about 2000 B.C. They made Babylon their capital city. Babylon then became the governing center of another large empire.

Hammurabi's Laws One of the greatest Amorite leaders was Hammurabi (HAH muh RAH bee). Babylonia was at its height between 1850 and 1750 B.C. For forty-two years during this period, it was ruled by Hammurabi, who was called the king of the four quarters of the world.

Hammurabi tried to unify his large empire. He believed that providing justice was one of his most important tasks as king. Previous rulers had tried to write down the existing laws. Building upon their work, Hammurabi provided a written set of laws for the whole empire.

A written law system is generally better than an oral system. With written laws, people know what their rights are.

Hammurabi's laws concerned property, marriage, crime, and other aspects of daily life. They outlined very carefully the relationship of merchants and their agents, debtors and creditors, landlords and tenants. These laws, plus others on interest, inheritance, wages, and prices, allowed the economy to function smoothly.

To us today, the 300 or more laws of Hammurabi appear severe and often brutal. The basis for Hammurabi's Code was the idea of "an eye for an eye." This meant that the loss of an eye to the injured person called for the loss of an eye to the person who caused the accident. If a builder built a house that collapsed and killed the owner of the house, the builder was to be put to death. Although these penalties were harsh, we do not know if the worst punishments were really enforced.

Justice, however, was not equal for all groups in society. If a slave were killed from a collapsed building, the builder would only have to pay for damages. Thus, harming lower-status people was not as serious as harming upper- or middle-class people. Sometimes, though, the penalties for crimes were harder on the wealthy. It was presumed that the wealthy were not ignorant of what they were doing.

Laws were ruthless toward farmers who did not maintain their dikes. Faulty dikes could cause other farmers to lose their crops. If the wrongdoer could not pay the damages, that person and even members of that household were sold as slaves to pay for the damages.

In other areas, Hammurabi's laws were more generous. An underlying idea of the code was that the strong should show mercy toward those in need. There were provisions for widows, orphans, and children, and limited rights for slaves. Slaves could engage in business, buy their freedom, and marry a free person.

Hammurabi's laws, based on previous laws, had enormous impact since they were used throughout the empire by different groups of people. Parts of the code influenced the Hebrews and are reflected in the Bible. Some of Hammurabi's laws also became a part of Muslim law.

Hammurabi's laws gave a degree of justice to a large number of people. Women had some legal rights such as the right to inherit property. They could also run businesses such as taverns.

Hammurabi's Code also shows the Babylonians as people concerned with economic justice here on Earth. Babylonians did not devote much attention to an afterlife. The goals of the Babylonians were to be successful in business, have many sons, and have good health.

Life in the Cities Babylon soon became one of the greatest cities of the ancient world. It was an important center of trade. The extensive trade probably reached as far as India, which provided spices and jewels. Lumber came from Phoenicia (fih NIH shee uh) on the Mediterranean coast.

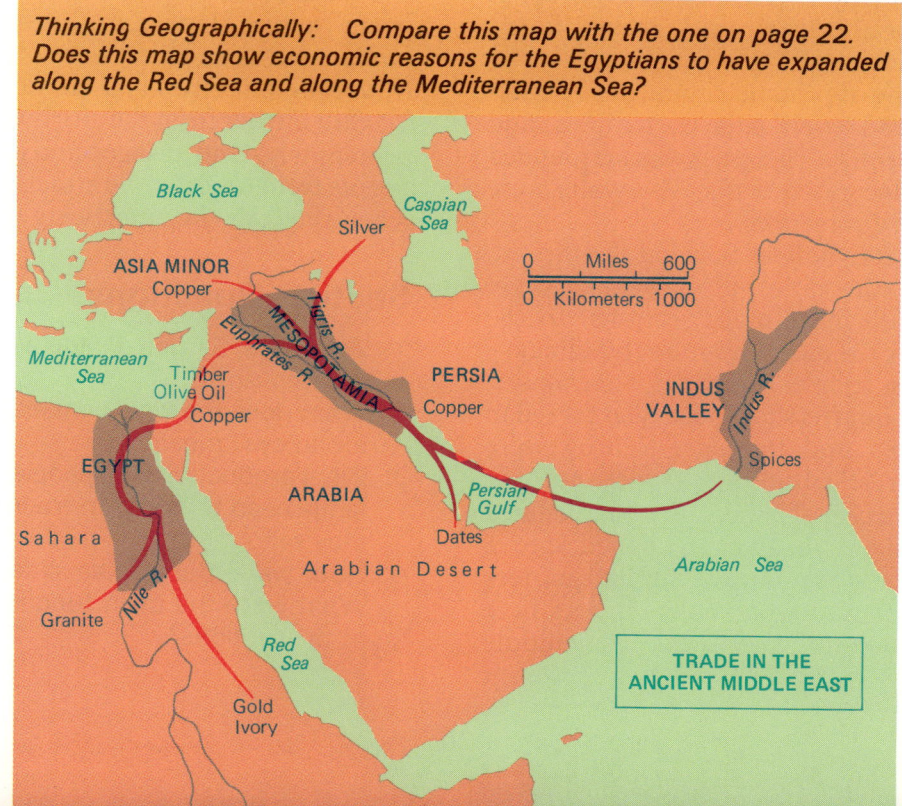

Thinking Geographically: Compare this map with the one on page 22. Does this map show economic reasons for the Egyptians to have expanded along the Red Sea and along the Mediterranean Sea?

TRADE IN THE ANCIENT MIDDLE EAST

A musical instrument from Ur, from about 2450 B.C.

Metals such as copper came from Persia. At first, donkeys were used as the beast of burden for the trade pack trains. Later, camels were used.

Like the Egyptian capital at Thebes, Babylon had lovely palaces, temples, and buildings. Unlike Thebes, it was surrounded by giant decorated walls. The walls were needed for protection.

Other cities besides Babylon also thrived. Typically, the cities of Babylonia were divided into three main sections. In the center were the most important buildings—the palaces, temples, granaries, storehouses, and living quarters for those who served in the palaces and temples. Nearby were crowded residential areas with narrow, winding streets. The wealthy people lived in two-story houses that opened into a courtyard. Alongside the living quarters were shops and workshops. It was here that the middle class lived. The middle class consisted of merchants, skilled workers, scribes, doctors, artists, and owners of large farms. Most of these people worked in the cities. Many had jobs related to trade.

Usually the central area of Babylonian cities was surrounded by thick walls. Beyond the walls were farmlands and villages. This section provided much of the food for the city. In some cities, this area was protected by secondary walls or forts. The vast majority of the people who lived here were farming families. Some were free, independent farmers who rented their land from the palace or the temple. Others were more like *serfs*, or slaves, who lived and worked on the land owned by their masters, the landlords. Besides the land owned by the kings and the priests, nobles also owned very large estates. Most people, both on the farms and in the cities, lived in small, dark, windowless huts.

The third section of Babylonian cities was the harbor area located on the major river. This was usually outside the city walls. The harbor area was the center of commercial activity. It had wharves for boats to land. It was in this section that foreigners lived. There were often traders from different cities and countries.

Still farther from the city lived nomadic peoples who tended sheep and goats. These people from time to time attacked the cities when they felt the cities were weak.

Section Questions

1. Who was Sargon I, and what did he accomplish?
2. What does the legal concept of "an eye for an eye" mean?
3. What products did the people of Mesopotamia need to get from trade? What did they sell?
4. How were Babylonian cities laid out? What were the main functions of each of the sections?

3. The Assyrians and Persians Gained Great Empires

The Babylonian empire did not last forever. This time it was the Hittites (HIH titz) who invaded the Middle East. The Hittites came from Asia Minor in what is now Turkey. They gained power because they knew how to make tools and weapons from iron. From 1600 to 1200 B.C. the Hittites controlled a large empire, including Babylonia.

Constant warfare with Egypt weakened the Hittites and allowed some smaller groups to become independent. One such group was the Phoenicians, who lived in what is now Syria, Lebanon, and Israel. The Phoenicians were the bravest and greatest sailors of the time. They traded all over the Mediterranean area—North Africa, Spain, southern France, Greece, and Italy. They even went beyond the Strait of Gilbraltar. The Phoenicians, strongly influenced by the Egyptian and Mesopotamian cultures, spread many ideas and products throughout the Mediterranean region.

To help in trading, the Phoenicians improved the older writing systems. About 1300 B.C., they developed an alphabet with twenty-two consonants and no vowels. Later the Greeks added vowels. In turn, the Roman and all Western alphabets borrowed from the Greek.

To us, the most significant of the smaller nations of this time was that of the Hebrews. The story of their background, their rise to power, and the loss of their nation is told in the Hebrew Torah, which also makes up the first five books of the Bible. The religious ideas that are explained in these are the foundation of Judaism and the base for Christianity and Islam. The Hebrews were the first to worship a single all-powerful, abstract God.

The Assyrians At the same time that the Hebrews were developing their religious ideas, the Assyrians were developing into a military power. The Assyrians were a mixture of many races. For thousands of years, they had lived in a hilly land north of Babylonia. This land did not give them any protection from their enemies. The Assyrians did not get much food from their hard, poor land.

Sargon I and Hammurabi conquered the Assyrians, but the Assyrians later fought back invaders and continued to be an independent people. After being invaded so many times, the Assyrians' first priority became protection of their land. So, the Assyrians became a military nation. All the farmers were drafted into the army. These farmer-soldiers became a strong military force. They expanded their territory

An Assyrian battle scene, showing some of their fearsome tactics and technology.

Did You Know?

The Story of the Hebrews

Unlike other peoples around 1800 B.C., the Hebrews did not worship idols or a god of nature. Their religion was based on moral ideas. If the Hebrews had faith and followed God's rules, they would be rewarded. If not, God would punish them. People's fates, then, were believed to be in their own hands.

By 1500 B.C. several Hebrew tribes settled peacefully in Egypt. After some years, though, the Hebrews were enslaved.

The Hebrews left Egypt around 1200 B.C. They were able to win their freedom because of Egyptian problems and because a strong Hebrew leader arose—Moses.

According to the Torah, the first five books of the Bible, the Hebrews wandered in the desert for forty years until reaching and conquering Canaan. Actually, it probably took them about 200 years to control Canaan. Then, under a king called Saul, the first Hebrew state began.

Saul was followed by King David and King Solomon. These were the days of greatest Hebrew power and wealth.

After Solomon's death, the kingdom split into two parts: Israel in the north and Judea (joo DEE uh) in the south. The word "Jew" comes from the name "Judea." This division weakened the Hebrews. The Assyrians conquered the north. The Babylonians conquered the south. The Judeans and Israelis were dispersed. But they kept their identity and religion.

After the state fell, the center of Jewish life was the meeting house, or *synagogue*. Synagogues were set up wherever Jews lived.

In Israel, an agricultural settlement from around 2000 B.C.

The Jews returned in 538 B.C. However, they were conquered again and again. In A.D. 70, the Romans banished them from Jerusalem, except for one day a year. On that day, Jews could, for a fee, weep at the ruins of their temple.

by raiding the surrounding areas. They demanded tribute from the conquered lands. The Assyrian army was successful for many reasons. They were the first to use many new weapons and equipment. They attached horses to a two-wheeled chariot. The horse-drawn chariot spread panic into the lines of the enemy's foot soldiers. They developed a disciplined *cavalry*, soldiers mounted on horses. They also designed the battering ram to destroy the walls of their enemies' cities. They used moving platforms for archers. Their iron weapons, borrowed from the Hittites, were much stronger than the bronze weapons of their enemies.

The lot of any people conquered by the Assyrians was terrible. Assyrian kings boasted of their cruelty to their victims. Prisoners and civilians were often killed in mass executions. Defeated cities were completely destroyed.

Around 800 B.C., the Assyrians raided lands in all directions. Within 100 years or so, they conquered Syria, Israel, Babylonia, and even far-off Egypt. The Assyrian empire became the largest empire of the time.

The conquered people hated the Assyrians. They would refuse to pay the tribute as soon as the Assyrian army left their lands. An Assyrian king's death often triggered a revolt. The Assyrians, therefore, began to institute a more permanent rule. The Assyrian king appointed a governor for each region. This was often the native king, and he was responsible for paying the tribute. A permanent Assyrian army was also placed in each region. The Assyrians improved communication by building roads. This allowed both troops and trade to move more swiftly. The Assyrians also started a postal service.

After 650 B.C., the Assyrian empire ran into difficulties. A succession of Assyrian kings spent more time at pleasure than on affairs of state. Also, sending troops to various parts of the empire depleted the number of soldiers. Foreigners were allowed into the army but they were not as zealous as the original Assyrian farmer-soldiers. In addition, the great wealth of the empire attracted other seminomadic groups. These people allied together and conquered the Assyrians. The Assyrian captial, Ninevah (NIHN uh vuh), was destroyed in 612 B.C. by Chaldeans (KAL dee unz), Medians (MEE dee uns), and Persians.

The Assyrian empire ruled the Middle East ruthlessly for 300 years. But the Assyrians did make some helpful contributions. They used a centralized system of government to hold the empire together. They encouraged trade and communication. The Assyrians excelled in architecture and sculpture. They borrowed heavily from the Sumerians and Babylonians. Their great cities had huge libraries and fine public buildings. Yet despite their contributions, the rest of the Middle East was glad when the Assyrians were defeated.

The Great Persian Empire The early Persians were a nomadic people who came from what is now southern Russia. By 900 B.C., they expanded into what is now Iran. They called themselves Aryans (AHR ee unz), from which came the name "Iran." Gradually, the Persians borrowed many ideas from their neighbors, especially the Assyrians.

In 612 B.C., the Persians joined with the Chaldeans and Medians to soundly defeat the cruel Assyrians. The Persians then quickly gained control of more and more territory. For about 200 years (550-330 B.C.), they ruled the largest empire the ancient world had ever known. It spread from Egypt and the Aegean (ih JEE un) Sea in the west to the borders of India in the east. It measured more than 8 million square kilometers (over 3 million square miles), an area about the same size as mainland United States today. The Persian officials treated their conquered people

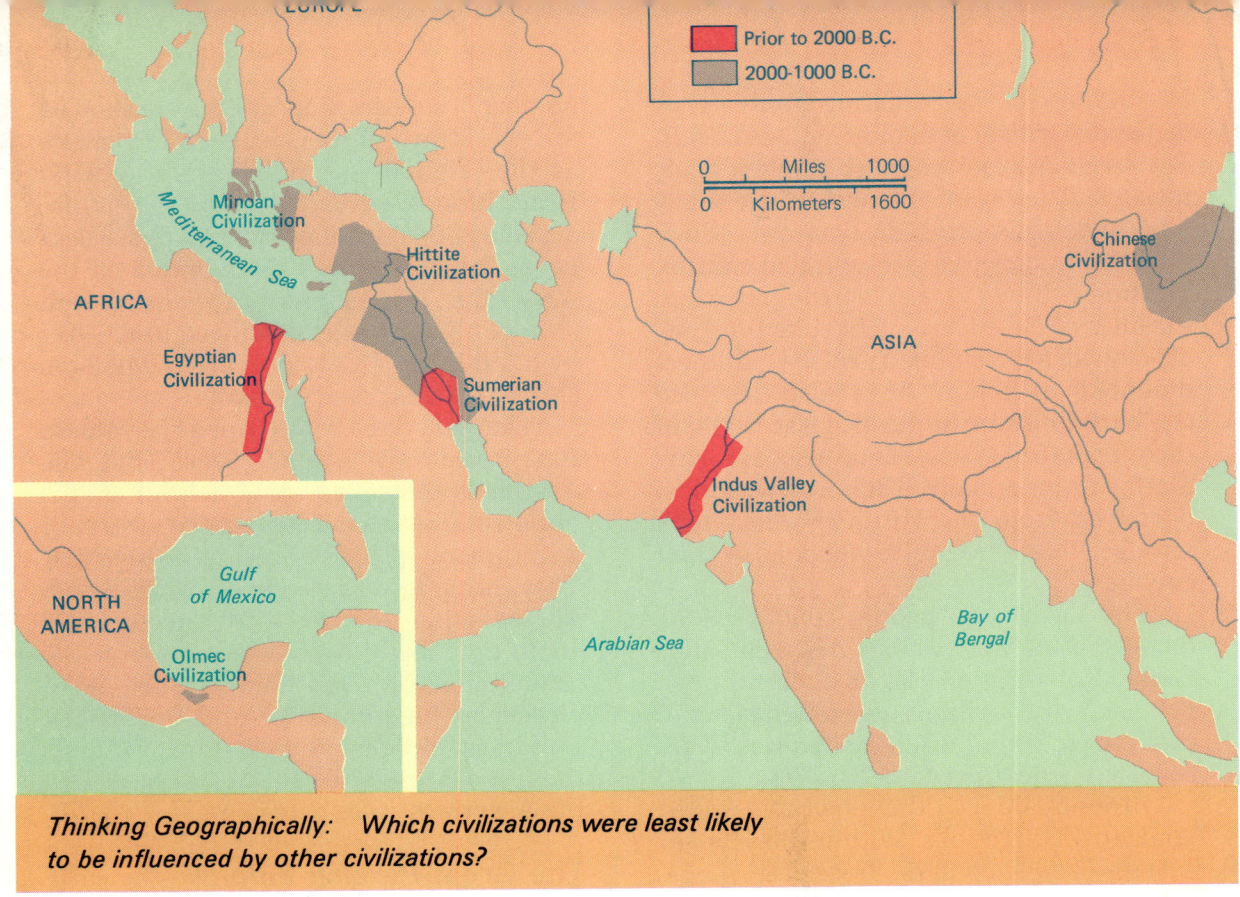

Thinking Geographically: Which civilizations were least likely to be influenced by other civilizations?

better than the Assyrians did. They did not kill defeated peoples. They allowed local groups to practice their own religion.

To rule effectively, the Persians divided their empire into large districts, called *satrapies*. Each satrapy had an appointed governor, often a member of the Persian royal family. The governor was responsible for maintaining order and justice in the district. From time to time, investigators from the royal court checked how each governor was doing. In addition, the Persians placed their army in strategic places to crush internal rebellions and to prevent outsiders from attacking their lands. The Persians used slave labor to build roads. The roads improved communication and increased trade in the large empire.

But the royal family declined in ability, and the royal court became corrupt. The army's strength was reduced. In 330 B.C., the defeat of the Persians by the armies of Alexander the Great of Macedonia (MAS uh DOH nee ya) led to the collapse of the Persian empire. Macedonia is an area of southern Europe that includes parts of Greece, Yugoslavia, and Bulgaria.

Another important Persian contribution was that made by Zoroaster (ZOR ruh WAH stur), a great religious leader. Zoroaster lived around 600 B.C. The details of his life are not known. But after living in the desert for about thirty years, he began to preach that there was only one supreme being, Ahura Mazda (AH hu reh MAZ deh), Lord of Wisdom, not six gods as in the Persian religion. Zoroaster also said that people had social and moral responsibilities. Thus, at about the same time that the Hebrew *prophets* were emphasizing

This statue of a man and woman was found in Nippur. It was probably made around 3600 B.C.

Although the Persians were not responsible for many new contributions, they helped spread the ideas of the civilized world into many lands.

A Crossroads In ancient times, there seemed to be endless wars. Thousands of people were killed. Defeated armies were generally enslaved. The main temple of the defeated city was completely destroyed in order to prove that the city's god had been defeated. Nevertheless, the invasions did spread ideas. People *migrated*, or moved, sometimes by force. As they moved, they exchanged ideas. The life-style of Mesopotamia became the model for many people living outside Mesopotamia.

The location of Mesopotamia helped spread ideas. There were three thriving civilizations in this part of the ancient

one god and social responsibility, Zoroaster, too, had arrived at this idea. (A prophet is a person who feels compelled to speak for God, telling people of God's plan for them.) In fact, many Biblical authorities believe that Zoroaster may actually have been one of the Hebrew prophets—perhaps Ezekiel (ih ZEEK yul), Nimrod (NIHM rahd), Seth, or Baruch (buh RUK).

The teachings of Zoroaster influenced the major religions. For example, Zoroaster introduced the idea of an evil force working against God. According to Zoroaster, Ahura Mazda had two sons. One chose good, and the other chose evil. The wicked one, Ahriman (AH rih man), was eventually seen as a separate, powerful force.

For a while, Zoroaster's ideas spread throughout the Persian empire. However, much later, the region was taken over by Muslims, a religious group that believes Allah (AH lah) is the only god. The Zoroastrians were then forced out. They fled to India, where the religion has been kept alive by a group called the Parsi (PAHR see).

LEGACY OF MESOPOTAMIA

- **Government:** city-states (Sumer), empires (Sargon I and Persians), centralized system of government (Assyrians), Hammurabi of Babylonia developed first written law system.

- **Writing:** Sumerians developed first writing system, the cuneiform. Phoenicians improved the system with an alphabet.

- **Inventions:** Sumerians developed potter's wheel and the use of a wheel as a machine. Assyrians developed iron weapons, new techniques of warfare.

- **Communication:** Phoenician sailors spread ideas and products throughout Mediterranean region. Assyrians developed a postal system. Assyrians and Persians developed roads.

- **Belief Systems:** Hebrews and Zoroaster contributed belief in one god, social and moral responsibility of individual.

world: Egypt, Mesopotamia, and the Indus Valley. Each of these early civilizations developed independently. But Mesopotamia was physically in the center and in contact with the others through trade and travel. The Egyptians, for example, borrowed written language and the use of the wheel from Mesopotamia. Long after the cities of Mesopotamia were in ruins and forgotten, their contributions remained alive.

Section Questions

1. Why did the Hittites become powerful?
2. What were two great contributions of the Phoenicians?
3. In your opinion, what are the most significant contributions of the Hebrews?
4. How did the Assyrians gain control of the largest empire of the time?
5. Who was Zoroaster? What were his ideas?

Chapter Summary

1. The first civilization in the world began in the city-states of Sumer, located at the southern end of the Tigris and Euphrates rivers. With irrigation, the Sumerians were able to grow a surplus of food. This supported the development of cities. Yet unpredictable floods and raids from nomadic peoples made Sumerians feel uncertain about the future. Because of these concerns and fears, the Sumerians turned to the priests for help. The priests acted as go-betweens for the gods and controlled the religious and economic life of the city-states. However, as more groups invaded Sumer, the people turned to military leaders for protection. Among the important contributions of the Sumerians were their writing system, advances in science and mathematics, the potter's wheel, and the use of the wheel for work.
2. The Amorites—a Semitic people—conquered all the cities of Sumer and other territories. One of the greatest Amorite leaders was Hammurabi. His great contribution was a system of written law. These laws show the interest of the Babylonians in trade and commerce. A typical Babylonian city had three main sections: the center with the important buildings surrounded by thick walls, the farmlands and villages on the outskirts of the city, and the harbor area, which housed the foreign traders who traveled to and from the city.
3. The Hittites, a people from what is now Turkey, conquered the Babylonian empire and spread out into a large area. Around 1200 B.C. the Hittites were weakened by constant fighting with Egypt and other enemies. The decline of the Hittites allowed the Phoenicians and Hebrews to form small, independent states. The Phoenicians, the great sailors living between the Mediterranean Sea and the mountains of Lebanon, spread ideas of civilization throughout the Mediterranean world. They improved Sumerian writing with the use of a twenty-two-consonant alphabet. Their alphabet, in turn, influenced the Greeks and the Romans. The Hebrews, a small group of Semitic nomads, made two great contributions to the world—their belief in one god and their book of laws, the Torah. Starting around 800 B.C., the warlike Assyrians conquered the entire Middle East and used a policy of terror. Through their conquests, they spread many ideas. In turn, the Assyrians were conquered by outside enemies. The strongest group became the Persians, who then gained control of the largest empire that the world had known at the time. From about 500 to 330 B.C., the Persians ruled all of the Middle East and other territories. The Persians helped spread the ideas of the civilized world and the ideas of their religious leader, Zoroaster. The great achievements of Mesopotamia influenced other ancient civilizations and are part of our lives as well.

Chapter 3 Review

Check Your Facts

1. Identify or describe the following:
   a. tells
   b. Moses
   c. Sargon I
   d. ziggurat
2. What clues gave an indication that ancient cities had existed in Sumer?
3. What were the two major problems faced by the people of Sumer? How did the Sumerians try to solve them?
4. For what purposes did the Sumerians use their writing system?
5. What was the cheapest means of transportation in Mesopotamia? What animals were used for land transportation?
6. Why was Hammurabi important?
7. To what areas did the Phoenicians sail?
8. Why did the Hebrews leave Egypt? Where did they settle?
9. Why were synagogues an important development for the Hebrews?
10. How did Persians differ from Assyrians in treating conquered people?

Words to Know

Define these words in one or two sentences. Then tell the significance of each.
   a. empire
   b. cavalry
   c. cuneiform
   d. city-state
   e. polytheism
   f. theocracy

Developing Your Skills

1. Identify the following places. Then find them on the maps on page 38 and in the Atlas.
   a. Mesopotamia
   b. Euphrates River
   c. Persian Gulf
   d. Babylon
   e. Israel
   f. Nineveh
   g. Turkey

2. Place a "1" on your paper if the event occured from 3500 to 2000 B.C. and a "2" if the event occurred from 2000 to 300 B.C.
   a. Assyrians use a policy of terror.
   b. Persians have the largest empire.
   c. Sumerians invent the potter's wheel.
   d. City-states are started in Sumer.
   e. Hammurabi establishes one of the first legal systems in the world.

Thinking It Over

1. Why do you think merchants had more power in Mesopotamia than in Egypt?
2. Compare the attitudes of the people of Egypt and Mesopotamia toward an afterlife, respect toward women, and the nature of the gods. Why did these differences exist?
3. Why were the Assyrians successful in gaining an empire, and why did their empire fail to survive for more than two or three centuries?

Special Activities

1. Sir Leonard Woolley (WOOL e), an English archaeologist, discovered the Sumerian city of Ur and found some of the greatest treasures of the ancient world. Learn more about Sir Woolley. Then write a brief report, or tell the class about him and his discoveries.
2. The Bronze Age arrived at different times in different parts of the world. Use your library to find out when the Bronze Age reached places such as England, France, China, and the Americas.
3. Begin making a chart of when and where human rights were first written down.

An excavation at Mohenjo-Daro showing the ruins of the Great Bath of Citadel.

Chapter 4 Ancient India

For over 3,000 years, the sand and the mud kept their secret. People worked, played, and died unaware of the fact that two cities lay hidden in their river valley. No one suspected that a large, well-organized civilization lay buried in the Indus Valley. The mystery began to unfold when a railroad track was being laid in the region of present-day Pakistan. The building contractor used thousands of ready-made clay bricks that lay scattered near the mounds. The age and quality of the bricks attracted the attention of British and Indian archaeologists and serious excavation began. Finally in 1921 and 1922, the ancient cities of Harappa (huh RAP uh)

3000-1500 B.C. (early dates approximate)

3000-2500   Pre-Harappan Indus Valley people
2500-1700   Harappan civilization
1800   Indo-Aryan invasion

VEDIC AGE—1500-1000 B.C.
1500-1000   Vedas composed
1300   Indo-Aryans migrate to Ganges area

EPIC AGE—1000-450 B.C.
600   Vedas are written down
563-483   Gautama Buddha

A.D. 1921-1922
Discovery of Harappa, Mohenjo-Daro

A clay toy from the Indus Valley.

and Mohenjo-Daro (mo HEN jo DAH ro), "mound of the dead," were uncovered. These cities had flourished at the same time as the ancient kingdoms of Egypt and Mesopotamia.

Archaeologists found the two cities to be remarkably similar in design and layout, though they were separated by nearly 640 kilometers (400 miles). Both had uniform streets and an elaborate system of drainage. Within the cities were found pottery, jewelry, and inscribed seals. From this evidence, scholars have been able to piece together much of the way of life of the people. But the important questions of who they were and what happened to them are still a puzzle.

The extent of the discovery is already quite impressive. The excavations have uncovered seventy sites. These sites are spread over an area of 4 million square kilometers (1.5 million square miles). The culture was uniform enough over this vast area to suggest that these were not just city-state societies but a unified empire. This ancient civilization was integrated into what was to become Indian civilization—along with the influences from later cultural periods.

1. A Complex Civilization Developed in Ancient India

The Indian subcontinent is shaped like a kite. Its lower half, a large triangular peninsula, is enclosed on two sides by water. The upper triangle is marked off from the rest of Asia by a wall of the highest mountains in the world—the Himalayas (hih muh LAY uhz) meaning "abode of snow." Below the mountains

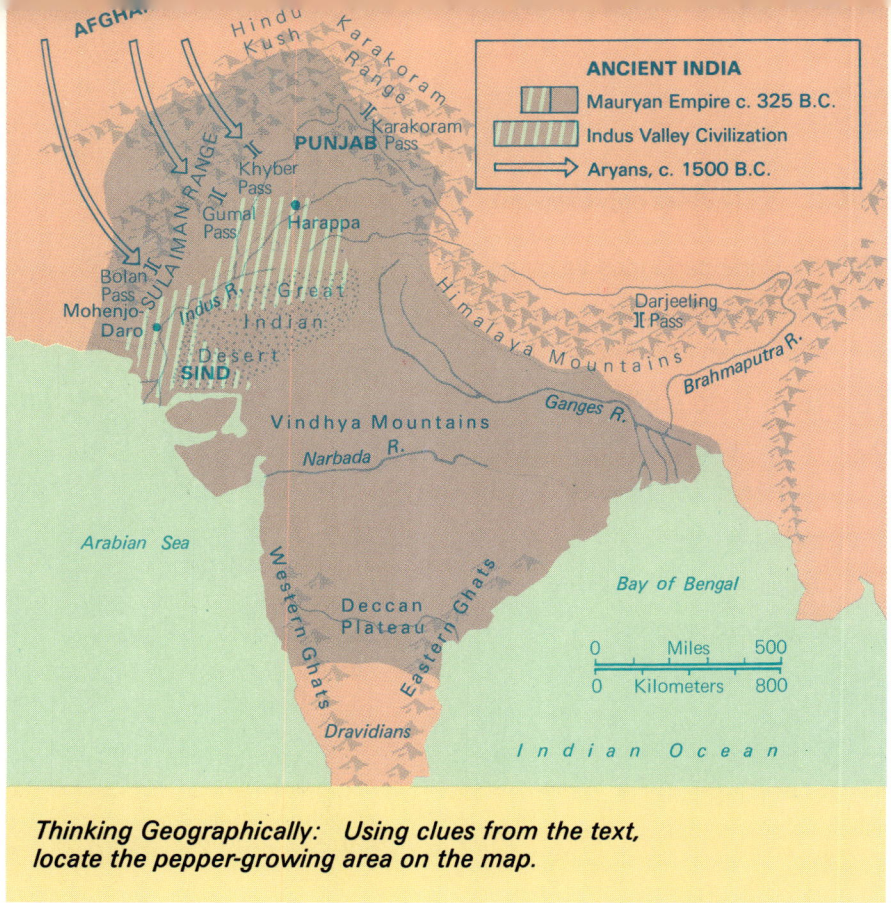

Thinking Geographically: Using clues from the text, locate the pepper-growing area on the map.

stretch fertile plains that are watered by two large river systems, both of which begin in the Himalayas. The river Ganges (GAN jeez), which flows south and east, forms a delta in the Bengal (ben GALL) area and empties into the Bay of Bengal. The Indus flows south and west through the Punjab (pun JAB) and Sind regions. It empties into the Arabian Sea. The only overland route to India was through two dangerous passes in the northwest through Afghanistan. Yet, over thousands of years, invaders from central and west Asia took the terrible journey to conquer India.

The physical features of the southern peninsula are dramatically different from those of the north. The southern area is a large plateau separated from the northern plains by the Vindhya (VIHN dyuh) Mountains. Deccan (DEK un), the name of the plateau, means "south." It is crisscrossed by several small rivers, which have divided the area into small wooded regions. This made travel and agriculture more difficult than in the north. The jungles and rain forest of the area supported only a thin population. The north had periods when it was unified into a large kingdom. The south was a region of small kingdoms that resisted being absorbed into a large political system. The narrow coastal strip in the west is the area where black pepper grows abundantly. It attracted ancient and medieval merchants, who came in search of this rare prize. The coast also had several natural harbors that were to make India an important link in the spice trade with Southeast Asia.

In modern India, bicyclists make their way against a monsoon rain.

The Monsoons During the winter months, the land mass of Asia is cold, and the air above becomes cold and heavy. The air falls, creating winds that blow outward. These winds, called winter *monsoons*, sweep across India and out toward the Indian Ocean. Because they come across land masses, they are dry winds and, therefore, bring little rain to India.

During the summer, it is a different story. The sun's rays heat up the land mass of Asia. The air over the land becomes warm and rises, drawing in wet air from over the oceans. This humid air drops its moisture in the form of life-giving rain over India.

Farming in India depends upon these summer monsoons. Ninety percent of India's rainfall occurs from May to October. When too much rain falls, farmers cannot work their fields. Seeds rot before they sprout, or dangerous floods sweep across farms, villages, and cities. When too little rain comes during the summer monsoon season, the land gets parched and does not grow crops. Plants wither in the fields, and famine is often the result.

It is not surprising, then, that water is important in Indian religious practices. Water is used to purify shrines, households, and worshipers themselves.

Early People The life of the prehistoric people who lived in the Indus Valley before the Harappan civilization is shrouded in mystery. The few pre-Harappan village sites excavated in the region suggest that these people had been hunters and gatherers who learned the principles of farming and herding over a long period of time. They also learned to make copper tools and wheel-made pottery. They lived in simple mud-brick huts and had domesticated sheep, goats, and oxen.

By 3000 B.C., these simple farmers lived throughout the area drained by the Indus and its tributaries. This area is bounded by the foothills of the Himalayas in the north and by the Arabian Sea coast in the south. It is almost twice as large as the settlement area along the Nile during the Old Kingdom and four times as large as Sumer in Mesopotamia.

Harappan Civilization Scholars estimate that sometime after 2500 B.C. the people of the Indus Valley had become civilized. They had progressed from a simple farming society to one with cities and an organized form of government. In addition to several small towns, two major cities developed in this area: Harappa (which has given its name to the civilization) in the Punjab, and Mohenjo-Daro in the Sind. The two cities appear to have been designed by the same group of architects, who preferred to build solid and practical structures rather than artistic ones. Both cities had a large *citadel*, or fort, enclosed by protective walls 12 meters (40 feet) thick and made of baked-clay bricks. These walls kept out invaders and floodwaters. In the citadel, the main structures were a large place with deep bathing pools, granaries to store surplus food, and a temple. Outside the citadel walls were the houses of the common people. (The population of Harappa is estimated to have been 35,000.) These were multistoried brick houses with rooms organized around an interior courtyard. Covered brick drains, better engineered than any others found in the ancient world until Roman times, were found inside homes and along streets. There were several public wells, and shops lined the main streets. The streets were in a tidy grid pattern running at right angles to each other. Every city block was the same size. The same standardization was found in the size of bricks, in the weights and measures used, and in house and street plans. This suggests that the government was strong and centralized.

The dominant way of life for the Indus people was still agricultural. The major food crops were wheat, barley, sesame, melons, dates, and peas. Cotton was cultivated, and the people had discovered how to spin yarn and how to weave and dye cloth. The use of cotton for clothing is one of India's contributions to world civilization. Even today, textiles is the leading industry in India. Herd animals included cattle, sheep, goats, water buffalo, and perhaps elephants. The Indus people were also one of the first to domesticate fowl into poultry. This made the Harappan diet rich and varied.

Artisans mass-produced wheel-turned pottery and worked with textiles, ivory, bone, and precious metals. Tools, such as saws, axes, swords, knives, and spearheads, were made from bronze. Several statues of men, women, and animals show a high level of artistic achievement. Thousands of soapstone seals, square or rectangular in shape and decorated with figures and writing, have also been discovered. The writing, however, has yet to be deciphered. When it is, we may learn a great deal more about the life and beliefs of these people. Harappan seals and other artifacts have also been found in Mesopotamia. This suggests that there was a lively commerce between the two peoples.

Government and Religion The crucial questions about the form of government and the religion of the people cannot be fully answered. The evidence points to a small ruling elite (of priests perhaps?) who controlled the artisans, metalsmiths, farmers, and street cleaners. There appears to have been widespread worship of a

This Mohenjo-Daro excavation shows a well in the foreground. A Buddhist stupa *(a cylindrical mound that serves as a shrine) is shown in the background.*

fertility goddess. It is also possible that the bull was considered sacred. Why this efficient government fell from power is also not clear. There is some evidence that prosperity declined, and there may have been a breakdown of the social order. Still, it is far more likely that the end was sudden and was caused by a natural disaster, such as a great flood.

Section Questions

1. Which mountains separate the Indian subcontinent from the rest of Asia? Which mountains separate northern India from southern India? What is the Deccan?
2. How do the monsoon winds affect farming in India?
3. What were the main occupations of the Indus Valley people in pre-Harappan times and after?
4. When did Harappan civilization develop? Why do scholars believe it was an empire and not just a series of city-states?
5. What evidence has been found that suggests that Harappan government was strong and centralized?

2. Invaders and Native Peoples Created a Lasting Culture

Sometime after 1800 B.C., a new group of people made their appearance in the Indus Valley. These were Indo-European peoples, or the Aryans. "Indo-European" is the name given to various tribes and clans that spoke similar languages. These languages include Greek, Latin, Celtic, German, Sanskrit, Hittite, and Iranian. The various Indo-European groups lived on the Russian steppes and on the plains of central Europe. From 3000 to about 1800 B.C., they migrated westward into Europe and southeast into Iran and northwestern India. Those Aryans who came to India have been called the Indo-Aryans, to distinguish them from those that went elsewhere. "Indo-Aryan," or "Aryan," refers to language and not race.

By 1300 B.C., the Indo-Aryans had migrated eastward in small groups until the entire plain of the Ganges was settled. This was to become the heartland of Hindu (hin doo) India. The Indo-Aryan era in Indian history is divided into the Vedic (VAY dik 1500 to 1000 B.C.) and Epic (1000 to 450 B.C.) ages. As a point of comparison, this time span of 1,000 years is five times as long as the history of the United States. It took 1,000 years to achieve a gradual synthesis of the way of life of the foreigners from southern Russia with that of the natives of India. This combination of traditions became the basis of early Indian culture.

The Vedic and Epic Ages Very little archaeological evidence has been unearthed for the Vedic Age. Our chief sources of knowledge for this age are the four Indo-Aryan *Vedas* (VAY duhz) or "books of knowledge," the most important of which is the *Rig-Veda* (RIGH VAY duh). The Vedas are a collection of thousands of sacred hymns. They are the oldest known examples of Indo-European literature. If we know about the Harappan people from the work of archaeologists, we owe to *linguists*, scientists who study language, our picture of Vedic times.

The Indo-Aryans were neither as civilized nor as technically advanced as the Harappans when they first came to India. They were a seminomadic people who settled in small villages. Their main wealth was in their cattle and horses. They lived in modest bamboo or wooden houses, since they did not know the art of firing bricks. They did not know how to build cities; so India had to reexperience the process of urbanization under the Aryans. The Aryans were a warlike people, with horse-drawn chariots, bows and arrows, and battle-axes. The Rig-Veda describes the Indo-Aryan conquest of the native people, the dark-skinned Dasas, a word which later came to mean "slave." There was frequent warfare among the different Aryan tribes as well. Disputes over the ownership of cattle, land, or pasture were settled by war.

Continuous wars led groups of tribes to band together. From among their chieftains, they elected a king and formed small kingdoms. As the tribes settled down, their occupations expanded from herding to raising crops. Their superior iron tools made it easier for them to clear forests and increase the land that could be farmed. Trade developed from the exchange of surplus food. By the time of the Epic Age, the Indo-Aryans had moved eastward to occupy the plains of the Ganges. Several market towns developed along the river. Trade appears to have remained within India. There is no convincing evidence of overseas trade.

Socially, the Indo-Aryans appear to have been an energetic people who loved music, song, and dance. They also gambled and drank a great deal. The games of dice and chess were invented in India. In one great epic poem which tells the story of feuding tribes, five princes gamble away not only their kingdom, but also their one shared and beloved wife. Gambling and music still make up an important part of the social life of village India today.

The Aryan age contributed a complex social organization to Indian culture. Two social institutions—the caste system and the joint family—became the foundations of Indian society. They exist to this day even though they have changed greatly over time.

The Caste System The *caste system*, the people's inherited class positions, slowly evolved from the traditional division of the Aryan tribes into warriors, priests, and commoners. According to the Rig-Veda, the Aryans were a "wheat-colored," or fair-

In modern India, two beggars of the lowest caste.

skinned people. Their migration to India brought them into contact with the dark-skinned Dasas, whom they conquered and enslaved. The Dasas were forced to perform all the menial tasks, such as tilling the earth and serving the ruling Aryans. They became a fourth category of people, but the division in this case was both occupational and racial. Of the Dasas, some were given jobs that were considered unclean and polluting—such as washing clothes, sweeping, disposing of garbage, and skinning dead animals for leather. This subgroup of Dasas were the untouchables of Indian society.

The Dasas were separated from the Aryans. The four main castes were Brahmans (BRAH munz), or priests; Kshatriyas (kuh SHAY tree yuhz), or warriors; Vaishyas (VISH yuhz), or traders, landowners, and

LEGACY OF ANCIENT INDIA

Social Institutions: caste system and the joint family

Belief Systems: Hinduism and Buddhism

Literature: The Vedas, thousands of hymns

Writing System: Harappan writing is still undeciphered

Government: Cities of Harappa and Mohenjo-Daro indicate a large, unified empire

hereditary groups. Individuals could not change caste; they were simply born into it. Each caste had several subgroups within it. For example, traders, carpenters, and landowners were distinct groups within the Vaishya caste. Thus, it was easy to absorb new groups that arrived in India and make them part of the society. Strict caste rules also evolved to preserve the system. Eating with members of other castes was forbidden and so was marriage.

The Brahmans and Kshatriyas were considered to be of equal rank in the early Vedic times. Later, the Brahmans made religious ritual more complicated. There was then a greater need for their knowledge, so their position rose. Over time, castes divided and subdivided so that Brahmans of one region were distinct from Brahmans of another. Today there are hundreds of subcastes within each main caste, and Hindu Indians identify themselves by their special subgroup rather than by caste.

The upper castes, particularly the warriors and priests, made the laws, interpreted the Vedas, and kept other groups in line. The Sudras lived in a segregated part of the village. Criminals were punished for a crime according to the social rank of their caste. Brahmans got off lightly for wrongdoing.

The Joint Family The other pillar of Aryan society was the joint family. As in any premodern society, the family was the basic unit of the social structure. Several families, tracing their descent from a common ancestor, made up a village. Several villages constituted a tribe. Just as the tribe was ruled by its chief, the family was ruled by the eldest male, or the *patriarch*. The family was comprised of descendants traced through the male line. The joint family included three or more generations. Typically, a grandfather lived in the same house and shared the food from the same hearth with his sons and grandsons. When the eldest male died, the authority of managing the family passed on to his eldest son. However, the property was divided equally among all the sons and remained within the family. In time, these males would set up their own joint families with their own sons and grandsons. Thus, the extended family was also the property-owning unit.

Male children were highly prized as they could bring honor to their family and their tribe. The position of women in a partriarchal society was a subordinate one. Women were born into the subcaste of their father. After marriage they were considered members of their husband's subcaste. The women did not inherit property. A father had to give the husband's family a *dowry*, or gift of currency or goods, when his daughter married. But even over this wealth, the woman had little control. Women were also not allowed to take part in sacrifices to the gods. They had to limit their religious role to performing simple rituals at home or making offerings in the temple. Even so, women were more privileged than they were to be in later times. There was, at least, no *polygyny*, a practice by which a man can have more than one wife. There were no child marriages, and widows were permitted to remarry. Child marriage, polygyny, and the ban on widow remarriage were probably pre-Aryan customs that came back into use as time went on.

Section Questions

1. What kind of people were the Indo-Aryans? How did they live?
2. What two institutions were firmly established during the Indo-Aryan era?
3. Which were the ruling castes, and what were their functions? Who were the Sudras, and what were their functions?
4. Who was a patriarch? Whom did he control?

3. Two Great Religions Were Born in Ancient India

We know more about the religious than the social features of the Vedic and Epic ages. Our knowledge of this 1,000-year period is based on several religious texts. The religion we call Hinduism today is a complex system of many schools of thought. The Hindus believed in several gods, whose importance rose and declined over the centuries. It is more a way of life than a religion. Hinduism did not have an organized church like the Roman Catholic Church. The Hindus also had no single text, like the Bible. The religion had no prophet, like Moses. It evolved over the centuries from Indo-Aryan and pre-Aryan ideas. Hinduism came in contact with Islam and Christianity when the Muslims and Europeans invaded India. But it was not wiped out by these religions. Hinduism proved flexible, so its gods have been worshipped continuously for over 4,000 years.

The Making of Hinduism When the Aryans arrived in India, they spoke an Indo-European language. This developed into Sanskrit (SAHN skrit). But they did not know how to write. How and when they developed an alphabet is not known for sure. However, we do know that the system of writing evolved from early business notations. A form of that writing is still used today in both Sanskrit and modern Hindi. The thousands of sacred hymns in the Vedas were passed down from father to son in Brahman families by word of mouth for hundreds of years. Great pains were taken to preserve each verse exactly. The priests memorized each line and each word backward and forward. A priest child could often perform these incredible feats of memory by age five. It was the world's toughest oral tradition. Even today, Hindu priests are judged by how many Vedas they know by heart.

By 600 B.C., Sanskrit had a written literature. The Rig-Veda ("hymns of knowledge") was the most important. It had 1,028 hymns of praise to at least thirty-three gods and to nature. The practice of

This text shows the development of Sanskrit.

TEXT AS IT READS IN THE ORIGINAL

एरस (बेरस इति वा) मद्दाराजस कलिंगाधिपतिनो महामेघवाहनस कदंप-
सीरीनो (कूदेव-सिरिनो इति वा) लेणं [१]

TEXT AS IT READS IN PĀLI

अयिरसस (बौरसस इति वा) मद्दाराजसस कलिंगाधिपतिनो महामेघ-
वाहनसस कदम्ब-सिरिनो (कूदेव-सिरिनो इति वा) लेणं [१]

TEXT AS IT READS IN SANSKRIT

आर्यस्य (बौरस्य इति वा) महाराजस्य कलिंगाधिपतेर्महामेघवाहनस्य
श्री-कदम्बस्य (श्री-कुदेवस्य इति वा) लयनं [१]

TRANSLATION

The cave (which is an excavation) of His Lordly Graceful Majesty Kadampa or Kudepa, the Great King, the Sovran Lord of Kalinga, whose vehicle is Mahāmegha (the great cloud-like state-elephant).

Did You Know?

How the Cow Came to Be Sacred

In early Vedic times, cows were slaughtered for special feasts, and beef was enjoyed even by Brahmans. Yet today, in most states in India, there is a total ban on cow slaughter. What brought about this change in the status of the cow? While the Indo-Aryans were still a herding and seminomadic people, the cow was one of their chief sources of food. It produced milk. Beef was eaten on special feasts. Bullocks were used in battle. Cattle also constituted the wealth of the tribe.

The cow came to be regarded as a mother, or *go mata* (cow mother), for two reasons. Not only was cow's milk given to children, but the cow was seen as the mother, or producer, of bullocks. Milk also had other uses. The most sacred of these was the conversion of butter into *ghee* (clarified butter), which was used in all rituals and sacrifices. But the cow's role as a producer of indispensable work bullocks brought her a very special esteem.

As forests were cleared away, cow dung became a main source of fuel. Dung was made into cakes. The dried cakes were later burned for both cooking and heating purposes. Dung was also a rich fertilizer for the crops. It served as cement for building mud huts.

After the animal died, it provided leather, hooves, and horns, which were used to make all kinds of ordinary goods such as clothes, sandals, and tools. To top it all, cows managed to graze on grass and other foods that were not consumed by humans. They cost little for upkeep.

The cows and bullocks supplied food and energy. They supplied cooking, cleaning, and building materials as well as clothing, shoes, and tools. In other words, common sense began to dictate that cows should not be killed for food since they provided so many of the needs of preindustrial people. To this was added the Hindu and Buddhist beliefs in the sanctity of all living things and, perhaps, a pre-Harappan veneration of the bull. When Krishna (KRISH nuh), the cowherd, became a deity in the Epic Age, the sacredness of the cow was reinforced, and beef became strictly forbidden. It was only eaten by the lower castes and people who did not consider themselves Hindus.

A decorated bullock.

Bathers in the River Ganges.

religion, at this early stage, centered around offering animal and food sacrifices to the gods. Pre-Aryan beliefs in a fertility goddess, in the holiness of life, and in sacred trees were absorbed. They formed the beginnings of Hinduism.

The Vedic gods were really like humans with magical powers. The great Indra was a handsome, hard-drinking, warrior-king god. There was a sun god and a moon god. The wind had a divine aspect; so had water. When the Aryans moved eastward, the River Ganges became a goddess. Her waters could cleanse sins. Great myths about these colorful gods were preserved in the literature of the Epic Age.

As the power of the Brahmans grew, the rituals and religious literature became more complex. A more questioning mood exists in the later parts of the Rig-Veda. For example, in earlier poems the creation of the world is described as a specific act of the gods. Later, it is discussed as a mysterious event.

Underlying the web of gods, ritual, and caste was the core of the Hindu "way of life." That was, basically, that all living things in the universe had a universal spirit in them. In other words, everything had a soul, or self, or *brahman*. This belief influenced the way Hindus regarded people of other religions, since everyone was part of the same universal soul. It also made lesser forms of life, especially animals, respected. It was a virtue to eat no animals.

The belief in the eternal, universal spirit, or brahman, led to the belief that the individual soul does not end after death. Instead it is reborn as something else. The position of the soul after rebirth, or its *reincarnation*, was determined by the actions of the previous owner of that soul. A man who had not lived by the laws of his caste and society, that is, had not lived by his *dharma*, would force his soul to be reborn as an untouchable, a dog, or even a stone. On the other hand, a man who kept strictly to his dharma would liberate his soul from the chain of rebirths. The Hindus tried to attain *moksha*, or freedom from rebirth. After liberation, the individual became part of the universal spirit. Women could only achieve moksha by being reincarnated as men first. Since moksha was so desirable, men began to discipline their bodies and minds. This art of self-discipline was called *yoga*.

Cremation, or burning the bodies, was the Indian way of disposing of the dead. Because of this, we do not have information about India such as that discovered in the royal tombs of Egypt.

The Buddhist Way By 500 B.C., two Kshatriya princes challenged the social and religious order. One of them founded the Jain (JIN) religion. Jain had only a small following. The more notable prince was Siddhartha Gautama (sihd HAR thuh GAHW tu mu). He later became the Buddha (BOO duh), or the "Enlightened One," and founded Buddhism. Born in 563 B.C. to royal Hindu parents, Gautama was brought up in the palace. He had a beautiful wife and son and spent his days in comfort.

However, all this changed suddenly. One day he decided to go out to see how the commoners lived. What he saw shocked him. He saw an old man starving to death. Another had a terrible disease. Then he saw a corpse. Finally, he saw a man in deep thought who looked as if he had mastered suffering. All these experiences troubled the young Gautama.

At age twenty-nine, Gautama went to the forest to think about the cause of human suffering. He spent the next six years with other holy men. He fasted, suffered self-torture, and meditated. He practiced yoga. But he remained troubled. So, Gautama decided to meditate only, alone under a sacred fig tree.

After fifty-nine days of constant meditation, the truth dawned on him. The root of suffering, he said, was human desire. Human desire for success, wealth, and power bound people to various kinds of pain. Ignorance about the cause of suffering kept humans from gaining liberation, or *nirvana* (nier VAHN uh). Nirvana could be achieved by following the Eight-Fold Path: right belief, resolve, speech, action, living, effort, thinking, and meditation. Deep meditation would define what was right for those who sincerely wanted to do right. Buddha rejected the caste system and its dharma. He rejected the Vedas and the required rituals and sacrifices. Buddha made people masters of their own fate. He kept the Hindu belief in reincarnation and stressed the need for nirvana (literally, "to blow out a candle").

A figure of Buddha from the Kanheri Caves in India.

Buddha spent many years teaching this new world view. He organized an order of monks, who spread his message. The monks and, later, nuns, took three vows: poverty, chastity, and total nonviolence. They lived in secluded monasteries and prepared themselves for nirvana. When their self-discipline was firm, they set out to preach. These Buddhist missionaries went barefoot, clothed in saffron-colored robes, with begging bowl and staff in hand to spread the message. By the time of Buddha's death in 483 B.C., his teachings had spread over northern and central India. For many centuries, Buddhism remained the dominant religion in much of India. However, by the year A.D. 1000, it was displaced by the revival of Brahmanic traditions, which were now heavily influenced by Buddhism. Buddhism was more permanent in southeast and eastern Asia. It traveled to the north and spread throughout Nepal (nu PAHL), Tibet, China, Japan, and Korea. It also traveled to south India and then to Sri Lanka (SREE LANG kuh), Vietnam, and Cambodia. India, the home of Buddha, became a place of pilgrimage for Buddhist monks.

Buddha did not write down his teachings. That task fell to his followers. The books of his teachings rank among the world's finest examples of rational thought.

Section Questions

1. Why do we know more about the religious aspects of life during the Indo-Aryan era than we do about the social or political aspects?
2. How were the Vedas preserved before the development of writing?
3. What was the brahman? How did it influence other Hindu attitudes and beliefs?
4. What caste did Gautama belong to? Why did he make such a radical change in his life?
5. How and where did Buddhism spread?

Chapter Summary

1. India is a kite-shaped area surrounded on two sides by water and on the north by the mighty Himalaya Mountains. There are mountains to the far north. River valleys with fertile plains stretch out below. There is a large plateau covered with forests and smaller rivers in the south. Its fertile soil, minerals, and spices made ancient India one of the world's richest regions.

Sometime after 2500 B.C., a large urban kingdom existed in the Indus Valley and modern-day Pakistan. The two main cities were Mohenjo-Daro and Harappa. The Harappan peoples were technologically and artistically advanced and had a thriving trade with Mesopotamia. Their writing system has not been deciphered. Many questions about this civilization remain unanswered.

2. Sometime around 1800 B.C., India was invaded by the Sanskrit-speaking Indo-Aryan tribes from southern Russia. They were a seminomadic people with superior warlike skills. They conquered and enslaved the native Dasas. They settled in small villages, rediscovering the process of agriculture, writing, and, eventually, city building.

They organized their society into a caste system. Priests and warriors had much greater status than the commoners. The ethnically different Dasas made up a fourth group. These divisions developed into the four-caste, hereditary system. The family was patriarchal and consisted of as many as three generations that held property jointly.

3. The four Vedas are the oldest collection of traditional beliefs. They contain hymns of praise to the gods and instructions for rituals performed by the Indo-Aryans. The chief beliefs of the Hindus centered on a universal spirit of which everything and everybody was a part. They believed that after death the individual soul was reincarnated in some other form. The object of life was to liberate one's soul from the chain of rebirths. Buddha rebelled against the caste system and the complicated rituals of the Vedas and founded a new religion. He claimed that desire was the root of human misery and the extinction of desire was the way to happiness. He founded a disciplined order of missionaries that preached his way.

Chapter 4 Review

Check Your Facts

1. Identify the following:
   a. Sanskrit
   b. Vedas
   c. dharma
   d. Mohenjo-Daro
   e. Siddhartha Gautama
   f. reincarnation
2. What two large river systems run through northern India? In which system did the first Indian civilization develop?
3. What were some of the important crops and domesticated animals of Harappan peoples?
4. Who were the Indo-Aryans? Where did they come from? Who were the Dasas?
5. Describe the joint family in ancient India. Explain how it was the property-owning unit.
6. What were the four main castes in ancient Indian society? What did each consist of?
7. What were the main beliefs of Hinduism?
8. What was Buddha's view of the world? How was one to avoid pain and suffering?

Words to Know

Write a paragraph discussing the role of women during the Indo-Aryan age. In your paragraph, use the terms *patriarch*, *dowry*, and *polygyny*.

Developing Your Skills

1. Draw a kite similar in shape to the map of India. On this "map" label the following:
   a. Indus and Ganges rivers
   b. Deccan Plateau
   c. rain forest area
   d. Afghanistan
   e. Himalaya Mountains
   f. Arabian Sea
2. Now examine your map and explain the difference between the north and the south of India. How did these differences affect early Indian history?
3. In which of these time periods—2500-2000 B.C., 2000-1000 B.C., or 1000-400 B.C.—did each of the following occur?
   a. Vedas are composed.
   b. Buddha is born.
   c. Indo-Aryans invade northern India.
   d. Harappan civilization flourishes.
   e. Written Sanskrit develops.

Thinking It Over

1. Why do we say that the Harrapan people of the Indus Valley were civilized? What had they achieved?
2. How does the Hindu belief in reincarnation give strength to the caste system in Indian society?
3. Would it be proper to refer to Hinduism as a religion? Why or why not?
4. Would it be proper to refer to Buddhism as a religion? Why or why not?
5. How are the concepts of moksha in Hinduism and nirvana in Buddhism similar and different?

Special Activities

1. Find a magazine or newspaper article dealing with life in India today. After reading the selection, list the economic, social, and religious patterns that had their beginnings before 400 B.C., or roughly the period covered by this chapter.
2. Learn about the ways in which the plains Indians of North America used the buffalo before the buffalo were almost all destroyed. Compare this to the uses of the cow during the Indo-Aryan era in India.

Workers excavating statues from Qin Shi Huang's burial ground.

Chapter 5 Ancient China

In the spring of 1974, peasant workers in the Yan Zai commune in the People's Republic of China made a startling discovery. Digging the reddish soil of the Huang He (Yellow) River Valley, they found a life-sized pottery statue of an ancient Chinese warrior. This 6-foot figure was dressed in full battle array.

Further excavations revealed an underground vault containing 6,000 life-sized figures—soldiers, servants, footmen, and attendants. No two people looked alike. Each of the faces seemed to be modeled after a different person. As the digging continued, they found pottery models of horses and chariots, jade, gold, linen, and silk.

The workers had uncovered the tomb of Qin Shi Huang (Shi Huang Ti), the first emperor of China. During his short fifteen-year reign, this strong leader brought the several states in China under one central rule.

50,000-202 B.C. (early dates approximate)

50,000	Stone Age settlements
10,000	Painted pottery
4000	Agricultural communities
2200	Xia dynasty begins
1766-1122	Shang dynasty
1122-256	Zhou dynasty
1122	Feudal states increased
551	Birth of Confucius
403-221	Period of the Warring States
221-207	Qin dynasty
221	China achieves unity
202	Han dynasty begins

This bronze of an acrobat with a balancing bear is from the Zhou dynasty, about 600-500 B.C.

Qin Shi Huang planned his extravagant burial dwellings when he became emperor. In earlier times, rulers buried live warriors, wives, servants, and animals with them for pleasure and protection in the afterlife. Qin Shi Huang's life-sized statues were symbols of or stand-ins for the living.

For thirty-six years, over half a million people dug the underground tomb. They built models of palaces, cities, and geographical features. They reproduced China's rivers in quicksilver. By a mechanical device, the rivers flowed. Artisans decorated the palaces with gold and jade.

When Qin Shi Huang died, the tomb was ready. His body was placed in the magnificent underground vault along with his protectors. The great jade door was sealed. Nothing was disturbed for 2,100 years.

What kind of civilization could afford such an extraordinary tomb? A civilization that has had the longest continuous history of any in the world. The civilization that engineered the architectural triumph of the Great Wall. The same civilization that gave the world the great philosophies of Confucianism (kun FYOO shun ihzm) and Taoism (DAHU ih zum).

1. Unity Was Achieved in China

Of the civilizations that began in ancient times, China's was the most isolated. Cut off from other parts of the world, it developed without the influence of other great civilizations.

China is bordered on the east by the broad Pacific Ocean and on the north by the immense Gobi (GO bee) Desert.

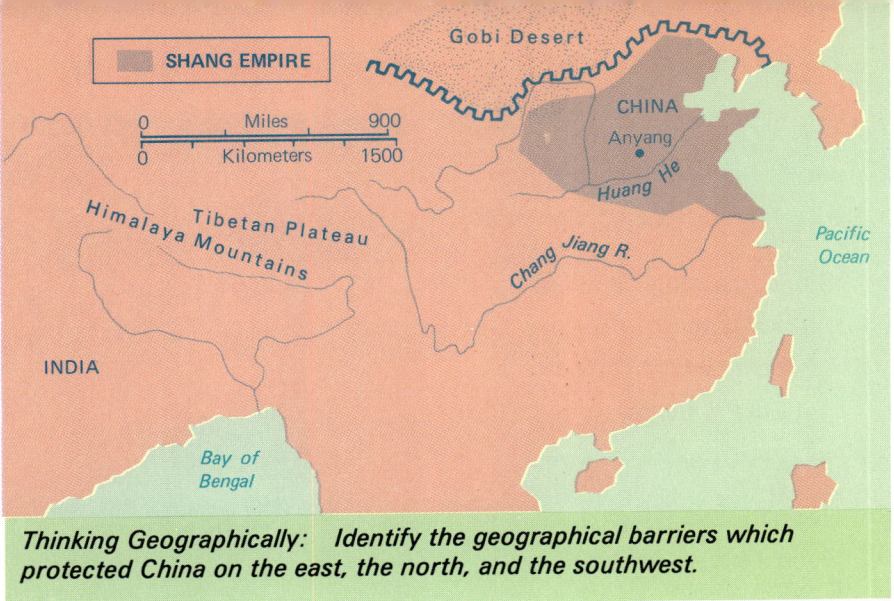

Thinking Geographically: Identify the geographical barriers which protected China on the east, the north, and the southwest.

PINYIN SPELLING

Since 1979, China has used the Pinyin system of spelling Chinese words and names. This system is a phonetic spelling based on Peking (or, rather, Beijing) pronunciations. The Pinyin system is now the world's standard. This book uses Pinyin spellings, with three exceptions. We use the old spellings for Peking, Sun Yat-sen, and Chiang Kai-Shek.

The first time a Pinyin spelling is used, the old spelling is shown in parentheses.

Southwest are the Himalaya Mountains and the Tibetan plateau. To the south are jungles, which for centuries seemed impenetrable to invaders.

The Land Within the vast land that is China, a crisscross of mountain ranges and rivers forms separate geographical regions—the main ones being the north and the south. Beginning in the high mountain ranges of the northwest, the Huang He River starts its 4,700-kilometer (2,900-mile) journey. Moving south, it picks up a heavy deposit of yellow silt, called *loess* (LES). Near the dry Gobi Desert, these rich mineral deposits have given life to people for centuries. But the Huang He River is also called China's Sorrow because it brought tragedy to millions. In the spring, when the mountain snows melted, China's Sorrow flooded hundreds of square kilometers. The floods made cultivation impossible for years after, and millions died from starvation. Only since 1949 has this problem begun to be conquered.

South China is watered in its northern parts by the enormous Chang Jiang (Yangtze) River. Many of its shorter rivers come together at what now is the city of Guangzhou (Canton). Here in southeast China, heavy rainfalls enable farmers to produce two crops a year.

The rivers in China were critical to its development. They provided water for irrigation and transportation. The loess of the Huang He, like the black soil of the Nile, provided a fertile land for farming.

A white pottery tripod jug from around 2000 B.C.

Early People At Zhoukoudian (Choukoutien), in northern China, archaeologists have excavated one of the earliest known sites of Homo erectus. There they found teeth and bones of at least forty men, women, and children. These primitive people have been named Peking man. They lived about 500,000 years ago.

Chinese agricultural communities began about 6000 B.C. in the Huang He Valley. These early farmers planted millet and other grains. They fished and raised pigs, dogs, and sheep. According to tradition, China had a series of wise rulers until the great ruler, Yu, founded the Xia (Hsia) dynasty about 2200 B.C. This dynasty is said to have lasted for about 400 years. So far, the legend of the Xia dynasty has not been confirmed. The next dynasty—the Shang (1766 to 1122 B.C.)—has been substantiated by many archaeological sites. By this time, two of the civilization's great achievements had appeared—bronze and writing.

Life Under the Shang The power of the Shang state was strong only around the capital city, Anyang. Though people spoke a common language and shared a way of life, they felt no unity as a nation. China during this period was a feudal state.

In the political system of *feudalism*, a country usually lacks a strong central government. Power is shared by many nobles. Each noble controls land that is worked by *vassals*. Vassals are servants who owe their allegiance to the noble.

The Shang rulers depended on the local feudal lords to control their areas. The local lords obliged until it interfered with their personal ambitions.

The Shang rulers failed to unify the country, but they did develop an advanced civilization. Among China's oldest and most beautiful artifacts are finely engraved bronze ceremonial containers created by Shang artisans. Archaeologists have found many writings on oracle bones. These bones from turtles or cattle were used in *divination ceremonies*. Questions were written on the bones. The soothsayer applied heat near a thin spot on the bone. When the bone cracked from the heat, the soothsayer read the god's "reply" from patterns in the cracks. The complex writings on these bones is close enough to modern Chinese for trained scholars to read many of them today.

People looked to Heaven to supply rain and fertile soil. The Shang rulers were the only intermediaries to the gods, so they were regarded as priests. A separate class of priests never became important in China as it did in Egypt, Sumer, and India.

The Shang rulers also offered sacrifices to their dead relatives. They believed that, after a person died, the spirit lived on to guide and protect his or her descendants. In times of trouble, the royal family communicated with its ancestors for guidance. Nobles and peasants began to copy these practices. Ancestor worship became an integral part of Chinese religion and culture.

On special occasions, such as a ruler's funeral, people were sacrificed to the dead as an offering of goodwill. Usually the victims were slaves or prisoners of war.

The Shang rulers never controlled the constant warfare among the nobles. Because of this, their power gradually weakened. In 1122 B.C., a neighboring state, Zhou (Chou), overthrew the Shang dynasty.

The Zhou Dynasty The Zhou rulers wanted continuity with the old regime and the cooperation of their new subjects. Their first step was to explain why there had been a change in leadership.

In a series of proclamations they stated that Heaven decreed certain people to be rulers of certain parts of the world. Heaven gave rulers a Mandate of Heaven, as long as they ruled with wisdom, justice, and honor. Shang rulers had proved cruel and wicked. Thus, Heaven took away their mandate and gave it to the Zhou rulers. The Zhou kings, called sons of Heaven, would keep this heavenly mandate as long as they ruled wisely. In later times, it was argued that natural disasters, such as earthquakes, were signals from Heaven that the current rulers were bad and that Heaven was taking away their mandate.

To further continuity, some Shang officials were kept in government service. Shang descendants were given the small state of Sun to guarantee them enough wealth for their costly ancestral practices. The Zhou rewarded their allies, nomadic people to the north, and their relatives by giving them land also. This strategy divided China even more. Now hundreds of feudal states, or *fiefs*, competed for land and power. Each fief consisted of a walled town or city surrounded by cultivated land.

The Zhou dynasty lasted longer than any government in China's history (1122 to 221 B.C.). Though its last centuries were dominated by constant warfare, its reign was also marked by great achievements. During these 800 years, the great philosophies of Confucianism, Taoism, and legalism appeared. Science and technology advanced. Farmers expanded cultivation to include two new grain crops: sorghum and buckwheat. Eventually, however, the lack of a unified country destroyed the dynasty.

In 771 B.C., several feudal lords stormed the royal palace and murdered the Zhou ruler. A new Zhou king set up court in another city. Though he and his descendants ruled for the next 500 years, they were *figureheads*, rulers in name only. By 403 B.C., the Period of the Warring States had begun. This was a period of constant warfare between the states and invasions of nomadic tribes from the north.

A bronze covered caldron from the late Zhou dynasty.

70

The Great Wall of China. Note how many people can walk side by side comfortably.

The Qin The Period of Warring States finally came to a close when the ruler of the state of Qin (Ch'in) assumed power in 221 B.C. The founder of the Qin dynasty called himself Qin Shi Huang, or first emperor. These words had only been used for gods and legendary rulers. Qin Shi Huang assumed absolute power. His subjects followed his edicts or were cruelly punished. He divided his empire into districts that were under direct control of a central government. He standardized measurements and money throughout the kingdom. To improve communication and trade, he had a network of roads built from his capital to the outlying regions.

Not content with the size of his kingdom, Qin Shi Huang sent his powerful army south to conquer the people near modern-day Guangzhou (Canton).

Several small walls had been built in earlier times. Now they were completed and connected. For fourteen years, more than one million workers built the Great Wall. The wall climbed over mountains, descended into the deepest gorges, and crossed over China's great rivers and valleys. It was 2,200 kilometers (1,400 miles) long, 5 meters (15 feet) wide at the base and 9 meters (30 feet) tall. This mammoth structure is one of the world's great architectural and engineering achievements.

In Qin Shi Huang's short reign, China was successfully unified. From his kingdom's name, the Qin, is derived the name China.

Qin Shi Huang expected his dynasty to last 10,000 generations. However, after his death, his son succeeded him and was assassinated within three years. Another civil war broke out, and in 207 B.C. a powerful noble, Liu Bang, became emperor. Liu Bang founded the Han dynasty, which ruled China for the next four centuries.

Section Questions

1. What physical barriers isolated China from the outside world? How did this affect China?
2. How did the Huang He River bring life? How did the Huang He River bring death?
3. Why did feudalism make it impossible to have a unified China?
4. What was the Mandate of Heaven? Why did the Zhou rulers claim this mandate?
5. What did Emperor Qin Shi Huang do to restore order and unify his empire?

2. The Chinese Produced Three Great Philosophies

The Period of the Warring States (403 to 221 B.C.) was a painful time. As a result, many philosophers were determined to find a way to transform this violence and conflict into peace and stability. Out of this situation came a man whose ideas would dominate Chinese culture for 2,000 years.

Confucianism The Chinese called him K'ung Fu Tzu meaning Master K'ung. We know him as Confucius (kun FU shes 551 to 479 B.C.).

Confucius was born in northern China in the state of Lu. Despite his father's early death, he managed to educate himself for political life. He became a scholar and adviser to a feudal lord in his state. As a statesperson, he hoped to put his ideas for reform into practice. When he realized that his influence was minimal, he left his job. Then he founded the first private school in China. He hoped to teach his ideas to young people, who would then put them into practice when they entered government service. His students numbered 3,000, and his reputation as a great teacher grew. However, in his own lifetime, his ideas received little notice.

Confucius believed that each person must adopt the ideal of *jen*, or humanity. Without virtue, there could be no hope of reforming the state. People must practice goodness and extend respect to others. In the *Analects*, a collection of short conversations between Confucius and his followers, his disciple Zi Zhang (Tzu Chang) asked him about jen.

"To be able to practice five virtues everywhere in the world constitutes humanity...courtesy, generosity, good faith, hard work, and kindness. He who is courteous is not humiliated, he who is generous wins the multitude, he who is of good faith is trusted by the people, he who is hard working attains his objective, and he who is kind can get service from the people."

Confucius looked to history for models to imitate, for rulers who represented goodness and humanity. He praised the early rulers of the Zhou dynasty who were able to control the feudal lords and who created solemn rites and music for people to follow.

Confucius saw these rites, or *li*, as visible expressions of wisdom and goodness. They were codes of behavior that represented harmony and order. The ideal ruler would combine the practice of li with the morality of jen. Virtuous and educated, this ruler would set high standards that everyone would follow. There would be no need for force. The ruler would use moral persuasion to achieve order.

Three hundred years after his death, the ideas of Confucius became the official doctrine of the state. All future government workers prepared for service by mastering his teachings.

Legalism Another philosophy, legalism, offered a different solution to the painful chaos of the times. Legalists rejected the Confucian ideal of jen. They said that such ideals had no practical value in political life.

"When little children play house together, they use dirt for rice, mud for soup, and bits of wood for slices of meat. But when sundown comes they all have to go home to eat supper. Dirt rice and mud soup are all right to play with, but they are no good to eat. Those who preach and praise the ways of the past do so with fine words but little sincerity. They can talk about the goodness and righteousness of the former kings but they cannot put the country on its feet again. Their doctrines are all right to play with too, but they cannot be used in governing."

This bas-relief from the Han dynasty shows the dipper part of the Big Dipper. It also expresses yin and yang through its emphasis on light and dark.

The legalists said that rulers could not rule by moral example, for people could not be trusted to be good. A ruler must derive power from strict laws and force. The ruler rewards those who conform and punishes those who do not. People's lives would be shaped by the interests of the state.

Under the reign of the Qin emperor, Qin Shi Huang, the legalists successfully put their ideas into practice. Qin Shi Huang's well-disciplined army triumphed over the remaining warring states. Scorning and fearing the ideas of the past, the emperor ordered the writings of Confucius and other thinkers burned. Scholars went into hiding, hoping to preserve these valuable works. In 207 B.C., when the Qin dynasty was overthrown, the Hans revived Confucianism and the other teachings.

Taoism   A third great philosophy flourished during the turbulent Period of the Warring States. It was called Taoism. This philosophy was very different from the moral and social teachings of Confucianism and from the harsh legal codes of legalism.

Taoism comes from the word "Tao," which means "the way."

"The great Tao flows everywhere:
It can go left; it can go right.
It blunts all sharpness,
It unties all tangles;
It is in harmony with all light.
It is one with all dust.
Deep and clear it seems forever to remain."

In this mystical philosophy, the individual is important. The individual seeks harmony with the universe, renouncing all artificial connections. Taoists saw government as out of harmony with nature for it created artificial ties.

Even when Confucianism became the official doctrine of the state, Taoism remained very popular. Its writings were vivid and poetic while the Confucian classics were often dull and moralistic in tone. Taoism also flourished because it

This drawing symbolizes yin and yang. Can you tell why?

suited another popular Chinese idea, the concept of *yin* and *yang*.

Chinese thinkers said that nature had a dual pattern. All actions in the universe could be explained by the interplay of yin and yang. Yin is female, dark, cold, and passive. Yang is male, light, hot, and active. Yin and yang are opposites that are not in conflict. They are complementary and exist side by side in all nature. We could not have light without darkness, big without small, or man without woman. We cannot appreciate life without appreciating death.

One might say Confucianism is the yang of Chinese thought and Taoism is the yin. The Chinese allowed room for both ideas in the universe.

Section Questions

1. Why did Confucius want to become a scholar? Why did he become a teacher?
2. How would Confucius' ruler maintain order?
3. What is jen? What is li?
4. How would a legalist ruler maintain order?
5. How was Taoism different from Confucianism and legalism?
6. How does the concept of yin and yang permit Confucianism and Taoism to exist at the same time?

3. China Created Lasting Patterns of Living

The Chinese civilization developed much later than those of Egypt, Mesopotamia, and the Indus Valley. By the end of the Qin dynasty in 207 B.C., however, the Chinese had made extraordinary gains. They had established political, social, and economic patterns that would serve China well for the next 2,000 years.

The Middle Kingdom The reforms of the Qin dynasty gave China a centralized government capable of better serving the needs of its people. Qin Shi Huang had broken up the feudal states and forced the nobles to live at his palace. Because they lost touch with their subjects, they gradually lost power. In this way, feudalism was destroyed in China several hundred years before it even began in Western Europe. In place of the nobles, the *scholar-officials* came to power. These were men, like Confucius, who had been trained in the principles of government. They knew how to keep careful records and how to apply the lessons of history to current problems. As advisers to the emperors, the scholar-officials were able to make China more modern.

Scholar-officials also helped standardize writing. This was an important contribution toward the unification of China. To make communication easier, scholars gradually developed common Chinese written symbols. By 500 B.C., an educated Chinese in one part of China could read a message sent from a person in another region. As before, people still spoke different dialects, but they read the same language.

As their government became more complex, the Chinese became more convinced of their own importance. They called their country Zhongguo (Chung-Kuo), or the Middle Kingdom. Because they were isolated, the Chinese saw themselves as the

Did You Know?

Chinese Pictographs

Chinese writing is pictographic. It works on the same principle as Egyptian hieroglyphics. Each Chinese *pictograph*, or character, represents an object or an idea, roughly the equivalent of an English word.

During the Zhou dynasty, the title "wang," or king, was used only for the supreme Zhou ruler. The pictograph describes his role. Three horizontal lines, called strokes, are written one under the

―

means one

other. When joined by a vertical stroke, "the king," they represent Heaven, Earth, and humanity.

=
means two

≡
means three

About 22 B.C., the word "huang" was used to designate the Qin emperor as the first and sole ruler of the empire. The symbol for antiquity, 曰 , was placed on top of the symbol for the king. The pictograph tells the story again. Huang possesses the greatness and wisdom of the famous ancient rulers.

When symbols are combined to produce ideas, they are called *ideographs.* The ideographs are logical and often picturesque.

In ancient times, this ideograph meant "what is good." The larger character on the left represents a woman, a wife. The

smaller symbol represents children. In China, the family was the most important social unit. "What is good" is a woman who perpetuates the family by having children.

The Chinese writing system is more difficult to master than the English phonetic system. Some characters require two strokes, and some require thirty or thirty-five. People must memorize 3,000 characters before they can read even the simplest material. In recent years, many of the commonly used characters have been simplified so that more people will learn to read.

The Chinese characters have a vitality missing from the phonetic systems. How graphic and appropriate is the character for "bright." It combines the characters for sun and moon.

King   Emperor

center of the world, surrounded by *barbarians*, or inferior foreigners. It was their destiny, they thought, to conquer the barbarians and absorb them into Chinese civilization. Therefore, the Chinese were slow to learn from other civilizations when they finally did come in contact with them.

Chinese Society The changes in government caused shifts in social structure. The emperors and their scholar-officials became recognized as the elite of Chinese society. Both groups were highly respected for their learning and their desire to serve the people. Their sincerity in running a good government was encouraged by the Mandate of Heaven. Any major failures would be seen as a justification of rebellion and the establishment of a new government.

The second level of society was that of the peasant farmers. They were generally poor and overworked. However, the farmers were respected because Chinese civilization depended upon the food that they provided. China has always prided itself on its agricultural productivity.

The lowest social level was occupied by the artisans and merchants. These groups became increasingly important. Still, they were looked down upon because they were considered unproductive.

At each of these levels, the family was the basic social unit. Other aspects of Chinese civilization have changed considerably since the Shang. But the family remained almost the same right up to modern times.

As in India, the Chinese family regulated and protected the lives of its individual members. Sometimes as many as five generations lived under one roof. Each family was expected to provide proper upbringing for its children and to keep them out of trouble. If one member committed a serious crime, the entire family could be enslaved or even killed.

Filial piety, the loyalty and respect of children toward their parents, was the cornerstone of the family. Children had definite obligations to their parents, and these did not end when the parents died. Good children were expected to provide parents with elaborate funerals. After the funeral, sons and daughters were supposed to stop work and observe a long period of mourning. The spirits of dead family members were worshiped as gods. This practice of ancestor worship led the Chinese families to show great respect to their older members. After all, today's grandparents would be tomorrow's ancestral spirit!

The family structure had its own *hierarchy*, or levels. Each position in the family had to humble itself to the ones above. The whole family group was under the authority of the eldest male. A young

A rectangular bronze food caldron from the Shang dynasty.

married woman, however, was dominated by her husband's mother. Thus, a Chinese woman faced many authorities. When she was unmarried, she was under the power of her grandfather, father, and brothers. Once married and moved into the house of her husband's family, she faced the authority of her husband; his father, grandfather, and ancestors; and her mother-in-law. These lines of authority helped maintain large families. But they also limited the achievements of women.

The Growth of an Economy The Shang people had many new ideas and did high-quality work. Their bronze work was not to be equaled anywhere else in the world for over 1,000 years. They made strong city fortresses. And they built a civilization upon their agricultural surpluses.

They were wasteful, however. In their hearts the Shang were still wild frontier people and great hunters. In one day, their royal hunting parties would sometimes kill more than 300 animals, including deer, tigers, and foxes. This practice was a misuse of the large game population of northern China. In addition, many animals, along with untold numbers of people, bronze vessels, tools, and other objects of wealth, were buried as sacrifices to the gods and the ancestors. This practice may have given them emotional comfort, but it was a continuous drain on their economy.

The Zhou and the Qin were more realistic in their attitudes toward the economy. The Zhou and Qin began large-scale projects to extend agriculture. Swamps were drained and planted with crops. Dams and irrigation canals were built.

These efforts were greatly helped by the introduction of iron during the Zhou dynasty. Iron plows, axes, hoes, and spades increased the efficiency of the workers. In the same way, iron weapons increased the power of the warriors. Chinese ironworking was particularly impressive because they

LEGACY OF ANCIENT CHINA

Economy: labor-intensive system

Social Institutions: filial piety

Philosophies: Confucianism, Legalism, Taoism

Government: feudalism (Shang dynasty), scholar-officials (Middle Kingdom)

cast their iron as they did their bronze. In the West, iron was forged until the 1300s. Forging is a slow process of repeatedly heating the iron and then hammering it into shape. The Chinese ironworkers, on the other hand, melted the iron and poured it into molds of whatever shape they wanted. This was an important innovation.

There were limits to the inventiveness of the ancient Chinese. In fact, they established a strong tradition that would in the long run slow the growth of progress in China. This tradition is called the *labor-intensive* economy. Instead of animals or machines, the ancient Chinese favored human labor.

Silkmaking was a typical labor-intensive industry. It was normally performed by women. Imagine a pound of silkworm eggs. When they hatch, they number about 700,000 worms. They are fed mulberry leaves by hand and tended for five weeks. The worms eat 11 metric tons of leaves while they weave their cocoons. After the weaving is complete, the cocoons are unraveled by hand, another time-consuming process. Of course, the thread must then be woven into fine cloth. Only 150 pounds of silk are produced from all this effort. Tea production and rice growing involve a comparable amount of hand labor.

With this kind of patient, hard work, the Chinese developed their economy. They had outgrown the wastefulness of the Shang. They had learned to make better use of their environment. The Chinese worked with nature in a way that allowed them to support a population of 50 million people on a limited amount of fertile soil. The Chinese were rightly proud of their labor-intensive economy and of the products of their people's efforts.

Section Questions

1. Why did the Chinese call their country the Middle Kingdom? How did this concept affect their attitude toward outsiders?
2. Who were the scholar-officials? Why were they important?
3. How did filial piety and ancestor worship help bind the Chinese family together?
4. What is labor-intensive work? Give an example of this process as it was used in ancient China.
5. How is Chinese writing different from our writing?

Chapter Summary

1. Cut off by physical barriers from other parts of the world, China developed a distinct civilization. Chinese historians date their civilization from 2000 B.C. One of the first dynasties, the Shang, is known for its finely engraved bronze vessels, its complex writing system, and ancestor worship.

The early dynasties, the Shang and the Zhou, were feudal states. The country lacked a strong, central government, and control of land and power was shared by many nobles. Not until the Qin dynasty (221-207 B.C.) did the constant warfare cease long enough for China to become unified. Under authoritarian Emperor Qin Shi Huang, order was restored, the government was centralized, and the Great Wall was constructed.

2. During the Zhou dynasty, great philosophies developed, each with its own ideas of how to restore and maintain order. Confucius believed that a virtuous and educated ruler would set high standards that everyone would follow. The legalists claimed that only strict laws and force maintain order. In the mystical philosophy of Taoism, the individual seeks harmony with the universe by rejecting such artificial institutions as government.

3. Throughout these chaotic times, one social unit offered security—the family. Families were bound together by love and by filial piety. Death did not break the tie. The children showed continual reverence by worshiping their dead ancestors. Between the ruling classes and the peasants and merchants, there emerged a class of advisers called scholar-officials. During the Qin dynasty, they began to administer the day-to-day activities of the government.

In ancient times and through much of China's history, agriculture, tea, and silk production were labor-intensive work. Human muscle did the work instead of animal muscle or machines.

Chapter 5 Review

Check Your Facts

1. Identify or describe the following:
   a. loess
   b. Qin Shi Huang
   c. Confucius
   d. Anyang
   e. vassal
   f. Peking man
   g. Middle Kingdom
2. Why is the Huang He River called China's Sorrow?
3. What institutions developed during the Shang dynasty?
4. Why was it important to standardize writing?
5. Give examples of yin and yang forces in nature.
6. What is the basic principle of Taoism?
7. What was the Period of the Warring States? What important developments came out of it?

Words to Know

1. Define these words in one or two sentences and explain their significance in the history of ancient China.
   a. pictograph
   b. labor intensive
   c. hierarchy
   d. filial piety
   e. fief
   f. feudalism
2. Look up the word "analects" in the dictionary. What does it mean? From what language does it come?

Developing Your Skills

1. Trace the route of the Great Wall. List the landforms (mountains, rivers, plains, deserts) that it crosses.
2. The early dynasties were Shang, Zhou, and Qin. In which of these periods did the following occur?
   a. origin of Confuciansim
   b. origin of Taoism
   c. implementation of legalism
   d. burning of philosophical books
   e. Period of the Warring States
   f. building of the Great Wall
   g. artistry of the bronze vessels

Thinking It Over

1. Compare the development of civilization in China and Egypt. In what ways were they similar and different?
2. How could the Zhou, Qin, and Han rulers use the concept of the Mandate of Heaven?
3. What groups of people in the United States today would be equivalent to the nobles, scholar-officials, farmers, artisans, and merchants in ancient China? How would you rank these classes in the United States? What are the bases for status in the United States today?
4. How do you think your friends would respond to the ideal of practicing filial piety? Explain.

Special Activities

1. In the last ten years, China's archaeologists have made some phenomenal discoveries. Go to the library and research the excavations at Zouhoudian, Ban Bei (Pan Pei), or Zhengzhou (Chengchow).
2. Over a two-week period, watch one family situation comedy on television. Compare the relationships in the TV family to an imaginary family in ancient China. Give examples of how each family relates to the concepts of filial piety, reverence for the dead, the role of women, and the role of mother-in-laws.

Unit 1 Review

Words to Know

1. Use the following words in a paragraph that discusses the religions of the early civilizations:
   a. reincarnation
   b. idols
   c. divination
   d. ancestor worship
   e. monotheism
   f. pyramid
2. Copy these words onto your paper and then put a "1" next to those that were found in only one of the four civilizations that you have studied. Put a "+" next to those that were found in two or more of these civilizations.
   a. irrigation
   b. caste system
   c. empires
   d. obelisks
   e. patriarchy
   f. surplus food
   g. bronze
   h. dynasties
   i. hieroglyphics
   j. ziggurat

Time and Place

1. Using the map on page 48, locate the sites where civilization developed in Egypt, India, and China. About how many kilometers was each of these from the civilization in Mesopotamia?
2. Describe the main route that could have been used in ancient times to get from each of these civilizations to Mesopotamia.
3. Make a time line that shows the approximate date when each of the following began:
   a. Sumer
   b. Shang dynasty
   c. Old Kingdom in Egypt
   d. Harappan civilization
   e. Indo-Aryan invasion of India
   f. Persian empire
   g. alphabet
   h. Qin dynasty

Putting It Together

1. Draw the chart at the bottom of the page on a piece of paper, and complete it with the appropriate information.
2. In your opinion, which of these civilizations accomplished the most? The least? Give evidence to justify your opinion.
3. Which was more important to the development of these civilizations: the nearby rivers, the development of writing, or the use of metal tools? Explain.
4. Do you think that people in these civilizations had better and happier lives than the nomads who lived around them?
5. What are the main similarities between the economies of these four civilizations? Why did these similarities occur?

	Geographical advantages	Major accomplishments	Products	Religions
Egypt				
Mesopotamia				
Indus Valley				
China				

Contemporary Parallel:
Who Is Civilized?

*I*n this unit, you have studied the rise of civilization. Human beings in ancient Egypt, Mesopotamia, India, and China came to be different from their ancestors. When we say that the ancient Chinese were civilized, we mean that they developed writing. They produced a surplus of food. They built cities. Art and literature flourished.

Today we often think of a civilized society as one with a high economic productivity; that is, a great deal of material wealth. Economic productivity is often a result of advanced technology—complex machines that help create surplus food, computers, nuclear missiles in silos, and so forth. To determine standard of living, social scientists also measure life expectancy. Life expectancy is the average number of years a person in a particular society can expect to live. Literacy rate, the percentage of people in a society who can read and write, is examined. The chart shows this data for several societies.

But many scholars argue that these measures may be inadequate. They argue that they do not show the quality of life. They point to the degree of violence in a society as one important measure of its level of civilization. They point to crime rates, to the amount of civil unrest, to the number of years of peace.

Many of us were taught that primitive people were uncivilized, cruel savages. This is clearly inaccurate. In 1971, the world discovered the Tasaday (TAW saw DI), a gentle people living in a rain forest in the Philippines. This small group of twenty-six people did not have weapons. They had no words to express fighting or enemies. Were they uncivilized?

	Per capita GNP (in U.S. dollars)	life expectancy at age one	literacy rate among people aged 15-35 (percent)
Afghanistan	137	47.9	8
Cuba	640	71.1	78
Brazil	912	55.9	34
USSR	2,380	70.0	100
Nigeria	297	49.0	25
United States	7,024	72.2	99
China	300	64.6	60
Sweden	7,666	74.6	99

QUESTIONS

1. As you can see, the definitions of "civilization" and "civilized" are controversial topics today. Examine the ways in which these terms were applied to ancient societies in this unit. Should we use these standards today? If not, what standards should we use?
2. Write your own definition of "civilization" and the standards you think we should use today.

800 B.C.	275	206	A.D. 27	395	476	A.D. 525
Sparta and Athens rise	Romans unify Italy	Pax Sinica begins	Pax Romana begins	Christianity becomes official religion of Rome	Roman Empire falls	Gupta empire ends

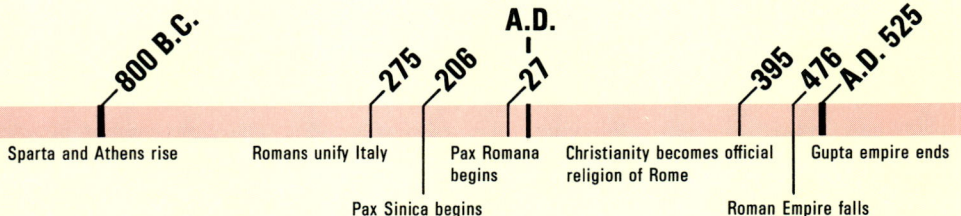

Unit 2
The Classical World

A Roman frieze showing the Roman emperor Augustus in an imperial procession.

In the year 10 B.C., a camel caravan wound its way through the great deserts that lie north of the Himalaya Mountains. It came from the Han kingdom of China, bound for the Mediterranean Sea. The camels were laden with silk, fruits, pottery, bronze, and delicate items made of ivory and jade.

The caravan's route was called the Silk Road. It formed a slender thread connecting the great empires of China and Rome. The Romans learned about new crops, like oranges, peaches, and pears. Soon these trees could be found on many parts of the Mediterranean coast. The Chinese gained, too, adding such foods to their diet as grapes and figs and walnuts. They were careful, though, not to share one of their great secrets—the origins of silk.

With the Silk Road, cultural ideas spread in two directions. This process is called *cultural diffusion*. The large regional empires of the Classical Age (800 B.C. to A.D. 600) led to a dramatic increase in the contact between peoples. Sea traders, like the Greeks and the Tamil (TAM ul) people of south India, became agents of cultural diffusion. So did empire builders like the Romans. And it worked in reverse. The groups who later invaded the Roman, Indian, and Chinese empires—Germans, Kushans (koo SHAHNZ), Huns, and others—quickly adopted many of the ways of these great civilizations. Christianity diffused throughout Europe and the Middle East within a period of 400 years. Buddhism expanded from its birthplace, India, to much of the Far East. Indeed, the world had become a smaller place.

83

The remains of the classic Greek Parthenon still stand, and are still an inspiration to architects throughout the world.

Chapter 6 Ancient Greece

Imagine yourself as a visitor to a Greek city-state in the sixth century B.C. People wander around the marketplace, engaging in lively conversation and enjoying the fresh sea breezes. Near the potter's workshop, a visitor consults with the public doctor about an injury that he got on his journey. At the barber's stall, five or six men exchange gossip about public affairs. One of them complains loudly about a politician who has argued that the pay of jurors serving the city-state should be increased to one drachma per day. The barber speaks his opinion as does a slave who has been drawn into the conversation. Rich and poor, citizens and slaves, residents and visitors—all mix freely. Leaving the marketplace, you pass by two open-air public buildings. The first contains

3000-1100 B.C. (early dates approximate)

3000-2000	Indo-European migrations
3000-1500	Minoan civilization
1900	Mycenae established
1100	Dorian invasions

HELLENIC PERIOD—800-400 B.C.

800-600	Sparta and Athens rise
600-500	Democratic reforms in Athens
490-468	Persian Wars
478-455	Athenian empire
450-320	Socrates, Plato, Aristotle
431-404	Peloponnesian War
357-338	Macedonia conquers Greece
336-323	Alexander the Great

"Girl with Doves," a marble grave relief.

a handful of people who are discussing the makeup of matter with a well-known philosopher. The second is being used by a boys' chorus as they practice for the competitions at the upcoming festival. The wealthy merchant who has sponsored them listens anxiously in the corner.

You then find your way to the public gymnasium. There some young men are practicing running, wrestling, and boxing. These are the winners of the local games. Now they are preparing for the Olympic Games, to be held at Olympia this summer. There, they will compete against athletes from other Greek city-states. If one of them wins a first place, he will receive free meals for the rest of his life.

City-states at war with one another often declare truces for the duration of the games. Although individual Greeks are loyal to their city-states, they value their Greek culture. Believing that they are unique, they refer to people who do not speak Greek as barbarians.

Is it any wonder that these Greeks consider themselves superior? Their city-states foster the growth of the mind, body, and public spirit of each of its citizens. Widespread participation in government and free discussion make active members of a community, not just subjects to a state. Out of these city-states will come many of our modern concepts of *democracy*—rule by the people.

1. The Greeks Developed Democratic City-States

Ancient Greece consisted of almost all the lands touched by the Aegean (ih JEE un) Sea. These included the mainland called Greece today, the western coast of Asia Minor, and the islands in between, as far south as Crete (KREET). Mainland and islands alike were marked by the same rugged mountain chain that ran from the northwest to the southeast. Consequently, the harbors and valleys of the peninsula opened to the southeast. This encouraged exchanges between the Greeks and the earlier civilizations of Egypt and Mesopotamia.

The land of Greece supported only a rather meager life-style. Most of its fertile soil was concentrated in the northern plains of Thessaly (THES uh lee) and Boeotia (bee O she uh). In other places, the people carefully cultivated corn, grapes, and olives in the occasional narrow valleys. Nearby uplands provided grazing for sheep and goats as well as timber for shipbuilding. There were small deposits of clay, limestone, and marble. These limited resources enabled the Greeks to build up a self-supporting civilization but only if they lived modestly and avoided waste. They were forced to look to the sea for trade and for additional land in the form of colonies. As a result, the Greeks became the greatest sailors of their age, the masters of the Mediterranean.

Origins The origins of the Greeks are difficult to trace. Scholars believe that, like the Indo-Aryans who migrated to India, the ancient Greeks were the descendants of Indo-European peoples. You may remember that Indo-European groups left their homelands in Central Asia between 3000 and 2000 B.C.

According to the legends of the ancient Greeks, their early ancestors belonged to three Greek tribes. The Achaian (uh KI un), the Ionian (i O nee un), and the Aeolian (ee O lee un) tribes were believed to have been led by heroes. Around 1900 B.C., the Achaians established themselves on the Greek mainland and formed their most important state at Mycenae (mi SEE nee) in the Peloponnesus (pel uh puh NEE sus), the southern part of Greece. The Ionians settled in Attica (AT ih kuh), a rocky peninsula that juts into the Aegean Sea. The Aeolians settled in the northern islands of the Aegean, which they named Aeolis (EE uh lus). The Achaians, or Mycenaeans, gradually became the dominant group. They gained control of Aegean

These rooms in Knossos may have been part of a burial chamber.

Did You Know?

Minoan Civilization

The first European civilization developed on the craggy, mountainous island of Crete. When the rest of Europe was living in simple hunting and gathering societies, the Minoan (muh NO un) people had produced a rich urban culture. That culture included the division of labor, a political system, a system of writing, and a calendar.

Minoan civilization flourished in the Aegean-Mediterranean region from 3000 to 1500 B.C. Crete is the largest of more than 2,000 islands in the region. It lies between the European mainland, Africa, and the Middle East. The Minoans made the best of this location. They developed the most extensive network of sea trade the world had ever seen. With ships powered with oars and sails, they came into contact with the advanced ideas of Egypt and Mesopotamia.

By 1600 B.C., Knossos, a town on the northern shore of the island, dominated Crete. Knossos had access to the sea, a good water supply, and fertile farmland. Artisans at Knossos were skilled in weaving, dyeing, shoemaking, pottery-making, and metalwork. Minoan art reflected Egyptian influence. It also showed a peace-loving people fond of bright colors, beautiful clothes, and the outdoor life.

Several great palaces were built in the towns of Crete. The palace at Knossos was the largest and most beautiful of them. Inside, the palace was a complex of royal apartments, living rooms, workrooms, corridors, tunnels, and a throne room. Majestic staircases linked the floors of the multistoried structure. Colorful *frescoes*—paintings made on wet plaster walls—portrayed the rich social life of the

This clay urn is from the Palace of Mallia on the island of Crete.

palace. Among them were pictures of court assemblies, dancing, boxing, the sport of bull-leaping, and other athletic contests. The palace was even equipped with an indoor plumbing system with running water and flush toilets. Outside, a large courtyard with wide, colorful terraces opened up the space to the sky and the countryside.

Around 1500 B.C. Mycenaeans from mainland Greece invaded the island of Crete. These invasions, as well as earthquakes and volcanic activity, weakened the Minoans. Around 1200 B.C., they were conquered by the Dorians. Although their civilization was destroyed, the strong influence of the Minoans remained.

The Acropolis of Athens, with the Parthenon in the background.

trade. About 1500 B.C., they captured the city of Knossos (kuh NAHS us) on Crete.

About 1100 B.C., the Dorians (DOR ee unz), a warlike people from the north, destroyed the fortresses of the Mycenaeans. The Mycenaeans either fled or eventually became part of the new culture, a mixture of Aegean, Mycenaean, Minoan, and Dorian influences. This mingling of groups and traditions formed the basis of ancient Greek culture. The people did not call themselves Greeks but Hellenes (HEL enz). They referred to their land as Hellas and their culture as Hellenic.

City-States and Democracy The Mycenaean political system had consisted of small kingdoms under the rule of a king. The term *acropolis*, or high city, referred to the fortress where the Mycenaean king had lived under the protection of a war goddess. After the Mycenaean centers were destroyed by the Dorians, the fortress settlements throughout the Aegean became centers of religious life. Each settlement was devoted to Athene (uh THEE nee), Hera (HIR uh), or Artemis (AR tuh mus), goddesses believed to protect settlements. As the villagers met to worship together in each religious center, they developed a sense of community. These political bonds led to the development of a new form of political community. The Greeks called this growing community a *polis*, or a city-state. Each city-state consisted of a temple, a seat of government, an *agora* (a marketplace), and a number of villages where the Greek people lived in households or family units. As described in the introduction, it was the free interchange of ideas in these city-states that gave birth to democracy.

Although the ancient Greeks developed democracy, not every city-state adopted that form of government. In the city-states that became democracies, rule by the people meant rule by the free adult male citizens. These Greeks considered their city-state a community of citizens who were members of the same family. Because of this, only Greeks who could trace their ancestors to the founders of the city-state were citizens.

Excluded from citizenship in every city-state were citizens of other city-states who had migrated in order to get work. Also excluded were slaves and women. Slaves usually outnumbered citizens. Slaves were non-Greek laborers from other regions in Europe and Greeks who had fallen into debt or had been captured in wars. Children of slaves were slaves from birth. But some slaves did win their freedom. Slaves worked in the silver mines, on farms, and in the homes.

Most scholars have concluded that women were considered citizens. But women did not participate in the outdoor life of the marketplace. Nor did they participate in the political life of the city-state. Except for family dinner parties, women did not dine with guests in their homes.

The development of city-states throughout Hellas produced some positive as well as some negative results. Many city-states provided citizens with the freedom to develop new ways of organizing the political, social, and cultural lives of their communities. But the sense of community that was the great achievement of the city-state prevented the Greeks from forming a united nation.

By 500 B.C., two city-states had become more powerful than any of their neighbors. They developed contrasting ways of life as they tried to influence the course of Hellenic civilization.

Athens Athens (ATH enz) was located on the coastal plain of Attica. By 700 B.C., the city-state of Athens had conquered all of Attica. However, instead of treating the people of Attica as subjects, the Athenians made them citizens. The soil of Attica was excellent for the cultivation of olive trees and grape vines. By 600 B.C., the Athenians were producing olive oil and wine for export to states in the Mediterranean region. Athens prospered through trade and commerce.

The political and economic life of Athens was at first controlled by wealthy landowners. Many smaller farmers lost their lands. And when they went into debt, they became slaves. This led to fear that the poor would rebel. In 594 B.C., an Athenian leader, Solon (SO lun), proposed a series of democratic reforms. He convinced the Athenians to stop the practice of enslaving debtors. He also persuaded them to admit less wealthy Athenians to the assembly of citizens and to the court. He created a council of 400 members representing all property owners. He proposed that the council draw up laws that would then be voted on by the assembly.

In 508 B.C., another Athenian leader, Cleisthenes (KLIS thuh neez), expanded the council from 400 to 500 members. The names of 500 citizens were chosen by lot.

Athenian boys were sent to school where they were taught to read and write and were educated in poetry, music, and gymnastics. Girls did not attend school. They were educated in household duties by their mothers.

The Athenians wanted to excel in

everything. Education and training were the means they used to reach that goal. Pericles (PER uh kleez), who governed Athens for more than thirty years (461 to 429 B.C.), maintained that excellence was the purpose of Athenian education:

> It is true that we are called a democracy, for the administration is in the hands of the many and not of the few. But while the law secures equal justice to all alike in their private disputes, the claim of excellence is also recognized; and when a citizen is in any way distinguished he is preferred to the public service, not as a matter of privilege, but as the reward of merit. Neither is poverty a bar, but a man may benefit his country whatever be the obscurity of his condition.

A bust of Pericles.

It can be said that Athenian life was typical of life in the Greek city-states of the fifth century B.C. Small farms dominated the plains and valleys of Attica. Each farm was owned by a single family. The men managed the farms. The women took care of the children and managed the household slaves. In the city, surrounding the magnificent public buildings of the polis were small, simple houses of sun-dried brick. Here lived the merchants and artisans who worked in the city. In the fishing villages of the seacoast, people fished in the waters of the Aegean. Many of their boys were to become sailors in the finest navy of Hellas. The herders on the mountainsides provided animals for sacrifice to the gods and meat for the households of Athens. In the forests, workers felled the trees for timber. Timber fueled the fires for cooking and provided the material for the ships that sailed in the Athenian navy.

Sparta Sparta (SPAR tuh) was located in the Peloponnesus. Although their origins are difficult to trace, the Spartans were probably descendants of mixed Aegean-Dorian peoples. In the 700s B.C., the Spartans conquered many of the Greek states in the Peloponnesus and reduced them to the status of subjects. About 100 years later, the Mycenaean Greeks rebelled against Spartan rule. After suppressing the rebellion, the Spartans gave all subject peoples the status of *perioeci* (per ee EE si), or "dwellers around." The perioeci were the merchants and skilled workmen. The Spartans were not interested in trade.

In the state of Sparta, before the Spartans began to colonize, a harsh class system separated citizens from noncitizens. Below the Spartans were the *helots*, thought to be descendants of Aegeans. Helots were considered the property of Sparta. They were enslaved farm laborers, assigned to toil on the farmlands of the Spartans

An infant undergoing public examination in Sparta.

Because they treated the helots so cruelly, the Spartans feared that the helots would rise up and overthrow them. Therefore, they assigned trusted perioeci to guard the helots and keep them in bondage. By 600 B.C., the helots outnumbered the Spartans by a ratio of ten to one.

The fear of rebellion by the perioeci or the helots led the Spartans to produce the most efficient army in Hellas. From birth, Spartans were subject to harsh training programs. When a Spartan baby was born, he or she was examined by five judges. If the baby was healthy and strong, it was allowed to live. If not, it was left on a mountainside to die. At the age of seven, Spartan boys left their families to live in barracks and begin military training. They were underfed and encouraged to steal. Those who were caught were punished severely, not for stealing but for getting caught. After fourteen years of hardship and training, the young Spartans went into the regular army. They were allowed to marry, but they had to live in the barracks until the age of thirty.

Spartan girls were allowed to live at home. They had more freedom than other Greek women. They were trained to be fit mothers of soldiers. To fulfill that role, they raced, wrestled, and boxed.

The Spartans never developed a democratic government. They were a severe people who developed no interest in philosophy or in the arts.

In the fifth and fourth centuries B.C., Sparta was ruled in wartime by two kings. These were descendants of the first Spartan rulers. Five *ephors*, or overseers, acted as guardians of the state. They had unlimited power. They enforced the laws and watched over the youth, citizens, perioeci, and helots. In peacetime, the kings had two functions. They acted as high priests and were members of the *council of elders*. The council consisted of twenty-eight men over the age of sixty who had retired from the army. The council proposed laws, tried criminal cases, helped the ephors, and conducted foreign affairs. An assembly of all citizens over the age of thirty approved the laws proposed by the council.

Colonization In the 700s and 600s B.C., almost all the important Greek city-states except Athens, Aegina (ih JI nuh), and Thebes established colonies. The lack of good farmland and food to feed growing populations led the Greeks to leave their city-states. They settled along the coasts of Asia Minor and the Black Sea and in Egypt, Italy, and southern France. Each Greek colony was independent of the parent city-state. But bonds of religion, language, family, and commerce continued to exist.

Proud of their culture and traditions, the Greek colonists continued to speak their own language and to practice their own customs. The colonists participated in the Olympic Games. Athletic competition led to commercial competition as well. The Greek colony of Syracuse in Sicily, for example, became a center of great commercial activity in the Mediterranean.

The Greeks brought a cultural unity to the Mediterranean world that had not existed before they arrived.

Section Questions

1. What was the polis? What did it consist of?
2. Why did Olympic Games take place in spite of city-state rivalries?
3. What is a democracy? What did "democracy" mean in the Greek city-states that developed a democratic government?
4. What were the main occupations of the Athenians?
5. How did Spartans train their youth? Why?

Thinking Geographically: Compare the shape of the Greek colonies with the shapes of ancient Egypt and Mesopotamia. How are they different? What caused the difference?

The Greek fleet defeating the Persians, 480 B.C.

2. The Greek City-States Failed

A series of wars led to the downfall of the Greek city-states. This section traces the failure of the political system established by the Greeks and the rise of the Hellenistic Age.

The Persian Wars In 546 B.C., Cyrus (SI rus) the Great, founder of the Persian empire, conquered the Greek cities on the coast of Asia Minor. Although the Persians were tolerant of Greek culture and traditions, these cities resented barbarian rule. Aided by Athens and other Greek city-states, they rebelled in 488 B.C. This rebellion was crushed by the Persian emperor, Darius (duh RI us). He realized that the western frontier of the Persian empire would never be secure until all of Greece was conquered.

In 490 B.C., Darius sent an army of 100,000 men to conquer the Greeks. Even under this great threat, the Greeks were unable to unite. Sparta refused to *ally*, or fight together, with its neighbors. Athens, with a few allies, formed an army that met the Persians on the nearby plains of Marathon (MAR uh thahn). Although outnumbered ten to one, the Greeks defeated the Persians. Darius and his army returned to Asia Minor.

As a result of this battle, the prestige of Athens rose in the Greek world. The Persians swore revenge. In 480 B.C., Xerxes (ZURK seez), Darius's successor, led an army of over half a million men into Greece. As it crossed over from Asia Minor and marched down the coast, a fleet of more than 1,000 ships accompanied it. Greek cities on the plains of Thessaly in the north quickly surrendered. Athens and Sparta finally united most of the Greek city-states against Xerxes. They formed a land and sea alliance dominated by Sparta. But time was running out.

The Spartan king Leonidas (lee AHN uh dus) stationed his troops along the narrow pass at Thermopylae (thar MAP uh lee), between northern and central Greece. Xerxes' army had to pass through this area, which was sandwiched between the sea and rugged mountain ridges. The pass was so narrow that Leonidas thought he could defend it with only several thousand men, 300 of whom were Spartan citizens.

Leonidas's small force held off the half million Persians for six days. Finally, a Greek traitor showed them another way through the mountains. Leonidas and his force could have escaped. But true to the Spartan tradition, they stayed until they were overcome. With the fall of Thermopylae, the people of Athens fled to the island of Salamis (SAL uh mus), off the coast. Xerxes' army marched into Athens and burned it to the ground.

Xerxes then ordered his fleet to attack the Athenian navy in the Bay of Salamis. In the confining space of the bay, the smaller Athenian ships outmaneuvered the bulkier ships of the Persian fleet. Xerxes, sitting on a golden throne on a mountaintop, watched the destruction of his navy. Xerxes' army lost its naval support, and he was forced to withdraw.

The Battle of Salamis was very important to the Greeks. Never again would the Persians attempt to conquer them. Had the Persians won, Greek civilization might have been destroyed.

The Athenian Empire Even though they rejoiced in their victory, the Athenians feared that the Persians would return. Their anxiety grew when Sparta decided to pull out its army. Athenian alarm was shared by other Greek city-states in the Aegean and along the coast. These cities felt especially threatened by Persia.

In 478 B.C., Athens organized a defensive alliance. The alliance had as its home base the island of Delos (DEE lahs) in the Aegean. The Delian league began as a loose union of equals to which all members, except Athens, contributed money. Because Athens donated ships that were essential to defense, it soon became the dominant power. As long as the allies believed that Persia was a threat, they tolerated Athens' position. However, in 468 B.C., the league defeated the Persian fleet and army. The league then liberated the Greek cities on the coast of Asia Minor. After this, some allies refused to make payments to the league.

Under the leadership of Pericles, the Athenians prevented their allies from pulling out of the league. In 454 B.C., they transferred the Delian treasury to Athens. Rebellious allies were forced to sign a treaty with Athens. The league had become the Athenian empire.

By the mid-400s B.C., Athens was at the height of its power. The city had been entirely rebuilt after the Persian Wars with the money collected from members of the league. The Athenian navy dominated the Aegean region and extended its influence from Egypt to Sicily. Pericles dominated the age. He tried to unite the Greek world under Athenian leadership.

This Greek vase from about 440-430 B.C. shows a battle scene, possibly from the Peloponnesian War.

The Peloponnesian War The growing power of Athens alarmed many city-states. They looked to Sparta as the only city-state that could check Athenian ambitions. By 435 B.C., the entire Greek world was divided into two armed camps. On one side was the Athenian empire, which consisted of Greek cities in the Aegean and on the coast of Asia Minor. On the other side were most of the mainland cities, which were under the leadership of Sparta. The Spartan army was supreme on land. Athens ruled the sea.

In 431 B.C., the Peloponnesian War broke out. It pitted the Athenian empire against Sparta and its allies. From the beginning, the war went against Athens. In 430 B.C. a great plague ravaged the city-state. It killed one-third of Athens' people, including Pericles. In 415 B.C., a badly planned Athenian expedition against Syracuse ended in defeat. Athens was unable to replace the men and ships that it had lost in the battle. Finally, in 405 B.C., the weakened Athenian fleet was trapped in a bay and destroyed. Athens surrendered in 404 B.C.

Athens never regained its military power. The Athenian empire was dissolved, and the walls of the city were torn down. Athens lost its dominant position in the Greek world.

Macedonian Conquest The defeat of Athens upset the balance of power in Greece. Sparta was not able to maintain order among the city-states. In 371 B.C., after fighting a series of wars, Sparta was defeated by Thebes. The stage was set for the rise of Macedonia.

Macedonia was a small kingdom north of Thessaly. Its subjects were half-barbarian and half-Greek. Under the leadership of Philip II, who ruled from 359 to 336 B.C., the area was unified. Philip reorganized the army into a powerful fighting force.

Gradually, Philip began to involve himself in the struggle of the various Greek city-states. In 338 B.C., he defeated a

These battling figures are from a sculpture on the sarcophagus (stone coffin) of Alexander the Great.

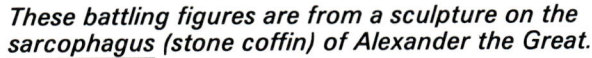

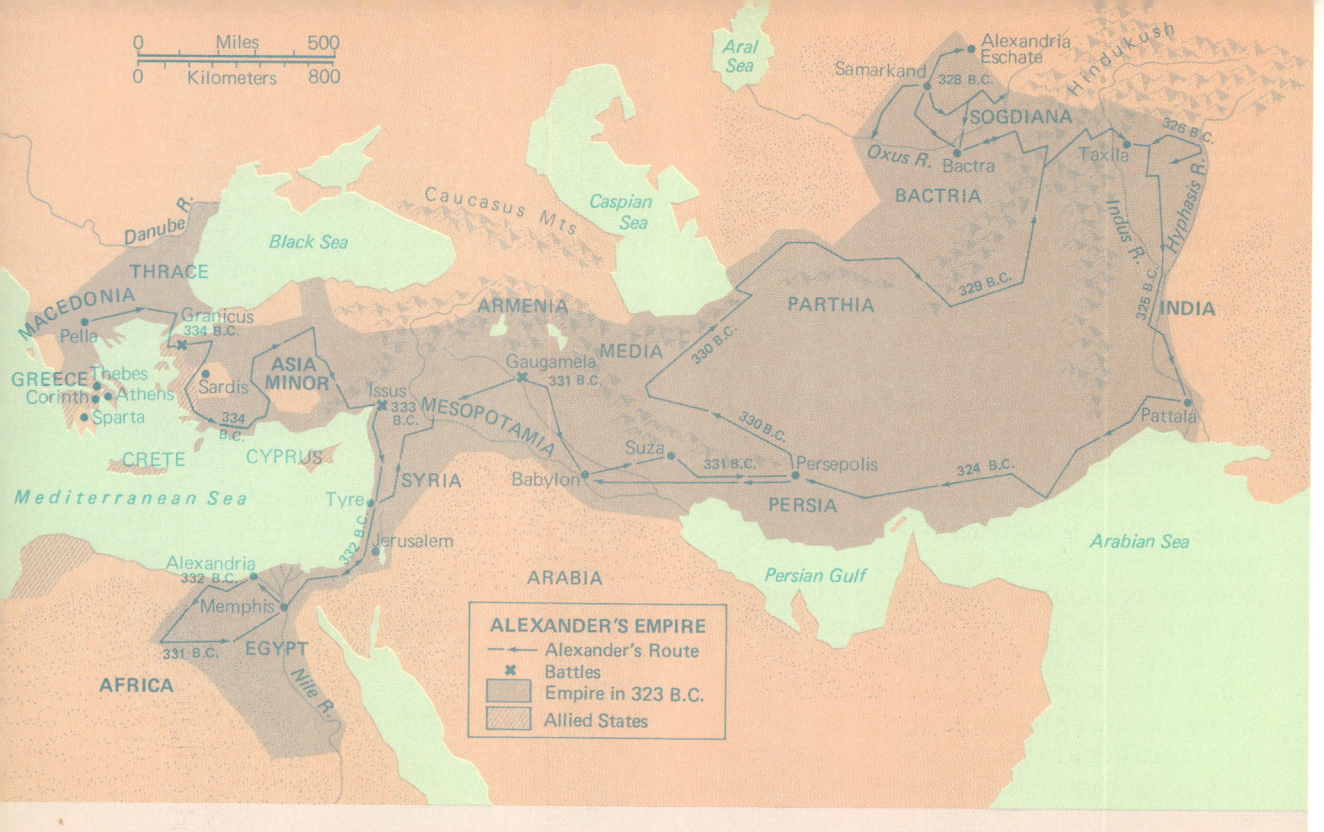

Thinking Geographically: Alexander's conquests spread Greek ideas and practices far beyond the borders of Greece. Study the map. Where would you expect to find the greatest Greek influence?

combined Greek force and gained control of the entire peninsula. Philip accomplished what the Greeks had been unable to do. He united them under a single ruler.

Philip allowed the Greek states to have an independent government. But they had to agree not to fight among themselves. Philip was a great admirer of Greek culture and civilization. In fact, his ambition was to invade Persia as a punishment for its invasion of Greece 150 years earlier. Before he could carry out his mission, he was assassinated in 336 B.C. At the age of twenty, Philip's son inherited an empire that was in open rebellion. The Greeks wasted no time. They, too, rebelled against Macedonia. A lesser leader would have given up the struggle. However, the son of Philip refused to accept defeat. His determination as well as his deeds earned him the name of Alexander the Great.

Like his father, the youthful Alexander admired Hellenic culture. As a boy, he had been tutored by Aristotle (AR uh staht ul), a great Greek philosopher. He developed an interest in war, politics, poetry, science, art, philosophy, medicine, and athletics. He mastered whatever task or study he undertook.

The Empire of Alexander Alexander began his rule by destroying Thebes, the city that had led the rebellion. So quick and total was his assault that it ended all resistance.

In 334 B.C., with a small army—no more than 40,000 men—Alexander crossed into Asia Minor. The Persian emperor,

Darius III, sent his army to meet Alexander's force at the Kocabas (kaw juh BAHSH) River. The Macedonian army quickly crushed the Persian force. With this victory, all of Asia Minor fell under Alexander's control. The following year, the two armies met at Issus (IHS us), in Syria, and Alexander was again victorious. Darius was able to save himself by fleeing. However, his family and personal fortune fell into Alexander's hands.

From Syria, Alexander marched south into Egypt, where he was proclaimed pharaoh by the Egyptian people. On the western delta of the Nile, he founded the greatest of his cities, Alexandria.

Returning to Asia, he met Darius for the last time in Mesopotamia. Once again, Alexander was victorious. Darius was assassinated by his own men. Alexander then took the title "king of kings." Alexander continued his march eastward. In 327 B.C., he crossed the northern Himalayas into the Indus Valley, where he defeated an Indian force. He planned an attack on the Ganges, but his soldiers refused to go on. It had been more than seven years since they had left their homeland. They begged him to return. Having granted their request, Alexander returned to Mesopotamia where he planned to reorganize his newly won empire.

Historians disagree about Alexander's political aims. Many believe that he had intended to build a world empire that would combine the best aspects of Greek and Persian culture. To support this idea, they point out that, after his return from India, Alexander began to wear Persian dress. In 324 B.C., in a great marriage ceremony in Susa (SOO zuh), a Persian city, Alexander married Statira (sta TI ruh), the daughter of Darius III. Thousands of his soldiers followed his example and married Persian women. Alexander kept the efficient Persian administrative system. He placed Persians as well as Macedonians and Greeks in government jobs. He also urged the Greeks to settle throughout the areas he had conquered. He founded many cities, such as Alexandria in Egypt, to encourage Greek settlement.

But Alexander never told his intentions. He died suddenly in 323 B.C. at the age of thirty-three. It had taken him only thirteen years to create an empire that extended from Greece to India.

The Hellenistic Age After Alexander's death, his empire broke apart. A series of wars erupted among his generals. By the time they ended, three states had emerged, each ruled by one of his generals.

The largest was the kingdom of Syria ruled by Seleucus (suh LOO kus). This kingdom extended from Asia Minor to the

A sketch of ancient Alexandria.

Indus. However, the area was too large to be ruled effectively. By 200 B.C., it had shrunk so much that it included only southern Asia Minor, Syria, and Mesopotamia.

The most powerful of the states was the kingdom of Egypt, ruled by Ptolemy (TAH luh mee). It was a Macedonian dynasty that controlled Egypt for 300 years. The seat of government was established at Alexandria, which soon became the largest city in the world.

The least stable of the states was the kingdom of Macedonia, established by Antigonus (an TIH guh nus). It consisted of Macedonia and Greece. Eventually, the Greeks developed a system of alliances that enabled them to break away from the kingdom.

The effects of Alexander's campaigns in the east were staggering. Thousands of Greeks left their homelands to settle the new cities of the east. They built temples, libraries, and schools. They spread Greek culture. It can be said that they Hellenized the east. But in the process of doing so, the Greeks adopted some aspects of Oriental culture. The result was a new culture, called Hellenistic.

As Athens had become the center of Hellenic culture in the fifth century B.C., so Alexandria became the center of Hellenistic culture. Alexandria also became the intellectual center of the Mediterranean and of the east. Greek became the language of all educated people and merchants who traveled in the area. This common language aided the growth of trade and the spread of ideas. Hellenistic civilization lasted for more than 100 years after Alexander's death.

Section Questions

1. What were several outcomes of the Persian Wars?
2. Why did the Peloponnesian War begin? Who was the victor of this war?
3. Why did Philip of Macedonia want to invade Persia?
4. What did Alexander the Great achieve that no one before him had achieved?
5. Name several ways in which the Hellenistic and Hellenic culture differed.

3. The Greeks Developed New Ways of Thinking

The questioning spirit of the ancient Greeks and the values nurtured by their culture led them to develop new ways of thinking. Their reliance on reason as a means to achieve knowledge and their drive for excellence had a profound effect on the development of Western civilization.

Greek Religion Almost every activity that the Greeks pursued was linked in some way to religion.

Like the gods of many ancient peoples, the Greek gods represented the forces of nature. But while the gods were believed to be immortal, they had human characteristics. They were not the abstract God of the Hebrews or the Persians. Greek gods had human weaknesses. They took sides in human conflicts. Sometimes they fought among themselves.

Most of the gods were said to dwell on Mount Olympus (uh LIM pus), a peak in northern Greece. The greatest of the gods was Zeus (ZOOS), god of the sky. Under Zeus was his brother Poseidon (puh SI dun), an important god to the ancient Greeks, for Poseidon ruled the sea. Aphrodite (AF ruh DI tee), one of Zeus's daughters, was the goddess of love and beauty. Athene, the protector of Athens, represented wisdom.

As nature seemed to follow orderly patterns (the seasons, for example), the Greeks believed that the gods demanded order from humans as well. They tried to attain this idea with their arts and philosophy.

In this view of Athene's palace, you can see the <u>caryatids</u>, female figures which serve as columns.

Literature, Art, and Architecture

Greek drama developed from processions in honor of the gods. It reached its height in Athens in the fifth century B.C. This period is sometimes called the classical age of Athens. Hundreds of plays were written. But only a few have survived. Most plays like those of the playwright Aeschulus (ES kuh lus, 525 to 456 B.C.), were tragedies. His famous play *Oedipus Rex* tells the story of a king of Thebes who killed his father and married his mother. The story is tragic because Oedipus was innocent of criminal intent. The gods had willed that he carry out those deeds. But Oedipus was guilty in another sense. He tried to outwit the gods by leaving his home. His pride in challenging the gods led to his destruction.

Not all Greek dramas were tragic. Aristophanes (ar ruh STAH fuh neez, 450 to 385 B.C.) wrote comedies that ridiculed democracy in Athens, politicians, and even the gods. These comedies show how much political freedom the Athenians had.

Some of the greatest works of art of the Greeks were also produced in the 400s B.C. The sculptures of this period were idealized representations of the human form in marble and in bronze. However, the statues revealed the artists' knowledge of anatomy. The wall paintings and building decorations show that the Greeks could create a sense of depth on flat surfaces. They could also create the harmonious blending of many vivid colors. The black-figured and the red-figured vases of the same period show mastery of detail. Skilled Greek potters were able to achieve works of true art.

Athenians created many beautiful public buildings. Perhaps the most beautiful was the Parthenon (PAHR thuh nahn), a temple built to honor the goddess Athene. The marble temple had eight columns at each end and seventeen on each side. The Greeks strove to attain perfect balance and perfect proportions. Many people believe that they achieved this ideal with the Parthenon.

A bust of Socrates.

Greek Philosophy In no other activity did the Greeks exert such a strong influence on future generations as in *philosophy*. The word "philosophy," which comes from the Greek, means "love of wisdom." Philosophy examines the basic questions about human values and the nature of reality.

The giant of the classical age of philosophy was an Athenian stonecutter named Socrates (SAHK ruh teez, 469 to 399 B.C.). Socrates spent most of his time talking and listening in the agora and in the homes of Athenian citizens. He believed that admitting ignorance was the first step toward discovering knowledge. Socrates developed a method of posing a series of related questions. It was a kind of never-ending debate that is known today as the *Socratic method*. Because Socrates questioned traditional beliefs, he made enemies. In 399 B.C., at the age of seventy, he was charged with teaching disbelief in the gods and with corrupting the youth of the city. At his trial, he could have escaped punishment by agreeing to leave Athens forever. He refused to do so and was condemned to death. His followers arranged his escape, but he refused to go. He carried out the sentence, drank a cup of poison, and died in the company of his friends.

Like so many great thinkers, Socrates never recorded his thoughts. What is known of his philosophy has been obtained from the writings of one of his followers, Plato (PLAY toh, 428 to 347 B.C.). Plato founded a school in Athens to educate students in philosophy and to train them in using the Socratic method.

One of Plato's books, *The Republic*, outlines the ideal city-state and discusses the meaning of justice. Plato limited the population of his ideal city-state to 5,000 citizens. Each citizen, in early childhood, was to be assigned to one of three classes based on natural abilities. The classes were the workers, the warriors, and the guardians. At the head of this ideal state was to be a philosopher-king. Plato's republic was not modeled on the Athenian democracy of the fifth century B.C. It was more like an *oligarchy*, or a government ruled by a small group. Plato believed that not all people were capable of understanding truth. The few who could understand the idea of a perfect state, he believed, were entitled to rule.

Plato's most famous student was Aristotle (384 to 322 B.C.). While Plato was most interested in things as they should be, Aristotle was interested in things as they are. Aristotle wrote about more subjects than any other Greek thinker. He had a special gift for *classifying*, for ordering information in a useful way. He dissected fish and shellfish. He broke open eggs at various stages to study the development of chicks. He collected more than 150 constitutions and arranged them according to systems of government. Aristotle was a firm believer in the Greek city-state. But like Plato, he said that the greatest good for all citizens could only be achieved in a state regulated by laws and governed by intelligent leaders.

In the field of logic, Aristotle used his skill in classifying to form an argument called a *syllogism*. A syllogism is based on *deductive* reasoning, that is, arriving at a conclusion through the use of reason. A syllogism consists of a set of *premises*, or assumptions, and a conclusion that follows from the premises. For example, if it is agreed that a good god does no evil and that Zeus is a good god, then it follows that Zeus does no evil.

Mathematics and Medicine The use of deductive reasoning and a passion for problem-solving made the Greeks great mathematicians. Greeks studied geometry, not because of its practical value, but because of its interest as a mathematical theory. In the sixth century B.C., Pythagoras (puh THAG uh rus) discovered the geometric theorem that now carries his name: The square of the hypotenuse (hi PAH tuh noos) of a right triangle equals the sum of the squares of the other two sides ($a^2 + b^2 = c^2$).

The Greek interest in nature led to many fascinating scientific discoveries. Much information was collected, observed, and analyzed.

The Greek physician Hippocrates (hih PAH kruh teez, 460 to 377 B.C.), made a study of disease. Many have called him the greatest physician of the ancient world. Hippocrates studied both the symptoms and the progress of each disease. He demonstrated that disease is caused by a problem within the body, not by a curse from the gods. He also opened a school to train students in medicine. His Hippocratic Oath is a solemn statement of medical principle to which graduating doctors commit themselves. It has continued to serve as the moral foundation of the medical profession.

In the Hellenistic Age, Greek science reached its height. Eratosthenes (er uh TAHS thuh neez) of Alexandria (275 to 200 B.C.) calculated the circumference of the Earth. Despite his lack of complex instruments, he was wrong by only 300 kilometers (200 miles). When you consider that modern scientists have only recently determined the circumference of the Earth, Eratosthenes's achievement is amazing. Euclid (YOO klud) of Alexandria wrote a textbook on geometry in which he developed forms and theorems that are taught today. Archimedes (ar kuh MEE deez) of Syracuse (287 to 212 B.C.) invented the water screw, a device for pumping water out of ships and flooded fields. He also calculated the value of *pi* (pie). In geometry, pi is the ratio of the circumference of a circle to its diameter.

The Hellenistic Greeks applied some of the scientific and mathematical discoveries of the Hellenic age. Among their inventions were clocks, washing machines, and even a steam engine. However, these inventions were forgotten until more modern times.

The Study of History The Greeks also were among the first people to write and study history in the modern sense of the word. The Greeks used history to learn about the actions and behavior of people. Systematic study, they believed, would help them evaluate the actions of historical figures and the significance of historical events.

The first of the Greek historians was Herodotus (hih RAH duh tus, 484 to 425 B.C.). He spent most of his life in Athens. He traveled to distant places, gathering information and comparing cultures. His greatest work, *The Persian Wars*, is perhaps the best account of that struggle. Herodotus has often been called the father of history.

Another Greek historian, Thucydides (thoo SIHD uh deez, 460 to 395 B.C.), was an Athenian. His great work, *The*

LEGACY OF ANCIENT GREECE

Literature: great dramatic tragedies and comedies

Art: emphasis on the human form in sculpture, sense of depth in paintings

Architecture: outstanding proportions

Philosophy: Socratic method, logic

Mathematics: Pythagorean theorem, Euclidean geometry, value of *pi*

Medicine: Hippocratic oath

History: first to systematically study history

Government: birth of democracy

Peloponnesian War, tells of the great struggle between Athens and Sparta. The work is remarkably free of *bias*, distorted or personal judgment. This is especially surprising since Thucydides fought in that conflict.

In history, philosophy, art, and science, the Greeks set standards that the Western world would pursue for centuries. They established themselves as a bridge between the ancient and the modern worlds.

Section Questions

1. Name several ways in which religion was linked to other aspects of Greek life.
2. What are some achievements of the Greeks that show that they were careful observers?
3. Describe the Socratic method in your own words. What was its purpose?
4. What kind of state did Plato describe in *The Republic*? Why did he believe that this was the ideal state?
5. Who was Hippocrates?

Chapter Summary

1. From Central Asia, Indo-European people migrated into Greece. In their new homeland, they were influenced by the rich cultures of the Mediterranean region.

The political unit of the Greek people was the city-state. The small size of each city-state and free discussion in the marketplace aided the development of democracy—government by the people. However, only free adult male citizens could participate in the political process. Two city-states gained predominance—Athens, a democracy which relied on sea power, and Sparta, a harsh militaristic state.

2. Athens and Sparta fought each other during the Peloponnesian War. The result was that many city-states were weakened. The political unity of the Aegean-Mediterranean region, which the Greeks did not achieve, was accomplished by Philip of Macedonia. These conquests and those of his son, Alexander the Great, produced a Hellenistic culture. Hellenistic civilization drew on the rich cultural traditions of Hellenic and eastern civilizations.

3. The common language of the Greeks, their worship of common gods, and their questioning approach to life led to the development of Hellenic culture. This great civilization reached its height in the city-state of Athens between the years 500 and 400 B.C. The Greeks produced great works of art, literature, painting, sculpture, pottery, and architecture. They made great advances in scientific methodology and systems of classification; in medical diagnoses, treatment of disease, and code of ethics; in the application of formal logic to mathematics; and in the recording and analysis of historical events.

Perhaps the greatest legacy of the Greeks was their achievement in philosophy. Greek philosophy reflected their questioning spirit and their faith in the power of reason.

Chapter 6 Review

Check Your Facts

1. What were the principal occupations in the Aegean region?
2. Who were the Minoans, Mycenaeans, and Dorians? When did each of these groups dominate the Aegean region?
3. What functions did the agora serve in the life of the city-state?
4. What contribution did Solon make to Athenian democracy? What contribution did Cleisthenes make?
5. Who were the perioeci? How did the Spartans use trusted perioeci?
6. Why did the Greeks establish colonies?
7. Why was Leonidas's behavior at Thermopylae characterized as true to the Spartan tradition?

Words to Know

1. Define these words in one or two sentences. Then tell how each relates to the accomplishments of ancient Greece.
   a. agora   c. deductive reasoning
   b. polis   d. philosophy
2. Explain what the Greeks meant by "democracy" and "oligarchy." List two disadvantages of each of these systems of government.

Developing Your Skills

1. Trace the map of ancient Greece on page 92. Then, using the map on page 43, draw arrows and write labels to show what goods would have come to Greece from other areas.
2. Study the map of Alexander's empire on page 96. List the peoples his empire included, and some of their customs, goods, or beliefs that might have been exchanged.
3. Change the following premises into syllogisms by adding a concluding statement.
   a. Cruel treatment leads to revolt. The helots were treated cruelly by the Spartans.
   b. Artists must know anatomy before they can portray realistic human forms. Athenian paintings show realistic human forms.

Thinking It Over

1. In modern terms, there seems to be a conflict between the Greek ideas of democracy and individual worth and the society's dependence on slaves. How do you explain this apparent contradiction?
2. What fundamental principle of city-state life did Pericles violate in trying to transform the Delian league into the Athenian empire?

Special Activities

1. Greece recently joined the European Economic Community (EEC). Research the EEC and prepare a report. Show why Greece's membership is a natural development of the commercial and political relationships entered into by the ancient Greeks.
2. Only on rare occasions did the Greeks give citizenship to alien residents. What requirements do immigrants to the United States have to fulfill before they can become citizens? If possible, interview a new American citizen.

Roman ruins in Tunisia.

Chapter 7 Ancient Rome

"They marched on their stomachs." So said the announcer in a television commercial for a breakfast cereal. The commercial showed the Roman army crossing a mountain leading to a field of grain. The theme of the commercial evoked a funny image. But it did suggest that Rome depended on the health of its army.

Every male citizen of Rome had to serve in the army when needed. Troops were organized into companies, and thirty companies formed a *legion*. Legions had about 4,000 soldiers. They were arranged into three lines of troops. Each soldier was assigned to a position about 2 meters (8 feet) from the soldiers in front

509 B.C.—A.D. 180	
390 B.C.	Gauls sack Rome
275 B.C.	Romans unify Italy
202 B.C.	Hannibal defeated
146 B.C.	Romans conquer Greece, sack Carthage
73 B.C.	Spartacas leads slave revolt
60 B.C.	Pompey, Crassus, Caesar form First Triumvirate
51 B.C.	Rome conquers Gaul
49 B.C.	Julius Caesar assumes power
27 B.C.	Roman Republic ends, Pax Romana begins
27 B.C.	Augustus assumes power
A.D. 14	Augustus' rule ends, instability begins
A.D. 96	Good emperors' rule begins
A.D. 180	Good emperors' rule ends

Bust of a Roman woman.

of, beside, and behind him. The first line of a legion contained recruits who had never fought before. The second line contained experienced soldiers who had fought in other battles of the war. The third line contained veterans of earlier wars who served as reserve troops.

Every soldier wore metal body armor and a metal helmet. He carried an oblong shield, two darts, and a short sword. The first line of soldiers threw their darts to stun and wound the enemy. Then the lines shifted position. The soldiers of the second line moved in and used their swords in hand-to-hand combat. The other line joined in combat whenever their help was called for.

As Rome developed from a small city-state on the banks of the Tiber River into a republic that dominated the Mediterranean world, the Roman army grew to four legions. It defeated the armies of the Etruscans (ih TRUS kunz), the Gauls (GALLS), and the Carthaginians (kahr thuh JIHN ee unz). Its armies kept order in the Roman provinces of western Europe, Africa, and Asia.

However, the conquests of the Roman Republic also led to revolution and civil war. Soldiers no longer fought as loyal citizens of the Republic. Instead, they transferred their loyalties to generals who tried to seize political power in Rome. In this way, the Roman army, which had contributed to the expansion of Rome, also contributed to the downfall of its republican form of government.

Thinking Geographically: Locate Rome on the map. What geographic features help explain its location?

1. A Republic Was Established

The country now called Italy is a peninsula that juts into the center of the Mediterranean Sea. To the north of the peninsula are the Alps. The most prominent feature of the Italian landmass is the Apennine (AP uh nin) Mountains. They extend the length of Italy toward the Adriatic (ay dree A tihk) Sea, making eastern Italy a rocky area fit mainly for cattle-raising. There are four large, fertile regions in Italy. One is the valley of the Po River in the north. The other three are the coastal plains in the west: Etruria (ih TRUR ee uh), Latium (LAY shee uhm), and Campania (kuhm PAY nyuh).

In the 700s B.C., the hills of the Latium region contained scattered villages overlooking the Tiber (TI bur) River. The mild climate favored agriculture. The hill people dug ditches to prevent erosion. They had little contact with outsiders, but their isolation was ended when the Etruscans invaded Latium about 575 B.C.

The Etruscans Many scholars believe that the Etruscans were a mixture of people from the eastern Mediterranean. Apparently, they came to Italy by boat during the 900s B.C. The Etruscans settled on the Etrurian coast between the Tiber and the Arno (AHR no) rivers. They turned the villages into city-states and made the Italian peoples citizens.

The Etruscans expanded south into Latium and Campania and north into the Po Valley. But the Greeks in the southeastern area of Italy checked their advance into the island of Sicily. The Etruscans never unified themselves into a nation.

The Etruscans developed an urban way of life. They built walls around their cities. They set aside a sacred place in each city-state for worshiping the gods. Using a central plan of construction, they dug ditches, drained marshes, and formed networks of connecting streets.

The Etruscans were farmers. They planted and harvested grapes, olives, vegetables, flax, and grain. They were also metalworkers. They mined iron, copper, and tin, and sold metal goods throughout the Mediterranean. They built large fleets of sailing ships.

Archaeologists have unearthed thousands of Etruscan tombs. The paintings decorating the walls of the tombs reveal the luxurious life of wealthy Etruscans. They also reveal the prosperous life of the middle class.

Scholars have concluded from the attitudes and positions shown in the wall paintings that Etruscan women and men were equals. Men and women wore fine clothes of linen and wool. Although both husband and wife wore jewelry, women's jewelry seems to have been more ornate. A woman wore snake bracelets, an armband, drop earrings, and a *diadem*, or crown.

On the tombs of the Etruscans were listed the names of both mother and father. The inscriptions suggest that the Etruscans honored and respected their fathers and mothers equally.

The Etruscans gradually lost their territory. The Greeks drove them out of Campania by 400 B.C. Shortly after 400 B.C., the Gauls drove them out of the Po Valley. The Romans expelled the Etruscans from Rome around 509 B.C.

This fresco of the three musicians is from an Etruscan tomb.

The sculpture shows Roman notaries at work.

Etruscan Contributions In building their city on the Tiber, the Romans developed the urban civilization that the Etruscans had given them. The Etruscans built Rome's forum (a large public square), the marketplace, and the civic center at the foot of the Palatine (PAL uh tin) and Capitoline (KAP uh tuh lin) hills. The Etruscans fortified the Capitoline and built a magnificent temple, which the Romans dedicated to Jupiter. From their membership in the Etruscan league of city-states, the Romans entered into trading relationships. Trade made them prosperous.

From the Etruscan social institution of the *gens*, the large family, the Romans developed two classes—the *patricians* and the *plebians*. The heads of the gens were called *patres*, or fathers. From the patres developed the patricians, nobles who served as the king's advisers, and priests who made elaborate sacrifices to the gods. The middle and lower classes made up the plebians. Many plebians attached themselves to patrician families as clients. The patricians protected their clients' legal rights in return for political support. This client system helped ensure the dominance of the patricians.

The Roman Republic The Romans date the founding of the Republic from the revolution of 509 B.C. After a long and bloody struggle, the patricians were finally able to wrest control of the government from the Etruscan king. The resulting loss of life and destruction of property may account for the hatred that generations of Roman senators expressed for the institution of monarchy. Their hostility led the Romans to create political institutions that they believed would prevent the development of rule by one person. The patricians established a *republic*, a government in which power is divided among various offices and institutions. Unlike the Greek city-states, which were pure, or direct, democracies because the people actually governed themselves, the Roman Republic was a form of indirect democracy. Although the people did not govern, they elected representatives, or officeholders, to govern for the benefit of all citizens.

To replace the Etruscan king, the patricians created the office of *consul*. They provided for two such offices to be filled by army generals. The consuls acted as the magistrates, or chief executives, of the Republic. They were members of the patrician class but were elected by the plebians to serve one-year terms. It was hoped that each consul would prevent abuses by the other.

The patricians also established the office of *pontiff*. Only patricians could become pontiffs. They interpreted the law.

The office of the *dictator* was established. The dictator was permitted to wield absolute power in wartime, which was expected to last no longer than six months. The dictator retired from office as soon as the army had defeated the enemy. The Roman story of Cincinnatus (sin suh NAT us) has survived centuries of retelling. Called from his farm to become dictator, Cincinnatus left his unplowed field. He reorganized the army, defeated the enemy, resigned from office, and returned to his farm, all in sixteen days.

The Senate was composed of 300 patricians. Senators were appointed by the consuls. Their primary responsibility was to advise the two consuls.

The assembly was composed of wealthy Romans who had fought in the army. They were selected by the consuls with the consent of the Senate. Their main responsibility was to vote on matters submitted to them by the consuls.

The Romans modeled these political institutions after parts of the Etruscan form of government. The idea for the consuls, the Senate, and the assembly all had their origins with the Etruscans.

The Plebians Versus the Patricians In 504 B.C., the patricians got a law passed that prevented the plebians from joining their ranks through intermarriage. In effect, the decree prevented the plebians from becoming consuls and senators. The plebians could not hold important political offices, but they were required to serve in the army, pay taxes, and pay high prices for goods imported by the Republic. They were sold into slavery when they failed to pay their debts. Because the laws were not written, the plebians had to rely on the pontiffs to tell them what their rights were. The plebians believed that the pontiffs were interpreting the laws for the benefit of the patricians.

Tradition dates the beginning of the plebians' revolt from 493 B.C. They withdrew from Rome to the Temple of Ceres (SIH reez). There they formed an assembly called the Tribal Council of the Plebs. It was to be the government of the city-state that the plebians intended to found.

The patricians gave in because they needed the plebians. They agreed to establish an office called the *tribune*. Two tribunes were to act as the protectors of the plebians. The Tribal Council of the Plebs was to elect the tribunes. The tribunes had the right to veto any oppressive act of the consuls.

During the next fifty years, the plebians used their influence to achieve other reforms. By threatening to veto the annual *levy*, the

Did You Know?

About Roman Women

A Greek observer of Roman life reported that, within the household, a wife was the equal of her husband:

> If a wife was virtuous and in all things obedient to her husband, she was mistress of the house to the same degree as her husband was master of it, and after the death of her husband...she was mistress of all he left, and if he had children, she shared equally with them.

One virtuous wife was honored in a Roman funeral speech. The husband's recollection of his wife's deeds suggests that mutual love and respect characterized their relationship. In praising the bravery of his wife, he described how far one woman was willing to go in exercising her rights as a Roman citizen:

> When I was on the run (in exile) you used your jewels to provide resources for me...During the civil war, when a gang of men... attempted to break into our house and pillage it, you successfully repulsed them and defended our home... When my civil rights had been restored, you went to Marcus Lepidus to ask him to honor this decision. You threw yourself on the ground at his feet and not only were you not raised up but you were dragged out like a slave... With the greatest courage you told Lepidus of Caesar's edict, begging him to ensure my recall from exile. You were insulted and wounded, and you let your wounds be seen so that people might know who was the cause of my misfortunes. Not long afterward he got into trouble over this matter.

A portrait of a wife and her husband. This couple was from Pompeii.

The civil liberties of Roman women did not include the right to hold office. Nevertheless, Roman women voiced their opinions about various issues. They had more freedom than Greek women. Girls from wealthy families had more education. With this knowledge, they were well prepared to speak out on public issues.

law that allowed the Republic to draft citizens into the army, the plebs convinced the consuls and the pontiffs to write and publish the laws of the Republic. The Twelve Tablets of Rome (450 B.C.) were displayed in the forum. The council became the tribal assembly of the Republic. Romans who were condemned to death were given the right to appeal their sentences to the tribal assembly. The law prohibiting intermarriage between patricians and plebians was repealed. The selling of debtors into slavery was prohibited and soldiers were paid for serving in the Roman legions. A law was passed that reserved to the plebs one of the consular offices.

In the following years, the government of the Republic changed considerably. The tribunes increased their power at the expense of the consuls. The tribal assembly acquired the authority to hear judicial cases and to declare war in times of crisis. New offices were created to administer the Republic. *Praetors*, for example, were authorized to administer justice and to govern the city in the absence of the consuls. *Censors* were elected to draw up the list of citizens on the tax rolls and to oversee work on public buildings and roads.

Family and Religious Life Unlike Crete, which was matrilineal, Rome was a *patrilineal* society. Romans traced their descent, or their family lines, from their fathers. Roman law gave to the *paterfamilias*—the father of the family—broad authority over family members.

The rights of a Roman father developed from his religious duties. He conducted religious services honoring the household gods. The *genius* was the spirit who guarded the family and represented the fertility of the father. The Penates protected the family storeroom. The Lar watched over the farm. Vesta was the guardian of the household fire. The Roman family included the father and the mother, sons and their wives, unmarried daughters, grandchildren, clients, and slaves. According to law, a father had the right to control every aspect of his children's lives. Like the elders of Sparta, a father had the right to decide whether a baby would live or be left in the hills to die. For serious offenses, a father could order the death of his child. In addition, fathers controlled the family estates. All money earned by children became the property of their fathers. Fathers had the right to choose husbands for their daughters. Marriage was supposed to be based not on love, but on the benefits that the marriage would bring to the fathers of the bride and groom. Nevertheless, most Roman fathers discussed likely partners with their daughters before they made their choice.

In practice, fathers rarely exercised the full authority given them by law. Children were considered important members of the household because they carried on the customs and traditions of the Roman people. Some fathers taught their sons reading, writing, and arithmetic. They also taught them how to manage their estates. Other fathers hired Greek tutors to teach both their sons and daughters. Poorer Roman families sent their children to local grammar schools.

Section Questions

1. Who were the Etruscans? How did they influence the political life of the Roman Republic?
2. What is a republic? How does it differ from pure democracy?
3. Give two examples of how the institutions of the Republic were designed to prevent officeholders from abusing their power.
4. Why did the patricians give in to the plebians? List at least three reforms that the plebians demanded.
5. Describe some of the ways in which Roman fathers exercised their authority.

The ruins of El Djem Colosseum, perhaps the greatest monument to Roman Africa.

2. Rome Dominated the Mediterranean

After the Romans defeated the Etruscans, they signed a peace treaty with the Latin League, an alliance of various towns in Latium. Instead of punishing their enemies for having helped the Etruscan king, the Romans treated the Latins as allies. The treaty provided for the creation of a Roman-Latin army. One year, the troops were to be commanded by a Roman general. A Latin general was to assume command the next year. Romans and Latins became trading partners. They were allowed to marry one another as well. The treaty formed the basis for the foreign policy that the Republic carried out during the next 200 years.

Unification of Italy The alliance between Rome and the Latin peoples did not bring peace to the peninsula. Neighboring hill people invaded Rome. The Romans drove them back and conquered their lands. Latins were sent to govern them. *Garrisons*, or fortified towns, were formed to defend these new colonies.

Then the Gauls in the Po Valley moved south and tried to seize the remaining Etruscan territories. Unlike the Gauls who had settled in present-day France and Switzerland, the Gauls of northern Italy were nomadic and warlike. Around 390 B.C., they crossed the Apennines and laid siege to Etruria. To prevent the Gauls from extending their territory into central Italy, the Romans gave aid to the Etruscans. The Gauls routed the Roman army at the Allia (AL ee uh) River. As most Romans fled their city, the Gauls moved in and sacked Rome.

Once the Gauls had finally been driven out of Rome and back into the Po Valley, the Romans rebuilt their city. They erected a strong stone wall around it. Then they conquered the Etruscan territories.

Fifty years after signing the treaty of alliance with Rome, the Latins demanded full political rights as Roman citizens. The

Romans rejected their demands. War broke out in 340 B.C. After defeating the Latins, the Romans disbanded the confederation and signed a separate treaty with each Latin town.

By 300 B.C., Rome dominated northern and central Italy. Then Rome broke its treaty with the Greek city-state of Tarentum (tuh REN tum), which was located in southern Italy. The Tarentines declared war and asked Pyrrhus (PIH rus), the king of Epirus (ih PI rus) in eastern Greece, for help. Pyrrhus defeated the Romans in two battles. But he lost so many troops that his army could not continue the war. Today, after more than 2,000 years, a victory at too great a cost is still called a *Pyrrhic victory*. Pyrrhus rebuilt his army but was defeated in 275 B.C. With the surrender of the last Greek city-state in Italy, Rome dominated the Italian peninsula.

Rome Versus Carthage Carthage (KAHR thihj) began as a Phoenician colony in North Africa. It eventually won its independence and established itself as a great naval power. Carthage controlled Sardinia (sahr DIH nee uh), Corsica (KAWR sih kuh), the western half of Sicily, and the southern coast of Spain. Rome and Carthage had become rival powers in the Mediterranean. When Carthage sent its fleet to Sicily to protect the city of Messina (muh SEE nuh), the Romans sensed a threat to their colonies in southern Italy. War broke out in 264 B.C.

The Roman dictator, Regulus (REG yuh lus), realized that in order to win the war, Rome had to build a fleet. According to Roman accounts, they seized a ship from the Carthaginian fleet. Their engineers studied its construction. Then the engineers had it torn apart and rebuilt it according to their own design. Under their direction, teams of carpenters were set to work. Working day and night, they built fleets of ships that were superior to those of Carthage.

Even though Rome won several battles on the high seas, the Carthaginian leader, Hamilcar Barca (huh MIHL kahr BAHR kuh), continued to fight. As the war dragged on, both sides became exhausted and dangerously close to bankruptcy. Finally, in 241 B.C., the Romans defeated a large Carthaginian fleet. Carthage gave up the struggle and signed a peace treaty, which ended the war. Since the Romans called the Carthaginians "Puni," or Phoenicians, this war became known as the First Punic War.

By the terms of the treaty, the people of Carthage were forced to pay most of the costs of the war. They had to withdraw from the entire island of Sicily. Rome took Corsica and Sardinia. Roman governors were sent to administer the islands as conquered territories under the control of the Senate.

In 225 B.C., the Gauls invaded central Italy for the second time in less than two centuries. The Roman armies drove the invaders back to the Po Valley. This time, however, the Romans conquered Gaul and founded colonies there. Rome extended its frontiers to the base of the Alps in 222 B.C. From their outpost on the southern coast of Spain, the Carthaginians rebuilt their fleets and army. Led by Hamilcar Barca, they had conquered most of Spain by 229 B.C. After the death of Hamilcar, his son Hannibal (HAN uh bul) continued to strengthen the Carthaginian forces. Little is known about the early life of Hannibal. According to Roman legend, Hamilcar took his son, at the age of seven, to the alter of Moloch (MAH luk) the god of Carthage. There he swore eternal hatred for Rome.

The Campaigns of Hannibal Hannibal set out to conquer the few remaining independent cities in Spain. He attacked a city on the east coast that was friendly to Rome. The Romans declared war in 218 B.C. Thus began the Second Punic War (218 to 201 B.C.).

Hannibal crossing the Rhone River.

The Romans believed that the war would be like the first—a long struggle fought mostly on the high seas. But Hannibal outsmarted his enemies. He marched his army and a large number of elephants across the Alps and into Italy. The Gauls joined his campaign.

In 216 B.C., Hannibal defeated a huge Roman force at Cannae (KAN ee) in southern Italy. Although his army was greatly outnumbered, Hannibal outwitted the Roman generals. By pretending to retreat, he was able to outflank the Roman troops. Then he sent his cavalry to attack the last line of the Roman legions. The Carthaginian army killed over 60,000 Romans. It was Rome's worst disaster.

After Hannibal's victory, most of the Greek colonies in southern Italy allied with him. So did Philip V, king of Macedonia. No one believed that Rome could recover. However, the Romans refused to accept defeat. They rebuilt their army and launched a series of surprise attacks on Hannibal's forces. They defeated their former allies on the Italian mainland.

In 210 B.C., Publius Cornelius Scipio (SIH pee o) was sent to Spain. His Roman legions defeated a Carthaginian army led by Hannibal's brother, Hasdrubal (HAZ droo bul). By 205 B.C., Spain was a Roman province.

The following year, Scipio invaded North Africa. Hannibal hurried home to defend his country. At the Battle of Zama (ZAY muh), 202 B.C., Hannibal and his army were defeated. Carthage was forced to sign a treaty of peace.

Did You Know?

The Celts

The Celts (SELTZ) were the prehistoric people who, around 700 B.C., spread over most of western Europe—from Ireland down to Spain and across Europe, including an area of Rumania. The term "Celts" actually refers to many different tribal groups, one of which was the Gauls.

Our knowledge about the Celts has been increasing, due to the archaeological evidence that has been accumulating. Their burial sites, hill forts, villages, and fields have given good evidence about their culture. Greek and Roman writers also described the Celts and their way of life. However, the Romans, who at times were defeated by the Celts, emphasized their warlike features—their bravery, their fearlessness, their skill as charioteers, and their weapons.

Although these war accounts present a colorful picture of the Celts, warfare was not their full-time occupation. Most Celts were farmers. Some were miners of salt. Like most farmers at the time, the Celts used iron tools. Both women and men tended the crops and cattle, wove, and made pottery.

At the top of their social structure were *druids*—leaders or sages. This group had many skills. They were the priests and the healers as well as the musicians. They memorized the poetry and legends of their group. Under the druids were the chiefs and warriors who were most skilled in fighting. Beneath them were the large mass of farm families and, at the bottom, some slaves.

The Celts worshiped many gods. Often the oak tree, certain pools, wells, groves, and rocks were the sites of religious ceremonies. Popular also was the practice

A remnant of a Celtic breastplace, from around 300 B.C.

of throwing dogs and other animals into deep pits as a sacrifice to the gods. A few human skeletons have also been found in these pits. The bloodthirsty image of the Celts probably resulted from their practice of displaying the heads of their fallen enemies.

Celtic artisans made richly decorated swords and jewelry. These objects were meant to startle the viewer with their colorful patterns.

Eventually the Roman armies conquered most of the Celts. The lives of these people changed under Roman influence. But the Roman armies did not conquer all the Celts. The Celtic world of Scotland, Ireland, Wales, and Brittany survived for many centuries. It was here that Celtic traditions and customs were preserved. But while living independently in these areas, the Celts were greatly influenced by the Christian Church.

Roman Supremacy in the Mediterranean Carthage was forced to disband its army and destroy its fleets. It had to pay great sums of money for war damages. Rome even controlled its foreign relations.

The Roman losses in the war were staggering. Thousands had died in battle. Over half the farms in Italy had been destroyed. Many of the towns on the Italian peninsula never recovered. But Rome was now the dominant military and commercial power in the Mediterranean.

Rome sent its armies to punish Philip V for allying Macedonia with Carthage. By 146 B.C., it had conquered Greece and Macedonia and made them into a Roman province. This expansion brought Rome into conflict with the Seleucid (suh LOO sihd) kingdom of Syria. The Romans defeated the Syrians in 133 B.C. and took control of Asia Minor. Meanwhile, Carthage had begun to recover some of its economic strength. The Roman Senate became alarmed. Cato (KAY to), the leader of the Senate, ended all his speeches with the phrase "Carthage must be destroyed." Finally, the Senate ordered all Carthaginians to leave their city. As expected, they refused.

Thus began the Third Punic War (149 to 146 B.C.). The Roman army sacked and destroyed the city and slaughtered thousands of Carthaginians. Showing burning hatred for the country that they believed had caused so much bloodshed and destruction, the Romans plowed the ground. Then they salted it and laid a curse on the land. The Senate reorganized the territory of Carthage into the province of Africa. By 133 B.C., the Roman state extended from Spain in the west to Asia Minor in the east.

Section Questions

1. How did the Romans treat their enemies, the Latins, in 509 B.C.? How did they treat their allies, the Latins, in 340 B.C.?
2. According to the Romans, how were they able to create such a good navy at the beginning of the Punic Wars?
3. What terms were the Carthaginians forced to accept at the end of the First Punic War?
4. Describe Hannibal's campaigns. Why was he so determined to defeat the armies of Rome?
5. What did Rome gain from the Punic Wars? What losses did it suffer?

3. The Republic Failed

The rise of Rome from a small republic in central Italy to a world power took approximately 400 years. It deeply affected the lives of Romans, Italians, and people living in the territories conquered by Rome.

Economic Changes Tribute collected from people living in the conquered territories allowed some Romans to become wealthy. They invested money in large estates called *latifundia*. These were used mainly for cattle grazing. Rome exported meat as well as wine and olive oil throughout the Mediterranean. This economic expansion created a new group of business people—the moneylenders. They lent money at high interest to wealthy Romans who wanted to increase the size of their landed estates. They also lent money to Romans who went to the conquered territories to build roads, aqueducts, and houses and to develop farms.

Small farmers, the backbone of the old Republic, were unable to restore the land that Hannibal had destroyed. Many of them moved to Rome. Unable to find jobs, they lived in shacks and nursed their grievances. While they waited for strong leaders who could help them regain prosperity, they looked to the government for food and entertainment. This unemployed population became a large, unruly force.

Rome's position as a world power led to a marked increase in slavery. Conquered Syrians, who were skilled in producing grain, were sold into slavery. They were sent to work on the great estates in Rome and in the provinces. Greek slaves, who excelled in cultivating grapevines, were sent to estates in the wine-producing regions.

New Ideas Before conquering Greece and Asia Minor, the Romans were noted for developing such practical arts as building roads and aqueducts, draining marshes, and adapting the shipbuilding methods of the Carthaginians. After conquering Greece, the Romans began to use Greek methods of architecture. Greek-style columns and pillars adorned all new public buildings.

Wealthy Romans began to learn Greek and to study Greek literature and philosophy. Influenced by the Greek writers, Roman writers began to write plays and poems in Latin. The introduction of Hellenistic philosophies, like Epicureanism (ep ih kyoo RE uh nihz um), weakened Roman values. By teaching that pleasure was the goal of society, the Epicureans angered some conservative Roman senators. Some wealthy Romans formed sects modeled on the Dionysian (di uh NIH zee un) cults of the Hellenistic world. As followers of Dionysus (di uh NI sus), the Greek god of wine, members of Dionysian cults engaged in drunken revelries. The Senate conducted investigations of the cults in 186 B.C. and declared them illegal. Twenty years later, the Senate banished Hellenistic philosophers from Rome.

The introduction of eastern ideas weakened the strong family bonds of the early republic. Knowledge of the Greek gods weakened the religious authority of the paterfamilias. This, in turn, weakened the father's authority as head of the family. The Romans had never given personalities to their gods. Used to impersonal, nonhuman gods, the Romans began to question religion when they read about the spiteful gods that caused Oedipus to kill his father and marry his mother. With the loss of religious

A Roman sculpture of the Greek philosopher Aristotle. One of Aristotle's disciples introduced Greek philosophy to the Romans.

beliefs, divorce, practically unknown before 300 B.C., became commonplace. Adultery was widespread, and prostitution flourished.

The Split in Roman Society Some Romans mourned the passing of the old republican society. Tiberius Gracchus (GRAK us), a tribune, was convinced that the only way to check the corruption of Roman society was to get unemployed citizens out of the cities and back on the farms. He proposed that public land in Italy, along with the latifundia, be divided and given to them. The Senate opposed him. Rioting broke out, and Tiberius Gracchus was killed (133 B.C.). Twelve years later, Tiberius's younger brother proposed the same kind of reform. He, too, was killed in a riot provoked by the Senate. The Senate, composed of wealthy patrician and plebian landowners, rejected every measure that would have reduced their land holdings.

In 107 B.C., the Roman consul, Gaius Marius (MER ee us), decided to create a professional army by recruiting the mobs in the cities. In armies of the past, soldiers had been small farmers drafted to serve the Republic for one year. Now, Marius's recruits were allowed to serve their commanders for sixteen years in return for bonuses, booty, and pensions. Inspired by Marius's example, General Lucius Cornelius Sulla (SUL uh) developed an army that was loyal to him.

For a time, Sulla and Marius vied with each other for control of Rome. The Senate and the wealthy backed Sulla. The urban mobs supported Marius. A bloodbath resulted as hundreds were killed on both sides. No longer did the republican constitution decide who would rule Rome. Armed force and political manipulation had become the new tools of power. Both Sulla and Marius died of natural causes. This left a vacuum that many ambitious politicians were anxious to fill. Such a man was Gnaeus Pompey (PAHM pee), one of Sulla's generals. In 76 B.C., the Senate sent Pompey to suppress a rebellion in Spain. Pompey's successes there boosted his prestige.

While Pompey was in Spain, a slave revolt broke out in Italy. Thousands of slaves had taken up arms and united under the leadership of a Thracian (THRAY shun) named Spartacus (SPAR tuh kus). The slaves plundered the countryside and defeated four Roman armies. Finally, they were overwhelmed by an army led by a wealthy Roman named Marcus Crassus (KRAS us). Over 6,000 of the slaves were crucified. Crassus' power grew considerably because of this victory, even though Pompey had returned home just in time to steal part of the credit. Both Crassus and Pompey were elected consuls in 70 B.C.

In 66 B.C., Pompey got himself appointed commander of the Roman forces in Asia Minor. He crushed pirates who had disrupted Roman trade and then routed Rome's opponents in Asia Minor. Pompey invaded Syria and defeated the last of the Seleucid kings. Then he led his army into Jerusalem. The kingdom of the Jews passed under Roman control. Feeling like a new Alexander, Pompey finally returned to Rome in 62 B.C.

Crassus had been working to undermine Pompey's popularity in the Senate. While Pompey was away, Crassus had financed Gaius Julius Caesar (SEE zur), a nephew of Marius, who was popular with the mob. Though they distrusted each other, Pompey, Crassus, and Caesar formed a political alliance. The alliance is known as the First *Triumvirate*, or rule by three. Crassus provided the money; Pompey provided the army; and Caesar provided the support of the mob.

The Triumph of Caesar Caesar used his new connections to get the Senate to declare him governor of the province of Gaul. The appointment gave him command of an army. In 58 B.C., he began an ambitious project—the conquest of the lands in western Europe settled by the Gauls. Caesar hoped that this campaign would make his troops the most experienced army in Rome. Caesar's Gallic Wars lasted eight years (58 to 51 B.C.). He wrote an account of his campaign, called *The War Commentaries*. It was published in Rome and won him great support from the people.

Crassus assembled an army in the east. He invaded Parthia (PAR thee uh) in 54 B.C. His army was defeated, and he was

Julius Caesar.

captured and killed. The death of Crassus broke the bond between Caesar and Pompey.

In 49 B.C., Pompey got the Senate to declare Caesar a public enemy. Leading his victorious army, Caesar returned home. Pompey fled to Greece. The Senate was terrified. Caesar controlled his troops and spared Rome another bloodbath. Caesar then crossed into Greece and defeated Pompey's army. He granted pardons to Pompey's men. Pompey fled to Egypt where he asked Ptolemy XIV, the thirteen-year-old king, for sanctuary. Ptolemy, waging a struggle for power with his sister, Cleopatra VII, and hoping to win Caesar's support, had Pompey murdered. After Caesar arrived in Egypt and was presented with Pompey's head, he wept.

Caesar became enchanted with Cleopatra. His army overpowered the Egyptians, and he made her queen of Egypt. Before Caesar left, Cleopatra gave birth to their son, whom she called Caesarion.

Caesar returned to Rome in triumph in 46 B.C. Armed with the powers of dictator, he prepared to reorganize the Republic. He reduced the powers of the Senate and increased its membership. He began a huge program of public works to beautify Rome and to provide jobs for citizens who wanted to work. He encouraged Romans to colonize the provinces. Using the calculations of Egyptian mathematicians, he revised the calendar (even naming one month, July, after himself). His calendar forms the basis for the calendar that we use today.

Caesar did not live long enough to complete his plans. Senators resented Caesar's power. They feared that he would use his army to destroy the Republic and crown himself king. A conspiracy, headed by Marcus Brutus (BROO tus) and Gaius Cassius (KA shee us), two Senate leaders, was formed. In March 44 B.C., sixty senators attacked and murdered Caesar.

A fragment of a Roman calendar.

Cleopatra.

The Struggle for Power The Roman mob rioted when they learned of Caesar's murder. The conspirators fled to Greece. Two of Caesar's generals, Mark Anthony and Marcus Lepidus (LEP ud us), restored order. But neither could obtain dictatorial power because the other commanded an army. And both of them faced another competitor, Gaius Octavian (ahk TAY vih uhn), the eighteen-year-old nephew of Caesar, whom he had named as his heir. The three formed a triumvirate, known as the Second Triumvirate, in 43 B.C.

Led by a distinguished Senator named Marcus Cicero (SIH suh ro), many Romans called for the restoration of the Republic. The triumvirate responded with force. Cicero and thousands of others were murdered.

Anthony and Octavian began to divide up the territory of Rome between them. Anthony accepted control over the east and went to Egypt. There he fell in love with Cleopatra and married her. Unfortunately, Anthony was already married to Octavian's sister, Octavia. Octavian delivered his wedding present in person. He sailed a fleet to Egypt and conquered it. Anthony and Cleopatra committed suicide.

Octavian was now the master of the Roman world. The Roman Republic was dead as were those who wished to restore it. Who would regret its passing? For the past 100 years, the Republic had been wracked by riots, slave uprisings, civil wars, conspiracies, and murders. Its constitution had been destroyed. It had degenerated into the rule of powerful generals and corrupt senators. An economy based on the productive work of small farmers had been replaced by one dominated by wealthy landowners and moneylenders. Its small farmers had become rootless and unemployed. The traditional Roman family and religion had been undermined. Divorce, prostitution, adultery, and corruption were widespread. All citizens longed for peace and order.

Section Questions

1. What role did the provinces play in the economic life of Rome? Why did the latifundia increase after 133 B.C.?
2. Why did slavery grow after 133 B.C.? Who was Spartacus? What did he do?
3. How did Greek philosophy and religion influence the life of Roman citizens after 133 B.C.?
4. What role did the mobs play in bringing about the failure of the Roman Republic? Who was Tiberius Gracchus? What did he want to do?
5. List Caesar's achievements. Why was he murdered?

Thinking Geographically: Compare this map with the map of the Greek and Phoenician colonies. How are they similar? How are they different?

4. Rome Brought Peace and Unity to the Mediterranean

The rule of Octavian, whom the Senate named Augustus Caesar in 27 B.C., began a period that historians call the *Pax Romana*. The Roman peace lasted 200 years.

The peace and order of these 200 years allowed trade and commerce to flourish throughout the empire and beyond. Italians sold their pottery, wine, olive oil, and metal goods in the provinces. Egyptians traded their linens, glassware, and papyrus. Syrians sold their purple dye, fruit, and wine. Spaniards mined silver, which was minted into coins for use throughout the empire. Vegetables, fruits, grains, and meats produced in Gaul, Africa, and Sicily fed the empire. The merchants of the Roman empire also shipped their wares to India, China, and Arabia. From these lands, they received precious stones, spices, pepper, silk, and gold.

The Roman Empire united two worlds: the Greek and the Roman. During the Pax Romana, the Romans improved their way of administering the provinces. They further developed military science and law. All these helped establish order and peace. This same order and peace made it possible

121

for Hellenistic civilization to thrive and expand throughout the empire. The Romans encouraged the Hellenization of Asia Minor and Syria. In Egypt, the Greeks continued to serve as merchants and business people. In the eastern empire, Greek was the language of daily life. In the west, Latin became the dominant language. However, many wealthy, educated Romans also spoke Greek.

Augustus Augustus ruled from 27 B.C. to A.D. 14. He planned to rule the empire himself. But he did not want to anger the Senate. So he announced that he was going to restore the Republic. Although the form of government that Augustus established was not a republic, it satisfied the Senate.

Augustus divided the provinces of the empire. He let the Senate govern the well-established provinces of the empire such as Macedonia, North Africa, and Spain. He kept the frontier provinces for himself. There he stationed the army and sent governors to enforce his laws.

Augustus reorganized the Senate. By reducing its membership to 600, he removed many corrupt individuals who had become senators during the civil wars. By establishing a pension system, he convinced many senators to retire. He announced that only citizens who owned large estates could become senators. By restoring the privileged status of the Senate, Augustus won the support of its members.

Augustus' Powers Augustus governed the city of Rome and controlled the grain supply. He was the commander in chief of the Roman army. He owned provinces and large estates. He was the wealthiest man in Rome. He nominated senators. He called the Senate into session and directed its meetings. He presented legislation to the Senate, which the Senate approved without change. The assembly had no power. Nevertheless, Augustus called it to order whenever he wanted to make an announcement. He was the final judge to whom all sentences and judgments could be appealed. He became the head of the Roman religion.

Imperial Administration Augustus ruled the empire through the army and the administrative offices that he created. He formed a permanent professional army. Eighteen-year-olds volunteered to serve for twenty-five years. At the end of their enlistments, they received bonuses or land. Augustus also reorganized the army. Stationed along the frontiers of the empire, the army established order, protected the provinces from invasions, and introduced Roman customs and the Latin language. By buying food and supplies from local merchants, the army also brought prosperity

Augustus.

The ruins of a Roman aqueduct in present-day Israel.

to the provinces. In peacetime, the troops built roads, bridges, and *aqueducts*, or tunnels for carrying water.

Augustus also formed an elite corps of troops called the *praetorian guard*. He selected 9,000 well-disciplined soldiers and trained them to act as his bodyguard. He stationed them in the vicinity of Rome.

To the provinces, Augustus sent governors who commanded the troops and supervised city officials. In the capital, Augustus created the central administrative offices of his empire. The office of state handled the emperor's correspondence. Other offices processed appeals, collected taxes, and managed the finances of the empire and of the emperor's estates. The empire had never before been so well administered.

Augustus secured the southern frontier of Egypt by conquering Ethiopia. He annexed several lands in the east and secured the frontier of Asia Minor. German tribes prevented the Roman army from extending the northern frontier to the Elbe (EL buh) River. But despite that defeat, the boundaries of the Roman Empire had been strengthened.

Augustus ordered the city of Rome and the temples of the gods rebuilt. Libraries, theaters, and public squares were erected. He ordered the construction of a system of roads that connected the provinces to Rome. He established penalties for adultery. He encouraged the institution of marriage and the creation of large families. After his death, the Senate named Augustus one of the gods of Rome.

Augustus' Successors Augustus failed to establish a system of succession to the office of emperor. This would be a nagging problem for the empire for the next three centuries. He finally named his stepson, Tiberius, to succeed him. But Tiberius seemed to lack the ambition needed to rule. Tiberius became emperor in A.D. 14 and quickly appointed one of his aides to rule in his name. Tiberius spent most of his rule in semiretirement in Capri (ka PREE). (Jesus was crucified during Tiberius's reign.) Tiberius named his nephew, Caligula (kuh LIHG yuh luh) to succeed him (from A.D. 37 to 41).

Historians believe that Caligula was insane. He considered himself a god. He ordered that a statue of himself be created and placed in the Temple of Jerusalem. He murdered people who displeased him. Caligula ordered wild games to be held. He spent all the money in the Roman treasury. He was finally murdered by the praetorian guard.

The praetorian guard then named Caligula's uncle, Claudius (KLAW dee us), to succeed him (from A.D. 41 to 54). Claudius was a scholarly man who proved to be quite a capable emperor. He replenished the treasury and built two aqueducts. He conquered southern Britain and made Thrace a Roman province. He was eventually murdered in a plot that many Romans believed was led by his wife. Her son, who took the name Nero (NEE ro), succeeded Claudius.

Nero, who ruled from A.D. 54 to 68, was a tyrant and a murderer. He killed his mother and two of his wives. He considered himself a genius. He wrote plays that he performed in public. He admired the talent of the Greeks. On a visit to the provinces, he declared that the Greeks were free to leave the Roman Empire. In A.D. 64, a fire almost destroyed Rome. Some of Nero's enemies accused him of playing his lyre while Rome burned. Others accused him of setting the fire. Nero charged a group of Christians with arson. He tortured them in public and then put them to death. To pay for rebuilding the city, Nero seized the lands of many senators and ordered their execution. The Senate finally declared him an enemy of the people. He fled from Rome. Evidently lacking the nerve to do the deed himself, Nero ordered one of his servants to kill him.

For the next thirty-two years, the praetorian guard and the armies of the east and west marched on Rome. They proclaimed their commanders emperors. After a reign of terror unleashed by the Emperor Domitian (duh MIH shun), the Senate asserted itself. Domitian was assassinated. The army accepted the Senate's authority. In A.D. 96, it supported Nerva (NER vuh), a senator, as emperor.

The Good Emperors With Nerva began an era known as the reign of the five good emperors (A.D. 96 to 180). Nerva reorganized agriculture. He granted low-interest loans to farmers who were too poor to improve their lands. During Trajan's (TRAY jun) reign, the Roman Empire reached its greatest extent. Hadrian (HAY dree un), an able and tolerant ruler, built a wall around the northern end of Britain and reorganized the army. He codified the edicts of the emperors and strengthened the civil service. For each position in government, specific duties and salaries were established. Antonio Antoninus (an tuh NI nus) established reforms that made females eligible for loans and aid from the state. Under Marcus Aurelius (aw REE lee us), the army turned back the German invaders who had reached the city of Rome. Marcus Aurelius, who spent much of his time protecting the empire, was also a follower of Stoic (STO ihk) philosophy.

Stoicism Hellenistic philosophers had introduced Stoicism into the Roman Empire. It seemed an appropriate philosophy to some wealthy Romans who considered themselves citizens of a world empire. Stoics believed that all the people of the world were born with certain rights, like the right to own property and to make personal choices. Taken together, these rights made up the natural laws of the universe. The Stoics sought to discover these natural laws through the use of reason. From these laws, they developed a moral code for both public and private behavior. They taught that self-discipline and personal responsibility were the highest virtues. Out of these Stoic ideas, the Romans developed the philosophy of law that they tried to establish in the late second century of the empire.

Roman Law Influenced by Stoicism, the Romans began to decrease the use of slaves on the estates. Notions of Stoic justice, as well as the example of farmers from the east who were more productive, finally changed the system of estate slavery into one of tenant farming. Laws were passed that made it easier for slaves to be freed. The Romans, influenced by natural law, extended civil liberties to women and to the accused in criminal and civil cases. Women were allowed to own and manage property. The principle that an accused person was innocent until proven guilty was written into Roman law. Roman law remained the foundation of the legal codes of most of Europe well after the Roman Empire had disintegrated.

Science, Architecture, Engineering It has been suggested that the Romans were so busy running their empire that they only found time to develop politics, military science, and law. The few great scientists who lived in the empire were Greek. The greatest physician was the Greek Claudius Galen (GAY lun, A.D. 130 to 200). He wrote a medical encyclopedia in which all known medical knowledge was compiled. He added a description of his discovery that arteries contain blood. The Romans established the first hospitals in the western world. They provided medical care for the poor as well as for the rich.

Some of the greatest achievements of the Romans were in architecture and

A Roman physician examining a patient.

engineering. Although they borrowed many ideas from other peoples, Romans built on a much larger scale. They were, perhaps, the first people to use cement and concrete as building materials. The roads they built for their armies connected the far reaches of the empire. Romans learned how to build the arch from the Etruscans. They used it to construct enormous bridges and aqueducts, which carried drinking water across rivers and valleys. Romans adapted the Greek amphitheater. The most famous of the Roman amphitheaters, the Colosseum, seated 45,000 spectators. Beneath the massive arena were dens, dressing rooms, and storage facilities.

Hundreds of public baths could be found in the city of Rome. The baths had dressing rooms, saunas, hot and cold baths, exercise rooms, lounging rooms, halls, and libraries. Wealthy Romans worked in the morning and came to the baths in the afternoon. There they met their friends, discussed politics and current events, bathed, exercised, lounged, and read.

The Roman apartment house had many levels. The first floor was reserved for shops and businesses. Above were apartments of different sizes and designs. Used in all Roman buildings were *arcades*—arched, covered passageways—that allowed Romans to enter and leave buildings easily.

This fresco illustrates Vergil's story of Dido and Aeneas.

The famous Colosseum of Rome.

Latin Literature By the first century, Rome had produced many great authors in poetry and in prose. Vergil (VER juhl, 70 to 19 B.C.) wrote the epic poem the *Aeneid* (ih NEE ihd). In it, he told how Aeneas, a legendary hero of the ancient city of Troy, escaped and settled in central Italy. There he founded the Latin race and the Roman people. Vergil has been called the greatest Roman poet.

The Odes of Horace (HAW rus, 65 to 8 B.C.) are delightful poems. Horace praised the simple life and encouraged the old Roman virtues. He recounted the pleasures of love and mourned the shortness of life. He also celebrated the greatness of Augustus. The poet Ovid (O vud, 43 B.C. to A.D. 14) wrote the *Metamorphoses* in which he told the great stories of Greek mythology.

The Roman historian Livy (LIH vee, 59 B.C. to A.D. 17) wrote a history of Rome from the time of the founding of the city to the reign of Augustus. Tacitus (TAS uh tus, A.D. 55 to 120), another historian, wrote a history of the first century of the empire. He also wrote about the Germans. He praised the simplicity of their lives and

LEGACY OF ANCIENT ROME

Social Institutions: father of family had broad powers.

Government: originally a republic, later replaced by emperors.

Law: based on philosophy of stoicism, Roman law extended rights of individuals.

Medicine: first hospitals established.

Architecture, engineering: probably first use of cement and concrete, extensive roads, aqueducts, amphitheaters.

Literature: great poems, mythology, history, biography.

condemned the immorality in Rome. Suetonius (swee TO nee us, *circa* A.D. 75 to 150) wrote biographies rather than histories. Only *Lives of the Twelve Caesars* has survived.

In Alexandria, Ptolemy, an astronomer, wrote a world geography that became the textbook for students throughout the Middle Ages.

Section Questions

1. What was the Pax Romana? How did it contribute to the prosperity of the empire?
2. What powers did Augustus exercise?
3. Why did the Senate call Nero an enemy of the people?
4. How did Stoicism contribute to the development of Roman law?
5. What contributions did the Greeks make to the development of Roman architecture, science, and literature?

Chapter Summary

1. The city-state of Rome expelled the Etruscan king in 509 B.C. and founded the Roman Republic. To the Etruscans, the Romans owed their political institutions, their family system, and their urban way of life. The republic that they created divided political power among a number of political institutions. They created the offices of consul and dictator to run the government. To represent the patrician class, the Romans established the Senate. To represent the plebians, they adopted the council that had existed under the Etruscans. Over the course of 250 years, the plebians won their struggle to achieve political equality with the patrician class. They won their fight to have Roman laws written and published. They won the right to be represented in the highest offices of government.
2. After the Romans defeated the Etruscan forces, they entered into alliances with their former enemies, the Latins. The Romans defeated the hill people around them. They established Latin colonies and cities in the conquered territories. On two occasions, the Gauls sacked Rome and damaged the city. The Romans finally conquered the territory of the Gauls north of the Po Valley. The Romans also broke their treaty with Carthage. And there began a series of wars that changed Rome from a small republic on the Tiber River to a power that dominated the Mediterranean world.
3. Tribute collected from the conquered lands poured into Rome. Added wealth created a class of business people and latifundia owners. The small farmers were uprooted. Many of them gathered in the large cities, where they formed mobs. The increase in the number of slaves taken as prisoners of war led to a number of slave uprisings. Strong leaders arose who either proposed land reforms or led their own armies. Julius Caesar eventually emerged as a Roman dictator. He accomplished some reforms but was assassinated. The struggle for power after Caesar's death resulted in the final victory of his nephew, Octavian. The Roman Republic had been exhausted.
4. From the Roman Empire created by Augustus, the Pax Romana (27 B.C. to A.D. 180) developed. The peace and order of this period permitted trade to flourish. Hellenistic civilization spread throughout the empire. Augustus exercised all the powers of the state. He reorganized the army and the Senate and secured the frontiers of his empire. Later, the rule of corrupt and insane emperors permitted the army to control the process of selecting emperors. Finally the Senate was able to select Nerva, who began the rule of the good emperors which lasted until A.D. 180. Among the lasting contributions of the Romans are their system of law and the Latin language.

Chapter 7 Review

Check Your Facts

1. Why did the Romans hate monarchy? How did this affect the system of government that they instituted after 509 B.C.?
2. Describe the economy of the Etruscans. Compare it with the Roman economy.
3. Explain the differences between the offices of the consul and the tribune.
4. What is a Pyrrhic victory? Where did the term come from?
5. How did the Romans get territory in Asia Minor?
6. Who was Cicero? What happened to him?
7. What effects did Greek drama and poetry have on Roman writing?
8. What changes in government did Augustus make?

Words to Know

Match each of these terms with its definition below: legion, triumvirate, republic, monarchy

1. an organization of soldiers positioned about 2½ meters (8 feet) from each other
2. a political system in which citizens elect officers who govern for their benefit
3. rule by a king
4. rule by three persons

Developing Your Skills

Make a time line that shows the chronology of the following events:

1. The Pax Romana begins.
2. Pyrrhus sends aid to his ally at the tip of southern Italy.
3. Hannibal defeats the Romans at Cannae.
4. The Etruscans invade Latium.
5. Augustus' death causes problems of succession.
6. The area ruled by the Roman Empire reaches its greatest extent.
7. Tiberius Gracchus is murdered.
8. Julius Caesar emerges as dictator.
9. Pompey is killed.
10. The Gauls sack Rome for the first time.

Thinking It Over

1. How did the introduction of Hellenistic religion contribute to the failure of the Roman Republic?
2. Evaluate the role of the dictator from the establishment of the Roman Republic in 509 B.C. to its failure as a form of government. Name two dictators and describe their contributions to the growth of the republic or to its failure.
3. Do you think Augustus was a good ruler? Explain your answer. Why do you think that the Romans got involved in so many wars?

Special Activities

1. Research Roman games. Prepare a report in which you describe to your classmates the Festival of Saturn held every December 17. Or describe the training, the dress, and the fighting techniques of the gladiators, or any other game that may interest you.
2. Pretend that you were a citizen of the Roman Republic. Write a series of diary entries that would reveal facts about your life-style.

This sculpture of a lion victorious over an elephant symbolizes the triumph of Hinduism over Buddhism in India.

Chapter 8 India and China

*I*ndia's reputation for fabulous wealth was well established in the west. The Greek historian, Herodotus, had described India as the land of "gold-strewn deserts where giant golden ants dug for gold"! The Bible mentioned the "ivory, apes, and peacocks" brought from India to the temple of King Solomon. Such legends inspired fresh waves of invaders from the west to come and conquer this vast land.

In contrast, China began a period of great cultural and scientific advancement, called the *Pax Sinica*, or Chinese Peace.

200 B.C.—A.D. 600

301 B.C.	Mauryan empire begins
206 B.C.	Han dynasty; Pax Sinica begins
184 B.C.	Mauryan empire ends
A.D. 50	Kushans conquer northern India
A.D. 220	Han dynasty, Pax Sinica end
A.D. 320	Gupta empire begins
A.D. 400s	India's classical age
A.D. 525	Gupta empire ends
A.D. 500s	Poet-saints popularize Hinduism

This bronze vessel in the shape of a duck is from the Han dynasty or earlier.

1. Strong Rulers United Most of India

In about 525 B.C., King Darius of Persia led his soldiers to the northwestern part of India. His army conquered the northwest and added it to the Persian empire as its twentieth province. Two hundred years later, the brilliant young general, Alexander the Great, defeated the Persians and then marched on to invade India in 327 B.C. He captured most of the Punjab region. Alexander left behind administrators and generals to look after the territory he had conquered. This kept India and the Mediterranean in close cultural and commercial contact. Alexander's invasion of India made no major impact on the life along the Indus. Yet, it is remembered in Indian history as a major landmark because the Greeks who accompanied him left detailed written accounts of conditions in western India at that time. Historians have relied heavily on these accounts for their knowledge of early Indian history.

Rise of the Mauryan Empire During Alexander's conquests, the warring kingdoms of the Ganges plains had combined to form four major kingdoms. These four kingdoms continued to compete for territory until the king of the Magadha (MUG ud uh) region managed to defeat his rivals. A bold young man named Chandragupta Maurya (chun druh GOOP ta MAY ur yah) then overthrew the king and seated himself on the throne. By 301 B.C., Chandragupta had united northern India, including the Indus plains. The Greeks were pushed northwest beyond the Hindu Kush (hin doo KUSH) Mountains. Chandragupta and the Greek general Seleucus made a treaty to trade peacefully and exchange ambassadors. Within a short time, Chandragupta trans-

131

formed several feuding kingdoms into a vast empire. He became an all-powerful ruler with divine right over his subjects—an emperor. He was helped in organizing his administration by a shrewd Brahman adviser.

Chandragupta ruled from his splendid capital at Pataliputra (pah tuh lih POO truh) on the banks on the Ganges. It was a well-fortified and planned city, not unlike Mohenjo-Daro. The empire was divided into four districts, and each district was ruled by a governor who belonged to the royal family. A large, centralized group of *bureaucrats* (government workers) and a well-trained army governed and protected the empire. Chandragupta was a low-caste person and tried to protect himself from the intrigues of the Brahman and Kshatriya castes. He depended heavily on spies to keep him informed about plots to overthrow him.

The Economy The majority of the people farmed the land and lived in villages. It was generally accepted that the land belonged to the emperor. He therefore had the right to collect taxes. Taxes ranged from one-sixth to one-fourth of the goods produced. This revenue gave stability to the government. It was used to pay the bureaucrats, to pay the army, and to maintain a luxurious court. New land was constantly being cleared by the Sudras and slaves, and larger areas were brought under

A view of a Buddhist stupa built by Asoka.

cultivation. Irrigation was highly developed and regulated. Dams were built to assure a supply of water.

While villages and cities were also taxed—for their cattle, manufactured goods, and trade—the wealth of the empire was built on the agricultural surplus from the countryside. Trade with the west flourished in the west of India. There was both overland and *maritime* (overseas) trade with Iran and the Mediterranean. The use of silver and copper coins for money and the strict standardization of weights and measures made trading easy. Inland trade also expanded. The Ganges provided a great waterway along which grew several trading towns. Land routes to the Deccan and along the east coast of India were opened. Commerce thrived. The artisan class expanded, and the subdivisions of the caste system became even more complex. Occupations were, in theory, hereditary. But Chandragupta himself, said to be the son of a potter, was a startling example of defiance of caste rules.

In 301 B.C., Chandragupta's son became ruler. He expanded the empire into the southern peninsula, after conquering the Dravidian- (druh VIH dee un) speaking peoples. However, it was Chandragupta's grandson, Asoka (uh SHO kuh 269 to 232 B.C.), who united the entire subcontinent.

Age of Asoka For the first eight years of his reign, Asoka led the life of a true Indian monarch. He hunted, feasted, and waged ruthless wars against his enemies to expand his empire. Then the bloodiest war of his reign, the conquest of Kalinga (kah LING uh), changed Asoka's life. To make certain that everyone knew of his accomplishments, Asoka had them inscribed on pillars of polished stone that were erected all over his kingdom.

Asoka's most lasting contribution to Indian history was his decision to help the spread of Buddhism. He sent delegations of monks and teachers to act as Buddhist missionaries in other nations. These missionaries reached as far west as Syria, Egypt, and Macedonia and as far south as Sri Lanka. (Sri Lanka is still primarily a Buddhist land today.) Yet, Asoka remained tolerant of the Brahmans. He did not persecute Hindus, who were still the majority in India. (See *Did You Know*, page 140.)

After Asoka's death in 232 B.C., the economic and spiritual strength of the empire declined. Conquered peoples within the empire began to reassert their independence. It took fifty more years, however, for the Mauryan empire to dissolve.

Disunity in India Indian history is marked by short spells of dynastic rule followed by long spells of disorder and disunity. The Harappan empire was separated from the Mauryan by 2,000 years of disunity. After the collapse of the Mauryan empire in 184 B.C., nearly 500 years of disunity followed. The Gupta (GOOP ta) dynasty would unite north India again in A.D. 320. In this interlude, south India was also divided into kingdoms ruled by Dravidian-speaking Hindu and Buddhist kings. The main Dravidian languages at this time were Tamil and Telugu (TE luh goo). The Telugu-speaking Andhra (AN druh) kings founded an empire that lasted from about 200 B.C. to A.D. 200. There were also three very prosperous Tamil kingdoms located farther south. All of them had a flourishing trade with Southeast Asia.

North India continued to experience fresh invasions from central Asia. The first of these after the decline of the Mauryas was the invasion of the Bactrians (BAK tree unz). The Bactrians had declared their independence from Alexander's successors, the Seleucid empire. They conquered the Punjab in 190 B.C. Their king, Menander (muh NAN dur), converted to Buddhism in 150 B.C. and proceeded to inscribe the Buddhist message on stone pillars, as Asoka had done. He wanted to influence his people to convert to Buddhism. Beautiful coins bearing the images of Greek gods and Bactrian monarchs have survived to tell the story of this dynasty. A unique blend of Greek and Buddhist art and culture was produced at this time. Greek and other western astronomers and healers strongly influenced the development of science in India. In turn, Buddhism had an important intellectual influence on western religions in the century before the birth of Christ. By about 100 B.C., Bactrian rule weakened, as new Asiatic tribes attacked the kingdom from the northwest.

The next set of invaders who succeeded in establishing a powerful kingdom in the northwest were the Kushans. By about A.D. 50, they drove other Asian tribes deeper into India. These periodic newcomers were "Indianized" fairly rapidly. The warlike people would adopt Kshatriya family names. From then on, they quickly mixed and intermarried with people of their "own" caste. These early invasions make Indians a very mixed and interesting people, ranging from fair to dark, with every possible combination of hair and eye color.

The Age of Commerce It was during this period, when the Kushans dominated the north and the Tamils dominated the

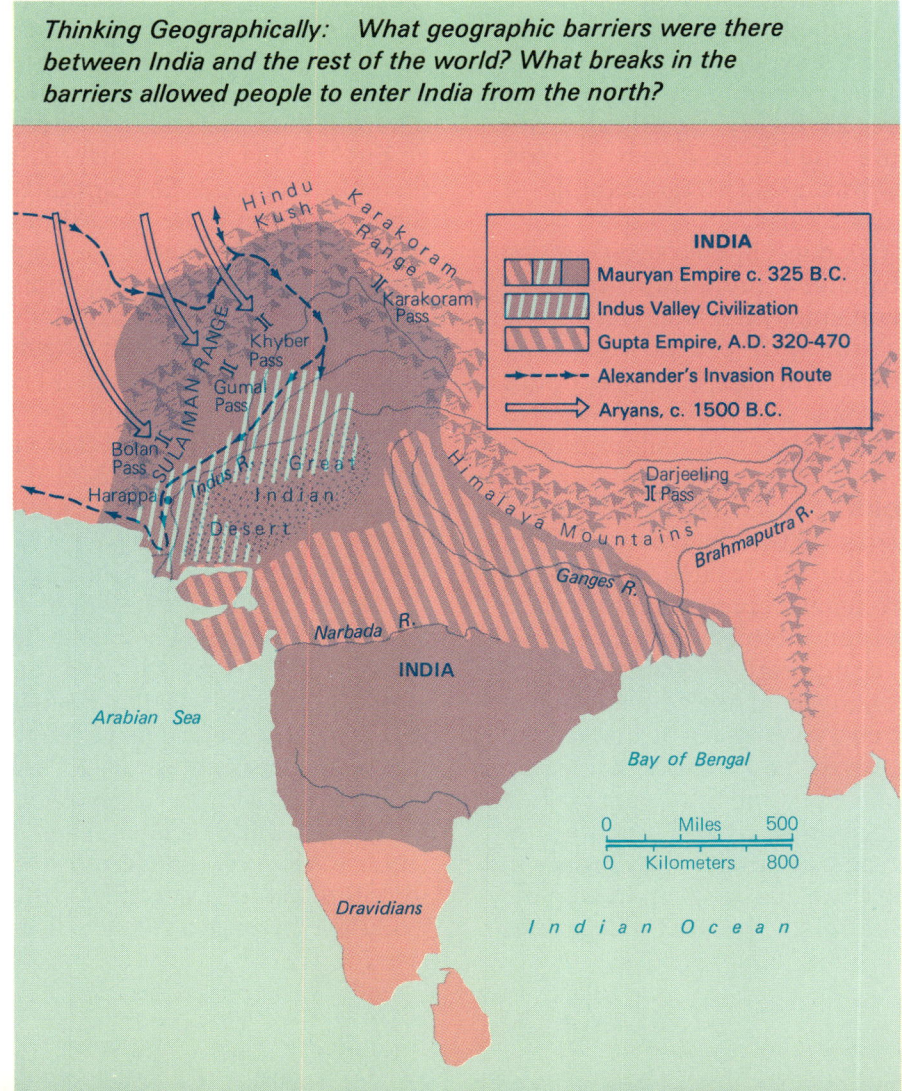

Thinking Geographically: What geographic barriers were there between India and the rest of the world? What breaks in the barriers allowed people to enter India from the north?

south, that trade and commerce with the west reached its height. The Kushans traded with the Romans through an overland route that crossed the kingdom of the Parthians. The Parthians grew wealthy by taxing this trade, since all caravans had to pass through their territories.

The Tamil kingdoms commanded the huge coastline of the Indian peninsula. They were a midpoint between the Far East and the Mediterranean lands. An important aid to navigation was discovered as early as the first century B.C. Sailors realized that the monsoon winds could be used to travel between the southern tip of India and the east coast of Africa at the mouth of the Red Sea. From May to October, the winds blew from the southwest, making the journey from Africa to India very easy. From November to April, the winds blew from the northeast, also shortening the return trip. The directness of this route, combined with the freedom from Parthian taxes, made it popular with merchants in both Egypt and the Tamil states.

When Augustus became Roman emperor, the Tamil states sent him a delegation with many gifts to honor the occasion. During his reign, Augustus, and later his successors, encouraged the use of this sea route from Egypt to India. As a result of this trade, Indian merchants lived in Alexandria and Roman merchants lived in the Tamil states. From India, pearls, precious stones, drugs, spices such as ginger and cinnamon, and works of art were shipped to the Mediterranean world. In return, Roman merchants sent wine, pottery, glassware, coins, and slaves.

To keep up with the western demand for spices, the Tamil states maintained close contact with the East Indies and Southeast Asia. Indian merchants lived along the Mekong (MAY KAHNG) River (in present-day Vietnam and Cambodia) and in Indonesia. Artifacts from the Mediterranean region have been found in these areas dating from that time. Eventually, this seagoing trade would reach into China itself.

In the third century A.D., the Kushan state declined, as did the Andhra and Tamil states to the south. This period of political disunity in both north and south India was in a large measure ended by the rise of the Gupta empire (A.D. 320 to 525). Many historians see this period as India's classical age.

A Tamil temple.

LEGACY OF CLASSICAL INDIA

Arts: Developed distinct Indian style in sculpture, painting, and music

Sciences: Astronomers proved that the Earth was round and rotated on its axis; calculated the length of the year; explained eclipses

Mathematics: Developed the number system we use today, including concept of zero, decimals

Commerce: Extensive trade, from China to Europe, spread ideas of different cultures

Section Questions

1. Name four invading groups who at one time or other conquered parts of northern India.
2. What impact did these invasions have on the development of northern India?
3. Who was Chandragupta Maurya? What did he accomplish?
4. Who was Asoka? What did he accomplish?
5. Describe the trade among the Tamil states, Egypt, and Southeast Asia. What was traded? By what routes did the goods travel?

2. The Arts, Learning, and Hinduism Flourished in India

The family origins of the Guptas are unclear. By 320, they had made themselves the rulers of Magadha in the Ganges Valley and had taken the title of great king of kings. From Magadha, the Guptas controlled the Ganges River, the main artery of trade in north India. They also controlled the rich iron mines of the valley, needed for making weapons. With these resources, Samudragupta (sah MOO druh GOOP ta) embarked upon a brilliant career of conquests. Historians today call him the Napolean of India. Samudragupta's army included many elephants. Elephants were the ancient Indian equivalent of the battle tank. War-horses were imported for his cavalry from Arabia and Persia because Indian breeds were not as strong.

In many parts of his empire, Samudragupta allowed defeated kings to rule as long as they paid him tribute and acknowledged him as supreme ruler. For the rest of his empire, he created a large bureaucracy, much like that of the Mauryans. Like all Indian kings, he depended mainly on agricultural taxes for his finances. To encourage the growth of agriculture (and his revenues) he ordered the building of wells, artificial lakes, and other irrigation projects. His state was also made rich by tribute, loot, and taxes on trade. He controlled the manufacture of salt and the mining of iron and precious gems.

India's Classical Age The empire reached its height under Chandragupta II (no relation to the first Mauryan). Chandragupta II (ca. 375-415) gained control of all of north India. But his empire never included the south. The old Andhra and Tamil dynasties were replaced instead by new regional kingdoms. Despite the political divisions in the south, foreign trade continued to thrive. Hoards of Roman coins have been discovered at archaeological sites in south India. Tamil literature flourished. The gradual blending of Dravidian and Aryan culture, which had begun centuries earlier, speeded up.

A palace scene from a fresco cave painting in Ajanta.

Chandragupta II is best remembered as a patron of culture rather than as a warrior. The wealth and learning of his court attracted many artists and scientists to his capital. Kalidasa (kal ih DAS uh), one of the greatest of India's poets and dramatists, wrote about the lively court life. Distinctively Indian styles emerged in all the arts. They owed little to the Greek influence of earlier periods. Sculptors made human shapes more curved and rounded. In painting and music, also, the styles that developed have influenced Indian art and music to this day.

In science, Aryabhata (AHR uh BUT ah), an astronomer, calculated the length of the year to be 365.5686805 days, which is very close to modern estimates. He also explained the nature of eclipses. Centuries before the Italian astronomer Galileo, Aryabhata proved that the Earth was round and rotated on its axis. We also owe our numbers, the idea of zero, and the decimal system to Indians. These were first adopted by the Arabs, and later by the Europeans.

The Guptas supported both Buddhism and Hinduism. But Hinduism was experiencing a revival. The great strength of Hinduism was its tolerance of diversity. Neighbors could believe in widely different ideas, for Hinduism holds that there are many paths to salvation. Another strength of Hinduism was the attention it gave to the daily aspects of people's lives. Sacred law books were prepared that described how society should be organized and how people should behave. Brahman astrologers became indispensable in determining the time for important events such as the start of a journey or a marriage. Religion even influenced what people ate. Vegetarianism became common because of the belief that living creatures should not be harmed.

Under the Guptas, temples were built out of stone for the first time. Some were carved out of mountainsides, such as the rock-and-cave temples at Ajanta (uh JUNT uh) near modern-day Bombay (bahm BAY). The first free-standing temples from rock were small and simple. But they became models for the grand temples found throughout India today.

India's artisans made beautiful silk and cotton textiles. They were also famous for their jewelry and their work in iron, copper, and bronze. India's trade with the west gradually lessened as Rome got weaker, but it did not end. The decline of the western routes was offset by the growth in the sea trade with Southeast Asia. Indian merchants also became regular callers at Chinese markets.

While most people still lived in villages, India had more cities than ever before. Some were political capitals or market centers. Others were built on holy spots and became the destinations for India's many pilgrims. Literature from the time describes a prosperous and bustling city life. Even those who were poor could count on charity. The government ran free hospitals and gave food to the needy. Religious orders built shelters where travelers could rest and eat.

Political Disunity in the North Around 450, nomadic Hun tribes attacked India through the passes in the northwest. At first, the Guptas beat the invasion back. But internal rebellions and fighting among the royal princes eventually left them too weak to defend their borders. The Huns overran most of the Gupta empire by 525. Former vassals and neighboring kings seized the rest.

In succeeding centuries, the idea of a universal empire continued to inspire India's kings. But none were able to duplicate the feats of the Mauryans or Guptas. North India was broken up into many states whose boundaries changed with the fortunes of war.

This sculpture from a temple shows a distinct Indian style.

Rebirth of the South Between 500 and 1200, south India was also split among kingdoms that were constantly at war. Disunity, however, did not hurt the region. The south flourished economically and developed rich regional cultures. Agriculture spread with the encouragement of kings who wanted to promote prosperity and strengthen their own finances. Settlers opened up new lands. Often they were Brahmans who received royal land grants. They had to depend on people of lower castes to do the work since it was prohibited for them to handle a plow.

Irrigation was the farmers' major problem. The south received heavy rains during the monsoons but not enough in the rest of the year. So villagers built large brick-lined tanks that caught the excess rains. In the dry season, water was distributed from these *reservoirs* through a network of canals.

Temples became important centers of south Indian life in this period. Besides serving as houses of worship, they were meeting places where people gathered to gossip and discuss community business. Schools were attached to them. The bigger ones were supported by money from kings, merchants, and pilgrims. The temples owned great amounts of land and owned the markets that grew around them. Many people worked for the temples—priests, musicians, singers, dancers, artisans, guards, gardeners, cooks, and cleaners.

South India remained the center of an international trade that stretched from China to Europe. Chinese records of the time speak of Indian colonies and Brahman temples in their cities. Muslim sources tell us that Indian ships were a common sight at the great ports along the Persian Gulf and Red Sea. South Indian cities were crowded with foreign merchants exchanging their wares for local goods.

Poet-Saints of Hinduism Most of the great intellectual developments in India, after the Guptas, began in the south and spread north. As the southern Dravidian culture was absorbed into Hinduism, it produced many remarkable people. By 820, a south Indian Brahman named Shankara (SHUNG kuh rah) had organized and written down the main philosophical ideas of Hinduism. While he appealed to the educated, his views were too complicated for the masses. The masses were attracted instead to holy people who preached a simple doctrine of devotion to the god of their particular sect. The first of these holy people were active in the Tamil region in the 500s. Similar people appeared in later years in other parts of India. To reach the people, they used India's spoken languages rather than Sanskrit. They spread their ideas through a poetry that was deeply moving. Their poems, in turn, were put to music, creating devotional songs of great power and persuasion.

These poet-saints mortally weakened Buddhism in India. They popularized Hinduism with their simple message of love and their inspiring poetic style. Buddhism was left with only a few followers who banded together in monasteries, isolated from the rest of society. In time, the monasteries became corrupt. They acquired great wealth despite their vows of poverty. Muslim invaders in the eleventh and twelfth centuries sacked the monasteries in search of loot. After that, Buddhism disappeared from India until the 1950s, when some people of the untouchable caste converted in an effort to improve their difficult lives.

Indian Influence in Southeast Asia In Southeast Asia, India's influence had been felt as early as A.D. 100. It became especially strong after 500. Many rulers in Southeast Asia converted to Hinduism or Buddhism. Some employed Brahmans from India as priests and government officials. Some rulers gave themselves and their cities Indian names. They adopted the

Indian calendar, weights and measures, and used Sanskrit. While Hindu influence in the royal courts reached its peak, Buddhism spread among the common people. In time, it replaced Hinduism in the region.

Indian culture spread peacefully in Southeast Asia. It was carried by merchants, missionaries, and colonists who brought their religion, language, and institutions with them.

Section Questions

1. What were three important achievements of the Gupta age?
2. Name at least two reasons why Buddhism disappeared in India.
3. Why did the south prosper after A.D. 500 while the north did not?
4. List two contributions of the poet-saints to Indian culture.

Did You Know?

The Reformer King

In 262 B.C., an Indian king named Asoka sent his armies to invade Kalinga, a state on the east coast of India. A terrible war took place. More than 100,000 people were killed and almost twice that number were made slaves to clear the jungles in the north. Asoka saw the bloodshed and destruction and was grief-stricken. He ended the war and slowly underwent a profound change in his philosophy.

He became a Buddhist and proclaimed his debt to all living creatures. Apologizing to the people of Kalinga, Asoka freed many prisoners of war. He drastically reduced the size of his army. He ordered government officials to be more lenient in their treatment of the Indian people.

Asoka banned animal sacrifices from the capital and forced those living at the palace to become vegetarians. While urging everyone to follow the Buddhist path, he also guaranteed freedom of religion. He had shade trees, wells, and inns placed along the roads for the benefit of travelers. Government workers gathered up seeds from useful plants and intro-

A statue of Buddha.

duced them into areas of India where they did not grow naturally.

The ancient world was changing. People of many backgrounds were moving to the cities, swelling their populations. Longer trade routes were opened, and people developed a taste for imported products. New religions became popular. All these changes created problems for the governments of this time. Asoka's reforms reflected his ideas about what the role of government should be.

The art above is from the Han dynasty. It is part of a landscape that was inlaid in gold on a bronze tub.

3. The Han Dynasty Ruled China for 400 Years

Emperor Qin Shi Huang expected his dynasty to last 10,000 generations. But one year after his death in 210 B.C., the first of many uprisings occurred. In 206 B.C., Liu Bang restored order and in 202 B.C. established the Han dynasty. The new dynasty lasted 400 years. It was a time of great cultural and scientific advancements. Western historians call this period the Pax Sinica, or Chinese Peace, and often compare it with the Pax Romana.

Confucianism, a New State Doctrine

Though uneducated himself, Liu Bang wanted educated people as his advisers. He believed they would ensure an efficient, smooth-running administration. He ended the persecution of Confucianism. Scholars reconstructed the ancient texts from memory and fragments. They wrote new commentaries on Confucius' ideas and reopened their schools.

In 124 B.C., Emperor Wu (or Wu Di, which means "emperor") set up a university dedicated to the study of Confucian thought. He encouraged the spread of Confucian ideas because Confucian models stressed respect for authority and for traditional ways. Gradually, Confucian ideas about ritual and etiquette were incorporated into the law. Confucianism became the state *doctrine*, or set of principles underlying government policy.

Written tests were set up to select the most qualified people for government work. The examinations did not test administrative ability. They tested understanding of Confucian ideas. Those who understood the great thinker's ideas were thought to be worthy for government service.

It took many years to prepare for these difficult tests. At six or seven, boys started studying the Confucian classics. These five books, written by Confucius and his followers, were considered a basis of wisdom and knowledge. The pupils memorized these books line by line and only later learned their meaning. When they knew the texts by heart, the teacher explained what the words meant. Though these examinations did not test administrative ability, the new scholar-administrators were selected by *merit*. They had proved themselves capable. With this system of examinations to identify government officials, China had created the first *civil service* in the world.

Inventions and Advances The Han dynasty was also marked by great scientific and medical achievements. Zhang Heng (Chang Heng A.D. 78 to 139) was a government official who was an accomplished mathematician and astronomer. He improved the precision instruments used to plot the heavenly bodies. He developed a *seismograph* that recorded the direction of earthquakes. By 200 B.C., the Chinese had developed a shoulder collar that increased the hauling capacity of horses. Chinese chariots were therefore larger than Greek or Roman models and carried more weight. By 100 B.C., the foot stirrup was used and the cavalry could mount and ride with greater ease.

As early as the third century A.D., the wheelbarrow was used to carry goods. This laborsaving device did not reach the west until 1,000 years later.

Remnants of rag paper from A.D. 100 have been found in China. Paper replaced the wood, bamboo, and expensive silk cloth that had previously been used for writing. During this time also, artisans developed early models of China's exquisite *porcelain*. Porcelain was a fine pottery made from white clay mixed with powdered rock and sand, what we call "china" today.

Medical diagnosis became more specific. Traditional Chinese medicine stated that good health was the balance of the yin and yang forces within the body. On each wrist were six pulses, which related to the condition of each of the twelve major internal organs. Doctors were instructed to feel and measure the pulse. Pulse types were categorized, and the doctor determined what was wrong by referring to these categories.

The doctor would then insert hot or cold needles at certain points along the pulse routes to release the yin or yang element that was out of balance. Sometimes the patient got relief from the first session. More often, the patient required more treatments. This technique is known as *acupuncture*. In ancient times, the needles were made of silver and gold. Today, they are also made of stainless steel.

Westward Expansion During the Han dynasty, China's isolation from other great empires was broken. After Emperor Wu (140 to 87 B.C.) unified the land under a powerful central administration, he set out on a campaign of foreign conquests. Wu Di is known as China's martial emperor. He conquered Korea (kuh REE uh) and Manchuria (man CHUR ee uh). He extended China's borders into Southeast Asia.

But his greatest campaigns were against the Hsiung-nu, or Huns, who constantly threatened China's northern border. These Turkish-speaking peoples were fierce warriors. They had abandoned farming and traded their fine horses for supplies. They also *pillaged*—looted and destroyed—neighboring agricultural countries.

Wu Di wanted to defeat them. To do so,

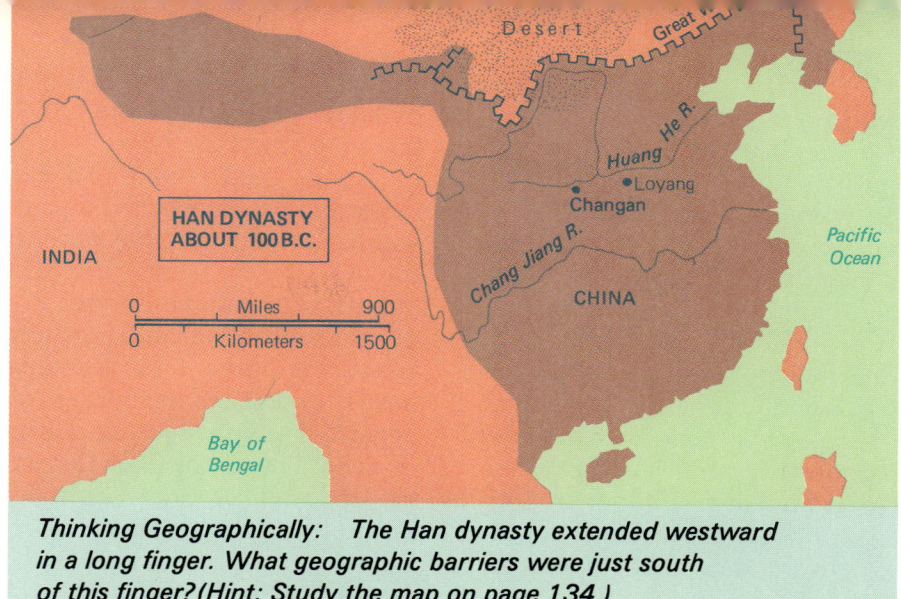

Thinking Geographically: The Han dynasty extended westward in a long finger. What geographic barriers were just south of this finger? (Hint: Study the map on page 134.)

he needed allies. In 139 B.C., he dispatched an officer, Zhang Qian, to make an agreement with the Yuezhi people who lived to the west on the other side of the Tarim (DAH REEM) Desert. But Zhang was captured by the Huns and kept as prisoner for ten years.

Finally, Zhang located the Yuezhi people, who had settled in what is now Russian Turkestan (tur kuh STAN) and Afghanistan (af GAN uh stan) but was then the Greek Kingdom of Bactria. The Yuezhi people were not interested in an alliance with the Chinese.

Zhang returned home. He amazed Emperor Wu when he told him that these people had built magnificent cities and mansions. Like the Huns, they had fine strong horses. Indeed, there was civilization west of the Middle Kingdom.

Wu Di wanted their horses. These powerful animals would help his army defeat the Huns. So he dispatched a military expedition to travel 3,000 kilometers (2,000 miles) to get horses. This was the first time the Chinese had traveled so far out of their empire. With these powerful horses and well-disciplined soldiers, Wu's army conquered the area north of the Himalayas and established control over the people of the Tarim Basin in central Asia.

Economic Reform Wu Di needed money to finance his military expeditions. He imposed heavy taxes and restored the government's control on minting copper coins. In 119 B.C., he seized the iron and salt industries so that the profits would go to the empire. Later he took control of beer and wine production.

In 110 B.C., Wu Di introduced the leveling system. Under this system, the government bought surplus grain in times of plenty to sell in times of shortage. Now greedy merchants could not hoard grain and then sell it for high prices. The leveling system stabilized prices and prevented inflation. But another economic problem developed that Wu Di did not solve. The peasant population was growing faster than the amount of available land. Most peasants had less land than their ancestors. Many of them rented land on large estates owned by wealthy nobles. Traditionally these estates were not taxed and so the government lost income from these peasants. To make up this lost revenue, peasants living elsewhere were taxed more heavily. In 22 B.C., a number of peasant revolts occurred.

In A.D. 9, Wang Mang, the nephew of an empress, usurped the Han throne and ruled in his own dynasty. Wang took dramatic action to end these large, nontaxable estates. He ordered the private estates nationalized. The land was given to those who worked it. But unfortunately, the administration of this plan was poor. Breakdowns in the water-control systems led to a series of bad harvests and then famine. In A.D. 18, another great peasant uprising started and in A.D. 23, Wang died at the hands of the rebels.

Order was partially restored two years later. Guang Wu Di reestablished the Han dynasty. The period from A.D. 25 to 220 is known as the Late Han.

Guang Wu Di did not have the difficult economic problems of the past. The civil war had wiped out many of the holdings of the aristocracy. Guang Wu Di turned his attention to foreign conquest. He reconquered south China and northern Vietnam. His successors continued expansionist wars until they reached the borders of India and Persia. In A.D. 89, the Chinese army marched across the Gobi Desert in Mongolia (mahn GOL yuh) and defeated the northern Huns.

The Silk Road With control over central Asia during much of the Late Han, the Chinese established trade with the west.

This simulated Chinese village is made up of Han dynasty earthenware tomb figures. It shows a trade caravan on the Silk Road.

Long camel caravans crossed the deserts and mountains of central Asia to the edges of the Middle East.

The Romans were most anxious to buy Chinese silk. Since no one else knew how to make silk, the Chinese had a monopoly on this luxury item. The Chinese charged high prices, and the silk was also taxed on its way. The west also liked the Chinese flowers; they wanted camellias, peonies, azaleas, and chrysanthemums. Westerners also learned to like the taste of oranges, peaches, and pears.

The Chinese bought fine horses from central Asia and glass objects from the Mediterranean area. They learned about new foods. They traded for grapes, alfalfa, chives, figs, and walnuts, but more goods were exported from China than imported. The west paid the difference in silver and gold. This helped further drain the gold reserves in the Roman Empire.

Disintegration of the Empire Despite this flourishing trade, the central government faced decreasing tax revenues. In the Late Han, rulers faced the old problem of controlling the owners of large private, nontaxed estates, who had become powerful again.

A strong ruler was needed to administer reforms and put them into practice. But after the first century A.D., there was a succession of weak Han emperors. Court life degenerated into a series of conspiracies and murders. Peasant revolts continued. Nomadic tribes north of the Great Wall threatened to attack. No one could maintain order. Power was decentralized.

The Han dynasty fell in A.D. 220 and China was divided into small kingdoms. Invasions and internal warfare continued. Barbarians from the north broke through the Great Wall and settled in northern China. Huge numbers of Chinese fled southwest to the Sichuan (Szechwan) region and areas south of the Chang Jiang.

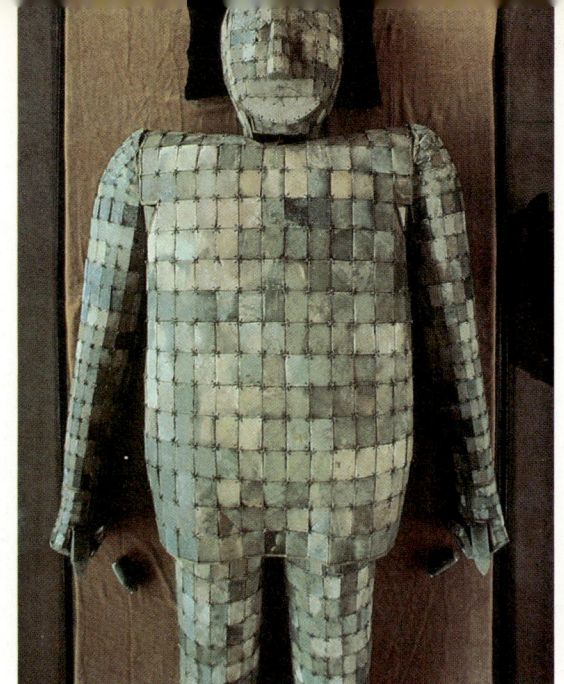

This shroud for a Han dynasty prince is made from jade.

The new cultural and commercial contact between east and west was broken. The fall of the Han coincided with the decline of the Kushan empire in India. It took place when Rome's Pax Romana was threatened by civil war and Germanic invasions.

Many successive dynasties ruled China between A.D. 220 and 589. During this time, the border peoples intermarried with the Chinese and became a part of the culture. Unity was not restored in China until the Sui dynasty in A.D. 589.

Section Questions

1. Why did Han emperors foster Confucianism? What is the significance of the examination system?
2. Why is the Han dynasty called by some historians the Pax Sinica?
3. Why were there great peasant uprisings in 22 B.C. and A.D. 23?
4. List at least four scientific advancements of the Han dynasty.

LEGACY OF CLASSICAL CHINA

Government: First civil service

Technology: Seismograph, horse collar, foot stirrup, wheelbarrow, rag paper, porcelain

Medicine: Acupuncture

Commerce: Exported silk, flowers, fruit; imported horses, glass, new foods

Chapter Summary

1. The warring kingdoms of northern India were united by Chandragupta Maurya, who established the Maurya dynasty about 300 B.C. The vast empire of the Maurya was ruled by a large, centralized bureaucracy. New land was brought under cultivation. The wealth of the empire depended on the surplus from the countryside. Another great Indian leader, Asoka, tried to apply Buddhist principles to the running of the state. The Maurya dynasty collapsed in 184 B.C. North India then experienced fresh invasions from central Asia, notably those of the Bactrians and Kushans. The period from A.D. 50 to 200 is known as the age of commerce for north and south India, since trade with the west reached its peak.

2. In A.D. 320, the Guptas united north India for the first time since the Mauryan empire. They ruled for 200 years. This was a period of peace, prosperity, and great cultural and scientific achievements. After invaders from central Asia overthrew the Guptas, India was divided among warring kingdoms for 600 years. Despite the constant fighting, India progressed economically and culturally. The most important developments occurred in the south. A new movement, believing in simple devotion to the gods, emerged. It gave new life to Hinduism and caused Buddhism to disappear from India. Indian cultural influences in Southeast Asia also reached their peak during this period.

3. The Han dynasty (202 B.C. to A.D. 220) in China was a time of great cultural and scientific achievements. Confucianism became the state doctrine. Written tests to select the most qualified people for government work were established. China's borders were greatly expanded during the Han. During this period, long camel caravans crossed central Asia and established a thriving trade with the west. A recurring problem during the Han was the distribution of land and taxes among the peasants and wealthy landowners. A succession of weak emperors brought the end of the Han in A.D. 220. The new period of disunity lasted until A.D. 589.

Chapter 8 Review

Check Your Facts

1. Identify or describe the following:
   a. Pax Sinica
   b. Asoka
   c. Aryabhata
   d. Wu Di
   e. Bactrians
   f. Tamil kingdoms
   g. acupuncture
2. Why is the Gupta age called India's classical age?
3. Why were temples important in south Indian life?
4. Name several reasons why Hinduism experienced a revival in India in the sixth century.
5. List four important achievements of the Han dynasty.
6. Why is Wu Di known as China's martial emperor?
7. What was the leveling system? What did it achieve?

Words to Know

1. Write a brief definition of each word below.
   a. bureaucrat
   b. civil service
   c. doctrine
   d. merit
2. Tell whether each of the following was helpful or harmful. Explain your answer.
   a. reservoir
   b. pillaging
   c. seismograph

Developing Your Skills

Draw an outline map that includes Europe, Africa, the Middle East, and Asia. You can trace it from a map in the Atlas.

1. On this map, plot the following places: Rome, Alexandria, Sicily, Syria, Ganges River, Tamil states, Southeast Asia.
2. With arrows, indicate the outer main avenues of trade during the period covered in this chapter.
3. The following events happened in India. Tell what was happening in China within fifty years of the same time. Then tell what was happening in Rome. (See Chapter 7.)
   a. Asoka died.
   b. Bactrian rule weakened.
   c. Kushans drove other tribes deeper into India.

Thinking It Over

1. Why do you think India's history is marked by short spells of unity and long spells of disunity? Review China's history. Can this be said about China? Why or why not?
2. Name at least one significant difference in the geography of China and India.

Special Activity

1. Compare the Pax Romana (Chapter 7) with the Pax Sinica. How were the two empires different? How were they similar?
2. *The Panchatantra* was an Indian textbook on "the wise conduct of life." Read some stories from *The Panchatantra* and compare them to Aesop's fables.

A fresco from the catacombs, or underground burial rooms, of Rome. The Christians held funeral and memorial services in the catacombs.

Chapter 9 *The Rise of Christianity*

*I*n A.D. 165, Justin (JUS tun), a Christian leader, and several members of his sect stood before a Roman prefect, Rusticus (RUS ti kus). They were charged with refusing to sacrifice to the gods. They also would not accept the divinity of the emperors.

Rusticus was angry at these Christians. How could they be loyal to a dead criminal Jew they had never seen! Jesus, Rusticus thought, must have been a madman. Had he not claimed to be the Son of God? Why had the authorities allowed him to preach for three years? Why had they not arrested and executed him the first time he opened his mouth in public? Now, more than 100 years later, Rusticus had to deal with the madman's followers!

The prisoners knew the horrible punishment that awaited them if they were convicted. Their willingness to die for a cause that made no sense upset Rusticus and many other Romans. To avoid

4 B.C.—A.D. 395

4 B.C.	Jesus is born
A.D. 35	Paul starts missionary work
64	Nero begins persecuting Christians
132	Jews' last revolt
180	*Pax Romana* ends
226	Sassanid empire begins
285	Diocletian becomes emperor
312	Constantine becomes emperor
313	Edict of Milan
325	Council of Nicaea
395	Romans accept Christianity

Detail from a fresco in Hagia Sofia Church, Thessaloniki, Greece.

the sentence, all the prisoners had to do was to offer a sacrifice to the Roman gods. Simply burning incense before a statue was considered an act of sacrifice. Surely even Christians could manage to do that!

Rusticus glanced at the prisoners. Their peaceful look told him that they would rather die than perform that small symbolic act. So be it, he thought. When they refused to carry out his order, he sentenced them to death. They were led away, singing and praising their god.

For Rusticus, dealing with Christians seemed a never-ending business. For well over a year, he had been sentencing them to death. Yet, instead of dying out, the number of Christians seemed to increase. He felt a curious mixture of despair and sorrow. We will never get rid of them, he thought. He wished that the emperor would set up special courts to deal with these people. Then he would not have to see them again. Maybe his nightmares would stop.

As more Christians were condemned to death, more Romans converted to Christianity. Eventually, even the chief judge of the Roman Empire came to believe in Jesus.

Within 400 years, Christianity became the official religion of the Roman Empire. Second to government, the Christian church became the empire's most powerful institution. How and why had this come about? Consider these questions as you read the lessons that follow.

An ancient synagogue in Djerba, Syria.

1. Christianity Developed in Judea

In 331 B.C., Alexander the Great took the Jewish state of Judea from the Persians. After his death, it became part of the Egyptian kingdom. In 198 B.C., Judea passed under the control of Syria.

Hellenistic culture had a greater effect on the Jews than the culture of any previous conqueror. When Greek became the language of the eastern Mediterranean, many Jews learned to speak it. But when the Syrians placed a statue of Zeus in the temple, the Jews rebelled. Led by Judas Maccabaeus (mak uh BEE uhs), the Jews launched a resistance movement that lasted twenty-five years.

The Jews succeeded in reestablishing an independent Judea. By 78 B.C., its borders extended north to Galilee (GA luh LEE), east to the Jordan River, and west into the Sinai (SI ni).

Judea as a Roman Province In 63 B.C., Pompey led his Roman legions into Judea and surrounded Jerusalem. Pompey earned the hatred of Jews for forcing his way into the *holy of holies*. This was the innermost sanctuary of the temple where only the high priest was allowed to enter. Before he returned to Rome, Pompey announced that Judea had become part of the Roman province of Syria.

During the civil wars between Caesar and Pompey (49 to 48 B.C.), the Jews again rebelled. Roman rule was not restored until Mark Anthony gained control of the east. He named Herod (HER ud) Antipater king. Herod was the son of a Jew who had helped Pompey in the east. Called Herod the Great, the king ruled Judea for over thirty years (37 to 4 B.C.).

Herod increased the process of Hellenization in Judea. He appointed many Greek advisers and ordered the construction of buildings in the Greek style. He also rebuilt the temple. Herod was loyal to Rome. The Jews, suffering under his heavy taxes, hated him. The religious leaders resented his program of Hellenization. Herod died in 4 B.C., mourned by few of his subjects.

Herod's three sons divided Judea into three regions. The Jews took advantage of this political division and rebelled. The Roman governor of Syria marched into Judea. He destroyed many towns and crucified thousands of Jews. He sold 30,000 Jews into slavery. The rebellion led Augustus to declare Judea a Roman province. He sent one of his officials to Jerusalem to govern the territory.

Throughout Jewish literature is the promise of a *Messiah*, a person inspired by God to deliver the Jewish people from oppression. Many Jews prayed that the Messiah would come to deliver them from Roman rule.

Realizing that the Romans were too powerful to be overthrown by force, some Jews, calling themselves Zealots, formed a terrorist organization. They waged guerrilla warfare, killing groups of Romans and Jews who worked with the alien rulers.

The Final Revolts In A.D. 66, the Jews revolted against the Romans because of the governor's handling of a case having to do with the temple. The Jews were so well organized and armed that they expelled the Roman troops. For the next several years, the Romans attacked Jerusalem. Finally, in A.D. 70, the city fell. Jerusalem

The Masada fortress was built on a huge rock. This location was difficult to attack, but also hard to supply.

was burned and the temple was destroyed.

The Zealots of Masada (muh SAH duh) held out against the Romans until A.D. 73. As the troops prepared to scale the cliffs surrounding the fortress near the Dead Sea, the Zealots decided to take their own lives. When the Romans stormed the fortress, they found seven people left alive. This Roman victory hastened the *Diaspora* (di AS puh ruh), the scattering of the Jews throughout the world, which had begun after the Babylonian exile. The Romans began to remove the Jews from Judea. They hoped that once the Jews were physically separated, they would become politically divided as well.

The final rebellion of the Jews took place in A.D. 132 to 135. After suppressing

This frieze on the Arch of Titus shows Romans with the spoils of the temple of Jerusalem.

the rebellion, the emperor Hadrian decreed that no Jew could enter the area where the temple had stood in Jerusalem. While some Jews continued to live in the Galilee and coastal areas, for almost 2,000 years the Jews would have no homeland.

Jesus in Judea During the reign of Augustus, around 4 B.C., Jesus was born in the town of Bethlehem in Judea. He grew up in the village of Nazareth (NAZ uh ruth). As a young man, he declared that he had been born to fulfill the Jewish prophecies and to renew Jewish law. To his followers, Jesus was the promised Messiah. Through the missionary activities of his followers, Jesus became the founder of a religion.

Most of our information about Jesus comes from the Gospels, the first four books of the New Testament of the Bible. Followers of Jesus wrote the Gospels many years after his death. Thus, there are some things about which the Gospels disagree and some things that disagree with other documents of the time.

According to the Gospels, Jesus began his public life when he was thirty years old. To the crowds gathered around him, he spoke in *parables*, simple stories that taught moral lessons. He appealed to the poor and to the oppressed. Because of his popular appeal, Jesus attracted the attention of the Roman authorities and of the religious leaders who ran the temple. They feared that his teachings would provoke a riot.

The Teachings of Jesus Jesus preached that God was deeply worried about human beings. He referred to God as "Father," and described God as loving and forgiving. Like the Jewish prophets, Jesus told of the coming of God's kingdom. He warned that there would be a terrible day of judgment: "The angels shall come forth, and sever the wicked from among the just, and shall cast them into the furnace of fire: there shall be wailing and gnashing of teeth." The just, he said, would be raised up to Heaven and would sit at the right hand of God.

Jesus urged people to put everything else aside in order to seek entrance into the kingdom of God. He told them to follow these two great commandments of the Jewish Bible: "You shall love the Lord your God with all your heart, and with all your soul, and with all your mind. You shall love your neighbor as yourself." Jesus repeatedly stated that love was more important than observing formal religious ceremonies. He criticized the leaders of the temple for expecting the poor to buy animals to sacrifice to God.

Jesus preached his message to people of all races and religions. He said that the kingdom of God was open to all who would follow him. Jesus chose to help people who were looked down upon, like servants and people with leprosy. He told his followers to do the same. He even urged them to love the people who persecuted them. In your dealings with others, Jesus said, you must treat them as you would want them to treat you. If someone strikes you, you should turn the other cheek.

Jesus summarized his message of justice and love in the Sermon on the Mount:

> Blessed are the poor in spirit,
> for theirs is the kingdom of heaven.
>
> Blessed are those who mourn,
> for they shall be comforted.
>
> Blessed are the meek, for they
> shall inherit the earth.
>
> Blessed are those who hunger
> and thirst for righteousness, for
> they shall be satisfied.
>
> Blessed are the merciful, for they
> shall obtain mercy.
>
> Blessed are the pure in heart,
> for they shall see God.
>
> Blessed are the peacemakers, for
> they shall be called children of God.
>
> Blessed are those who are persecuted
> for righteousness' sake, for theirs
> is the kingdom of heaven.

The ruins of the first temple of Old Jerusalem are now being excavated.

To preach his message after his death, Jesus chose twelve simple men to be his disciples. In selecting ordinary, uneducated men, Jesus emphasized that his teachings could be understood by everyone.

The Death of Jesus Jesus went to Jerusalem to preach. His preachings had dramatic impact.

To the Jews, Jesus's calling the temple his father's house smacked of *blasphemy*, an insult to God. They felt that Jesus was claiming to be the Son of God.

To the Romans, the preachings of Jesus were a call for the overthrow of the government. Jesus was arrested and brought before the governor of Judea, Pontius Pilate (PAHN chus PI lut). Jesus was sentenced to death by crucifixion. Three days after his death, Jesus's disciples spread the news that Jesus had risen from the dead. Forty days later, they announced that Jesus had risen to Heaven. They called him "Christ," the Greek word for "messiah" or "redeemer." Led by Peter, the disciples set forth to spread the message of Christianity.

Section Questions

1. What were the reasons why Jews rebelled against their conquerors?
2. What is the Diaspora? Name two occasions in which it took place.
3. What are the Gospels?
4. How did Jesus describe his mission? What were some of his teachings?
5. Why did Jesus speak in parables and choose simple men as disciples?

2. Christianity Grew as Rome Decayed

The missionary activities of the disciples provoked persecutions in Judea and in Rome. So the followers of Jesus concentrated their work in the east.

The dome of the great Hagia Sophia Church in Constantinople.

The Spread of Christianity One of the greatest missionaries in the east was a Jew named Saul of Tarsus (TAHR sus), which is a town in southern Asia Minor. After his conversion, Paul (his Greek name) spread the message of Christianity to both Jews and *gentiles*, or non-Jews. He traveled to the Near East, Greece, and Italy, gaining converts and establishing churches. Through Paul's efforts, Christianity became a religion distinct from Judaism.

Paul contributed to the development of *Christian doctrine*, a system of beliefs and principles based on the teachings of Jesus. Paul preached that Jesus was the Son of

God. He maintained that the sufferings, death, and resurrection of Jesus had *redeemed*, or atoned for, the past sins of humankind. He preached that believing in Christ, rejecting sin, and doing good works would assure Christians' entry into the kingdom of Heaven.

There were many reasons for the success of the early Christian missionaries. First, Christianity appealed to the oppressed. It taught that all people were equal in the eyes of God. It promised a reward in an afterlife which made the sufferings of life on Earth easier to bear. The Roman Empire, which had many unemployed workers and slaves, was fertile ground for gaining converts. Second, Christianity gave people a sense of belonging to a holy community founded by God. The only ritual needed to become a member of the community was *baptism*. Baptism was the act of submerging the body in water. It symbolized the washing away of sins. Third, Christianity shared some common themes with Greek philosophy. For example, the importance of living a good life, based on the principles of love and justice, appealed to the Stoics. Fourth, the Christian missionaries began their work in the first century of the Pax Romana. Peace and the system of roads built by Rome made it possible for missionaries to travel safely and quickly. By A.D. 100, there were Christians in almost every city of the empire.

Structure of the Church At first, churches were communities of Christians where one could meet in fellowship and where the poor and the sick were cared for. In time, a strong church organization

Thinking Geographically: What is the largest area of Christianity shown on the map?

developed. The people who served the community and performed the rites of the church were the priests. Above them in the hierarchy were bishops. Through the ceremony of *ordination*, bishops appointed the priests. Bishops could accept new members into the church and authorize their baptism. They also had the power of *excommunication*, of banishing sinners from the community of the faithful. Bishops were the financial officers of the church. They collected donations from the members of the community and directed the charitable work of the priests. The bishops met in congresses to develop church policies and to resolve problems.

The pope, the bishop of Rome, claimed special authority as the head of the church founded by Peter. The pope claimed the right to settle disputes among the bishops and to hear appeals submitted by the communities. The bishops agreed that the pope occupied a position of honor as the successor of Peter. But they refused to accept his right to exercise special powers.

Rome Versus Christianity The rapid growth of this new religion alarmed the Roman authorities. Some Christians had refused to serve in the army. The authorities feared that if the Christians preached against army service, before long Rome would be unable to defend itself against the "barbarians." The Christians refused to participate in certain public ceremonies and festivals. They were against such Roman customs as the games. Thus, Christianity was considered anti-Roman and a danger to the state. Persecutions began during the reign of Nero (A.D. 54 to 68). Christians were hunted, captured, and told to sacrifice to the gods. When they refused, they were convicted and sentenced to death. But as some historians have concluded, several emperors encouraged the persecution of Christians to gain popular support during periods of economic trouble.

The End of the Pax Romana The last of the five good emperors, Marcus Aurelius, chose his son, Commodus (KAH muh dus), as successor. Commodus thought of himself as a gladiator. He spent so much money staging games and contests that the treasury went broke. In A.D. 192, Commodus was murdered. The praetorian guard offered the throne to the highest bidder. Once again, in an effort to block the emperor's guard from controlling the throne, the armies on the frontier acted. The army on the Danube (DAN yoob) frontier won the power struggle and declared its general, Septimius Severus (su VIH rus), emperor.

Septimius (A.D. 193 to 211) was a shrewd ruler. He stripped the Senate of its administrative powers and rewarded his troops for their support. He increased their pay, pensions, and other benefits.

After the death of Septimius, his family managed to hold onto the throne for more than twenty-five years. In A.D. 238, the last Severan emperor was assassinated. A civil war broke out which lasted fifty years. Several legions declared their commanders emperor. During that time (A.D. 238 to 285), there were twenty-six emperors. Only one died of natural causes. The others were murdered or died in battle.

Invasions and Economic Disruption East of the Rhine and the Danube frontiers lived the Germanic tribes. The Germans lived in thatched houses in small, self-contained villages. Most were farmers, and their lives were hard. Their homelands were covered with forests. In order to feed their increasing population, the Germans had to work long hours to clear land on which to raise more crops. The growing season was short, and the winter was usually severe. The Germans wanted to settle in the Roman Empire because they had heard of the mild climate and good soil in the south. They had also heard about the wonders of Roman civilization.

This frieze shows Romans fighting off the German invaders.

While the armies on the frontiers were busy making their commanders emperors, Rome's neighbors took advantage of the chaos. During the third century, German tribes invaded deep into Gaul and sacked cities in Spain and northern Italy. Goths (GAHTHS) from across the Danube invaded Macedonia and Greece, sacked Athens, and crossed into Asia Minor. In the east, an old enemy posed a new threat. The Parthian empire collapsed in A.D. 226. The Persian rulers, dominated by the Sassanid (suh SAH nud) family, set up a state on the ruins of Parthia. They declared that they intended to recapture all lands that had belonged to the Persian empire. Those lands included the Roman provinces of Egypt, Judea, Syria, and Asia Minor. War between the Sassanian and the Roman empires seemed unavoidable.

The civil wars and the Germanic invasions disrupted trade and commerce. Olive oil, wine, and pottery, the main exports of the empire, were in short supply. Meeting the needs of the many soldiers in the army left exporters little to sell to civilians.

As the Roman authorities continued to send export goods to the troops, the demand for goods increased, forcing prices to rise. Thieves and bandits, few in number during the Pax Romana, threatened merchants and travelers. Artisans and shopkeepers fled the cities. They set up their small businesses on the latifundia, or large estates.

The Reforms of Diocletian In A.D. 285, during this period of chaos, an outstanding commander of the praetorian guard became emperor. Diocletian (di uh KLEE shun) restored order and reorganized the empire. He also defeated the Sassanians. Diocletian declared Maximian (mak SIH mee un) Western Emperor. Instead of Rome, Maximian chose Milan as the site for his capital. He wanted the seat of his government to be closer to the Rhine-Danube frontier where fortifications separated the people of the Roman Empire from the Germanic tribes. Diocletian ruled the east. The long-standing cultural division of the Roman Empire (Greek east and Latin west) became a political one as well.

Diocletian believed that one of Rome's greatest problems was its lack of procedure for selecting successors to the emperor. To solve this problem, he declared that both he and Maximian would bear the title of *augustus*, or emperor. Each augustus would appoint an assistant, who would be called *caesar*. The caesars would succeed the emperors when the emperors gave up their offices. The new emperors would then appoint caesars to act as their assistants and eventual successors.

Diocletian also doubled the size of the army. He imposed an effective draft. He made army service a hereditary obligation, forcing the sons and the grandsons of soldiers to become soldiers.

Once the frontiers were secure, Diocletian began to reorganize the government. In the most important provinces, he separated the civil from the military administration. The purpose of this reform was to create a team of well-trained specialists in each area.

Diocletian tried to stop inflated prices by imposing price controls. Prices on almost every good were fixed by the government. The attempt failed. Merchants held back large quantities of their goods from the marketplace. They developed black markets, where they sold goods at the highest prices customers would pay. The illegal markets flourished, and prices of goods soared.

The costs of increasing the efficiency of the government and securing the frontiers were huge. Diocletian imposed taxes on every citizen, animal, and piece of property in the empire. To make sure that taxes would be collected, he ordered a census of everyone. He decreed that no one could leave her or his community to find a job elsewhere. The decree led to the creation of a caste system based, not on the ability to do a job, but on birth. Locking workers and their descendants into jobs lowered their morale and productivity.

Diocletain believed that the patriotism of Romans would be strengthened by reviving worship of the traditional gods of Rome. He encouraged the old rituals. He issued four *edicts* (orders with the force of law) against the Christians. Churches were closed and church property was seized. Priests were arrested and Christians were forced to sacrifice to the Roman gods. The edicts were enforced in some provinces of the west from time to time until A.D. 313. In the east, persecutions were carried out without mercy. Many martyrs were created during the ten-year campaign to crush Christianity.

Section Questions

1. List several of Paul's contributions to the growth of Christianity.
2. What functions were performed by Christian bishops during the first and second centuries?
3. Name at least three problems that the empire faced in the third century.
4. What did Diocletian hope to accomplish by fixing prices? Did his reform succeed? Explain.
5. What effects did Diocletian's taxes have on people's lives and productivity?

3. Christianity Became the Religion of the Roman Empire

In A.D. 305, Diocletian and Maximian gave up their thrones after ruling for twenty-one years. Diocletian's system of succession failed. Civil war broke out. Generals fought against one another for the thrones in the east and west.

Achievements of Constantine Constantius (kon STAN shee us), the caesar in the west, died in 306. His army declared his son, Constantine (KON stun teen), emperor. In an effort to defeat his main rival, who had seized power in Rome, Constantine led his army toward the former imperial capital. According to Christian writers, on the night before the battle Constantine saw a flaming cross in the sky. The next morning he ordered his soldiers to place a Christian symbol—the initial Greek letters for Christ—on their shields. Leading his outnumbered army into battle, Constantine defeated his rival.

As the only recognized emperor of the west, Constantine helped his friend Licinius (luh SIH nee us) become emperor of the east. In 313, they jointly issued the Edict of Milan. This proclamation extended religious freedom to all Christians in the empire.

By 324, Constantine and Licinius were competing for power. Constantine defeated Licinius in battle and forced him to give up the throne. Constantine then became the sole emperor of the Roman Empire. For the first time in fifty years, the empire was reunited.

Instead of reestablishing the imperial capital at Rome, Constantine moved his court to the old Greek city of Byzantium (buh ZAN shee um). It was an ideal site from which to administer his far-flung empire. The city was located midway between the Danube and the Euphrates rivers—natural frontiers of the reunited Roman Empire. It had been built on a strip

The Arch of Constantine, located in Rome.

of land that jutted into the water between the Mediterranean and Black seas. It had an excellent harbor and a series of roads that extended into the eastern and western regions. These allowed Constantine to communicate with and control both sections of his empire.

Over a period of six years, Constantine fortified the city. He ordered the construction of magnificent churches and public buildings. He imported art treasures from the Hellenistic cities of the east. The new capital was given the name of Constantinople (KON STAN tun O pul), or "city of Constantine." It became the dominant city in the empire.

Constantine appointed Christians as his ministers and counselors. He gave the church vast tracts of land and large supplies of corn to feed the *clergy* (the individuals ordained for religious service) and the poor. He excused the clergy from serv-

159

ing in the army and in the government. He decreed that the church could not be taxed. He gave bishops the authority to hear appeals and to make slaves into citizens. In 325, Constantine called a council of bishops at Nicaea (ni SEE uh) in Persia to settle a dispute over doctrine that threatened the unity of the church. Despite his lack of religious training, Constantine proposed the text that the council adopted. He then enforced the council's interpretation of Christian doctrine throughout the empire.

Did You Know?

In Praise of Constantine and Kingship

Eusebius (yoo SEE bee us) became Bishop of Caesarea (see ZEH ree uh), Palestine, about 315. As a scholar of Christian doctrine, he attended the Council of Nicaea. He helped persuade the other bishops to accept Constantine's interpretation of the relationship between Christ and God.

Eusebius was also the first historian of Byzantium. As an adviser to Constantine, he was commissioned to provide the first fifty bound copies of the New Testament. He wrote a study of Judaism and a history of the Christian church. He also wrote *A Life of Constantine*.

Eusebius was a political theorist. As the following excerpt from his writing shows, Eusebius provided the justification for the first Christian emperor's claim that he ruled as the deputy of God:

A giant head of Constantine.

> He (God) is the standard of kingly power; and it is He who determines the establishment of a single authority for all men. Monarchy is superior as a system of government for all states. *Polyarchy* (many states) is chaos rather than a form of government. So there is one God—not two or three or more. For *polytheism* (many gods) is in reality *atheism* (belief in no gods). And there is one King; and the Word and the law that proceed from Him (God) are one, expressed as God's Word. The king governs the Kingdom of the Father for all who are under him. The king, beloved of God, will already share in the heavenly kingdom. For he is crowned with the virtues which are in God and he has received in his soul the grace that comes from God. He has become rational from the Universal Reason, wise by participation in Wisdom, good by fellowship with the Good.

Constantine also enforced the reforms of Diocletian. But unlike Diocletian who strengthened the military posts, Constantine increased the number of troops to create a field force that could move quickly to protect threatened areas. He appointed German generals. And he gave them the authority to recruit from the German tribes that had been allowed to settle in the Roman Empire.

After giving so much to the church, Constantine finally considered himself worthy of becoming a Christian. He was baptized just before his death.

The Christian Roman Empire With the exception of one ruler, Julian (JOOL yun), every emperor after Constantine was a Christian. Constantine's decision to call a council of bishops set a pattern that affected relations between the state and the church. Emperors now were able to interfere in the affairs of the church.

The church came to depend on the emperors' grants and rulings. Maintaining good relations with the emperors became so important that bishops assigned priests to the court to represent the interests of the church. In time, the bishops' representatives began to influence the political decisions of the emperors. As the political influence of the church grew, it attracted people who considered Holy Orders the first step toward building a career in the empire.

The loss of a sense of belonging to a community led by simple men weakened the unity of the church. Many disagreements over doctrine broke out. Bishops competed with one another to convince emperors to enforce their interpretations of Christian doctrine. In 395, Emperor Theodosius (THEE uh DO shee us) the Great (379 to 395) declared Christianity the official religion of the empire. Many non-Christian temples were closed. The games were ended. The baths were abolished. The church had become one of the most influential institutions of the Roman Empire.

Three Centuries of Change Augustus would not have recognized the Roman Empire of the fourth century. Rome was no longer the seat of imperial power. It was no longer the main center of religious activity. The thriving city life in the west had been replaced by the unchanging life of the great estates. Independent farmers had become tenants, or they were unemployed in the decaying cities of the west. The citizen army led by members of the

Some of the ramparts surrounding Byzantium, or Constantinople, still stand.

Senate was expanded to include "barbarian" generals and soldiers. The gods of the Roman Empire had been replaced by Jesus, who had been born in a province of the empire during Augustus' reign.

Section Questions

1. Why was Byzantium a good site for the new capital of the empire?
2. Describe the influence of the emperors on church affairs during the fourth century. Then tell how the church gained some influence over politics.
3. Why did Constantine appoint German generals? Can you think of some additional reasons not mentioned in the text?
4. Name at least five changes that distinguished the reign of Augustus from that of Constantine.

Chapter Summary

1. The history of the Jewish people in Judea was not a peaceful one. Persian, Egyptian, and Roman conquerors tried to impose their rule on the Jews. The Jews rebelled whenever their oppressors were weak or when their temple was defiled. In this climate of political tension, Jesus was born. His message of love and justice appealed to the slaves, the poor, and the oppressed. The Roman rulers suspected that Jesus was a revolutionary. Jesus was tried, convicted, and crucified. Three days after his death, his disciples said that he had risen from the dead. Forty days later, they claimed that Jesus Christ had risen to Heaven.

2. Paul, a convert to Christianity, preached the faith to both Jews and gentiles (non-Jews). He also helped develop Christian doctrine. By A.D. 100, Christianity had spread throughout the Roman Empire. Among reasons for its success were its appeal to the poor and oppressed, the security and ease of travel of the Pax Romana, and the heroism of the Christians who died for their beliefs.

The civil wars of the third century led to political and economic problems. The armies on the frontier determined who ruled Rome. Germanic tribes sacked several provinces of the empire. The Sassanids threatened the Roman provinces in the east. The resulting chaos caused many Roman artisans and merchants to abandon the cities. They fled to the estates, where they were offered protection and markets for their goods.

Diocletian became the emperor in 285. He fortified the frontiers. He increased the number of administrators and imposed taxes on every person and piece of property in the empire. Diocletian tried to curb inflation by fixing prices. But his economic reforms led to the creation of a caste system. Tenant farmers, soldiers, artisans, and administrators were forced to remain in their jobs.

3. Diocletian's system of succession did not work. After he died, Constantine, son of one of the caesars, conquered his rivals in the west. He and the new eastern emperor issued the Edict of Milan. It granted freedom of religion to all Christians in the empire.

After defeating the eastern emperor in 324, Constantine became the sole ruler. He moved the capital to the site of the old Greek city of Byzantium, later called Constantinople. Constantine carried out many of Diocletian's policies. He further increased the size of the army and appointed many German generals and soldiers. Constantine also gave gifts of land and food to the church. He freed priests from military and public service. The church was not to be taxed. Fifty years after Constantine's death, Theodosius the Great declared Christianity the official religion of Rome.

Chapter 9 Review

Check Your Facts

1. What did Pompey do that earned him the hatred of Jews in Judea?
2. Who was Herod? Describe some of his policies.
3. What event completed the Diaspora? When had it begun?
4. Why did Christianity spread in the Roman Empire?
5. Name several reasons why Romans at times persecuted Christians.
6. Why did many German tribes want to settle in the Roman Empire?
7. What special powers did the bishop of Rome claim? Why? Did other bishops accept his claims?
8. Name three reasons why Constantine founded a new capital at Byzantium.

Words to Know

Define or describe the following words. Then explain the significance of each in the development of Christianity during its first 400 years.

    a. gentiles
    b. parables
    c. Gospels
    d. baptism
    e. bishops
    f. excommunication
    g. edicts
    h. clergy
    i. Christian doctrine

Developing Your Skills

1. Examine the maps on page 155 and in the Atlas. Then list the modern-day countries in which Christianity had spread by A.D. 400.
2. Make a time line that shows the approximate dates for the following events:
    a. Judea passes under Syria's control.
    b. Parthian empire collapses.
    c. Nero persecutes the Christians.
    d. Paul converts gentiles.
    e. Pompey invades Jerusalem.
    f. Christianity becomes the official religion of the Roman Empire.
    g. The Pax Romana ends.
    h. The Council of Nicaea meets.

Thinking It Over

1. In what ways were Jewish ideas about the messiah similar to those later accepted by Christians? In what ways were they different?
2. Why do Christians consider the Resurrection of Jesus so important? In what way does baptism relate to the Resurrection?
3. In what ways was the Roman caste system that developed during Diocletian's reign similar to and different from the Roman system of slavery? How was it similar to the caste system in India?

Special Activities

1. The current name for Constantinople is Istanbul (IS tum BOOL). Locate Istanbul, Turkey, on the map in the Atlas. Is Istanbul as important now as Constantinople was in the fourth century? Explain your answer.
2. The political conditions in first-century Judea sparked the formation of the Zealots. Political conditions in the Middle East after 1948 led to the Palestine Liberation Organization. After doing library research, compare the goals and tactics of these two organizations.

Unit 2 Review

Words to Know

1. Explain the difference in meaning for each pair of words below.
   a. democracy/republic
   b. triumvierate/monarchy
2. Use a dictionary if necessary to determine the present meaning of *spartan*. Then explain why that meaning could have arisen from the natives of Sparta.
3. Explain the importance of aqueducts and reservoirs.
4. Both the Greeks and the Chinese considered certain people to be barbarians. Would the Chinese and Greeks agree as to who were barbarians? Explain.

Time and Place

1. How were elephants important to Rome? To India?
2. How were horses important to India? To China?
3. Make a time line for 800 B.C. to A.D. 500. On it, show the religious beliefs of the early Greeks, the early Romans, the Indians, and the Roman Empire in the time of Constantine.

Putting It Together

1. Draw the chart at the bottom of the page on a piece of paper. Then complete it by writing "stable" or "unstable" and a brief explanation. Two examples are shown. Refer to Unit 1 for early dates if needed. (Not all are given.)
2. What sorts of government did most countries have during their stable periods?
3. Did the greatest cultural diffusion occur during stable times or unstable times? Give reasons for your answer.
4. Did cultural diffusion occur more often through land travel or sea travel? Give reasons for your answer.

Date	Greece	Rome	India	China
600 B.C.	stable, city-states		(not given)	stable, Zhou dynasty
300 B.C.				
100 B.C.	(not given)			
A.D. 100				
A.D. 300	(not given)			

Contemporary Parallel:
Cultural Diffusion

Conquests, trade, and missionary zeal all helped scatter new ideas during the Classical Age. The conquered peoples of the Roman Empire, for example, had to accept Roman law. But few ideas really spread by force. Most were accepted because they filled a need. Egyptian and Chinese paper were found useful by many other peoples. Buddhism must have filled a need in Southeast Asia, for within a short time it spread through much of the region. Cultural diffusion remains a vital element of modern life. With the speed of modern travel and communications, the diffusion of ideas can be worldwide and almost instantaneous. Radio, television, and films spread news, songs, and ideas. A new style by an Olympic high jumper can be copied by jumpers in 100 countries. Or more slowly, we can watch the spread of nuclear technology from one nation to many. Travelers crisscross the globe. Libraries contain literature and research discoveries from around the world. Engineers and scientists meet to exchange ideas.

Let's take one object that you are familiar with—blue jeans. Blue jeans were developed by the Levi Strauss Company in San Francisco during the early days of the Gold Rush of 1848. Miners needed tough pants that would not easily wear out when scuffed against rocks or washed in mountain streams. Miners found blue jeans useful. Legions of workers adopted blue jeans for the same reason. The cotton denim cloth and the stitching were tough and long-lasting. They became part of the uniform of ranch hands, farmers, and factory workers.

In the 1950s, young people began to wear jeans as inexpensive, long-lasting clothing. In the 1960s and 1970s, middle-class Americans adopted blue jeans for casual wear. Blue jeans became a status symbol. The new "in look" swept across the western world. Today, a consumer can buy blue jeans in almost any major city of the world.

QUESTIONS

1. Some writers have complained that the world's cultures are becoming too much alike. These people value the rich diversity of the Earth's people.
   a. Do you think the people of Earth are achieving a monoculture? Give evidence to support your statement.
   b. If they are, is this good or bad? Why?
2. Is it easier to diffuse a new and useful product (for example, a steel plow or chemical fertilizer) or new idea (for example equality for women or a new religion)? Give reasons for your answer.

500	641	768	1066	1215	1347	1485
Byzantine civilization emerges	Arabs conquer Persia	Charlemagne begins rule	Normans conquer England	Magna Charta signed	Black Plague begins	War of Roses ends

Unit 3
The Medieval World

In the eastern Mediterranean, Islam rapidly developed as a major religion. It united people by the belief in a common faith. Through conquest and conversion, Islam forged a mighty empire.

As the Roman Empire crumbled, a power vacuum was left in the lands that had been part of it. There was no government, no real authority thoughout Italy, Spain, and the areas to the north.

People's need for security led to a new power system. A family whose house was well protected could offer protection to others. The latter could give some of their crops in return for that security. As you will see, this became a highly complex feudal system that established order over wide regions of Europe. Some rulers began combining regions. In that way, they established new kingdoms. This was a major step toward the development of modern nations. By 1450, rulers in England, France, and Spain were consolidating their power and creating a new sense of loyalty.

Later, people would look back on the early part of this period as the "Dark Ages." The light of classical civilization was out. Europe entered a period of ignorance and darkness. While the beginning stages of feudalism were not peaceful, they were not a dark age. New cultures were being shaped in the shadows of the old. They would eventually become the cultures of modern Europe.

One other power gave unity to Europe—the Roman Catholic Church. People thought of themselves as members of Christendom, not as members of a nation or a society.

The month of April in feudal Europe.

A mosaic showing the court of Theodora, Empress of Byzantium.

Chapter 10 The Collapse of the West

The Germanic invasions of the fourth and fifth centuries led to the collapse of the Roman Empire in the west. Romans called the invaders barbarians because they spoke neither Latin nor Greek. The Germans also behaved differently. And they looked different, too.

Earlier German settlers had adopted Roman dress when they became part of the empire. The new Germanic invaders, however, wore trousers, the hallmark of barbarians according to the Romans. Made of animal skins, the pants were shaped to the legs like tights. They were held by crisscrossed straps and a belt worn at the waist.

370-900

378	Visigoths defeat Roman emperor
410	Visigoths sack Rome
451	Attila the Hun attacks Gaul
455	The Vandals sack Rome
476	Roman Empire falls
481	Clovis begins rule
533	*Corpus Juris Civilis* completed
527	Age of Justinian begins
565	Justinian dies
500s	Byzantine civilization emerges
732	The Battle of Tours
756	Donation of Pepin
768	Charlemagne begins rule
late 800s	The Carolingian empire ends

The Goths sack Rome.

The Germans wore mantles of rough colored wool, bronze collars around their necks, and fur caps. Regional variations, such as fur-trimmed mantles, fur-trimmed jumpers, and plaid mantles, distinguished one tribe from another. But to "elegant" Romans, all Germans looked alike.

The standard Roman dress in the west included garments adopted from the Greeks. The main garment was the *toga*. The toga was a cloak that was draped around the body in folds. Most Romans wore simple togas of white wool. Chief judges wore purple-bordered togas.

Under a toga, both men and women wore a *tunic* adapted from the Greek. A tunic was a woolen or a linen garment sewed at the sides and held at the shoulders by clasps. Women's tunics were set off with embroidered bands at the neck and at the hemline. Senators' tunics had wide purple bands from the neck to the hem. Such bands showed that they were members of the imperial government.

The rulers of the Germanic states that were created after the collapse of the west swore allegiance to the emperor in the east. Before long, many Germans were wearing the tunics of the west or styles typical of the east. Coarse woolen fabrics were replaced by linen and silk.

These changing styles reflected the great changes that were taking place in the Roman Empire. In the period between 370 and

Roman soldiers destroying German huts.

600, the western empire collapsed and came under the rule of the Germans. The culture that developed in the west was a blend of Latin and German traditions. The Christian church became more powerful. Meanwhile the eastern Roman Empire gradually became a separate entity. But it managed to preserve Greco-Roman culture, which it blended with the rich traditions of the Middle East.

1. The Western Roman Empire Fell to the Germans

There was a general feeling in the middle of the fourth century that the Roman Empire would last forever. Had not the empire survived the chaos of civil wars, barbarian invasions, and economic problems? Most people believed that the reforms of Diocletian and Constantine had restored the empire. The frontiers had been secured, and the barbarians had retreated. The empire seemed safe and strong.

But the reforms of the fourth century did not solve the basic problems of the Roman Empire. Stagnation affected every aspect of life in the west. The estates failed to increase the amount of food produced. Fewer people actually farmed the land. The numbers of unemployed had increased. Prices soared as the government imposed price controls and then increased the amount of money in use. This weakened the value of money. Force still determined who became ruler of the empire.

Barbarian Invasions By the end of the 300s, the German tribes had become powerful and well organized. Centuries of contact with Rome had given them knowledge of military tactics. In spite of this, however, the German tribes failed to stop the Huns who poured into their territories in the late 300s.

In 372, nomadic horsemen from Mongolia crossed the Volga (VAHL guh) River north of the Caspian Sea. Their appearance provoked horror and fear. According to historians, they had hideous scarred features. They arrived in Europe as a vast shock wave of plunderers. The Huns conquered the Ostrogoths (AHS truh GAHTHS), the east or "bright" Goths, who lived along the Dnieper (NEE pur) River in southern Russia. Fearing that they would suffer the same fate, the Visigoths (VIZ uh GAHTHS), the west or "wise" Goths, fled to the Danube. They appealed to the emperor in Constantinople for permission to cross the frontier and settle in Thrace. In 376 they were allowed to enter the empire.

Roman officials in Thrace took advantage of the Goths. They sold food to them at high prices and even sold some of them into slavery. The Goths fought back. Emperor Valens (VAY lunz) assembled an army and marched against them. The Romans were defeated in 378 at the Battle of Adrianople (AY dree uh NO pul), and the emperor was killed.

The Sack of Rome The new emperor in the east, Theodosius the Great, lacked the resources to punish the Visigoths. Instead, he made them Roman allies and gave them land along the Danube.

In 392, Theodosius became emperor of the west as well. He died three years later, leaving the empire to his two sons. The eastern emperor's advisers persuaded him to cut off annual payments to the Visigoths. The Visigoths were encouraged to seek their fortune in the west. In 401, led by their leader Alaric (AL uh rihk), the Visigoths invaded Italy. The western emperor's capable general, Stilicho (STIH lih ko), a German, defeated Alaric and forced the Visigoths to withdraw. Then, fearing Stilicho's growing power, the emperor ordered his execution. Now Alaric demanded territory, gold, and food. When the emperor rejected his demands, Alaric and his soldiers marched on Rome, captured the city, and sacked it (410).

Romans were shocked. Few had expected the Visigoths to do what the Gauls had done 800 years before. Non-Christians blamed the sack of Rome on the Christians. They claimed that the acceptance of Christianity had angered the Roman gods to whom the capital had been dedicated. One of the church's great scholars, Augustine (AW guh steen), a bishop in North Africa, wrote *The City of God* to deny the charge. He claimed that the institutions created by people do not last; only those made by God endure.

This detail from a church painting shows Saint Augustine.

Barbarian Triumph After sacking Rome, Alaric died. Led by his brother, the Visigoths headed north into southern Gaul. The Roman legions were ordered to abandon Britain in order to reinforce the military posts on the Rhine-Danube frontier. Despite these reinforcements, another German tribe, the Vandals (VAN dulz), broke through the fortifications. The Vandals pillaged Gaul and crossed into Spain. The emperor made a surprising decision. He paid the Visigoths to drive the Vandals out of Spain. But when they did, the Visigoths refused to leave the province. Although they claimed to rule Spain in the emperor's name, the Visigoths had set up their own state within the empire.

The Vandals crossed into North Africa. They completed their conquest of the province by 439. From the rebuilt city of Carthage, the Vandals pirated ships in the Mediterranean. The new western emperor, Valentinian (val un TIHN ee un) III, accepted the Vandals as allies. But he realized that another chunk of the western empire had been taken from Rome.

Now the Huns, united under the rule of Attila (AT ih luh), crossed the Danube and invaded Thrace. The eastern emperor paid Attila to leave the region. In 451, Attila's forces crossed the Rhine and invaded Gaul. He was met by a combined Roman-German force under the command of Aetius (ay EE shee us). At the Battle of Chalons (shah LON), Aetius repulsed the Huns. But it was a Pyrrhic victory. Aetius lost so many troops that he could not pursue Attila into Italy.

The Huns proceeded to sack cities in the Po Valley. Nothing stood between them and Rome. The Huns advanced on the capital, where they were met by the bishop of Rome, Pope Leo I. Leo persuaded Attila to spare the city. In 452, Attila withdrew beyond the Danube. He died the following year, and his confederation broke up. During the next century, the Huns merged with

Attila burning a township during the invasion of Italy.

the peoples of central Europe. The term "Hungarian" refers to the descendants of these mixed peoples.

Valentinian III blamed Aetius for failing to destroy the Huns. He had Aetius executed in 454. This was the second time that an emperor had blamed a capable general during a crisis. Aetius's lieutenants reacted by murdering the emperor. Taking advantage of the chaos, the Vandals marched into Italy and sacked Rome. So great was the damage that an eighteenth-century French bishop coined the term *vandalism* to describe willful destruction.

The Saxons invading Britain.

Britain was taken by the Angles (AN gulz), the Saxons (SAK sunz), and the Jutes (JOOTS). Other Germans had claimed to accept the authority of the western emperor. But these three tribes proclaimed themselves conquerors. They destroyed all traces of Roman civilization on the island. The Britons (BRIT unz) waged a losing guerrilla war against the invaders. Some Britons escaped into the swampy western fringes of the island, where their descendants, the Welsh, live today. Others fled the island. They crossed the channel and settled in the coastal region of northern Gaul. The region—Brittany—still bears their name in modern France. Under the Germanic conquerors, such Roman institutions as law, centralized administration, language, and for a time, Christianity, disappeared.

The End of the Western Roman Empire Gaul was seized by two German tribes. The Burgundians (bur GUHN dee unz) invaded the Rhone (RON) Valley, and the Franks took most of the north. After 455, only Italy was under the authority of the western emperor.

But the emperor did not actually rule Italy. The Germans, who controlled the army, controlled the emperor. In 476, Odoacer (OD uh WAY sur), a German chieftain, asked the eastern emperor to recognize him as Italy's ruler. The eastern emperor agreed. Many Romans hailed the action as a step toward reunifying the empire. But most historians claim that it marked the end of the Roman Empire in the west. A German who had been willing to act as the power behind the throne was

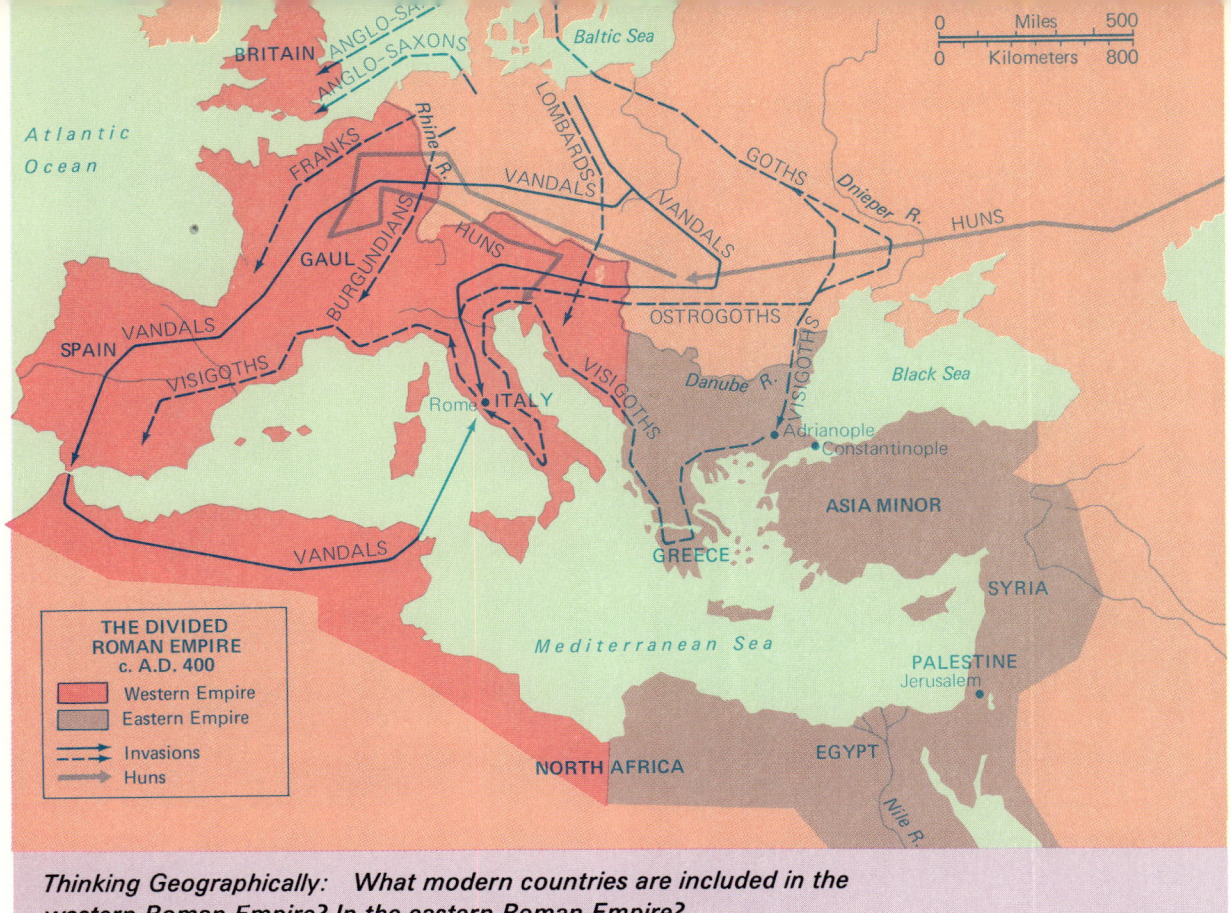

Thinking Geographically: What modern countries are included in the western Roman Empire? In the eastern Roman Empire?

no longer willing to mask his role. In 476, he claimed the right to declare himself king. Other German rulers followed Odoacer's example. The Roman Empire in the west had ceased to exist.

A New Europe Britain was ruled by the Angles, the Saxons, and the Jutes. Gaul was under the control of the Franks and the Burgundians. Spain and southwestern Gaul were dominated by the Visigoths. North Africa and islands in the Mediterranean were ruled by the Vandals. Italy was under the control of the Ostrogoths.

Life under the German kings appeared to go on as it always had. With the exception of the German tribes in Britain, the German rulers admired Roman civilization. They modeled their administrations and legal systems on those of the empire. Latin was the official language of the new states. The non-German people were still subject to Roman law. German officials had Roman titles and carried out the same functions as before. The German kings had pledged their allegiance to the emperor in Constantinople.

The only apparent change was in the distribution of land. One-third of the farmland was taken away from Roman nobles and given to German settlers.

However, the damage caused by the invasions of the 400s further weakened the cities. The remaining libraries and schools were forced to close. But the texts of classical culture were not lost. The church took over the responsibility of preserving Greco-Roman civilization.

The Church Church leaders modeled the administrative structure of the church on the hierarchy of offices in the empire. By the year 400, the pope was using the special powers that popes had claimed hundreds of years earlier. The pope settled disputes among the bishops and made final decisions in matters relating to church discipline. Until Constantine established the imperial capital in the east, the bishops of Alexandria (a lig ZAN dree uh), Antioch (AN tee ahk), and Jerusalem had had a place of honor second only to the pope's. With the founding of Constantinople, the capital city became the second most important church district. Roman law formed the basis of *canon* law, or church law. Canon law included the interpretations of Christian doctrine approved by the councils and rules for the monasteries that developed in the west.

During the late 200s, some Christians had left their homes to live simple lives in the Egyptian and Libyan (LIB ee un) deserts. They wanted to be alone in order to pray and fast. They believed that these activities would help them become better followers of Christ. In time, other Christians gathered around their caves. These small groups of *hermits* founded simple religious communities called monasteries. The rapid growth of monasteries may have been a reaction against the growing complexity of the church.

In 520, Benedict (BEN uh dikt), a member of a noble family, founded a monastery at Monte Cassino (MAHN ti ku SEE no) in the hill country between Rome and Naples. He formed a rule based on poverty, *chastity* (virginity), and obedience. The monks lived according to this rule. Their day was divided into prayer and work. Monte Cassino was a self-sufficient community devoted to cooperative work. The Benedictine order owned villas, serfs, and vineyards. The monks developed healthier strains of plants and improved crop yields.

This manuscript illumination shows a monk copying a text.

They fed the poor. They provided hospitals for the sick and inns for travelers and for the homeless. Some monks were scholars and teachers. They copied the texts of the New Testament and the classics of Greco-Roman culture. They wrote histories of earlier civilizations. Pope Gregory (590 to 604), also a Benedictine monk, sent Augustine and other Benedictine missionaries to convert the Anglo-Saxons in Britain. Many became Christians. Now Anglo-Saxon missionaries worked among the Celts and Germans. Patrick, a native of Britain, converted the Celtic people of Ireland in the 300s. Irish missionaries then crossed the channel and worked among the Franks. Boniface (BAH nuh fus, 672 to 754) traveled from Wessex (WES iks), England, to

Did You Know?

A Fascinating Question

Why did the western Roman Empire collapse? This question has intrigued historians for more than 1,500 years. Many theories have been advanced.

The eighteenth-century historian Edward Gibbon (GIB un) and the twentieth-century historian H. M. Jones concluded that the German invasions caused the collapse of the west. Jones came to this belief despite criticism directed at Gibbon's older theory. Jones said that, true, the middle class was stronger and more land was owned by independent farmers in the east. But the east suffered from the same kinds of political, economic, and social problems that beset the west. In his judgment, the shorter frontier of the east—the lower Danube—was defensible. The longer frontier of the west—the Rhine and the Danube—was not. Geography, not a moral decay in the west or a less rigid class system in the east, was what enabled the eastern empire to last 1,000 years longer than the west.

The fourth-century Roman historian, Marcellinus (mahr suh LI nus), claimed that the reason for the collapse was, in fact, moral decay. Montesquieu (MAHN tus kyoo), the eighteenth-century French philosopher, noted that the laws passed during the Republic were simply not effective when Romans gained an empire. A. E. R. Boak maintained that the population loss caused by the outbreak of plague during the second century led to the underpopulation of Rome. The lack of people to defend the frontier made it possible for the Germans to break through, plunder the empire, and become the rulers of the west.

Alaric entering Rome.

Another historian claimed that the class struggle between the wealthy and the poor was responsible for the collapse. Still another claimed that the crushing burden of taxation and the regulation of every part of economic life weakened the spirit the Romans needed to resist the Germans.

Probably no one theory alone can explain the decline of the western empire. As you know, historians specialize. Some concentrate on political history. Others on economic or social history. Taken together, their theories can help us understand the complexity of events. Probably the interaction of several of these forces caused the collapse of the west.

present-day Germany, where he established monasteries. He is known as the Apostle of the Germans.

The Benedictine rule of poverty, chastity, and obedience was to become the model for other monasteries later founded throughout western Europe.

The Fate of Rome Italy suffered devastation from 400 to 600. The peninsula was ravaged by Visigoths, Huns, Vandals, Ostrogoths, Byzantines, and Lombards (LAHM bahrdz). By 568, almost all the farmland in Italy was destroyed. By 600, Rome had become a poverty-stricken settlement. The great aqueducts broke down and disease threatened the lives of many.

Rome's last center of power was the church, led by the bishop of Rome. Pope Gregory acted like the governor of Rome. He gave refuge in the churches to people fleeing from bandits. He supervised the police. He tried offenders and punished criminals. He arranged for the aqueducts to be repaired. By entering into an alliance with the leader of the Franks, the Pope became the ruler of a state in Italy. Through that alliance, he tried to build a Christian empire based on Greco-Roman civilization and German protection.

Section Questions

1. What caused the Visigoths to rebel in 378? What was the result of that rebellion?
2. Why did Augustine write *The City of God*? What was his argument?
3. What is the significance of the year 476?
4. In what ways did life remain pretty much the same under German control of the western empire? What things changed?
5. What major reasons or events caused the fall of the western Roman Empire?
6. What impact did monks and monasteries have on religious, social, and economic activities during the fifth and sixth centuries?

2. The East Turned Away from the West

The eastern empire lasted almost 1,000 years after the collapse of the west. The empire drew strength from its secure geographical position. Its capital was surrounded by water on three sides. On the land side were two rows of very high walls. Unlike Rome, which was located on an open plain, Constantinople was a fortress. Different groups did, at times, attack the empire and gain portions of it. However, Constantinople was not successfully invaded until 1204 and finally in 1453.

The eastern empire also had a healthy economy with a fairly large middle class, especially in Constantinople. Located at a crossroads between Asia and Europe, the capital was a bustling center of trade and manufacture. From Russia (via the Black Sea) came furs and fish. Jewels and spices arrived from the east. The cities of the empire controlled trade in the eastern Mediterranean at a time when trade in the west had come to a near standstill. A great cloth industry developed. Workers created exquisite gold-embroidered tapestries, carved ivory, leather, and jewelry. The government was administered by a highly centralized, well-trained bureaucracy. The bureaucracy managed to keep services going even during times of weak emperors.

The Age of Justinian Although the eastern emperors did not control the city of Rome, their armies carried Roman symbols. Judges enforced Roman law. The emperor was advised by a senate that sat in Constantinople.

Roman influence reached its height in the east during the reign of Justinian (ju STIN ee un, 527 to 565). He was the last emperor who spoke Latin fluently. Justinian dreamed of ruling over a unified Roman Empire.

Early in his reign, groups in the

Hippodrome (HIP uh drom), the massive theater where gladiator contests were held, rioted and stormed the palace. Because most of the army was fighting the Sassanians, Justinian prepared to escape. His strong, convincing wife, Theodora (thee uh DO ruh), refused to leave. She told her husband, "If there were left me no safety but in flight, I would not fly. Those who have worn the crown should never survive its loss. Never will I see the day that I am not hailed empress. If you wish to fly, caesar, well and good. You have money, the ships are ready. The sea is clear; but I shall stay. For I love the old proverb that says: 'The purple is the best winding-sheet.'" Encouraged by her attitude, Justinian ordered Belisarius (bel uh SAR ee us), the commander of the guard, to gather the troops remaining in the city. They attacked the mob in the Hippodrome, killing 30,000 to 40,000 people.

Justinian rewarded Belisarius by sending him to retake the west. Belisarius first tried to reconquer North Africa. His forces then invaded the Ostrogoth kingdom of Italy. By 540, Italy was again a part of the empire. But misrule and high taxes sparked a revolt that Belisarius finally put down. This ten-year war destroyed much of Italy. Rome was captured five times, starved, and looted. The liberators had become conquerors. The eastern forces also defeated the Visigoths in southern Spain.

However, the military campaigns drained the treasury. In 541, while Belisarius was completing the reconquest of Italy, the Sassanian forces took the city of Antioch in Syria. Only a hefty payment from the eastern treasury convinced the Sassanid ruler to withdraw. In 568, three years after Justinian's death, the Lombards from central Europe invaded Italy, and the Visigoths recaptured most of the eastern territory in Spain. Justinian's costly wars convinced the new eastern emperor that reuniting the east and west was a lost cause.

A mosaic showing Emperor Justinian.

Justinian's Code The most enduring of Justinian's achievements was the *codification*, or the organization in systematic form, of Roman law. In 528, Justinian appointed the best lawyers to review all Roman laws and legal writings. Their work resulted in the publication of the *Corpus Juris Civilis* (Latin for "body of civil law").

This collection of laws was divided into four volumes. The *Codex* included more than 4,000 Roman laws. The fifty books of the *Digest* contained the writings of legal scholars arranged alphabetically by idea. It explained how the laws had been interpreted over time. The *Institutes*, a textbook for students, explained the basic principles underlying Roman law. Finally, the *Novellae* collected the legislation of Justinian. This great work preserved the legal knowledge of Rome. The *Corpus Juris Civilis* formed the basis of west European law.

Byzantine Civilization Most scholars have concluded that the patterns of development in the eastern empire after 500 or 600 point to the emergence of a distinct civilization. They call it Byzantine, for the ancient city of Byzantium where Constantinople was built. The eastern empire had always been a Hellenistic environment. Most of its people were Greeks, though there were also Syrians, Jews, and Slavs. After Justinian, the eastern emperors spoke Greek. Byzantium, then, drew on the cultural achievements of its Greek and Middle Eastern peoples. Another significant part of the civilization was the Christian church, which developed differently from its counterpart in Rome.

The Church The organization of the church was modeled on the organization of the state. The patriarch of Constantinople was the highest church official. Under him were several levels in the hierarchy. There were the metropolitans and archbishops, who ministered to the cities and provincial centers. Then there were the bishops, priests, and other individuals who helped perform the services of the church. Although the patriarch was supposed to be elected by the bishops, he was nominated by the emperor and was subject to his control. In the Byzantine Empire, the emperor was, in fact, the head of the church. The religion that developed in the east was based on the New Testament and on the seven councils. The seven councils had been called to settle disagreements over doctrine. *Heresy*, a religious opinion contrary to church doctrine, was considered a crime against the state. In 1,100 years, seven councils proclaimed the three most divisive beliefs: Arianism (A ree uh NIZ um), Nestorianism (ne STOR ee uh NIZ um), and the Monophysite (muh NAHF us SIT) beliefs. These heresies differed from the councils about the natures of Christ and God the Father.

Rifts with Rome As the Roman pope tried to impose his will in matters relating to faith and morals, the struggles between the main bishops of the church became more intense. The patriarch of Constantinople stated that only the bishops meeting in councils could resolve matters of doctrine. When the pope asked for protection from the Carolingian kings, he entered into an alliance with Pepin, who gave him Byzantine lands in Italy. By proclaiming Charlemagne emperor of the Romans, the pope again angered the Byzantine emperor. In 800, Pope Nicholas and Patriarch Photius (FO shee us) excommunicated one another, that is, each expelled the other from the church. Two hundred years later, in 1054, Pope Leo IX and Patriarch Michael Caerularius (see roo LAIR ee us) excommunicated one another. This later resulted in the separation of the two churches into the Roman Catholic in the west and the Eastern Orthodox in the east.

Missionary Activities Church missionaries from Byzantium converted the peoples of Caucasia (kaw KAY zhuh), the northern Balkan (BAWL kun) peninsula, and the Russian plain. They taught these peoples a modified Greek alphabet called the Cyrillic (suh RIL ik) alphabet. It is still used today in some form by Slavic groups such as Serbs, Bulgarians, and Russians. These missionaries also diffused the Greek and Roman classics. The patriarch of Constantinople allowed the clergy of the new churches to conduct services in their native languages.

Art and Architecture Byzantine art mirrored the religious intensity of the Byzantines and the contributions of Greek, Syrian, and Persian artists. Greek painters portrayed natural-looking figures bending and sitting in easy poses. Greek calligraphers used figures from classical literature to illustrate manuscripts. Persian artists con-

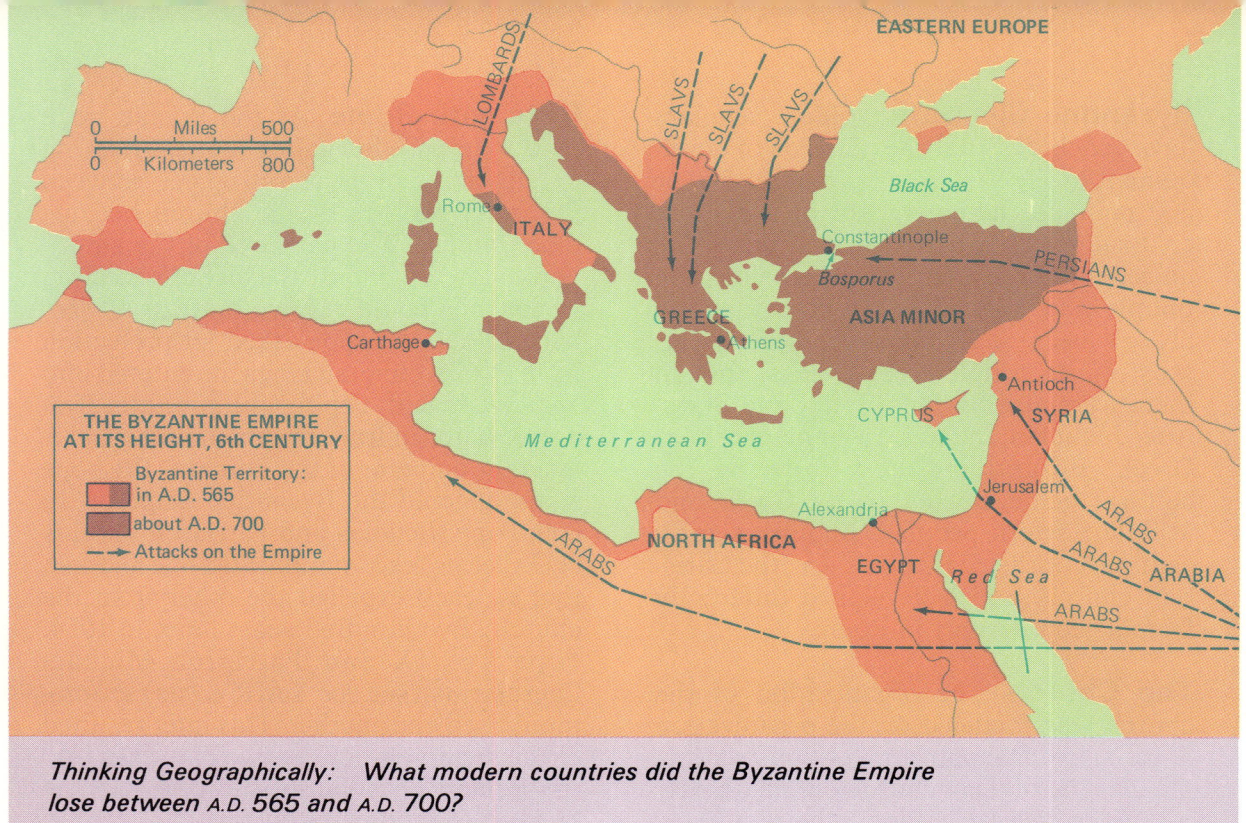

Thinking Geographically: What modern countries did the Byzantine Empire lose between A.D. 565 and A.D. 700?

tributed a form of symbolic art that used ornamentation, geometric designs, animal themes, and rich fabrics. They used gold extensively, even to highlight the backgrounds of their paintings.

Silk in dazzling colors showed religious themes, the emperor and his court, exotic birds, and other animals. According to legend, two Persian monks, during a trip to China, hid silk worms and bamboo shoots in their hollowed-out staffs. On their return to Byzantium, they presented these treasures to the emperor, Justinian. The manufacture and distribution of silk became an imperial monopoly. The looms used to produce the fabric were placed in the empress's rooms at the Grand Palace.

The fortifications, aqueducts, and bridges of the Byzantine Empire were modeled on Roman ones.

Greek and Armenian architects learned and perfected the technique of balancing a dome over a square. That technique became the model for the construction of magnificent basilicas such as those of Galla Placidia (GAL la PLACH ee deah) in northern Italy, Hagia Sophia Constantinople, and the Greek church at the monastery of the Holy Land.

The construction of the church of Hagia Sophia was ordered by Justinian. It was part of the building program he launched after the rioting mobs had destroyed many of the buildings in Constantinople. The church is considered a masterpiece of Byzantine art and architecture. The floor plan is in the form of a cross. The interior walls were built with various tones of marble to form a continuous color scheme. Above was a huge dome 54 meters (179 feet) from the floor. The altars and floors were decorated with gold, silver, ivory, marble, and precious stones. *Mosaics*, pictures or patterns made with bits of colored glass, stone, or enamel, were placed on the walls.

The Defense of the Empire The fortifications of Constantinople held up against the advances in 591 of the Avars (AH vahrz), a Slavic people from across the Danube, the Sassanids in 671, and the Arabs in 717. But the Byzantines were not successful in preventing the Arabs from seizing Palestine and Syria in 640, Alexandria in 642, and Carthage at the end of the 700s. Constantinople suffered a devastating attack by the crusaders in 1204. But the empire managed to survive until Muslim Turks stormed the capital in 1453.

Section Questions

1. Examine your map on page 180. What lands were part of the Byzantine Empire in the year 565? What groups of people lived in the empire?
2. Why was restoring the Roman Empire in the west considered a lost cause after Justinian?
3. What is the *Corpus Juris Civilis*? Why is it considered the most enduring achievement of Justinian?
4. Name several things that made life in the Byzantine Empire different from life in the west in the sixth to ninth centuries.

3. Franks Ruled Much of Western Europe

After the collapse of the western empire, the Franks were unified by a shrewd leader. Clovis (KLO vus) ruled as king of the Franks from 481 to 511. He was a master of intrigue. He used marriage, treachery, and assassination to achieve his ends.

In 496, Clovis became the first important German leader to convert to Christianity. Accompanied by 3,000 Franks, Clovis was baptized on Christmas Day. A popular story credits his conversion to the influence of his wife, Clotilda (klo TIHL duh), who was a Christian. Whatever his rea-

Clovis being baptized.

sons, Clovis won the support of the Pope by accepting Christianity. He considered that support necessary for the conquest of other German peoples.

Clovis united most of northern Gaul. He conquered the Visigoths in southern Gaul and gained control over some areas east of the Rhine River. By the time of Clovis's death, the Franks had become the most powerful people in western Europe.

The Mayors of the Palace Clovis's family ruled Frankland for the next 250 years. Because they were constantly fighting one another, the kings lost real control over their kingdoms. In the 600s, a political struggle resulted in the division of the kingdom into three territories. Each territory had a king. And each king had a *mayor of the palace*. The mayor of the palace ran the royal home and estates for the king. In 687, Pepin (PEP un), one of the mayors, reunited and ruled the three territories. When he died, his son, Charles Martel (mahr TEL) (martel means "the hammer") succeeded him as mayor. Arabs had conquered most of North Africa and parts of Spain. Charles met the invading Arabs at Tours (TOOR) in northern Gaul. He defeated the Arabs and forced them to withdraw to Spain.

181

Thinking Geographically: Compare this map with the map on page 174. What parts of the Roman Empire had the Germans taken over?

The Carolingian Empire In 741, Charles' sons succeeded him. After his brother had retired to a monastery, Pepin the Short decided that he had earned the right to be recognized as the king of the Franks. He wanted the pope's support. In a ceremony performed by the pope's representative, Pepin was made king. To show his appreciation, Pepin gave the church some lands in his kingdom.

In 751, the Lombards, who ruled most of Italy, seized a province of the eastern empire in central Italy. Pope Stephen II begged Pepin for help. Pepin led his armies into Italy and defeated the Lombards. He forced the Lombards to give the captured territory to the pope. This deed in 756 is called the Donation of Pepin. The pope became ruler of a small area that formed the Papal States, land that the popes ruled until 1870. Pepin had become the protector of the Church of Rome.

When Pepin the Short died in 768, the crown passed to one of his sons, Charlemagne (SHAHR luh mayn). Charlemagne means "Charles the Great." From his Latin name *Carolus Magnus* comes the name of his dynasty, Carolingian (ka ruh LIN jee un).

Charles quickly expanded the boundaries of his kingdom. He conquered the Lombards in 774 and waged a long war against the Saxons across the Rhine. By the end of the 700s, Charles' kingdom included modern France; a part of Spain; modern Holland, Belgium, and Austria; a part of modern Czechoslovakia (CHEK uh slo VAH kee uh); and most of Italy.

Charles had become the most powerful ruler in western Europe since Constantine. On Christmas Day 800, Pope Leo III crowned Charlemagne Emperor of the Romans. The king of the Franks recognized the significance of the event. Setting aside his usual trousers, his crossed straps,

Charles Martel at Tours.

his fur-trimmed mantle, and his fur cap, he dressed himself in a magnificent costume of Byzantine design. Charlemagne wore embroidered garments. One had an elephant pattern set off in circles of blue, green, and gold flowers and another, a pattern of squares adorned with rubies. The pope placed on his head a crown covered with jewels. The pope's crowning of Charlemagne was important. It meant that the emperor ruled by the grace of God and with the approval of the church. It also showed that the church wanted to create a Roman empire that would unite all Christians—Romans and Germans. The pope asked the emperor in Constantinople to return the *insignia*, or emblem, of the western empire. The emperor refused. Charlemagne was considered a barbarian who was not worthy of the honor that the Pope had given him.

Despite the attempt to revive the western Roman Empire, Charlemagne's empire was mainly Frankish. It was a blend of Latin and German cultures. Charles ruled his empire not from Rome, but from Aix-la-Chapelle (ayk slah shuh PEL) in northern France.

Accomplishments and Failures

Charlemagne encouraged culture and learning throughout his empire. He had the songs of his people written down. He tried to put together a grammar of the Frankish language. But he finally had to drop the project because he could not master the art of *calligraphy*, beautiful handwriting. He brought scholars, poets, historians, and architects to his court. Education was centered in the palace school, where classical courses were taught: grammar, speech, philosophy, math, geometry, music, and astronomy. Charles also formed an academy at his court that his sister and his daughters could attend. The members of the academy read poetry and classical literature. All members of the academy spoke Latin.

A detail from a silver sarcophagus, showing Charlemagne.

Charles encouraged the growth of monasteries. Manuscript copiers developed a style of writing called Caroline minuscule. It became the standard for most of western Europe. Charles asked his architect to build his palace church on the model of Hagia (AH ee uh) Sophia in Constantinople. He also modeled the administration of his empire on that of Constantinople. He appointed two representatives—a member of the clergy and an imperial administrator—to travel across the kingdom and supervise local officials. Charles' government reflected the German concept of rule based on a strong personal bond between the ruler and his subjects. Charles created rules of conduct for the monasteries and for the clergy. He also appointed bishops and abbots. Some members of the church, including the pope, believed that the emperor was wrongfully seizing their power. But they did not challenge him.

Charles gave faithful nobles land that they eventually passed on to their sons. The land was worked by serfs, who were also transferred from father to son. The economy was based on self-sufficient estates. Thus, it promoted the growth of local, not central, government. Trade was limited to the exchange of goods at markets that met only once a week. *Barter*, or trade of one good for another, was the principal means of exchange. Although there were administrative centers, such as Rome and Aix-la-Chapelle, they were not like the earlier cities. There were no set arrangements for the promotion of trade and industry. There was no city council or government.

Division and Decline After Charlemagne's death in 814, his son, Louis the Pious, became king. Lacking the forceful personality of his father, Louis did little to check the power of the nobles. Before he died, Louis announced that he would divide the empire among his three sons. After his death, Louis's sons quarreled over the divi-

Vikings invading Normandy.

sion. With the aid of groups of nobles, they waged a power struggle that lasted three years. Under the terms of the Treaty of Verdun (ver DUN) in 843, Charles the Bald received West Frankland, the home of Franks who spoke a form of Latin similar to French. Louis the German received East Frankland—most of the land east of the Rhine River. It contained German-speaking peoples. Lothair (lo THAIR) received the title of emperor and the Middle Kingdom, which extended from the North Sea to Rome. The Middle Kingdom contained many different peoples who spoke various forms of German and Latin.

Because it lacked defensible boundaries and cultural bonds, Lothair's kingdom broke up after his death. Louis and Charles divided the Middle Kingdom north of the Alps.

None of the kingdoms survived. After 840, Europe suffered a series of invasions that proved more devastating than those of the fifth century. From the north, an adventuresome seafaring people, called Vikings or Northmen, raided the coasts of Europe. They sacked villages and plundered monasteries. From the east came the Magyars (MAG yahrz), a seminomadic people from the Eurasian steppe near the Ural (YUR ul) Mountains. They devastated eastern and central Europe and invaded Italy. From the south, the Arabs began to make raids on the coasts of Italy.

The Carolingian kings could not defeat the invaders. They had no armies. They could only request troops that were loyal to individual nobles. By the dawn of the tenth century, against a backdrop of destruction, western Europe had become a region of many private estates.

Section Questions

1. What did Clovis gain by converting to Christianity?
2. What was the Donation of Pepin? How did it come about?
3. Name several of Charlemagne's accomplishments.
4. How did Charlemagne's empire become a region of many private estates? Name at least four things that led to this state of affairs.

Thinking Geographically: Read the text description of the way Charlemagne's empire was divided after the death of Louis the Pious. Which section shown on the map went to Charles the Bald? To Louis the German? To Lothair?

Chapter Summary

1. Most historians consider 476 the year in which the Roman Empire in the west collapsed. In that year, the German general Odoacer declared himself king. By 493, different German groups controlled Europe and North Africa. Scholars have developed a number of theories to explain the collapse of the west. Some claim that the barbarian invasions brought about the collapse. Others say that moral decay, or underpopulation, or class struggle, or too much taxation, inflation, and regulation mortally weakened the empire.

The daily lives of the people living in the new Germanic states seemed not to change. The major change involved the distribution of land. The German rulers took away from Roman nobles about one-third of their lands. The church copied the administrative structure of Rome. The monasteries that began in the 300s may have been a reaction against the new complexity of the church. The monks preserved Greco-Roman civilization by copying the classics. Monks and missionaries converted Anglo-Saxons in Britain, the Celtic people of Ireland, Franks, and Germans.

2. Scholars date the transformation of the east into the Byzantine Empire at 500. Its religious tradition and its Greco-Roman-Middle Eastern culture made it clearly different from the west.

Roman influence reached its height in the east during the reign of Justinian. He tried to reunite the west under his rule. But after his death, various German groups retook the western territory. Under Justinian's direction, the *Corpus Juris Civilis* was published. This work preserved the legal knowledge of Rome. It formed the basis of west European law.

The organization of the church of Constantinople was modeled on the organization of the state. The patriarch was supposed to be elected by the bishops. But he was nominated by the emperor and was under the emperor's control. Byzantine art reflected the religious intensity of the Byzantines and the contributions of Greek, Roman, Syrian, and Persian artists. Several magnificent basilicas were created. The fortifications of Constantinople proved effective in stopping the Avars, Sassanids, and Arabs. However, the Byzantines were not successful in preventing the Arabs from seizing Palestine, Syria, Alexandria, and Carthage.

3. Clovis united the Franks. By 496, he had united most of Gaul. In that year, he became the first important German leader to convert to Christianity. During the 600s, divisions among Clovis's descendants led to the division of Frankland. Pepin, one of the mayors of the palace, declared himself king and reunited the empire. His son, Charles Martel, defeated the Arabs at Tours in 732 and forced them back into Spain. In 751 Charles' son, Pepin the Short, was crowned king. Pepin was the first Carolingian king. He gave the Pope lands in central Italy that came to be known as the Papal States. Charlemagne became king in 768 and conquered still more lands in Europe. In 800, Pope Leo crowned Charlemagne emperor of the Romans.

Charlemagne encouraged culture and education in his empire. After his death, his empire was divided among his three sons. The lack of cities, an economy centered on private estates, and a powerful class of nobles promoted disunity in the empire. The Carolingian kings were unable to stop the invasions and raids of the Vikings, Magyars, and Arabs.

Chapter 10 Review

Check Your Facts

1. Identify the following. Then in one or two sentences, tell the significance of each in the history you have just studied.
   a. Huns
   b. Alaric
   c. Franks
   d. Clovis
   e. Pepin the Short
   f. Theodora
2. Name three groups who sacked and helped destroy the city of Rome. Who ran the old imperial city when there was little else left?
3. What was the *Digest*? Why was it written?
4. What German tribes conquered Britain? What did they proceed to do?
5. What role did monasteries play in preserving Greco-Roman civilization?
6. How did the eastern empire protect itself from the Germans?
7. What goods were produced in the Byzantine Empire?

Words to Know

Complete the following statements with the most appropriate word: *heretic, mosaics, vandalism, patriarch, missionary, canon.*

1. A _____ went to other countries to teach a faith to others.
2. A _____ was the highest church official in the Byzantine Empire.
3. The councils' interpretations of Christian doctrine and rules for monasteries formed the basis of _____ law.
4. A _____ rejected the Christian doctrine approved by the councils.
5. _____ was coined by a bishop to mean willful or mindless destruction.
6. _____ are bits of colored glass or stone used to make whole pictures.

Developing Your Skills

1. Carefully examine the photos of Byzantine art on pages 154 and 178. Then look at the examples of Greek and Roman art on pages 94 and 110. Compare the two sets and list the major differences you find. (Consider materials, function, subject matter, size, style, use of color.)
2. Examine the map on page 185. What modern-day countries were part of the Carolingian empire?

Thinking It Over

1. What was the attitude of the Franks toward the Byzantines? How did this compare with the attitude of the Byzantines toward the Franks? Why do you think most groups of people consider those who are different as inferiors?
2. In your opinion, what achievements of Greek and Roman civilization added the most to the Byzantine Empire? Give reasons for your answer.

Special Activities

1. The citadel in Moscow, where the Kremlin is located, is noted for its architecture. After studying photographs in the library, write an essay tracing the Byzantine influences in its design.
2. The Byzantine mosaics are some of the most beautiful works of art in the world. If you are a microcomputer fan, you might try to duplicate one of their mosaic pictures, or perhaps just a part of one. Present the resulting picture to your class.

Muslim pilgrims at Mecca.

Chapter 11 Islam

In the morning light, men from many places were circling a shrine. After the seventh circle, they stooped to kiss a black stone set into the corner of the shrine. Each man wore a simple white cloth, wrapped loosely about his body. Each chanted: "Lord God, from such a great distance I have come to Thee...Grant me shelter under Thy throne." Although they had their own native languages, they all chanted in Arabic.

These men were in Mecca (MEK uh) on a *pilgrimage*, a trip to a holy place for religious reasons. They came from Egypt, Africa, India, Ceylon (si LAHN), Persia, and other distant lands.

570–1258

570	Muhammad born
622	Muhammad leaves Mecca
641	Arabs conquer Persia
644	Arabs reach India and Libya
661	Umayyad dynasty begins
732	Arabs defeated at Tours
750	Abbasid dynasty overthrows Umayyads
756	Abd-er-Rahman I invades Spain
1055	Seljuk Turks take over Baghdad
1258	Mongols sack Baghdad

Muhammad.

They had different backgrounds, were of different races, and spoke different languages. Yet, something pulled these men together and brought them to Mecca.

The force that pulled them was Islam (is LAHM), a religion that sprang up in Arabia during the seventh century. This religion inspired Arabs to create a vast empire and civilization. It united Arabs and, as the faith spread to other non-Arab groups, it unified people who were culturally different. Today, that common bond of religion continues, almost 1,000 years after the Islamic empire vanished.

To understand the development of this new religion and what it became, we have to begin with a remote desert area populated mainly by nomadic tribes and scattered townspeople. It was in this region that Muhammad (Mo HAM ed) received his vision and founded Islam. It was from this region that the Islamic civilization swept forth. And it was here that Muhammad, on his last pilgrimage to the sacred shrine in Mecca, declared, "Every believer in Islam is a brother to every other believer." This ideal of fellowship was meant to provide unity and purpose to all believers, Arab and non-Arab. We must turn to history to see what happened to this ideal.

1. Muhammad Offered Arabs a New Religion

Early in the seventh century, Semites lived on the Arabian Peninsula. Old trade routes crossed their lands. But the ancient empires had passed them by. Most Arabs were never ruled by outside peoples or by a central government very long. They lived in small tribal groups bound by family ties and a common language, Arabic. They agreed upon many rules about how people should behave. Often the rules did not

189

This old photograph shows a group of Bedouins having a meal in front of their tent. Their daily life was not much different from the time of Muhammad.

work and conflicts between tribes boiled over into warfare.

Most of the Arabs wandered across vast deserts seeking food and water for their animals and themselves. They lived on the meat of camels, goats, and sheep. They bought cloth, dates, and tools from villagers. Villagers farmed around an oasis. Other Arabs settled in farming areas in the valleys near the Red Sea. Here towns developed and prospered. Even in towns, the Arabs were grouped into tribes, and conflicts arose among them.

The town of Mecca, in west-central Arabia near the Red Sea, was a crossroad for the caravan trade. The caravans carried spices, gold, and other luxury goods on camels from Africa to Jerusalem and other cities to the north. Meccans prospered by supplying these caravans with water, food, and a safe place to rest. They also prospered because people came to worship at the Kaaba (KAH buh), a small black stone set in the side of a temple. Arabs made long trips across the desert to kiss the sacred stone and to worship the many gods and spirits that they believed in. The temple in Mecca was so important to the Arabs that all warfare between groups stopped for four months each year while pilgrims traveled to the Kaaba.

The Birth of Islam Islam began in the visions of a camel driver from Mecca named Muhammad. Muhammad was born in Mecca in 570 to a family that belonged to the ruling tribe of that city. His father died before he was born, and his mother died when he was six. The young orphan was finally raised by his uncle. He tended flocks of sheep in the hills around Mecca.

Later, Muhammad became a camel driver on the routes between South Arabia and the cities to the north. He was successful and married his employer, the widow Khadija (kah DEE ja). She ran a very large trading business on her own.

Muhammad, though successful, became restless. His attention turned to religion. On his many trips, he had met Jews, Christians, and Zoroastrians. He learned about their belief in one god and he thought about the religion of his people. He was tired of the tribal quarrels and greed in Mecca. He regularly saw merchants cheat pilgrims and caravan drivers. He knew they did little for the poor, the orphans, the slaves, or the sick. These unfortunates suffered in the streets. The religion of his fellow Meccans did not make them compassionate.

The Arabs believed in one god spirit called Allah ("the god"). But they were more concerned about personal gods—the mother goddess and the gods of the morning star and the moon. They also saw a world that was filled with three kinds of powerful spirits: fairies, who did nice things; jinns, who played tricks; and ghouls, who led people to evil. People worshiped at the Kaaba to please these gods and spirits. Muhammad was no longer moved by them.

One night in about 610, Muhammad felt that an angel appeared to him in a cave outside Mecca. The angel told Muhammad to carry God's word to others. "Read," commanded the angel. "In the name of your Lord who created man from a drop of blood. Read: Your Lord teaches man that which he did not know."

Muhammad believed that God had chosen him to reform the religions earlier revealed to Abraham, the prophets of Israel, and Jesus. He thought that he was chosen as the twenty-eighth and last prophet of God.

Muhammad went forth to preach his new faith. His message was simple. God hated the Arabs' evil ways. Worshiping idols, gambling, drinking alcohol, stealing, cheating, and fighting were forbidden. He told them that they had to submit to the will of God (Allah) and that Allah would one day pass judgment on them. Muhammad made a few converts, mostly from the poor and slaves, but most Meccans laughed. When Muhammad continued to preach, interfering with business, the Meccans persecuted his little band of followers.

After several attempts on his life, Muhammad thought about leaving Mecca. People from Yathrib (YATH rub), 400 kilometers (250 miles) north of Mecca, visited him. They wanted his leadership to stop political quarrels in their city and make it as rich as Mecca.

One year later, in 622, Muhammad escaped from Mecca with a few followers. He moved to Yathrib, which he renamed Medina (muh DEE nuh), meaning "the city of the prophet." Muhammad's flight from Mecca to Medina was a turning point. For Muslims, this year marks the first year of their calendar—1 A.H. (*anno hegirae*, or "year of the flight").

Muhammad became the religious and political leader of Medina. He stopped the tribal quarrels and the worship of spirits. He had the first *mosque* (MAHSK) built. A mosque is a place of worship. At the mosque, he began Friday services to the one God, Allah. Believers washed themselves and removed their shoes. The men then prayed together. Women prayed in a special section. Believers were divided only by sex, not by wealth, race, or anything else. These Friday services were dignified, simple, and effective. The community of believers grew.

In Medina, Muhammad not only preached and taught, he led an army that

Pilgrims arriving at port in Jeddah, Saudi Arabia, on their way to Mecca.

protected the Medinans' trade and raided Meccan troublemakers. Finally, in 630, after several years of war, Muhammad's army brought Mecca under his control. Only four people lost their lives in this final battle. Muhammad preferred to win people to Islam rather than to subdue them with weapons. So he granted mercy to all Meccans who accepted Islam.

Muhammad immediately cast out all spirit worship and idols in Mecca. The Kaaba became the central shrine in Islam.

A pilgrimage to Mecca became a duty for all believers who could manage it. Mecca was declared the holiest city in Islam. This attitude toward Mecca and the mercy shown in victory eased Meccans' acceptance of Islam.

The Faith of Islam Muhammad's teachings are the core of Islam. Central to it is Allah, the one god who knows all, sees all, and guides all. The word "Islam" means submission. A Muslim is one who submits to the will of Allah.

All Muslims must be ready to face the day of judgment. On judgment day, those who win Allah's approval go to paradise. The condemned ones are forced into the fires of hell. Muhammad set forth strict rules about charity. He prohibited cheating, gambling, and drinking alcohol.

According to Islam, Allah is a judge of persons—but a compassionate one. Allah shows mercy by sending prophets to warn people. Allah also gave believers a code of practice, called the Five Pillars of Islam, which is a simple set of rules. The first pillar is the profession of faith: "There is one God, and Muhammad is his prophet." The second pillar is prayer. Five times a day, Muslims kneel and face Mecca. This reminds them of Allah and their duty.

The third pillar is fasting, as Muhammad did during *Ramadan*. Ramadan is the ninth month of the Muslim calendar and the month when Muhammad had his first revelation. During this month, the faithful do not eat or drink during the day. The fourth pillar is charity. Muslims are expected to help care for the poor. The fifth pillar is the pilgrimage to Mecca during the lifetime of each believer.

To these pillars, some Muslims would add a sixth—*jihad* (juh HAHD). Jihad means holy war, or the struggle against the enemies of Islam. At the time of Muhammad, jihad meant taking up arms against enemies. But it also meant struggling against evil in one's own life. Thus jihad covers missionary activity and personal improvement.

The Prophet as a Teacher With Mecca and Medina secure, Muhammad continued to preach about the ways Islamic society should be run. He worked to end the tribal quarrels, using devotion to Islam as a common bond.

Muhammad was both a religious and a political leader. In Islam there is not supposed to be a separation between the religious and the political community. Allah's word was law. Believers were equal, whether poor or rich. Christians and Jews, while not believers, were respected as people to whom God had sent earlier prophets. They were to be tolerated within all Muslim communities.

Muhammad's teachings improved the status of Arab women. Women were no longer property but persons. Men were limited to four wives at a time. Women could inherit money, own lands, and conduct business. They were to be educated. Divorce was carefully regulated.

As problems arose, Muhammad responded with sermons explaining what the law should be in the community. He was well on his way to reforming Arab society when he died in 632. His followers immediately began writing down the revelations Muhammad received from Allah. This collection is known as the Koran (ku RAN). It is a sacred book, similar to the Bible. Muhammad's followers also collected and wrote down what they could remember about his personal statements or practices on rules and policies in the Islamic community. These collections—the sayings of Muhammad—are an important source for understanding the Koran.

Thus, Muhammad, upon his death, left Muslims with a sacred text offering direction for a better society on Earth and for paradise afterward.

An open copy of the Koran showing beautifully illustrated pages.

Section Questions

1. Who was Muhammad? Why was he a prophet?
2. Why did Muhammad flee Mecca in 622? How is this flight remembered by Muslims today?
3. Why did Meccans finally accept Islam and Muhammad?
4. What are the Five Pillars of Islam?
5. What does jihad mean?

Arabian cavalry sweeping across the desert.

2. Islam Spread Rapidly

After the death of the prophet, Islam was without a religious and political leader. Since Muhammad did not have a son and had not named someone to succeed him, some tension arose. It was decided that Muhammad's friend and early convert, Abu-Bakr (ah BOO BAK ur) would be his successor, or *caliph*. For twenty-five years after Muhammad's death, Muslim leadership was continued under four caliphs. Their skilled leadership led to the expansion of Islam. Arab armies seized eastern Arabia and moved northward. Wherever the armies found resistance, they offered three choices: Choose Islam as the true religion; surrender and pay special taxes to the Muslim community; or stand and fight against the Islamic army.

The Byzantine empire and the Sassanid empire in Persia were weak from warfare with each other. Christianity was torn by differences among competing groups. Thus, the Arab armies were often welcomed, and large numbers of Christians converted to Islam. When the Arabs attacked Jerusalem, the Byzantine defenders were forced to ask for peace. The caliph came personally to accept the surrender and to protect the people and churches of Jerusalem. Jerusalem was a holy city for Muslims because they included Abraham, Moses, and Jesus among the twenty-eight prophets.

The Arab armies moved on. Between 637 and 650, they conquered all of Iraq and Persia. In Egypt, a fortress on the site of modern Cairo fell in 641 after a seven-month siege. Within eighteen months, all of Egypt was under Arab control, and the armies were moving across North Africa. By 698, North Africa was largely under Islamic control. The Arab armies successfully conquered and converted the Berber (BUR bur) tribes of modern Algeria, Tunisia (too NEE zhee uh), and Morocco.

The Egyptians and Syrians helped the Arabs at sea. With their ships and sailing ability, the Egyptians took the Arab armies to the island of Cyprus in 649. The Arabs seized this island from the Byzantines and then, in 655, defeated a Byzantine fleet of 500 ships. The forces of Islam were in control of a large portion of the Mediterranean Sea and its commerce.

In 711, a Berber army under Tariq (TAH rik) attacked Spain. Other forces were added under Arab leadership, and the Visigoths were defeated. City by city, the Muslim forces won Spain in six years of war. But in 732, exactly 100 years after the death of Muhammad, the armies of Islam were defeated by Charles Martel in the Battle of Tours, France. While the Muslim armies continued raids into France, they never again mounted a major invasion into western Europe.

The Muslims also failed to take Constantinople, the Byzantine capital. Long assaults were mounted, but the sieges failed.

However, the Persians were conquered, and so Arab armies reached far into central Asia. Even faraway India was invaded by Muslim armies led by a 17-year-old general.

The Muslim advances into Europe were stopped at Tours.

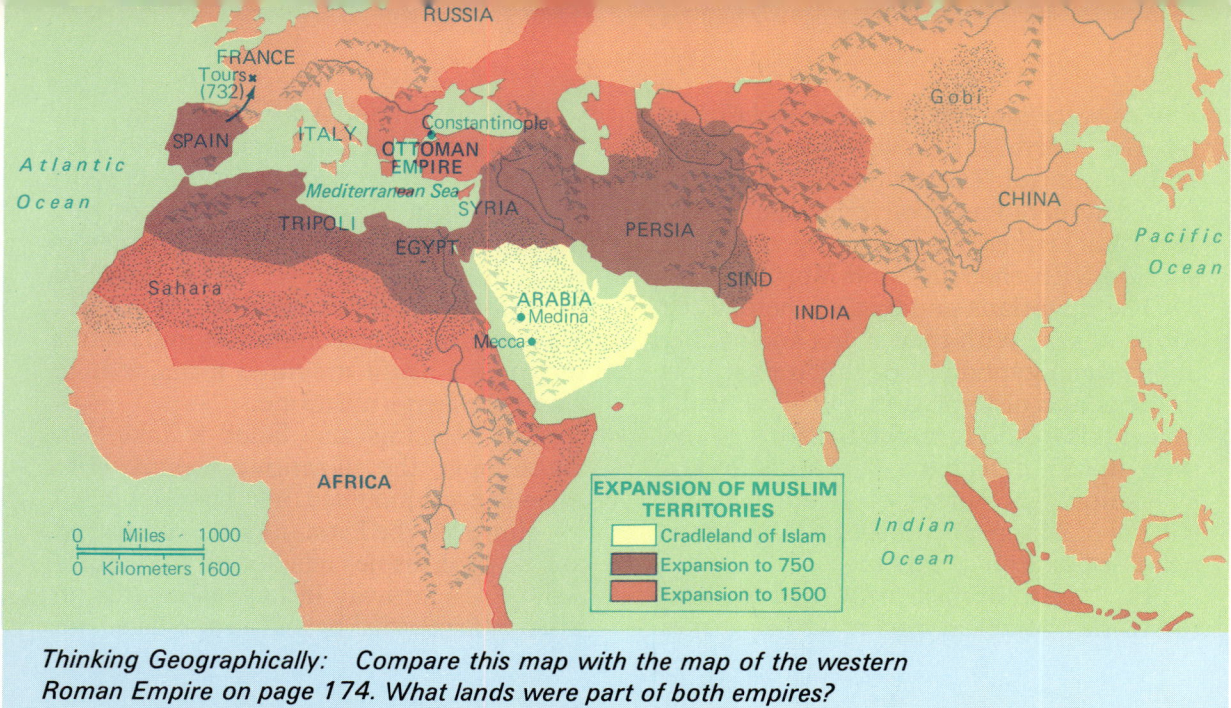

Thinking Geographically: Compare this map with the map of the western Roman Empire on page 174. What lands were part of both empires? What lands did the Arabs conquer that the Romans did not?

Arab Successes It is hard to find the reasons for the speed and the vastness of the Muslim conquest. In 100 years, the Arab armies won an empire more than twice the size of the Roman Empire. No single cause explains this successful expansion. To a large extent, it could be because of faith—the belief that one was performing the will of Allah. Death in battle held little fear for people confident of doing God's work. In addition, there were the new military tactics of the Arabs. Their camel cavalry could move swiftly across vast deserts. Their enemies were often unable to react quickly.

The Arabs were skillful, fierce fighters. Courage was a key value in their code of honor. Military victories also brought considerable wealth to the army, to the religious community of Islam, and to the various Arab tribes sending troops to battle. They had strong incentives.

The Sassanid empire (Persia) was on the decline when the Arabs brought Islam to its borders. Barbarian attacks and a devastating war with Persia had exhausted the Byzantine empire. To its former subjects in the Middle East, Arab rule seemed benevolent. Taxes were reduced. Religious toleration was welcomed by Jews and members of heretical Christian churches, who had been discriminated against by the orthodox Byzantine church. The Arab conquerors offered benefits for joining their faith and their armies. Furthermore, the new Islamic sense of community and fellowship was appealing.

Governing the Empire Disciplined troops proved they could win battles. But the caliphs had to rule the empire that had been won. To gain insights on how to rule, the caliphs appointed scholars to write down the Koran and to establish a correct text for the sayings of Muhammad. These texts were used as government books. In the conquered lands, local converts might be used as soldiers, but they were under Arab command. To keep them loyal, Arab troops were settled in communities—

actually fortified cities. There the soldiers lived a life much like the one they had back in Arabia.

The Arabs were still organized by tribes and lived as tribes in the fortified cities. Tribal customs continued along with Islamic rites and duties. Each soldier and tribe received part of the taxes of the area where they were settled.

In this way, the Arabs controlled their new empire without upsetting many local customs or making drastic changes. As long as the conquered peoples paid their taxes, they were usually allowed to govern themselves.

Changes and conflicts, however, did arise among the Arabs. The Islamic community and individual tribal leaders received vast sums of money from their empire. Squabbling began over riches, and the tribal loyalties again became divisive.

Like the prophet, the early caliphs had been humble leaders inspired by faith. But conflicts arose over who should succeed each caliph who died. The conflicts often followed tribal divisions among the Arabs. The third caliph was murdered for favoring his tribe over others. The fourth caliph was also murdered, and political power swung to the Arab governor of Syria. This governor seized power and moved the capital of the empire to Damascus (duh MAS kus) from Medina in 661. Mecca remained the holiest city, attracting pilgrims. Medina also remained holy as the place of the *hegira*, or migration. But Damascus, away from tribal feuds, was the capital.

The Umayyad Dynasty This new dynasty ruled Islam for almost 100 years, until A.D. 750. The Umayyad (oo MI yed) caliphs continued to expand the empire. They adorned Damascus and Jerusalem with beautiful mosques. Damascus flourished as a center of religion, trade, and government.

It was under the Umayyads that Muslim armies reached as far as France in the west and India in the east. In 751, an Arab army defeated the Chinese in a battle in Turkestan.

The Umayyad caliphs continued the Arab fortress-city style of administration. But now the Arabs were a minority in their own empire. They were outnumbered by non-Arab converts to Islam—Syrians, Persians, Egyptians, Berbers, and many others. These people resented the special status of the Arabs, who received greater pay in the army, held lands tax-free, and received greater respect. These non-Arab converts expected to be treated as Muslims in fellowship, not as second-class citizens.

Early in the Umayyad rule, another dispute arose over the succession to Muhammad. The first four caliphs had been known as the companions of the prophet. After them, the Umayyads established a hereditary dynasty. However, a rival group of Muslims thought that the caliphs should be related to Muhammad through his daughter Fatima (FAT i muh), and her husband, Ali, who was Muhammad's cousin.

These supporters of the house of Ali called themselves Shi'ites (SHEE itez). In 680, the Shi'ites tried to install Hasan (ha SAN), Fatima's son, as caliph. A fierce battle resulted in which the Umayyad army was successful. Hasan and his army were massacred in Iraq.

A basic division in Islam occurred which continues until today. The Umayyads became the orthodox, or Sunnites. They believed that the caliph could be appointed by the consent of the Islamic community. The Shi'ites claimed that only the descendants of Ali and Fatima were guided by Allah and therefore qualified to be caliphs. The last of these descendants disappeared during the ninth century. Since then, the Shi'ites have waited for a true descendant to reappear and end Sunnite control of Islam. Today, Shi'ites mourn the death of Hasan and the massacre of his army during

Ramadan. Large Shi'ite communities live in Iran, Iraq, and Pakistan.

Section Questions

1. Examine the map on page 196. What areas had been conquered by Arabs by the year 750?
2. What four reasons help explain the Arab success in establishing an Islamic empire?
3. How did the Arabs control their empire?
4. Why did the caliphs want the Koran and the sayings of the prophet collected and an accurate text written down?
5. What is the difference between Sunnite and Shi'ite Muslims?

3. The Golden Age of Islamic Civilization

In 750, after a long civil war, the Umayyad dynasty at Damascus was violently overthrown by the Abbasid (uh BAS ud) dynasty. The Abbasids were descendants of Muhammad's uncle, Abbas (a BAS), and, like the Umayyads, members of Muhammad's original Arab tribe. Much of their support, however, came from non-Arab Shi'ite Muslims in Persia and central Asia.

The Abbasid Dynasty In 762, the caliph al-Mansur (AL man SOOR) moved the capital from Damascus to a new city, Baghdad (BAG dad). He set the site for Baghdad in Mesopotamia, between the Tigris and Euphrates rivers. As a major trading center between west and east, Baghdad grew rapidly. There the Abbasid caliphs had their court, their administrators, their religious leaders, and their armies. Taxes and tribute flowed into the city as the empire prospered. Fifty years later, Baghdad was the largest city in the world.

Baghdad reached its peak under Harun al-Rashid (hu ROON AL ruh SHEED), caliph from 786 to 806. Muslim vessels sailed the east coast of Africa, to India, and to the East Indies. There were Muslim merchants in the Chinese port of Guangzhou (Canton) trading for porcelain and silk. Papermaking was brought back from China and carried as far as Spain by 900. Besides trading, Muslim merchants made many converts to Islam in east Africa and Southeast Asia.

The Abbasids replaced Arab aristocrats with trained administrators. These were Muslims who came from many areas of the empire. In the army, non-Arab troops became widespread. The caliphs rarely appeared in public. They lived in luxury in

"The City of Baghdad," from a minature painting dated 1536.

Baghdad. They ruled, collected taxes, crushed rebellions, and defended the empire.

In religious matters, the Abbasids turned to a growing and powerful group of Islamic scholars, the ulama (oo luh MA). The ulama took over much of the religious authority of the caliphs. They often disapproved of the Abbasids' luxury and abuse of power.

Under the Abbasids, Muslim cities became great centers of learning and art. The caliphs built a huge library at Baghdad. They had hundreds of Greek, Persian, Jewish, and other scholars translate their ancient works into Arabic.

Baghdad had several medical schools and the world's first free public hospital. The works of classical Greek physicians and surgeons were translated and studied. But the Muslims went far beyond the Greeks in medical knowledge. Al-Razi (AL RAY zee, 860 to 925), better known as Rhazes (RAY zeez), wrote over 200 medical books. He studied smallpox and measles and recommended treatments.

Muslim scientists studied optics, astronomy, and chemistry. In 771, an Indian scholar introduced a number system that had been developed by the Hindus: these were what we now call Arabic numerals. The Muslims added the symbol of 0, which made possible the decimal system. Mathematical problems could be solved much faster with these new numbers and decimals. Muslims borrowed and developed the compass, which locates magnetic north. They improved on the astrolabe, which is used to determine the location of stars. Both the compass and the astrolabe were a great help to sailors.

The Abbasid caliphate was the classical period of Arabic literature—especially poetry. Abu-Nuwas (ah BOO nu WAHS), who died in 815, was Persian, but he wrote in Arabic. His poems described the pleasures of love, wine, and hunting. Abu-Tammam (ah BOO ta MAHM), who died

A manuscript illustration of Arabian astronomers at work.

in 845, wrote a famous poem celebrating the capture of a Byzantine fortress in 838. The astrologers at Baghdad had told the caliph that the fortress could not be taken. He ignored them. Abu-Tammam praised the caliph's boldness:

> The sword is truer than what is told in books:
> In its edge is the separation between truth and falsehood,
> In the white sword-blades, not the black pages of texts,
> Is found the clarification of doubt and uncertainty.

Al-Mutanabbi (al MOO tan AHB bi, 915-965) is usually considered the greatest classical Arab poet. Many of his lines are still quoted in the Arab-speaking world:

> Honor the man of noble soul and he becomes your slave,
> But the mean-souled man when honored grows insolent.
> He who desires the ocean makes light of streams.
> Men bury and are buried, and our feet Trample the skulls of those who went before.

Another great poet was Firdausi (fihr DOW see), who died in 1020. He was a Persian who was Muslim but anti-Arab. He wrote an epic poem about the mythical rulers of ancient Iran from the creation to the Arab conquest.

Philosophy and religious study were important activities in Baghdad and other Abbasid cities. Learned people wanted to unite Greek ideas and knowledge with Islamic beliefs. However, the philosopher al-Farabi (AL fah RAH bi), who died in 950, boldly declared that the arguments of

Did You Know?

Sindbad the Sailor

Under Persian influence, poetry during Abbasid times was elaborate and elegant. About A.D. 942, Persian and other legends were written into poetry under the title *A Thousand and One Arabian Nights*. None of these legends is more famous than that of Sindbad the Sailor.

Sindbad was a superhero—an adventurer. At a time when European sailors stayed close to shore, Arab sailors plied sea routes to India, Ceylon (Sri Lanka), Africa, and south China. They brought back to Baghdad the riches of those other lands: silk, gold, ivory, gems, tools, spices, and porcelain.

The Sindbad stories are based upon the dangerous voyages of these Muslim sailors. In these stories, Sindbad sails to Africa, India, and China. Along the way, he meets and overcomes many monsters, demons, and accidents. He is carried from one island to another by a huge bird. He visits the splendid diamond mines of Ceylon. He buys timber and ivory from traders in India. Sindbad discovers tin in Malaya (muh LAY uh) and barters for monkeys in India.

This illustration shows the Old Man of the Sea leaping on Sindbad.

Near the close of his adventuresome life, Sindbad is "reported" to have said: "I wait only for my last journey, upon which a man takes nothing to sell, and no money to buy and no ship to go in. And no man has ever come back!" Death was the only enemy that Sindbad could not conquer.

Islamic theology were not as good as the logical methods of the Greeks. On the other hand, Abu-Hamid al-Ghazali (ah BOO Hamid al GHA za li), a religious scholar who died in 1111, insisted that increasing knowledge was less important than moral awareness and doing the right thing.

In all the major branches of learning, the Islamic world was far ahead of Christian Europe. Later, Europeans were able to acquire the knowledge of classical Greek civilization because the Muslims had preserved that knowledge and added to it over the centuries.

Muslim Spain When the Umayyads were overthrown in Damascus, the new Abbasid caliph ordered all male members of the family killed. One Umayyad escaped, however, and fled to the Berbers of Morocco. This young leader, Abder-Rahman (ahb DUR ra MAHN) built an army and crossed over to Spain. There he seized control in the name of the Umayyad dynasty and established his capital at Cordoba (KORD uh vuh).

Abder-Rahman III took over the title of caliph. During his reign, Cordoba became a great city with 500,000 inhabitants, 3,000 mosques, and 300 public baths. With its magnificent Great Mosque, gardens, paved streets, and piped water, Cordoba was considered one of the most beautiful and comfortable cities in the world.

Under the Umayyad caliphs, Muslim Spain became the most prosperous country in Europe. Weaving and papermaking were important industries. Cordoban leather goods and Toledo (tuh LEE do) steel were world famous. Wheat and olives were grown in the dry south, and a massive irrigation system supplied water for fruit, vegetables, sugarcane, rice, and cotton. Foreign trade routes reached east to India, north into Europe, and south into the Sahara (suh HAR uh) Desert.

Cordoba, Toledo, and other cities of

This delicately carved arched doorway in Granada, Spain, shows the Muslim influence in Europe.

Muslim Spain were centers of learning. Cordoba in particular, with its fine university and famous library of more than 600,000 volumes, attracted scholars from all over the Islamic world and from Christian Europe. One of the greatest thinkers was Averroes (ah VER uh weez, 1126-1198). He was a physician and philosopher who wrote about Aristotle and other classical Greek thinkers. He argued that people had the right to use reason to test ideas and denied that the individual soul was immortal. This brought him into conflict with orthodox Islam, and he was exiled to

This marble mosque in Cairo was built by Mohammed Ali.

Morocco. After the death of Averroes, his books were translated into Latin. They were widely read in Christian Europe.

Several great thinkers who lived in North Africa were born or educated in Muslim Spain. Maimonides (mi MAHN uh deez, 1135 to 1204), a Jew, was from Cordoba. He settled in Cairo, where he wrote a book, *The Guide to the Perplexed*. This work tried to resolve the differences between classical Greek thought and Judaism.

Ibn-Khaldun (IHB un kal DOON, 1332 to 1406), a famous Muslim historian, was born in Granada (gruh NAH duh). Though he lived in Tunis, he wrote about events in Spain. Ibn-Khaldun developed a theory of history. He argued that the life of a civilization is like that of an individual: it is born, grows up, ages, and decays.

The most famous Muslim geographer, Ibn-Batuta (IHB un buh TOO tah), came from Morocco but was educated in Spain. He traveled across North Africa, through Egypt, Arabia, and Persia, to India. He spent eight years in Delhi (DEL ee) and also visited Ceylon and China. After returning to Morocco in 1349, he went to the famed city of Timbuktu (tim buk TOO) and to the Niger (NI jur) River area below the Sahara. Ibn-Batuta left excellent accounts of his many trips. One scholar estimated that he traveled over 120,000 kilometers (75,000 miles).

The Umayyad caliphate fell in 1031. Muslim Spain then broke up into several smaller states. Beginning in the early thirteenth century, these were gradually conquered by Christian Spain. In 1492, the sultan of Granada, Spain's last Muslim ruler, had to flee to Morocco.

North Africa In 909, a Shi'ite movement, the Fatimids, revolted against the Abbasids in North Africa. A new caliphate was begun in Tunisia. In 969, Fatimid armies conquered Egypt. They founded the city of Cairo and made it the capital of an empire which spread from Morocco to Syria. In Cairo, the Fatimids built the al-Azhar (al az HAR) mosque. This mosque is still a seat of Muslim learning. The Fatimids fell in 1171. In 1250, the Mamluk (MAM luk) commanders of the Egyptian army took power. They ruled for nearly 300 years until Egypt was conquered by the Ottoman (AH tuh mun) Turks.

In the eleventh century, Morocco, Algeria, and Spain were seized by a Berber dynasty, the Almoravids (al MO rah vidz), who reigned from 1050 to 1140. They were succeeded by another Berber empire, that of the Almohads (AL mo haydz), who extended their rule all through North Africa. Meanwhile, Berber nomads carried Islam along the Sahara trade routes into west Africa and the Sudan (soo DAN). They traded luxury goods and salt for gold, leather, and slaves. Gold from Africa was a major source of the wealth of the Islamic world in this period.

The Decline of the Abbasids While Islamic culture flourished under the Abbasids, the unity of the Islamic empire was shattered. In 874, Persia regained its independence. By the beginning of the tenth century, Spain, North Africa, and Egypt were in the hands of other caliphs. Governors in the Abbasid territories were carving out their own states. At the court in Baghdad, Seljuk (sel JOOK) Turks, rough, nomadic tribesmen brought in to provide a trusted palace guard, grabbed power in 1055. The Seljuks took the title of *sultan*, or king, and left the Abbasid caliphs with symbolic power over religious matters. Thereafter, the Abbasid caliphate existed

Ruins of a church built by the Seljuk Turks.

in name only. The Seljuks used Arab and Persian religious and government leaders as administrators. These officials maintained the irrigation system, farm productivity, and commerce. The sultans enjoyed the lavish life at the court in Baghdad while collecting taxes and tribute. But with the rise of the Seljuks, Arabic civilization had definitely entered a period of slow decline. The invasion in 1258 of the Mongols, a nomadic group from Mongolia, was the final blow to the Abbasids. Libraries were plundered, art destroyed, and people massacred. The irrigation system, which Mesopotamian civilization had depended upon from ancient times, fell into decay.

In time, the Mongols were converted to Islam and were absorbed into Islamic society. Meanwhile, in 1260 their advance was stopped by the Mamluks. But while Muslims were fighting Mongols, they also faced invasions from the Christian kingdoms in Europe, which launched a series of Crusades to seize the Holy Land.

In what is now modern Turkey, the Ottoman Turks turned back the Mongol invasions and began to increase their territory. The Ottoman Empire was now established, an empire which would continue into the 1900s.

Section Questions

1. At the end of the Umayyad caliphate, what divisions appeared in the Islamic empire?
2. How did the Berbers of North Africa help make the wealth of the Islamic world possible?
3. What were the major achievements of the Spanish Umayyad caliphate after 756?
4. Who were the Seljuk Turks? What did they achieve? How did their rule compare with that of the Mongols?

Chapter Summary

1. Late in A.D. 600, Muhammad taught a new religion, called Islam, in Arabia. He hoped to reform Arabian society using truths that he felt were revealed to him by Allah, the true god. After leaving Mecca in 622, Muhammad built support in Medina and took Mecca by force in 630. Controlling Mecca and Medina, Muhammad began a series of conquests. These were continued after his death in 632 by dedicated followers. Muhammad's teachings were written down in a sacred book, the Koran. The prophet preached that Allah had a plan for humankind to follow that would yield paradise for Muslims.

2. The first four caliphs, successors to Muhammad, organized the Arabs along religious teachings. They continued the conquests and conversions. In 661, the Umayyad caliphate began with its capital at Damascus. The building of an empire continued, sweeping as far as southern France and the Atlantic in the west and as far as India in the east.

3. When the Umayyad caliphate at Damascus was overthrown, the empire of the Arabs crumbled. The Abbasids took the east and established a lavish capital in a new city called Baghdad. They promoted a flourishing culture and intense commercial activity. In Spain, a member of the Umayyad family established a caliphate with its capital in Cordoba. The Fatimids, a Shi'ite group, took control of North Africa. They based their caliphate in Egypt and were eventually succeeded by the Mamluks. The Abbasid caliphate declined under the domination of the Seljuk Turks and was finally destroyed by the Mongol invasion. The Islamic world remained bound together by a common religious and cultural tradition, but its political unity was shattered.

Chapter 11 Review

Check Your Facts

1. Identify or describe the following:
   a. Shi'ite   c. Allah
   b. Kaaba   d. Koran
2. Describe the religious beliefs of the Arabs before Islam. What changes were made by Muhammad?
3. What are some of the Umayyads' major accomplishments? Why did their caliphate end in 750?
4. What are some of the Abbasids' major accomplishments? Why did their empire fall?
5. Name four important writers in Muslim civilization. What did they write about?
6. Why was the Spanish Umayyad caliphate held in such high regard? What were its acomplishments from 756?

Words to Know

Complete the following statements with the most appropriate word:
1. A Muslim who journeys to Mecca is on a _____ .
2. A holy war is a _____ .
3. The numerical symbols 1, 2, 3, 4, 5, 6, 7, 8, 9, and 0 are called _____ numerals.
4. A leader of the Muslim world was a _____ .

Developing Your Skills

1. Place each of the following in one of these time periods: 500 to 650, 650 to 800, or 800 to 1300.
   a. Baghdad is sacked by Mongols.
   b. Muhammad is born.
   c. Damascus becomes the seat of the Umayyad caliphate.
   d. The Abbasid caliphate is established.
   e. The Koran is written down.
2. In what modern countries are the following places located?
   a. Cairo   e. Constantinople
   b. Damascus   (Istanbul)
   c. Baghdad   f. Tours
   d. Cordoba   g. Medina

Thinking It Over

1. Think about the many reasons people accept a new idea or belief. What reasons did people have for accepting Islam between 622 and 1250?
2. It has been said that the Arabs continued where the ancient Greeks left off. In what ways was this true?
3. At the time of Muhammad, did the new religion raise or lower the status of women? How? Why?

Special Activities

1. The following words and many others come to our language from Arabic and Persian words: tambourine, admiral, lemon, satin, guitar, coffee, average, bazaar, arsenal, ream, zenith, nadir, algebra, traffic, risk, magazine. Look them up in an unabridged dictionary and write down their roots.
2. Americans generally believe in the separation of church and state. Read about one of the following predominately Muslim nations: Pakistan, Jordan, Egypt, Iraq, Syria, Libya, Saudia Arabia, Iran. Does that nation practice separation of church and state?

A grape harvest at a feudal manor.

Chapter 12 Feudalism and Faith

What was Medieval Europe? What were the Middle Ages? When did the Classical Age end and the Middle Ages begin? Historians divide time into different periods as a convenient way of organizing and interpreting history. Often, an important political or economic event is used as a dividing point between periods.

The word "medieval" comes from Latin. It means "between the ages." Some European historians, looking back at the course of history, identified the civilizations of the Greeks and Romans as the earlier or classical period. The fall of the Roman Empire in A.D. 476 was given as the end of Roman civilization.

800-1233

c. 800	Feudalism begins in Europe
c. 840	Viking and Hungarian invasions
c. 900	Improved plow
910	Foundation of Cluny
1054	Split between Roman Catholic and Greek Orthodox Church
1198-1216	Reign of Pope Innocent III
1209	Order of St. Francis founded
1212	Poor Clares founded
1233	Inquisition begins

The legendary King Arthur, as shown on a French tapestry.

Some historians think of the Middle Ages as starting about 476 and lasting until about 1500. These historians sometimes call the early part of the Middle Ages the "Dark Ages." This was the time when waves of barbarians were destroying the Roman civilization. In the period from the 400s to the late 900s, few people knew how to read and write. Only a few monasteries and schools kept alive the ideas of the ancient Greeks and Romans. Western Europe was "dark," since little advancement was made in knowledge and in the arts. However, the Byzantine Empire retained many features of the Classical Age. At the same time, the civilization of the Arabs flourished, and the long-lasting civilization of China continued.

Other historians think of the Middle Ages as starting around A.D. 900 or 1000 It was then that feudalism began in Europe. Some historians also divide the Middle Ages into two main time periods. They consider 1000 to 1300 as the "High Middle Ages," marked by the growth of towns, trade, and the arts. They regard the years 1300 to 1500 as the decline, or waning, of the Middle Ages. In that time period, western Europe suffered from plague, long wars, and economic recession.

The year 1492 or 1500 is often thought to mark the beginning of the modern period of history. Starting about 1500, western Europe began to expand its power throughout the world. In addition, the modern state became more powerful. Furthermore, the Roman Catholic Church, the major belief system of Europeans for about a thousand years, lost influence as Protestant Christianity gained supporters. The High Middle Ages (1000-1300) are covered in Chapters 12 and 13 and the decline of the Middle Ages (1300-1500) is covered in Chapter 14.

Thinking Geographically: What lands did the Norse invade?

1. Europe Developed Feudalism

After Charlemagne's empire split into three parts in 1843, the kings of these areas were not able to provide protection for their people. Gradually, power fell into the hands of lords who held large amounts of land. Each of these great lords had his own army. By the late 800s, Germany was divided into about nine different kingdoms or *duchies*, areas ruled by dukes.

During this time, invaders were a constant threat all over Europe. The Arabs (the Moors) were still in Spain and had control of many islands in the Mediterranean. The Vikings, with their seaworthy vessels, were plundering from the north. Hungarians, or Magyars, on horseback were making raids from the east. In one sense, these raids were disasters because of the destruction they involved. In another way, however, the raids served a constructive purpose. The new groups, especially the Muslims, brought in new ideas.

tive purpose. The new groups, especially the Muslims, brought in new ideas. Later, the Vikings colonized new areas.

A New Political Organization Europe faced two threats—invasions from the outside and warfare from within. To meet these threats, a new system of political and military organization developed: feudalism. (Although China had a feudal system as early as the Shang dynasty, feudalism was new to Europe.) The feudal system was a private arrangement reserved for the few nobles. The main element of feudalism was personal loyalty—the loyalty of vassals to their lord. Feudalism did not properly include the peasants, the mass of the people living in western Europe.

To control invaders and to gain some internal stability, some of the kings and powerful lords started to grant a fief, or source of income, to each of their vassals, or loyal followers. A fief typically included land, the buildings on it, and the services of the peasants. In return, the vassal, who was most often a knight but sometimes a church leader, owed military and political support to his lord.

According to the theory of feudalism, the king was on the top of the social ladder. People believed that the king had been granted the power to rule by God. The king then gave fiefs to his vassals, such as the dukes in his kingdom. In turn, a duke had his own vassals. The whole system was like a pyramid, with only the powerful few on the top.

Feudalism quickly spread to many parts of Europe. It started in the 700s and 800s in what is now France and Germany. The Normans (the French of Normandy) conquered England in 1066. The successful leader of the conquest of England was William (now called William the Conquerer). He thoroughly feudalized England by claiming all the land. His nobles had to pledge their loyalty to William and his successors. From England, feudalism spread to Scotland. In the south, it developed in Italy. The Crusaders introduced it into Jerusalem and the surrounding area. Feudalism was at its height from about the 800s to the 1200s.

Feudalism varied somewhat from one region to another. Nobles might be called dukes, counts, earls, or barons, depending on the particular area. In England, the king had great power over his barons. The king of France had vassals who were more powerful than he.

The main problem with feudalism was private wars. The system had no way of settling disputes between vassals of two different lords. Often, a petty quarrel erupted into a small war. As one group of knights fought another group, the peasants' crops and animals were often destroyed.

The Knights Feudal wars were fought by armies made up of knights. No longer could a ruler successfully field an army of peasant volunteers on foot. Knights in armor would make devastating cavalry charges through such lines of troops. The knight had become a more effective fighter because of two new inventions. Stirrups allowed a rider to sit firmly on a horse and thus fight from it. Metal horseshoes allowed the horse to carry the greater weight of a heavily armored knight.

The knight, wearing about 14 kilograms (30 pounds) of armor, was like a human tank. He usually carried another 14 kilograms of weapons. With all this heavy equipment, a knight now needed years of training to be able to ride a horse and use his weapons effectively. War was no longer a part-time occupation. It now required a trained warrior class.

To become a knight was expensive. A war horse and armor cost about as much as twenty oxen. Generally, only nobles

Did You Know?

Of Knights and Chivalry

A boy from a noble family started training to become a knight when he was seven years old. At that young age, he was sent away from his parents' home to another castle. The boy first became a *page*. As a page, he learned good manners —courtesy to the ladies of the court and respect for elders. He also learned to ride and to hunt. Then, at about the age of fourteen, the young man became a *squire*, a personal servant to the knight who was his master. Now he began serious training in the use of weapons, among them the sword, the lance, and the battle-ax.

After this training, the squire was ready for the important ceremony of becoming a knight. At first, the master who had trained the squire simply tapped him on the shoulder and dubbed him a knight. Later, being made a knight became a religious ceremony. The young squire confessed his sins and fasted. He also took a ritual bath of purification to wash away the sins of his past life. Then he spent an all-night vigil in church, standing or kneeling before his armor. In the morning, the squire put on a white linen robe and a scarlet cloak. In front of a priest or a bishop, he swore his vows, promising to be loyal to his lord and the Roman Catholic Church.

From the rough ways of the knights there developed *chivalry*, a code of honor or proper conduct. The knight was to be honorable and to fight according to fair rules. He was to be loyal to the lady he loved and to protect all those in need.

During the Middle Ages, many paintings were made of St. George, the patron saint of knights. He was shown fighting a dragon, which represented evil. St.

A painting of St. George and the dragon.

George was thus a symbol of the ideal of knighthood.

Of course, in actual practice, not all knights were true to their vows and followed the rules of chivalry. Moreover, their code often only extended to members of their own social class and not to the peasants. While we may disagree with parts of the code, chivalry was an improvement over the rough and violent ways of earlier times. Chivalry reinforced Christian ideals of treating people with goodness and kindness.

could become knights. Most rulers could not afford to keep many knights stationed in their own courts. Furthermore, for strategic reasons, it made sense for the king or lord to place his knights in different parts of his realm. *Castles*, with heavy walls and high lookout towers, were built as forts for security and protection. In a castle, a few knights could hold off the enemy until reinforcements could arrive.

Services of the Knights or Vassals
Vassals were supposed to perform three main services in return for their fiefs. The most important service was military. Each vassal promised to come to the aid of his lord when called. He was to bring a certain number of knights and soldiers.

The second service of the vassals was political. Several times a year, the lord was supposed to summon his vassals to his court. There, the lord was to get the advice and consent of his vassals in military and political affairs. Along with feasting and entertainment, important work was done at the court. One such task was the settling of disputes. Two vassals might have a quarrel with each other. Since most agreements were oral, there were a lot of misunderstandings. The lord and his vassals met as a court. The lord presided as chief judge. Vassals acted as a jury and decided if the charges were true. Vassals had the right to a trial by a jury of their *peers*, that is, their equals or fellow vassals. This was the beginning of the British court system, which is also used in the United States.

In reality, of course, justice was not always done. Sometimes, justice was determined by a trial of combat. The two knights would fight each other. The stronger knight would win the case. When there was a weak king or lord, the vassals often ignored the decisions of the court. However, because both the lord and the vassals gained something from the feudal contract, it was often honored by both.

Knights jousting in a tournament.

The third service of the vassals was financial. The vassals were expected to pay certain sums of money to their lord. For example, if a lord were captured in a battle, his vassals were expected to pay any ransom needed to free him. The lord could ask for money for the dowry of his eldest daughter when she married or for the knighting ceremony of his eldest son. Many vassals raised money for their lord by collecting taxes from their own peasants.

A man and woman duel to settle a marital dispute.

Feudalism declined in Europe when new methods of warfare developed. Kings turned to infantry and cannons fired by gunpowder. Nonetheless, feudalism gave Europe some degree of internal stability during many centuries. It helped check the advances of outside invaders. Starting about 1100, the political stability and military power it fostered enabled western Europe to take the offensive against the Arabs, Slavs, and Byzantines. Probably the greatest contribution of European feudalism was the idea that nobles (and later all citizens) had rights no king could take away.

Section Questions

1. Under what conditions is feudalism most likely to develop?
2. Why did the knights require training?
3. What was a chief cause of quarrels between a lord and his vassals or between vassals? How were these quarrels settled?

2. Manorial Agriculture Became Common

Manorial agriculture was the economic system that accompanied the political and military system of feudalism. By the 900s, most of northern Europe had been divided into farming units called *manors*. The lords and the knights protected the peasants who lived on the manors. In return, the peasants gave goods and services.

A manor was usually controlled by a knight. A lord might have a number of manors. In addition, the Roman Catholic Church gradually came to hold many manors. A large manor could have several hundred people living on it. A small manor might include only ten families. Almost all the people in Europe were farmers who lived on manors. When feudalism and manorial agriculture had their beginnings between 700 and 800, there were few towns and cities.

Changes in Agriculture Northern Europe has more rain than southern Europe. The soil becomes wet and heavy. This makes it hard to plow in the spring. Because of these conditions, the Germans developed a heavier kind of plow about A.D. 900. This heavier plow was pulled by six or eight oxen. Usually, it had wheels. It cut into the soil with a sharp blade and created ridges and ditches. These ditches allowed the water to drain off better. As a result, spring planting could be started earlier. Plows were so important in the Middle Ages that the wealth of a manor was often measured by the number of plows its farmers possessed.

Using a heavier plow led to more changes. Few farmers could afford all the animals needed for plowing. Thus, the farmers pooled their resources and worked as a plowing team. A group decision was made about the dates on which the fields should be plowed and planted.

Plowing the manor fields.

Turning the heavy plow was difficult. Consequently, it was better for the animals to plow long strips of land than to change direction frequently. Thus the land was divided into long, narrow strips. A few of the strips might be reserved for the needs of the priest of the village. The rest of the strips were "owned" by the peasants.

The most important result of the improved plow was an increase in the amount of grain—wheat, rye, and oats—grown in northern Europe. The typical peasant family in northern Europe could work about 12 hectares (30 acres) of land. This was much more land than the average family worked in southern Europe. As a result, northern Europe became a center of agricultural production.

As forests were cut down in northern Europe over the next several hundred years, more and more land was put under cultivation. Horses replaced oxen in many places. Such inventions as the hard horse collar and the horse harness helped make this possible. The use of horses further improved agricultural productivity. The larger food supply led to a great increase in population in northern Europe. Towns grew because farmers could produce extra food for the people who lived in them.

Parts of the Manor A typical manor had two main parts: the village and the outlying fields and other lands. The houses of the peasants were clustered together in the village. The knight and his family usually lived on the outskirts of the village. In earlier times, a lord's house was often a one-story wooden structure designed for defense rather than comfort. Later, it was often made of stone or bricks. The powerful and wealthy usually had a fortified castle. It was ideally situated more or less in the center of the various manors that the family controlled.

In the manor house, there was usually one great hall used for eating and sleeping. During the day, rushes were placed on the floor. At night, fresh rushes or mattresses were put down. To sleep on a mattress of feathers instead of one made of straw was considered a great luxury. Because of the cold winters, the whole family, as well as the servants, dogs, and cats, usually slept near the warm fireplace in the great hall. Later in the Middle Ages, the nobles often used canopied beds with curtains for more privacy. The manor house also had a kitchen and storerooms.

In addition to his house, the lord of the manor usually had barns to house animals and store grain, orchards with fruit trees, and beehives for honey. The lord's stream served as the water supply for the community. There was a mill near the stream

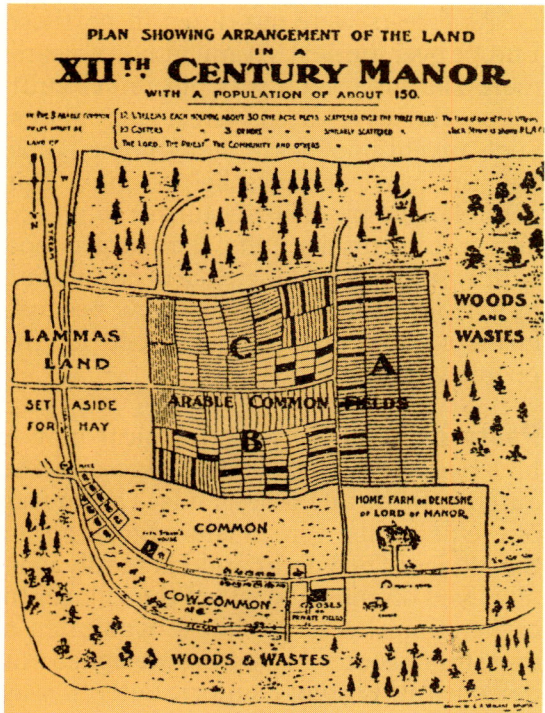

A diagram showing a twelfth century manor.

for grinding grain. There was also an oven for baking bread that was used by the whole community. In warmer climates, there might also be a press for making wine. Sometimes, there was a wall around the manor house and its outbuildings. A small church might stand nearby if the community were large enough.

The small thatched huts of the peasants often lined a single unpaved lane. They had dirt floors and usually only one or two rooms. Since there was no chimney, the hut was smoky and dirty. In winter, the farm animals shared the space or were close by. Each peasant family also had a vegetable garden, a beehive, and a few chickens.

The farmers of the Middle Ages knew that they had to let some fields "rest" between growing seasons in order to have fertile soil. It was necessary to allow part of the fields to remain *fallow*—plowed but not seeded. Often, the plowed land on which the crops were grown was divided into three parts. One field was planted for spring grain, another for winter grain, and the third left fallow. Then, in the next year, the fallow field would be planted with grain and another field would be left fallow. Finally, in the third year, the field planted the previous two years would be fallow. The rotation would then continue. In some areas, especially on lands owned by monasteries, fertilizers were also used to replenish the soil.

Social Classes on the Manor At the beginning of the Middle Ages, there were only two main social classes: nobles and peasants. Social class was inherited. People belonged to the same class their parents did. Only in the Roman Catholic Church did a bright peasant youth have much chance to rise in social prestige. Over 90 percent of the people were peasants. They were on the bottom of the social ladder. A few of them were free peasants, but most were serfs. A serf was midway between a free person and a slave. Serfs came with the land they lived and worked on. They were regarded as part of the property. A serf could not leave the land without the lord's consent. Thus, when a new lord took over property, he also got a group of serfs.

The serfs had heavy obligations to the lord of the manor. Typically, both men and women worked about two or three days a week for the lord. At harvest time, they worked longer and harder.

In addition to working in the fields, peasant men repaired roads and built fences and bridges. They also gathered firewood, dug ditches, and butchered pigs. Peasant women ran the dairy and textile industries of the manor. They milked the cows and made the cheese. They also spun thread, wove cloth, and sewed clothing. The manors

Blacksmiths at work.

were almost self-sufficient economic units, supplying most needs of the small community. Thus, the furniture, bricks, food, clothing, and other goods were made on the manor. Only a few items such as salt or iron might have to be bought outside. The nobles also purchased expensive items such as weapons and armor, fine cloth, war horses, falcons, and jewelry.

The workers with the highest prestige on the manor were those with special skills. Among them were the miller, the blacksmith, the mason, and the carpenter. If the lord of a manor did not live there, he appointed a steward or bailiff to supervise the community. The job of the steward was to see that all tasks were done and that the lord was not being cheated by the peasants.

In addition to controlling the economy of the manor, the lord also had complete political control over the peasants. It was he who settled disputes and judged wrongdoing. The decision of the lord was final, and there could be no appeal. For breaking the law, peasants were often fined. A common offense was *poaching*, hunting or fishing on the lord's land. Peasants poached to add to their simple diet of brown bread, cheese, eggs, cereals, vegetables, soup, bacon, and beer.

The serfs had a hard life. Even so, being a serf offered some security in an uncertain age. In return for providing food and services to the lord of the manor, they got military protection. Many lords also helped the peasants in times of need, as when food was short.

A weaver and a butcher at work.

Daily Life The peasants—both men and women—worked long hours, toiling from dawn to dusk six days a week. They worked especially hard during the harvest season. They often became old before their time. They had little medical care. Many peasant children died before they reached adulthood. The average life-span was only about thirty years. The peasants had only simple clothing to wear. They were given no education. They sometimes suffered from hunger and disease. Typically, they lived all their lives in the same village and were buried in the village churchyard. They enjoyed simple pleasures, such as drinking beer, dancing, singing, and playing games. Yet, in the early part of the Middle Ages, they seldom rebelled. They were told—and most believed—that there was a better life for them after death.

The contrast between the lives of the peasants and the nobles was striking. The nobles ate better. Because of this better nutrition, they were healthier and often taller than the peasants. However, the lives of the knights were often cut short by war. The nobles enjoyed going hunting often. Hunting allowed the men to practice their military skills, and the meat was a welcome addition to the table. Sometimes, the women of the family also accompanied the men on hunting expeditions. However, the noble women were usually too busy with their work. They had the responsibility of running the household—from preserving food to managing a large staff of servants. In some cases, they were in complete charge of the manor when their husbands were away or when they became widows. However, though many noble women had major responsibilities, they had few rights. Legally, they were subject to their husbands.

Section Questions

1. Describe the improved plow invented by the Germans about A.D. 900. What advantages did it have? How was it important in the Middle Ages?
2. What type of living quarters did the typical peasant family have?
3. What did the farmers do to keep the soil fertile?
4. What was the only way to rise in social class at the beginning of the Middle Ages?
5. What obligations did the peasants owe to the lord of the manor?

3. The Roman Catholic Church Held Great Power in Feudal Society

During the Middle Ages in Europe, the Roman Catholic Church was a very important institution. People were taught that their time on Earth was only a brief interval between birth and an eternal life in Heaven. They believed that the church would help them gain the reward of salvation above. The hope of a happier life after death was a source of comfort to many, particularly the peasants, who led hard lives in the here and now. Because most people believed in its teachings, the Roman Catholic Church was a great unifying force in Europe.

The Church and Politics About the year 900, however, the influence of the pope was in decline. In past years, the kings had been a strong source of support for the church. Thus, the decrease in the power of the kings under feudalism also weakened the church.

Political events greatly affected the Roman Catholic Church. Otto, a warrior-king, greatly expanded the territory of the Saxon Germans in the 900s. In the east, he defeated the Hungarians and started the drive of the Germans into the Slavic world. He also expanded into the Frankish kingdom. Otto had become the strongest ruler in western Europe. He marched into northern Italy and in 962 was crowned by the pope as the first emperor of the Holy Roman Empire. Otto I, or Otto the Great, ruled an empire that included the lands from Germany through northern Italy.

After the foundation of the empire, the Holy Roman emperor often selected the pope. This tended to corrupt the church.

Gradually, the pope became more powerful. In addition to being the supreme religious leader, he became one of the most

This painting is called "The Dream of Pope Innocent III."

important political figures in Europe. The church owned a great deal of land. Church officials were virtually the only educated people. Thus they became active in government. Because the German bishops were so important in running the government, the Holy Roman emperors wanted to appoint all of them.

The appointment of the German bishops led to a bitter quarrel between the popes and the emperors. In 1059, the church established a new procedure for electing the pope. No longer was the German Holy Roman emperor to have a say in the election. The pope was now to be chosen by the cardinals, the highest church officials below the pope. To gain control over appointing the German bishops, the popes tried to undermine the emperor's power both in Germany and in Italy. In 1077, Emperor Henry IV was forced to humble himself before Pope Gregory VII.

The height of the church's power came during the reign of Pope Innocent III (1198-1216). Pope Innocent III claimed supreme authority in both *spiritual* (religious) and *secular* (everyday) affairs. As pope, he felt responsible for the souls of all Christians. Therefore, he asserted the right to supervise the activities of kings and other rulers as they affected the spiritual welfare of the people. As a result, Innocent III involved himself in the affairs of European rulers such as King John of England.

At the very time that the pope's influence was increasing in western Europe, it disappeared in the east. As you read earlier, in 1054, a permanent split occurred between the western Roman Catholic Church and the eastern Greek Orthodox Church.

Internal Problems In addition to problems with kings and emperors, the church had problems within its own organization. Many men obtained such positions as bishop by paying for them. The local parish priests were often uneducated. Many of them married despite the church rule against this practice. Religious standards had declined among the monks and nuns in the monasteries. It seemed to many people that there was an urgent need for reform in the church.

Those shocked by conditions in the church included both devout clerics and lay people. Some monks wanted to purify the monasteries and the church. Lay people demanded higher religious standards in churches and monasteries. If they had paid money to have masses or prayers said, they wanted it done. They were concerned about relatives in the monastic life.

In 910, a group of monks at Cluny in France started a reform movement to clean up the church. The Cluny, or Cluniac,

St. Francis.

movement helped make stricter rules for those religious men and women who lived apart from society as monks and nuns. The Cluny movement gave new life and spirit to the monasteries and, indirectly, to the church as a whole.

New religious orders were founded to strengthen the Roman Catholic Church. One such order was started by Francis of Assisi (later St. Francis). St. Francis (1182-1226) was the son of a wealthy Italian wool merchant. After an intense religious experience in which he believed he

A monk working in a wheat field.

had a vision, he gave up all that he owned. He then led a simple life. St. Francis felt that to truly follow Christ, a person should seek salvation not in the monasteries, but in preaching to and tending the poor and the sick. He tried to be humble and helpful, and he had a love for all creatures. St. Francis worked with the sick, including lepers.

St. Francis' beliefs and personality attracted many followers to him. In 1209 he founded a religious order for men, the Franciscans.

Clare of Assisi (later St. Clare) founded a related religious order for women, the Poor Clares. This group lived on alms, made clothes, and helped the sick. These orders gave the people a fine example of the Christian life. The Franciscans and Poor Clares helped alleviate the poverty and disease common in the growing towns.

Another major religious order was the Dominican order. The Dominicans stressed learning and teaching. Dominicans soon became prominent at the recently established universities. Because of their knowledge, the Dominicans could argue against the heretics who challenged the authority of the Roman Catholic Church.

Not all people could be persuaded by the example of the Franciscans or the preaching of the Dominicans. As a result, the pope set up the Inquisition in 1233. This was a court that was to find and root out heresy. At first, the heretics were encouraged to change their views and way of life and confess their sins. But people who would not change were then handed over to the civil government for punishment. They might be tortured until they died or confessed. Or they might be burned at the stake. Many people died as a result of the Inquisition. Because of its power to punish dissent, few dared to challenge the Roman Catholic Church openly. Nonetheless, some people continued to resent the church's taxes and what they saw as its failure to respond to their needs. Protest movements recurred until the Protestant Reformation began in 1517.

In spite of its problems, the Roman Catholic Church of the Middle Ages had a great many sources of strength. It touched the lives of most people in Europe through the *sacraments*, rites believed necessary to achieve salvation.

The Roman Catholic Church was also involved in conducting court cases. It had the power to try and to punish offenders. Marriages, wills, and contracts also came under the authority of the church courts.

The Roman Catholic Church was also in control of education. The church had almost a monopoly on knowledge. Members of the clergy were about the only people in the early Middle Ages who knew how to read and write. The clergy ran most of the schools. At the universities, all the teachers and many of the students were members of the clergy.

The local parish church was the social center of the community. People gathered at the church on Sundays and feast days to worship, meet their friends, and learn the latest news. The special ceremonies of life took place at the church. Baptisms, marriages, and funerals were held there. If a person was excommunicated, he or she was entirely cut off from the community.

In many ways, therefore, the Roman Catholic Church shaped people's lives. When its moral power failed, the church could rely on the force of the Inquisition and its courts. In 1300, the Roman Catholic Church seemed mighty. It had great political and economic power, as well as power over people's hearts and minds.

Section Questions

1. Why was the power of the pope and the Roman Catholic Church in decline in the 900s?
2. What was the Cluny movement?
3. What rights did Pope Innocent III claim?
4. What were some of the strengths of the Roman Catholic Church?

Chapter Summary

1. Feudalism was the political and military system that evolved after the fall of Charlemagne's empire. It arose as a response to the unsettled times of invasions and internal wars. Lords gave the use of land to their vassals. In return, the vassals, often knights, had to perform military service when called on by the lord, give political service such as advice and jury duty, and provide financial resources. Feudalism was based on loyalty and was reserved only for the nobles. Feudalism first developed in France and Germany and later spread to the rest of Europe. Its greatest contribution was the idea that nobles (and eventually all people) had certain rights that the king could not take away.

2. Manorial agriculture was the economic system that accompanied feudalism. The lords and knights provided protection for the peasants. The peasants repaid their lords by giving them goods and services. Agriculture improved with the invention of a heavier plow, a horse collar and harness, and other changes. The population grew as more land was planted and food production increased. The lords and ladies of the manor had a higher standard of living than the peasants. The peasants, who were mostly serfs, had to pay part of their crops and give their time to the lord of the manor. They were also charged fees for using the lord's facilities and had to give gifts to the lord. But manorialism was based on mutual dependence, so the lord often helped the peasants in times of need. The peasants, women and men, worked hard through life. Among the nobles, the men hunted and fought and the women ran the household.

3. The Roman Catholic Church had a great deal of control over the lives of most people living in medieval Europe. The church's influence was declining about 900. But a reform movement plus stronger popes made the church more powerful. To help the unfortunate, new religious orders were started. The Inquisition was established to root out heresy. The church shaped people's lives through its wide-ranging powers.

Chapter 12 Review

Check Your Facts

1. Identify the following:
   a. Pope Innocent III
   b. St. Francis
   c. Dark Ages
   d. Inquisition
2. Why did knights become important in the Middle Ages?
3. What advantages did the knights have in fighting?
4. How did the system of trial by jury begin?
5. For the peasants, what were the benefits of manorialism? What were its costs?
6. Why were the manors mostly self-sufficient about 900?
7. In what ways did the heavier plow change the community life of the peasants?
8. What was one reason the peasants usually did not rebel during the Middle Ages?
9. Why was hunting important to the knights?

Words to Know

1. Write a brief paragraph (or paragraphs) about life in the Middle Ages. Use these words: *manors, peers, fallow, castles*.
2. Write a brief paragraph or two about the Roman Catholic Church in the Middle Ages. Use these words: *spiritual, secular, sacraments*.

Developing Your Skills

1. Place the following events in the proper chronological order:
   The Inquisition starts.
   Order of St. Francis is founded.
   Cluny reform starts.
   Vikings attack Europe.
2. Use the maps in the Atlas. Find the latitudes of modern England, Germany, and France. Then find places in North America that have the same latitude. Check an encyclopedia to see if crops raised in the two areas are similar.

Thinking It Over

1. In what ways did the feudal king have to share his powers with the vassals?
2. In what way was every noble a member of both the feudal system and the manorial system?
3. The judges of the Inquisition thought that they were doing the right thing by punishing heretics. Why did the Inquisition think its role was necessary? Do you think that the Inquisition harmed or helped the Roman Catholic Church?
4. In what ways were St. Francis and his order indirectly criticizing the role of the Roman Catholic Church?

Special Activities

1. Because their heavy armor hid their faces, knights used a "coat of arms" as a symbol of who they were. Such figures as lions and eagles were used to suggest strength or power. Design your own coat of arms showing your interests and values.
2. Write a poem or song pretending that you are a peasant working on a manor.
3. Make a time line of the most important events in a person's life. Can you find a middle period? What key events signal its beginning and end? Why?

This fresco showing city life in the Middle Ages is called "Good Government in the City."

Chapter 13 The Revival of Europe

The typical romantic image of the Middle Ages may include knights on white horses rescuing fair maidens, impressive Catholic cathedrals, Robin Hood, and monasteries. However, one of the most important contributions of Europeans during the Middle Ages was their improvements in tools and ways of using them. This is usually a very unromantic and down-to-earth area.

The medieval Europeans were very practical inventors. They made enormous improvements in agriculture. These included ways of growing crops, a better plow, irrigation, the wheelbarrow, better animals. In industry, they made increased use of mills powered by

1000-1291

1000	Many in North and East Europe become Christians
1066	Normans conquer England
1096-1099	First Crusade
1100	Rise of guilds
1147-1149	Second Crusade
1189-1192	Third Crusade
1202-1204	Fourth Crusade
1218-1221	Fifth Crusade
1228-1229	Sixth Crusade
1248-1254	Seventh Crusade
1270	Eighth Crusade
1291	Last Christian stronghold in Holy Land falls

William the Conqueror.

wind and water for grinding grain and sawing wood. It is true that the Europeans borrowed many of their ideas from the more advanced cultures of the time, such as China, India, and the Muslim world. But they often markedly improved an idea and made more use of it than its original inventors. Indeed, Europeans became known for their mechanical inventiveness.

Let us look at just one example, gunpowder. By the 1000s, the Chinese knew how to make gunpowder. They used it for firecrackers in their colorful festivals. The invention of gunpowder caused no major changes in Chinese society. Gunpowder was introduced into Europe in the 1300s and was widely used by the 1450s. Unlike the Chinese, the Europeans used gunpowder in cannons. Cannons fired cannonballs at the thick walls of castles and cities. At first, the cannonballs often missed their targets. But the noise and smoke of the firing cannons badly frightened people and horses. The very prospect of cannonfire was enough to make some people think of surrendering. Cannon were soon able to knock down tall towers and strong walls. The use of gunpowder completely changed the nature of warfare.

The Europeans, even in the so-called Dark Ages, were more practical and inventive than the ancient Greeks and Romans. With their improved technology, they were able to expand farming. They reclaimed the Low Countries (now the Netherlands and Belgium) from the sea with dikes. They increased mining and milling. By 1500, they were sailing in improved ships to seek control of the world. The supremacy of European civilization in later centuries had its roots in the technological progress of the Middle Ages.

1. Western Europe's Influence Widened

Towns and trade began growing within western Europe. At the same time, its influence started to expand far beyond its traditional borders. This expansion grew from the activities of missionaries and merchants, and from increased use of military force.

Missionaries and Merchants The Roman Catholic Church had long been engaged in missionary activities. However, after about the year 1000, more missionaries moved beyond the borders of western Christendom. This increased activity was partly due to the revival of the church in western Europe.

One important missionary area was the Scandinavian countries of northern Europe. At this time, the various bands and tribes of Norse were consolidating into states such as Denmark, Norway, and Sweden. From Scandinavia came the Vikings, who raided and colonized far from their homeland. The Swedes moved east and south, deep into Poland and Russia, eventually reaching the Black Sea. The Danes and Norwegians moved west and south to the British Isles and France and, eventually, to Iceland and Greenland. Under Leif Ericson, they even established a short-lived colony, Vinland, in the New World, probably on what is now the coast of Newfoundland.

In many cases, the missionaries were able to convert the Scandinavian rulers to Christianity. In about the year 1000, King Olaf of Norway was converted, and, as a result, his people also accepted Christianity. About the same time, the Danes were also converted under Canute the Great. The king would simply announce that all should be baptized. Thus, these conversions were accomplished without persecution or bloodshed.

This wooden church is typical of the first churches in Scandinavia. Compare it with the cathedral on page 225.

As a result of these missionary activities, schools were established by the clergy in Scandinavia. The clergy wrote down the Scandinavian laws. Previously, they had existed only in oral form. The clergy also encouraged the arts. In effect, the missionaries brought the culture of western Europe into Scandinavia. The Scandinavian peoples accepted many of the religious, political, and technological ideas of the western Europeans.

At the same time that the missionaries were being successful, more trade was developing between Scandinavia and the areas to the south. Eventually, most of this trade fell into the hands of German merchants, who established themselves in some of the important Scandinavian towns.

Did You Know?

The famous Notre Dame cathedral in Paris.

Cathedrals: Symbols of Their Times

Christian faith was symbolized in the Middle Ages by the building of large, magnificent churches and *cathedrals*. A cathedral is the main church of a bishop. People considered these buildings to be monuments to God and a way of knowing and glorifying God. In addition, a great church or cathedral was a source of pride for a town or city. The entire community helped to build it. Often, they contributed free labor and money.

The typical cathedral had a floor plan in the shape of a cross. There was a long nave where the people gathered. At the far end of the nave was the high altar. There were also the two arms of the cross, the wings.

In the early Middle Ages, most churches were built in the relatively simple style called Romanesque. This style used Roman features such as rounded arches and heavy walls.

Later, people wanted more light and cathedrals that would soar upward. Thus, the Gothic style was born. There was a problem of how to support a tall roof. The architects built flying buttresses outside of the church to carry the weight. This allowed them to build a higher cathedral with pointed arches. The walls became thinner. Some of the stone was replaced with beautiful stained-glass windows. The windows helped explain the teachings of the Roman Catholic Church to non-readers, who made up the vast majority of people.

Now cathedrals were taller and lighter. A cathedral seemed to be reaching toward Heaven itself. However, the cathedrals were not all the same. There was a great diversity in styles among regions and even within a region.

In addition to symbolizing the faith of the Middle Ages, the cathedrals also showed the enormous range of talents of the skilled workers of the time. They also showed that the Europeans were capable of excellent organization and coordination.

Missionaries also traveled east from western Europe. The Germans expanded into the Slavic lands, especially into what is now East Germany, Poland, Czechoslovakia, and Austria. By about 1100, the German nobles were settling these lands with peasants. They eventually took over Prussia and came into contact with the Lithuanians and Finns who lived along the Baltic Sea.

Eastern Europe contained a wide variety of peoples, though most were Slavs. The Poles, Czechs, Hungarians, Bulgars, and others spoke different languages. They had little unity among themselves and were often hostile to each other. Roman Catholic missionaries converted the peoples of Poland, Bohemia, and Hungary in about 1100.

In spite of some missionary successes, however, Roman Catholicism was not the unifying force in eastern Europe that it had been to the west. The Greek Orthodox Church had also expanded and converted the Slavic Russians and Bulgars to its faith. The Orthodox Church was dominated by the Byzantine emperor at Constantinople. The Orthodox patriarch and bishops had less power than the Roman pope and bishops. Moreover, many national Orthodox churches achieved independence from the Greek Orthodox Church. Eastern Europe thus lacked the common cultural experience of the west. Nonetheless, trade and towns grew there too. There was increased contact between western and eastern Europe, particularly fostered by German traders in what is now Austria and Czechoslovakia.

Military Conquests The influence of western Europe expanded not only by means of trade and religion, but also through military force. This was directed particularly against Islam and Byzantium. The Normans of northern France were leaders in military expansion. In 1066, William the Conqueror crossed the English Channel with about 5,000 knights to conquer England. The Battle of Hastings was the decisive engagement. In addition to their conquest of England, the Normans moved south into Muslim areas. They secured control of Sardinia and Corsica. By 1090, they had completed their conquest of Sicily, a center of Arab civilization, and of some Byzantine lands in southern Italy. After the Norman conquest of Sicily, many Arab ideas spread into western Europe. Norman control of these areas in the Mediterranean increased security for European ships.

Spain Western Europeans continued to expand their holdings in Spain. The Muslims, called the Moors in Spain, had conquered much of Spain in 711. The Spanish Moors spread their language and religion. Having borrowed from the Greek, Persian, Byzantine, Syrian, and even Hindu civilizations, the Moors imported advanced ideas from the Near East and Asia. From

This picture shows another view of the Alhambra in Granada, Spain.

cities such as Baghdad, Cairo, and Alexandria came both ideas and products. Fusing all of these elements, the Moors in Spain produced a unique civilization and a number of brilliant scholars.

The few Christian states in the north of Spain, such as Leon and Navarre, tried to reconquer the rest of Spain. They had more success after the Moors in Spain became divided into separate kingdoms. By 1300, only Granada remained under Moorish rule. In the reconquered areas, the kings of Leon and Castile, Aragon, and Portugal divided the land into fiefs. New monasteries were also started.

There was little unity among the three religious groups—Christians, Muslims, Jews—living in Spain. There was a growing feeling among the Christians that, as a result of the fighting in Spain and Sicily, Christians could not compromise with the Muslims. Since Roman Catholic missionaries had generally been unsuccessful among the Muslims, many Christians felt that military force was their only alternative.

Knights on the First Crusade.

The Crusades The most striking feature of western European expansion was the Crusades. These were wars against the Muslims to regain control of the Holy Land. The idea of fighting the Muslims had already been established in the campaigns in Spain and Sicily. In 1095, the emperor of Byzantium asked for help from the pope and the rulers of western Europe in fighting against the Seljuk Turks. These Turks had been gradually taking over the lands of the Byzantine Empire and had won an important battle against the Byzantines in 1071. They now had conquered about half of the Byzantine Empire.

Pope Urban II carefully considered the Byzantine appeal. He was concerned by reports that Christian pilgrims visiting the Holy Land had been ill-treated. The Holy Land (Jerusalem and the surrounding area) was regarded as a sacred place for Christians to visit. It was now said that the Turks were not allowing Christians to make visits and were, in some cases, robbing and even enslaving and killing the pilgrims. Urban wanted the holy places to be under church control.

Pope Urban II was also eager to settle the quarrel between the Roman Catholic Church of the west and the Greek Orthodox Church of the east. The two branches of Christianity had been separated since 1054. The pope hoped that by helping the Byzantine emperor and gaining control of the Holy Land, he might bring the two churches together. Thus, in 1095, Urban II gave a stirring speech calling for Europeans to free the Holy Land from Muslim rule. Other preachers repeated this message, asking the nobles to put aside their personal quarrels and fight for the church in a holy war.

Thousands of knights responded to the pleas of the preachers. Religious motives were important for many who chose to make the long, dangerous march to the far-away Holy Land. The Crusaders were promised remission of their sins for fighting in the Crusades. They sewed a cross on their garments as a symbol that they were Crusaders.

Some also chose to go on the Crusades because they were searching for adventure. Some wanted to gain both land and glory in the Holy Land. As in Spain and Sicily, they hoped to get a fief in return for their service in war. In spite of the potential benefits, going to the Crusades was expensive. Some of the lesser nobles allowed their serfs to buy their freedom in order to raise money for the Crusades.

After many difficulties and delays, the knights of the First Crusade managed to capture Jerusalem in 1099. They were aided in their victory by political divisions among the Muslims. The successful Christians then established a feudal state called the Latin Kingdom of Jerusalem. The long, narrow surrounding territory was divided into fiefs.

Italian merchants gave financial and naval support to the First Crusade. Italian ships maintained the lines of communication between the Holy Land and western

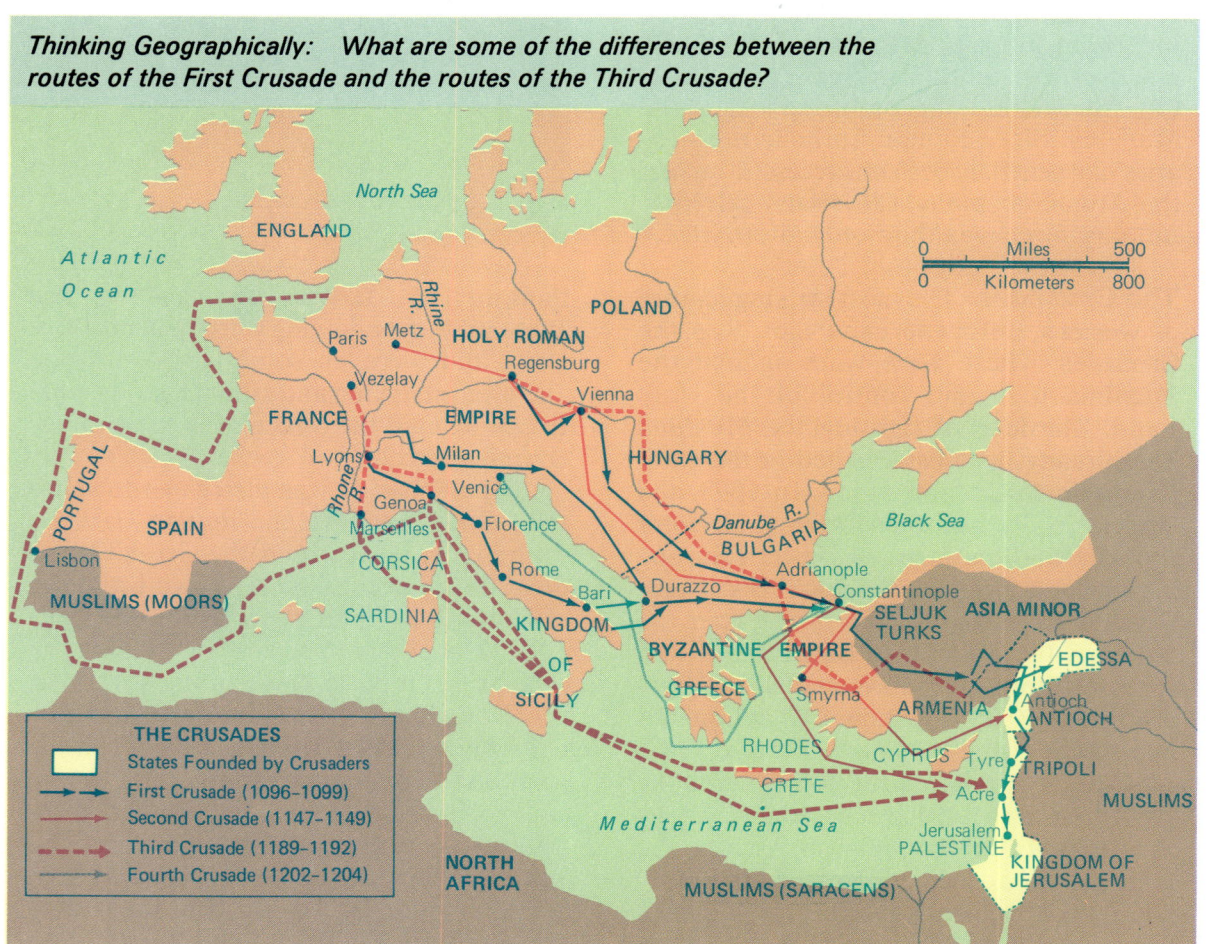

Thinking Geographically: What are some of the differences between the routes of the First Crusade and the routes of the Third Crusade?

Europe. In return for this support, the Italian cities were granted trading privileges in the Holy Land. This greatly increased the power of the Italian cities in the whole area of the Mediterranean.

Despite their victories, the Crusaders were in a weak position in an alien territory. They did build castles and station knights in them. However, the Turks would soon recapture a city and reestablish their control. Therefore, for almost 200 years other popes had to ask Christians to try to regain control of the Holy Land.

The most dubious of the Crusades was the Fourth Crusade (1202-1204). The Fourth Crusade was diverted from its goal by an offer of transportation from Venice, and the knights never reached the Holy Land. Instead, the Crusaders attacked Constantinople, capital of the Byzantine Empire. Thus, Christians were fighting Christians. Western Europeans took over the Byzantine Empire and made it into a feudal state. The Venetians were awarded trading rights. Later, the Byzantines were able to throw out the western Europeans. However, the Fourth Crusade permanently weakened the Byzantine Empire. It was eventually conquered completely by the Turks.

There were eight Crusades plus a Children's Crusade. In time, the gains of the Crusaders in the Holy Land were wiped out. The last Christian fortress fell in 1291. The Crusades were not a military success. However, they were very important in other ways.

The First Crusade strengthened the power of the pope. It showed the pope's influence to the world. It demonstrated that Europeans could cooperate, even though with difficulty, in a joint effort. The Crusades drew off the more adventurous knights and probably contributed to peace.

Some knights died in the Crusades and others lost their fortunes. The Crusades thus weakened the position of the lesser knights and increased the power of the kings. Partly as a result of the Crusades, the knights were more sharply divided into different social ranks on the basis of wealth. They were no longer considered equal brothers in arms.

Trade had started to increase in Europe even before the Crusades. However, the Crusades did contribute to its further expansion. Italian ships carried people and horses to the Holy Land. The merchants then loaded up the empty ships with goods to sell back in Europe. The Crusades increased the need for money among the nobles. They had developed a taste for the new foods of the East such as rice, sugar, and apricots, as well as for other goods. Italian cities such as Venice and Genoa secured control over the new trade. The Italian merchants now had access to the trade of central Asia and China. The Crusades had an influence on European dress, introducing the tunic without sleeves. A more delicate, rounded arch and domed roofs were introduced into European architecture. The use of *heraldry*—coats of arms and other symbols—increased.

By the 1300s, the influence of western Europe had expanded north into Scandinavia, east into the Slavic and Byzantine lands, and south into Spain and the Mediterranean. Western Europe was no longer weak and isolated. Its neighbors were beginning to feel the effects of its growing power.

Section Questions

1. Why was converting a Scandinavian king important in spreading Christianity?
2. Why was there less unification in eastern Europe than in western Europe?
3. What was the importance of the Norman conquests in the Mediterranean?
4. Why was Spain not culturally unified?
5. Why did Pope Urban II issue a call for a Crusade against the Muslims in the Holy Land?

Thinking Geographically: The Hanseatic League was a confederation of merchants from the German cities along the North and Baltic seas. What other countries were included in the League's trading area?

2. Town Life Grew in Europe

From about 1000 to 1300, a remarkable new civilization based on town or city life developed and flourished in western Europe. The food supply of western Europe increased. In addition, there was more security under feudalism. No major plagues occurred between 700 and 1300, and malaria may have lessened. For these reasons, the population grew. It is estimated that in the year 700 there were about 27 million people living in western Europe. By 1300, the population had increased to about 73 million, almost three times the number in 700.

Trade The growth in the food supply meant that there was often surplus food that could be traded for other goods. No longer did everyone have to live on manors and grow their own food.

Starting about 1050, trade and manufacturing revived rapidly in Europe. Of course, trade, both local and international, had not completely disappeared during the barbarian invasions and "Dark Ages." Nonetheless, the volume of trade had been small.

Because of increased trade, towns expanded in size and number. Some of the growing towns were old Roman towns that had survived through the centuries. Some were the sites of castles, monasteries, or cathedrals. Others were located at convenient places along trading routes. At first, most merchants merely brought their goods to local towns to barter. They bought more cheaply in areas and times of plenty and sold more dearly in areas and times of scarcity. Soon, however, there was trading in finer goods that came from the Byzantine Empire and other distant lands to the east. Spices, dyes, medicines, silk, and cotton began to be sold.

The towns also increased in size and importance as more skilled workers, such as smiths, metalworkers, and stonecutters settled in them. These workers had previously lived on the manors. The more specialized among them had traveled from one manor to another. Now they stayed in one place, a town or city, and the buyers came to them. The growth in trade meant not only that more goods were exchanged, but also that more were manufactured. The western Europeans paid for the goods from the Muslim lands and the Byzantine Empire with gold or with such products as timber, furs, metals, and, particularly, woolen cloth. Some raw wool cloth came from England and was finished in the cities of Flanders (now mostly in Belgium) and in northern Italy. England also manufactured some of its own cloth.

Trade was centered in two areas. One was the cities of northern Italy, such as Venice and Genoa. The northern Italian cities had never declined as much as cities in other parts of Europe during the Middle Ages. Thus, they were the largest cities in western Europe between 1000 to 1300. The Italians also had a strategic position on the trade routes. They successfully challenged the sea power of the Muslims. Soon, they controlled the trade of the Mediterranean, the Byzantine Empire, and North Africa. In addition to trading, the Italian cities also started to manufacture their own specialities, such as glass and leather goods.

The second important trade area was the towns of Flanders and northern Germany. From these trading cities, goods could be moved easily by water across the Channel to England, north to Scandinavia, deep into Germany, and into the Baltic area. Between these two areas—the Italian cities and the Flemish and German towns—there arose a great overland trade route that utilized rivers whenever possible. This route was adequate for small luxury goods. Later, when there were fewer Muslim pirates around the Straits of Gibraltar, bulk goods like grain, wine, fish, and lumber were carried by regular fleets. These sailed from Italy to the Flemish cities and returned with Flemish goods. Inland water routes such as the Rhine and the Danube were also widely used.

In the 1100s and 1200s, before the cities grew larger, international fairs (the Champagne Fairs) were held near Paris, France. Buyers and sellers traveled there to exchange their goods. Later, in the 1300s and 1400s, goods were always available in the shops of the cities, and the international fairs were not needed. However, fairs still continued to be important in local areas.

Towns The rise of the towns greatly altered and weakened the old feudal society. The most obvious change was in the appearance of the towns themselves. The towns continued to be dominated by their walls, their churches, and the large homes of the rich. Now everything was larger. The churches and chapels were bigger. The residences of the wealthy were larger and more opulent. New structures such as guild houses, the town hall, and university buildings began to appear. The typical building in the now-crowded towns was a tall, narrow wooden house. It usually had a shop on the ground floor, living quarters above it, storage space above that, and, on top,

Did You Know?

Merchants, entertainers, and onlookers crowd the streets at a fair.

Come to the Fair!

Fairs have a very ancient history. There were fairs in ancient Greece and Rome, fairs among the Chinese, Aztecs, and Russians, and many others.

In western Europe in the Middle Ages, the fairs centered around the holy days of the Roman Catholic Church. Often the fairs were held in an open area, near the church. It was hoped that the traders would not quarrel and fight with a church nearby.

The most famous fairs of the Middle Ages were those held in the 1100s and 1200s in France by the counts who ruled Champagne. The fairs took place in the four cities of Troyes, Lagne, Bar, and Provens. Champagne was located on the route between the two great trading centers of Flanders and northern Germany to the north and the northern Italian cities to the south.

Merchants came from all parts of Europe to the fairs at Champagne. There was a wide assortment of goods from the East, such as spices, silks, and velvets. There were money changers to deal with the huge variety of coins issued by feudal lords. The fairs were so popular that they also attracted visitors who today would be called tourists.

Even if a person did not buy anything, the fairs were entertaining. There might be tightrope walkers, jesters, jugglers, acrobats, animal trainers with dancing bears, magicians, and fire eaters.

A person had to be very wary at the fair. The merchant who sold an item might never be seen again. Though most merchants were honest, some rural people were taken advantage of by the "city slickers." At the fairs, there were also often quacks selling bogus medicines.

The good times to be had at the fair, however, usually outweighed any disadvantages. The festive spirit was increased by the dancing, drinking, and eating that went on. After a fair ended, people eagerly looked forward to going to another.

a loft where the children, apprentices, and servants slept. More choices in food, clothing, and occupations were now available in the towns. Entertainers and artists began to be seen there.

Thus, between 1000 and 1300 the process of urbanization that typifies the modern world had started in western Europe. On the average, only about 10 percent of the people now lived in towns and cities. The typical town had only about 5,000 to 10,000 people. However, these small groups influenced the whole society far out of proportion to their numbers.

A second way in which the rise of the towns affected feudal society was in the creation of a new powerful social class. This was the middle class, also called the *bourgeoisie* or the burghers. This group included the merchants and skilled craftworkers and their families. In status, they were below the nobles. The nobles looked down on the members of the middle class because of their practical interest in business rather than in chivalry. However, the members of the middle class regarded themselves as free persons. They wanted the opportunity to make their fortunes and better their positions. They also wanted more say in running their towns. They felt that they were the energetic people with the new ideas. They used new techniques such as bookkeeping and banking.

At first, the Roman Catholic Church looked with suspicion and disfavor on people of business because they charged interest on loans. In the early Middle Ages, the Jews, not bound by the church law against interest, had controlled the lending business. Later, however, Italian bankers such as the Medici displaced the Jews. They charged high interest to finance the church's own building projects and the wars of the kings.

Town Government Usually, the middle-class people of the towns tried to secure a *charter*. This was a written document giving the town or city the right to make its own laws and have its own courts. In many cases, a noble on whose lands a town was located received a good income as a result of its growth. The noble often collected part of the money from fines and a sales tax on trade. In northern Italy especially, some towns freed themselves entirely from the lord or a king and became independent city-states.

In some places, such as England, the king became the protector of a town or city. In effect, the king and the wealthy merchants developed an alliance against the feudal lords. The merchants wanted the king to provide safe roads, a sound coinage system, and laws to encourage trade. The king liked the towns because he collected taxes or other income from them. With this

The merchants with street stalls became part of the middle class, or bourgeoisie.

233

money, he could hire his own army and administrators. No longer did he have to depend on the often uncooperative nobles.

Most of the towns and cities evolved a similar kind of government. Officials such as a mayor and a council were elected to rule the town. In general, the government was controlled for the benefit of the merchants and skilled workers. The officials were responsible for taking care of the streets and the walls of the town. If the town was not under a king or feudal lord, the officials also had to hire professional soldiers to protect the town. The city officials also settled conflicts and tried to maintain order and safety. The latter was difficult in the crowded conditions. Thieves were a particular danger in the dark, narrow streets at night.

In addition to the town government, people in the various occupations organized *guilds* to protect their common interests. Thus, the merchants, the bell ringers, the tailors, and the cabinetmakers would each have their own guild. The members of the guilds did not want anyone in their trade or occupation to lower prices or increase competition. Thus, the guilds regulated the prices to be charged for goods and the quality of the goods produced. They restricted entry into the professions and trades. They enforced rules on the training of new workers, setting limits on the number of apprentices and journeymen a master might employ. They did not want too many workers in their occupation since this could lower their income.

The guilds had political importance

Members of the tailors and clothing makers guild at work.

Coins from Venice.

since the heads of the major guilds were often members of the city council. The guilds performed many social services for their members, such as looking after the dependents of deceased members. They sponsored significant events such as processions.

Opportunities There was a third way in which the growing towns and cities of western Europe changed feudal society. They offered more opportunity for discontented serfs. Many ran away from the manor to the towns. The towns depended on these runaway serfs for unskilled labor. It became an established tradition that if a person lived one year and one day in town, he or she was freed from service to a feudal lord. This caused many lords to treat their serfs better.

Women also had more opportunities in towns and cities. They could get jobs as shopkeepers, weavers, and the like. Women in towns also had more opportunities to learn to read, which was important in doing business. Many women helped their husbands operate the family business. A widow might then take over the business.

Money The towns had another important influence on both peasants and nobles. The trade and manufacturing in the towns resulted in an increased use of money— gold and silver coins. Thus, people began to pay for goods and services instead of bartering for them. Of course, there had been some money during the early Middle Ages. But now the use of money was more widespread. Wealth came to be defined partly by the amount of money a person had. Before, it had been measured only by the amount of land a person owned.

The peasants as well as the lord of the manor could now sell their surplus food directly to the towns. In turn, the peasants and nobles used the money they got for the food to buy goods the townspeople had imported or manufactured. Now everyone wanted more money. Expectations were rising. For example, what people considered an adequate diet called for more food in the year 1300 than it had in the year 1000.

The nobles desired a more comfortable— and more costly—standard of living. They wanted fine cloth, fine weapons, spices. In order to raise more cash, many lords, especially in France, England, and Germany, changed the obligations of their serfs from performing labor on the manor to paying rents. In addition, some serfs were allowed to pay a fee over a period of years to gain their freedom. The peasants could now use their own time as they wanted. Since their annual rents and fees were fixed, the peasants also gained at the expense of their lords as monetary inflation occurred. Often, there was a gradual rise in the peasants' standard of living. The peasants came to be regarded as tenants, which represented a rise in social status. On the other hand, many nobles, especially the lesser ones, suffered a reduction in real income. However, some greater lords did receive more money from the towns.

The use of cash payments also increased mobility among the peasants. More could now legally move to the towns since they were not tied to the land. In some cases, the feudal lord, anxious to earn more money, dispossessed his serfs from the land. He would then set up a more specialized farming system, such as sheep raising, that did not require as large a labor force. He now used hired labor, often his former serfs.

Thus, both the peasants and the nobles were concentrating more on raising a surplus. They were no longer content to have enough food to feed themselves and their families. They wanted to sell their surplus agricultural products to get money to buy goods and services in the towns and cities. Manorial agriculture was changing to meet the needs of the towns and cities.

Towns were thus a force for change. They contributed to the decline of feudalism and serfdom. By 1200, the growth in population, trade, and town life was widespread. There were also changes in attitudes. The towns challenged the older ideas. No longer was a person's station in life necessarily set at birth. More people sought to rise to a higher social position. The social order was not as fixed as before.

Section Questions

1. What contributed to the population growth in western Europe from 1000 to 1300?
2. Where were the two great trading centers of western Europe during the Middle Ages?
3. Why did the Roman Catholic Church dislike the people of business in the Middle Ages?
4. What were the purposes of the guilds?

Chapter Summary

1. Christian missionaries converted the Scandinavians and the peoples of eastern Europe. Unlike western Europe, however, eastern Europe did not have a common cultural experience. The Normans conquered England in 1066 and later Sicily and other lands. In Spain, the Moors were being driven back. The Crusaders attempted to secure the Holy Land for the Christians. The First Crusade was successful, but after about two hundred years, the Christians were completely driven out of the Holy Land. However, the Crusades had a significant influence by encouraging more trade, making Europe less isolated, and strengthening the power of the kings at the expense of that of the lesser nobles.

2. Population increased in western Europe. There was a revival of trade and manufacturing in towns and cities. Old and new towns grew in size and influence. The centers of trade were the northern Italian cities and the towns of Flanders and northern Germany. The Champagne Fairs were important in the 1100s and 1200s. A middle class arose in the towns. Towns secured charters giving them limited rights. In return, they paid fees to the king or a feudal lord. Local governments and guilds developed. Serfs and women had more opportunities in towns. The use of money increased.

Chapter 13 Review

Check Your Facts

1. Identify the following:
   a. William the Conqueror
   b. Pope Urban II
   c. Battle of Hastings
   d. Latin Kingdom of Jerusalem
2. In what ways was eastern Europe different from western Europe during the Middle Ages?
3. Why did some Europeans go to the Crusades?
4. What goods did the western Europeans want from the East?
5. What products did the western Europeans produce to pay for the goods they wanted from the Muslims and Byzantium?
6. Why were the Italians able to gain control of the trade in the Mediterranean?
7. Why were the Champagne Fairs important in the 1100s and 1200s?
8. In what ways did the towns and cities change the lives of the serfs? The lesser nobles? The kings and the great lords?

Words to Know

Define these words in one or two sentences. Then tell the significance of each in the Middle Ages.
   a. cathedral   d. Crusades
   b. guilds   e. charter
   c. Romanesque   f. bourgeoisie

Developing Your Skills

1. Identify the following places. Then find them on the maps on pages 228 and 230.
   a. Jerusalem   d. Poland
   b. Constantinople   e. Sicily
   c. Sweden   f. Hungary

2. Place the following events in chronological order:
   Fall of last Christian stronghold in the Holy Land
   Separation of the western and eastern Christian churches
   Fourth Crusade
   Conversion of Norway to Christianity
   Norman conquest of England
   Moorish invasion of Spain

Thinking It Over

1. Argue for and against this idea: The Crusades were unsuccessful because they did not fulfill their goals.
2. In what ways were guilds similar to unions? How were they different?
3. Should any organization be able to restrict entry into an occupation or profession? How do trades and professions today regulate the entry of newcomers?
4. Describe a typical medieval city. Would you have liked living in such a city? Why or why not?

Special Activities

1. Check on one of these famous people and events. Prepare an oral or written report.
   The Children's Crusade (1212)
   Richard the Lionhearted of England
   Stephen of Vendom
   Nicholas of Cologne
   Saladin
   Bernard of Clairvaux
   Frederick I Barbarossa
2. Dramatize a discussion on whether interest should be charged on loans.

This painting from the time of the Black Plague is called "The Triumph of Death."

Chapter 14 The Late Middle Ages

The *plague*, often known as the bubonic plague, or "Black Death," is a very serious epidemic disease. In 1347, a black plague, probably imported from Constantinople by ship rats, spread rapidly through most of Europe. It is estimated that one-fourth to one-third of the total population was killed. The death rate was even more severe in the crowded towns.

It is now known that the bacteria *Pasteurella pestis* is generally carried from rodent fleas, especially those that live on rats, to human beings. The symptoms of the plague appear very suddenly. The victim suddenly has chills, a very high fever, rapid heartbeat,

1138-1485

1138	Hohenstaufens begin rule of Holy Roman Empire
1215	Magna Charta signed
1309-1377	Avignon papacy
1323-1328	Peasant revolts in Flanders
1338-1453	Hundred Years' War
1347-1350	The Black Plague
1378	Wycliffe condemns church structure
1415	John Huss burned at the stake
1431	Joan of Arc executed
1455-1485	War of Roses

King Henry VII of England.

stupor. The most noticeable symptom is inflamed lymph nodes, which become filled with pus and drain. These small bleeding spots in the skin, which turn black, have given the disease the name Black Death.

During the Middle Ages, people could do little about the plague. It was realized, however, that it was a little safer in the rural areas than in the crowded towns and cities. So some people fled to the countryside.

The plague demoralized the population. Some saw it as the wrath of God, punishing people. These people focused even more on religion. Others felt that the plague meant they should live only for the pleasures of today. Participation in black magic increased. Authorities persecuted witches. There was preoccupation with death in the arts. The loving Virgin Mary, who had formerly radiated hope to all, was now shown as sorrowing at the foot of the Holy Cross.

The plague also affected the economy and politics. There was an economic recession and a slowdown in trade. Kings gained power. The pope and the Roman Catholic Church lost authority as the clergy, particularly the monks, were decimated by the plague.

1. Western Europe Faced a Time of Crisis

As the thirteenth century came to an end, western Europe seemed powerful and prosperous. The continued growth of towns and trade predicted a bright future. Not only was the economy expanding, but creative thought was also blossoming in the new medieval universities. In the arts, the great churches and cathedrals showed that the High Middle Ages were a time of great change and achievement. More progress was being made in Europe than at any time since the fall of Rome.

There were, nevertheless, strains in western European society. The Roman Catholic Church was fighting against the rising power of the kings. The middle class wanted more privileges and rights. The nobles and kings were quarreling with each other. Some of these conflicts became sharp during the 1300s and 1400s, a period often described as the decline of the Middle Ages or the end of feudalism.

Problems, Problems, Problems In the 1300s and 1400s, most people were still peasants living on manors. The rural population was increasing. People whose labor was not needed on the manors went to the towns. The people of the growing towns had to be fed. Farmers increased their holdings, often expanding into marginal lands that would only be profitable if the price of food remained high. Soon, there was too large a surplus of food, and the price of food dropped. Marginal farmlands were abandoned. There was unemployment in the countryside and, eventually, in the towns.

Many European farmers lacked good places to store crops for use during poor years. Famine had been rare in western Europe from 1000 to 1300. However, a famine occurred in 1315 when constant summer rains ruined crops all across Europe. In some towns, perhaps ten percent of the population died. There were general crop failures several times during the 1300s. The climate in some regions of northern Europe was getting colder and wetter, making the growing season shorter.

International trade stopped expanding. In 1291, the Holy Land fell completely into the hands of the Muslims. The Ottoman Turks increased their power in the Middle East. The Turks were not against trade, but they wanted a greater share of the profits from the goods passing through their area. They did not encourage the expansion of European trade into Asia. As a result, the prices of spices and other luxury goods went up, reducing the amount of foreign trade.

Chronic wars, principally the Hundred Years' War (1338-1453) between England and France, ruined crops and damaged towns. Wars were now bloodier and lasted longer. They were being fought by paid troops who lived off the land. To keep the enemy from getting food, the troops burned crops. Bandits also roamed the land.

European society, already weakened by famine, economic problems, and war, was hit by plague. The Black Plague ravaged most of Europe between 1347 and 1350. The plague continued to haunt Europe, striking different areas during the next few centuries. Never again, however, was it so severe as in 1347-1350. Terrorized by the tragedy, people felt that their whole world was crashing down upon them. Population growth and economic expansion stopped. No longer did people feel confident in the future.

Long-term Effects of the Plague At first, the huge death toll from the plague raised wages, since labor was in short supply. Serfs often won more freedom from their lords. However, farmers no longer had as large a market for their food since the towns and cities had fewer people. There was also a general shrinking of trade and manufacturing. This increased competition among groups in the towns. The guilds made rules excluding the products of outsiders.

As a result of these economic developments, social unrest increased. Many workers in the towns who had formerly been artisans were now just hired laborers. They felt they were being exploited by the few wealthy owners who were cutting wages or not employing them. Throughout Europe—in England, France, and Italy—

Did You Know?

The Mechanical Clock

How many times a day do you look at your watch or at a clock? Watches and clocks are now very widely used. Being on time is important in our modern society. Clocks, instruments for dividing time into fixed intervals, were first introduced in the Middle Ages.

A need for clocks was felt in the monasteries that followed the rule of St. Benedict. The monks had to get up to pray at certain times: midnight, 3 a.m., dawn, sunrise, and so on. Something or someone had to ring a bell to tell them when to rise to pray.

During the day, people could tell time with sundials or by observing the position of the sun. There were also water clocks in which water flowed from one vessel to another. The amount of water that flowed could then be measured to tell the time. However, the sun could not be used to tell time when it was cloudy or dark, and water clocks were not very convenient. Thus, monks designed the first mechanical clock, which then provided an alarm for the community.

In the 1300s, clocks began to appear in church towers and town squares. These clocks would often strike bells on the hour. It was the pride of a town to have a large public clock. However, no one could carry around the town clock. Later, small watches, clocks that can be carried, were developed for the wealthy. The first watch was made about 1500 in Germany. It was so heavy that it had to be hung around the waist. Later, during the age of Louis XIV, skilled workers, especially in Switzerland, gained more skill in making fine and often very expensive watches.

A clock from the 1400s.

there were violent riots as workers tried to fight their misfortunes with force.

Revolts occurred in the countryside as well. The peasants, because of the decline in the prices they received for their products, felt that their standard of living was falling. In addition, they had to pay more taxes both to the king for his wars and to their lords. There were more peasants who lacked land and worked as laborers.

After centuries of relative harmony between the peasants and their lords, the peasants began to feel a new hostility toward the rich. The old feudal tradition of helping the peasants in times of need was vanishing. The peasants resented the life style of the nobles. They felt that they were losing their hard-won status as free people. The peasants particularly hated any form of serfdom and payments to the lord that had survived. A folk hero of the late Middle Ages was Robin Hood, who robbed the rich but never harmed the peasants.

These frustrations of the peasants, made worse by warfare in the countryside, led to riots and rebellions against the authorities. The revolts were the first by the lower classes against authority since the fall of Rome. Officials and nobles were murdered and castles and other property were damaged and destroyed. Serious peasant revolts occurred in Flanders (1323-1328), in France (1359), and in England (1381). There were also uprisings in other parts of Europe during the 1300s and 1400s. The riots and rebellions were eventually put down by the nobles and the rich.

These worker and peasant rebellions were not successful for several reasons. First, the upper classes—the king, the nobles, and the higher clergy—had better military resources and were more united. In the face of what they regarded as a common enemy, the king and the nobles forgot their differences. Secondly, the rebels, by contrast, were unable to maintain unity. In the towns, the various guilds found it

The folk hero Robin Hood is still popular today.

In this painting, a peasant is about to be executed for taking part in a rebellion.

difficult to cooperate. In the countryside, the peasants were scattered and communication was poor. Finally, though the lower classes knew what they were against, they had no agreed-upon program of what to do if they did get power. The rebels had a vague goal of a paradise on Earth. However, they did not know how to translate their goal into reality.

The cries of the peasants and workers for economic justice thus went unanswered. The revolts were put down ruthlessly, sometimes with the loss of thousands of lives. Restlessness did not decline until economic recovery came about 1450. However, in some areas previous levels of prosperity were never regained. The peasants of eastern Germany, in particular, remained poor and embittered. There, the landlords trying to protect their interests imposed heavy rents. Many formerly free peasants were reduced to working as hired laborers.

Section Questions

1. What contributed to crop failures after 1300?
2. Why did trade stop expanding around 1300?
3. Why were workers in the towns dissatisfied in the fourteenth century? Why were peasants dissatisfied?
4. Why were the riots and rebellions of the workers and peasants not successful?

Thinking Geographically: What states on this map would later become part of Spain?

2. Kings Expanded Their Power

During the Middle Ages, rulers in various nations tried to create a stronger and larger state out of their fragmented feudal domain. To achieve more power, they used feudal laws to help them expand. The need of the towns for protection furthered the development of stronger central power. These townspeople found it easier to support one king than to work out arrangements with many nobles. Feudalism, the importance of the lesser nobles, and serfdom all declined as the power of the king increased.

Holy Roman Empire In 1138, the crown of the Holy Roman Empire passed into the hands of the Hohenstaufen (HOH un SHTOW fun) family. The Holy Roman Empire was then at its highest point of prestige, but its weaknesses were growing more serious.

Frederick I, or Frederick Barbarossa (bawr buh RAWS uh 1152-1190), tried to rebuild the empire in Italy. He fought unsuccessfully against the pope and the northern Italian cities. Having failed to subdue the cities, he granted them more independence in return for an annual payment. In 1254, the Hohenstaufen family lost the crown. In 1274, the first member of the Hapsburg family became emperor.

The Holy Roman emperors had many lands but too few resources to control them. Distracted by Italy, they failed to create a strong kingdom in Germany.

By 1400, Germany was split into about 300 independent states and cities. The only link between these various states was the Holy Roman Empire. Eventually, seven important German states gained the right to elect the Holy Roman emperor. However, after 1438, all emperors except one were members of the Hapsburg family.

Although Germany lacked unity, German influence in eastern Europe continued. The Germans kept moving into the more sparsely settled lands to the east. This movement was in some ways similar to the westward movement in the United States in the 1700s and 1800s. Peasants, knights, and feudal lords imposed their German way of life on many of the Slavic peoples of eastern Europe.

The eastern European nations of Poland, Lithuania, and Hungary did not have strong, effective governments. What power the governments did have was based more on force than on acceptance. The rulers often found it difficult to control the nobles. However, the Germans were resented. In 1410, the Polish people defeated the German knights at the Battle of Tannenberg.

England After William the Conqueror seized England in 1066, he divided up much of the land among his knights. These barons supplied the king with military and other services. No one baron was powerful enough to challenge the king. The king also controlled the appointments of high church officials. In addition, the king chose the *sheriffs*, local nobles who collected his taxes and maintained the peace. William had no major opposition and was the real master of England.

William the Conqueror thus laid the

A medieval lawcourt in session under City Oak.

groundwork for royal power in England. During the next century, the 1100s, the English kings consolidated this power. They began to appoint traveling justices to settle disputes. Previously, there had been only local courts, with each noble in effect acting as a judge for his community. The traveling judges consulted with each other on how they were settling cases. Soon, they were following one common law that applied to all of the people in England. Common law was based on custom and traditional rights. It is the foundation of the present-day legal systems of Britain, the United States, and other English-speaking countries.

The kings gradually increased the number of courts and judges. In this way, a king could expand his authority at the expense of feudal lords and the Roman Catholic Church, which ran its own courts. It became a custom that all free persons (not serfs) could, by paying a fee, get their cases heard. It also became a tradition for a judge to call together a jury of local people to decide a case. Initially, the kings used their courts as a way of raising money, since they collected fees for hearing cases and fines from those found guilty. Soon, however, the royal courts became a way in which free people could seek justice. Plainly, a system with a judge, common law, and jury was far superior to trial by combat. It was also much better than various methods used in the Middle Ages to let God show who was innocent.

In the 1100s, the English kings found that they needed more soldiers than their feudal vassals could supply. The kings thus started to depend more on a paid army. However, the kings were chronically short of money. They were therefore always seeking ways to gain more income and impose more taxes. They soon came into conflict with the Roman Catholic Church, which held much of the country's wealth. The struggle between the king and the church, however, did not develop into long, costly wars like the conflict between the Holy Roman emperors and the pope.

Limits to the King's Power The nobles and higher clergy of England became resentful of the power assumed by the king. They felt that the king's power was limited by feudal law. During the reign of King John (1199-1216), this issue came to a head. John, a stubborn and tyrannical ruler, was not well-liked. Furthermore, the French defeated his army in 1214, lowering his prestige. The barons then successfully rebelled against John in 1214. The only way John could save himself and his crown

King John reluctantly signs the Magna Charta.

was to sign the Magna Charta, the "Great Charter," in 1215.

In the Magna Charta, King John promised to respect the rights of the nobles, the Roman Catholic Church, and the townspeople. The Magna Charta said that the taxes of the king would have to be approved by the upper classes. Later, the Magna Charta was interpreted to give specific rights to the upper classes. More important than any specific rights such as trial by jury, however, was the fact that the Magna Charta implied that there were real limits to the king's power. Nevertheless, it should be noted that the Magna Charta initially was only concerned with the rights of the upper classes. Only much later was it interpreted to include the rights of all English subjects.

The signing of the Magna Charta did not end the conflict between the king and the barons. Disputes over the meaning of the Magna Charta were frequent. The nobles were also angered when the Scots under Robert the Bruce won their freedom at the Battle of Bannockburn in 1314. Thereafter, there was an independent kingdom of Scotland separate from England.

There were frequent uprisings of the barons. To keep the peace, the English kings started the practice of regularly calling together a *parliament*, or council of state. Parliament eventually split into two parts. There was a House of Lords, to which the nobles and the upper clergy belonged. The House of Commons was for the wealthy townspeople and the lesser nobility (or gentry).

During the 1300s and 1400s, the king frequently had to ask Parliament for money to fight wars against Scotland and France. These were long, drawn-out campaigns. The Hundred Years' War against France actually lasted, off and on, for more than a century (1338-1453). Parliament followed the practice of granting the money for only a specific time period. Several powers of Parliament became established during these years. Parliament gained the right to approve all money matters. In addition, Parliament acquired some control over royal officials. The right of Parliament to petition the king was also established. If the king signed such a petition, it became the law of the land. In effect, the English Parliament gained control over making laws.

The stability of the English government was shaken when a long civil war broke out in 1455 between the houses of Lancaster and York, two branches of the royal family. This conflict is known as the War of the Roses. It is called this because a white rose was the symbol of the Yorkists and a red rose was later erroneously thought to have been the symbol of the Lancastrians. Many nobles were killed in the struggle, reducing the power of Parliament. After 30 years of intermittent fighting, Henry VII became king in 1485. Henry VII belonged to the house of Tudor, an offshoot of the Lancastrians, but he married the Yorkist heiress. A nation weary of civil war allowed the new king to assume great powers. Parliament tended to automatically approve laws desired by the king.

France Compared to the England of William the Conqueror, France in 1066 was not a unified, powerful nation. France had originated in the division of Charlemagne's empire. The French king was Count of Paris, ruling directly only a small area

A view of the House of Commons, with Henry VIII on the throne.

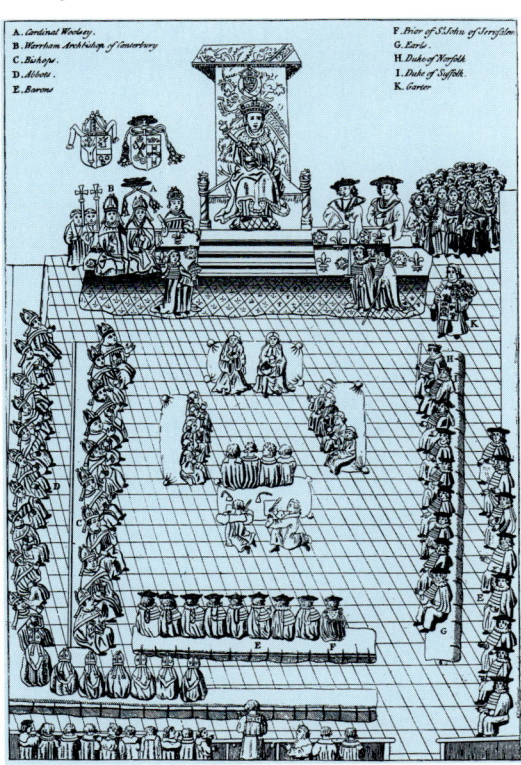

A French vassal honors his prince.

around that city. This area was, however, an important trading center and thus a source of income for the king.

The rest of France was divided into many territories. Not a few were both larger and richer than those owned by the king. These territories were ruled by feudal lords who were largely independent of the king. The nobles gave the French kings no military service. France was, in effect, a collection of feudal states with a weak king.

The biggest obstacle to making France a powerful nation was England. Since William the Conqueror was a Norman, England actually had extensive lands in northern France. For a long time, the English king held a large section of southern France as well. However, over the centuries, the French kings gained more control over their original territory. They had a far more manageable domain than the Holy Roman emperors. The French kings enlarged their holdings by means fair and foul—by conquests, by alliances, and by seizing feudal territories that lacked male heirs.

One of the most important French kings in the Middle Ages was Philip II, or Philip Augustus (1180-1223). Philip II tried to give his subjects a better rule than the feudal lords. He protected merchants from attack while they were on his roads and from exploitation by the nobles. During his rule, Paris became the most important city in France.

In addition to increasing his control in the immediate area of Paris, Philip II sought to break the power of the English in France. In 1214, he decisively defeated King John of England in the Battle of Bouvines. As a result, Philip II took over the lands of the English kings in northern France. By greatly enlarging his territories, Philip II made France the most powerful nation in Europe. This power was demonstrated in the bitter quarrel between Philip IV and the pope. Pope Boniface VIII tried to prevent the French and English kings from taxing the Roman Catholic Church and trying clerics in their own courts. In 1303, Philip IV arrested the pope. He wanted to try the pope on charges before a general council of the church. The pope, broken and humiliated by this event, died shortly thereafter.

In 1305, a French pope, Clement V (1305-1314), was elected. He moved the papal court to Avignon, a town on the French border. The pope appointed many French cardinals. Clement V and his successors lived in Avignon for about 70 years, a period sometimes called the "Babylonian Captivity." Many Christians regarded the Avignon popes as being pawns of the French king. They felt that the pope should live in Rome, the historic seat of the papacy.

Philip II and his successors tried to strengthen their power in other ways. They made laws for the whole nation and set up royal courts. They devised various ways to raise money, levying taxes on the Roman Catholic Church, on Jews, on foreigners such as bankers, and on their own subjects.

Like the English kings, the French kings were constantly in need of money for wars. The taxes that the French kings collected made the nobles and people suspicious and resentful. Despite their enlarged territories, the French kings had to share power with the nobles at the local level. As they added new lands, the French kings usually let

The papal palace at Avignon.

the local customs and laws remain. Thus, France never developed the unified laws that England had.

Hundred Years' War The increasing power of the French kings ended with the outbreak of the Hundred Years' War (1338-1453). This conflict was really an extension of the struggle that had been going on between England and France for centuries. Control of the rich wool trade of Flanders had long been a major issue in this fight. The war officially started when the English king Edward III claimed the French throne after the king of France died without a direct male heir. The Hundred Years' War was actually a series of wars. Each peace treaty, often negotiated by church leaders, was broken and fighting would start up again. The long war was fought entirely in France, as the English controlled both sides of the channel.

At first, the English were brilliantly successful at the battles of Crecy (1346) and Poitiers (1356). There the trained English archers with their powerful longbows and pikes slaughtered the French nobles on horses. The days of the feudal knights were disappearing. The longbow could pierce armor at a short distance and the pikes could stop a cavalry charge. The courage of the French knights was no substitute for the experience and new military techniques of the English soldiers. Towards the end of the long war the French did use cannons, another military innovation, to retake castles and towns.

At the Battle of Poitiers, King John of France, his youngest son, and dozens of nobles were captured. A huge ransom had to be paid for their return. Meanwhile, France was in a state of chaos. There was no effective ruler. Nobles tried to gain control in their own areas. Peasants, suffering from the effects of the war, were rebelling.

In 1415, King Henry V of England won control of the northern part of France. He married the daughter of the French king and signed a treaty giving France to himself and his heirs.

Joan of Arc At this darkest hour for France, a young uneducated peasant girl came to the fore. Joan of Arc claimed to have had visions from God. The visions said that the French should drive the English out of France. In 1429, she managed to get a hearing at the French court. She convinced the young prince, Charles, that he was to rule France and should be crowned king. Openly defying the English, he assumed the throne as Charles VII in 1429. Joan rallied the French troops and they were successful for a time. However, in 1430, she was captured by the English. She was tried by an English court on the charges of being a heretic and a witch. Convicted, she was burned at the stake in 1431. However, Joan of Arc had inspired the French nation. The French began to slowly push back the English. By 1453, they had regained all of France except Calais.

The destruction done in France during

The English and French battle at Crecy.

Joan of Arc triumphantly enters the liberated city of Orleans.

the long war was severe. However, the French were united by their hatred of the English. They developed a sense of nationhood. The disorder in the land showed the need for a strong central government. French kings assumed more power.

From time to time, the French kings called together the *Estates General*. This body was made up of the representatives of three *estates*, or social classes—the clergy, the nobles, and the wealthy townspeople. But the Estates General was a tool of the king. In part, this was because the French nobles could never unite long enough to oppose the king. The Estates General, therefore, never developed the powers of the English Parliament. The French king, beginning with less power than the English king, in the long run gained more. The French king had complete power over taxation and was thus able to support an army without the assistance of the Estates General. The French king was becoming an *absolute monarch*. In other words, there were no limits to his power.

Section Questions

1. In what ways was the system of judges appointed by the English kings a better method of obtaining justice?
2. Why was Parliament in England able to assume power in lawmaking?
3. Why were the Estates General in France not as successful in gaining power as Parliament was?

Did You Know?

Clothing in the Middle Ages

The clothing worn in the Middle Ages was adapted from what the ancient Romans wore. Roman women and men wore togas, usually long, loose gowns. Trousers for males were introduced into Europe from Central Asia, where men who rode horses found them convenient. Moreover, in the colder climate of northern Europe, trousers made of cloth or leather were warmer because they fit closer to the body. Trousers were held up with a belt at the waist.

However, males in powerful or respected positions—priests, teachers at the universities, monks, doctors, lawyers—still continued to wear long gowns, especially at important ceremonies. This is true even today, as kings wear robes at coronations, the clergy often wears robes at religious ceremonies, professors and graduates wear academic robes at graduations, and judges wear robes in courts.

To protect their regular clothing, peasants and workers—both men and women—often wore smocks over everything. Even so, changing clothes was not common. The very neat might change their clothes about once every two weeks. Of course, many people slept in their clothing. For example, monks in strict orders had only two robes. They wore the same one day and night.

In the 1000s and 1100s, people started to wear fitted, rather than loose, clothing. Women laced their dresses at the waist. About 1300, people began to use buttons, which also contributed to making clothing more close-fitting.

To keep warm, people wore a cloak, often with a hood, or a surcoat, a loose outer coat without sleeves. The rich had

High style in the 1300s.

their cloaks lined with costly furs. The poor lined their with sheepskin, rabbit, or squirrel. Legs and feet were covered with hose and with boots or shoes.

In the late Middle Ages, the emerging middle class began to devote more money and attention to their clothing. However, the nobles did not like the middle class copying their fancy dress. Laws were passed in some places outlining what was proper for women and men in the different social classes to wear. The nobles wanted to keep everyone in the proper social class and clothing was one way of identifying social class in the Middle Ages. Do you think this is true today?

3. The Roman Catholic Church Grew Weaker

During the Middle Ages, the popes were the most important religious leaders of western Europe. In addition to their religious power, the popes had political importance. They could influence the politics of the European nations. The popes directly ruled lands in central Italy—the Papal States. During the 1300s and 1400s, the power of the papacy was declining. Though the Roman Catholic Church still possessed much wealth and influence, gone were the days of Innocent III, when the pope had been supreme in both spiritual and secular affairs.

Scandal of Avignon From 1309 to 1377 the popes lived in Avignon. People believed that the papacy was controlled by the king of France. Many Christians wanted the pope to live in Rome. The life of the papal court at Avignon gained the reputation for being worldly and luxurious. People particularly complained about the taxes the pope was trying to collect from the clergy. Often, the clergy in a given country did not want to pay these taxes and looked for support from their own kings and nobles. Thus, the pope could no longer count on the support of some of his own clergy. Many Christians were now more loyal to the French king or the English king than they were to the pope. The prestige and power of the papacy suffered.

In 1377, Pope Gregory XI returned to Rome. At that time, the whole of Italy was divided into warring cities and states. There was no single, central authority. The popes had begun to lose power in Italy when the papacy had moved to Avignon. They now had to struggle to regain control over their Italian lands. To many people, the popes appeared little different from the secular rulers. Like the secular rulers, the popes seemed preoccupied with raising taxes, expanding their territory, and leading worldly lives.

Scandal of the Great Schism A great scandal further weakened the papacy and shocked the whole of the Christian world. In Rome in 1378, the cardinals elected Urban VI, an Italian pope. The cardinals later claimed that they were forced into this action when a Roman mob threatened them with violence. Meeting a second time, the cardinals then elected a Frenchman, Clement VII. Both Urban and Clement refused to give up their claims. Urban stayed in Rome, and Clement lived in Avignon. Thus, there were two rival popes, and the authority of the Roman Catholic Church was hopelessly divided. Both popes tried to gain support among European rulers, and each criticized the other. The Great Schism of the church, with its two lines of popes, had thus begun.

This scandalous situation lasted for almost forty years. Indeed, at one time there were three popes. At last, the Council of Constance managed to reunify the Roman Catholic Church under a single pope, Martin V, in 1417. While the church council did solve the problem of multiple popes, it failed to institute other reforms and to check heresy, a major problem for the church.

Many devout people now regarded the monasteries as being corrupt. The monks had a reputation for breaking their vows and being idlers rather than hard workers. The reputation of the local priests was not much better. Both groups were accused of not performing their duties and of failing to serve the needs of the people.

Heresies In spite of the scandals and abuses in the Roman Catholic Church, religion was still very important in the lives of many people. During the 1300s and 1400s, some people became *mystics*. Mystics believed that people could know

God directly, without the aid of the church, by looking within themselves. Some of the important saints of the Middle Ages, such as St. Bernard, St. Francis, and St. Catherine, had also been mystics, but they had remained close to the church. In the 1400s, many people who believed in mysticism began to preach and write openly. People like Thomas à Kempis (1380-1471) said that union with God could only be achieved by those pure in heart. Indirectly, this emphasis amounted to an attack on the sacraments of the church.

Of great concern to the Roman Catholic Church were the ideas of John Wycliffe (1320-1384), an English professor and scholar. He attacked many of the church's beliefs and practices and its structure. Wycliffe favored a literal interpretation of the Bible, believing that the scriptures were more important than the teachings of the church. Asserting that each person could be his or her own priest, he viewed the hierarchy of pope, bishops, and so on as unnecessary. Wycliffe's ideas spread from England to Bohemia. There John Huss (or Hus), a priest at the University of Prague, preached these ideas and was charged with heresy. In 1415, John Huss was burned at the stake for his beliefs. However, his followers in Bohemia were not successfully suppressed, and a rebellion broke out. The ideas of Wycliffe and Huss were like those of the Protestant Reformation a century later.

The Roman Catholic Church had, therefore, been gravely weakened by the fifteenth century. The clergy were being strongly criticized. Many people were listening to new religious ideas. The church seemed unable to reform itself.

Section Questions

1. What two areas were supposed to be controlled by the Holy Roman Empire?
2. Why did the prestige of the popes decline during the time they lived in Avignon?
3. Why did papal prestige decline during the Great Schism?

Chapter Summary

1. In the 1300s, famines appeared. Trade stopped expanding. The Black Plague killed at least one-fourth to one-third of the Europeans. All these events produced much social unrest. Both workers and peasants rebelled, but these revolts were put down by the upper classes.

2. Kings during the Middle Ages tried to expand their power. The Holy Roman emperors were not able to control their extensive territories. Both Germany and Italy became divided into many cities and states. The Germans did continue to expand into eastern Europe. The English kings increased their power by setting up courts. However, the Magna Charta set limits on the king's authority. The English kings needed money to wage war. It became their practice to ask money from Parliament, which developed into a law-making body. However, the War of the Roses reduced the power of Parliament.

The French kings expanded their territory, and France became a powerful nation. But the power of France and its kings was broken for a time by the Hundred Years' War between England and France. The French were finally able to drive the English out of France. The long war increased the need for a strong central power, which the French kings supplied.

3. The popes lost power in the 1300s and 1400s because of the Avignon papacy, the Great Schism, and other scandals. The Roman Catholic Church seemed unable to reform itself. Mystics, heretics, and other critics threatened the authority of the church.

Chapter 14 Review

Check Your Facts

1. Identify the following:
    a. Holy Roman Empire
    b. Robert the Bruce
    c. Philip II
    d. Henry V
    e. Hundred Years' War
    f. War of the Roses
    g. John Huss
    h. Edward III
    i. Joan of Arc
2. Why did the Holy Roman emperors and the popes quarrel?
3. Why did the barons rebel against King John of England?
4. Why was Magna Charta an important document in English history?
5. What did the arrest of Pope Boniface VIII show about the power of the Roman Catholic Church? The power of France?
6. Why were the English at first successful in the Hundred Years' War?
7. How did the ideas of John Wycliffe threaten the Roman Catholic Church?

Words to Know

Define these terms in one or two sentences. Then tell the significance of each in the Middle Ages.
   a. plague
   b. absolute monarchy
   c. mystics

Developing Your Skills

1. Use a world atlas that has a detailed map of France. Trace enough of the map to show Calais, Crecy, and Poitiers.
2. Place the following events in the proper chronological order from the earliest year to the latest.

   Battle of Bouvines
   John Huss put to death
   Start of Hundred Years' War
   Black Plague hits Europe
   Popes start to live at Avignon
   King John signs the Magna Charta
   Hundred Years' War ends

Thinking It Over

1. What century, up to 1500, would you have liked to live in? Why? What century seems the worst? Why?
2. It is often said that the Holy Roman Empire was not holy, Roman, or an empire. What does this statement mean? Give some evidence to support it.
3. Why do you think the people of Rome wanted the pope to live in their city? In what ways would they benefit?
4. What evidence do you think we now have that the climate turned colder in parts of northern Europe during the Middle Ages?

Special Activities

1. Check what policies people today want the government to follow when there is an economic recession. Compare these present policies with those used by the guilds during the late Middle Ages when there was a recession.
2. Many people think that all danger of the plague has passed. But in the western United States, rodents such as squirrels may be carriers of the disease. What steps are taken today to make sure that the plague does not spread?

Unit 3 Review

Words to Know

1. In one or two sentences, compare or contrast the following.
   a. Crusade/jihad
   b. patriarch/pope
   c. cathedrals/mosques
2. How was chivalry similar to the Five Pillars of Islam? How was it different?
3. How were ulmas like monks? How were they different?

Time and Place

1. Indicate how the following events influenced the development of towns and cities.
   a. The Black Plague
   b. Improvements in agriculture (plow, use of horses, etc.)
   c. The Crusades
   d. Increased population in the countryside
   e. The growing power of kings
2. Use a scale of 1 to 5 to rank the power that each king below had. Assign 1 to the king who had the most power. Be prepared to defend your choices.
   William the Conqueror
   John
   Edward III
   Henry V
   Henry VII

Putting It Together

1. Copy the chart below on a piece of paper. Fill in dates for the rise, peak, and decline of each group, then give brief reasons for the declines. You may have to refer to Unit 2 for some dates.
2. Did geography seem to affect the rise and fall of some groups? How?
3. How did people inside the groups affect some groups? How did outsiders affect some groups?

	rise	peak	decline	reason for decline
Rome				
Byzantine empire				
Carolingian empire				
Umayyad dynasty				

Contemporary Parallel:
Power

Power is the ability to control, the potential to punish or reward. An individual can have power, for example, as a king, a mayor, or a bishop. A group, a parliament or a band of robbers such as that led by Robin Hood, can have power.

In every society, there is agreement among the majority of the people on who has power or authority in certain areas. Thus, parents typically have authority over their own children. Administrators are usually given legal authority to run the schools.

In Europe in the Middle Ages, as in some parts of the world today, young people did not usually have the power to arrange their own marriages. The woman usually had to have a dowry. An individual's wishes about whom to marry typically were given little consideration.

Young people in the Middle Ages were also less powerful than today in the choice of occupations. In the towns of the Middle Ages, parents often had their son(s) apprenticed to learn a trade, such as that of a silversmith. Those who lived on manors had even less opportunity to choose their occupations.

In the early Middle Ages, little money was in circulation. Instead, agreements involving goods or services were often made with a landlord. This meant that young people did not have many opportunities to earn their own income.

In addition, most young people in the Middle Ages did not have many opportunities to learn to read and write. Often, the clergy were the only ones with these skills.

Thus, in many ways, young people in the Middle Ages had less power than young people do today. A young person today has more choices in lifestyle, occupation, marriage, and education.

QUESTIONS

1. What can those in power do to enforce their decisions?
2. What are the advantages of a marriage system in which a wife needs a dowry? The disadvantages?
3. What are the advantages of the apprenticeship form of education? The disadvantages?

300	618	1000	1250	1370	1450	1550
Mayan classic period	Tang dynasty begins	Muslims in India; Ghana strong	Mongols and Mali strong	Mongol empire fallen; Aztecs strong	Incas, Zimbabwe strong	Portuguese in Africa; Spanish in New World

Unit 4

Africa, Asia, and the Americas

An Aztec temple in Mexico.

The period from A.D. 600 to 1450 might well be called the "age of regional unity." Human societies were still very much isolated in some ways. Entire regions like the Americas, Australia, and central Africa were cut off from the rest of the world, yet new civilizations, new religions, and new social systems were creating a sense of unity and belonging over wide regions.

While the Western Roman Empire had collapsed, other established empires like the Byzantine and Chinese remained intact. China, in fact, continued to be one of the most advanced civilizations. Early in this period, the invention of gunpowder and of printing were added to China's list of contributions.

New African kingdoms established unity over large areas of that continent. Three great city civilizations emerged in the Americas.

In Europe, disintegration of the Carolingian empire led the way to the establishment of a new social system, with unity provided by the Christian religion. A similar system also created new stability in Japan.

In each of these regions, new patterns and new traditions were taking shape. In this unit, you will be studying these emerging patterns in the non-European world.

Arab travelers approaching Timbuktu.

Chapter 15 Africa

One of the Five Pillars of Islam called for the faithful to make a pilgrimage to the holy city of Mecca. When Muslim rulers made these holy journeys, they also used them as a way to show the rulers of other states their wealth and power.

An eyewitness recorded the parade into Mecca of Mansa Musa (MOO sah), ruler of the kingdom of Mali (MAH lee), in the year 1324: No less than 500 servants, each carrying a 2-kilogram staff of pure gold, marched ahead of their king. Behind wound a caravan of thousands, including the emperor's military escort, secretaries,

900 B.C.—A.D. 1550 (early dates approximate)

900 B.C.	Early kingdom of Cush
400 B.C.	Africa steel furnaces operating
A.D. 1	Bantu groups begin migration
1076	Ghana's capital conquered
1235	Sundiata takes throne of Mali
1312	Mansa Musa becomes ruler of Mali
1400	Zimbabwe empire arises
1400	Kongo kingdom at its height
1440	Arab traders spread Swahili culture
1464	Sunni Ali becomes ruler of Gao
1482	Portuguese come to Kongo
1550	Portuguese take over Arab trading empire

A bronze figure by a Benin artist (see page 279).

porters, and servants. Eight camels carried more than 11,000 kilograms (24,000 pounds) of gold to pay the cost of the trip.

Mali was located in North Africa, south of the Sahara Desert. Timbuktu, capital of this Muslim state, was a center of Islamic culture. Its brick buildings included mosques, palaces, and universities. The city impressively displayed the arts, learning, and comforts that wealth from trade can provide.

Timbuktu was only one center from which spread the Arabic language, complex political and social ideas, the Islamic religion, and foreign trade goods. The eyewitness account of Mansa Musa's pilgrimage, however, was the report that led Europeans to understand that the continent of Africa was far from the dark continent they thought it was.

1. African Geography Was An Important Influence

Africa, a huge land mass, is the second largest continent in the world. The continental United States could fit into Africa more than three times over. The northern coast of Africa and southern coast of Europe share the Mediterranean Sea. But Africa's closeness to Europe has not prevented Europeans from seeing Africa as a dark continent. Until recent times, even educated people thought of Africa as a land with no history.

We now know that Africans, during the reign of Mansa Musa, had much contact with the rest of the world. In fact, Africans had more mobility than Europeans would have for the next several hundred years.

Mirror Images The equator divides the continent of Africa in half. In general terms, the climate regions below the equator are a mirror image of those above it. The rain forest along the equator is bordered on both sides by areas of *savanna*, or tropical grasslands. Both savanna regions in turn give way to deserts. The deserts are rimmed by coastal plains along the Mediterranean Sea in the north and along the Cape of Good Hope in the south.

The rain forest typically gets so much rain that fields cleared for farming begin to sprout trees, tangled vines, and thick jungle ground cover as soon as farmers set aside their chopping knives. The rain, as much as 2 meters (7 feet) per year, washes valuable minerals from the soil. This makes the soil useless for farming. Inhabitants must hack out new fields every few years.

Historically, people in the rain forest regions lived by fishing, hunting, and gathering. Among the foods they gathered were root crops brought to Africa from the farming cultures of southern Asia. Today, as then, the kola nuts from which soft drinks are made and the palm oil used in soaps and cosmetics are typical rain forest crops. Others are cocoa beans, yams, and bananas.

Trees in the savanna are shorter than in the rain forest because there is less rainfall. They share the land with thick green grass, ideal for raising cattle. Here are found most of the herds of wild game that have become symbolic of Africa: giraffes, antelope, elephants, and zebras. Here also live the lions, hyenas, and other animals that prey on the grazers.

In the north, the savanna is called the *sudan*. In the south, it is called the *veld*, after the Dutch word for field. This is a reminder that the first maps of Africa were made by Europeans who settled there. Modern African nations are gradually replacing these colonial terms with the names native people have been using throughout their history.

As the savannas stretch toward the desert regions, there is less and less rainfall. Grass becomes harder to find. This marginal land, called the *sahel*, often sees widespread tragedy. Its inhabitants live as nomads in order to move their cattle on when the grass is gone. As recently as the 1970s, during a period of lower-than-normal rainfall, these people became the victims of mass starvation. They also lost their carefully developed herds of cattle. Herders in the savanna cannot move their cattle into the lush rain forest when the grass dries up because the forest houses the tsetse fly, which causes sleeping sickness in humans and kills cattle.

Above and below the savanna lie vast regions of arid desert. In the north is the Sahara (the Arabic word for "desert"), and the smaller Nubian (NOO bee un) Desert. It is often rocky rather than sandy. In the south are the Namib (NAH mib) and the Kalahari, often so dry that the Bush people have developed the skill of inserting long straws into the land in order to drink what little moisture lies far beneath the surface. When rain does come to the desert, it brings floods that sweep along dry river beds and fill oases. Rains alone restore the levels of lakes like Lake Chad in the northern sahel, an enormous body of water that has no outlet.

The northern fringe and the southern tip of Africa have a Mediterranean climate similar to that of southern Italy and California. These coastal plains have rainy winters, dry summers, and mild temperatures. The climate is especially favorable to the growing of grapes, fig and olive trees, grain, and livestock. Farms and orchards flourish here, and the coastal location encourages trade. Today, modern cities in these areas are visited by ships that carry away agricultural products. The ships also carry away loads of gold, iron, and other metals as well as the diamonds that are mined in the interior of Africa.

Barriers to Travel The geography of Africa has made trade, communication, and the movement of people difficult in all but the coastal areas. Even the west African coast has few natural bays. Shifting sandbars prevent the formation of good harbors at the river mouths. Boats must often be unloaded far offshore amid a roaring surf.

Another feature has isolated many of Africa's regions and made African history different from that of Europe. This is the

Did You Know?

Can Deserts Move?

The Sahara region was not always what it is today. About 65,000 years ago, heavy rains supported lush vegetation. The Sahara was a tropical rain forest. Then as recently as 6000 to 2500 B.C., the region had a period of savanna climate. Regular rainfall helped willow, ash, sycamore, and cedar trees grow tall in the Sahara region. Small bands of nomadic people hunted lions, elephants, giraffes, and other game. Rock paintings made by these people have given us permanent records of how they lived.

The period of savanna climate began to fade about 2000 B.C. when the pattern of winds shifted. The moisture-heavy winds moved across Africa farther south than they had before. Over hundreds of years, the nomadic tribes and the grass-eating animals retreated from the region as the desert continued to grow.

In our century, the Sahara reaches from the border of the Mediterranean Sea in the north to the grasslands of the sudan. Only a few oases and the amazing endurance of the camel have enabled people to maintain contact across the spectacular dry Sahara.

An oasis in the desert.

Beautiful Victoria Falls blocks river traffic on the Zambezi River.

fact that Africa is a *plateau*, high, relatively flat land that rises sharply from the land around it. More than 90 percent of Africa's land is over 150 meters (500 feet) above sea level. This means that the great river systems carrying rainfall to the sea often drop suddenly in giant waterfalls or rush along through dangerous rapids. The Zambezi (zam BEE zee) River is 3,500 kilometers (2,200 miles) long, but is blocked to travel by Victoria Falls. The Nile is navigable only in lower Egypt. The Niger and the Congo (KAHN go) tumble and foam for much of their length. During dry seasons, the level of some rivers drops too low for navigation.

Movement between north and south on this long continent is not easy because of the thick rain forest that divides it. The rain forest also harbors insects that bring sleeping sickness, malaria, yellow fever, and other illnesses to humans and animals.

Perhaps the greatest barrier to trade and communication is the Sahara. This desert is so vast that it was almost impossible to cross until the camel was introduced. Camels were not native to Africa. They came from southwestern Asia sometime between 500 B.C. and A.D. 400. The Sahara is very nearly the size of the United States. Its size reminded its explorers of an ocean. To this day, the camel is often called the ship of the desert.

Africa's Prehistory Many archaeologists have dug below the surface of Africa to find clues to the continent's prehistory. Most of them now believe that the earliest humanlike creatures developed in Africa. Scientists are carefully examining tools, bones, and seeds that have been buried for millions of years in the Rift Valley of east Africa.

Anthropologists have learned much about earlier times by studying African art, music, dance, religions, and languages. They know that Southeast Asian cowrie shells were used as coins all over Africa.

These shells, Chinese porcelain, and other objects found at archaeological sites along the east African coast tell us the extent of early African trade. So does the presence in Africa of cattle, camels, and Asian fruits and vegetables.

Historians trace early African history through reports written by traders and explorers. They also listen to the stories Africans have kept alive by retelling them to each new generation.

Section Questions

1. What are the major climate zones of Africa?
2. What plants and animals have been most important to Africans living in each of the climate zones?
3. Define savanna, veld, sudan, and plateau.
4. What are the major geographic barriers to trade and communication in Africa?
5. Name several ways in which scientists and historians learn about Africa's past.

2. African States Developed Under Muslim Rule

Permanent settlements of African people developed in Egypt before the Sahara had entirely dried up. As villages grew too large for the farms around them, people moved south into upper Egypt along the Nile.

One society that developed there was known as Cush. The Cushites had already learned about ironmaking. In about 800 B.C., the Cushites conquered Egypt.

After the Babylonians destroyed the capital of Cush, in about 600 B.C., the Cushites moved south to where there was iron ore. Soon their new capital, Meroe (MER uh wee), became one of the largest iron-producing areas of the ancient world.

The Cushites set up a lively trading empire and helped spread ironmaking to all of Africa. They also spread their ideas of religion and government. As in Egypt and Sumer, the government of Cush was a theocracy. The Cushites also developed a written language that, unlike the Egyptian hieroglyphics, has not been deciphered.

The Cushite empire reached its height about A.D. 400. At that time, a new empire was rising in the western Sudan.

Ghana People who live in hot climates must have salt. They eat it to replace the body salts lost through perspiration. They also use it to preserve meat. A simple skill like salting meat lets populations grow. Communities can then develop into cities. Exchanging gold from mines in the sudan for salt from desert tribes was an important function of the trading kingdom of Ghana (GAH nuh).

At first, silent trade was the custom. Tribal miners would leave their gold ore at a central point, like a river crossing, and leave. Berber traders would then leave as much salt as they thought the gold was worth. They would depart, leaving the gold untouched. The miners would return and take back the gold if they thought the payment was too small. If not, they would carry away the salt.

Ghanans organized this primitive trade into a well-developed system. Their long camel caravans brought in salt, copper, and cloth. To the Mediterranean world, Ghanan traders exported gold, ivory, and leather. They also traded slaves that had been seized from the rain forest to the south of Ghana.

Trade cannot be carried on safely when people and the land they work are disrupted by war. The king of Ghana kept the peace with a huge army. One observer wrote that this army numbered 200,000 warriors, each bearing a spear tipped with iron.

Ghanans did not welcome foreign peoples or ideas. In A.D. 1000, their capital,

Kumbi-Soleh (KUM bee SAH luh), consisted of two towns about 10 kilometers (6 miles) apart. One town housed foreign merchants and traders. The walled king's town enclosed the royal palace and the public buildings. Well-guarded vaults held the empire's great wealth.

The king and his nobles ran the state. They collected taxes from all the little kingdoms and villages in the empire and administered justice under Ghanan laws. The king, wrote one reporter, "sits in a pavilion around which stand ten guards holding shields and golden swords. At his right sit the sons of nobles, and his ministers sit on the floor around him. Dogs guard the king on his throne. At a drum beat the people come to listen to the king. They fall on their knees and show respect by sprinkling their heads with dust."

The king had a *monopoly* on almost all the gold in Ghana. This meant that he controlled the source of the gold, the amount of it to be traded, the price it should bring, and who could buy and sell it. A clever king sold only as much as he needed to sell. That made gold harder to get, so that people would pay a high price for it. It also kept the supply from running out.

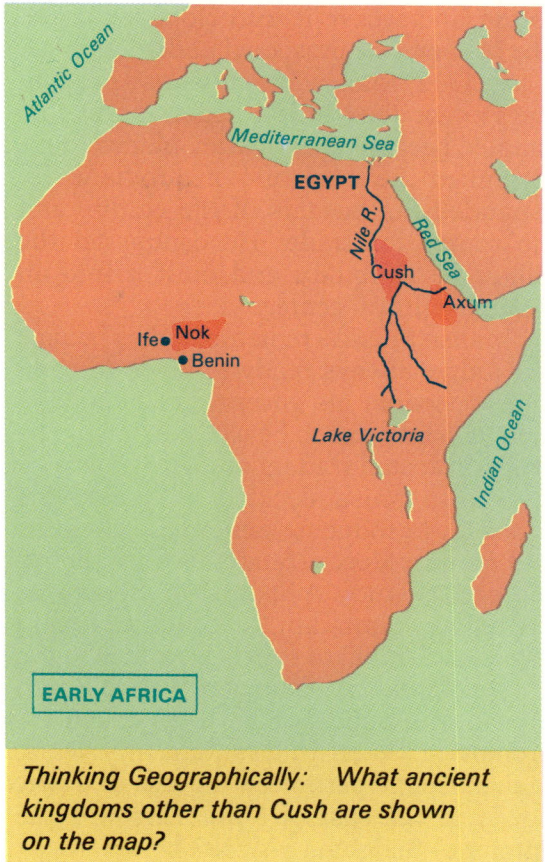

Thinking Geographically: What ancient kingdoms other than Cush are shown on the map?

Mali Ghana was conquered in 1076 by Muslim reformers. With Ghana's loss of power several other kingdoms rose. One was Mali. Mali began as a small group of villages peopled by Mandingos (man DING oz) who converted to Islam. It was located in the savanna farther from the desert and therefore could develop better agriculture.

In 1224, the king of neighboring Sosso, who had taken over the weakened Ghana kingdom, conquered Mali. He murdered eleven of the twelve sons of the Mali ruler. The remaining child, Sundiata (SAHN dee AH tuh), was spared because he was badly crippled. Legends tell that Sundiata overcame his disability by painful exercise. He even became a soldier and hunter.

The king *exiled* (sent away) Sundiata to prevent him from leading the conquered Mandingos in rebellion. In 1234, Sundiata returned at the head of an army of followers. One kingdom sent 1,500 archers to help his troops defeat the Sosso power. Within a year, Sundiata had taken the Mali throne. In the twenty years of his reign, he extended the Mali empire to include the salt mines of the Sahara, all the land westward to the Atlantic, and the gold-bearing regions to the south. This empire was much larger than Ghana ever was.

Sundiata was an able administrator. He divided the empire into small provinces and set up one of his generals to govern each one. He encouraged people to plant cotton and weave it into cloth for trade. The Mali empire prospered under Sundiata.

In 1312, Mansa Musa, whose pilgrimage is described in the beginning of this chapter, became ruler of Mali. Mansa Musa continued the wise rule of Sundiata. He expanded the borders of the empire and the routes for trade. He conquered the village of Timbuktu and built it into an Islamic cultural center.

Mansa Musa is remembered as being a fair judge, always ready to listen to complaints against his governors. His government workers had to be well educated. His army protected traders on their travels.

Mansa Musa decided to benefit his people by introducing some of the things he had seen in Mecca. Students were sent to Morocco to study. A Spanish architect was invited to Timbuktu to build beautiful mosques. Timbuktu streets were lit at night.

Unfortunately, the rulers who followed Mansa Musa did not have his talent for promoting peace. In less than fifty years, Mali's decline permitted the rise of a new power to the east of Mali. This was the empire of Songhai (SAWNG hi).

Songhai Songhai began as a small kingdom on the Niger River. The people fished, raised cattle, and traded. Gao (gow), its capital, was the end of three major caravan routes in the Mali empire. When Mali became weak, Gao broke away in 1375.

In 1464 Sunni Ali (SUN ee AHL ee) became the ruler of the small but wealthy Gao kingdom. During his twenty-eight-year reign, he created an enormous army of cavalry and infantry as well as a naval fleet. Many of his conquests were easy. The people of Timbuktu, for example, begged him to free them from the Mali ruler that had taken over their region.

Sunni Ali governed his conquered empire shrewdly. He understood that people are less likely to rebel against a great power if their local rulers remain unchanged. So he

The oldest mosque still standing in Timbuktu.

kept the defeated kings as governors. The governors had to share the taxes they collected with his imperial government.

If any group resisted the rule of Sunni Ali, he used another tactic: fear. One report says that Sunni Ali hated one enemy group so much that he had almost every man and woman killed. Those he left alive "could have gathered under the shade of one tree." The Muslim religious leaders protested that Sunni Ali was not acting according to the beliefs of Islam.

But Sunni Ali was not able to completely unify his empire. He drowned mysteriously while returning from one of his wars. His throne was seized by his most trusted general, Muhammad Askia (as KEE uh). In order to keep his power, Muhammad Askia had all of Sunni Ali's family killed. Then he went on a pilgrimage to

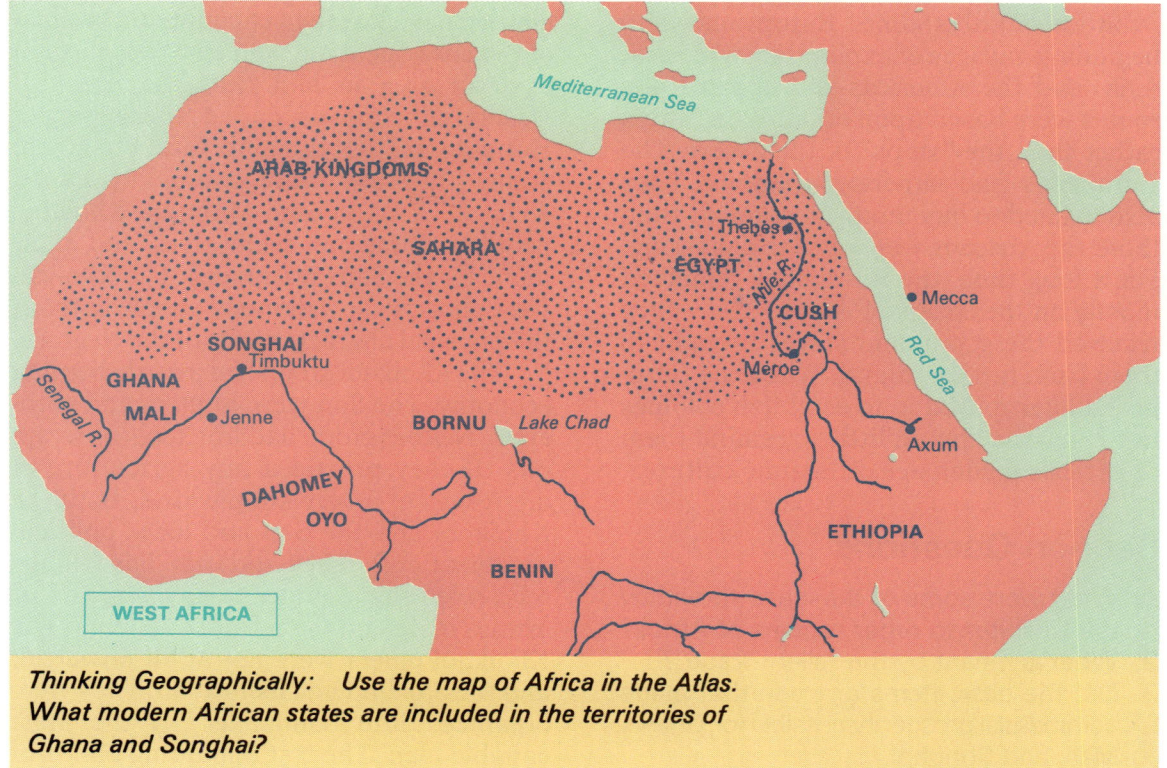

Thinking Geographically: Use the map of Africa in the Atlas. What modern African states are included in the territories of Ghana and Songhai?

Mecca to show that he intended to defend the laws of the Muslim faith.

Muhammad Askia was an effective king. He restored peace and made the trade routes safe again. He encouraged judges to convict officials who charged illegal taxes. Scholars were encouraged to recreate a great education center at Timbuktu. Muhammad Askia's own wealth supported a court of doctors, judges, Muslim priests, and professors.

Only sixty years after the death of Muhammad Askia, the empire of Songhai fell. The Songhai army was attacked by the army of a Moroccan king who wanted to control the Sahara caravan trade. According to one account, the Songhai army numbered 18,000 warriors on horseback and 9,700 foot soldiers armed with bows and arrows, spears, swords, and clubs. It was totally defeated.

The much smaller Moroccan forces were made up in part of well-paid Turks, Portuguese (por chuh GEEZ), and Spaniards. The Moroccans had armed 2,000 soldiers with an early type of portable gun called an *harquebus*. Five hundred gunfighters were on horseback, and some carried muskets. The report says that the Songhai warriors were so terrified of the strange noise and smoke of the guns that they fled in all directions.

Most of the Songhai empire was made up of separate kingdoms united into one empire. When Muhammad Askia was defeated, these kingdoms became independent almost immediately.

The sultan of Morocco and his successors did not establish a system of government to replace the Songhai federal system. They did not support religion and learning. Soldiers looted the Songhai cities.

At about this time, Europeans were beginning voyages of exploration to Africa, Asia, and the Americas. European trade routes were based upon ocean-going ships rather than the "ships" of the desert. The Europeans had superior weapons. They also wanted to buy many more goods than those the Africans were used to delivering. For a long time, the Europeans remained mostly on the coasts of Africa. There they received the goods and slaves brought to them from farther inland. When the Europeans later moved in to establish colonies in Africa, they found little to remind them of Africa's golden age of Islamic culture.

Section Questions

1. What were some of the ideas spread by the Cushites to other regions of Africa?
2. What is meant by the "silent trade"?
3. List the basic items of trade that made commercial prosperity possible for Ghana, Mali, and Songhai.
4. In what ways did Mansu Musa, Sundiata, and Muhammad Askia strengthen their empires?
5. What are some techniques used by Mansa Musa, Sundiata, Sunni Ali, and Muhammad Askia to keep local kingdoms in their empires loyal?
6. What technology destroyed the great Songhai empire?

3. Peoples in the Interior Developed Differently

The African groups of the interior, whose histories are being traced by anthropologists today, are named for the languages they developed.

The Khoisan The first groups known to have lived in much of eastern and southern Africa spoke related languages that included click sounds. When Europeans arrived in southern Africa, they encountered the last of the click-speaking peoples. They lived in a small area in and near the Kalahari Desert. Europeans called these people Hottentots (HAH tun tahtz) and Bushmen. Today they are more commonly called Khoisan (KAW ih sahn), from the Khoikhoi people's name for themselves and their name for the San (Bushmen). The Khoisan were short, yellow-skinned people without the physical characteristics of the Negroes.

The Khoikhoi group had a cattle-herding economy. The San were hunters and gatherers. Neither group had iron tools or weapons. If they practiced any agriculture at all, it was of a very simple kind. Both the Khoikhoi and the San had loose political organizations. They did not have kings who ruled them, states to pay taxes to, or armies to defend them from outsiders. The Khoikhoi chiefs were not at all powerful, and the San had no chiefs at all. They were organized into bands, led by the most capable men. The last remaining bands of the San, or Bushmen, exist today in the Kalahari Desert.

The Bantu Linguists can trace the origins and migrations of the peoples who pushed the primitive Khoisans out of their original lands. Linguists call the later inhabitants the Bantu (BAN too). Bantu is the parent language of most of the black peoples in Africa south of the Sahara. The Bantu people differ widely from region to region in body structure and size, in culture, and in social organization. However, they all speak related languages. One interesting form that all Bantu languages have is the way they make words plural. English speakers usually add an *s* or change the ending of a word, such as "woman" to "women." Bantu speakers change the beginnings of words. Thus, in Bantu languages, uMUntu means "person," and aBAntu means "people." (This is the origin of the name for the people called Bantu.)

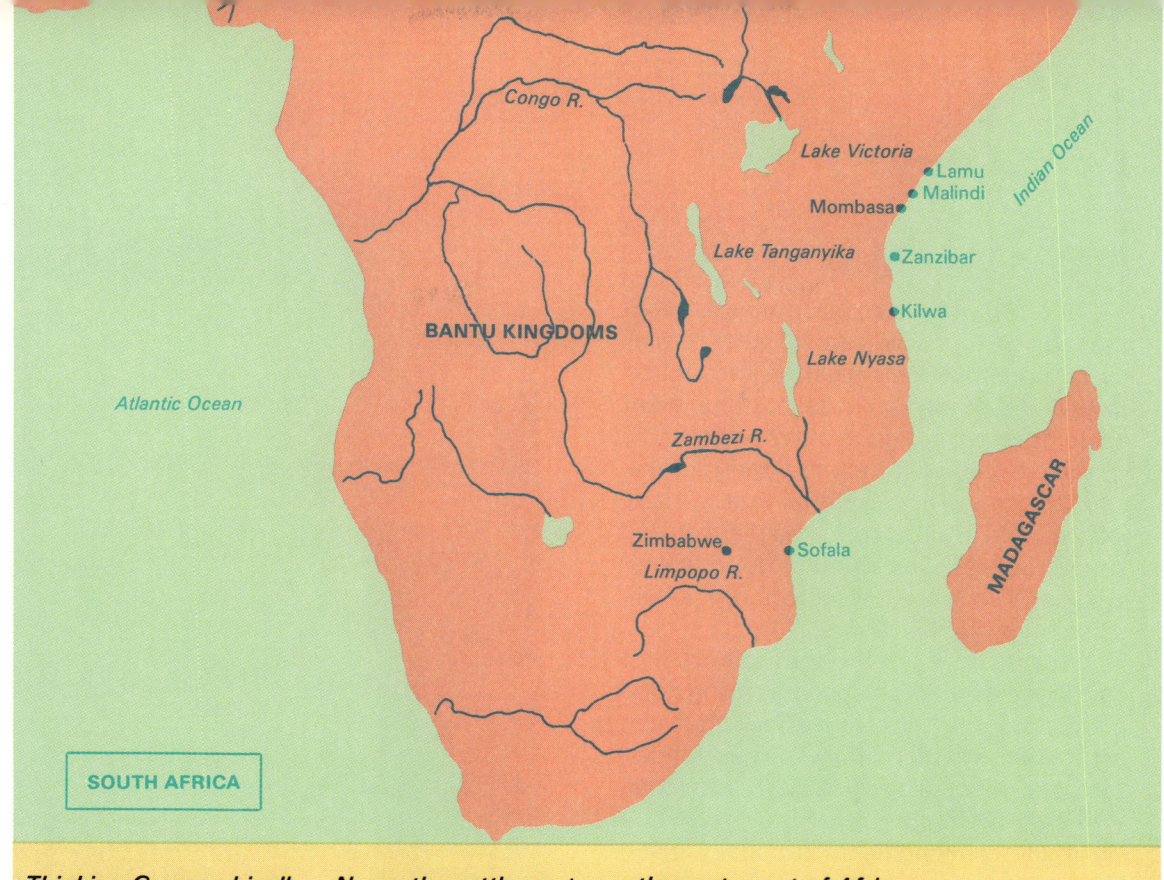

Thinking Geographically: Name the settlements on the east coast of Africa.

Today the Bantu peoples live in about one-third of the African continent, below the equator. When the Bantu population began expanding, many people moved outward from what is now Nigeria and the Cameroons (kam uh ROONZ) or from the upper reaches of the Congo River. Historians are still arguing Bantu origins. Probably the Bantu population grew rapidly because the knowledge of ironworking made them such successful farmers. Also, iron-tipped weapons made them militarily superior to the Khoisans. Most historians now believe that the Bantu learned the secret of ironworking from survivors of the fallen Cushite kingdom of Meroe.

There is also strong evidence that the Bantu already had crops from what is now Malaysia (muh LAY zhee uh). Bananas, yams, oil palm, and other products enabled them to exist profitably in the forest. Cereal crops such as millet and sorghum enabled the Bantu to expand into the veld, or southern savanna. Wherever they practiced agriculture, the Bantu borrowed heavily from the people of the earlier Cushite kingdom.

The cultivation of certain cereal crops is not the only custom borrowed from Meroe. The original Bantu from the rain forest did not have a complex political structure. Land was plentiful, and the Bantu had no property to protect. No early Bantu chief was strong enough to force the neighbor chiefdoms to unite. By the time the Bantu had expanded deeply into the savanna, however, many Bantu groups lived as members of highly complex states. By that

Did You Know?

African Steel Mills

One of the hardest and strongest metals that can be manufactured is steel. Wherever huge steel mills exist, in the United States and other industrial nations, giant cities have grown up around them.

These mills with their towering smokestacks turn out the material that is made into trucks, trains, ships, airplanes, and space rockets. Skyscrapers are made of steel, and so are the elevators that whisk us to their highest floors.

Europeans were thought to have first developed the technology for making good quality steel. It takes a furnace that can create the very high temperatures needed to make steel from iron ore and coal. Wilhelm Siemens (1823 to 1883), a German-born engineer, is usually given the credit for designing such a furnace. Recently, however, thirteen steel-making furnaces were discovered in Africa on the shores of Lake Victoria. These furnaces are between 1,500 and 2,000 years old. Africans must have had the technology for making steel tools sometime before A.D. 400.

The ancient African steel furnaces were cone-shaped. Each was about 1.5 meters (5 feet) high. They were made of mud, and each of them had eight hard-clay pipes rising from the bottom. Workers would build a fire with charcoal and blow warm air into a furnace through the pipes to make the fire very hot. They would add iron ore and charred swamp grass. (In modern times, we use coal instead of grass for carbon.) Then the workers would force more air into the furnace. When the temperature inside reached 1,800°C (3,275°F), the molten iron and carbon combined to make steel. Later, African artisans heated the steel again and shaped it into tools.

Historians are not entirely certain how the steel-smelting technology was learned and later lost to the culture of these inventive African people.

These ruins are from the Cushite kingdom. The Cushites probably spread the skill of ironmaking to other parts of Africa.

time, also, many Bantu accepted the idea of divine kingship. That is, they did not elect the kings who ruled over them, and they believed those kings to be gods.

Nilote Expansion Several groups of people speaking Nilotic (ni LAH tik) languages lived north of the equator above the rain forest barrier. From about 1350 on, a series of them moved south and east into areas populated by the Bantu. The Nilotic people were greatly outnumbered by the Bantu. They soon dominated the Bantu, however, because of their political organization and their military power. The Nilotes had developed these strengths in order to protect cattle and grasslands from raiders. They also used their power to capture pasture lands from rival states. Their own surplus population had created the need for more grazing land for their herds.

The Nilotes dominated the agricultural Bantu by adding the small Bantu chiefdoms to their states. Some of the recent independent nations of Africa bear the names of these Nilotic states. Uganda (yoo GAN duh), Rwanda (ru AHN duh), and Burundi (bu ROON dee) are three examples.

The Bantu remained second-class citizens under the domination of the Nilotes until very recently. But they have, in a sense, dominated the Nilotes. Except for a few remaining Nilotic groups, such as the tall, cattle-herding Masai (mah SI) warriors of the plains, the Bantu absorbed the Nilotic minority. They took the customs and the technology they could use and added it to their Bantu culture.

Zimbabwe Farther to the south, in what is today the modern state of Zimbabwe (zihm BAHB wee), a Bantu people did form a state of their own. The people were called the Shona (SHO nuh). They had originally migrated from the Congo basin. By 1400, a group of Shona *clans* (communities of people related to each other) dominated what is now southern Zimbabwe. They were organized under the chief of the strongest clan who ruled with the support of the high priest of their religion.

At least 200 years earlier, Muslim traders had settled on the east coast of Africa. There they built a thriving Islamic culture. These Arabs operated trading posts throughout the region. Through these agents, the Bantu exchanged gold, ivory, and copper for salt, cloth, beads, porcelain, and glassware from northern Africa, the Middle East, India, China, and Southeast Asia.

About 1440, the Arabs had an unusual opportunity to extend their trading network. The Bantu king Mutota (moo TO tuh) had begun a major military campaign. He wanted to control a large region of southeast Africa. The king paid his soldiers with cloth bought from traders. He invited the Arabs to set up trading posts as the army advanced into the interior. Less than 200 years later, the Portuguese found it easier to occupy these Bantu regions because Arabs had gone there before them.

The Arabs had built a Muslim culture among the Bantu. Bantu languages spoken in east Africa became heavily influenced by Arabic. Even some of the languages of the Asian traders influenced Bantu speech. A new language began to develop. That language is called Swahili (swah HEE lee). It is spoken by most people in east Africa today.

After Mutota died, his son Matope (muh TOW peh) continued military conquest of the southern African interior. But, as with other empires before his, shortly after Matope died the empire broke into pieces. Matope had placed relatives and Rowzi chiefs in control of conquered areas. After his death, they fought for control of the empire. This conflict helped the Portuguese in the late 1500s because it made the provinces weak and disunited. By 1628, the Portuguese had replaced the Arab traders and dominated the entire region.

The ruins of a walled compound in Zimbabwe.

The Kongo Along the west coast of Africa, where the Congo River empties into the Atlantic Ocean, a different group of Bantu lived. In fact, the Bantu language group may have originated very near this area. Historians believe that the Bantu were surrounded at first by tribes of non-Negro hunters and gatherers called Pygmies. Soon the agricultural Bantu dominated the region. The group who occupied the coastline at the Congo River's mouth were called the Kongo. The Kongo possessed the skills of ironworking and were powerful as hunters and warriors, as well as farmers.

The Kongo people received a visit from Europeans in 1482. The country of Portugal was eager to expand its trading empire and to spread the Christian religion. By 1490, Portuguese missionaries were living in the kingdom of the Kongo. Within a year they had converted a Kongo prince. After his conversion, he used the name of his baptism, Alfonso. In 1507, Alfonso became king of the Kongo.

Alfonso sent for Portuguese priests, teachers, carpenters, and masons. He believed they had skills to improve the lives of his people. Alfonso also sent many young Kongolese to Portugal to be educated. He paid for these improvements by raiding neighboring Bantu chiefdoms, capturing their warriors, and selling them as slaves to the Portuguese.

The Portuguese, in the meantime, had established a colony in Brazil. Alfonso was called upon to step up his supply of captured warriors. But to capture as many slaves as the traders wanted would have taken an army far greater than Alfonso could provide. The army would have had to travel far to find that many villages to raid. Too late, Alfonso tried to limit the trade in slaves. The Portuguese moved into his kingdom, made war in his name, and soon made enemies of every group in the Kongo. In 1660, the Kongo declared war on the Portuguese. The Europeans won, and the Kongo kingdom was soon reduced to a few villages.

Section Questions

1. What three language groups are represented by the peoples described in Section 3?
2. What technology enabled the Bantu people to spread over so many different regions of Africa? From what culture do historians think the Bantu learned these skills?
3. Why were the Nilotic peoples able to dominate the Bantu?
4. What caused the breakup of the Zimbabwe empire?
5. How did the Portuguese win control of the eastern and western coasts of Africa south of the equator?
6. Why do you think the Kongo ruler was unable to limit the slave trade?

4. African People Developed Unique Cultures

Africa's people have spread across the continent from many different homelands. Africans' skin colors, hair textures, body structures, facial features, and languages differ widely from region to region. It is not possible to make many general statements that would be true for all the peoples of Africa.

But throughout African history, one thing has been true for almost every African group. It has been true for people smelting iron in Cush, packing camels in Mali, digging yams in the rain forest, planting sorghum in the savanna, and tending cattle in the sudan. Their social organiza-

This ivory mask was worn on the belt of a ruler. It is probably from Benin.

tion was built upon the foundation of family. Africans might have lived in mud hut villages in a tiny chiefdom or in brick cities ruled by a king. Their ultimate loyalty, however, was to their family relatives.

Lineage The key to understanding the African family structure is to understand the importance of *lineage*. A lineage consists of all people who can trace their descent to a common ancestor. In most African societies, individuals traced their descent through the father's family. These societies are called *patrilineal*. Societies that trace descent through the mother's side are called *matrilineal*. An African's family tree contained only the one direct line, a patrilineal line or a matrilineal line. Most

275

societies in Europe and America today do not place much importance on knowing one's ancestry beyond a few generations. But those who draw a family tree track the lines from both parents. Thus their societies are *bilateral* ones.

Lineage membership meant both security and responsibility for an African. A lineage was responsible for the welfare of its members. If a family's crops should fail, other relatives of the father or the mother would help the family make a new start. They might share their harvest or give gifts of cattle and tools. A lineage also sent warriors to defend relatives from outside enemies.

Africans defined the word "family" differently from the way Europeans did. This is because Africans practiced polygyny. African men could marry more than one woman. They usually married as many as they could afford to house and support. Most husbands provided separate homes for each wife and their children. All lived in the same *compound* (a fenced-in group of dwellings) in the large village. A typical family would consist of one husband, several wives, their unmarried daughters, and all the sons and their wives and children. African wives may not always have enjoyed sharing one husband. But they were usually happy to have the help of the other wives in preparing food and farming the land. They were also used to having many people around to talk with.

Polygyny was practiced everywhere in Africa because it was important to have many children. Children increased the power of a lineage. They provided more workers and more soldiers. It was expected that a woman would marry as soon as she could care for a child. This usually meant that girls married around the age of thirteen.

A lineage was also responsible for arranging the payment of *bridewealth*. In Europe, brides usually brought gifts of money, land, or other possessions to their new husbands. This payment was called a dowry. In Africa, the husband's family paid cattle, weapons, pieces of iron, or other goods to the family of his new wife. This bridewealth payment proved the husband's ability to care for his wife and their children. It also showed his understanding that the bride's family was losing a valuable member.

There was another kinship level above the lineage. This was the clan. A clan is all of the people who believe they are descended from a common ancestor. But they can no longer trace the lines of descent. Often clan members shared a common name. They also shared a set of rituals, a *totem* (clan symbol), and the rules of behavior expected of the members of that clan.

Community Life African children grew up quickly. They were not separated from adults in work or games. However, they were expected to remain quiet during meetings and storytelling sessions. In these sessions, children learned their lineage history and its obligations. The stories were often acted and sometimes sung. By twelve or thirteen, girls had learned to farm and prepare meals and boys had learned to hunt and tend cattle. Both girls and boys were expected to care for younger children. Boys usually did not marry at thirteen. They had to prove first that they were able to assume responsibility for a family.

The size of a community determined what work African men could choose to do. Larger villages having many food producers could support a division of labor, at least part time. They typically had artists, jewelry makers, priests, traders, and tax collectors. Those Islamic societies that developed complex states and trade empires prepared young people for careers as professors, camel drivers, and bricklayers, to name a few. Some societies supported toolmakers, fishers, sculptors, and slavecatchers.

In modern-day Africa, workers tend vineyards.

Political Organization In a patrilineal society, every lineage group was headed by the eldest male descendant of the eldest male ancestor. In a matrilineal society, the eldest brother of the first born daughter ruled. Even in matrilineal societies, women did not hold the title of ruler. Members of a lineage usually lived in the same village or nearby villages. But women members did not. They lived with their husband's people.

Usually several lineages joined together to strengthen their defense against attack. They united also to increase the number of food providers and to make available to their children a supply of future wives and husbands. The most powerful lineage would provide the ruler for this chiefdom. If two lineages were equal in power, their chiefs shared the ruling position between them. The ruler of a chiefdom acted as a judge in disputes among the people. He organized the army and called upon men to serve in it. He distributed the land among families to use for growing crops or grazing cattle. No African actually owned the land. A family was granted only the right to use it temporarily. The chief acted as priest or supported priests to practice the rituals necessary for good harvests and safety from enemies. The people paid tribute to the chief in food, cattle, craft goods, and in labor. When the chief needed soldiers or builders, he called upon donations of men. The payment in goods supported the chief, his advisers, and the priests.

Chiefdoms were the most typical political structure in Africa. When the population expanded and a chief became more powerful, his relatives and the heads of some of the smaller lineages in the chiefdom shared power as his *council of elders*. They could not make final decisions, but they spoke for their people. A group of chiefdoms that joined together by choice or by conquest became a kingdom. A group of kingdoms became an empire. But the loyalty of the people was to their lineage head. They always belonged first of all to their chiefdom.

A chief could not rule for long without the respect of those he governed. Proof of this is the fate of the states of Mali, Zimbabwe, and the Kongo. Their histories show how African empires fell apart whenever kings became weak or failed to reward chiefs by keeping them in office as governors of their own people.

Religion Most African groups shared a number of common religious beliefs. Africans often treated their king as if he were a god. But it would be more accurate to say that most African groups believed the office of chief or king was god-given. Often the king could not actually sit upon the royal throne. This chair or stool remained empty. The king's duty was to guard it. The chair was the symbol of an office that he could hold only so long as he followed the rules of good leadership.

Africans believed that family members who died went to live in the world of their god or gods. Because the ancestors now lived nearer to the gods, they could deliver messages more easily. Africans called upon their ancestors in prayers and ceremonies. They asked for good harvests, relief from epidemics of sickness, or help in overcoming enemy attacks. Most appeals were sent to ancestors who had died recently. It was felt that these ancestors would remember living relatives and care more about their welfare. Individuals might send messages about a sick child or their hope to give birth to a healthy baby. Prayers from an entire community or chiefdom were sent during great festivals. Hundreds of people

Women spectators at a Dama festival, a masked dance of the Dogon tribe.

danced to music and joined in storytelling dramas and pageants. They brought offerings to the god and the lineage ancestors.

The Arts of Africa The ceremonies of religious festivals were an important artistic expression for a people who, for the most part, had no written language. Storytelling developed into the highest form of theater. Performers acted out tales of ancient deeds and conquests. The audience contributed by singing, dancing, and cheering. African dancing and African music developed together into very complicated forms. African music combines many different rhythms. The rhythms are played against each other at the same time. Africans dancing to such

An ancient Ife head made of terracotta.

music may move their feet in time to one beat, their body to another, their arms to another, and their heads in time to yet a different rhythm.

Much of early African art has been lost because it was crafted in wood. Wood eventually rots and is attacked by termites. Festival rituals required carved statues and sculptured animal forms. Plays and dances required masks. Ceremonial meals required special bowls with certain designs. Dancers required drums, flutes, banjos, and other musical instruments. Because wet climates and insects quickly destroyed these between festivals, Africans copied them again and again over the centuries. This is how historians know what the early art forms looked like.

The best-known African art form is its sculpture. The Ife (EE fay), who lived in present-day Nigeria, sculpted outstanding bronze heads with the *lost-wax method*. Ife artists began by delicately sculpting a wax figure. They then covered the figure with a clay that bakes very hard. When the pieces were heated (fired), the wax melted and drained out through straws. Molten bronze was then poured to replace the wax. After cooling, the clay was cracked, and the original wax figure appeared in bronze. The Ife created their magnificent sculptures around A.D. 1200.

The Bini (buh NEE) group of Benin (buh NIHN) from the Lake Chad region sculpted bronze heads and wall plaques. They used them in religious ceremonies. The art of the Bini was at its height when the Europeans arrived at their inland kingdom. Soon their bronze plaques were showing Portuguese in armor, carrying harquebuses and crossbows.

African art has had enormous impact on the arts of Europe and the Americas. Fabric designers, potters, music composers, dancers, and other artists are continually rediscovering Africa's artistic heritage. Some say that modern art owes a great deal to Picasso's visit to a Paris museum collection of African carvings in 1907.

Section Questions

1. How does a lineage group differ from a clan? Why were lineage groups important in Africa?
2. How did African children learn the history of their people?
3. How did African children learn the skills they would need as adults?
4. Why were African ancestors called upon in prayers and ceremonies?
5. What roles did music, dance, drama, and wood carvings play in African religious ceremonies?

LEGACY OF ANCIENT/MEDIEVAL AFRICA

Social institutions: Social organization built upon the family

Government: Usually chiefdoms

Technology: Steel-smelting technology developed but lost

Arts: African music, dancing, and sculpture developed unique, complex forms

Commerce: Extensive trade with Asia and Mediterranean areas

Chapter Summary

1. The geography of Africa has made communication between peoples difficult. Much of Africa is on a plateau, so that rivers suddenly drop in moving toward the sea. The resulting waterfalls and rapids make the rivers unsuitable for travel. The thick rain forests near the equator and the deserts in the north and south, particularly the Sahara, were extremely hard to cross.

Study of Africa prehistory had led many scientists to believe that the earliest human-like creatures developed in Africa. Artifacts show that early Africans traded with other countries.

2. The Cushite society conquered Egypt in about 800 B.C., but moved south after the Babylonians destroyed their capital. Their new capital, Meroe, became one of the largest iron-producing areas in the world as well as a trading center. The Cushites developed a written language that has not been deciphered.

Ghana developed an extensive trading system, based on salt and gold. Ghana was conquered in 1076 by Muslim reformers. Several kingdoms arose in Ghana's place. Mali became a strong empire, led by Sundiata, and later by Mansa Musa. After Mansa Musa's rule ended, Mali became weak, and the empire of Songhai became strong. When Songhai's leader, Muhammad Askia, was defeated, Songhai broke up into small kingdoms.

3. The first groups known to have lived in eastern and southern Africa spoke a click language. Today's Khoikhoi and Bushmen are members of the click-speaking peoples.

The Bantu people inhabited most of Africa south of the Sahara. About 1350, several groups of Nilotic-language-speaking peoples began moving from north of the equator into Bantu territory and soon dominated the area. Further south, in what is now Zimbabwe, a Bantu people called the Shona dominated the area. Working through Arab trading posts, the Bantu exchanged goods with other nations. The Kongo group of Bantu lived on the west coast of Africa, at the mouth of the Congo River. In 1507, Alfonso of the Kongo set up a slave trade with the Portuguese. By 1660, the Kongo lost a war with the Portuguese and the Kongo kingdom faded away.

4. Almost every African group built their social organization around the family. Lineage membership meant both support and responsibility for an African. Several lineages might join together. This group was a chiefdom. The ruler was chosen from the strongest lineage. A group of chiefdoms formed a kingdom, and a group of kingdoms formed an empire. Africans believed that family members who died went to live with their god or gods. They called upon the deceased to speak to the gods on their behalf.

Storytelling, music, and dance were important in African religious ceremonies. Early wooden art has been lost to decay, but has been copied for generations, so we know what it was like. The Ife produced magnificent bronze sculptures through the lost-wax method.

Chapter 15 Review

Check Your Facts

1. Use each of the following names or terms in a sentence about Africa:
   a. Mansa Musa   d. Nilotic
   b. Bantu   e. Swahili
   c. Khoisan   f. Sundiata
2. What was the basis for the wealth of Ghana, Mali, and Songhai? What else did these states have in common?
3. What different things did the Bantu learn or borrow from the Cushites?
4. To whom did most Africans owe their ultimate loyalty? How was that loyalty rewarded?

Words to Know

1. Explain the difference between the following pairs of terms:
   a. silent trade/caravan trade
   b. chiefdom/kingdom
   c. patrilineal/matrilineal
   d. coastal plain/plateau
   e. sahel/savanna
   f. iron/steel
2. How did the king of Ghana have a *monopoly* on most of the gold in Ghana?

Developing Your Skills

1. Read about the four major river systems of Africa. What are the barriers to navigation? How might these become advantages to African nations that want to develop industries?
2. Describe the "mirror images" of Africa. What imaginary line separates them?
3. What is the Sahara? How has it changed in the past 65,000 years? Why?

Thinking It Over

1. African empires remained strong only as long as a strong leader was in power. Why did this happen? Why does a nation like the United States retain its strength even though its leader dies in office or is replaced by a new leader?
2. The African nation that until recently was called Rhodesia was named for an Englishman, Cecil Rhodes. Why is this nation now called Zimbabwe? Why do you think most Africans would prefer its new name?

Special Activities

1. Sleeping sickness (*trypanosomiasis*) is a disease that is spread by insects. In Africa, it is spread by the tsetse fly. Read more about this disease. Why is it called sleeping sickness? Where else does the disease exist? Outline on a map the area in Africa where the tsetse fly is found and describe the geography of this part of the continent. Find out what modern nations (and the United Nations) and their health agencies are doing to prevent this disease.
2. Visit a museum or study a book of photographs that features African art in pottery and wood carving. Write a report that attempts to answer the question: "Why do modern artists and art collectors find African art interesting and meaningful?"
3. Write a diary entry of your visit to one of the following kingdoms during the height of its power: Cush, Ghana, Kongo, Zimbabwe.

A golden Sikh temple in Amritsar, India.

Chapter 16 Asia

"Before we had decided the problem it was already 7 P.M. and the east wind was blowing fiercely, and the waves were raging high. The ship was suddenly dashed up onto a *shoal* (sandbar). In trepidation we immediately lowered sail. But the corners of the rudder snapped in two places, while the waves from both east and west battered the ship and rolled it back and forth.... The men were desperate. All from the head of the mission down to the sailors stripped and bound their loin cloths fast about them. Since the ship was about to break in the middle, we rushed to the stern and bow.

500–1368	
500–700	Turkic empire
587	Prince Shotoku begins rule
618–766	Tang dynasty
794–1185	Feudal period in Japan
960	Song dynasty begins
971	Muslim raids in India begin
1069	Wang Anshi becomes prime minister
1160–1227	Genghis Khan
1185–1333	Kamakura period in Japan
1206–1526	Delhi sultanate in India
1211–1368	Mongol empire
1276	Yuan dynasty begins
1368	Ming dynasty begins

Genghis Khan.

Each of us looked for a place that remained intact. Because of the shock of the waves the structural joints of the ship were all falling apart...."

These words were written by a Japanese Buddhist monk. The year was 838. The monk was on a ship going from Japan to China. He knew how dangerous this trip was because he had tried to make this crossing twice before. Each time his ship had been turned back by similar storms.

Why did Japanese people leave their island and risk such a hazardous journey? What did they expect to learn in China that was so important?

As in the lands of Islam, regional unity in Asia increased during the period you are about to study. In India, Muslim domination united much of the subcontinent for about 400 years. A golden age in China, the Tang dynasty, made China an even stronger magnet for the societies existing around it. Through conquest, trade, and example, its influence spread to the north and west, to Southeast Asia, and to Korea and Japan. This had an enormous impact on the development of that important crescent of islands in the Pacific.

Then in the thirteenth century, Mongol conquests brought together the largest empire the world had yet seen. The *Book of Marco Polo*, which documented the wealth of this great empire, made Europeans aware of the splendor of the East.

1. Muslims and Hindus Influenced Each Other

For hundreds of years, Arab traders had come to India for spices, cloth, and rare gems. By Muhammad's time, a large colony had settled on the southwestern tip of India. They converted to Islam and lived peacefully—buying, selling, and worshiping as they pleased.

However, not all Indian kings treated them well. The ruler of Sind allowed pirates to plunder their ships. Umayyad rulers in Iraq tried twice to punish the Sindhi ruler but failed. A third army was put together in 711 under the command of Muhammad ibn-Qasim (KAH sihm), a youth of only 17 years. The army had a 12,000-horse-and-camel cavalry, a supply train of 3,000 camels, and some of the best soldiers in the Arab empire. Muhammad ibn-Qasim easily defeated and killed the Sindhi king, captured his cities, and married his widow. His conquests raised a question Muslims would face for 1,000 years: How should they, a small group, govern their subjects, who believed in a religion the Muslims considered false?

Muhammad ibn-Qasim's solution was one that most Muslim kings would choose. His invasion was not a "holy war" against unbelievers. Once they submitted, he protected the Hindus and taxed them lightly. He let them build their temples and worship their gods. He also used many Hindus in his government, although the highest posts went to Muslims. In this way, he tried to gain his subjects' cooperation. Thus began a long period in which Islam and Hinduism had a powerful influence on each other.

Muslim Conquest of North India The invasion of Sind did not lead to more Arab conquests. For the next 200 years, Sind was important mainly as a bridge between the Islamic and Indian worlds. Indian astronomy and mathematics influenced the scientists of Baghdad and Damascus. Indian physicians were called to the court of the caliphs. Some of the tales of the *Arabian Nights* are believed to have come from Indian stories. The main impact of Islam on India in this period was made by peaceful Arab merchants who spread the ideas of Islam.

By the year 1000, Muslim attacks on India began again. These were led by Muslim Turks from central Asia rather than by Arabs. One Turkish dynasty gained control of Afghanistan. From there, Sultan Mahmud (ma MOOD, 971 to 1030) led seventeen raids into northwest India. Mahmud called himself the sword of Islam. He boasted of killing nonbelievers by the thousands, smashing idols, and destroying temples. He may have acted out of religious feeling, but he was also attracted by India's wealth. In one famous temple raid, he carried off huge amounts of gold, silver, gems, cloth, and grain. It was 150 years after Mahmud's death that his dynasty was overthrown by Muhammad of Ghor (GAWR).

Ghor began as a small Turkish kingdom in the hilly central part of Afghanistan. But Sultan Muhammad turned it into a large empire. After slowly conquering the Punjab and Sind, he defeated the most powerful king of north India in 1192. Within ten years, his generals overran the other Hindu kingdoms of north India.

The speed of the Muslim conquests did not mean that they were easy. Indians resisted fiercely and won many battles. In the end, however, the generals of Ghor were better than their opponents. Their central Asian horses were superior to those of the Indians. With a fast cavalry, they could outmaneuver the elephants on which the Indians relied. Also, the Hindu kings never united against the Muslims. So the Muslims defeated them one by one.

The Delhi Sultanate At first, the Muslims felt they were part of a larger empire centered in central Asia. In 1206, Sultan Muhammad was killed. His successors were too weak to keep his empire together. Soon after, the Mongols under Genghis Khan (jen gus KAHN) burst into central Asia. They destroyed entire cities in a once-great area of learning. India's Muslim conquerors were cut off from their former homelands. Thousands of central Asians—nobles, soldiers, scholars, artisans, and villagers—fled to India.

After Sultan Muhammad was killed, his main general established the sultanate of Delhi. More than thirty sultans succeeded him before the sultanate fell in 1526. Many sultans were killed, and the dynasties changed five times. The land under the sultanate varied from one ruler to the next. Under strong sultans, it controlled all of north India. Under a few very able rulers, it even expanded into the south. When the sultan was weak, many areas broke away and powerful nobles ruled.

In the 1200s, the sultans concentrated on building a strong government in north India. Through skillful diplomacy and a strong defense, they kept the Mongols out. They crushed rebellions by Hindu princes and reduced the power of Muslim nobles. They also set the stage for a strong administrative system.

One sultan, Raziya (ra ZEE yuh), was a woman. An observer wrote this about Raziya: "She was endowed with all the qualities befitting a king, but she was not born of the right sex and so, in the estimation of men, all these virtues were worthless." Muslim women were expected to stay home with the family. Outdoors, they hid behind veils. Thus, Raziya acted improperly. She was quickly overthrown and later killed.

In 1296, the sultanate's armies crossed into the south. Under Ala-ud-din Khilji (kihl JEE), who ruled from 1296 to 1316, its armies almost reached India's southern tip. Ala-ud-din let the kings he defeated rule in his name.

The beautiful Qutab Minar tower in Delhi, India.

Ala-ud-din strictly controlled his nobles. To keep them from plotting against him, he had spies report on their activities. He taxed them heavily, regulated their marriages, and did not allow social gatherings or the drinking of alcohol. On the other hand, he was fair with the common people. He tried to control the price of food and other necessities. He also reformed the tax system. Instead of squeezing as much as he could from peasants, he had his officers measure their fields and take only a fixed percentage of their crops. The weak rulers after Ala-ud-din discarded this system. They went back to giving land grants to nobles in return for the promise of revenue and troops. In the confusion that followed Ala-ud-din's death, the south regained its independence.

This statue of Tamerlane shows him in battle armor.

In 1398, the sultans faced a powerful enemy from the northwest. Their capital, Delhi, was sacked by another Mongol leader, Tamerlane (TAM ur layn), and the sultanate never recovered. In 1526, it was overthrown by Tamerlane's great-great-grandson, Baber (BAH bur), who founded the Mogul (mo GUL) empire.

Hindus Under Muslim Rule The sultanate was ruled by Muslims, but most subjects were Hindus. Sultans did at times persecute Hindus. Some forced Hindus to pay a special tax. Others tore down temples and killed Hindus. These rulers, however, were exceptions. The government felt that the worst sin Hindus could commit was rebellion, not idol worship. As long as they obeyed the law, most sultans let Hindus live their own way.

Since there were few Muslims, they needed Hindu help to rule India. Great tracts of land often remained under Hindu princes, who paid tribute to the Delhi sultan. All the sultans used Hindu officials as tax collectors, accountants, record keepers, and clerks. A few Hindus became generals and governors of provinces.

In the countryside, where most Indians lived, people rarely, if ever, saw a government officer. Hindu villagers were organized into castes. Each caste had a ruling council to keep its members in line. These councils enforced rules about marriage, work, eating habits, and other aspects of daily life. When members broke the rules, the council fined them or had them beaten. For more serious violations, it would banish the offenders and their families from the caste.

Most villages were dominated by one caste whose members owned most of the land. The dominant caste left the affairs of the other castes to their councils. But it settled conflicts between castes and punished criminals. Its council also collected taxes for the sultan. It represented the village whenever it had any business with government officials.

Hinduism and Islam Although forced conversion was rare, the Muslim population in India grew steadily under the sultanate. Some Muslim immigrants came from Persia and central Asia. Most new Muslims, however, were Indians who chose to accept Islam. Some high-caste Hindus converted in hopes of receiving government jobs. Many more were untouchables who saw in Islam the chance to improve their lives.

Under the challenge of Islam, attempts were made to strengthen Hinduism. Some Hindus, deeply moved by Islam, tried to unite the best of the two religions. The most successful was Guru Nanak (NAH nuk, 1469 to 1539), who founded the Sikh (SEEK) religion. Others were hostile to Islam. They tried to purify Hinduism and give it new energy to resist foreign influences.

Indo-Muslim Culture India's Muslims and Hindus influenced more than each other's religious beliefs. They also borrowed customs. Muslims, for example, wore turbans and jewelry in the Hindu style. They seasoned their food with Indian spices. They enjoyed Indian games, such as chess and backgammon. Many high-caste Hindus dressed in Muslim trousers and jackets. They adopted the Islamic custom of strictly separating women from all men except those in their immediate family.

Many gifted writers added to a rich literature in Persian, the court language of the sultanate. The greatest was Amir Khusrau (kah SROW, 1253 to 1325) who is said to have written ninety-nine books on everything from history to music to poetry. He is also believed to have been the first to write in Urdu. The Urdu language developed as a means of communication between common Indians and foreign Muslims. At first, it combined elements of Persian and Arabic with Hindi, the main north Indian language, in an ungrammatical way. Muslims in the south began to write in Urdu in the fourteenth century. From there, the written form gradually spread to the north. It ended up replacing Persian as the literary language of Indian Muslims.

Important works were also written in India's many regional languages. In the arts, new styles of music and dance developed. Muslim kings ordered many fine mosques, tombs, and palaces built. These combined Islamic style with many Hindu elements.

Section Questions

1. Who was Ala-ud-din? How did his treatment of the nobles differ from the way most other sultans treated them? Why were sultans so concerned about Hindu princes and Muslim nobles?
2. What impact did the Mongols have on the Delhi sultanate?
3. How did the sultans in Delhi treat the Hindus in their territory?
4. List three influences of Indian culture on Islam and three ways in which Muslims influenced Hindus.

2. Mongols Ruled an Enormous Empire

The Great Wall of China zigzags along China's northern Mongolian border. Beyond the wall and the Gobi Desert, there lived for many centuries China's most feared enemy.

They were cattle herders who lived in felt tents, or *yurts*, which they moved as needed to find good pastures. Mounted on strong shaggy ponies, they roamed the grassy plain, or *steppe*. The steppe stretched across southern Russia, from Manchuria in Asia to Hungary in eastern Europe. Like the early Arab tribes, these nomadic herders recognized no state borders. Their loyalty was to the family and tribe. Their animals provided transportation, clothing, food, and felt for tents. They traded horses and skins to townspeople for grain, weapons, and luxuries. The nomads' joy was hunting and warfare. They considered the settled people fair targets for plunder.

Turkish was the most common language on the steppe, followed by Mongol and Tungus (TUN goos) in the east. Despite common languages and life-styles, there was little unity among tribes. The Chinese played one against another. They rewarded allies with gifts and privileges to keep their enemies divided.

Once in a while over the centuries, a chieftain was able to unite many tribes into an empire. These nomadic empires have left few written records. We know of them mostly from songs, art, coins, and objects they made and used. The steppe empires often invaded and sometimes ruled surrounding countries. To write the full story of these kingdoms, a historian must read what the Arabs, Persians, Chinese, Russians, Indians, and western Europeans have written about them.

The Turkic Empire One great empire, the Turkic (TUR kihk, 500 to 700) left an account written in stone—the Orkhon (AWR kahn) inscriptions found in Mongolia. The Turkic empire ruled the steppe from Mongolia in the east to the Caspian Sea in the west, an area that came to be called Turkestan. It dominated the silk trade between China and Byzantium. By the middle of the 700s, torn by internal quarrels, the empire had fallen. The small successor Turkic states were now threatened by Islamic conquerors, who were pushing into the steppe. Some Turks appealed to China for help. China was then struggling against the Tibetan empire, which was about to cut China off from central Asia. When the Chinese finally did help the Turks in 751, their army was beaten by the combined forces of the Islamic Abbasids, Tibetans, and Turks. China was never again a power in Western Turkestan. The Turks in the west soon were converted to Islam. They gradually drifted south and westward.

The central and eastern tribes, which included Mongol and Tungus people, continued their nomadic life. Many adopted Buddhism and Nestorian Christianity. From this group, 400 years later, came the world-conquering Genghis Khan.

Mongols and Genghis Khan The Mongols took over their world by surprise. The Chinese Tang dynasty (618 to 907), about which you will read later, did control the steppe tribes for a while. But after China was weakened by civil war, strong seminomadic kingdoms developed along its borders. Some came to be considered Chinese dynasties. Neither they nor the Chinese were paying attention toward the end of the 1100s as Temujin (tem YOO jihn, *circa* 1160 to 1227), the future Genghis Khan, began to collect followers.

Temujin's father, a tribal chief, was poisoned by a rival tribe while Temujin was still a boy. During this time, Temujin's bravery won friends to his cause. In time he married Borte, a woman from another tribe.

Later, in a surprise enemy attack, Borte was carried off as a captive. With the help of a ruler who had been a friend of his father, Temujin recovered his wife. Gradually, Temujin overcame all his rivals, including the ruler who had helped him earlier. In 1206, the Mongols gathered to elect him supreme ruler of all the Mongols with the title Genghis Khan.

Now, too late, the Chinese took notice. By this time, the Khan had formed a cavalry with a speed and endurance that was almost unbeatable. Their principal weapon was the deadly bow and arrow. Stirrups enabled archers, skilled since childhood, to shoot as they rode. Troops were drilled in tactics. Tricks, such as fake retreats, trapped and cut off pursuers. Information was collected from merchants, travelers, and spies. The Khan knew more about his enemies than they did about him. He depended on his followers and rewarded courage and loyalty. In return, he demanded obedience.

Mongol women kept the fighting clothes ready: a doubled-layered sheepskin coat, boots worn under heavy felt socks, and a leather helmet. With supplies of dried horsemeat, milk curd, and millet, a soldier could ride for days, eating and sleeping in the saddle.

Nomad women worked hard. But unlike many other Oriental women, who lived isolated from nonfamily males, they were free to move about. They could buy, sell, and trade their belongings. They often served as head of the clan or even ruler in case of a husband's absence or death.

Mongol Conquest To the nomads, China was a fabled land of riches. It had always been a goal for conquest. But Genghis knew that, even with his superb warriors, he would need careful preparation to conquer such a large, well-defended country. To avoid crossing the Gobi Desert, the Mongols conquered a people along China's northwest border. The attack on China began in 1211. By 1214, the Mongols controlled the north Chinese city of Zhangdu.

The Khan was angered when the members of a Mongolian mission to a central Asian emperor were murdered. Leaving his generals to complete north China's conquest (1234), the Khan turned west. His troops were now helped by several Chinese military engineers who had joined them. The engineers were skilled in the use of battering rams, *catapults* for hurling boulders, and flame throwers. To fight a war on two

Yurt tent homes at a horse collective in the steppes of central Mongolia.

fronts, the Khan needed good communications. His "arrow" messenger, body and head bandaged for protection, rode night and day. By changing horses at special outposts, he covered thousands of kilometers.

Terror was part of Genghis Khan's plan to get cities to surrender. Those who surrendered were spared. In others, artisans and skilled workers were taken along with the army. Young women were shipped off as slaves. Healthy men were used as shields in front of regular troops to storm the next town; some joined the regular army. All others were put to death, and the city was looted and burned.

At the Khan's approach, the rash central Asian ruler who had provoked the invasion fled west to Persia. Mongol commanders who had chased him then raided the Caucasus and southern Russia. Jalal-ad-Din (ja LAH loo DEEN), the son of the central Asian ruler, organized his forces in Afghanistan and gave the Mongols one of their few defeats. Genghis drove him into India, but he admired the prince's courage.

Though the Khan's soldiers had won many battles and slaughtered millions, he died in 1227 without fulfilling his dream of world conquest. Under the rule of his sons, the Mongols completed the conquest of Russia. They galloped across Europe almost to the borders of Italy and Germany. The courts of Europe were paralyzed with fear.

By 1258, the Mongols had conquered Persia and the Abbasid caliphate. They were welcomed as liberators by Christians, Jews, and Shi'ites, who were second-class citizens under Islam. The nature-worshiping Mongols were tolerant toward other religions.

The Mongol Empire Except for Mongolia, where most Mongols remained, they were a small minority in their empire. To help run this huge state, Genghis Khan and his sons chose the wisest men from twenty countries. A Muslim governed Peking. An adviser from the Chinese royal family was responsible for many of the Khan's good policies. When a general suggested that Chinese peasants be killed to provide more pasture land, the adviser pointed out that taxes would then be lost.

In the years of peace after the Mongol conquest, trade flourished. Roads were repaired and policed. Cities were rebuilt. Genghis' law code, the Yasa, was enforced.

Genghis Khan gave each of his sons a part of the empire. To Jochi (JOO jee), the eldest, went the most distant. It included part of southern and western Russia. This group came to be called the Golden Horde.

Chaghatay (jah guh TI), the second son, got part of central Asia. There the Mongols were soon absorbed by the local Turkic population. From this area came another world conqueror, the Turkic-Mongol Tamerlane. In the late fourteenth century, he smashed the Golden Horde.

In Mongolia where Ogadai (ah guh DI) succeeded his father as great khan, riches poured in from all corners of the empire. Officials of other governments, traders, and missionaries visited the Mongol court, the most important political and economic center of the world.

Kublai Khan When Genghis' grandson, Kublai (KOO BLI), was elected great khan in 1260, he moved his capital to Peking and called his new Chinese dynasty Yuan. A young Venetian nobleman, Marco Polo, spent many years at Kublai's court. He traveled through Asia as the Khan's representative. Marco Polo's book describes the splendor of the Khan's marble palace set in a park of rare birds and animals. The Khan drank the milk of snow-white mares from golden cups. His summer palace was made of gold-painted bamboo, which, like a yurt, could be folded up and moved. Marco Polo also noted the success of Kublai's policy of rebuilding cities and helping farmers after years of war.

This stone tortoise at Karakorum, Mongolia is believed to be one of the remains of Genghis Khan's capital. (The tortoise is a symbol of good luck.) The Buddhist monastery and Tibetan stupas in the background were built in the sixteenth century.

Kublai's expeditions to invade Japan and Southeast Asia failed. But he did reach his chief goal: to unite China under his rule. The Song (Sung) dynasty finally surrendered in 1276. Kublai became the first foreigner to rule all of China.

End of the Mongol Empire About 100 years after the Mongols had built the largest empire of all times, it was in ruins. The Mongols in China returned to the steppe. And the Yuan gave way to the Ming dynasty. The Mongols in Persia (who had become Muslims) were replaced by small kingdoms. The central Asian state had split in two. The Golden Horde in Russia had passed from the original line to another of Genghis' descendants.

But the world was changed. In joining east to west by force, the Mongol empire had opened up unimagined possibilities for trade, art, and science. Western Europe, spared the devastation of the east, quickly seized the advantage. Seeking a direct route from Europe to the land of Kublai Khan, Europeans launched a new age of discovery.

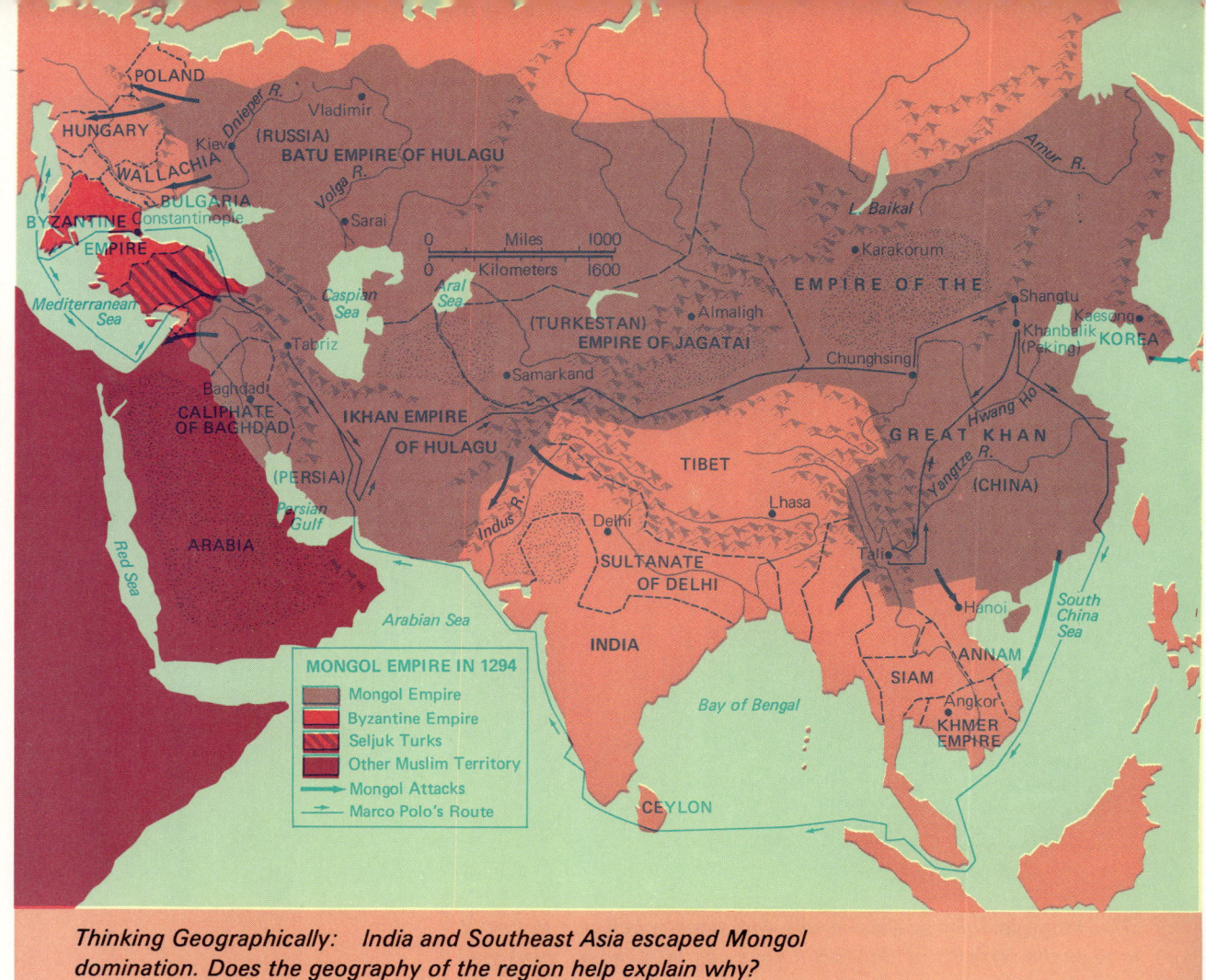

Thinking Geographically: India and Southeast Asia escaped Mongol domination. Does the geography of the region help explain why?

Section Questions

1. The steppe people were nearly always outnumbered by the settled societies around them. What provided the steppe armies with their military advantage?
2. Genghis Khan has been described by some historians as a successful robber chieftain. Others see him as one of the world's greatest military geniuses. How would you evaluate him and why?
3. What was the role of women in nomadic society? How did it compare with that in India or the lands of the Arab caliphate?
4. An Arab historian described the Mongol invasion as "a tremendous disaster such as had never happened before." Was this true? Can you name any benefits that came from the century of Mongol rule?

These four musicians are tomb figures from the Tang dynasty.

3. China Prospered During the Tang and Song Dynasties

Much of China's history was marked by periods of first turmoil and then relative stability. In 589, after 300 years of disunity, Yang Qian, a general, unified the realm and founded the Sui dynasty. Yang Qian reestablished a strong central government. But wars of conquest drained the treasury. Massive public works took workers away from their fields and crafts.

In 612, after an unsuccessful military campaign in northern Korea, revolts took place. In 615, eastern Turks defeated the Chinese army. The second Sui emperor was assassinated in 618. A new dynasty began which, like the Han, was to be one of the golden ages of China.

Unity and Expansion in the Tang The reign of Emperor Tai Zong (626 to 649) marked the first great period of the Tang dynasty. Its centralized government and cultural achievements were admired and copied by neighboring peoples.

Through military force, Tai Zong extended the borders of the empire. The army defeated the Turks and the Tibetans. The Tang empire stretched from southern Siberia at the north to Southeast Asia. It stretched west through Tibet and central Asia to the Caspian Sea. China was larger than it had ever been.

Land Reform Land reforms, begun under the Sui dynasty, were continued. Under the equal-field system, the highest ranking families received a maximum of 554 hectares (1,370 acres). These nobles also received additional official lands, depending on their position in the government. The rest of the land was divided among the peasants. Each man between 18 and 59 received 5.5 hectares (13.7 acres). Only a small part of that land stayed in the family. Much of it had to be returned to the government when the peasant died.

The government set up a careful census. It counted all the people. It also recorded every piece of land and its size and all taxes paid in grain or silk. The peasants gave twenty days of free labor to the central and local governments. They were also expected to join the army when asked. Thus, the empire had ample tax income. The free labor and military service of millions of peasants were part of this wealth.

For the equal-field system to work, the land had to be redistributed regularly among the peasants. But the population grew faster than the available land. Many peasants considered all 5.5 hectares (13.7 acres) as permanent. The rulers often gave land to their ministers that should have gone to the peasants. Thus, most farmers inherited less land than they believed was rightfully theirs.

By the early 700s, this carefully designed land and tax system was breaking down. Some historians believe that the eventual collapse of the Tang government was partly caused by the decline of this system.

Foreign Influences The bustling capital city, Changan, was the center of the powerful Tang empire. The overland trade routes that crossed central Asia met at Changan. Over two million people lived within the walled city and in the surrounding countryside.

As in the Han period, contact with the outside brought profit, new products, and new ideas. From Southeast Asia came tea. The western chair became so popular that gradually it replaced sitting pads and mats.

Foreigners from all over Asia came to Changan. Here were priests from India, merchants from central Asia and Arabia,

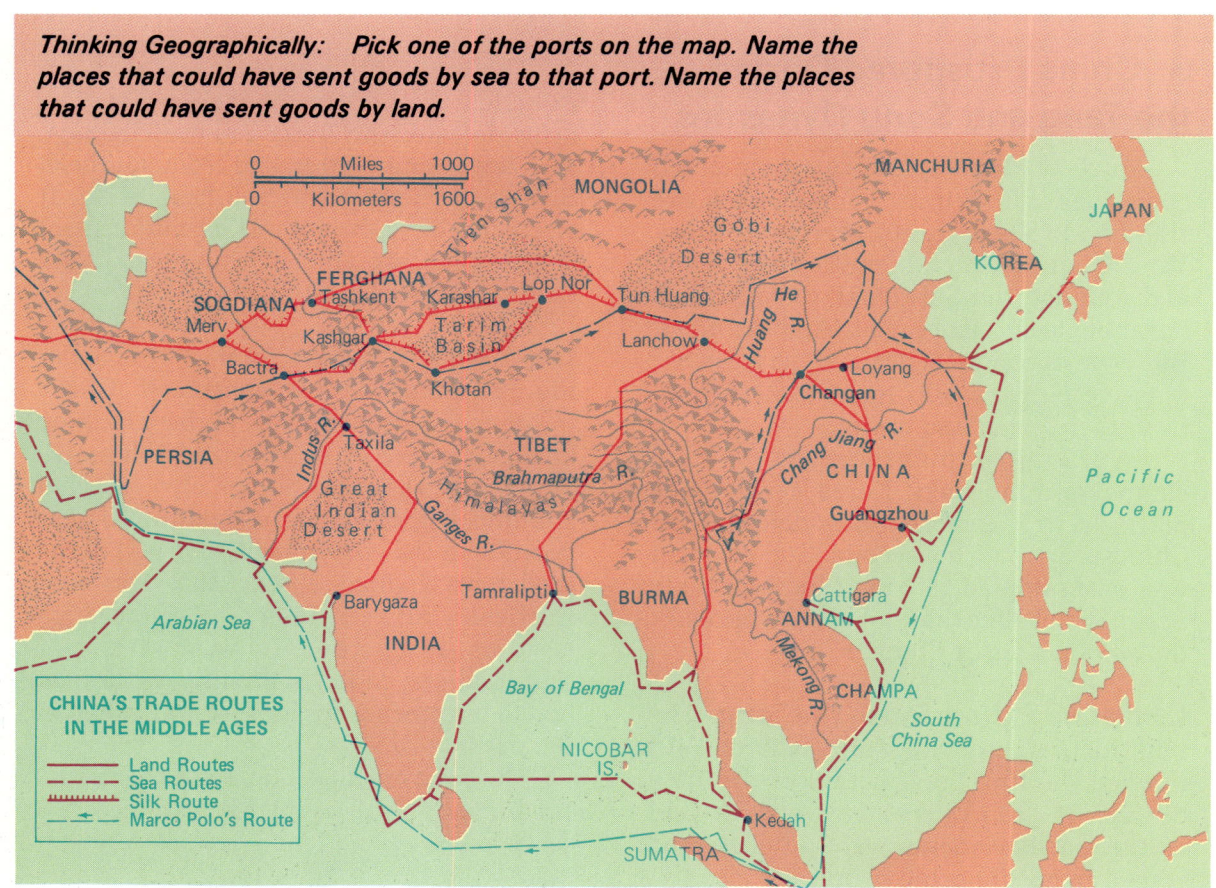

Thinking Geographically: Pick one of the ports on the map. Name the places that could have sent goods by sea to that port. Name the places that could have sent goods by land.

and travelers from Korea and Japan. As a Taoist, the first emperor believed that "the way" had more than one name. The practices of Zoroastrianism, Islam, and Nestorian Christianity were welcome. Chinese Buddhist scholars received Buddhist pilgrims from Japan and Korea. Buddhism had the zealous support of Empress Wu (690 to 705), who had been a Buddhist nun. She was also the only woman in China to rule as empress.

Despite the official policy of religious tolerance, some Chinese worried about the growing strength of the Buddhists. Taoist priests saw Buddhism as competition. Confucian scholar-officials disapproved of such Buddhist practices as not marrying and cremation. Not marrying threatened the continuation of family. And cremation was forbidden under ancestor worship.

Government officials were displeased because the Buddhist monasteries, lands, and art treasures were not taxed. By 729, the state created a system to control the number and size of monasteries and the number of Buddhist nuns and monks. As with attempts to control the landholding of wealthy families, this system did not always work. However, from 841 to 845, under a fanatical Taoist emperor, 4,600 monasteries and 40,000 Buddhist shrines were destroyed. Still Buddhism, which had many followers in China, survived.

The Golden Age of Poetry The Tang emperors supported musicians, poets, and scholars. Woodblock printing, developed by Buddhist monks, aided the growth of literature and scholarship. Chinese characters were carved on blocks of wood. The surface of each block was wet with ink and then pressed on paper. At first, the great works were printed on scrolls. Later they were put in book form.

Two of the greatest poets of the period, Li Bai (699 to 762) and Du Fu (712 to 770) knew one another. Their world outlook, however, was often different. Li Bai was Taoist by nature. When he was young, instead of preparing for the civil service exams, he left school and lived for a couple of years with a Taoist hermit. From 742 to 745, he was at the court at Changan, writing poetry for the emperor. Li Bai's poems recorded his feelings about life in the capital. He wrote of his longings for nature.

> My friend is lodging high in the Eastern Range,
> Dearly loving the beauty of valleys and hills.
> At Green Spring he lies in the empty woods,
> And is still asleep when the sun shines on high.
> A pine-tree dusts his sleeves and coat;
> A pebbly stream cleans his heart and ears.
> I envy you who far from strife and talk
> Are high-propped on a pillow of grey mist.

Li Bai did not like the constant politics of court life. Eventually he left the capital and returned to study Taoism. Li Bai is said to have drowned when, in a drunken ecstasy, he tried to embrace the moon's reflection in the water.

Du Fu was a Confucian moralist. He was disturbed about the increasing disorders of the late Tang dynasty. He commented on the harm that military campaigns and internal chaos brought.

> Now a little gang of military
> adventurers have seized the country
> so that people have become
> of no more account than fish
> for the table
> out on the land made
> desolate by war, the sound of ghosts
> in the wind and rain;
> while sad-eyed wives,
> mourning their husbands, horses
> riderless, are forced into revelry
> with the butchers.

A giant sculpture of a celestial king at a Buddhist grotto.

The Weakened Empire Despite the wealth and achievements of the late Tang dynasty, Du Fu clearly saw the signs of a weakened empire. The cost of maintaining the splendor of the imperial court had grown. The equal-field system had broken down. Peasants' holdings were smaller but were taxed so heavily that peasants often fled their farms or transferred their land to wealthy men. It was less expensive to rent land than to pay taxes on it.

By 723, a system of paid soldiers had replaced the old system of drafted peasants. These permanent professional armies cost money and were loyal to their commander, not to the dynasty. The more ambitious generals wanted power, as had the ancient feudal lords.

As you have read, in 751, the Arabs defeated the Tang armies in central Asia. In 755, a frontier commander in the north led a rebellion for control of the empire. This bitter civil war (755 to 766) devastated north China. The golden age of the Tang dynasty was over.

The Song Dynasty Disunity and warfare in the north ended in 960 when a general seized the throne and founded the Song dynasty. This dynasty endured for more than 300 years. It made lasting contributions to Chinese civilization.

Zi Ki, the first Song emperor, knew that Chinese unity depended on reducing the power of local military chiefs. He limited their areas of control to one district. When they died, he replaced them with government officials who were loyal to the throne.

The Song dynasty was constantly challenged by the barbarian peoples in the north and west. One of these groups, the Qin, conquered north China in 1127. The Song rulers fled south, where they established a new capital at Hangzhou (Hangchow). Despite the military weakness of the later Song dynasty, cities grew as trade expanded between China and Southeast Asia, India, and Arabia. Southern ports, such as Guangzhou (Canton) became important centers of commerce.

The Reforms of Wang Anshi

One Confucian statesperson wrote proposals for reforming many of China's institutions. Wang Anshi (1021 to 1086), prime minister during the northern Song, was a brilliant scholar and an able administrator. He believed that the government was losing money from untaxed lands and that the poorer peasants were too heavily taxed. He also wanted the education system and the civil service tests changed.

> In recent years, teaching has been based on essays required for the civil service examinations, but this kind of essay cannot be learned without extensive memorization and strenuous study. Such proficiency...is at best of no use in the government. Even if students remained in school until their hair turned gray...when finally appointed to office, they would not have the faintest idea of what to do.

Wang Anshi believed students should examine Confucius's ideas instead of memorizing them. He wrote a new interpretation of the classics and designed a new test.

Among other reforms, Wang Anshi offered crop loans to the peasants. These spring loans to buy seed and tools would be repaid at harvest time. The loans protected poor peasants from lenders who charged high interest. Wang also set up granaries throughout the provinces, where tax grain, or tribute, was stored. He gave government officials the power to resell this grain when people needed it. Before this reform, the grain had been sent to the capital. It did not often reach starving peasants in the provinces.

Wang's ideas were not startling, but people feared change. Reforms changed practices that had been going on for hundreds of years.

Song Landscape Painting

As in the Tang, the Song was a period of great artistic and literary accomplishment. Porcelain-making became an art form. Exquisite vases, plates, and cups were created. People read the poems of Su Dungbo and Li Qingzhao. The painting of natural scenery, or landscape painting, outdistanced all earlier painting. Art had once been only a medium for religious themes — but no longer. It was now valued for beauty's sake. Painters were respected. They were people of education with high social status.

Landscape paintings were not designed to be hung on walls. They were scroll paintings. As the scroll was unrolled, the painting unfolded. With each unrolled length, the viewer saw some new scene of nature.

Some artists did not paint large landscapes. They selected a detail in nature and focused on it. They painted a spray of bamboo or a peach blossom on hand fans or book leaves. The brushwork gave the paintings their vitality. There are short strokes, delicate strokes, thick strokes, and circular strokes.

Another development of the Song was the use of gunpowder. At first, it was only used during festivals for great firework displays. The Chinese also invented a mechanical clock. A magnetic compass was widely used, especially by the trading ships that left from the thriving southern ports.

The Yuan Mongol Dynasty

With Genghis Khan's conquest of north China in 1234, the Mongols became the new rulers in the north. The southern Song held out until 1276, when Kublai Khan brought all China under his rule. Kublai set about rebuilding China's war-torn agriculture and trade. An excellent organizer, Kublai adopted a form of Chinese administration but kept

This painting from the Song dynasty, "Landscape with Egrets," is done with ink on silk.

firm control. China was prosperous under his rule.

Later, under weaker Yuan rulers, court feuds broke out. Taxes rose again. And, as a result of natural disasters, food was in short supply. This led to inflation and rebellion. The Mongols could no longer govern China. In 1368, the new rulers, the Ming, seized Peking without a fight. The Mongol rulers had abandoned it.

Section Questions

1. Name three major achievements of the Tang dynasty.
2. Reread the poem excerpts on page 295. In what ways does Li Bai's poem reflect Taoist philosophy? In what ways does Du Fu's poem reflect Confucian philosophy?
3. What reforms did Wang Anshi offer for education and land distribution? How were these reforms received by other administrators?
4. How are scroll paintings different from the single-canvas paintings Westerners are used to?
5. What recurring problems helped bring the downfall of the Tang, Song, and Yuan dynasties?

4. Japanese Culture Was Influenced by China

Mountains cover much of Japan. The climate is mild in most of the country, and there is almost always plenty of rain. Thus, rice has always been an important crop to Japan.

A chain of 3,000 narrow islands stretches north from the southern tip of Korea. As a series of islands in the Pacific Ocean, Japan was well protected from outsiders and was able to develop its own institutions. Still, it was heavily influenced by the Middle Kingdom. The land bridge to Asia was Korea. And for much of its history, Korea was allied with China and dominated by it.

Early Japanese Archaeologists believe that small tribes or clans lived in Japan 20,000 years ago. These family groups became known as *uji*. Each group had a hereditary chief and worshiped an uji god thought to be its ancestor. The families who owned the most land were the most powerful. Ranked below the nobles in the uji were farmers, fishermen, weavers, and potters.

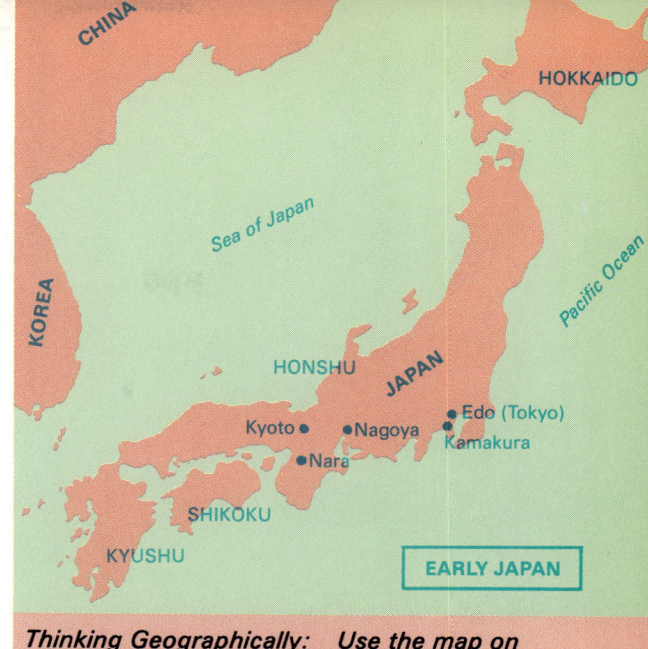

Thinking Geographically: Use the map on page 294. What Chinese trade routes could reach Japan by way of Korea?

In modern Japan, an ancient Shinto religious dance.

299

The oldest pagoda, or temple, in Japan.

When stronger uji conquered weaker ones, the conquered would worship the ancestral god of the conquerors. Thus clusters of uji were created. By the fifth century, one clan, the Yamato (yah mah to), became the dominant uji. Its ancestral god, the sun goddess, reigned over other gods. Eventually, worship of the sun goddess became a national religion called Shinto. Until the end of World War II, most Shintoists believed that the emperor of Japan was descended from the sun goddess.

Beginnings of a Unified Country In 587, Prince Shotoku (sho to koo) began to rule Japan. The prince was half Yamato and half Soga (SO gah), a rival clan. Just as early Chinese rulers needed to weaken the power of feudal lords, the prince needed to weaken the power of the uji. He wanted to promote unity among rival families.

Shotoku wanted his people to adopt Chinese ideas. He thought these ideas would help unify his country. The prince believed that China had a superior civilization. So did most other Japanese.

Shotoku patterned Japan's religion, art, and government after Chinese models. He promoted Buddhism, which spread through Japan over the next several hundred years. The success of Buddhism in Japan was due in large part to its ability to adapt to Japanese traditions. For example, Buddhism adopted the many gods of the uji in its ceremonies. Prince Shotoku also promoted Confucianism because it stressed loyalty to authority.

To strengthen the power of the central government and weaken that of the families, Shotoku issued a set of principles that stressed the supremacy of the imperial ruler. A new bureaucracy was established that took orders from the central government. The ruler now had more power than before. However, the wealthier families still had control of large areas of the provinces.

Prince Shotoku also adopted the Chinese calendar. He sent groups of Japanese to China to learn the Chinese ways. Buddhist monks, scholars of Chinese culture, painters, and musicians studied there. They brought back knowledge of Chinese language, literature, and rituals. Tang orchestral music and dances are still performed at the Japanese court today.

The Taika Reforms In 645, a Yamato prince, who later became Emperor Tenchi (ten chee), sped up the patterning of Japanese society on Chinese models. He proclaimed an edict, the Taika reforms, which outlined ways in which the society would be reorganized. The central government became the owner of the rice lands and gave land to those who worked it. Uniform laws and taxes were established, patterned after those of the Tang dynasty.

Did You Know?

Japanese Literature

Though Japanese writers studied Chinese literature, many Japanese writers wrote poems and novels that showed little Chinese influence.

One extraordinary collection of poems is *Man'yoshu*, or *Collection of Ten Thousand Leaves*. These twenty books contain 4,516 poems, written during the Fujiwara and Nara periods. The poems cover many subjects—the brilliance of city life, the charm of country life, love. The poets wrote ballads on legendary heroes but did not write any war songs. There is only one poem about a battle.

Most of the poems in the collection are five lines long. These short poems, tanka, have thirty-one syllables. The tanka below is reproduced in phonetics on the left and in English on the right. If you read the phonetics, you can hear the thirty-one syllables.

Haru tateba	When spring comes
kiyuru koori no	the melting ice
nokori naku	leaves no trace;
Kimi ga kokoro mo	Would that your heart too
ware ni tokenan	melted thus toward me.

Members of the imperial family wrote many of the poems in the Man'yoshu. In the eleventh century, one court woman, Lady Murasaki (moo rah sah kee), wrote a book, *The Tale of Genji*, which is still popular in Japan and has been translated into many languages.

In this excerpt, the hero, Prince Genji, goes to visit his foster mother, who lives in a poor part of town.

The gate...made of a kind of trellis work...stood ajar, and he could see enough

An illustration from The Tale of Genji.

of the interior to realize that it was a very humble and poorly furnished dwelling. For a moment he pitied those who lived in such a place...(On a) fence...some ivylike creeper spread its cool green leaves... Among the leaves were white flowers with petals half unfolded like the lips of people smiling at their own thoughts. "They are called Yugao, evening faces," (his) servant told him; "how strange to find such a lovely crowd clustering on this deserted wall!" And indeed it was a most strange and delightful thing to see how on the narrow tenement in a poor quarter of town they had clambered over rickety eaves and gables and spread wherever there was room to grow.

Central government ministries were set up to carry out the laws and collect taxes in the provinces.

Naniwa (NAH nih wah), a Chinese-styled capital with palaces, temples, and broad avenues, was built on the present-day site of Osaka (o SAH kuh). After Tenchi's death, a new capital was established in Nara (NAH ruh), which was near by. In 794, Kyoto (kee O to) became the capital and home for the court until 1868. The Japanese modeled the capitals at Nara and Kyoto after Changan, the Chinese capital.

Tenchi and later Japanese emperors achieved a more uniform system of government than before. But many families continued to act independently of the emperor. The higher ranking families still kept their own land. Provincial officials were members of these families and were loyal to them, not to the emperor.

Chinese ways, art, sculpture, and painting continued to influence the Japanese until the early 800s. Most literature and scholarly works were written in Chinese. Buddhism enjoyed a wider popularity. Many different Buddhist sects developed.

A Feudal System In the ninth century, as the Tang dynasty in China began to lose its vitality, its influence in Japan lessened. Leading families began to exert more influence. As high officials of the court, they collected land taxes and controlled the income from these lands. They started to keep most of these taxes and claimed more land as their own. So did officials of the Buddhist monasteries and Shinto shrines. These families and religious groups acted as minigovernments. The families still respected the emperor as the descendant of the sun goddess. But they did not often follow his orders.

The Fujiwara (foo jee wah rah) family was the most powerful family at the Kyoto court. They owned the largest number of estates. Fujiwara women often married emperors. In 858, Fujiwara Yoshifusa (yo she foo sah) named his seven-year-old grandson emperor. He named himself regent, or acting ruler, and controlled the country while his grandson was growing up. He was the first regent who was not a member of the imperial line.

The court had less political and economic power, but it did remain the center for learning and the arts. During this period there was a revival of Japanese poetry and prose.

Rival families fought for government posts and for land. Some families banded together in the provinces for mutual protection, as in the earlier uji society. They organized small armies of provincial warriors. Emphasis on the military grew. The provincial warrior class became known as the *samurai*. To become a member of the samurai was costly. A warrior

A Japanese warrior.

needed a horse and servant. He wore armor of steel strips and carried a bow, arrows, and curved sword. Because of the expense, warriors had to be members of the ruling families.

The samurai developed a brotherhood with a stern code of conduct. One might call it spartan. The code stressed bravery, self-discipline, and death before dishonor. Every day, samurai practiced the martial, or military arts—horseriding, archery, and sword fighting. Each warrior owed complete loyalty to his lord.

Of the families that banded together, the Minamoto (mee nah mo to) and Taira (tah EE ruh) families became the most powerful. In 1156, the Taira family defeated its rivals and ruled Japan for the next thirty years. In 1185, Minamoto Yoritomo (yo ree to mo) defeated the Taira armies and became the new ruler.

The Kamakura Period (1185 to 1333)

The emperor, while still claiming that he had real authority, gave Yoritomo the title *shogun*, "supreme military commander." Instead of ruling from the court in Kyoto, Yoritomo set up a second government, called shogunate, at Kamakura (kah mah kuh rah) near the clan estates in eastern Japan. Now there was a clear division between the symbolic, but powerless, imperial government and the military government, which actually controlled Japan.

The shogun's rule was nationwide. He owned many new estates taken from the defeated Taira family. Other families gave him their estates in return for protection. He rewarded his samurai with the jobs of running these estates and the provincial governments. He also assigned his warriors to protect the provinces. These protectors chose local warriors for guard duties and led them in war. Now, men loyal to the shogun were in both civil and military posts. Yoritomo had the most effective central authority that Japan had ever known. After he died in 1199, the shogunate lasted another 700 years.

During this period, China was under the rule of Kublai Kahn's Yuan dynasty. In 1281, the Mongols tried to take Japan. But their ships were destroyed by a typhoon at sea. This came to be known by the Japanese as "divine wind," or *kamikaze*. It was proof that the gods had protected them from the Mongols.

The Ashikaga Period (1338 to 1573)

The power of the Kamakura shoguns gradually weakened as their warriors spread out all over Japan. These warriors became local military leaders and vied with one another for power. In 1338, a warrior from the Ashikaga (ah shee kah gah) family established his shogunate in Kyoto.

The days of a strong shogunate were over. Major families did not feel loyal to the Ashikaga shogunate. They kept the income from their own estates rather than paying it to the shogunate. Thus, the Ashikaga were limited to income from their own lands and what taxes they could collect from a few loyal families.

Families all over Japan fought each other for land and local leadership. The years 1467 to 1568 are called the Epoch of a Warring Country.

The Daimyo During this civil war period, local leaders began to control small areas. They were called daimyo (DI mee o). Some came from powerful old families. Many were new warrior-class leaders who had overthrown local protectors. Daimyos ran their regions, using their own codes. They organized peasants into tax-paying villages.

The daimyo was lord over all the military families in a region. He hired them to lead large bodies of foot soldiers in battle against rivals. All resources went toward increasing the daimyo's military power.

This period was chaotic on a national level. But locally, the daimyos set up very efficient administrations. These local kingdoms provided a solid base for the central government that later evolved.

Section Questions

1. Why did Japanese rulers want to model their country after China?
2. In what ways did Chinese civilization influence or shape life in Japan? When did this influence weaken? Why?
3. How did the samurai class develop? How did it contribute to the establishment of the shogunate?
4. In what ways did the daimyos succeed? In what ways did they fail?
5. Would you say that Japanese history before the 1500s was characterized by unity or disunity? Explain.

Chapter Summary

1. The first Muslims in India were peaceful Arab traders. They were followed by an Arab army that conquered the region of Sind in northwest India in 711. Three centuries later, Muslim Turks from central Asia invaded north India and established the Delhi sultanate. At its peak, it brought almost all of India under a single government. For the most part, the Delhi sultans followed a policy of religious tolerance toward their Hindu subjects. Even so, the number of Muslims grew steadily as Hindus converted to the new religion. Under the sultanate, a rich and flourishing culture developed that combined Hindu and Islamic influences. The sultanate fell to new Muslim invaders from the northwest in 1526.

2. In the early 1200s, Genghis Khan unified the Altaic tribes living on the Mongolian steppe. The Mongol armies under Genghis Khan and his sons conquered China, central Asia, Persia, the Arab caliphate, Russia, and eastern Europe. By 1258, the Mongols ruled the largest continuous empire in the history of the world. During the years of peace that followed the Mongol conquest, trade flourished between Europe and the East. After the mid-1300s, the Mongol empire had practically ceased to exist. But it had altered the course of history for countries both within and without the empire.

3. In 589, after 300 years of turmoil, the Sui dynasty was founded. Its public works projects and expansionist wars eventually weakened it. During the Tang dynasty (618 to 906), a golden age in China, people from all over the world traveled to the capital at Changan. These foreigners brought new religions, such as Buddhism and Zoroastrianism, and new products. The Tang was also marked by great literary and artistic achievements, especially in poetry. By 700, land and tax reforms had broken down. Ambitious regional chieftains fought for power and land. The Song dynasty was founded in 960. While barbarian invasions remained a constant threat, the Song thrived culturally and economically. In 1276, Kublai Khan conquered the Song. The Yuan Mongol dynasty lasted until 1368, when the Chinese established the Ming dynasty.

4. Japan is part of east Asia. As a remote series of islands, it developed its own institutions at the same time that it adopted foreign ways.

Japan's early ruler, Prince Shotoku, wanted his people to adopt Chinese ways. He thought this would help unify the country. Shotoku promoted Buddhism, set up a bureaucracy based on merit, and sent students to China to study. Emperor Tenchi continued many of these practices. He centralized his power through ministers who carried out the laws and collected taxes. But in Japan, as in China, rival families often acted independently of the emperor. Rival families fought for land and power. A pattern developed by which the emperor remained a figurehead while the country was ruled by the most powerful family or military ruler.

Chapter 16 Review

Check Your Facts

1. Identify or describe the following:
   a. Delhi sultanate
   b. Urdu language
   c. Temujin
   d. equal-field system
   e. uji
2. Name two reasons why the Muslims were able to defeat the Indians in the twelfth century.
3. What was life like in the typical Indian village during the Delhi sultanate?
4. Why were land reforms necessary during the Tang and most other Chinese dynasties?
5. How did people live on the steppe? What were the three main language groups of the region?
6. What were the Taika reforms? How did they affect Japanese life? What did they fail to do?

Words to Know

1. Define these words and explain their significance:
   a. census
   b. yurts
   c. shogun
   d. steppe
2. Use the following words in a brief paragraph about the history of Japan: *samurai, kamikaze.*

Developing Your Skills

1. Examine the map on page 292. Describe the borders of the Mongol empire at its greatest.
2. During which Chinese dynasty did each of these people make a contribution?
   a. Wang Anshi
   b. Empress Wu
   c. Kublai Kahn
   d. Li Bai

3. Arrange the following in the order in which they happened:
   Ming dynasty begins in China.
   Taika reforms proclaimed in Japan.
   Yoritomo gets title of Shogun.
   Tang dynasty is founded in China.
   Mongol empire is at its height.
   Delhi sultanate begins in Delhi.

Thinking It Over

1. In Unit One, you learned one definition of the term "civilization." Consider what you have read about the Mongols. In your opinion, were the Mongols civilized? Explain.
2. In the Tang and Song dynasties, peasants had to give twenty days of free labor to the government. How do you think Americans would react to this requirement?
3. Among other things, the Japanese adopted the religions, government systems, and written language of the Chinese. What Japanese traditions and social systems survived the period of Chinese cultural dominance?

Special Activities

1. Several religions and philosophies are mentioned in this chapter: Islam, Buddhism, Zoroastrianism, Shinto, and Confucianism. Find out if there are any followers of these religions in your community.
2. Read about karate or judo. Report on its origins, its purpose, and how it has changed.

This fresco shows Mayan warriors.

Chapter 17 The Americas

Over 1,000 years before Columbus landed on San Salvador (san SAL vuh DAWR), a great American civilization was at its height. These people were astronomers, architects, and mathematicians. They developed a complex system of picture writing, or hieroglyphics. Centuries before the Europeans, they invented an accurate calendar and used the concept of zero. They correctly predicted eclipses. And they built towering pyramids in tropical rain forests without using the wheel.

These people were the Maya. In early 1980, archaeologists pushed Mayan history back by 6,500 years. They were exploring

40,000 B.C.—A.D. 1532

40,000-24,000 B.C.	People cross Bering Strait
9000 B.C.	People in southernmost South America
3400-3000 B.C.	Farming begins
1200 B.C.	Olmec culture in Mexico
A.D. 300	Mayan civilization classic period
	Teotihuacan civilization in Mexico
950	Toltecs rise in Mexico
1100	Incas found Cuzco
1325	Aztecs rise in Mexico
1438	Inca empire begins
1519	Cortes conquers Aztecs
1532	Pizarro conquers Incas

A Mayan carving of a warrior.

over sixty sites in the lowlands of Belize (buh LEEZ) along the Caribbean (kar uh BEE un) coast. There, as elsewhere, clues to early cultures lie buried in the earth.

Dr. Richard S. MacNeish headed the 1980 expedition. Based on early findings and long experience, he identified five new stages of pre-Mayan culture. In the earliest stage, Lowe-ha (9000 to 7500 B.C.), the people were big-game hunters. They left behind chipped stones, called fishtail points. Such stones have been found at other sites with the bones of giant ground sloths and wild horses. So archaeologists think the points were used on hunting weapons.

In their second stage, Sand Hill (7500 to 5500 B.C.), the people had become gatherers. They used stone tools for grinding seeds. They also had woodworking tools and may have begun to build boats.

In the third stage, Belize (5500 to 4200 B.C.), the people gathered wild plants inland and shellfish along the shore. Lobsters, crabs, and oysters became part of their diet. Then in the fourth stage, Melinda (4200 to 3300 B.C.), they built large seaside fishing villages.

In their fifth stage, Progresso (3300 to 2500 B.C.), the population grew, and people started moving into river valleys. There the former fishers became planters, raising corn, squash, and beans.

The human history of the Western Hemisphere appears to have begun long before Lowe-ha. It stretches back beyond 20,000 B.C. to a time when Asians crossed a land bridge to Alaska. Thousands of years later, and much farther south, this history was to flower in the Mayan, Aztec, and Incan civilizations.

1. Wandering Hunters Settled the Americas

Columbus had set sail in search of India. So when he arrived in San Salvador in 1492, he called the people "Indians." This mistaken name came to be applied to many different peoples of the Americas. Actually, these people differ in looks, language, and culture as much as the people of western Europe do.

Where did the Indians of the Americas come from? Most experts believe that they are descended from the peoples of eastern Asia. These experts also agree on how the earliest wanderers got to America. They crossed the Bering Strait to Alaska. Even today the Innuit (IN yuh wut) and Aleuts (uh LOOTZ), or Eskimos, can cross the Bering Strait by raft. But in the distant past, during the Ice Ages, the sea level was lower. Some of the ocean water was frozen in huge glaciers. This exposed a bridge of dry land between the continents. Wandering hunters could walk across this land bridge to North America. The glaciers may have blocked their way south for a time. But eventually, they made their way down to warmer climates.

Early Migrations Apparently, the Asian hunters followed herds of big animals to North America. They hunted mammoths, bison, and horses. From the Bering Strait, small bands of hunters pursued the herds southward through Canada. Then they traveled down the continent into what is now the United States and Mexico. Some remained in North America. Others continued south, to Central and South America.

Scientists are less certain about when these wandering hunters came. They left no written records. All we have are traces of their campsites, found along their route. Carbon 14 dating can be done on plant and animal remains found with their tools. This has shown that people were in northern Alaska around 24,000 B.C. Carbon dating shows that toolmakers had reached southern Mexico at least by 2,000 to 4,000 years later. As more research is done, earlier dates may be discovered.

Tools and Weapons Other clues are furnished by the types of tools and weapons the people used. By 10,000 B.C., the hunting bands were skillfully chipping flint to make special spear points. Excavations in Clovis, New Mexico, revealed nineteen of these Clovis points, along with other tools for hunting large game. But many campsites have been found with only crude stone tools and with no spear points. This leads some scientists to believe that migrants may have left Asia as early as 40,000 B.C. They would have left Siberia before people made spear points there.

For thousands of years, the people of the Americas followed a hunting and gathering way of life. Then, between 10,000 and 8000 B.C., the Ice Age ended. Gradually, the climate grew hotter and drier. There were fewer forests, rivers, and grasslands. The herds of big grazing animals began to disappear. At first, the hunters shifted to smaller game. The people lived on whatever food their area provided. They caught fish and speared or trapped small animals. They also gathered wild plant foods, which they learned to dry and store.

Shift to Farming The shift to farming was a major change. Miniature corncobs found in Mexican caves show that wild corn existed around 5000 B.C. After 3400 B.C., the cobs were larger. People had improved the corn by choosing and planting the larger seeds. Then they crossed corn with related plants to improve the corn further. By 3000 B.C., the improved corn was feeding many more people. By 2000 B.C., farming was a way of life in Mexico and Central America. People settled in small villages and raised corn,

A cliff dwelling at Mesa Verde, Colorado.

squash, and beans. Given this steady source of food, the population grew larger. Labor became more specialized. Some community political control was established. A settlement would have a central leader and a council.

North American Cultures The different cultures that people developed in North America varied depending on where they lived. In the dry southwestern United States, the Pueblo Indians built with *adobe* (sun-dried brick). Their homes look like large apartment buildings. They were built several stories high, with ladders leading to entrances in the roof. The Pueblo people needed to irrigate their croplands. So they changed the course of streams and built ponds to store water.

In the east, the Woodland Indians farmed in fertile river valleys. Southern Woodland Indians settled in places like Ocmulgee (ok MUL gee), now Macon, Georgia. There they developed religious and political leadership, a division of labor, and a religion tied to corn production.

On the Pacific Coast, people settled, not to farm, but to fish and gather acorns in the forests. Where the climate was too dry or cold for farming, the old tribal ways of life went on. Hunting of bison continued on the western plains and prairies. And in the sub-Arctic north, the Innuit and Aleuts hunted seal, whale, elk, and walrus, traveling by canoe and sled.

In areas with forests, the craft of wood-carving developed. Along coasts and rivers, pottery was made of clay. On islands off the coast of Georgia and South Carolina, shells were piled high to form gigantic circles. Near the Great Lakes, native copper was hammered into knives and spears.

A prehistoric rock effigy of an eagle, left by mound builders in Georgia.

Mound Builders As people settled down, they began to make art and ornaments as well as weapons. They also honored the dead and developed ceremonies. Consider the influence of the Woodland Indians of the Ohio River Valley. The Adena (uh DEE nuh) people began building burial mounds and other earthworks around 1000 B.C. The Hopewell people continued the practice. Huge hills of earth were heaped over graves. Some earthworks were shaped like animals, and others were in geometric forms. Sometimes, rich offerings to the dead were placed inside the tombs.

The Hopewell people traded for materials, such as shells and copper for their crafts. Their trade network stretched from the Gulf of Mexico to the Great Lakes and from Yellowstone in the northwest to the southeast Appalachians (ap uh LAY chunz). Those who traded with them picked up their ideas and art styles. Many other groups began to build burial mounds and to copy the Hopewell's pottery and ornaments. Through trade, the different North American cultures passed their arts and customs on to one another. As you will learn, this was true in Central and South America as well.

Section Questions

1. Why did wandering bands of people come to the Americas? How did they come?
2. Why is it hard for scientists to determine when these wandering peoples first arrived? What evidence of these people is left?
3. Name three changes that took place when people turned from hunting and gathering to farming.
4. What did geography have to do with the development of different ways of living among groups in North America?
5. What effect did trading have among settled peoples in North America?

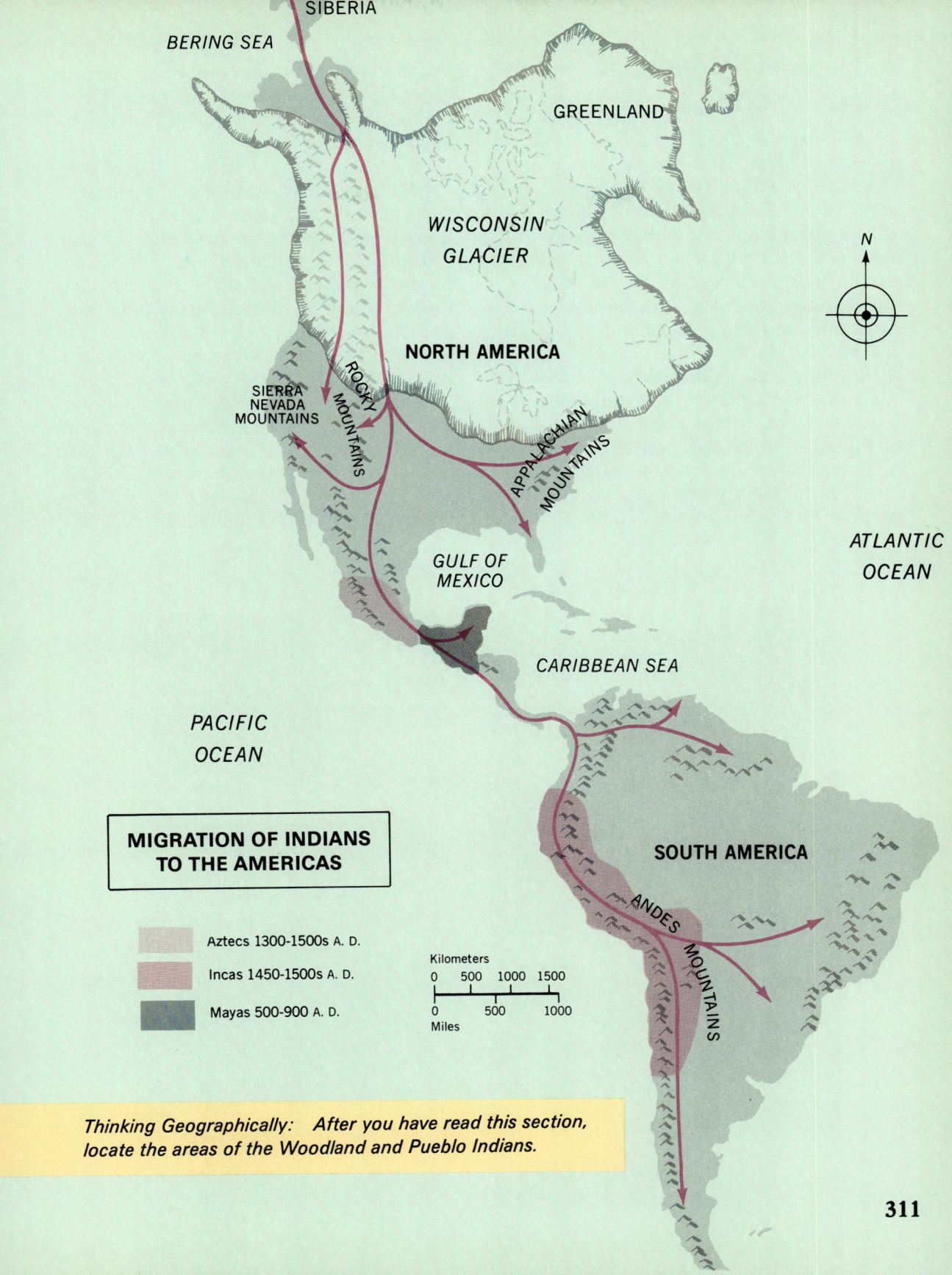

2. The Maya Created a Great Civilization

A hook of land juts up and out between the Gulf of Mexico and the Caribbean Sea. This is the Yucatán (yoo kuh TAN) Peninsula. Today the peninsula is shared by Mexico, Belize, and Guatemala (gwah tuh MAH luh). But the Yucatán and the region around it are still known as the land of the Maya. In thick rain forests and sunny plains, their palaces and pyramids still stand.

You have read about the ancestors of the Maya. By 2500 B.C., these people had begun to farm. It was not until then that they started to make pottery. You also know what it means to have a civilization. People need writing and numbers to keep records. They need a government to make and enforce laws. They need a division of labor, with experts in different fields. Art, architecture, and trade are also signs of civilization.

Archaeologists have found a Mayan date that was carved in stone during the first century B.C. This shows that the Maya had invented a number system before the birth of Christ. During the next three centuries, the Mayan civilization developed further. Its great classic period was from A.D. 300 to 900. For those 600 years, the Maya had the most advanced civilization in the Americas.

In many ways, the Maya were unique. But they probably borrowed some ideas from the Olmec (AHL mek) of Mexico. The Olmec culture dates from around 1200 B.C. Their religious system, with its powerful priests, seems to have influenced the Maya.

Mayan ruins of the Castillo, in Yucatán.

The Olmec built ceremonial centers to worship the gods. And their crude picture writing may have led to the complicated Mayan system.

But the Maya went far beyond these borrowings. They became expert in astronomy, mathematics, arts, and architecture. These cultural achievements were shaped by their religious beliefs. The Maya believed that the gods controlled all aspects of their lives. Chac (chahk), the hook-nosed rain god, often appears in their stone carvings. Rain and a good harvest were needed for survival.

The needs and beliefs of the people made the priests very powerful. The priests studied the movement of the sun, moon, and planets. This helped them predict the best time for planting crops and the time when the rains might come. They advised the people on everyday decisions. They also planned a constant round of ceremonies to please the Mayan gods.

The Ceremonial Centers We know a great deal about the Maya through the cities they built and left behind them. Many archeologists believe these places were not cities for people to live in. The rooms in the palaces seem too dark and damp for daily living. There are no windows for fresh air or chimneys to let out cooking smoke. Water may have oozed in during the rainy season.

Experts believe these places were built as ceremonial centers. The palaces were probably used only by the priests and nobles. Some rooms may have been government offices. Some may have been used by priests to prepare for ceremonies. Other rooms may have sometimes housed rich and powerful families, but this is uncertain. A wall in a palace in Palenque (puh LEN kay) shows scenes from the life of the nobles.

Archaeologists have had to reclaim remains, such as the Mayan center of Tikal (tih KAHL) in Guatemala, from the rain forest around it. Roots and vines once covered the steep pyramids. Trees grew out of temple tops. Many monuments were ruined by the jungle.

In classic Mayan times, temples were not choked with jungle growth. Then, the people used the slash-and-burn system of clearing land for farming and building. They cut down and burned trees, vines, and underbrush. The ashes fertilized the soil. Crops could be grown for a few years until the soil was exhausted. Then a new field had to be cleared. A small religious center would have a paved courtyard, a pyramid, and a few other buildings. A great center, such as Tikal or Copán (ko PAHN), covered a large area of land. There were many great plazas were people could gather on special days. Temples, palaces, and pyramids faced these central plazas. These buildings were richly decorated with sculptures, carvings, and wall paintings.

The most impressive buildings were the pyramids. A Mayan pyramid had steep, narrow stairs leading up to a temple on top. This temple was usually crowned with a painted crest or roof comb. Ceremonial centers also had ball courts where the Maya played a ball game. Their rules allowed them to hit the rubber ball with their bodies but not with their hands. Carvings show that the players wore helmets, knee pads, and chest protectors.

The Peasant Farmers Most of the Maya were farm families. They lived in villages in the countryside, near the cornfields. They had small houses with thatched roofs to keep out the rain and hot sun. About 75 percent of their food came from corn. This made corn very important to the Maya. One of their legends teaches that the gods made people out of corn. It was important to show respect for the gods. So people made offerings at various stages of the corn crop. The Maya also ate squash, beans,

A Mayan palace at Palenque.

fruits, chili peppers, and pumpkin. They gathered honey, and sometimes they had meat. The only animals they tamed were dogs and turkeys. Farming was hard work. They did not have plows or wheels and did not use animals to pull loads.

The farm families came into the cities for religious festivals and market days. Then the cities were crowded and busy. Markets were held every five days. Cacao beans and jade beads were used as money. The Maya traded for food, pottery, dyed cotton cloth, and salt from the coast. They could also buy luxury products, such as chocolate, jaguar skins, and colorful feathers. Courts of law were held in the city on market days. Then lawbreakers could be tried, and disagreements over goods could be settled.

After a market day or a festival ended, the farm people left the city. But they supported the ceremonial centers with their work and their offerings. Experts estimate that a typical family of five produced a surplus of food. This surplus helped maintain the upper class. It also fed the workers who built the pyramids, temples, and palaces. Without the Mayan peasants and their religious feelings, the ceremonial centers would not have been built and could not have survived.

The Class System The Maya had a strict class system. As in the city-state society of Sumer in Mesopotamia, the priests ranked highest. Next came the nobles, or lords. They made the laws, managed the government, and kept the priests in power. Priests and nobles belonged to the ruling families. On festival days, they wore jaguar skins, tall headdresses, and brightly colored feathers to show their power and importance.

The Maya had a small middle class. Some were engineers and minor officials who directed building projects. Some were artists who decorated the buildings. Others were skilled workers who made fine clothing and jade ornaments for the priests. Merchants and traders also belonged to the middle class.

But most people were peasants. Besides farming, they did the building. They had to cut heavy blocks of limestone and roll them on logs to the building site. Then they had to grind the stones and fit them into place. Only slaves ranked lower than the peasants. Some slaves had been taken in war. Others were made slaves for breaking the law.

The Scholar Priests In Mayan society, high positions were inherited. Only members of the ruling families could be trained as priests. They studied astronomy in special observatories on top of temples. There, they learned to measure time by a 365-day solar calendar as accurate as our own. It had eighteen months of twenty days plus a special month of five days. There was even one extra day every four years for leap year. Long before the Europeans, the Mayan priests knew that the solar year was slightly less than 365 days long. Openings in their observatories marked various points in the orbit of the sun, the moon, and the planet Venus. From their studies of the heavens, the priests were able to predict eclipses. At Copán, they even held meetings on astronomy.

Mayan Numbers and Hieroglyphics The Maya also had the concept of 0. Their system of mathematics was easier to use than Roman numerals. They counted by 20s and used dots and bars to write numbers from 1 to 19. A dot equaled 1. A bar equaled 5. A zero was drawn as a shell symbol. It was used to multiply dot-and-bar numbers by 20.

Using this system, the priests were able to count large blocks of time, such as 144,000 days. They recorded dates on monuments called *stelae* (STEE luh ee). These were standing slabs of stone covered with carvings and picture writing. Stelae show Mayan counts of dates extending into millions of years.

Besides the power of numbers, the Mayan priests had the power to write. They developed a highly detailed system of picture writing. Each symbol had a special meaning. The priests wrote about astronomy, religion, and history. Only a few of their books on bark paper have been preserved. But written records are also carved on the Mayan stelae, and centuries of history may be recorded on the hieroglyphic stairway at Copán.

Until recently, people found Mayan writings hard to read and understand. Now computer experts have helped translate them. Writings on monuments often tell about rulers of the past and what they did.

End of the Classic Period Suddenly, in the ninth century, the classic age of the

> The Maya used dots and bars to count from 1 to 19. They used zero to multiply numbers by 20. How would the Maya write the number 40?
>
> —— = 5   • = 6
> •••• = 4   == = 10
> ••• = 3   ••••= = 14 (dots over two bars)
> •• = 2   •••≡ = 18 (dots over three bars)
> • = 1   •• over • = 22
>
> ⬭ = zero = × 20
>
> • over ⬭ = × 20 → 1, 20
>
> ≡ over ⬭ = × 20 → 15, 300

Maya ended. The priests stopped keeping their solar calendar. Temples were left unfinished. Great Mayan centers such as Tikal and Copán were abandoned. What happened remains a mystery. Did disease strike? Did the climate change? Did the crops fail? There are no signs of natural disaster.

Some scholars think the peasants may have revolted against the priests and nobles. Perhaps they were no longer willing to maintain the great religious centers. Whatever the reasons, in the south, Mayan civilization simply collapsed.

The Mayan cities in the northern Yucatán were not abandoned. They survived until the Spanish arrived. But there, the peaceful Maya came under the power of the warlike Toltec (TOL tek) people from Mexico. The symbols and gods of the Toltec invaders can be seen in the Mayan center of Chichén Itzá (chuh chen ut SAH). The Maya had been a peaceful people. The Toltecs were fierce warriors and practiced human sacrifice. The great days of the Maya were not to return. But from their art and artifacts, we know much about their gods, their customs, and their daily lives. Today in the Yucatán, the descendants of this great people keep their religion and myths alive. Even now, they have not forgotten their Mayan gods.

Section Questions

1. What features of the Mayan culture made it a civilization? Give specific examples from classic Mayan life.
2. In what ways did peasant farmers help Mayan civilization develop?
3. How were the Mayan ceremonial centers of Tikal and Copán like modern-day cities? How were they different?
4. Why were the Mayan priests so powerful?
5. Explain the Mayan calendar and number systems. How were they like the systems we use today?

3. The Aztecs Built an Empire in Mexico

In the centuries after A.D. 700, Mexico was subject to waves of invasions. Periodically, warlike tribes from the north would attack defenseless cities and settlements. Later, those tribes settled down to build cities of their own. But they brought their war gods with them. Both the Toltecs and the Aztecs (AZ teks) first appeared as aggressive invaders.

The Toltecs The Toltecs built their city of Tula (TOO luh) around A.D. 950. Tula stood on a hill, where it could be defended against attack. The columns of its temple were shaped like warriors. Carvings at Tula also show racks of human skulls and an eagle eating a heart. The Toltecs practiced human sacrifice.

After founding Tula, the Toltecs invaded the Yucatán Peninsula. There, they absorbed the peaceful Maya into the fiercer Toltec world. Until the latter part of the twelfth century, the Toltecs continued to spread their control over central Mexico.

The Aztec Island-City Then, in the thirteenth century, Aztecs invaded from the northwest. They brought with them their sun-and-war god, Huitzilopochtli (WEET see lo POCH tlee). At first, they were like a wandering band of outlaws. According to legend, they first settled near a Toltec city. But they started a war with the Toltecs and were defeated and driven away. They fled to Lake Texcoco (tes KO ko). The god Huitzilopochtli told them to look for an eagle perched on a cactus and eating a snake. They found this eagle on an island in the lake. There, in 1325, they founded their city of Tenochtitlán (tay nach teet LAHN), meaning "near the cactus." This city was to become the capital of their empire. Over its ruins, Mexico City now stands.

Living on an island gave the Aztecs

Aztec priests preparing a sacrifice.

some advantages. They were safer from attack. They could form alliances with different cities on the mainland. And they could use canoes to carry people and goods. This was easier than moving things on land. Like the Maya before them, the Aztecs did not use animals to pull or carry loads. And except for toys, they had no vehicles with wheels.

The Aztecs figured out a way to make their island larger. They drained swamps and built up low-lying marshland with rocks and soil. They also built small islands where they planted gardens and grew vegetables and fruits. They would fill in swampy areas with reeds, dirt, and refuse, much as we use landfill today. Silt and mud from the lake bottom made this land very fertile. Walls and tree roots kept it from washing away.

These small artificial islands circled the central city. The city itself was crisscrossed by canals built for transportation.

It was also linked to the mainland by several long, narrow roadways. In the center of the city, the Aztecs built a tall pyramid with two temples on top. There they worshiped the gods of sun and rain. Smaller pyramids were built around this very tall one. Tenochtitlan also expanded to take in a twin Aztec city nearby. Each city had a central market. There, a variety of foods, clothing, fine jewelry, weapons, and crafts were sold.

The Aztec Religion To understand the Aztecs' way of life, it is necessary to know what they believed. A number of religious stories were handed down to them by their ancestors. These stories taught them two main ideas. They taught that the universe was constantly threatened with death and destruction. And they believed that sacrifice to the gods would keep the universe going.

The Aztecs believed that they had been created by the sacrifice of gods. Two more gods had sacrificed themselves to give the Aztecs the sun and moon.

Mayan priests studied the sun to understand the gods and predict what was going to happen. But the Aztecs thought the fate of the sun depended on their actions. They believed the sun had to be fed with human hearts. It needed blood for strength to battle against the dark forces of night. They thought of themselves as the people of the sun. Thus, to the Aztecs, human sacrifice was a religious duty. They fought wars and took prisoners to give the sun its food. Huitzilopochtli was both god of the sun and god of war. He promised them victories in return for victims.

In a sacrifice to the sun god, priests forced the victim down backward onto a special stone slab. Four priests held the victim's arms and legs. Another priest cut out the heart with a knife. Then the heart was burned in a stone urn. On special occasions, a sacrifice could go on for days.

Thousands of captives waited in line to be killed. Tens of thousands might be sacrificed in a year. There were also sacrifices to the god of spring. His priests danced in skins that they had stripped off human victims. The Aztecs believed that life after death was a reward for fighting well and for keeping the universe going. Dying as a sacrifice was supposed to guarantee eternal happiness.

The Aztec Empire To the Aztecs, religion provided a reason for war. To serve Huitzilopochtli, they had to conquer other

Did You Know?

The Pyramid of the Sun

The largest pyramid in the Americas stands in a plain near Mexico City. The Pyramid of the Sun is larger than two United States capitol buildings. From a huge base, it rises 65 meters (213 feet) above the ground. It is as tall as a nineteen-story building.

Once, priests climbed the broad steps of the Pyramid of the Sun. They went from level to level up to the temple that stood on top. From there, they could look down onto a long, broad avenue. At one end was the smaller Pyramid of the Moon. At the other end was the temple of the god Quetzalcoatl, the feathered serpent.

These buildings stand in what was once the center of a great city. The Aztec name for this city is Teotihuacán (tay o tee wuh KAHN), which means "Place of the Gods." The pyramids of the sun and moon were also given their names by the Aztecs. We do not know what their original builders called them. In fact, experts are not even sure who the builders of Teotihuacán were. But they were great architects.

The heart of the city was the ceremonial center. Beyond this center was a zone of palaces. Still farther out, small adobe houses were crowded close together. As many as 50,000 city workers could have lived in them. In A.D. 600, when

The Pyramid of the Sun.

Teotihuacán was at its height, 125,000 people may have lived in and around it. It was the largest city in the Americas.

Then about A.D. 750, the people deserted the "Place of the Gods." Some think the city was conquered and burned by barbarian invaders. Perhaps it had been weakened by internal power struggles. Its fall remains a mystery. But twelve centuries later, visitors still climb the Pyramid of the Sun.

peoples. At first, their settlement at Tenochtitlan was dominated by larger towns nearby. But the Aztecs were fierce fighters. Other groups wanted them as allies. In 1428, after their king was captured, the Aztecs joined a revolt that defeated the groups in power. Then they formed an alliance with two neighboring towns. This brought the central valley of Mexico under one government controlled by one king. It also became the basis for further conquest and expansion. And the Aztecs became the dominant force.

The Aztecs built their empire the way they built their island. They extended outward from a central base. Their strategy for conquest was simple but brilliant. They allied with larger groups to defeat smaller enemies. Then they fought their former allies. That way, they put together a collection of conquered peoples. These defeated tribes were loosely linked to the Aztecs but were subject to their control. The Aztecs let them keep their leaders and their gods. But this "freedom" had its price. Defeated tribes were forced to send the Aztecs tribute in the form of food, cloth, pottery, weapons, and other goods. The Aztecs needed these imports to support their priests, nobles, armies, and officials. They also needed a supply of captives to support their gods.

By 1519, the Aztec empire covered 120,000 square kilometers (75,000 square miles) in central and southern Mexico. It had a population of 5 to 6 million people. At least 100,000 people lived in Tenochtitlán alone.

The Social System Like the Maya, the Aztecs had social classes. First came the king and his top officials. Kingship was usually inherited. Next came the upper class of priests and nobles. The nobles were a warrior class. They owned their own estates. Young nobles were educated by the priests, who taught them Aztec ideals. The priests had palaces and temples, as in the Mayan world.

The middle class was made up of merchants and government officials. They worked to keep trade and tribute flowing. This kept the Aztec empire rich. There were also craft workers and experts in different fields. All the Aztec men could be called on to serve as soldiers.

At the bottom of the social order were peasants, serfs, and slaves. The peasants farmed lands that were owned in common by Aztec tribes. Each family could work a piece of land but could not give it away or sell it. The serfs worked in the farmlands on the nobles' estates. When land was sold, they came with it, as though they were trees or buildings. The slaves, who were mostly conquered peoples, had the lowest status. They did the hardest jobs on farms and in trade. They also were the labor that built religious centers and public buildings. Sometimes, slaves were bought for the purpose of sacrifice.

Although social class was important in Aztec society, ability was important too. A fine soldier could improve his position by success in battle. Through hard work and talent, a government official could rise to higher positions. Clan leaders were elected from powerful families, but they could be removed if they were not effective. So there was more social mobility than in the Mayan world.

Aztec Culture The Aztecs brought their fierce energy to their art and architecture. But they borrowed heavily from other cultures before them and around them. Their ceremonial cities and social structure were much like those of the Maya. The Aztecs adopted the Mayan calendar, renaming the days and numbering system. Their great round calendar stone can be seen in the National Museum in Mexico City. Their language, Nahuatl (NAH wah tl), gave us such words as "chocolate" and "tomato."

Aztec agriculture made use of stone tools and was very productive. The island gardens and mainland fields yielded a surplus of 18 million kilograms (20,000 tons) of food. This food found its way into the empire's trading network. However, there is evidence that, by the early 1500s, the population was growing faster than the food supply.

The Aztecs also passed down many legends from the people who came before them. One Toltec legend had a great influence on Mexican history. This was the story of the god Quetzalcoatl (ket SAHL kwah tul). Quetzalcoatl was a peaceful god of learning and civilization. His name meant "feathered serpent." The Toltec ruler-priest who served him brought his civilizing influence to Tula. But the followers of the Toltec war god rejected the god of learning. So the priest of Quetzalcoatl went into exile. Legend has it that the god himself left Mexico and sailed out to sea. But Quetzalcoatl promised to return from the east with the rising sun. He even gave the date for his reappearance.

Over 500 years later, at that promised time, ships with white sails appeared from the east. They carried fair-bearded men. In 1519, Hernando Cortés (kawr TEZ), the Spanish conqueror, landed in Mexico. And the emperor, Montezuma II (mahn tuh ZOO muh), first greeted him, not as a new enemy, but as a returning god.

Section Questions

1. Where did the Aztecs build their capital city? What were the advantages of that location?
2. What did it mean to the Aztecs to be the people of the sun? How did their religion encourage them to conquer other peoples?
3. How did the tribes that the Aztecs defeated help support the Aztec empire?
4. What were the main classes of people in the Aztec social system?
5. Name three ways in which the Aztecs were like the Maya. Name three ways in which they were different.

4. The Incas Governed in the Andes Mountains

The Andes Mountains run down the Pacific coast of South America like a curving spine. This is a region of rugged peaks, cool highlands, fertile valleys, and a dry coastal plain. Here, beginning in Peru, the legendary Incas built their empire. For a century, their power stretched over much of the longest mountain chain on Earth. From archaeological records, we know that wandering tribes had reached the southernmost tip of South America by 9000 B.C. On their way south, these groups passed through what was later the Incan empire. Some settled in the region. One great center of civilization was built high in the Andes near Lake Titicaca (tih tih KAH kuh). Its arts and religion had spread widely by A.D. 800 when the Incas were only a small tribal band.

Rise of the Incas According to legend, the first Incas were children of the sun god. Four brothers and four sisters set out from the house of dawn to found a kingdom. The eldest brother was Manco Capac (MAHNG ko KAH pahk). He carried a golden rod. This rod was supposed to sink into the ground when the Incas found the right place to settle. (It may have been used to test for fertile soil.) Manco Capac's brothers died during the journey. But he went on to sink the golden rod into the ground at Cuzco (KOOS ko) in Peru. One of his sisters, Mama Huaco, helped win a battle to claim Cuzco. Another sister, Mama Occlo, married Manco. Thus Cuzco became

Machu Picchu in Peru.

the capital city of the Incas. And Manco was the first Inca ruler.

Archaeological evidence shows that the Incas came to Cuzco about A.D. 1100. It was not until around 1438 that they began to conquer other areas. Then it took them less than 100 years to build an empire. By 1463, they ruled the highlands of Peru. By 1471, they conquered the great coastal city of Chan Chan. By 1493, the Incan empire extended from the equator in Ecuador (EK wuh dawr) halfway down through Chile (CHIL ee). This stretch of land was about 4,000 kilometers (2,500 miles) long.

Government Organization The name "the Inca" has three meanings. It can refer to all the people of the Incan empire. It can mean only the nobles. Or it can be the title of the king, the Inca. The Inca traced his family back to the legend of Manco Capac and Mama Occlo. His chief wife was always his sister, but he had many other wives as well. When he died, the next Inca was chosen from among his sons. The Inca was the head of government and had unlimited power. People believed he was descended from the sun god. Male members of the Inca's family served as a council of advisers and top officials. The center of government was Cuzco, the capital.

As the empire grew, it was divided into provinces. Each province had a royal governor who lived in Cuzco and served on the Inca's council. A second official was like an acting governor and lived in the province itself. Both officials carried out the Inca's orders.

Lesser officials were usually chosen from their own local areas. Sometimes the Incas took over new territory without having to fight. If local leaders cooperated, the Incas often kept them in office.

There were many different levels of local officials. They were ranked by the number of taxpaying families in their district: 10; 100; 1,000 or more. As the empire grew, more local officials were needed. The Incas looked for new talent and rewarded loyalty and service. If local chiefs were not

Incan nobles by birth, they were made honorary Incas. These Incas by privilege then became part of the *aristocracy*, or ruling class.

The Management System The Incas were expert at organizing people and managing resources. To build their empire, they needed a good army. To control such a long stretch of territory, they needed good communciations. To support their population, they needed to farm every possible piece of land.

When the Incas took over new areas, they made a model of the land in clay. Using this map, they decided where roads and irrigation canals were needed. To defend the land, they built forts. To reeducate the local people, they sent loyal Incas in as colonists. Their spoken language, Quechua (KECH uh wuh), was used for official business.

The Incas also took a census. They counted by 10s. Since they had no written language, they kept records by tying knots in string. Each knot represented 10. Thanks to the census, the Incas could draft soldiers for the army. They also had thousands of workers to call on for public projects. Using these workers, they built irrigation canals to water fields in dry coastal regions. They cut terraces into steep slopes so that crops could be grown on the sides of mountains. They built a winding road through the mountains and a straight one along the coast. These were not roads for carts or wagons. The Incas did not have the wheel. These were highways on which messengers ran and armies marched. The messengers were relay runners. They memorized their messages.

The armies used animals, the llamas, to carry supplies. Both messengers and armies could stop at rest houses along the route. In the mountains, sections of road were sometimes connected by swaying rope bridges. And in the steepest sections, highways could be steps cut into rocks. The Incas built with stone in the mountains and with adobe near the coast. They cut, shaped, and fitted heavy stones together so closely that not even earthquakes could shake them. Their cities had temples, palaces, plazas, and government buildings. You can still visit the great granite city of Machu Picchu (mah choo PEEK choo). It was built on a ridge between mountaintops, at a dizzying height.

The Economy The Incan economy did not use money. It was based on work and credit. The empire owned most of the animals, crops, goods, and lands. In exchange for their work, people had their basic needs taken care of. Farmers were given enough farmland to feed their families. First, though, they had to plant the empire's public lands. Food from the public fields supported priests, nobles, soldiers, and officials, along with workers in special trades.

Farming in the Andes region was not easy. Yet the people of the Incan empire raised more than forty kinds of crops. They planted each crop in the climate where it grew best. High altitudes were good for growing potatoes. In fact, the Irish potato originated in the Andes. Corn was the main crop in warm coastal valleys. Besides corn and potatoes, they raised squash, beans, tomatoes, chili peppers, pumpkins, peanuts, and avocados. The government stored food surpluses for use in the dry years when crops were poor. The people also raised ducks, guinea pigs, and llamas for their meat supply.

The Incas raised a cotton crop and their herds of llamas and alpacas were a source of wool. Crops from fertile valleys fed families who tended herds in the highlands. Wool from the herds was given out to the weavers. Farm families were given wool for their own clothing. People who could not work because of age or illness were also provided for.

Social Control While the Incas provided security, they also controlled people's lives. Families could be moved from their homes and sent to settle a new region. But they could not move or change jobs on their own. Young people were told when to marry—women by age eighteen, men by age twenty-four. They usually had to marry someone from their local village. Then they would be given land, and the community helped them start their home.

At a very early age, certain girls were chosen for special training. Such a girl might later be sent to serve in a temple. Or she might be made one of a noble's many wives. Sons of nobles studied to prepare for posts in the Inca's administration.

Incan Religion The religion of the Incas reflected the importance of farming in their lives. They were the people of the sun god. But officially, their most important god was the creator, who was thought to have a human form and to live in the sky. A lesser sky god was the protector of crops. Another was the god of thunder, who controlled the rain.

The people also worshiped the moon goddess. It was she who regulated the all-important farming cycle. Festivals were held in her honor and in honor of the goddesses of the earth and sea.

The Incas felt that snowcapped mountains were close to the sky gods. This made them sacred places. Certain springs, caves, and hills were considered sacred, too, along with the Inca's palaces and the city of Cuzco.

Incan Crafts To the Incas, weaving, pottery, and metalwork were art forms as well as jobs. Women ran the textile, or cloth-making, industry. They spun thread and used hand looms to weave wool and cotton cloth. Incan women knew almost all the weaving methods and patterns that factories use today. And they made every type

An Incan mask of gold.

of fabric, from delicate gauze to rich brocade and heavy tapestry.

The Incas were also famous for their metalcraft. They melted, molded, and joined metals and knew how to make bronze from copper and tin. They used the bronze and copper for tools and weapons. And they used gold and silver for cups and plates and for jewelry and ornaments. They also hammered sheets of gold and used them for decoration. Their gold-plated palaces and temples glittered in the sun.

The End of the Empire The Incas valued gold for its shining beauty. To them, wealth meant workers, animals, food, goods, and land. But gold itself was wealth to the Spanish conquerors. And their search for treasure brought them to the Incas' lands.

In the 1490s, the Incas had built a second capital city at Quito (KEE to) in northern Ecuador. Having two capitals helped divide the empire. When the reigning Inca died around 1525, two of his sons—one at each capital—fought a civil war. One son emerged as the Inca. But when Francisco Pizarro (puh ZAH ro) and his troops arrived in 1532, the empire was already weakened from within. The Spanish only had to seize the Inca, and the empire was helpless. The government fell apart without its head.

Section Questions

1. Describe the government of the Incas. What were its national, state, and local units?
2. How did the census help the Incas control and develop their land?
3. Name an advantage and a disadvantage of life in the Incan empire.
4. How did the Incan economic system work without using money?
5. Name three things that helped bring the Incan empire to an end.

Chapter Summary

1. During the Ice Ages, Asia and North America were connected at the Bering Strait. Wandering hunters crossed from Siberia to Alaska and traveled south, following herds of mammoth, bison, and horses. At first, these people were hunters and gatherers. Then, between 3400 B.C. and 2000 B.C., they shifted to farming and raised corn, beans, and squash.

The cultures that people developed in North America depended on where they lived. In the Southwest, the Pueblo Indians built houses of adobe and irrigated their fields. In the east, Woodland Indians farmed in fertile river valleys and built burial mounds. On the coasts, people settled to fish, and hunting continued on western plains. Through trade, different groups passed on their arts and customs to one another.

2. Ancestors of the Maya lived on the Yucatán Peninsula as early as 9000 B.C. But the classic age of Mayan civilization dates from A.D. 300 to 900. The Maya had a 365-day solar calendar. They had a number system that counted by 20s and used the concept of 0. They also had a system of hieroglyphics, or picture writing. To worship their gods, they built great ceremonial centers, with plazas, palaces, and pyramids.

Scholar-priests had the highest rank in Mayan society. Most people were peasant farmers. Around A.D. 900, ceremonial centers in the south, such as Tikal and Copán, were suddenly deserted. In the north, the peaceful Maya came under the power of the Toltecs of Mexico. But later civilizations were influenced by the Mayas' knowledge and ideas.

3. Like the Toltecs, the Aztecs began as a tribe of fierce fighters and invaders. They established their capital at Tenochtitlán, where Mexico City now stands. There they enlarged a small island and built their city out over a lake. They also built small artificial islands to use as gardens to grow crops.

The Aztecs formed alliances, fought wars, took many prisoners, and practiced human sacrifice. Between 1428 and 1519, the Aztecs extended their control over much of central and southern Mexico. They borrowed such ideas as the ceremonial center, with pyramids and temples, and the Mayan calendar. They were later conquered by the Spanish.

4. From their capital at Cuzco in the Andes of Peru, the Incas developed, between 1438 and 1493, a powerful and efficient empire. The Incan economy was based on work and credit. People used llamas for wool and for carrying loads. They raised potatos, corn, cotton, and other crops. The Incas took a census and drafted people from the army and for public works. They made maps of their lands and built roads, irrigation canals, and terraces for crops. They also built stone cities and were famous for weaving and metalwork. But after 1525, a civil war weakened the empire. And when the Spanish came in 1532, it quickly fell apart.

Chapter 17 Review

Check Your Facts

1. Identify or describe the following:
   a. Clovis points
   b. Tikal
   c. ceremonial center
   d. Tenochtitlán
   e. Nahuatl
2. How did archaeologists learn about the following?
   a. the wandering hunters from Asia
   b. the ancestors of the Maya
3. Name five major accomplishments of the Maya.
4. How did the following people prepare land for farming?
   a. Pueblo Indians in the southwest
   b. Maya in the rain forests
   c. Aztecs on their island
   d. Incas in the mountains
5. Name two ways in which the Aztec and Incan empires were alike. Name two ways in which they were different.

Words to Know

Match each of these terms with its definition below: *adobe, solar year, stelae.*
1. the number of days it takes Earth to revolve around the sun
2. sun-dried brick
3. monuments on which dates are recorded

Developing Your Skills

1. Examine your maps on page 311 and in the Atlas. What modern-day countries were these part of:
   a. the land of the Maya
   b. the Aztec empire
   c. the Incan empire
2. Make a time line that shows the order of the following events. Give each event an actual date or approximate time span.
   a. Cortes conquers the Aztecs.
   b. The Aztecs found Tenochtitlán.
   c. Hunters cross from Asia to North America.
   d. Pizarro conquers the Incas.
   e. The Maya abandon their ceremonial centers in the southern Yucatán.
   f. Farming begins in Mexico.
   g. The Incas settle at Cuzco.

Thinking It Over

1. The sun had a central place in the religions of the Maya, the Aztecs, and the Incas. What did each group believe or know about the sun?
2. "Knowledge is power." "Might makes right." Match one motto to the Aztecs and the other to the Maya. Then write a paragraph for each motto, explaining why it fits. Give examples.
3. One scholar has said that the Maya compared with the Aztecs were like the Greeks compared with the Romans. In what ways is this true?

Special Activities

1. Look up the words in the list below. Use a dictionary that gives word origins. From what Native American language does each word come? Canoe, chipmunk, chocolate, coyote, jaguar, kayak, maize, opossum, persimmon, potato, raccoon, skunk, squash, toboggan, tomato.
2. Compare life in the Incan empire 500 years ago with life in the United States today. Include at least four things that are similar and four things that are different.

Unit 4 Review

Words to Know

1. Compare a steppe and a plateau. Use a dictionary if you need help.
2. Explain why the savanna in Africa is called the sudan in the north and the veld in the south.
3. How did the harquebus and the catapult affect events in Africa and Asia?
4. How was a samurai warrior like a knight? How was he different?

Time and Place

1. Look at the maps on pages 292 and 311. Why would messengers be important to the Mongols and the Incas?
2. For each group and date below, state whether or not the group was in contact with Europe. If the answer is yes, state whether the contact was helpful, harmful, or neutral.
   a. Mali   1312-1324
   b. Kublai Khan's court   1260
   c. Tang dynasty   700s
   d. Maya   700s
   e. Inca   1530s
3. Use the Atlas. Find the shortest distance between each of the following.
   a. Europe and North America
   b. Europe and Africa
   c. Asia and Africa

Putting It Together

1. Compare the attitudes of the Chinese, the Africans and the Mayans toward families.
2. If you were a woman in the 1200s would you rather be a Muslim in India, a Mongol, or a native of China? Explain your choice.
3. Compare the attitude toward land ownership of the Africans, Chinese, and Mongols.
4. For each group below, state whether trade was very important, somewhat important, or not very important.
   a. Ghana
   b. Hindu villages
   c. Mongol empire
   d. Incas
5. For each group below, state how easy it was for people of high ability to rise in social status: almost impossible, very difficult, quite possible.
   a. Hindu villages
   b. Mongol tribes
   c. China during Wang Anshi's ministry
   d. Mayans
   e. Aztecs
   f. Incas

Contemporary Parallel:

The Search for Roots

A sleek sports car sped along the highway out of Kuwait. Then it turned off to race across the burning desert sands. The man behind the wheel and the teenager next to him wore traditional Bedouin robes.

Every year they did this, the man and his grandson. For two weeks they lived in the desert, finding their own water and food. "We are Bedouin," the man would say. "We must not forget the ways of our people."

At first the boy went only to please his grandfather. He was much more interested in learning to drive the sports car. But now he was beginning to see things differently. His grandfather was showing him another side of Kuwait—and of himself. He was thrilled when his grandfather showed him where a fierce battle had been fought. Part of him, he realized, was Bedouin.

The Kuwaiti youth was taking part in a ritual that has been important to people throughout history. In many ways, our heritage is important to our sense of belonging.

Around mid-century, Americans wanted to build a "modern" society. Old buildings were neglected or torn down. Creating tomorrow was more important than preserving yesterday.

During the 1950s and 1960s, social scientists found that many Americans felt rootless. David Riesman called Americans "the lonely crowd."

Americans in the 1970s felt a new curiosity about their roots. People began learning about their family histories. The book and television movie *Roots*, by Alex Haley, helped inspire them. It told how a Black American traced his family's origins back to Africa.

This awareness of one's heritage is one way we establish continuity—a connection between the past and present. Rooted by this sense of continuity, we are better able to cope with change.

QUESTIONS

1. Americans collect antiques and build colonial style houses. We struggle to have old buildings preserved as historical landmarks. What does this have to do with an individual's concern about roots?
2. Consider the Kuwait story of the boy and his grandfather. What would be an American version of the story? What would the heritage include?

1237	Tatars conquer Russia
1368	Ming dynasty begins
1451	African overseas slave trade begins
1492	Columbus lands in New World
1517	Luther's 95 *Theses*
1588	Spanish Armada defeated
1613	Michael Romanov Czar of Russia
1648	Thirty Years' War ends

Unit 5
Changes and Discoveries

An early map of the world.

Change is always occurring. A drought, a change in the physical environment, may cause changes in people's lives—the social environment. Normally, however, changes in the physical environment are slow and not very noticeable. Social change typically has far more immediate influence on people.

One change often leads to many other changes. The invention of the printing press led to the education of more and more people. In turn, educated people learned quickly the new ideas of the time.

This unit is concerned with the time period 1350-1650, when there was a great speed-up in change. Often, this period is called modern history, as contrasted to the Middle Ages or the medieval world. Many fundamental changes occurred in the lives of Europeans. Protestants rejected the teachings of the Roman Catholic Church. Nations such as Spain and England increased their power. Europeans explored and established colonies throughout the world. Russia expanded its territory as the Ottoman Turks gradually lost power. Meanwhile, the highly civilized empires in India and China, formerly very powerful, were becoming subject to the influence and trade of western Europeans. In Africa, the slave trade increased, bringing black people into the New World.

All these great changes—in thought, in religion, in politics, in trade—were going on at the same time. However, for convenience, the chapters of the unit are divided into separate topics, such as religious changes or exploration and trade.

Leonardo's "Adoration of the Magi."

Chapter 18
Renaissance and Reformation

*R*enaissance is a French word that means rebirth. The Renaissance in western Europe was a time when the ideas of the ancient Greeks and Romans were rediscovered. It was a new way of thinking that questioned many ideas of the Middle Ages. The Renaissance started first in Italy. Many of the ideas of the Renaissance are found in the works of one of the greatest figures of that time, Leonardo da Vinci.

Leonardo, along with the other great artists of the Italian Renaissance, broke completely with the past. During medieval

1307-1632

1307	Dante begins *Divine Comedy*
1452-1519	Life of Leonardo da Vinci
1454	Printing press invented
1475-1564	Life of Michelangelo
1517	Luther's 95 Theses posted
1534	Henry VIII heads Church of England
1536	Calvin in Switzerland
1543	Copernicus' theory published
1545-1563	Council of Trent
1546	Death of Luther
1602	Shakespeare writes *Hamlet*
1605	Cervantes' *Don Quixote* is published
1632	Galileo publishes findings

Michelangelo's statue of Lorenzo de Medici.

times, most painting was stiff, formalized, and flat. Now, inspired by Greek and Roman art, Italian artists like Leonardo moved far beyond their ancient models. They developed a whole new style of painting.

During the late Middle Ages, many people had found fault with the Roman Catholic Church. As you have read, many people tried to make reforms. However, little was changed.

In 1517, a young German priest, Martin Luther, nailed a document to the door of a church.

Immediately, a controversy arose. Luther was convinced that some of the teachings of the Roman Catholic Church were both wrong and harmful. Luther's clash with the church started the *Reformation*, a religious movement to reform or purify the Roman Catholic Church. The result of the Reformation was a split between Roman Catholics and *Protestants*, those who protested against the teachings and practices of the Roman Catholic Church. This represented an immense change in the lives of the people in western Europe. The Protestant Reformation shattered the unity of the Roman Catholic Church. Western Europe was now divided into many Christian faiths instead of just one. These religious divisions have not only lasted to the present, they have grown.

1. The Renaissance Began in Italy

The Renaissance, a rebirth of interest in Greek and Roman culture, began in Florence, Italy, and spread rapidly to other Italian cities. Italy's location helps to explain why the Renaissance started in such Italian cities as Florence, Venice, and Padua. These cities had become wealthy from the rich international trade.

Florence and the other Italian cities admired the ideas of the ancient world for two important reasons. First, Florence, like the ancient Greek cities, was actually a city-state, a small independent country centered on a city. Despite their small size, the Italian city-states like Florence and Venice had great wealth and power. Each ran its own political, diplomatic, and economic affairs. The political concerns of the Greek city-states—war, the duties of citizens, social tensions within the city—seemed very similar to the problems the Italian city-states faced at the time.

Secondly, the people of Florence and the other Italian cities were living in the land of the ancient Romans. They admired the Romans for uniting all of the Italian people. Many of the city-states were republics, political entities without monarchs. They thus felt that they were the true heirs of the Roman Republic.

Another cause of the Renaissance was the rise of a new class of powerful bankers and merchants in the Italian cities. People like the Medici (MED uh chee) family in Florence had both the money and interest to support the arts. They built beautiful homes filled with art. These wealthy families supported many artists and writers who lived in Florence. Such wealthy people thought that living in a city was much better than living in a monastery or in an isolated castle in the countryside.

The main source of the ideas of the Renaissance was the rediscovered ideas of the ancient Greeks and Romans. A passionate interest developed in learning more about the ancient past. The supporters of the Renaissance greatly admired the achievements of the ancient Greeks and Romans. During the Renaissance, scholars were finding, translating, and editing the works of that era. Of course, the ideas of the ancient world had never been completely forgotten. However, the recovery of the past now became almost an obsession among educated people.

Main Ideas of the Renaissance In contrast to the older medieval emphasis on God and salvation, the people of the Renaissance placed more importance on human

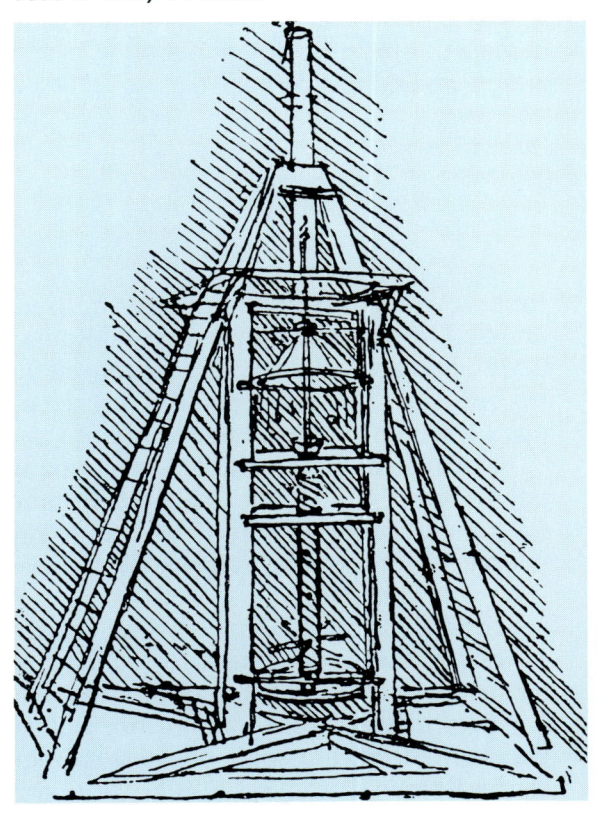

A drilling tower suggested by Leonardo. It is similar to the drilling towers used in early oil fields.

beings and their achievements on Earth. The people of the Middle Ages saw this life as a preparation for the next world. The ideas of the Renaissance, on the other hand, led to a stress on the pleasures of life. Possession of wealth was acceptable, not suspect. It was considered appropriate to acquire things of beauty. A person could show good taste by collecting works of art. The joys of the physical world were also praised. The senses were allowed to feel pleasure at the beauties of nature, of the human form, and of art. Life should be enjoyed. Human beings were also judged capable of understanding and changing their world. People, no longer thought to be just subjects of God's mercy or wrath, could control their own lives.

Another aspect of Renaissance ideas was the discovery of the self, or *individualism*. Individualism encouraged pride and ambition. This part of the Renaissance is reflected in the great popularity of the artists of the time. Unlike the humble, unknown artists of the Middle Ages who worked on the great cathedrals, the Renaissance artists willingly signed their names to their works. These artists competed with each other for the reputation of being the finest.

Individualism also furthered the idea that a person's prestige and position in society should be based on merit, not birth. It was felt that a person's ability should count the most in gaining honor and prestige. The old system of fixed class positions in which the nobles held most power was rejected. This idea of social advancement was popular among the rising middle classes in the cities, who were fighting for power against the feudal lords.

Another quality emphasized in the Renaissance was that of being skilled in many areas. The ideal Renaissance figure was an all-around, complete person, not a narrow specialist in one field. The ideal Renaissance man was a scholar, a gentleman, an athlete, and a soldier. He was a man of action and affairs, not a person confined to a monastery. It was also felt that a man had obligations to society. A person should participate and hold office in the government.

To help people achieve these skills—from fencing to writing a love poem—private schools and academies were established. In these schools, the young studied languages and literature, especially Latin and Greek. *Rhetoric*—the art of persuasion—also was judged important for use in public affairs. History, moral philosophy, and poetry were part of the curriculum. Religion was deemphasized.

At this time, a few wealthy women became educated. They received the same education as men. Especially in Italy, a few women became poets, painters, and writers. However, they were still expected to be wives and mothers.

Conflict with Religion? Were the ideas of the Renaissance a sharp break with Roman Catholic beliefs? The answer partly depended on the individual. Most writers and artists of the Renaissance accepted the faith of the Roman Catholic Church. For example, the paintings of the Renaissance reflected the artists' sincere interest in religious subjects. This focus on religious subjects was also strengthened by the popes and other wealthy church leaders. They hired the major artists of the day to work for them. However, though the theme was often religious, the spirit of realism and naturalism was also evident in many works.

Other Renaissance people were more interested in human than divine affairs. They were not as devoted to religious topics as the scholars of the Middle Ages. Because of this new emphasis, a little more tolerance developed for other religious beliefs. However, there were few people in western Europe who did not believe in God.

Raphael's "School at Athens."

There were also some Renaissance people who were critical of the Roman Catholic Church. However, most of them were not interested in seeing the church destroyed. They wanted to change or reform the church.

Most people were able to harmonize the ideas of Christianity and the Renaissance. Only a few were not. However, the inherent conflict between the two value systems caused strains. No longer was there just one set of standard beliefs that everyone in the society shared. Of course, most people accepted the traditional values of the Roman Catholic Church. The ideas of the Renaissance were adopted mainly by the intellectuals and the middle-class people in the cities. The vast majority of people were little affected by the ideas of the Renaissance.

The Great Italian Writers and Artists

The Italian Renaissance made its greatest contributions in the arts of writing, sculpture, and painting. Italian writers were leaders of the movement. During the Middle Ages, most literature had been written in Latin. There was no unified Italian language. Instead, many local dialects were spoken.

Three great giants in the literature of the Italian Renaissance actually helped create the modern Italian language. They were Dante (DAHN tay), Petrarch (PEE trark), and Boccacio (Bo KAWT cho)—all from Florence. These men established the dialect of Tuscany, the area around Florence, as the main literary language of Italy. They also developed new literary forms, such as the sonnet, for using the Italian language. Dante (1265-1321) wrote the great work *Divine Comedy*, a long poem about a journey through hell, purgatory, and paradise. Petrarch (1304-1374) expressed human emotions such as love, loss, despair, and hope in his sonnets. Boccacio (1313-1375) was one of the great storytellers of his time. His earthy characters—successful or unhappy lovers, unfaithful wives or husbands—expressed values that were not completely in accord with Christian ideas.

The great political writer of the Italian Renaissance was Niccolo Machiavelli (MAK ee ah VEL ee). In his book *The Prince* (1532), he advised a leader who wanted to stay in power not to follow Christian morals. The prince should manipulate and trick the people. This should be done, according to Machiavelli, because people are basically corrupt and self-seeking animals. For Machiavelli, therefore, success, not ideas, was what counted in politics.

The highest achievements of the Italian Renaissance were in the visual arts. The four towering Italian geniuses were Leonardo da Vinci (1452-1519), Michelangelo (MI kel AN je lo 1475-1564), Raphael (RAF a el 1483-1520), and Titian (TISH an 1477-1576). Leonardo was a many-sided, talented person. Michelangelo was probably the greatest of all sculptors of the Renaissance. Popular Raphael was best known for his many gentle pictures of the Virgin and the Christ child. Raphael also painted large frescoes such as the "School at Athens," which shows the high esteem in which the Renaissance held the world of ancient Greece. Like many other leading Renaissance artists, he was greatly in demand. The popes and other wealthy people all wanted Raphael to paint for them. For a time, Raphael was also the chief architect of St. Peter's. Titian, another great painter, is best known for his rich, colorful treatment of topics and for his portraits of famous people. Titian's paintings of Charles V and Phillip II show real insight into character.

Leonardo is the perfect example of the versatility of a Renaissance person. He was skilled in many areas. Leonardo was an artist, musician, inventor, engineer, botanist, astronomer, and geologist. He designed everything from war equipment to canals. Leonardo made exact drawings of the human body. In his notebook, he outlined ideas for scientific experiments. His masterful paintings include the "Mona Lisa," "Adoration of the Kings," and "Virgin of the Rocks." He is also known for "The Last Supper," which shows the emotions of Jesus' disciples.

Titian's "The Young Englishman."

Did You Know?

Michelangelo

Michelangelo was probably the greatest of all sculptors of the Renaissance. Sculpture almost started anew at the time. In medieval cathedrals, sculptures of humans were draped under heavy folds of clothing. During the Renaissance, there was a new understanding of the human anatomy. Nude figures became more popular. Often, the sculpture was placed in a central position, such as in a town square, and could be viewed from all sides.

Many of Michelangelo's well-known works, such as his statue of David, are of active, powerful males. Yet these strong figures are graceful. His work shows both fidelity to the form of the human body and the spirit of the Renaissance. In the "Pieta" in St. Peter's in Rome, the mother of Jesus expresses her deep sorrow at his death. She seems to be a human figure with human emotions.

Michelangelo, like many of the great Renaissance artists, did not restrict himself to one field. He was hired by the pope to work as a painter on the Sistine Chapel at the Vatican in Rome. For about four years, he painted the ceiling while lying on his back on a tall scaffold. He depicted nine scenes from the Bible. These included God creating the world, Adam and Eve, and Noah and the Great Flood. He painted over 300 figures of power and beauty. Some believe this to be the greatest single painting of all time. Much later in the same chapel, Michelangelo painted a view of the Last Judgment, a somber, disquieting work.

Michelangelo's statue of Moses.

Leonardo's paintings show three main trends among Renaissance artists. One was an interest in *chiaroscuro* — variations in the shades of light and dark. The second idea was *perspective*. Perspective gives an appearance of depth in a two-dimensional medium such as painting. It adds a suggestion of the third dimension, depth, to the dimensions of length and width. Perspective helps the artist portray what is really seen by the observer. To the eye, distant figures look smaller than they really are and closer figures look larger. Thirdly, there was a movement toward more *realism* in showing the features of individuals. People in paintings were portrayed more as human beings. Even in religious scenes such figures as the Virgin Mary and Jesus were more lifelike.

In architecture, the Italians liked to use old classical models such as columns, domes, and arches. The best and largest example of Renaissance architecture is St. Peter's Basilica in Rome, the largest Christian church in the world. In 1506, Pope Julius II demolished the old structure. It then took about 150 years to rebuild St. Peter's. Ten different architects were used. Many changes were made. However, the architects mainly used Greek and Roman motifs for this large and imposing building. St. Peter's shows the spirit of the Renaissance. The building conveys a sense of confidence and pride as well as beauty. It was officially dedicated in 1626, but other parts were added later.

Section Questions

1. Why did the Renaissance start in the Italian cities?
2. What groups of people adopted the ideas of the Renaissance?
3. What skills did the ideal Renaissance person possess?
4. Name four great writers and four great artists of the Italian Renaissance.

An aerial view of Vatican City, with St. Peter's Basilica in the foreground.

A drawing of Gutenberg showing the first proofs from his new printing press.

2. The Renaissance Moved to Northern Europe

About 1500, long after the Renaissance had begun in Italy, it spread from there to the rest of Europe. Because Italy was the center of the Renaissance movement, many students and intellectuals were attracted there. They wanted to see the new art and hear about the new ideas. They visited Italy and then returned home to their native lands. Often, scholars set up their own schools to reflect the new ideas. Some of the returned visitors now changed the courses they taught at their old universities.

The northward movement of the Renaissance reflected changes in trade. The nations on the Atlantic seaboard—Portugal, Spain, France, and England—were becoming more powerful. Cities in these areas were becoming more prosperous. New ideas were welcomed in these booming cities.

The Printing Press The greatest single discovery of the Renaissance originated in the north. This was the invention of the first practical printing press using movable type. This invention is credited to a German craftsman, Johann Gutenberg (GOO ten burg). In 1456, he published the first printed Bible. The new printing press actually involved putting together many separate steps, each a complete invention in itself.

Before the printing press, books were written by hand, a very slow and costly process. The printing press greatly increased the number of books that could be made. The use of the new invention spread rapidly. Printing presses were soon set up in almost all parts of Europe.

By 1500, a thousand printing presses were at work. All European countries except Russia had at least one press. It is estimated that by 1500, less than fifty years after the first successful printing press, about ten million books had already been printed. By contrast, it is estimated that in 1450 there were only about 100,000 handwritten books in Europe. In 1450, a large library had only about 200 books.

At first, most of the books printed were religious or ancient classics. Soon, books were available on almost all subjects, ranging from technology to medicine. It was now easier to transmit information. New ideas spread faster. In addition, the use of native languages in place of Latin grew and spelling became more standard.

Changes in the Renaissance The northern Renaissance was different from the Italian Renaissance. In the north, there was less emphasis on architecture and sculpture. Few really imposing Renaissance buildings were constructed. The northern Renaissance was more involved with learning than art. However, painting did flourish in Holland. The brothers Hubert and Jan van Eyck (IK) painted realistic portraits and landscapes. Later, Peter Breughel (BRUH gel 1520-1569) painted many scenes of peasants as well as biblical scenes. He is known for the clarity of detail in his people and their tools.

The northern Renaissance was marked by great achievements in literature. Many writers used their own language—English, French, or Spanish. They expressed a wide range of feelings in a wide variety of forms, including drama, poetry, and essays.

These Renaissance authors had much in common. They were proud of their own countries. They focused on human beings and were not interested in religious topics alone.

In England, the Renaissance flourished during the Elizabethan period, named after the reign of Elizabeth I (1558-1603). Many English writers, such as Ben Johnson and Christopher Marlowe, appeared. The greatest was William Shakespeare (1564-1616).

van Eyck's "Saint Barbara."

A scene from Shakespeare's <u>Midsummer Night's Dream</u>.

He is considered the world's greatest playwright. Using borrowed stories, he was most successful in the creation of characters—moody Hamlet, tragic Macbeth, and jealous Othello. The focus of Shakespeare is the human being. According to Shakespeare, humans like Macbeth are responsible for their successes and failures. In portraying character, Shakespeare showed a wide range of human emotions. In rich language, he colorfully set forth many of the conflicts that human beings experience. Shakespeare greatly influenced the literature of England, Europe, and the world.

The greatest French writers of the Renaissance were François Rabelais (RAB e LAY 1494-1553) and Michel de Montaigne (Mon TANE 1553-1592). Rabelais was a witty but serious writer. His books show a great appetite for life. He was a good storyteller. His advice to the reader seemed to be this: Do as you like and try new things. In other words, he suggested, forget the restraints of the medieval period.

Montaigne came from a wealthy family. He wrote a large number of witty essays on many topics. These essays show quiet, balanced judgment. He promoted a moderate and reasonable life. In religion, Montaigne was tolerant in an age when most people were not. His style greatly influenced French literature.

In Spain, the outstanding writers were Miguel de Cervantes (Sir VAN tez 1547-1616) and Lope de Vega (VAY guh 1562-1635). Cervantes' *Don Quixote* is considered by some as the finest novel ever written. It recounts the adventures of Don Quixote, a poor middle-aged, confused knight. He is accompanied by his faithful and practical servant, Sancho Panza. In this work, Cer-

A drawing of Don Quixote studying to become a knight.

vantes made fun of knighthood and romance. But on a deeper level, he was depicting the contrast between a person's hopes and dreams and the reality of life.

Lope de Vega produced more than 400 excellent Spanish plays. Often the themes of these plays are the conflicts of passion and the Spanish honor code. The dramatic situations are exciting. De Vega was a master of many kinds of writing. His works greatly influenced the style of other Spanish writers.

Science The Renaissance was a new way of thinking. In addition to changing literature and art, it laid the foundation for modern science. Artists and scholars were encouraged to be careful observers. The Renaissance also fostered doubts about existing authorities. As a result of these trends, people began to think anew and to reject older ideas. Nicolaus Copernicus (1473-1543) offered a theory that the Earth was not the center of the universe. This encouraged others, such as Galileo and Kepler, to do more work in astronomy. In addition, progress was made in mathematics and biology and in knowledge of the human body.

The Renaissance was not an age of total progress. The Renaissance chiefly affected the elite or the few educated people. Many peasants saw little change in their lives. Despite the high regard in which human beings were held during the Renaissance, there were still wars and oppressive rule. There were still fears about witchcraft.

In spite of problems, however, there also was a spirit of renewal and a concern for the present — living here and now. These ideas helped shape people's view of the world. The Renaissance served as a transition from the religion-centered world of the Middle Ages to the more secular world of today.

Section Questions

1. Why was the invention of the printing press important?
2. How did the Renaissance change as it moved away from Italy?
3. Who were the important Renaissance writers in England? In France? In Spain?
4. In what ways did the Renaissance encourage science?
5. Did the reference to the Renaissance as being the "discovery of the self" also apply to the Renaissance in northern Europe? In what way?

Martin Luther.

3. Martin Luther Started the Reformation

Martin Luther (1483-1546) was born into a peasant family in Germany. His father, Hans, moved to a town and became a prosperous mine owner. Hans Luther wanted his son to be well-educated and to become a lawyer. Although religious, Luther followed his father's wishes and studied the law. He was an excellent student. At the age of twenty-one, Luther was in a forest during a terrifying lightning storm. He cried out: "St. Anne help me; I will become a monk." Shortly thereafter, he entered an Augustinian monastery over his father's objections.

Martin Luther was a very serious priest. By fasting and praying, he tried hard to do everything pleasing to God. However, he was often bothered by self-doubts. He was not sure if he was worthy of salvation. He tried good works, the sacraments, and other religious practices without gaining peace.

In 1515, in the midst of one of his doubting periods, he gained hope. In the New Testament, he read a phrase from St. Paul: "The just shall live by faith." Luther interpreted this to mean that salvation was not based on good works, the sacraments, or rituals. It was also not based on the merit of the individual. Luther came to believe that salvation was instead a free gift from God. God gave salvation to those who had faith in him. Faith was attained by accepting God's words as found in the Bible.

Luther's Statements Luther was in his early thirties when in 1517 he nailed his 95 *Theses*, or statements, to the door of a church. He was outraged by the selling of *indulgences*, the remission of temporal punishment for sins, by the Roman Catholic Church. He thought that selling indulgences was just a way of making money for the church that was harmful to people.

Luther sent copies of his statements on indulgences and other practices of the Roman Catholic Church to his friends. His writings were widely printed. They spread to many parts of Germany and were even translated into other languages.

In addition to indulgences, Luther challenged many of the other ideas and practices of the Roman Catholic Church. He denounced the pope and said that the pope did not have any more authority than any other Christian. Luther believed that people could directly communicate with God and did not need priests to gain salvation.

In 1520, Luther was declared a heretic by the Roman Catholic Church. In 1521, he appeared before Charles V, the Holy Roman Emperor, and his court in Worms, Germany. There he was asked to give up his ideas.

He refused to do this. Luther then was exiled from the Holy Roman Empire. However, Frederick, the ruler of Saxony, hid Luther in one of his castles. While in hiding for a year, Luther translated the New Testament from Greek into German. This translation was important. Both Roman Catholic leaders and Luther's followers believed that the Bible justified their own ideas. In addition, Luther's excellent translation provided a written standard for the German language.

The Growth of Lutheranism Lutheranism was growing in strength and numbers. At this time, and especially in Germany, there was much discontent against the Roman Catholic Church. Germans and other northern Europeans resented sending money to the Italian pope at Rome. Many people—rulers, townspeople, and peasants—wanted to reduce the church's influence. It is estimated that the Roman Catholic Church owned about one-fifth of all the land in Germany at the time of the Reformation. In addition, some people were not satisfied with what they regarded as the formal and empty rituals and ceremonies of the church. They wanted a more direct and emotional encounter between the individual and God. They also criticized the behavior of some among the clergy who neglected their religious duties. They were shocked by the actions of the pope, who seemed to be more of a wealthy ruler than a church leader. They were appalled by the fact that many bishops purchased their offices.

Lutheranism also became firmly established in the German states because Emperor Charles V, though a Roman Catholic, was very busy at this time. He was fighting major wars against both the Turks and France. He had no time or money to put down the growing religious rebellion in Germany.

Luther's religious ideas were revolutionary. They caused social as well as religious turmoil. In 1524 and 1525, the peasants in southern and central Germany rebelled against their landlords. They interpreted Luther's teachings to mean that they should have more freedom. Many of the peasants were being squeezed financially by their landlords who were themselves under financial pressure. The peasants presented a list of moderate demands to the landlords.

The landlords did not agree to the peasants' demands. The peasants then roamed the countryside seizing lands. At first, Luther urged both sides to show restraint and avoid violence. Eventually, however, he sided with the landlords. Luther felt that people did not have the right to revolt against the authorities. He rejected the peasants' claims. He said that they should be suppressed without mercy. This the landlords did as they turned their fury on the peasants. As a result of the Peasants' War, Luther lost support among the peasants in southern Germany.

Political conflict also increased as a consequence of Luther's ideas. Luther called on the German princes to seize the property of the Roman Catholic Church. Wars broke out. In 1555, after a long controversy, a treaty, the Peace of Augsburg, gave the three hundred or more German princes the right to choose between Lutheranism and Roman Catholicism for their territories. The people in each region had to follow the prince's choice. By this time, Lutheranism was well established in northern Germany, in Scandinavia (Denmark, Norway, and Sweden), and in some of the Baltic nations that were then under Swedish control. Lutheranism, like Roman Catholicism before it, became the state religion in these places. However, Luther was not influential only in the places that adopted his specific religious beliefs. Luther's writings spread throughout western Europe. His ideas were powerful in shaping the thought of other Protestant reforms.

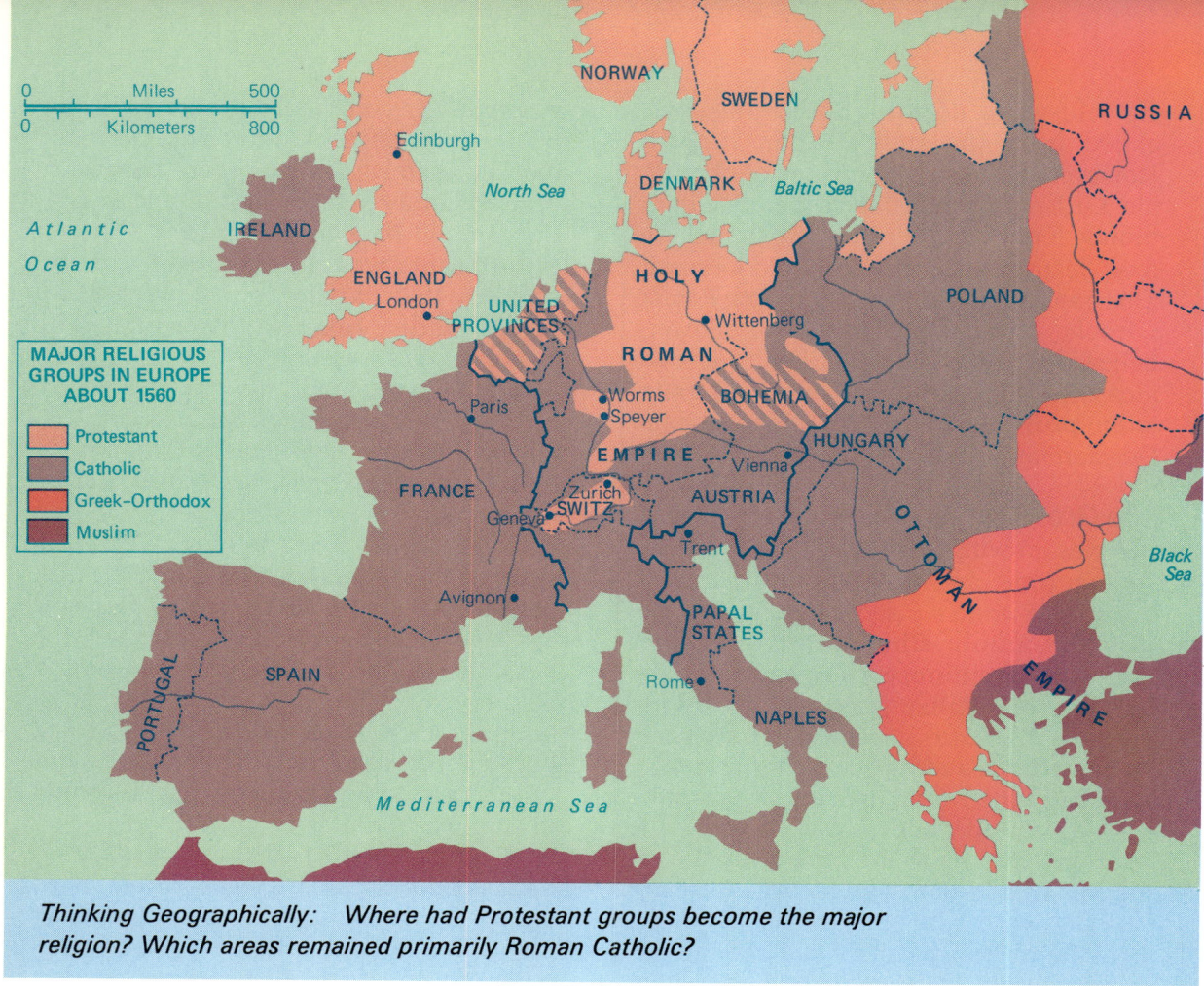

Thinking Geographically: Where had Protestant groups become the major religion? Which areas remained primarily Roman Catholic?

John Calvin The Protestant Reformation quickly spread outside of Germany. After Luther, John Calvin (1509-1564) became the most important leader in the Protestant Reformation. John Calvin was born in northern France into a middle-class family. He was an intelligent child. His father, like Luther's father, wanted his son to become a lawyer. Calvin received a fine education in France. In his early twenties, Calvin became a Protestant. Fearing for his safety, he fled to Switzerland.

In Switzerland, while still a young man, John Calvin wrote the *Institutes of the Christian Religion* (1536). This was the best statement of what Calvin and his followers believed. Calvin accepted many of Luther's ideas, such as the importance of the Bible. However, in many areas Calvin departed further from Roman Catholicism than Luther had. According to Calvin, God had created the whole world for all eternity. Therefore, God knew all things. God knew which individuals were going to receive salvation. Those who were saved, the chosen, had faith and the desire to live a good Christian life.

Calvinism In the ways he organized his churches, Calvin was also more radical than

Did You Know?

The Anabaptists and Other Sects

The ideas of Luther and Calvin had great impact. However, some felt that their reforms did not go far enough. These were the "radical" Protestants. They questioned the whole social and political structure.

During the years from 1520 to 1561, these groups became active in Switzerland, in Germany, and in what is now the Netherlands. They are generally called Anabaptists. Actually, there were many different sects with varied ideas. However, common to most of these groups was the idea of adult baptism. Infant baptism was practiced by both the Protestant groups and the Roman Catholics.

For the Anabaptists, a church was a group of people who had been "born again" in adult baptism. Baptism was a sign of conversion. Often, it was a deeply emotional experience.

Even more radical than the Anabaptists' idea of adult baptism was their belief in the separation of church and state. The Anabaptists thought that all governmental institutions were evil. It was the state, they reasoned, that waged war and committed other violence. Therefore, the Anabaptists asserted that it was sinful to serve in the army. They also considered it wrong to pay taxes. Because of these beliefs, the authorities treated the Anabaptists both as heretics against God and as rebels against the state. They were severely persecuted by both Protestants and Roman Catholics. Nonetheless, they stuck to their beliefs.

Persecuted by almost everyone, the Anabaptists sought refuge in any place that would accept them. Some settled in what is now Czechoslovakia, in Poland, and in Russia. Much later, some settled in the tolerant American colony of Pennsylvania.

This engraving shows persecution of the Huguenots.

These groups were few in number. However, they were a challenge to the accepted thinking of the day. They were one of the first religious groups to support freedom of worship. It was a long time before either Roman Catholics or Protestants granted these groups the right to practice their religious beliefs.

Luther. Calvinist churches were not under bishops or other higher authorities. Instead, each church had its minister(s) and a board of elders, called *presbyters*. In theory, this form of organization represented a move toward democracy, the rule of the many. In practice, the ministers dominated the new churches. Calvinist religious services were simpler than Lutheran services. Calvinists worshipped in plainer church buildings. Statues, crucifixes, stained-glass windows, organ music, and the elaborate garments of the clergy disappeared. The Calvinist services emphasized preaching, Bible reading, and hymn singing. Like Luther, Calvin kept only two sacraments: baptism and Holy Communion.

At first glance, it might appear that Calvin's ideas would promote a passive attitude toward religion. After all, people could not do anything to change their salvation or damnation. However, Calvinism actually encouraged good behavior among church members and in the community at large. If the Calvinists were in the minority in a community, they strove to set a good example. In some places, Calvinists obtained political power. There, as at Geneva in Switzerland, they dictated the whole life of the community. There were many strict rules of behavior. There was to be no card playing, because it wasted time. Gambling, swearing, singing, and dancing were forbidden. Lawbreakers were punished.

Geneva became a major base for Protestantism. Calvin set up an academy that later became the University of Geneva. Geneva was a haven for Protestant refugees from Catholic countries. Students came there from all parts of Europe to learn from the important Protestant reformer. Trained in Calvin's ideas, they returned to their homelands and spread his influence. One student was John Knox, who converted Scotland to Protestantism.

Calvin and the Lutherans were not, however, able to reconcile their differences. In 1561, shortly before his death, Calvin split with the Lutherans. This became the first major division among the Protestants.

The changes that took place in Germany and at Geneva showed that the Protestant leaders were not just attacking the abuses of the Roman Catholic Church. Both Luther and Calvin criticized the popes. However, they did not merely wish to reform the papacy. They wanted to abolish it. Luther and Calvin did not want just to reform monastic life. They wanted to eliminate the monasteries. The Protestant Reformation was, therefore, more than a simple attempt to purify the Roman Catholic Church. It was more of a revolution, a major change in religious thinking and practices.

The religious revolution that Luther began did not die with him. John Calvin gave it the ability to expand. Lutheranism was able to survive only if it became the state religion. It needed to be the majority in a nation. Calvinism, on the other hand, was able to survive as a minority religion. The Calvinists were a majority in Switzerland, in Holland, and in Scotland (the Presbyterians). They were a minority in France (the Huguenots), in England (the Puritans), and in parts of Germany, Hungary, and Poland. The Christian unity that the Roman Catholic Church had represented in western Europe had now been completely destroyed.

Calvinism may also have influenced economic attitudes. The ideas of Calvin encouraged people to work hard and to live simply. This helped some people save money that they could then invest in businesses and trade. In addition, many Protestants came to feel that success in business was a sign of God's approval. All of these things may have promoted the development of *capitalism*, an economic system in which individuals own most capital goods. This new economic system was rising in western Europe at the same time, and in many of the same places, as the Protestant Reformation.

Section Questions

1. Why did many of the German princes support Luther?
2. Why did Geneva become an important base for Protestants?
3. Why may the Protestant Reformation be considered a revolution?
4. In what ways were the ideas of Luther and Calvin similar? In what ways were they dissimilar?

4. The Roman Catholic Church Fought Back

The growth of Protestantism was much more gradual in England than on the European continent. This was due to the way in which it started. It was not a popular movement as in Germany. The Church of England, the Anglican Church, developed in its early years according to the political and personal wishes of Henry VIII, king of England from 1509 to 1547.

The English reformers had been critical of the power and abuses of the Roman Catholic Church. However, few seemed attracted to Lutheranism. The king and the country remained loyal to the Roman Catholic Church. Indeed, in 1521, the pope conferred the title of Defender of the Faith on Henry VIII because he had criticized the teachings of Luther. However, the English did not feel too strongly linked to faraway Rome.

Henry VIII The circumstance that turned England away from Roman Catholicism was the lack of a male heir to the throne. In 1509, the young and popular Henry VIII had married a Spanish princess, Catherine of Aragon, the daughter of King Ferdinand and Queen Isabella of Spain. After eighteen years of marriage, Henry VIII and Queen Catherine had only one living child, Princess Mary.

Henry VIII.

Now Henry VIII wanted to marry Anne Boleyn, a young woman at his court. He asked the pope to *annul*, or set aside, his marriage to Catherine. However, the pope was unwilling to do this, in part because the Holy Roman Emperor Charles V was Catherine's nephew. Charles V urged the pope not to grant the annulment.

Henry VIII was a powerful king who dominated Parliament. In 1534, Henry asked Parliament to give him the authority to be the supreme head of the English church. This meant that all would owe allegiance to Henry instead of to the pope. Parliament did this and, again acting according to Henry's wishes, also annulled his marriage to Catherine.

Henry VIII then married Anne Boleyn, who was already pregnant. However, their

347

marriage produced only one child, Princess Elizabeth. There was still no male heir. Tiring of Anne, Henry VIII tried Anne and her "lovers" on charges of adultery. In 1536, he had them executed. Henry then married Jane Seymour.

Meanwhile, the pope excommunicated Henry VIII for his actions against the Roman Catholic Church. The pope also declared the marriage of Henry and Anne Boleyn invalid. However, the English people generally supported their king. This was particularly true of members of Parliament and other wealthy people. Many had purchased, at a low price, lands of the church that Henry had seized. The townspeople also liked Henry's policy of encouraging trade and peace with other nations.

Only a few openly objected to the religious policies of Henry VIII. One was Sir Thomas More, a brilliant Renaissance man and a personal friend of the king's. He had been lord chancellor, a judge, a member of Parliament, and an ambassador. Sir More and a few others were beheaded.

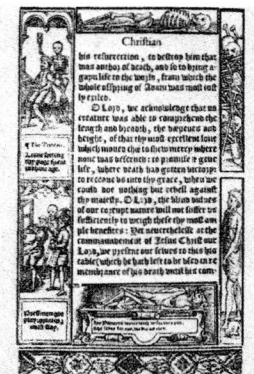 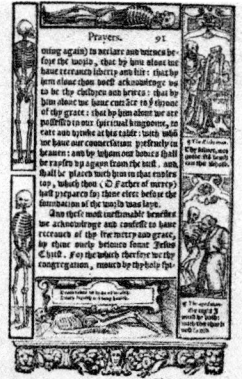

The Church of England First Prayer Book.

Sir Thomas More and his daughter Margaret.

Acting under Henry's instructions, Parliament broke off all relations with the Roman Catholic Church. Henry VIII was now in complete charge of the Church of England. However, he was not really a Protestant. In 1543, the king had a document drawn up that outlined the teachings of his church. These teachings were thoroughly Roman Catholic except for a somewhat greater emphasis on the authority of the Bible. Those who disagreed with Henry were persecuted. This group included a few Roman Catholics who would not recognize Henry as being supreme over the pope. It also included Protestants influenced by the ideas of Luther and Calvin.

Henry's Successors When Henry VIII died, he was succeeded as king by his young son, Edward VI (1547-1553). Edward was the son of Henry's third wife, Jane Seymour. During his short reign, Edward was guided by regents, older people who really ruled for him. The regents issued the First Prayer Book. This described how the rituals of the Church of England should be conducted. It had a Calvinist flavor. However, the Church of England remained under the control of the crown.

Edward VI died at the age of fifteen. Mary I (1553-1558), Henry VIII's eldest daughter, became queen. Many of the English people felt sorry for her because of the way she had been treated as the daughter of Queen Catherine. Mary had remained a devout Roman Catholic.

At first, Mary was tolerant of religious differences. However, Mary married Philip II of Spain, England's traditional enemy. She lost support among the English people because of her pro-Spanish policy. Having become unpopular, Mary felt that the Protestants were plotting against her. She had about 300 Protestants put to death. Because of this, she came to be called "Bloody Mary." Mary I died without children. Her half-sister, Elizabeth I (1558-1603), was then proclaimed queen. Elizabeth's reign was to be long and successful.

Elizabeth I Elizabeth herself had no strong religious feelings. She wanted stability in her kingdom more than anything else. Changes in the state religion were introduced gradually. Parliament adopted the Thirty-nine Articles (1563), a statement of the faith of the Church of England. The articles represented a compromise. The religious beliefs and the views on the sacraments were Protestant. However, the communion ritual and the church organization based on rule by bishops were modeled on those of the Roman Catholic Church.

The Thirty-nine Articles were binding on all. However, the articles were vague in some areas. This allowed many Protestants, whatever their specific beliefs, to remain officially in the Church of England. However, some Protestants and Roman Catholics rejected the articles. Roman Catholics were not allowed to practice their religion openly. Concerned with plots against her, Elizabeth I had some Roman Catholic priests executed. The number of Roman Catholics in England declined.

Elizabeth I, like all rulers of her time,

Elizabeth I.

wanted religious conformity. It was considered an act of treason not to support the religion of the monarch. Therefore she opposed the Puritans as well as the Roman Catholics. The Puritans wanted to "purify" the Church of England by ridding it of Roman Catholic influences. They disliked Anglican rituals. They objected to the rule of the bishops. The Puritans became increasingly unhappy about the religious situation in England.

By 1600, England was a firmly Protestant nation. However, England had achieved this status gradually. The English Reformation was mainly a triumph of the monarchy over the Roman Catholic Church.

The Roman Catholic Reform In 1540, the Roman Catholic Church was in disarray. Much of northern Europe had completely broken away. Protestants were in power in northern Germany, in much of Switzerland, in part of the Low Countries, and in Scandinavia. There were also growing numbers of Protestants in France, Poland, Bohemia, Hungary, and other areas.

Long before Luther, some Roman Catholics had pressed for change. They were as concerned as Luther and the other reformers about the need to improve the church. However, until the pope and other church leaders came to support reform, the efforts of individuals remained ineffective.

The spread of Protestantism caused the Roman Catholic Church to heed the cries for reform at last. In part, the reformers felt that the church needed to be cleansed so that the Protestants could not use the abuses as arguments against Catholicism. For a while, some reformers continued to hope for a reunion of the Protestant and Roman Catholic churches. However, the two groups had already drifted too far apart. Both sides had gradually hardened their viewpoints. No compromise between Protestants and Roman Catholics seemed possible. At that point, a new, aggressive spirit swept the Roman Catholic Church: the Catholic Reformation or the Counter-Reformation. The first objective of the Catholic Reformation was to purify the Roman Catholic Church. The second goal was to win back the Protestants.

This new spirit was evident at the church council held in Trent, a city in northern Italy. Church leaders met on and off there between 1545 and 1563. Their work involved two main areas. One was a restatement of the doctrines of the Roman Catholic Church. The council asserted that tradition as well as the Bible supported certain practices of the church. The second area of concern was reform. The days of the pleasure-loving popes and other high officials of the church were over. Now every member of the clergy, from the pope to the local parish priest, was to be more responsive to the needs of the people and more faithful to the church's teachings.

People who were more devout were placed in important positions. More responsibilities were given to the bishops. Each bishop had to establish a *seminary*, a school for training priests. More emphasis was placed on choosing good men for the priesthood. Monasteries and religious orders were also held to higher standards.

The religious orders were partly responsible for the success of the Catholic Reformation. Some orders placed a new stress on helping the poor and needy. New religious orders were founded to fight Protestantism.

The Jesuits The spirit of the Catholic Reformation was most fully embodied in a new religious order, the Society of Jesus, or

Ignatius of Loyola, founder of the Jesuits.

Jesuits. The Society of Jesus was founded in 1540 by Ignatius (Ig NAY shus) of Loyola (1491-1556), later made a saint. Ignatius was a Spanish officer. He was wounded in 1521. During his painful recovery, he became convinced that it was his calling to serve the Roman Catholic Church and the pope. He obtained a better education. Then, with a few friends, he started his new religious order.

Ignatius formed the Jesuit order along military lines. He stressed obedience and action. No longer were the soldiers of Christ to remain in the monasteries. They were to defend and spread the Roman Catholic faith throughout the world.

Ignatius believed that the struggle against Protestantism was mainly a battle of ideas. Therefore, all members of his order had to be educated and trained well. Ignatius and the Jesuits established many new schools. Soon, the Jesuits had the reputation of being the best-educated religious group. Many became teachers at the universities. By 1600, four-fifths of them were teachers in schools they had established. In their teaching, they used newer methods. These included textbooks, different grade levels instead of one mixed group, and regular examinations. Instead of physical punishment, they tried to motivate their students by prizes and competition. They also attempted to instill a strong devotion to the Roman Catholic Church.

The Jesuits became powerful at the courts of the Roman Catholic rulers. They became the confessors of important people. They influenced government policy. Because of the high standards in the Jesuit schools, many wealthy parents sent their boys to them.

The Jesuits also became active missionaries. They helped convert Poland and parts of central Europe back to the Roman Catholic Church. They kept the Protestants from making further gains. They also sent missionaries around the world—to the

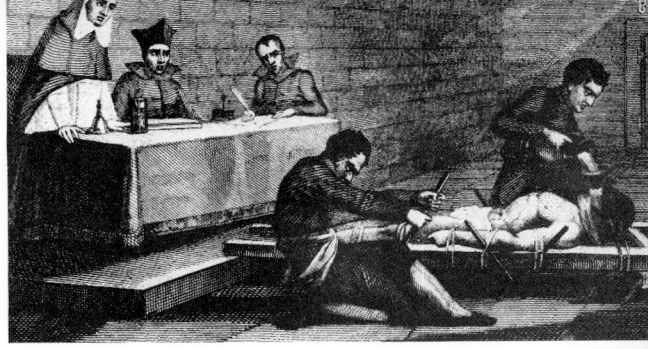

Suspected heretics were tortured during the Inquisition.

Amercias, to Asia, and to Africa. Their greatest missionary was Francis Xavier (1506-1552), who won many converts in Asia.

During the Catholic Reformation new efforts were made to keep all Roman Catholics loyal and faithful. It was felt that they needed to be instructed and guided. *Catechisms*, books that summarized the teachings of the church, were used to help children learn religious doctrine. In Spain and Italy the Inquisition, a church court that tried heretics, became more active. By persecuting dissidents, the Inquisition eliminated opposition to the church. Those found guilty were turned over to the state for punishments such as death or imprisonment.

The Catholic Reformation made the Roman Catholic Church better organized than it had been for centuries. The spread of Protestantism was halted and some gains were made. However, the Roman Catholic Church was not able to regain its position in places where the Protestants were in the majority. The church also gave up some of its powers to the French and Spanish rulers. This was the price the church paid to win their cooperation.

The Protestant Reformation thus caused the Roman Catholic Church to reform itself. The church now had less land and less political power. However, it was better suited to meet the religious needs of its people. It could concentrate more on its spiritual mission.

Section Questions

1. Why did Henry VIII want to divorce Queen Catherine?
2. Which two groups were persecuted by Elizabeth I? Why?
3. What was the purpose of the Catholic Reformation?
4. In what areas did the Jesuits achieve some successes?

Chapter Summary

1. The Renaissance was a new way of thinking. It was a rediscovery of the ideas of the ancient Greeks and Romans. The Renaissance began in Florence, Italy, and spread to the Italian cities and then to the rest of Europe. The new rich in the cities supported the Renaissance artists. The Renaissance placed more importance on human beings and their achievements on Earth. The Renaissance also encouraged the discovery of self, or individualism. This fostered pride and ambition. The Renaissance ideal was also that a person should be skilled in many areas. The ideal Renaissance person had, like Leonardo, many talents in many fields. The Renaissance served as a transition from the religion-centered world of the Middle Ages to the secular modern world. The ideas of the Renaissance were adopted mainly by the intellectuals and the middle class in the cities. During the Italian Renaissance, some of the most beautiful literature and art of the world was produced.
2. The Renaissance moved from Italy to the rest of Europe. People visited Italy and returned to their own lands with the new ideas of the Renaissance. The greatest invention of the time was the printing press, which allowed information to spread rapidly. The northern Renaissance placed less emphasis on architecture and sculpture. It was more concerned with religion and literature. Writers of the northern Renaissance made great contributions to world literature. The most outstanding English writer was William Shakespeare. The Renaissance also encouraged science. However, the Renaissance was not an age of total progress. Problems such as war, oppression, and fear of witchcraft continued.
3. Martin Luther started the Protestant Reformation, a movement to purify the Roman Catholic Church. The result of the Reformation was a split between Roman Catholics and Protestants. The unity of the Roman Catholic Church was destroyed, and Europe became divided into many Christian faiths. The ideas of Luther gained support for many reasons. Lutheranism led to a peasants' revolt in Germany. Political rulers gained more control over the religious affairs of their subjects in both Protestant and Roman Catholic countries. John Calvin's ideas allowed Protestants to survive even if they were in the minority. Calvinist Geneva became a Protestant base, but Lutherans and Calvinists separated. The Protestant Reformation had actually become a religious revolution. Calvinism may have influenced economic attitudes and encouraged the development of capitalism in western Europe.
4. England gradually became a Protestant nation after Henry VIII became the head of the Church of England. Mary I failed to restore Roman Catholicism. Elizabeth I wanted stability and religious compromise and conformity. She disliked both the Roman Catholics and the Puritans. Gravely weakened, the Roman Catholic Church tried to reform itself and stop the spread of Protestantism. The Catholic Reformation took shape at the Council of Trent and in religious orders such as the Society of Jesus. The Jesuits became influential in education and at Roman Catholic courts. Catechisms were used, and the Inquisition was more active. However, even in the Roman Catholic countries the church lost power to the rulers.

Chapter 18 Review

Check Your Facts

1. Identify the following:
   a. Elizabeth I
   b. St. Peter's Basilica
   c. Michelangelo
   d. Dante
   e. Luther
   f. Calvin
   g. Gutenberg
   h. Henry VIII
   i. Cervantes
   j. Medici family
2. Why was Leonardo da Vinci the ideal Renaissance person?
3. In what ways were the ideas of the Renaissance in conflict with the teachings of the Roman Catholic Church?
4. What helped Protestantism survive after Luther's death?
5. In what ways could it be said that Calvinistic ideas affected the economy?
6. Why did most of the English people support Henry VIII against the pope?
7. What reforms were made as a result of the Catholic Reformation?
8. What did the Roman Catholic Church do to make sure that its members remained loyal and faithful?

Words to Know

Define the following words in one or two sentences. Then tell the significance of each during the Renaissance.
   a. perspective
   b. rhetoric
   c. individualism
   d. indulgences
   e. Protestants
   f. catechism

Developing Your Skills

1. Study the legacy charts in the early chapters of this text. Then make a chart of the legacy of the Renaissance.
2. Trace part of the map on page 344. Label the map with the names of people or groups who spread Protestantism to each area.

Thinking It Over

1. In the Renaissance, talented artists were highly respected. Do you think artists are respected today?
2. During the Renaissance, the wealthy few supported the artists. What are the advantages of this system? The disadvantages? Should the arts today be supported by the public? Who should make the decision on which artists should get support?
3. What are the advantages of having a state religion? What are the disadvantages?

Special Activities

1. In small groups, discuss the positive effects of the Renaissance on society. Then discuss the negative effects of the Renaissance on society.
2. Hold a debate on the following issue: Compared to the time of the Protestant Reformation, is religion increasing or decreasing in importance in our society?
3. How might society change if religion increases or decreases in importance in the future?
4. Sects are small religious groups that are intensely devoted to their religious beliefs. Find out more about new sects that have appeared in the United States.

The Escorial, the largest Renaissance building outside of Italy, was built by Philip II.

Chapter 19 Modern States

During the same centuries that the Renaissance and the Reformation were altering the cultural and religious life of Europe, the rise of the modern state was transforming European politics. These three developments, plus discoveries in the Americas and other places, changed the way Europeans viewed the world. The state was now coming to have more power and authority. The influence of religious leaders declined. The use of a professional army and navy and trained government officials helped make the modern state more unified.

1237-1725	
1237-1240	Tatars conquer Russia
1368	Ming dynasty begins
1453	Ottoman Turks capture Constantinople
1486	Ivan the Great defeats Tatars
1519	Charles V becomes Holy Roman Emperor
1526	Mogul empire begins
1559-1589	Religious wars in France
1588	Spanish Armada defeated
1598	Edict of Nantes
1613	Michael Romanov chosen Czar of Russia
1618-1648	Thirty Years' War
1644	Manchu dynasty begins
1689-1725	Peter the Great

Charles V.

A strong ruler whose life illustrates the rise of the modern state, as well as other changes of the time, was Philip II of Spain (1527-1598). Philip II was the most powerful Roman Catholic ruler of his time.

To combat the Reformation, Philip II sent both his army and navy to fight against Protestant nations. Protestant critics have portrayed Philip II as a religious fanatic who waged war against the Protestants as if he were on a religious crusade. It is true that Philip II was a devout Roman Catholic. However, he was also concerned about the political and commercial interests of Spain. He did not focus totally on religious issues. During Philip's lifetime, Spain had its greatest colonial empire. His forces weakened the power of Muslim Turks in 1571 in a sea battle at Lepanto (lay PAHN to).

Among earlier historians, Philip II generally had a poor reputation. This was particularly true of English historians. Many condemned his attempt to invade England. Philip II also had a poor image in other areas. In Verdi's famous opera *Don Carlos*, Philip II is shown as ready to turn his own son over to the Inquisition. This was not true. Modern historians see Philip II as no better or worse than other rulers of his age, whether Protestant or Roman Catholic. At that time, few rulers were tolerant of religious differences. In the context of his age, Philip II was an intelligent and hard-working ruler.

1. England and France Challenged the Hapsburgs

During the late Middle Ages, from about 1300 to about 1500, kings gained more power. The nations on the Atlantic seaboard—Spain, Portugal, England, and France—were becoming strong, modern national states. These states differed from those of medieval Europe in that the king had more authority and control over the people living within the nation's boundaries.

Modern States During the 1500s, most kings were able to consolidate their growing power for two basic reasons: (1) they controlled a professional army, and (2) they used trained government officials throughout their kingdoms. No longer did the king depend on feudal lords or volunteers to defend the nation against outside enemies. Instead, the king had at his command a hired army and, later, a navy. In addition to using the army to ensure the security of the nation, the king could employ it to put down enemies from within.

The government officials were responsible to the king, not to the local feudal lords. These officials enforced the royal laws. All people in the nation now had to obey the laws of the king. In addition, judges tried cases in royal courts. Formerly, justice had been administered by the local lords and the Roman Catholic Church.

As the European monarchs gained more power, people became more loyal to the king and nation than to the local lord. The nation thus became more unified, supporting one leader, the king, instead of many lords.

The modern national states became more concerned about foreign affairs. The nations of Europe wanted to prevent any one power from dominating the whole continent. During the 1500s and 1600s, the European nations particularly sought to reduce the power of the Hapsburgs, the most powerful royal family in Europe.

The Hapsburgs In 1519, Charles V inherited the huge Hapsburg empire. These territories included the Holy Roman Empire, Spain, Austria, the Low Countries (now the Netherlands and Belgium), parts of Italy, Sardinia, and Sicily. Within the Holy Roman Empire were the 300 or so independent German states and cities. Charles did not inherit a true empire. His lands were not unified by language, customs, or geography. After Luther defied the Roman Catholic Church, the lands of the Roman Catholic emperor were further divided by the violent split between the Protestants and Roman Catholics.

To better manage his vast lands, Charles V divided the Hapsburg empire into two parts. In 1521 and 1522, he gave his younger brother, Ferdinand I, the rule of the Austrian Hapsburg empire. This mainly included Austria, Bohemia, and Hungary. Charles V then concentrated on ruling the rest of his territories, the Spanish Hapsburg empire.

For almost forty years, from 1519 to 1556, Charles V and his brother faced three major problems. The first was to keep the Ottoman Turks from invading central Europe and from attacking ships on the Mediterranean Sea. In 1529, the Turks reached the outskirts of Vienna in Austria. However, they were stopped and pushed back into Hungary.

The second challenge came from the ideas of Luther and Calvin. The Protestant German princes wanted to be free of the rule of their Roman Catholic emperor. The French aided the German princes.

France represented Charles' third major problem. The French kings felt encircled by the Hapsburg empire. France fought four wars against the Hapsburgs, mainly in Italy. Charles V retained control of parts of Italy but France gained a few cities near the border.

Worn out by these problems, Charles V retired, giving the Spanish Hapsburg

The Great Armada as painted by an unknown artist.

empire to his son, Philip II. Along with his lands in Europe, Philip II inherited the rapidly growing Spanish possessions in the Americas and Asia.

Philip II tried to increase the power and influence of Spain and to further the cause of the Catholic Reformation. As you read earlier, his forces broke the power of the Turks by a great naval victory near the town of Lepanto in Greece. In 1580, Philip II also conquered Portugal. However, he failed to put down the revolt of the Dutch Protestants or to conquer England. In 1588, he sent a huge fleet of 130 ships with 27,000 men—the Great Armada—against England. The plan was for the Armada to defeat the English navy and then invade England. However, the English won the sea battle by better seamanship. Storms also struck the Spanish fleet. Only a few Spanish ships made it back to Spain.

The defeat of the Spanish Armada showed that the power of Spain was declining and the strength of England was rising. Spain still controlled much territory but England was now stronger on the seas. This naval power was vital in trade and colonization.

France By 1550, France had almost reached its present-day boundaries. With about fifteen million people, it had the largest population in Europe. France was the great land rival of the Hapsburg empire. However, from about 1559 to 1589, France was torn apart by religious civil wars. As a result, the French kings were unable to expand the size of their kingdom.

The ideas of Luther and Calvin were attractive to many of the French nobles who wanted to be more independent of the king. About two-fifths of the nobles came to support the Huguenots, the French Calvinists. In addition to the nobles, the Huguenots also won the support of many middle-class people in the towns.

Although the Huguenots numbered only about one million, they were well-organized and disciplined. They controlled many of the towns in the south and west. Conflict broke out between the Roman Catholics and the Protestants and continued on and off for many years. However, the conflict had almost been settled. Then Charles IX permitted a massacre of the Huguenots in Paris on the eve of the Feast of St. Bartholomew, August 24, 1572. About 20,000 Huguenots were killed. As a result of the massacre, the savage war continued.

Peace finally came in 1593. Henry IV, a Protestant and the first of the Bourbon line of kings, agreed to become a Roman Catholic. He thereby won the loyalty of most of his subjects. A few years later, in 1598, Henry IV issued the Edict of Nantes. This recognized Roman Catholicism as the official religion of France. However, it provided for some toleration for the Huguenots. This law eased religious tensions and allowed France to become prosperous and powerful again.

The Thirty Years' War All the religious and political conflicts of the time came to a head during the Thirty Years' War (1618-1648). The war started in 1618 when the Protestant nobles in Bohemia rebelled against the Austrian Hapsburgs. The Hapsburgs put down the Bohemian rebellion by 1623. They then outlawed Protestantism in Bohemia. Hundreds of the Protestant rebels were executed.

The war then spread to Germany. In 1625, when the Roman Catholics appeared to be winning, the Protestant Danes sent troops into Germany. The Protestant Swedes sent troops in 1630. By 1632, there was a deadlock with neither side strong enough to win. By 1635, the Hapsburgs were ready for peace. However, Roman Catholic France then entered the war on the side of the Protestant Swedes against the Roman Catholic Hapsburgs. France entered the war for political, not religious reasons. It had long been worried about being surrounded by the powerful Hapsburgs. The fighting now spread to France's northern border and its border with Spain in the south.

Finally, after many years of negotiation, the Treaty of Westphalia (1648) brought the war to an end. France received Alsace and Lorraine, bringing its frontier to the Rhine River. The Swedes obtained control of important waterways in the areas of the Baltic Sea and the North Sea. The Calvinists won the right to be recognized as an official religion in Germany. They were now equal with the Roman Catholics and the Lutherans. However, the Anabaptists and other sects were not allowed to practice their religions openly.

The war more or less settled the boundaries of the European nations. The Netherlands and Switzerland won recognition of their independence. The German states remained divided. The power of France was growing at the expense of that of the Spanish and Austrian Hapsburgs.

Section Questions

1. What two features of a modern state made it different from a medieval nation?
2. Why was Charles V's empire not really an empire?
3. What successes did Philip II of Spain have? What were his failures?
4. What was the Edict of Nantes? What was its significance?
5. In what way was the Thirty Years' War not strictly a struggle of Roman Catholics against Protestants?

A painting of the Byzantine Empire, the empire which greatly influenced Russia.

2. Russia Arose as a New Nation State

From the time of the ancient Greeks, Slavic people lived in loosely organized bands in what is now eastern Europe. From one of these Slavic groups came the Russian state, now the Soviet Union. It is the largest nation in the world in land area. Today the Soviet Union has many ethnic and racial groups, but the Russian nation was originally Slavic. By 800, these Slavic people had established an agricultural system in which wheat, rye, barley, and oats were the main staples. The Slavs also raised cattle and were good hunters and fishers. They were skilled in carpentry and woodwork. They mined metal, extracted salt, built in stone, and tanned skins. The Slavs worshiped the forces of nature and their ancestors.

In the ninth century, the Slavs came to be dominated by Vikings from Sweden. These Vikings were probably called Rus, and thus gave their name to Russia. The Rus expanded trading activities and created stronger political organizations, centered in the towns. Soon, they were absorbed by the Slavs.

The first Russian "state" was really a loose federation of tribes. It was centered on Kiev (KEE ef), a fort on the Dnieper (NEE per) River. From this fort, founded in the 800s, the grand princes of Kiev controlled the surrounding area. They demanded tribute, gifts or taxes, from the other princes of the area. At the height of Kiev's glory, the grand prince probably controlled over a million people. It was the most important trading center in what later became Russia. There the merchants traded raw materials such as furs, wax, and honey for the luxury goods from the Middle East and Asia: spices, glass, jewels, and fabrics such as silk.

About 988, under the influence of the Byzantine Empire, the ruler of Kiev adopted the Christian religion. Monasteries were founded. The monks fostered learning and the arts. The Russians also borrowed writing from the Byzantines. The Orthodox Church obtained land and took over such charitable tasks as helping the sick and providing shelter for travelers.

Russians battling the Tatars.

The Rise of Moscow The Tatars allowed certain princes to collect the taxes in their immediate area. The prince would then turn over the taxes to the Tatars. Gradually, the princes around the city of Moscow became more powerful. This happened for several reasons. Moscow was at the headwaters of four major rivers: the Oka, Volga, Don, and Dnieper. Water was the best and cheapest means of transportation at the time. Thus, Moscow had a geographical advantage for trade and communication. In addition, Moscow was at the center of a great landlocked plain that had no natural barriers. This allowed the princes of Moscow to expand their territory easily. Moreover, the princes of Moscow lived long lives. Thus, a ruling family did not have a young, weak child inherit the title.

Gradually, the princes of Moscow increased their territory. Sometimes, they

Dark days came between 1237 and 1240, when the fierce Tatars (TOT urs) attacked Kiev and other Russian cities. In some towns, the entire population was killed. During their 250 years of rule, the Tatars made the Russians pay tribute every year. Life under the Tatars was harsh. There were setbacks in education and the arts. Russia was also cut off from the Byzantine Empire and western Europe, so it lagged behind the rest of Europe in technology and ideas.

The Tatars established a capital, Sarai (saw RI), in the area of the lower Volga River. This shifted power away from Kiev to the east. However, the Tatars allowed the Russian people to keep their ruling princes and did not interfere too much with religion and daily life. They kept apart from the Russians and were mainly interested in collecting the annual tribute.

A painting of early Moscow.

Did You Know?

The Ottoman Turks

The Ottoman Turks were warlike Turkish nomads. As the power of the Mongols declined during the 1300s, the Ottoman Turks expanded their territory in Asia Minor. In 1453, the strong Ottoman army seized weakly defended Constantinople. Constantinople was the center of the Greek Orthodox Church and the Byzantine Empire. Constantinople was renamed Istanbul by the Ottoman Turks.

The Ottoman Turks continued to expand. By 1481, they had conquered most of southeastern Europe. The Ottoman empire reached its height in 1566, when it had conquered much of North Africa.

The Ottoman Turks had an effective military organization and civil administration. However, their leaders were unable to adopt new ideas. In the Battle of Lepanto (1571), the better-designed European ships defeated the Turkish navy. As a result of this defeat, the Ottoman Turks were less able to defend the Mediterranean area. In addition, the Portuguese, and later the English and the Dutch, gained control of the trade between Europe and Asia. This trade had been a good source of income for the Ottoman Turks when it had moved overland through their territories.

At the same time that trade revenues were declining, the Ottoman empire population was growing. This led to a shortage of land and large-scale unemployment. The government could not pay the salaries of its troops. The unpaid soldiers wandered in bands and began to loot. Between 1595 and 1610, rebellions and civil disorders broke out. The battles often ravaged the lands of the peasants.

Constantinople, renamed Istanbul, in 1462.

The Ottoman government increased taxes. This imposed a heavy burden on the people. Now more people, especially those living at the fringes of the empire, wanted their independence.

By the 1580s, the Dutch and the English controlled the Indian Ocean and the Mediterranean. By 1618, the Ottoman Turks were barely able to defend their lands. The Russians pressed down toward the Black Sea. The Arab states of North Africa became more independent. By about 1700, the Hapsburgs had gained control of most of Hungary. The days of the greatness of the Ottoman empire were passing.

did this through military force. At other times, they bought land. By clever diplomacy, they entered into favorable economic agreements with other princes. They also encouraged peasants to settle in their relatively peaceful area. These peasants then produced food for those in the towns.

The growing role of Moscow as the center of Russia was solidified by the accomplishments of Ivan III, the Great (1462-1505). About the time that Columbus was discovering the New World for Europe, Ivan III achieved independence from Tatar rule. He refused to pay the money due the Tatars. The Tatars then sent their army to destroy Ivan III, arriving at the outskirts of Moscow in 1480. The Russians started to retreat, but then the Tatars turned back, apparently worried about an attack on their capital, Sarai. The Tatars lost control of the Moscow territory.

Ivan III also strengthened his position through his Greek bride, Sophia Palaeologus (pay lee OL o gus). Sophia was the niece of the last emperor of Byzantium. Since the Greek Orthodox Church was now located in an area controlled by the Ottoman Turks, Ivan made himself the supreme head of the Russian Orthodox Church. This event was very important. As it had been during the Middle Ages in western Europe, religion was central in the lives of most people. Ivan III built up Moscow with impressive buildings and churches. Moscow was now the seat of religious, as well as political, power.

Ivan III had unlimited power. By gaining control over other cities such as Novgorod (NOV go rod) north of Moscow, Ivan effectively eliminated opposition. He was at the top of the social structure. Below him were the *boyars*, or nobles. The boyars owned the large estates. Formerly, they had collected the taxes and administered justice in their own territories. However, Ivan reduced their power. In contrast to nobles in other European nations they had no firm rights or privileges. Below the nobles were a few traders and skilled workers who had no political power. The vast majority of the people were peasants.

Ivan IV, the Terrible Ivan IV (1533-1584) further increased the power of the Russian ruler over the people. Ivan was only three years old when his father, Basil III, died in 1533. The young grand prince soon became aware of plotting around the palace. When he was eight, his mother died, perhaps because she had been poisoned. The boyars took away Ivan's favorite servants and friends. Some of these people were executed or imprisoned. Ivan's early childhood was very painful and bitter. It probably contributed to his later emotional instability.

Suddenly, at the age of thirteen, Ivan threw out the regent who was ruling in his behalf. In 1547, Ivan IV was crowned the first *czar* of all Russia. This title meant that he was the caesar, or supreme ruler, of

Ivan III, the Great.

Ivan IV, the Terrible.

About 1553, Ivan IV changed. He began to think that the boyars were plotting against him. In 1560, his beloved wife Anastasia died. Ivan suspected that she had been poisoned. His wrath then turned on everyone. Some historians believe that he was insane at times during these years. This was the "bad" period, when he became known as Ivan the Terrible.

Ivan IV crushed the boyars and started a reign of terror. He organized a secret police that was absolutely loyal to him. The police killed thousands of people whom Ivan suspected of disloyalty. Sometimes, entire towns were wiped out. Ivan even killed his oldest son and heir. After his outbursts of rage, Ivan would feel ashamed

Ivan IV with his dying son.

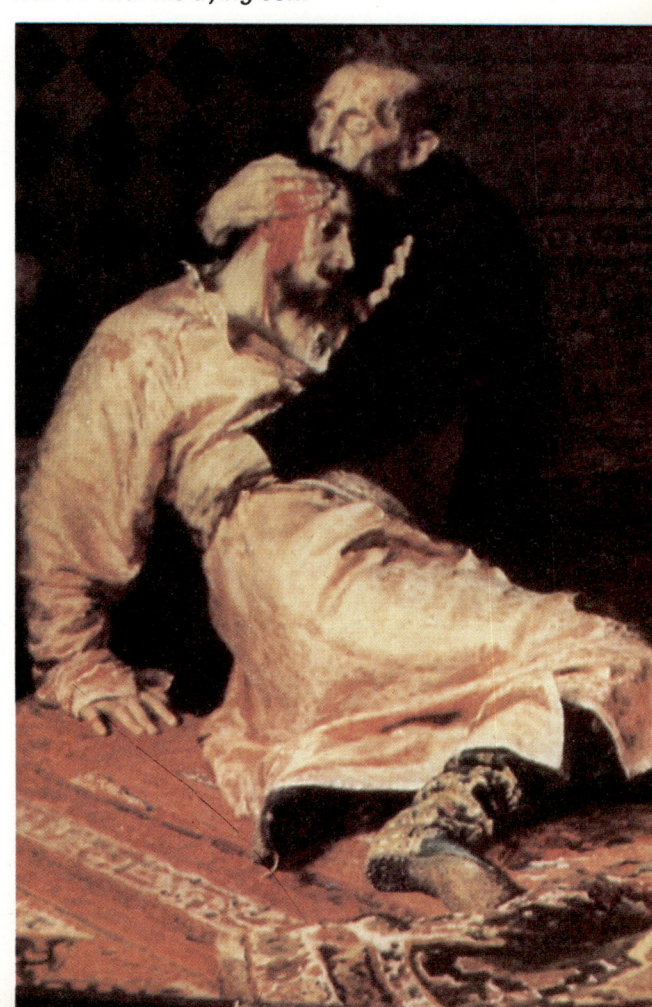

all the Moscow territory. Ivan continued the policy of expansion of his predecessors. He conquered the remaining outposts of the Tatars in the east and southeast. This gave him control of the Volga River. Russians also began to explore Siberia, the vast area to the east.

Ivan's rule is often divided by historians into two parts, the "good" period and the "bad" period. During the good period, when he was a young man, Ivan IV married Anastasia. She was a kind and supportive wife and their marriage was happy. Ivan followed her good advice and that of wise advisers. He tried to make reforms in the army, in the Russian Orthodox Church, and in local government. He sent diplomats from isolated Russia to the outside world.

and repent. However, the cycle of violence would soon start up again. Ivan died in 1584, perhaps by poison.

Before Ivan died, he broke the power of the boyars. He created a new group of nobles, or *gentry*. They served the state as military officers or government officials. With the expansion of Russia, their services were needed in the newly conquered territories. Ivan granted estates to the gentry. However, the large estates were of limited value without workers. There was a great demand for workers, since Russia was not densely settled. This was especially true in Siberia. Like the West in the United States in the 1800s, Siberia offered more opportunity and freedom for new settlers.

Originally, even in the early days when Kiev was dominant, the peasants worked under agreements with the nobles. In return for grain or the use of tools such as plows, the peasants agreed to pay the landlord in some combination of labor and goods. These agreements were often made for a long time, typically ten years. However, unless the peasants could completely pay off the debt by the end of that time, they could not leave the land. Because of disasters such as poor crops, it became increasingly difficult for peasants to leave.

During the reign of Ivan IV, the peasants were legally reduced to serfs. The government stated that, in certain years, no peasants could move, not even those who could pay off their contracts. Serfdom was thus established, and the serfs were at the mercy of their landlords. They had no rights and were almost slaves. By the late 1500s, about ninety percent of the Russian people were serfs. Serfdom lasted in Russia until 1861, much later than in western Europe.

Troubled Times, 1584-1613 After the death of Ivan IV, Russia faced many problems. Ivan was followed by weak rulers, and the ruling family died out. There was then a struggle over the throne. With Russia weakened internally, the Poles and the Swedes attacked. So many boyars had been killed by Ivan IV that there were not enough leaders for the army and the government. Then famine hit Russia from 1601 to 1603. Many of the hard-pressed serfs, losing all hope, revolted, increasing the violence and anarchy.

Finally, in 1613 a group of nobles chose young Michael Romanov (ROH muh noff) as czar. He was the first of the Romanovs to rule. His family reigned for about three hundred years, until overthrown by revolution in 1917.

Under Czar Michael's direction, the foreign invaders were repulsed. The czar and his successors also made agreements with the gentry and the Russian Orthodox Church. For supporting him, the gentry received strict control over the peasants, whose revolts were put down. Thus, at the end of the troubled times, the czar and the gentry had reasserted their power, while the peasants had gained nothing.

Peter the Great By 1689, Russia had expanded across Siberia to the Pacific Ocean. It had become, in land area, the largest nation in the world. However, compared to the nations of western Europe, Russia was backward. Peter I, the Great (1689-1725), speeded up the modernization of Russia and successfully sought a seaport for his landlocked country.

Peter I was a giant of a man, almost seven feet tall. He did not have much formal learning and could barely read and write. However, he had a great deal of energy. Peter visited several nations in Europe, becoming the first Russian ruler to travel widely. During his travels, Peter absorbed many ideas. He learned best in informal situations. He particularly liked visiting shipyards and learning about mechanical things. He enjoyed doing things with his hands, such as practicing dentistry

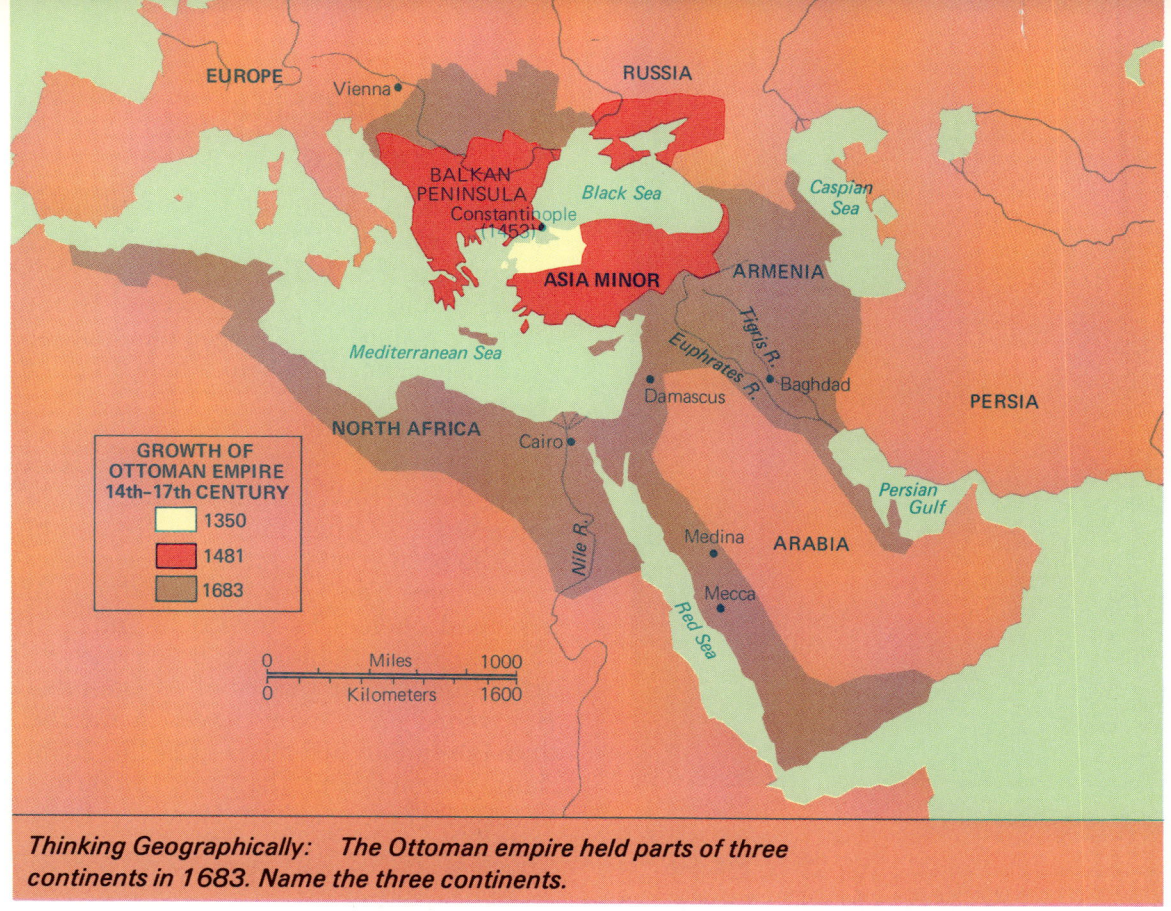

Thinking Geographically: The Ottoman empire held parts of three continents in 1683. Name the three continents.

and making shoes. After his tours of Europe, Peter became convinced that Russia should become as modern as western Europe.

Throughout his reign, Peter's first priority was to obtain a warm-water seaport for Russia. Russia bordered mostly on land areas or on oceans that were frozen for much of the year. Peter sought a port on the Black Sea, an area then held by the Turks. His long war against the Turks eventually proved unsuccessful. However, to fight his wars, Peter I built Russia's first modern army and navy. Peter won a port on the Baltic Sea from Sweden after a long struggle.

Peter's second priority was to change the lifestyle of the Russian gentry. Despite protests, he ordered that French customs be adopted in his imperial courts—including French manners and clothing and the French language. The women of the nobility became more active in social and public life. Peter I encouraged the nobility to become better educated. He forced male members of the gentry over the age of sixteen to serve in the military or the government.

Peter I sought a modern and strong Russian state. Most of his demands for change directly affected the aristocrats. However, he made some changes in the lives of the peasants. Each village now had to send a certain number of recruits to serve in the army. Peter spent heavily to encourage science and industry and build a new capital, St. Petersburg (1703). Thus, Peter was pressed for money. Under his rule, the peasants were taxed even more heavily and treated more severely.

Peter the Great.

Peter's changes caused him to be both praised as a hero and damned as a person who was trying to destroy old Russia. Westernization was now a state policy, and Russia gradually became more European. Meanwhile, the other European nations were beginning to worry about the growing power of Russia as it became more important in European affairs.

Section Questions

1. What kind of people started the Russian nation? In what area did they live?
2. Why did Moscow become a power center?
3. What two things did Ivan III do that made him important in the history of Russia?
4. What happened to the peasants during the reign of Ivan the Terrible?
5. What were the two main goals of Peter the Great?

3. India and China Had Strong Leaders

The Delhi sultans of India had fallen on hard times by 1500. They ruled only a part of northern India. Even there, rebellious Muslim nobles and powerful Hindu princes constantly challenged their authority. This weakness invited a new invasion from central Asia.

The Moguls The Mogul invaders were led by Baber (BAW bur), a brilliant general and a writer of great fame. His first ambition had been to rule central Asia. However, rivals drove him from his homeland. As a second choice, he turned to India. In 1526, he came thundering down with his army through the passes of Afghanistan. His troops were many fewer in number than the Indian defenders at Delhi. Historians estimate that he had only 12,000 men to 100,000 for the sultan. However, Baber had muskets and artillery. These were more than a match for the sultan's many elephants. Baber routed the sultan's army and quickly conquered northern India.

The Moguls were a mixed group of Turkish Muslims. They should not be confused with the Mongols of Mongolia, the area north of China. The Moguls ruled over one of the most powerful empires in the history of India. At about the time Baber invaded northern India, the Portuguese were gaining control of key ports along the Indian coast. The Portuguese were but the first wave of a flood of adventurous Europeans who came to Asia in search of wealth and glory. As long as the Mogul empire was strong, the Europeans would confine themselves to trading activities.

Akbar After living for only four years in India, Baber died. His empire at once declined. His son was driven out of India. It was fifteen years before he regained his throne. The Moguls' fortunes revived under

This picture shows the birth of Akbar's second son.

Akbar (1556-1605), a grandson of Baber. He became emperor at the young age of thirteen and ruled for forty-nine years.

Akbar was one of India's greatest rulers. He reconquered northern India and Afghanistan and added part of southern India to his empire. Akbar was a shrewd and ambitious ruler. He wanted to make sure that his empire remained strong and stable. To achieve this goal, he used several methods.

One was to ensure that no one could challenge his power. The emperor recruited his nobles from many different groups so that they could not unite against him easily. Many came from outside India. Akbar never allowed a noble to remain in one office for long. After a noble had served for two or three years in one area, he was often sent to a post on the other side of the empire. This kept him from establishing a power base independent of the emperor.

Despite this frequent switching of personnel, Akbar's administration was efficient. He drew upon the best talent available, regardless of ethnic and religious background. Reforms in the tax system ensured his government a steady flow of revenue. Large expenditures on public works, especially roads, made the area more prosperous and united than it had been for centuries.

Akbar also neutralized the religious conflicts in India. He married a Rajput princess to win the loyalty of the most important group of Hindu warriors in northern India. In addition, Akbar tried to give all people in his domains equal rights.

Akbar was tolerant of all religions, especially if they were practiced privately. He was a deeply spiritual person. He had Muslims at his court, and he invited Hindu, Parsi, and Catholic priests to instruct him on their faiths. However, Akbar demanded that people respect his authority. When he was challenged, he was not always merciful. Both Muslims and Hindus who defied him were executed.

Thus, Akbar conquered a large territory and gave it a strong and just government. This was the most solid achievement of his long rule. In addition, he and later Mogul emperors made outstanding contributions to the arts, especially architecture.

The best-known example of Mogul architecture is the famous Taj Mahal. Completed in 1653 at great expense, it was built by Akbar's grandson, Shah Jahan, as a tomb for his beloved wife. This building incorporates a lovely balance of Muslim ideas and Hindu materials. There is an extensive use of marble and a graceful dome. The building is decorated with Arabic passages from the Koran, etched into its walls with inlaid stone. *Minarets*, or slender towers, on the sides and reflecting pools in front enhance the structure.

The Taj Mahal.

The Decline of the Mogul Empire The good administration that Akbar set up held the diverse peoples of India together for about 100 years. This was true even though his heirs were less talented than he. His son and grandson both increased the size of the empire. Under Aurangzeb (AW rung zeb 1658-1707), the next ruler, the empire reached its greatest size. The last two important kingdoms in the south were conquered.

However, these conquests were not lasting. Aurangzeb spent the last 26 years of his life in the south fighting costly wars that never seemed to end. As soon as one area was subdued, rebellion broke out in another. The most serious resistance came from the Marathas. These were a hardy people who lived in the highlands in the western part of the Deccan. They became a constant source of trouble for Aurangzeb. They used hit-and-run tactics to wear down the Moguls.

While Aurangzeb was trying without success to defeat the Marathas, rebellious groups began to throw off Mogul authority in other parts of the empire. After his death, the Mogul empire rapidly broke up into smaller political units. The strongest of these was the Maratha confederacy. At its height, the confederacy ruled most of southern India and extended into the north. By 1739, the Moguls had become so weak they could not resist an invasion by Persians.

Delhi, with its marvelous buildings and jewels, was sacked and the emperor was blinded.

There were many reasons for the decline of the Moguls. Aurangzeb, a strict Muslim, discriminated against Hindus. He excluded them from his government and reimposed the *jizya*, a special tax on non-Muslims. He was a stern ruler who severely punished anyone who opposed him. Preoccupied with the wars in the south, Aurangzeb allowed Akbar's administrative system to weaken. Nobles in many parts of India began to set themselves up as independent rulers. The tax system also broke down. The peasants were harshly oppressed by both nobles and bandits. The common people were often innocent victims of the constant warfare that accompanied the end of Mogul power.

The Ming Dynasty As you read earlier, the Mongols were driven out of China by native Chinese. A new ruling family, the Ming dynasty (1368-1644), came to power. The Ming dynasty showed the effects of the earlier occupation of the Mongols. The Chinese developed a sense of superiority in driving out the Mongols. In addition, as a result of the Mongol invasion, the Chinese had become afraid of foreigners and foreign influence.

Chinese government was practical and efficient during the Ming dynasty. The Chinese were stronger than they had been for many centuries. They controlled all the territory of what we now consider China proper. Up to 1500, there was peace and prosperity. Many bridges, city walls, and temples were built. Roads, reservoirs, and irrigation canals were improved or extended. The Great Wall was largely rebuilt.

Agriculture also improved during the Ming dynasty. The most important change was the introduction of a new kind of rice from Indochina. It was resistant to drought. Later, the Chinese developed a variety that

A view of China in the 1500s.

could mature in only sixty days. This meant that farmers could plant two rice crops a year instead of just one. People began to keep fish in the rice fields to provide food and to produce fertilizer. The fish also helped control the malaria-carrying mosquitoes. The mosquitoes formerly had rendered large sections of southern China uninhabitable. The old system of cultivation that allowed some fields to remain fallow each year was abandoned. It was replaced by a system of crop rotation.

The population started to increase as a result of these improvements. By 1400, there were at least 65 million people in China. The European nations were just recovering from the Black Plague. They had relatively small populations. Germany, the largest European country west of Russia, did not reach a population of 60 million until after 1900, more than 500 years later.

During the Ming dynasty, the Chinese began to trade by sea as well as by land. Chinese ships now traveled all the way from Indonesia to the Persian Gulf. Some reached the east coast of Africa.

About 1431, because of the threat of Japanese pirates, among other reasons, the Ming government prohibited overseas commercial voyages. Chinese ships were restricted to trading along the Chinese coast. The Chinese no longer had direct knowledge of the outside world. They remained within their secure borders. The imperial court became more conservative. It did not encourage new developments in ideas, literature, or art.

The Chinese resisted outsiders. They felt that the Portuguese and all other Europeans were barbarians. After some difficulty, the Portuguese were allowed to use one port, Macao, near Guanzhou (Canton). There the foreigners were carefully supervised. The Chinese also permitted a few Jesuits to come to China. One, Father Matteo Ricci, was very learned. The imperial court liked the scientific information he imparted more than his religious ideas. In general, however, the Chinese thought that most foreigners, especially merchants, murdered and plundered.

About 1550, problems began to multiply for the Ming dynasty. Japanese pirates looted cities and swept inland. In addi-

A porcelain vase from the Ming dynasty.

tion, the Ming rulers became increasingly incompetent. In part, this was because the emperor was secluded behind the palace walls in Peking. The only information that the emperor received was from his advisers. Few were frank, since the emperor could order the death of anyone who had shown "disrespect" to him. Too often, emperors spent their time in search of pleasure. Administrators increasingly became corrupt and incompetent. With more corruption, the small tenants were hard pressed to pay their taxes. In the 1600s, peasant revolts became more common. The Ming dynasty had grown very weak.

A porcelain plate.

The Manchu Dynasty As in the past, a new group came from outside China to assume power. The Manchu, a nomadic tribe from Manchuria, founded the new Ching dynasty. This imperial house ruled from 1644 to 1912. Before their conquest, the Manchu had already adopted many Chinese ideas and customs. Thus, unlike the Mongols, they were not completely foreign.

During their long rule, the Manchu expanded China to its greatest size. They ruled over China proper, Manchuria, Mongolia, Tibet, and Sinkiang. In addition, the Chinese had loose control over large sections of Southeast Asia and Korea. China was prosperous during the early years of the Manchu dynasty.

To perpetuate their control, the Manchu, who were few in number compared to the Chinese, tried to keep separate from them. They kept military power in their own hands. However, they allowed the Chinese to enter government service. All male Chinese had to wear part of their hair in a braided pigtail, a *queue,* as a sign of their loyalty to the Manchu. The Manchu also passed laws against intermarriage between themselves and the Chinese. Despite these restrictions, the Manchu retained the traditional Chinese ideas and customs. They continued the policy of isolation of the Ming dynasty. Among the few new things introduced into China at this time were corn and sweet potatoes from the New World. These helped feed the rapidly growing population.

The traditional society of China began to come under great pressure from foreign powers about 1800. Russia now represented a threat. Europeans, especially the British, wanted more trade with China. They were eager to buy such Chinese goods as tea and porcelain. The Chinese empire would soon be shaken by wars with the European powers.

Section Questions

1. How did Akbar make his empire strong and stable?
2. Why did the Mogul empire decline?
3. In what ways did the Mongol invasion influence the Chinese during the Ming period?
4. How did agriculture improve under the Ming dynasty?
5. What steps did the Manchu take to retain their power?

Chapter Summary

1. During the time that the Renaissance and Reformation were changing Europe, the modern state also appeared. The kings who headed these newly powerful states depended on professional armies and trained government officials. In 1519, Charles V inherited the huge Hapsburg empire. Charles and his brother, Ferdinand I, faced three main problems: (1) the Ottoman Turks, (2) the Protestant Reformation, and (3) France. When Philip II became head of the Spanish Hapsburg empire in 1556, Spain was the most powerful nation in the world. However, with the defeat of the Spanish Armada in 1558, England became more powerful on the seas. France settled its religious quarrels under Henry IV, first king of the Bourbon line. France successfully entered the Thirty Years' War against the Hapsburgs and became the leading land power of Europe. At the end of the war in 1648, the Treaty of Westphalia solidified the religious and political boundaries of modern Europe. In Germany, Prussia was becoming more powerful. However, the empire of the Ottoman Turks was declining.

2. Russia's early center was at Kiev. Kiev was weakened by the invasions of the Tatars. Gradually, the princes of Moscow became more powerful. In 1480, Ivan III threw off the Tatar yoke. He and his successors continued to expand into the surrounding territories. Ivan IV, the first czar, further increased the power of the Russian ruler over the people. He destroyed the power of the boyars, or nobles. After his death, Russia suffered from internal and external wars. A new royal family, the Romanovs, finally took over in 1613. Russia continued to expand. Peter the Great speeded up the process of westernization in Russia. He gained a port on the Baltic Sea from Sweden and built there a new capital, St. Petersburg.

3. In 1526, Baber, the leader of the Moguls, conquered northern India. His grandson, Akbar, extended the territory of the Mogul empire. Akbar ruled wisely and reduced the hostility between the Muslims and the Hindus. One of the most important contributions of the Moguls was in the arts, especially architecture. Akbar's heirs were not as talented as he, and after about a hundred years, the Mogul empire declined.

The Mongols were driven out of China by native Chinese. A new dynasty, the Ming, started in 1368 and lasted until 1644. Initially, the Ming dynasty was successful. Agriculture improved and the population started to increase. However, under the Ming dynasty, the Chinese began to be more isolated and to resist outsiders, whom they considered barbarians. About 1550, problems began to increase for the dynasty. There were invasions, incompetent rulers, and peasant revolts. Another group, the Manchu, started a new dynasty. The Manchu expanded the size of China. They kept separate from the Chinese, but did allow the Chinese to participate in the government. However, by the 1800s, China was being pressured by foreign nations such as Russia and England.

Chapter 19 Review

Check Your Facts

1. Identify the following:
    a. Ivan III
    b. Michael Romanov
    c. Charles V
    d. Ivan IV
    e. Ottoman Turks
    f. Treaty of Westphalia
    g. Akbar
    h. Baber
2. Why was France concerned about the Hapsburgs?
3. Why was the Spanish Armada unsuccessful?
4. What groups supported the cause of the Huguenots?
5. How did the Thirty Years' War start?
6. What were the terms of the treaty ending the Thirty Years' War?
7. In what ways were the Tatars a destructive force in Russia?
8. Why was the policy of isolation from other nations harmful to the Chinese?
9. What was the greatest achievement of the Manchu dynasty?

Words to Know

Define the following words in one or two sentences.
    a. Huguenots
    b. boyars
    c. minaret
    d. queue

Developing Your Skills

1. Trace a map of Russia. Show the direction in which Ivan III expanded his territory from Moscow. Show where Peter the Great built a new capital.

2. List an important event in Asia and in Europe for each time period shown below.
    a. 1450-1499
    b. 1500-1549
    c. 1550-1600

Thinking It Over

1. Ivan IV, the Terrible, has his defenders. Some say that he was similar to Henry VIII and other European rulers in his ways of dealing with his nobles. List some similarities or differences between Henry VIII and Ivan IV.
2. Discuss in small groups the advantages and disadvantages of a ruler ordering modernization of a nation.
3. Why do you think that the Atlantic seaboard nations such as England and France were becoming more powerful than other European nations?
4. Was Akbar's empire a modern state?

Special Activities

1. Check the plot of the opera *Boris Godunov*. What does it show about the troubled times in Russia?
2. One characteristic of modern states is the use of trained government officials, whom today we call civil servants. Make a list of all the services provided by the government for your local community.
3. Look up information in the library on Catherine the Great, a Russian ruler.

A French warship.

Chapter 20 Exploration and Commercial Expansion

About A.D. 1000, Leif Ericson, a Norseman, discovered land in North America. This event had little effect on Europe or Asia. Europeans then had a very limited view of the world. Their knowledge was a blend of facts from ancient geography, fanciful stories, and more recent discoveries. For example, the Portuguese wanted to find the kingdom of Prester John. Prester John was supposed to be the Christian ruler of rich lands in Africa. He was said to rule over seven kings and have an army of one million soldiers. Prester John was even thought to have a magic mirror

1451-1664

- 1451 First African slaves to Europe
- 1488 Dias rounds Cape of Good Hope
- 1492 Columbus lands in New World
- 1498 da Gama reaches India
- 1500 Portuguese reach Brazil
- 1513 Magellan goes around the world
- 1521 Cortes conquers Mexico
- 1532 Pizarro conquers the Incas
- 1534 Cartier claims St. Lawrence
- 1607 English settle Jamestown
- 1608 French found Quebec
- 1620 Pilgrims reach New England
- 1664 English capture New Amsterdam

Prince Henry of Portugal.

that allowed him to see everything that was going on in his vast kingdom.

The accounts of European travelers provided more recent and somewhat more accurate information. Thus, Europeans were familiar with North Africa even though no European had been to the African interior. European geographers were aware of the land east of the Black Sea. India and China were recognized as large land masses to the far east. Their maps showed the lands of Europe, Africa, Asia, and what was labeled as unknown territory. The maps did not show the true size of the Atlantic and Pacific oceans because no one knew how large those oceans were.

The great discoveries around the time of Columbus had a huge impact not only on Europe, but on the rest of the world as well. The age of discovery affected Europe, Africa, Asia, the Middle East, and the Americas.

Europe became the dominant region of the world. The nations on the Atlantic seaboard—Portugal, Spain, England, and France—became the most powerful in Europe. A new economic system and new technology also led to further changes.

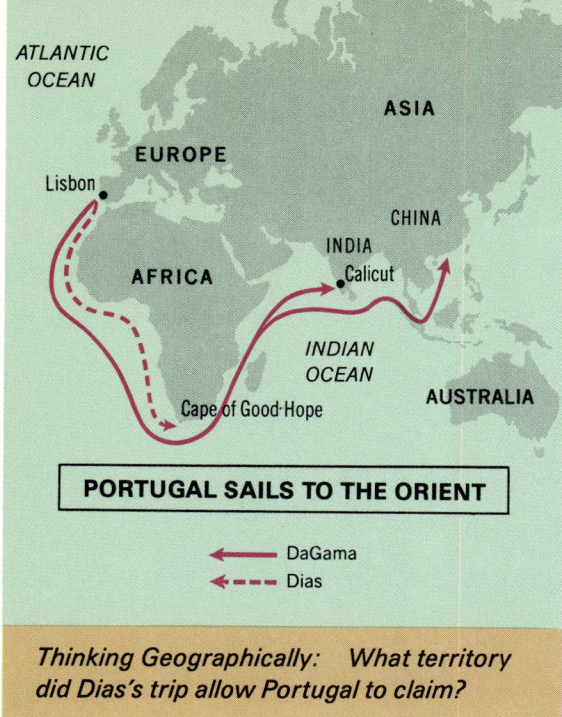

Thinking Geographically: What territory did Dias's trip allow Portugal to claim?

1. The Portuguese and Spanish Made Discoveries

During the late Middle Ages, improvements in navigation were made. European seafarers borrowed the magnetic compass from the Chinese to tell directions. Two new instruments, the *quadrant* and *astrolabe*, were developed to determine *latitude*, the distance north or south of the equator. These inventions allowed Europeans to sail far away from land. Thus they could make longer voyages. Improvements were also made in shipbuilding. These included better sails, straight keels, and stern rudders. Ships became faster, more stable, and safer. More accurate maps were also available to Europeans.

Many Europeans wanted the spices, drugs, perfumes, jewels, and silks of Asia and the gold and ivory of Africa. Now they had the means to obtain them by sea.

Portuguese Discoveries About 1400, Portugal tried to gain control of the gold trade in Africa. At that time, the gold was mined in Mali in West Africa. However, the gold trade was in the hands of the Muslims. It moved north across the Sahara Desert to the Mediterranean Sea and then flowed into Europe.

The Portuguese also wanted to find a new water route to Asia. They then could by-pass the Italian merchants and others who controlled the land trade with Asia. To promote this goal, Prince Henry, a son of the king, established a school for sea captains. These sea captains, like those influenced by the Renaissance, had a spirit of adventure and a desire for fame.

The Portuguese also hoped to find Christians in Africa and India. They believed that people in those areas had been converted to Christianity in past centuries. They wanted to reunite them with the main body of Christendom.

The Portuguese had the advantage of a good geographic location on the Atlantic Ocean and near Africa. Bit by bit, they pushed south along the coast of Africa. Finally, in 1488, Bartholomeu Dias (DEE as) rounded the southern tip of Africa, the Cape of Good Hope. The Portuguese also secured islands off the coast of that continent—the Azores, Canaries, and Madeiras. In 1500, one of their sea captains even touched on the coast of Brazil.

The most important of the Portuguese discoveries was made by their great sea captain, Vasco da Gama (GAH mah). Da Gama's two-year trip, 1497-1499, was one of the greatest sea voyages in history. He and his men sailed half-way around the world to India and back, about 38,600 kilometers (24,000 miles) in all. Da Gama and his sailors encountered many hazards. They were out of sight of land far longer than Columbus was on his voyage to the New World. Da Gama's voyage more than paid for itself. His cargo of spices was sold

The wealthy of Europe had developed a taste for spices.

for sixty times the cost of the expedition. However, only 44 sailors from the original crew of 170 returned. The rest had died.

Having discovered a water route to India, the Portuguese pressed on into Asia. In 1516, they reached China. Later, they forced the Chinese to allow them to trade. The Portuguese gained control of Macao, near Quangzhon (Canton) in China. In 1542, the Portuguese also visited Japan. Later, they sent both merchants and missionaries to Japan.

Thanks to their rapid discoveries, the Portuguese soon controlled the European trade in both Asia and Africa. They established trading posts along the coasts of Africa, India, Persia, and the islands of the East Indies. Their ships brought back rich cargoes of Asian goods. In Africa, the Portuguese traded iron, cloth, and guns for gold. Until 1530, gold was the most important trade item for the Portuguese in Africa. After 1530, slaves became more important than gold.

Portugal had a small population and limited resources. Except for Brazil, their power never extended inland from their trading posts. The Portuguese did not seek political dominance in Africa and Asia. They were mainly concerned with acquiring a rich trading empire. Theirs was not a true colonial empire. Spain, seeking its share of gold and glory, did found a colonial empire.

377

Spanish Exploration The year 1492 is an important date in world history. In that year, Granada, the last Moorish stronghold in Spain, fell to the Christians. With the Moors defeated, King Ferdinand and Queen Isabella of Spain were now willing to finance Christopher Columbus. That visionary navigator wanted to find a new water route to the rich Indies by sailing west from Spain.

In 1492, Columbus and his men sailed west and discovered not Asia, but America. On this and his later voyages, he explored the Caribbean Sea and its major islands. He also touched the mainland of South America. However, he was unwilling to admit that he had found a new continent. Until his death, Columbus insisted that he had reached the edge of the Indies.

Others were not as fixed in their views as Columbus. The news of his voyages was printed, and soon spread throughout Europe. The imagination of the Spanish rulers was stirred by Columbus' voyages. They had visions of new lands, new peoples, and new oceans. Columbus' voyages led to further Spanish explorations. Spain sent the first permanent European settlers to the New World. At first, these settlers in Cuba and the other West Indies looked for gold. Later, they started to farm and to raise cattle. The settlements provided the Spanish with bases from which other expeditions could be launched.

Daring Spanish explorers set forth on journeys to new places. In 1513, Vasco Nunez de Balboa (bal BO uh) became the first European to cross American land to the eastern shore of the Pacific Ocean. Between 1519 and 1522, ships commanded by Ferdinand Magellan (ma JEL an) became the first to sail around the globe. Magellan's crew suffered thirst, starvation, scurvy, storms, and attacks from natives. Only one of the five ships and very few of the men made it back to Spain. Magellan's voyage gave Europeans a much better idea of the true dimensions of the continents and the oceans.

Within the few short years from 1492 to 1522, the Spanish had made enormous discoveries. Many more followed as they concentrated on the great land mass of the Americas. The Spanish established only one significant colony in Asia, the Philippines. The Spanish, like the Portuguese, had several motives for exploration. Most important were the search for wealth and the desire to save souls.

Spanish Conquests Between 1519 and 1521, a Spanish expedition under the ruthless Hernando Cortes (1485-1547) conquered the Aztec state in Mexico. With four hundred men and seventeen horses, Cortes made his way from Vera Cruz on the coast to Tenochtitlán in central Mexico. The Indians that Cortes' force encountered on the way did not offer much resistance. They were afraid that Cortes might be a god. They were also frightened by the horses and arms of the Spanish.

The emperor of the Aztecs, Montezuma II, was fearful about the arrival of the Spanish in his land. However, he cordially received Cortes into his beautiful capital. The Spanish were amazed at the temples, the palaces, the canals crowded with canoes, and the bridges built to join the city together.

Cortes seized Montezuma. Later, Montezuma was killed. The Aztecs then attacked Cortes and his troops. Cortes and his men had to abandon the city. They tried to escape with the treasures of Montezuma. This retreat was a disaster. Most of the soldiers were killed and the treasure was lost in the lake.

Later, Cortes returned with more soldiers and Indian allies. For almost three months, there was a fierce battle for control of the city. The Aztecs were weakened by a severe epidemic of smallpox. Cortes completely destroyed the beautiful capital, taking much booty.

Pizarro leading his troops against the Incas.

In 1532, Francisco Pizarro began to conquer the Incas, who lived along the west coast of South America. At a conference, the crafty and deceitful Pizarro seized Atahualpa, the Inca ruler. To secure his freedom, Atahualpa agreed to fill a room with gold and silver. Pizarro collected the treasure but had Atahualpa killed.

From these and other conquests, Spain acquired an enormous empire populated with millions of people. Except for Portuguese Brazil, the Spanish conquered all of Central and South America. They also had control of the West Indies and the southern part of North America, including part of what is now the United States.

Spain, like all European nations at that time, looked upon its new empire as a source of wealth. The first major industry in the new lands was mining. Improved European mining techniques were introduced into Mexico and Peru.

At first, the successful Spanish conquerers retired to Spain with their newfound wealth. Later, more permanent Spanish settlers arrived. Spain then developed a true colonial empire. The Spanish imposed their culture—language, religion, laws, and customs—on the Indians.

The Indians The Spanish conquest was a disaster for the Indians. War and European diseases such as smallpox lowered the Indian population. Some groups were entirely wiped out. Irrigation systems such as that developed by the Incas in Peru were not maintained. Thus not enough food could be produced to feed all the people. Famine and hard work in the mines caused many more deaths.

Gradually, new foods and animals were introduced on each continent. To America, Europeans brought wheat, rice, sugar cane, vegetables, and fruits. From the Americas came valuable crops such as potatoes, tomatoes, peanuts, chili, corn, cacao, red beans, tobacco, and others. The new European foods helped the population to increase again. Black slaves from Africa were imported into the areas where the number

Did You Know?

Sister Juana

In 1651, Juana Inés de Asbaje (as bah he) was born into a wealthy family in New Spain (Mexico). She was very bright and learned to read when she was only three. Her family allowed her to read as many books as she could. Thus, she learned Latin as well as Spanish.

Because of her family's position, she later was allowed to live in the viceroy's palace in Mexico City. The viceroy was the king's representative so he had the most power in colonial New Spain. The viceroy was amazed at her brilliant mind. He became interested in her when he found that she wrote beautiful poems.

Juana (WHA nah) wanted to attend the university. However, at that time, women were not admitted to the university. Her mother did not give in to Juana's requests for a formal education. Juana left the viceroy's court at the age of sixteen and entered a convent. For women of her position there were only two choices in life: to marry or to become a nun. It may be that Juana was not interested in marrying and wanted to dedicate her life to the study of literature. The religious life of some orders was not too strict, and she would have time to study and to write poetry. It is also possible that she had fallen in love with someone she could not marry.

After Juana became a nun, she was known by her religious name, Sor Juana Ines de la Cruz, or Sister Juana. For almost thirty years, Sister Juana wrote some of the most beautiful and original poetry in the Spanish language. In some of the verses, there are hints of an ill-fated romance. However, others see her poetry as illustrating the problems that are caused in a society where intelligent women have few choices.

Sister Juana.

of native people had drastically declined. Some degree of stability was established.

Spanish missionaries from the Roman Catholic religious orders also came to the New World. Most of the Indians, having no choice in the matter, adopted the religion of their Spanish conquerors. After some instruction, hundreds of thousands were baptized. However, the Indians blended into the Roman Catholic religion many of their own beliefs.

A few of the Spanish tried to improve the lot of the Indians and the black slaves. These reformers, many of them priests, publicized the problems of the Indians. Laws were eventually passed to free the Indians from manual labor on the large estates. In actual practice, the owners of the estates demanded labor from the poor in payment for debts. It seemed that the poor were always in debt to the landowners.

Most Europeans were hostile to the religions of the Indians. They quickly destroyed all their "idols" and practices. A few Europeans, however, were curious about these people who lived so differently from them. These Europeans gathered up the artifacts of the Indians. They talked to the natives and wrote down their histories. These few amateur anthropologists described the Indian cultures. To them we owe much of our knowledge of what life was for the Indians before the arrival of Columbus.

Harmful Gold and Silver? In 1550, Spain was at the height of its power. It controlled vast lands both in the New World and in Europe. However, the vast amounts of gold and silver from the New World really did not help Spain. Instead, they caused *inflation*, a sharp increase in the prices of goods and services. Inflation upset the traditional economic and social relationships. People like the landed nobility and wage earners whose income was fixed suffered the most. However, middle-class townspeople such as merchants and bankers became more important. They gained from inflation. The use of money increased and more loans were made.

Much of the gold and silver came to the Spanish king, who used it to support expensive wars in many parts of Europe. On those occasions when the precious metals did not arrive on time, the king was almost bankrupt and could not pay his troops or sailors.

Many of the profits from the Spanish New World flowed to the cities of northern Europe. The Dutch bought the goods that arrived in Lisbon and Seville. They then shipped them where they were needed at a nice profit.

Antwerp (ANT wurp) became the center of business activity in the north. Antwerp is in the north part of Belgium, just south of the Netherlands. From about 1460 to 1560, its population doubled. Antwerp was then destroyed by the Spanish. As a result, Amsterdam and London became the leading trade centers. From those two cities the products of Asia and the Americas were distributed to all parts of Europe. Northern Europe also produced the goods needed for trade in Africa and Asia—cloth, weapons, tools, and so on. The gold and silver of the Spanish was siphoned off to foreign cities to the north as Spain failed to develop its commerce and industries. In the long run, the gold and silver of the Americas did not help Spain.

Section Questions

1. Why were European sailors able to make longer voyages in the 1400s and 1500s?
2. What were the main motives of the Portuguese and Spanish explorers?
3. In what ways were the Indians in the Americas hurt by the European conquests?
4. Why did the gold and silver of the Americas not really help Spain?

An advertisement seeking English colonists for Virginia.

2. Other Nations Wanted Trade and Colonies

Explorations were expensive. In the beginning, only kings could finance them. The discoveries opened up many new trading opportunities but only if enough money could be secured to equip ships.

Capitalism This need for money, or *capital*, led to the further development of capitalism. Capitalism can be defined in several ways. Most authorities agree that capitalism is an economic system in which money and resources are put into business and industry to make more money. The goal of the system is to make a profit. Capitalism is also founded on private property. Under the capitalist system, those who own property may decide what to do with it. For example, a person with money may put it in a bank or risk it buying real estate.

To finance explorations and trade, people pooled large amounts of capital. This spread the risk. For example, it is safer to put one-fifth of your money into each of five different ships than to risk all of your money on one ship. At the beginning, an investment partnership was limited to one journey. Later, more permanent associations came into being. One form was the stock company. In such a company, each person had a certain share of the total stock. If in a given year, there was a profit, the investors shared it in proportion to the amount of stock they owned. Similarly, they shared in any loss.

Stock companies were not just limited to trading ventures. They were also being used to support growing industries. For example, printing was spreading throughout Europe. There was a great need for more paper. Stock companies were used to organize paper manufacturing. Other industries, such as mining, were also expensive to operate. They needed capital in the form of money or materials. Gradually, larger industries began to get their capital by selling stock.

Mercantilism Even as capitalism was growing, many governmental leaders thought that a nation's wealth was determined by the amount of gold and silver in the country. This idea is called *mercantilism*. Under the mercantilist system, the parent country manufactured goods and sold them to its colonies. In turn, the colonies produced raw materials. They were forbidden to manufacture their own goods or to get them by trading with foreign countries. The goal of the parent country was to obtain more gold and silver. These precious metals had an almost magical quality to the Europeans.

The Spanish were able to finance further expeditions from the silver and gold they discovered in the Americas. The Portuguese used money they made from their trading empire.

The Italians and Germans were also interested in exploration and trade. There were many Italian explorers, geographers, and map-makers. However, the Italian city-states were too small and divided to support expensive exploring and trading ventures. Exploration and large-scale trade also depended on a certain degree of stability in a nation. At that time, both the Italians and the Germans lacked a unified national state. Their sea captains had to go to other countries for financial support.

England, France, and the Netherlands also sought the power and profits that Spain and Portugal had won. In 1497, King Henry VII of England sent John Cabot to explore the New World. Cabot discovered present-day Newfoundland, Nova Scotia, and the eastern United States. However, the English did not immediately follow up on these discoveries. They found no gold in North America. There were no docile Indians to work for them. Only European fishers began to use the coast of northern America.

France The French also made some efforts at exploration. In 1523-1528, Giovanni da Verrazano (VAR raw ZAH no), an Italian sea captain, sailed for France. He reached the coast of North America. Like many other explorers, he was looking for a short route to the Indies, a "Northwest Passage" to China. A more important explorer for France was Jacques Cartier (KAR tyay). On two trips between 1534 and 1536, Cartier also tried to find the Northwest Passage. Instead, he discovered the west coast of Newfoundland, Prince Edward Island, Chaleur and Gaspé bays, the St. Lawrence River, and the sites of Quebec City and Montreal. The French thus had claims to large sections of what is now Canada.

Amsterdam at the time capitalism and mercantilism began to develop.

The French, like the English, did not immediately follow up their discoveries. The French civil war between the Huguenots and the Roman Catholics was not settled until 1598. Moreover, Canada was a cold land and no valuable metals were found there.

The Dutch Henry Hudson, an Englishman, explored the New World for the Dutch. In 1609, many years after the first English and French voyages, he touched Newfoundland and sailed down the coast to Virginia. This expedition gave the Dutch a claim to the Hudson River region. Hudson too was searching for the Northwest Passage.

Hudson was sailing for the English when his crew mutinied. Hudson, his son, and a few loyal crew members were left to die. However, this ill-fated expedition did give the English a claim to the Hudson Bay area in Canada.

As cities like Amsterdam brought in wealth, the Dutch were in a position to become more powerful on the seas. At the end of the Thirty Years' War, the independence of the Netherlands was officially recognized. Now the Dutch could devote even more of their energies to trade and colonization.

By the 1600s, the Netherlands was a leading sea power. The Dutch used mass production methods in shipbuilding. They used standard parts and mechanical devices such as wind-driven sawmills. The number of Dutch merchant ships tripled between 1600 and 1650. The Netherlands supplied about half of the world's shipping.

The Dutch were expanding at the expense of the Portuguese. Portugal had become part of Spain in 1580. The Spanish had little interest in defending the Portuguese trade routes. As a result, the Dutch replaced the Portuguese in many areas, including what is now Indonesia. Unlike the Portuguese, the Dutch realized that they needed more than a few trading posts.

In 1619, they settled Java and the entire island soon came under their control. The Dutch colonized the southern tip of Africa, New Netherland (what is now New York), islands in the West Indies, and Surinam in South America. The Dutch also established trade with Japan.

The Dutch also tried to gain more control of the Spanish trade in the Americas. Spain tried to enforce a system in which trade was completely restricted to the Spanish. For example, sugar produced in Cuba had to be sent first to Spain even if it was going to be sold to Peru. There was a death penalty for any person who traded with a foreigner. However, this law was not enforced. The Dutch and the English sold manufactured goods that Spain could not supply to the Spanish colonies. They made trade deals with local Spanish officials in the New World. In these ways, the English and the Dutch began to reduce, little by little, the power of Spain and Portugal.

New Colonies In the 1600s, long after Spain had established its empire in the New World, England, France, and the Netherlands tried to develop colonies. Companies obtained permission from their governments to control settlement and trade in a particular area. The most important English groups were the East India Company and the two Virginia companies of London and Plymouth. In the Netherlands, the Dutch East India Company and the Dutch West India Company were also organized. In 1607, the first successful English colony, Jamestown, was started in Virginia. The New England colonies and Maryland followed soon. The English also settled in the West Indies, where they had profitable sugar-producing colonies.

In 1624, the Dutch established a permanent settlement, New Netherland, in the Hudson River area. New Netherland was captured by the English in 1664 and renamed New York.

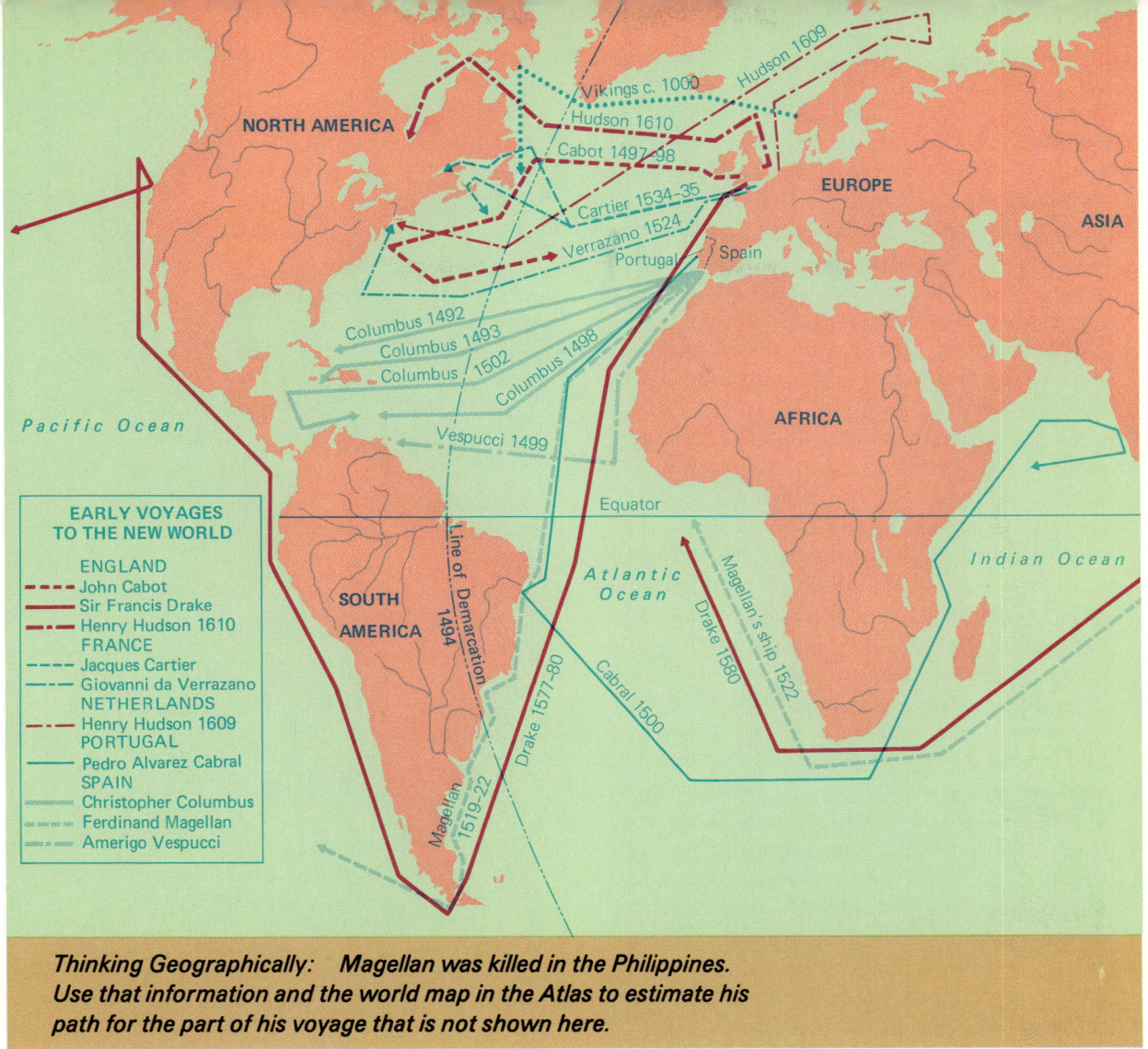

Thinking Geographically: Magellan was killed in the Philippines. Use that information and the world map in the Atlas to estimate his path for the part of his voyage that is not shown here.

In 1608, a year after Jamestown was founded, the French began to settle Canada. The French also had colonies in the West Indies. They were rivals of the English in India. However, the French king gave only one trading company at a time the right to establish colonies. This slowed colonial development. The French also had great difficulty in getting French families to move to Canada, which had a colder climate than France. By 1763, when French rule ended, there were only about 60,000 people in Canada. However, the French did establish a profitable fur trade there.

The English colonies were more successful in attracting settlers. Most colonists were seeking to better their economic situation. In England, landlords were driving farmers off the land and enclosing fields to use as pastures for sheep. A few people also settled in the English colonies in order to practice their religion freely.

The English, and, to a lesser extent, the French, had a different pattern of colonization from that of Spain. The territories claimed by the English and French had relatively few native Indians. They thus had to bring their own people to America. They killed or pushed back the Indians as they settled the continent. By contrast, in Latin America, intermarriage among the Europeans, Indians, and Africans was far more common. As a result, a new population of mixed races came into being in Latin America.

The European settlement of the Americas started the greatest mass migration the world has ever known. Millions of people would eventually come from all over the world, especially Europe, to settle in North and South America. With the Europeans came their culture. This culture changed somewhat in the new environment, but remained fundamentally European.

The discovery of the Americas and of the new trade routes to Africa and Asia had a tremendous impact on the Europeans. They now had a more accurate knowledge of what the world was like. The Atlantic seaboard nations—Portugal, Spain, England, France, and the Netherlands—explored many areas. They established colonies where there was a small native population, such as in the Americas, Australia, and Southern Africa. Where there was a heavy concentration of people, as in Asia, they began to control trade and acquire increasing political influence.

Section Questions

1. Why did investors pool their resources, as in a stock company?
2. What was the Northwest Passage? Why did explorers want to find it?
3. Why did France not immediately follow up on its explorations in the New World?
4. What helped the Netherlands become a sea power?
5. How did English colonization differ from that of the Spanish?

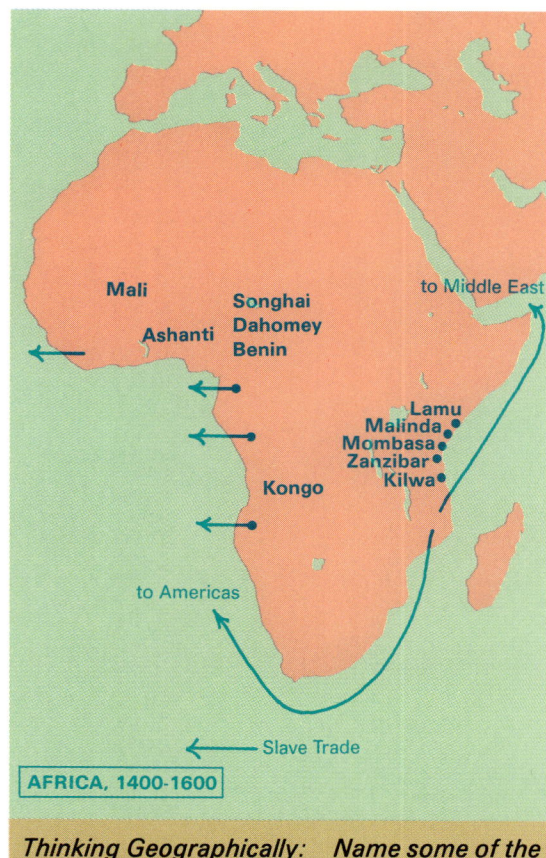

Thinking Geographically: Name some of the city-states that made up the land of Zanj.

3. The Slave Trade Affected Africa and the World

By 1400, three areas of Africa south of the Sahara Desert had large kingdoms, some as large as European states of the time.

One group of kingdoms was the Western Sudanic states, located west and south of the Sahara. As you read earlier, the Ghanaians gained control of the African trade in salt, gold, ivory, and slaves by about A.D. 1000. Later, Ghana was superseded by Mali. After about 1400, Mali began to decline, and Songhai became stronger. In the three decades after Columbus' first voyage to the New World in 1492, Songhai was at the height of its power. It had large cities and universities.

A second group of African kingdoms was concentrated much further south. The states of Benin, Ashanti, and Dahomey were forest kingdoms located along the coast of the Gulf of Guinea. At the time of the Portuguese explorations in the 1400s, Benin, now in southern Nigeria, was the most powerful state in the area. When the Europeans arrived at Benin, they were amazed at the wide variety and high quality of the goods they found there.

The third group of kingdoms were the city-states on the east coast of Africa, called the land of Zanj. This area was the center of a wide-ranging trade involving Asia, Arabia, and eastern Africa.

The Portuguese The coming of the Portuguese affected the different African communities in different ways. The Portuguese were impressed by the riches of the communities on the east coast of Africa. The Portuguese fought for control of these trading cities and quickly subdued them. There the Portuguese established trading posts. These posts were not colonies or missionary centers, but merely places where a few Europeans lived so as to control the trade. As such, the trading posts did not greatly disturb the Muslim, Arab, and African cultures of the area. However, the profits from the trade now went to Portugal.

The coming of the Portuguese resulted in a shift of trade. Songhai lost power as trade routes across the Sahara became less important. At first, Benin became more important. Then, in the 1700s, the states of Ashanti and Dahomey rose to power. The Guinea coast developed into the center of the slave trade. There were few natural ports and no true cities on the coast itself. Large ships often had to dock at the islands off the coast. Small boats then ferried people and goods back and forth between ship and shore. The African rulers along the Guinea coast typically had a large military force to back their authority. The rulers did not encourage the Europeans to settle in Africa. They often made the Europeans stay on their boats or required them to live in special areas on the coast. Thus, there was little cultural exchange between the Europeans and the Africans. The European presence certainly had an impact on Africa. However, it did not lead to the destruction of the native culture. Indeed, the nations along the Guinea coast prospered as they became more heavily involved in the slave trade with the Europeans.

The Slave Trade Slavery had existed in Africa for hundreds of years before the arrival of Europeans. Slaves were often prisoners of war. They might also be criminals or debtors. However, slavery originally existed on a small scale. The children of slaves did not always have to remain in slavery. It was possible to get out of slavery by marriage or hard work. Slaves could even own and inherit land.

In 1451, the first Portuguese ship with slaves returned to Lisbon. The slaves were bought to work on farms or to become household servants in Portugal. However, the slave trade did not become important in Europe proper. Since Europe had a sizable labor force of its own, there was not that much need for slaves.

However, by 1530, there was a great demand for labor in the New World. The Spanish and the Portuguese found that there were not enough Indians to do the work in their colonies. The Spanish and other Europeans found that sugarcane could be successfully grown in the West Indies. Sugar and, later, tobacco were in great demand in Europe. Sugarcane was grown on large plantations with many workers. The workers had to cut down the cane and get the juice out of it within twenty-four hours. Field workers also needed other

Captured slaves in central Africa.

workers to produce their food and clothing. The hard, regimented work on the plantations seemed to require slaves. Africa seemed the only likely source for these workers.

The demand for a labor force in the Americas thus led to an expanded slave trade in Africa. However, the Europeans were not usually interested in capturing the slaves themselves. Africa was considered a graveyard for Europeans. Tropical diseases killed many of those who ventured there. As a result, the Europeans encouraged the Africans to secure the slaves for them. The powerful black states along the Guinea coast conducted raids to obtain more slaves. They used guns, which they got from the Europeans. This gave them an advantage over tribes.

By 1600, with Portugal now under Spanish control, the Portuguese lost control of the African slave trade. The Dutch, English, and French took it over. Slaves were now the important and valuable product of Africa.

The Europeans were eager to engage in the slave trade because it was so profitable. The human cargoes made the traders rich. The profits of the slave trade could then be put into other investments. From the beginning of the African slave trade, there were Europeans who protested against its inhumanity. However, those who made profits—the plantation owners, the shippers, and the African rulers—did not want it to end.

The number of slaves sent from Africa to the New World steadily increased. By 1550, about 12,500 slaves had been landed in Spanish America. Between 1600 and 1650, about 7500 slaves were imported each year. By 1700, the average was about 24,000 a year. By 1776, at the beginning of the American Revolution, the number was up to about 65,000 a year.

Some historians believe that about ten million black slaves had been sent from Africa to the Americas by 1870. About one-third went to Brazil, where there were many large sugar and coffee plantations. Another third went to the West Indies, where the sugar industry was so important. About a half million were sent to the United States before and after independence.

In addition to the ten million slaves from Africa who were sold in the Americas, about another two million were sold in the slave trade along the east coast of Africa. These numbers, however, do not tell the whole story. Thousands of slaves were killed in the raids. Some died on the way from the interior of Africa to the coast. Packed tightly together inside the slave ships, many slaves died on the dreaded journey overseas. Slaves unable to adjust to their new environment also died. From the raids to the plantations, slavery was brutal. It may be that for every two slaves that were captured, only one survived. This means that as many as twenty million Africans were captured as slaves.

Effects in Africa The slave trade reduced the population in Africa. However, with a few exceptions, the population was apparently able to regain its former size. New foods, such as corn from America, helped to increase the food supply. Africa lost its most important resource—human beings—but it did not become depopulated.

The African rulers who became wealthy from the slave trade purchased European goods such as guns, ammunition, and luxury items. Africans now depended on European iron, cloth, and other goods, since they no longer made as many of their own products. The slave trade thus distorted the economic development of Africa.

The slave trade also increased tribal warfare within Africa. Whole villages were destroyed. Fear and insecurity increased. Those likely to be attacked wanted weapons to defend themselves. In order to get the money to buy weapons, they sold slaves. Some tribes moved into the deep interior, where they were likely to be more safe from capture.

One of the most long-lasting effects of slavery was the development of *racism* among the Europeans. Racism is the belief that one *race*, or group, of people is superior to another. At first, the Africans were treated as equals by the Portuguese traders. African states were considered to be like European states. European and African kings considered each other to be monarchs and addressed each other as such.

With the development of large-scale slave trading, Europeans began to try to justify enslaving fellow human beings. They used the following arguments: (1) the blacks were pagans and under slavery they could become Christians; and (2) blacks were less intelligent since they were only seen doing manual labor. These attitudes continued even after the slave trade was abolished by Britain in 1807.

One of the most important effects of the slave trade was that it gave Europeans a foothold in Africa. The African states did hold their own in the 1700s. However, in the 1800s, the trade would lead to further European control in Africa.

Section Questions

1. Where were the three areas of African kingdoms in the 1400s?
2. What kind of trade came to be most important in Africa in the 1500s?
3. In what ways did the states of West Africa try to discourage Europeans from settling in the area?
4. What was the main reason Europeans engaged in the slave trade?

Chapter Summary

1. Leif Ericson discovered North America in A.D. 1000, but this discovery had little impact. During the late Middle Ages, ships became safer and faster. The Portuguese were the first to explore. They moved gradually along the coast of Africa. Da Gama in 1497-1499 made his way to India. The Portuguese also set up trading posts in Africa and Asia. In 1492, Columbus led the first of the Spanish expeditions to the New World. From later explorations, Spain gained control of almost all of Central and South America and parts of what is now the United States. The Spanish started permanent European settlements in the New World. The conquest by Spain was a disaster for the Indians. They lost much of their culture as the Spanish language, religion, laws, customs, and values were imposed on them. Finding gold and silver did not ultimately benefit Spain, since Spanish commerce and industry did not develop. Instead, the cities of northern Europe gained at Spain's expense.

2. To finance the expensive voyages, people put their money into stock companies. This spread the risk. Capitalism was becoming established in the European countries. Rulers also believed in the idea of mercantilism. According to this theory, colonies existed for the benefit of the parent country.

The English and French did not immediately follow up on their early explorations of the New World. The Dutch became a sea power and took over much of the trade that Portugal had formerly controlled. In the 1600s, England, France, and the Netherlands made permanent settlements in the New World. The European settlement of the Americas started the greatest migration the world has ever known.

3. There was a great diversity of peoples in Africa. In the 1400s, three areas of Africa south of the Sahara had large states or kingdoms: the Western Sudanic states, the kingdoms of the Guinea coast, and the city-states on the east coast of Africa. The Portuguese established trading posts on the east coast. Benin became the most important trade center on the west coast. The African rulers did not encourage Europeans to settle in Africa. The slave trade increased in scale as the demand for slaves grew in the Americas. The Europeans engaged in the slave trade because it was so profitable. However, the whole system of slavery was brutal. The slave trade distorted the African economy, increased tribal warfare, promoted racism, and gave the Europeans a foothold in Africa.

Chapter 20 Review

Check Your Facts

1. Identify the following:
   a. Henry Hudson
   b. Prince Henry
   c. Vasco da Gama
   d. Jacques Cartier
   e. Montezuma
2. Why didn't Portugal establish a colonial empire?
3. Why did the American Indian population decline?
4. Why didn't the Italians send out expeditions to the New World?
5. In what ways did the slave trade hurt Africa?

Words to Know

1. Write a paragraph about the explorations in this chapter. Use these words: *quadrant, astrolabe, latitude*.
2. Write a paragraph about how the explorations described in this chapter were financed. Use these words: *capitalism, mercantilism*.

Developing Your Skills

1. Use the map on page 389 and the Atlas to determine what explorers reached the farthest point south. About what latitude did they reach?
2. What explorer reached the farthest point north? About what latitude did he reach?
3. Place the following events in the proper chronological order.
   Da Gama reaches India.
   Quebec is founded.
   Cortes conquers Mexico.

Thinking It Over

1. If you were an investor or a king or queen, what qualities would you seek in an explorer?
2. What might have happened if China had discovered Europe by a water route before the Portuguese discovered Asia?

Special Activities

1. What exploration is going on today? Who normally pays for it? Is it a good investment of money?
2. Find out what are the most important exports of China, India, and Africa today. Compare the situation now to the period discussed in this textbook. What has caused some of the changes?
3. The map on page 389 shows the Line of Demarcation. Prepare a brief report on the Line of Demarcation.

Unit 5 Review

Words to Know

1. In what way was the jizya like a queue (see Chapter 19)?
2. The city of Istanbul has also been called Constantinople and Byzantium (see Chapter 10). Explain the significance of each name.
3. Explain the difference between capitalism and mercantilism.
4. Explain the significance of each of the following documents.
    a. Luther's 95 Theses
    b. Thirty-Nine Articles
    c. Edict of Nantes
    d. Catechisms

Time and Place

1. Compare the ideas of the Middle Ages and the Renaissance in the following areas:
    a. Importance of salvation
    b. Role of pride and ambition
    c. Importance of the present
    d. Enjoyment of life
2. In what ways did the following historical developments change people's views?
    a. The Renaissance
    b. The Reformation
    c. Development of nation states
    d. The discoveries of the Americas
    e. The slave trade

Putting It Together

1. Copy the chart on a piece of paper. Tell briefly what was happening in the places listed during each time period.
2. Look through Unit 5 for the names of important people. Which three of all those mentioned in the unit do you think were the most important? Why? (Examples: Luther, Akbar, da Vinci, Elizabeth I)
3. Of the important people found in Unit 5, name three who you think did not achieve the goals they sought. Why were they unsuccessful?

	1450-1550	1550-1650
India		
Western Europe		
China		
Africa		
The Americas		
Russia		

Contemporary Parallel:

Change and the Media

*I*n 1456, Johann Gutenberg used movable type for the first time to print the Bible. Within a short time, millions of books and pamphlets were being printed in Europe. Thus, as just one example, news of the voyages of Columbus and other explorers spread rapidly through Europe. The earlier trips of the Norse to the New World had had little impact, partly because communication was so slow and expensive.

Change continues in communication. We now often use the words *mass media* or *media*. These include television, radio, films, newspapers, magazines, books, and billboards, the main communication devices used today.

Television, because of its extreme popularity, is frequently discussed. The effect of television on children is of particular interest. Some experts think that television stretches children's minds and increases their speaking and hearing vocabularies.

Other experts are disturbed about the effects of television on children, especially those who are heavy watchers.

Evidence suggests that violence on television has harmful effects on some children. These children become more aggressive and more fearful as a result of watching violence.

Some experts claim that children who are heavy viewers are easily distracted. They have difficulty concentrating on their schoolwork.

For better or worse, television is here to stay. In the future, school children may use a television set to do their homework. Television may offer more choices on more channels. Thus, the rapid change that has come to characterize the media in general and television in particular may accelerate. Television may end up having more influence than the printing press.

QUESTIONS

1. How did the printing press affect communication?
2. What kinds of influence do the media have on our lives?
3. What do experts say about the effects of television on children?

1543	1648	1689	1783	1789	1804	1815	1824
Copernicus publishes his theory	Civil War in England ends	English Bill of Rights	United States wins independence	French Revolution begins	Haiti achieves independence	Napoleon defeated	All of Latin America independent

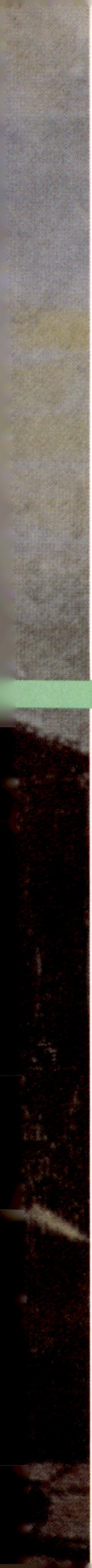

Unit 6
Quest for Liberty

In 1215—more than four centuries before the age you will study in this unit—a band of English nobles faced their king on the plain of Runnymede. They came to force King John to govern more fairly. He yielded to their demands and signed the Magna Charta. In doing so, John admitted that some law was above even the king.

In the centuries that followed, strong monarchs pulled in one direction, striving for absolute power. The people pulled in the opposite direction, seeking more freedom.

The struggle required courage and sacrifice. Sometimes the battle was waged in a parliament, sometimes in the streets. Those who dared take part often risked prison or the gallows.

People gradually gained more rights—the right to vote, the right to a trial by jury, the right to freedom of speech, and more. By the late 1600s, a new idea was taking shape: the government had a duty to protect people's basic rights. If it failed to do so, it had lost the right to rule. The people were then at liberty to create a new government.

This was an explosive idea. It meant, really, that government depended on the consent of the governed. The powerful monarchs would not let such an idea go unchallenged. That made it a revolutionary idea—people were willing to take up arms against an unpopular government.

The siege of the Bastille.

395

The Battle of Bunker Hill.

Chapter 21 Revolutions and Rights

Just before he was beheaded in 1649, King Charles I of England said:

"For the people,...I desire their liberty and freedom as much as anybody whatsoever: but I must tell you that their liberty and freedom consists in having government, in those laws by which their life and goods may be most their own. It is not their having a share in government; that is nothing pertaining to them. ... If I could have given way to have all changed according to the power of the sword, I needed not to have come here; and therefore I tell

1603-1824

1603	James I becomes King
1642-1648	Civil War in England
1648-1660	Cromwell's rule
1688	Glorious Revolution
1689	English Bill of Rights
1776	Declaration of Independence
1783	United States wins independence
1804	Haiti achieves independence
1816	Bolivar liberates Venezuela
1817	San Martín liberates Chile
1821	Mexico gains independence
1824	All Latin America independent

Oliver Cromwell.

you (and I pray God it be not laid to your charge) that I am the martyr of the people."

Thus, Charles I maintained to the time of his death that he had certain rights as a king and that people should be subject to his laws. However, Parliament wanted a more active role in law making. The friction between the crown and Parliament developed into a civil war. This revolution led to a rethinking of what kind of government the English really wanted.

In contrast to Charles' views, John Locke said in 1690 that "whenever government tries to take away and destroy the property of the people, or reduce the people to slavery, it puts itself in a state of war with the people. The people are freed from any further obedience to that government...and have the right to establish a new government." Thomas Jefferson repeated Locke's ideas in 1776. He said in the American Declaration of Independence "That whenever any form of government becomes destructive of these ends, it is the right of the people to alter or to abolish it."

The idea of the right to revolt against an unjust government had an enormous impact on the world. It helped lead to the French Revolution in 1789. It was a factor in the rebellion of the Latin American colonies in the 1800s.

1. The English Revolted Against Their King

Elizabeth I, Queen of England, died in 1603 after ruling with great popularity for forty-five years. Elizabeth was the last member of the House of Tudor, having no children or immediate heirs. The English crown then passed to James Stuart, her Scottish first cousin twice removed. He was already King James VI of Scotland. Thus, when he became King James I of England, the two countries were united under his rule. Scotland had been independent from England since 1314, when Robert Bruce had defeated an English army at Bannockburn. The Stuart family had ruled Scotland since 1371.

James I James believed that his power as a king was a divine right from God. James did not go through the motions of sharing power with Parliament. He was tactless and overbearing. He constantly lectured members of Parliament about his divine right to rule.

Actually, it was not clear what the king could do and what Parliament could do. Tradition said that the king controlled foreign affairs. Parliament had a long history of power over taxation. However, fighting a war cost money. Thus, there was no clear-cut line between the authority of the king and that of Parliament.

James's expenses were twice those of Elizabeth. James had a large family. His court expenses involved the running of several palaces. In addition, at that time, the king himself paid for the upkeep of the army, navy, ambassadors, and other royal officials. Inflation, caused partly by the influx of silver from the Americas, also increased the royal expenses. Moreover, James was more extravagant than Elizabeth.

The members of Parliament thought that James I wasted money. They believed that his ministers were incompetent and

James I.

corrupt. Each time James demanded funds, Parliament gave him little money but a large list of grievances.

James I also had difficulties with Parliament over foreign affairs. Parliament did not like his pro-Spanish policy. The members thought that England should be helping the Protestant nations against the Roman Catholic Hapsburgs in the Thirty Years' War. James told Parliament not to meddle in foreign affairs. Parliament criticized the king's foreign policy and defended its right to debate any government policy.

Puritans and Presbyterians were strong in the House of Commons. The House of Commons represented the landed gentry, merchants, and professional people. The House of Lords consisted of the nobles and the bishops.

Religion was the greatest source of conflict during the reign of James I. The king supported the Church of England, the Anglican Church, of which he was the head. He wanted everyone to conform to the rituals of the Church of England. He insisted that the church should continue to be governed by bishops. However, the English Puritans wanted to "purify" the church ceremonies by ending the use of candles and elaborate clerical vestments. These practices reminded them of the Roman Catholic Church, which they detested. The Puritans also wanted to remove the bishops and increase the power of the local churches. Nevertheless, the Puritans remained within the established church. They were trying to reform the Church of England from within.

James I could not get his way with Parliament, so he dismissed it. Then he tried to raise money by selling hundreds of monopolies. This practice increased the prices of everyday goods such as coal and soap. The merchants in Parliament and throughout the nation particularly resented these monopolies. By the time James I died in 1625, he was very unpopular.

Charles I trying to arrest five members of the House of Commons.

Charles I Charles I was 25 when he succeeded his father, James I. Like his father, Charles needed money. Thus he was dependent on Parliament. Parliament demanded a say in how the money should be spent and criticized Charles' ministers.

In 1628, in order to get tax money from Parliament, Charles I agreed to sign the Petition of Right. This document said that the king could not levy taxes without the consent of Parliament. In addition to limiting the power of the king, the Petition of Right gave some civil rights to individuals. It stated that people could not be imprisoned without due process of law.

Parliament continued to criticize the king. In 1629, Charles I dismissed Parliament for eleven years. He tried to govern by himself, raising money by any means. New taxes, imposed without the consent of Parliament, angered the gentry and merchants. They challenged the legality of a ship-money tax that normally was imposed on coastal areas in emergency situations only. The royal judges upheld the legality of the ship-money tax in 1638. However, the tax could not be collected because of rising discontent.

A religious issue caused the most conflict. The archbishop of Canterbury, William Laud, insisted that every church in the land follow all of the details of worship of the Church of England. These included organ playing at services, reading the Book of Common Prayer, and less preaching by the clergy. These practices outraged the Puritans. Three men who protested the archbishop's policy had their ears cut off and were sentenced to life imprisonment by the Court of Star Chamber, a royal court. These three men became martyrs and popular heroes.

Charles I also tried to impose the Church of England on the Presbyterian Scots. The Scots declared in 1638 that they would not change or give up their religious practices. Furthermore, the Scots defeated Charles' weak army and marched into northern England in 1640. Needing money desperately for defense, Charles was forced to call Parliament into session in 1640. This was the beginning of the famous Long Parliament. It was so called because it remained in session for 13 years.

Charles I was in a weak position. He had no money, no effective army, and almost no support in the country. Parliament was not in an agreeable mood. The members would not grant Charles money unless he agreed to certain limitations on his power. Parliament sought the right to meet at least once every three years. The king would not be able to dissolve Parliament without its consent. Parliament would have to vote on all taxes. In addition, the king was to abolish the special royal courts. These had been punishing people who had not paid Charles' taxes or had criticized Archbishop Laud. These provisions amounted to a sharp reduction of the king's power and authority.

Charles I had no choice but to agree to the demands of Parliament. Parliament was successful against the king, but there were divisions among its members. The Puritans wanted to change the Church of England and to limit the king's power even further. They were opposed by the staunch Anglicans and the supporters of the king.

In 1642, Charles I tried to take advantage of this split within Parliament. He felt that the discontent was due to just a few troublemakers. Charles thus charged into the House of Commons with his troops and tried to arrest five Puritan leaders for treason. This act outraged Parliament. London was in an uproar. Mobs roamed the streets and the king fled from London for safety.

In June 1642, Parliament sent Charles I a plan by which Parliament would have supreme power. Charles rejected this plan. Parliament then asked for troops to enforce its authority. The king asked his supporters to rally around him. The English Civil War had started.

The English Civil War People sided with one group or another for a variety of reasons. There were no clear-cut class divisions. However, upper-class people tended to support the king and middle- and lower-class people tended to support Parliament. The Anglicans and the Roman Catholics generally sided with Charles I. The aristocrats of the court, the House of Lords, and the gentry from the north and west also supported the king. These people were called royalists or *Cavaliers*. The Cavaliers were named for their dashing appearance—many wore shoulder-length hair and fancy clothes. These people supported the king and wanted to restore him to power.

Parliament was backed by the Puritans and Presbyterians. In fact, this war is also called the Puritan Revolution. The poor and the working class, especially in London, also supported Parliament. The working class hoped to gain certain bene-

Cavaliers and Puritans. Note the differences in clothing and hair styles.

developed a disciplined army under the leadership of Oliver Cromwell. He became their most important general.

Cromwell Before the war, Cromwell had been a country squire and a member of the Long Parliament. He was completely committed to the cause of Parliament. He infused the parliamentary army with a sense of purpose, an awareness that they were fighting for a just cause. The strongest assets of the army were its high morale and dedication.

Cromwell and his army defeated the king's forces in a decisive battle in 1645 at Naseby. The king was captured in 1646. The war was essentially over by 1648. However, Parliament and its victorious army were divided over what kind of government England should have. The parliamentary army had the real power. Cromwell was the link between Parliament and the army.

The majority of the members of Parliament were Presbyterians. They favored a limited monarchy and a national Presbyterian church. The Puritans were the second largest group in Parliament. They did not want a state church. A third group, not strongly represented in Parliament, spoke for the radical Protestant sects. They demanded full religious freedom. These people—small urban shopkeepers, artisans, apprentices, soldiers—wanted the right to vote and more participation in government. Some sects wanted to abolish privilege and even private property. However, not many of these people were in positions of power.

Cromwell was worried that Charles I would plot against Parliament. He expelled the Presbyterian members from Parliament, forming the so-called Rump Parliament. This Parliament abolished the Church of England and the House of Lords. In January of 1649, it charged Charles I with treason and ordered him tried in court.

fits, such as the right to vote and improved education for their children. London, the larger towns, and the southeastern part of England favored the forces of Parliament. The Parliament forces were called *Roundheads* because of their short hair.

Parliament was in control of the wealthy commercial areas. This included London, the richest city in England. Therefore, Parliament was able to impose taxes to raise an army. In fact, Parliament taxed more heavily than Charles I had ever tried to.

At first, Charles I controlled more territory. However, the king lacked money and troops. By 1645, the Roundheads

Cromwell and his group had already decided that Charles was guilty. The purpose of the trial was to demonstrate the guilt of the king to the whole world. Charles was found guilty and was publicly beheaded. The king conducted himself with dignity at his last hour. He defended until the last moment his views about the rights of a king.

Few thought that the Civil War would end with the death of Charles I. Many of the English people were shocked at the execution of their king. This daring act also horrified all the monarchs of Europe.

Cromwell's Government Cromwell had charge of the parliamentary army and the army had much to do. In 1649, his army ruthlessly put down a revolt in Ireland. In 1650-1651, the army conquered Scotland. By force, England, Scotland, and Ireland were unified into one nation.

Cromwell then imposed his vision of the "good" society on all of England. Forms of amusement such as theaters, dancing, and some sports were forbidden. There was to be no gambling or swearing. Hard work, honesty, and a sober life were emphasized.

Cromwell sincerely wanted to restore order in England. However, his Puritan

Charles I at Nottingham, after he had fled from London.

supporters were a minority. Like James I and Charles I, Cromwell found that Parliament did not always cooperate. In this case, they could not agree on a new constitution to replace the monarchy. Using his troops, Cromwell dismissed Parliament saying, "It is not fit that you sit here any longer!...You shall now give place to better men." The other generals named Cromwell Lord Protector of England. He ruled as a dictator until his death in 1658.

To maintain the large army with which he controlled England, Cromwell had to impose more taxes than Charles I had ever demanded. These taxes were imposed on the middle and working classes, and they were greatly resented. However, Cromwell and his advisers did curb the power of the Dutch and the French. They passed laws called the Navigation Acts. All goods entering or leaving England were to be carried in ships that were built and manned by English crews. These laws promoted English trade.

However, Cromwell was not popular. His army-backed rule was resented by the English people. The Anglicans and Presbyterians were outraged by their lack of power. Most of the English people were tired of Puritan rule.

The Restoration Cromwell's son was not able to rule effectively after his father's death in 1658. In 1660, a new Parliament invited the handsome thirty-year-old son of Charles I to return. Charles II had fled to Europe when his father was arrested. He eagerly accepted the invitation to return.

Charles II's return was a triumph. He was greeted with great enthusiasm by the people. Weary of the strict rule of the Puritans, the English were happy to be back in merry England. The tone of social life completely changed. Charles II's own behavior set the standard. He was fun-loving, and his court was lively. Elegant French fashions became popular.

Oliver Cromwell dissolving the Long Parliament.

The new king, however, had greatly diminished powers. In one way, the English Civil War was the last of the religious wars. More importantly, however, the English Civil War was the first of the modern revolutions. It raised the issue of who should rule a nation. The English Civil War served as a model for peoples throughout the world and greatly influenced America and Europe.

Toward the end of Charles' reign, Parliament began to worry about the problem of the succession to the throne. Charles II had no legitimate children. At his death, he was succeeded by his Roman Catholic brother, James II. James II put many Roman Catholics into positions of power and appeared to support French foreign policy. When a son was born to James in 1688, Protestants were greatly upset. This meant that the English crown would pass to a Roman Catholic instead of to one of the Protestant daughters, Mary and Anne, of James' first marriage.

The Glorious Revolution James II's daughter Mary was married to Prince William of Orange, the leader of the Netherlands. A group of leading Protestants invited Prince William to England. In 1688, William landed in England with an army and James II fled. Parliament then offered the crown jointly to William and Mary. This event is known as the Glorious Revolution.

Parliament insisted that William III and Mary II sign a Bill of Rights. This Bill of Rights provided that Parliament control taxation. It prohibited the monarch from suspending the laws of Parliament, or interfering with freedom of speech and debate in Parliament. The Bill of Rights thus guaranteed Parliament a share in decision making. The document also granted basic civil rights to individuals. These included prohibition of excessive bail and fines and of cruel and unusual punishment. In addition, the Toleration Act of 1689 gave religious freedom to Protestants, though not to Roman Catholics. However, Roman Catholics in England did not suffer much persecution after 1689. In Ireland, on the other hand, the Roman Catholic majority was prevented from having their

James II receiving the news that the Prince of Orange has landed in England.

own schools and priests and from holding public office. They also had difficulty in obtaining good jobs.

William III occupied himself largely with foreign policy. He left most domestic affairs in the hands of a small group of leaders in Parliament, the *cabinet*. He generally let them do what they wished. The practice developed that the majority party in Parliament had the right to make key decisions.

Mary II died in 1694 and William III in 1702. They were succeeded by Anne (1702-1714), Mary's younger sister. Anne had no living children. Parliament arranged that after Anne's death the crown would go to a German branch of the Stuart family, the house of Hanover. The family of the Roman Catholic James II was to be excluded from inheriting the throne. In 1707, during Queen Anne's rule, England, Wales, and Scotland were legally united into a single kingdom, known as Great Britain.

The Prime Minister The first two Hanoverian kings, George I (1714-1727) and George II (1727-1760), were German speaking. They left most decision making in the hands of the cabinet. The party in power in Parliament was recognized as having the right to select the *prime*, or first, minister. The prime minister and his cabinet then made the important decisions on how the British government would be run.

This system of government proved to be quite flexible. It allowed the voting public to express its ideas. The elections of members of Parliament communicated the general will of the public. Change became an orderly process, and the British never again had a civil war.

Some civil rights, such as freedom from unreasonable searches and the right to a fair trial, were now protected. However, Britain was not yet a democracy. Power was in the hands of wealthy and educated males—the country squires and the merchants. Women and working men could not vote. Married women had no legal control over their property or earnings. They could not make a will or ask for a divorce. It was assumed that husbands would look after their wives' interests.

The Protestant work ethic dominated British society. This contributed to making Britain the center of a strong commercial empire.

Section Questions

1. Why was James I unpopular?
2. What incident started the English Civil War in 1642?
3. Why did the Roundheads win the war?
4. Why was the English Civil War important?
5. How did the rule of foreign kings (William III and the first two Georges) affect the development of the British government?

2. The North American Colonists Rebelled

Thirteen British colonies were established on the eastern coast of North America. These colonies grew rapidly and prospered. Most people came to the British colonies for better economic opportunities. Some groups came for religious freedom. These included Puritans, Roman Catholics, Huguenots, and Protestant sects such as Quakers, German Mennonites, and Dunkers. Religious strife in Europe led to an increase in immigration. One part of the work force, the African slaves, were brought to the colonies against their wills.

Different colonies developed different economic systems. The southern colonies had economies based on slavery and crops like tobacco and rice. The middle colonies were the grain-growing "bread colonies." They also began to manufacture goods

Early colonists in a Maine fishing port.

such as iron, textiles, glass, and paper. The New England colonies depended heavily on trade and fishing.

In 1763, Britain's thirteen colonies had one of the highest standards of living in the world. What caused them to revolt? Revolution, it has been said, starts in the hearts and minds of people.

European Wars Throughout the 1600s and 1700s, Great Britain and France were rivals. In 1667, Louis XIV of France embarked on a lifelong battle to expand the borders of his kingdom. The English were concerned about France's growing power. The two nations were also competing for overseas empires in India, North America, and the West Indies.

There were constant wars between Britain and France. In 1756 the Seven Years' War began. It was fought in several parts of the world. In North America the British called it the French and Indian War.

France was defeated in both North America and India and forced to give up almost all of its overseas empire. Both France and Britain were left with huge debts at the end of the war.

In Britain, King George III and Parliament decided that the colonies should help pay for the costly war. They reasoned that the American colonists were now safe. The French and their Indian allies were no longer a threat. The British government decided to make the colonies pay more taxes by enforcing the old trading laws.

Fears of Oppression By 1763, New England and the middle colonies were not following the trade pattern that Britain desired. The southern colonies sent their exports—tobacco, rice, and *indigo* (from which blue dye was made)—to Britain. Britain needed these raw materials. The South was thus tightly linked to the British trading system. However, New England and the middle colonies had little to sell to Britain. They traded their fish, timber, grain, and animal products with many other parts of the world. They were directly engaged in commerce and trade, including the profitable slave trade. The New England and middle colonies also manufactured some of their products. Thus, they did not buy all of their manufactured goods from Britain.

Parliament tried to force the colonies into the trading pattern that would most benefit Britain. It passed many laws restricting trade. However, these trade laws were not obeyed. The American colonists constantly broke the laws by trading with the Spanish and French in the West Indies. Smuggling was common.

Things began to change after the French and Indian War. Within a few years, Parliament passed a series of laws that the American colonists saw as oppressive. The old trade laws were to be enforced. *Writs of assistance* (broad search warrants) were used to combat smuggling. Taxes were levied on goods from the Spanish and French West Indies. The colonies were prohibited from issuing paper money. In 1765, the Stamp Act provided for a tax on all legal documents, newspapers, and other printed materials. The act got its name from the tax stamp that had to be placed on these things. By 1770, this unpopular tax was repealed. In 1767, new taxes were placed on many everyday items, such as paper. This law was also repealed in 1770 after the colonists *boycotted*, or refused to buy, these goods.

The Stamp Act Riots in New York, 1765.

The American colonists were hurt in the pocketbook by the British trade and tax laws. New Englanders especially saw the disadvantages of being part of the British Empire. They felt that the laws were a form of oppression. The laws passed after 1763 were also seen as an invasion of the colonists' rights as British subjects.

Actually, the American colonists had more freedom in many ways than the people in Great Britain. About 50 to 75 percent of the white males in the colonies could vote for their representatives in the colonial legislatures. Less than 10 percent of the British subjects could vote for members of Parliament. The class system in the colonies was also more open than in Britian, with much opportunity for upward social mobility.

The American colonists had become used to making laws for their own benefit in their own assemblies. They resented Great Britain's attempts to interfere with their way of life. The colonists did not know how far Parliament might go. When 10,000 British troops were stationed on their soil, some Americans became concerned about religious freedom. There had been talk in the House of Lords about strengthening the Church of England in the colonies.

These economic, political, and religious factors transformed many loyal colonists into rebels. Many American colonists came to believe that King George III and the British government were planning to destroy their liberties. Fear of oppression united the different groups within each colony and united the colonies as a whole. Thus, the seeds of revolution had been planted. It took only a series of specific events to destroy the remaining loyalty to Great Britain.

Steps to War The Stamp Act of 1765 and the taxes of 1767 had produced a storm of protest in the American colonies. They had stirred up so much trouble that Parliament had finally repealed them in 1770. Nevertheless, in 1773, a tax was levied on tea. To the American colonists, this was another example of taxation without representation. The colonies had no representatives in Parliament to vote on such taxes. Some refused to buy the tea. In other places, the tea was stored in damp places so as to ruin it. Ships with cargoes of tea were not allowed to unload. Under the leadership of the radical Samuel Adams, a group of men dressed as Indians dumped the tea from three ships into Boston harbor. This event became known as the Boston Tea Party. It produced a political crisis.

The British were furious over the destruction of the tea. In the heat of anger, Parliament passed laws to punish the people of Boston. The American colonists called these laws the "Intolerable Acts." Then the Quebec Act of 1774 gave the coveted western lands across the Appalachian Mountains to Canada. Many colonists who wanted to move to the frontier thought they were being denied the opportunity for a better life.

A few American colonists began to think of independence. The British government was determined to rule the colonies as subordinate parts of a world empire. The two sides were unable to compromise.

In 1774, the First Continental Congress met in Philadelphia. It asked Britain to repeal the Intolerable Acts. It also urged the colonists to arm and train themselves. The chances for a peaceful settlement were reduced as the colonists began arming.

Tension was high. On April 18, 1775, British soldiers were sent out of Boston. They were to capture two American leaders, Sam Adams and John Hancock, and seize military supplies. *Minutemen*, armed colonists, were warned. The British soldiers were met by the Americans at Lexington, outside of Boston. Shooting broke out. The War for American Independence had begun.

In 1775, the Second Continental Con-

The Battle of Lexington.

gress gave George Washington the powers of commander-in-chief. On July 4, 1776, Congress adopted the Declaration of Independence, making a final break with Great Britain. This document, written mainly by young Thomas Jefferson of Virginia, spelled out the reasons for the rebellion. The Declaration of Independence was not just for the Americans. It said to the world that any people had the right to revolt against their government if it failed to protect their rights.

Winning the War Great Britain did not want to lose the largest and richest part of its colonial empire. However, the War for American Independence had a heavy cost in lives, money, and energy.

On the seas, American privateers did real damage to the British merchant fleet. Those who captured a British ship were allowed to keep the ship and the cargo. Privateers seized about six hundred British ships during the war and sold them for profit.

There were several major land battles. The British had certain disadvantages. They were fighting in a largely hostile land. Troops and supplies had to be sent across the Atlantic Ocean and then overland to the military areas. British officers constantly complained about a lack of good maps. They were even more dismayed by the American style of fighting. The British officers would have preferred European style confrontations, in which troops marched openly in straight lines and then fired.

The Americans were fighting in their own land. However, they lacked adequate supplies. Money to pay the army was scarce. There was a lack of cooperation among the new states.

Loans from foreign nations became available when the Americans won the Battle of Saratoga in 1777. In 1778, France,

409

Did You Know?

Note the American soldiers in trees and behind rocks.

Guerrilla Warfare

The American Revolution was similar to many modern-day wars of independence in that much of the fighting was *guerrilla warfare*. In guerrilla warfare, small armed forces make surprise raids and then flee before the enemy can capture them. Guerrilla fighters must be very mobile—able to hit and run. The fighters also have to know where to hide. Some of these techniques of fighting were learned from the Indians.

One of the best guerrilla leaders of the American Revolution was General Francis Marion, whose nickname was the Swamp Fox. His name gives a clue to his activities. He and his small group of armed men hid in the swamps and marshes in South Carolina. They would make quick raids on the British supply areas, often seizing the ammunition they needed. Then the Swamp Fox and his men would melt back into the safe area of the swamps.

Guerrilla warfare depends on support from the civilians in the area. Guerrilla fighters normally cannot grow their own food. They often do not have enough money to pay for the food and other goods they need. The guerrilla fighters also need to get information from trusted civilians about the enemy's movements. In guerrilla warfare, the guerrillas are typically in charge of the countryside, while their enemy controls the urban areas. Guerrilla fighting does not usually itself lead to a direct military victory. However, guerrilla fighters can gradually wear down the strength of an enemy. It can then be more easily defeated by more conventional military forces.

eager to get even with Britain, declared war on its old rival. Later, Spain and the Netherlands also entered the war against Great Britain. This forced the British to use some of their troops, supplies, and ships outside of America.

French aid was especially valuable to the American cause. France granted loans to the struggling Americans. A French army and fleet were sent to help the American forces. With the help of the French, General Washington forced Lord Cornwallis to surrender a large British army at Yorktown in 1781. This was the last significant battle of the war.

A peace treaty was signed in 1783. The United States of America had won its independence from Great Britain. The principles of the Declaration of Independence and the American Revolution were to serve as models for nations around the world.

The new republic ratified the United States Constitution in 1788. The Constitution was also an example for other peoples throughout the world. The new form of government was based on the American

The French soldier Lafayette leading troops at Monmouth.

Lord Cornwallis surrendering at Yorktown.

experience as members of the British Empire. Americans believed in protecting the rights of citizens and in placing limits on the power of the central government. They had no king in an age in which almost all nations had monarchs. The Americans were concerned that no person or branch of the government should get too much power. Thus, they devised a government in which authority was divided into three main branches: the executive, the legislative, and the judicial. Each branch also had the power to check, or stop, the other and to balance its power. The Constitution stated both what things the government could do and what things it could not do. These limitations on the power of the government were further strengthened by the first ten amendments to the Constitution. These amendments are known as the Bill of Rights. The Bill of Rights outlines the basic rights of all citizens.

Section Questions

1. What were the results of the Seven Years' War?
2. What made the American colonists fearful of oppression by Britain?
3. Why did the Americans win the war?
4. Why did the Americans divide power in their new government among three branches?

3. Latin America Fought for Independence

In 1776, when the United States declared its independence from Britain, colonial Latin America seemed to be prosperous and stable. Population and trade were increasing. The *elite* — the top government officials, the important church leaders, and the wealthy — lived a comfortable life in fine cities. They seemed to be contented and loyal to the distant king of Spain or Portugal. The cities, Mexico City and Lima, and smaller ones such as Quito, Arequipa, and Guadalajara, were elegant. They compared favorably with the dirty English-speaking cities such as Philadelphia or with European cities such as Madrid. Latin American cities had attractive cathedrals, convents and seminaries, customs buildings, acad-

This photograph shows a room in the house of Simón Bolívar.

Ouro Prêto, Brazil.

emies and universities, city halls, and theaters. The wealthy few had large, tasteful townhouses. The wealthy plantation and mine owners of Latin America lived and spent most of their time in the city. A wealthy Virginia planter, on the other hand, usually lived almost the whole year on his own plantation. He and his family would spend only a few weeks at Williamsburg, the capital of the Virginia colony. The homes on the *haciendas*, or estates, of the elite were, therefore, large but uncomfortable and sparsely furnished places. Most of the rural churches were small and unimposing.

The Social Structure In Latin America, the social class system was much more rigid than in the United States. There were the few members of the elite, a small middle class of shopkeepers and artisans, and the great mass of mostly poor, nonwhite people—Indians, blacks and those of mixed blood. There were few opportunities to move ahead. Wages were low because labor was plentiful. Partly because of the large supply of cheap labor in Latin America, few white people did physical labor. Poorer white men struggled to secure government jobs so they would not have to work with their hands. Despite this rigid class structure, few riots or disturbances arose among the lower classes. This peaceful scene in colonial Latin America soon was to change violently.

The Creoles Spain controlled most of Latin America. The Portuguese had the large colony of Brazil. The French, British, and Dutch had a few small colonies, mostly in the West Indies. All these colonies had much in common. Discontent was growing in Latin America. One social class, the *creoles*, or *criollos*, especially resented what they felt was discrimination from the Spanish. The creoles were people of Spanish ancestry born in Latin America. In some parts of Spanish America, *mestizos* who had gained some wealth were closely allied with the creoles in seeking higher social standing. Mestizos were people of mixed white and Indian backgrounds. However, the poorer mestizos' interests were closely tied to those of the *peons*, or peasants.

The creoles were angered because they could not get high-ranking government positions. Typically the government sent out natives of Spain to occupy these jobs. They were called *peninsulares* because they were from the Spanish peninsula. The creoles regarded these Spanish as their social inferiors. The creoles respected only the Spanish viceroys and the archbishops as of

Workers in Peru.

equal social status. They disliked the "invasion" of lower-status people from Spain such as army officers and clerks. At the same time, they envied the power of these Spanish-born officials. They felt that they, the creoles, were the heirs of the early conquistadors and should not be blocked from promotion. There was a growing rift between the creoles and the European Spanish. There were several reasons that the Spanish government favored the native-born Spanish for important positions in the colonies. It felt that Spanish-born officials would not be as likely to bow to local pressures. Unlike the creoles, who favored the interests of their relatives and friends, the Spanish-born could be more objective. Such fairness was important in affairs such as promotions and court cases. In addition, the Spanish government felt that the creoles were too harsh in their treatment of the Indians. Spain hoped that the Spanish officials would give the Indians some protection.

The creoles also resented not being able to rise to the highest positions in the Roman Catholic Church. On the local level, there were no problems. The parish priests of the time were usually creoles, mestizos, and sometimes even Indians. The main struggle was over who would lead the wealthy religious orders that owned large tracts of land, an important source of income. In many cases, a religious order was split between those favoring a creole monk and those favoring a Spanish monk as head of the order. Sometimes, compromises were made, such as a rotation of the office between a creole and a Spaniard.

Economic Problems By the time of the French Revolution, which you will read about in Chapter 23, the Spanish government had eased many of its trading restrictions on the Spanish colonies. Ports were open to foreign merchants. Members of

Creole men riding for pleasure.

the elite were able to secure manufactured goods and other items from other nations. However, Spain was also attempting to reform its colonial system by tightening imperial control and exacting more revenues. The creoles felt a sense of economic injustice. They believed that the powerful merchants in Seville and other Spanish cities had more influence than they did. The creoles resented the taxes.

Political, religious, and economic issues were dividing the creoles and the Spanish. The ideas of the Enlightenment (Chapter 22) were spreading among the creoles. Intellectuals gathered together to discuss reforms to improve Latin American society. After 1776, the ideas of the American Revolution spread through the upper and middle classes. The Declaration of Independence and Thomas Paine's *Common Sense* were read by literate Latin Americans. The news of the violent French Revolution, with the beheading of the French king, received even more attention.

Did You Know?

General Toussaint L'Ouverture

Toussaint (too SAN) was born in 1743 as a slave on a plantation in the French colony of Saint Domingue (san do MANG). This colony was located on the western half of the island of Hispaniola (his pun YO la). The Spanish controlled the eastern half, the colony of Santo Domingo (sant uh duh MING o).

Fortunately for Toussaint, his owner was a kind man. Toussaint learned to read. Later, he took over his father's job as a coachman. Toussaint was a slave for almost fifty years. In 1789, at the beginning of the French Revolution, there were about eight times as many black slaves—around 500,000—as French colonists.

The news of the French Revolution threw the island into turmoil. In 1791, a great slave rebellion started. Toussaint became the leader of the rebellious slaves. At this time, Toussaint gained the name of L'Ouverture (LOO vur tur), the French word for "opening." This referred to the fact that he seized the advantage of any opening to break through the enemies' lines. In 1793, the blacks learned that the National Convention in Paris had outlawed slavery. They were now free and independent.

Toussaint controlled the French part of Hispaniola. In 1801, Toussaint defeated the Spanish and seized the entire island. Toussaint was master of all of Hispaniola, though he officially ruled in the name of the French Republic. Toussaint's power annoyed Napoleon. In 1802, Napoleon sent an army of 30,000 to Saint Domingue.

A scene from the revolution in Haiti.

The blacks, recently freed and unwilling to be governed by outsiders, resisted. Toussaint was tricked into coming to a conference and was arrested. He was sent in chains to France and left in a cold, damp prison near Switzerland, where he died in 1803.

Although Toussaint had been eliminated, the French did not succeed in Saint Domingue. Yellow fever spread rapidly through the French army, killing about 25,000 troops. Seeing the weakened condition of the French army, the blacks again revolted. They drove out both the French and the Spanish. In 1804, Saint Domingue became an independent nation. Its name was changed to Haiti, an Indian word meaning "high ground." Haiti was the first Latin American nation to become free.

Haiti In 1804, the blacks of Haiti successfully won their independence from France. The success of the blacks and *mulattos*, people of mixed African and European background, worried the creoles. They did not want to grant more social rights to the lower classes. The creoles wanted a political, not a social, revolution. They did not want to lose their property and position in society. The creoles believed they were racially and socially superior to the masses. The French Revolution also worried the Spanish officials in Latin America. They too did not want ideas about the rights of people to spread among the poor Indians and mestizos. The Spanish officials began to prosecute critics who spoke for change in the Latin American colonies. In many cases, these "malcontents" were exiled from the Spanish colonies. From exile, the rebels continued to plot against the Spanish government.

The wars of Napoleon triggered independence for the Latin American colonies. In 1808, Napoleon drove the Spanish king from his throne. Napoleon then made his own brother, Joseph Bonaparte, king of Spain. This sparked a revolt not only among the Spanish at home but in Latin America as well. However, until Napoleon's defeat in 1814, the true Spanish king could not send troops to Latin America to curb any rebellions there. From 1808 to 1814, the time of turmoil in Spain, the independence movement in Latin America gained strength. One by one, the Spanish colonies on the continent declared themselves free from Spanish rule. Most of the revolutions were led by the creoles, who wanted to free themselves from Spanish rule. However, the creole leaders needed soldiers so they turned to the mestizos, Indians, and blacks for help. Thus, the creoles talked of liberty and equality. However, after independence they generally forgot about rights for the common people. Unlike the French Revolution, the Latin American revolutions were not true class struggles. They were more like the American Revolution in that they involved a shift in political power from the parent country to the wealthy local leaders. The one important exception to the pattern was Mexico. There the revolution started as a revolt of the landless peasants against the wealthy creole landowners.

Mexico Many groups in Latin America wanted independence after the Spanish king was driven from his throne in 1808. The plotters had a good excuse. They could say that they did not have to obey Napoleon's brother because he was not the legal ruler.

Miguel Hidalgo.

In many places, there were several pro-independence groups. They often quarreled with each other. One group of plotters in Mexico included Miguel Hidalgo (E dal go), an idealistic priest in the town of Dolores. Hidalgo learned that his plot had been discovered. On September 5, 1810, before he could be seized by the authorities, he ordered the church bells to be rung. The people in the community wondered why the bells were ringing and rushed to the church. Hidalgo then spoke to the people and incited them to rebel. Responding to Hidalgo's call, the Indians seized many haciendas, towns, and cities. They killed the estate owners whether they were native-born Spaniards or creoles. The land-hungry peasants regarded the big landowners as their real enemies. This was not the way the creoles in Mexico had planned the revolution. As Hidalgo's army of thousands approached Mexico City, the creoles joined forces with the Spanish officials and defeated the rebels, capturing Hidalgo. In 1811, Hidalgo was executed. The officials placed his head on the wall of his native city to serve as an example to the people.

Nevertheless, small bands of guerrillas scattered across Mexico continued to fight even after the defeat of Hidalgo's army. After the Spanish king regained his throne in 1814, experienced Spanish troops were sent to the Americas. The Spanish reestablished control in many areas, but their authority was weak. Finally, about 1820, the creoles joined with the mestizos in Mexico. By 1821, the Mexicans had completely defeated the Spanish. Mexico gained its independence from Spain. However, the vast majority of the Mexican people still lacked rights and the opportunity to better themselves.

Bolívar and Martín Two men, Simón Bolívar (bo LEE var) and José de San Martín (sawn mar TEEN), were the outstanding independence leaders south of Mexico. Bolívar (1783-1830) was an intellectual creole leader. He was convinced that Spanish control of Latin America must end. He united many quarreling groups to fight together for the cause of freedom from Spain. His personality made many admire him, and his magnetic leadership inspired others. In 1816, Bolívar put together an army of English and Irish soldiers, runaway slaves, Indians, mestizos, and cowboys. Eventually, the Spanish government in what is now Venezuela, Colombia, and Ecuador was overthrown. Out of this area, Bolívar fashioned the Republic of Great Colombia. He was elected the first president.

José de San Martín (1778-1850) was a professional soldier. He drove the Spanish

Simón Bolívar.

José de San Martín leading his army through a pass in the Andes.

from Argentina in 1817. San Martín followed this victory by leading a miraculous march over the Andes Mountains. This resulted in the liberation of Chile. By 1820, he helped Peru to secure independence.

In 1824, the Latin American rebels defeated the last large Spanish force in the hemisphere at Ayacucho (I uh KOO cho), Peru. Most of Latin America was now independent. Only Cuba and Puerto Rico remained in Spanish hands.

Brazil had a more peaceful revolution. In 1807, John VI of Portugal fled from Portugal to Brazil when Napolean's forces invaded Portugal. After fourteen years in Brazil, King John returned to his country. He left his son, Dom Pedro, behind as regent. In 1822, Dom Pedro declared Brazil independent. The Brazilians defeated the small group of Portuguese troops. In December 1822, Dom Pedro became Emperor Pedro I of Brazil. The country also adopted a new constitution.

Thus, almost all of the nations on the mainland of Latin America were independent by 1824. The small armies of the rebels had fought bravely.

The final victory in the independence movement was also aided by the intellectuals in the cities. The intellectuals supplied the revolutionary slogans and raised the money to pay and feed the rebel armies. They helped make Latin Americans feel patriotic and desire independence. Thus, both soldiers and civilians contributed to winning the wars of independence. Nonetheless, independence did not solve the many problems facing Latin America.

Section Questions

1. What groups were most discontented in Latin America in 1789 ? Why?
2. In what colony did the blacks revolt against French control?
3. Who were the important leaders in the movement for independence in Latin America?
4. In what ways did the intellectuals help in the wars for independence in Latin America?

Chapter Summary

1. Friction developed between James I, King of England, and Parliament, the law-making body. James' son, Charles I, also had difficulty in dealing with Parliament. Charles supported the Church of England. His archbishop of Canterbury tried to force the Anglican services on the Puritans and Presbyterians. The Puritans and Presbyterians were strongly represented in Parliament. Parliament was reluctant to give the king money unless he acted according to the laws and gave Parliament a voice in government policy. The English Civil War began when Charles tried to arrest the leaders of Parliament. Charles lost the war and was beheaded. Oliver Cromwell then ruled as a military dictator. The English people, tired of Puritan rule, put Charles II on the throne. He was succeeded by his brother, James II, a Roman Catholic. Parliament, not wanting a Roman Catholic dynasty, invited William and Mary to assume the throne. They did so, but, in signing a Bill of Rights, agreed that Parliament had power and that English subjects had civil rights. After the reign of Queen Anne, the British crown was inherited by the German Hanoverians. Gradually, the cabinet system developed and Parliament began to determine government policy and make the laws.
2. The thirteen British colonies on the Atlantic seaboard had one of the highest living standards in the world. After 1763, in order to help pay for a costly war with France, Britain began to try to exert greater control over the colonies. The colonists saw the new taxes and the enforcement of old trade laws as restrictions on their freedom. They feared the loss of other liberties. The unpopular Tea Act led to further strains between the colonists and the British government. The colonists began to organize themselves for war. Fighting broke out at Lexington in 1775. The War for American Independence had started. In 1776, Congress approved the Declaration of Independence. This document stated the reasons why the colonies had to separate from Britain. It also influenced other peoples who wanted to revolt against their established governments. After a long struggle and with the help of foreign nations, the United States of America won complete independence from Britain in 1783. The Constitution of 1788, which established a secure foundation for the new republic, also served as a model for the world.
3. In 1776, colonial Latin America seemed to be loyal to the parent countries. However, discontent was growing. The creoles resented the Spanish-born officials sent out to rule. They also resented not getting high positions in the Roman Catholic Church and felt a sense of economic injustice. In addition, the upper and middle classes became familiar with the ideas of the Enlightenment and of the American and French revolutions. In 1804, the blacks in Haiti won their independence from France. The Mexican drive for independence started in 1810, when Miguel Hidalgo incited the peasants to rebel. His rebellion was put down and he was executed. Later, in 1821, Mexico achieved independence from Spain. Bolívar and San Martín were the outstanding independence leaders in the rest of Latin America. In 1822, Brazil became independent from Portugal under Emperor Pedro I.

Chapter 21 Review

Check Your Facts

1. Identify the following:
   a. George Washington
   b. William III and Mary II
   c. James II
   d. Charles I
   e. Miguel Hidalgo
   f. George III
2. How did King James VI of Scotland become King James I of England?
3. Which groups in the English Civil War generally supported the king? Which supported Parliament?
4. Why did Cromwell and his supporters want to execute Charles I?
5. Why did the English people generally not like James II?
6. In what way was the Declaration of Independence important beyond the borders of the United States?
7. Why did France help the American colonies win independence?

Words to Know

1. Define the following words in one or two sentences.
   a. Roundheads
   b. Writs of Assistance
   c. Cavaliers
   d. boycott
2. Write a paragraph about Latin America. Use these words: *mestizos, creoles, haciendas, mulattos, peninsulares.*

Developing Your Skills

1. Trace a map of eastern United States. Mark the sites of the battles of Lexington, Sarasota, and Yorktown.
2. Place the following events in the proper chronological order:

   William III and Mary II agree to a Bill of Rights.
   Mexico gains independence.
   The Stamp Act is passed by Parliament.
   Charles II assumes the throne of England.
   Shooting begins at Lexington.

Thinking It Over

1. During the 1600s and 1700s, people worried about trying to limit the power of the government. Now the government of the United States tries to protect the rights of its citizens in areas such as racial or sexual discrimination. Why do you think this shift occurred?
2. After 1814, do you think it would have been possible for Spain to make concessions and keep most of Latin America in the Spanish empire?

Special Activities

1. In small groups, discuss the meaning of treason. Should a person always be loyal to the existing form of government? If there are exceptions, what are they?
2. Thomas Paine's words stirred the colonists to revolt and boosted their spirits during the American Revolution. He wrote: "These are the times that try men's souls." He also said: "The summer soldier and the sunshine patriot will, in the crisis, shrink from the service of their country." How important was the press in the American Revolution? In the English Civil War?

Milton looking through a telescope in Galileo's observatory.

Chapter 22 The Age of Reason

How can we harness solar energy? How does the human body fight off disease? Answers to such questions depend heavily on the findings of science.

Many scientific explanations are now commonly accepted. This was not true in past centuries. People believed in common-sense ideas. The Earth looked flat, so it must be flat. People also relied upon the beliefs of their culture—the ideas passed down from one generation to another or given by some authority figure. Often, these views were not based on accurate information.

1543-1789

1543	Copernicus publishes his theory
1590	First microscope
1616	Galileo discovers some of Jupiter's moons
1628	Harvey discovers circulation of blood
1643	Torricelli invents barometer
ca. 1675	Van Leeuwenhoek observes bacteria

AGE OF REASON 1687-1789

1687	Newton's *Principia*
1690	Locke justifies revolution
1747	Montesquieu advocates separation of powers
1762	Rousseau's *Social Contract*
1789	Beginning of French Revolution

Isaac Newton.

The growth and acceptance of science revolutionized peoples' ideas about the world. Scientists, using the *scientific method*, search for data and their meaning. They prize careful observation and objective collection of data. They demand verification of the accuracy of a finding or an assertion. Through the use of this method, scientific knowledge grows. Because new data are uncovered, science changes. In biology, for example, it was about 1675 that a microscope was first used to identify bacteria. Today, scientists are using new technologies, such as gene splicing, to discover much more about biology.

The century from 1687, when Newton's *Principia* was published, to 1789, the beginning of the French Revolution, is called the Enlightenment or the Age of Reason. The Enlightenment was marked by the growth and acceptance of science. The thinkers of the Enlightenment, rejecting the medieval reliance on faith, stressed that people could use reason to improve themselves and society.

1. Science Uncovered New Ideas

One field of science that changed greatly even before the Age of Reason was astronomy. The founder of modern astronomy is considered to be Nicholaus Copernicus (1473-1543). Copernicus was a Polish priest who had studied in Italy. He questioned the ancient theory of Ptolemy of Alexandria that the Earth was the center of the uni-

423

Johannes Kepler discussing his theories with his sponsor, Emperor Rudolph II.

verse. Most people had accepted Ptolemy's views for more than a thousand years.

Copernicus' Theory Copernicus was the first astronomer to claim that the Earth revolved around the sun. People on the Earth do not see or feel this motion because they are traveling with the Earth.

These startling new ideas were outlined in Copernicus' book *Concerning the Revolutions of Celestial Spheres*, published in 1543. These ideas did not match the commonly accepted belief that the Earth stood still and the planets and stars revolved around it. In addition, religious leaders thought that the Bible implied that the Earth was the center of the universe. Both Roman Catholic and Protestant leaders denounced Copernicus' theory as false. At first, even the few scientists of the day did not pay attention to Copernicus' ideas. Copernicus had made some mathematical mistakes, since he thought that the orbits of the planets were circular.

Tycho Brahe (BRA eh 1546-1601), a Danish astronomer, was a careful observer. Night after night, with his unaided eyes, he faithfully watched the positions of the planets. He gathered the most accurate data on astronomy thus far available. Tycho

An engraving illustrating the concept of Earth revolving around the sun.

Brahe's assistant was Johannes Kepler (1571-1630), a German mathematical genius. For years, Kepler worked with Brahe's careful observations. From these data, he discovered three laws or principles about the motion of planets. First, every planet follows an *ellipse*, or oval-shaped path, as it revolves around the sun. Second, the planets do not move at the same speed all the time. They move faster when they are closer to the sun and slower when they are farther away. Third, the time taken by a planet to make one complete trip around the sun depends on how far away it is from the sun. Kepler's laws upheld Copernicus' theory. They also showed that the natural world behaves in an orderly way that can be measured mathematically.

More data supporting Copernicus' theory came from Galileo Galilei (1564-1642), an Italian scientist. Galileo made his most important discoveries in mechanics. However, he is most famous for his telescopes. Galileo improved on the Dutch invention of the *spyglass*, or telescope, an instrument for enlarging the range of a person's view. Galileo built the most powerful telescopes of his time. With these, he was able to observe many new things in the heavens. He found that the moon was not a smooth sphere shining by its own light. Instead, he saw that it had mountains and valleys that reflected light. Galileo was also the first person to see the rings around Saturn. His most sensational discovery, in 1616, was of four moons that revolved around the planet Jupiter. This provided concrete evidence to support Copernicus' theory because it proved that not all heavenly bodies revolve around the Earth.

Galileo's scientific ideas were accepted throughout western Europe. This alarmed the leaders of the Roman Catholic Church.

They asked Galileo not to write about the theory that the Earth revolved around the sun. Years later, in 1632, Galileo did write that the Copernican theory was true. For this, Galileo, now an old man, was brought before the Inquisition. Under pressure, but not torture, Galileo was forced to deny in public his belief in Copernicus' theory.

Newton The great genius of the scientific age was Sir Isaac Newton (1642-1727), an English astronomer and mathematician. Building on the work of others, he made enormous contributions in many fields. In optics, Newton discovered why objects appear to be colored. He also invented an important branch of mathematics, *calculus*. Calculus deals with changing quantities. For example, it allows one to calculate the volume of irregular shapes such as bottles.

Newton's greatest achievement was the Universal Law of Gravitation. Legend has it that Newton got the idea of gravity when he saw an apple fall in his garden. Newton's law explains why the Earth, the planets, and even apples move. To Newton,

An experiment on the speed of falling bodies. The objects were "seen to fall evenly."

Newton analyzing a ray of light.

everything has a force that he called *gravity*. Gravity pulls objects together. The gravitational pull of anything—an apple or a planet—depends upon its weight and how far it is from another object. The sun's gravity holds the Earth near it and prevents it from flying out into space. The apple, when the tree lets it go, falls toward the heavier object, the Earth.

Newton's work on motion and gravitation remained unnoticed for about twenty years. Then Edmund Halley, an English astronomer, found that Newton had some real evidence to support the law of gravity. Halley convinced Newton to publish *Mathematical Principles of Natural Philosophy* in 1687. The book came to be called *Principia*, the first word of its Latin title.

Principia was immediately recognized as a masterpiece. It combined the ideas of preceding scientists into one theory. The book was very technical, but others popularized Newton's ideas for the general public.

Newton did not do all the calculations needed to prove his theory. Others continued the work. Scientists worked under his set of principles for 250 years. His theory was superseded only in the twentieth century by that of another great genius, Albert Einstein.

Newton was recognized as the most notable scientist of his day. In 1705, he was knighted by Queen Anne. He was also made president of the Royal Society of England. This society brought scientists together and also granted them money for their work. The royal scientific academies in cities such as London and Paris were the centers of scientific learning.

When he died in 1727, Newton, the son of a farming family, had a state funeral. He was buried in Westminster Abbey with the kings and queens and other famous people of Britain. At his death, science was the wonder of the age. The universe seemed like a giant clock that ran in perfect order.

Mathematics, Chemistry, and Physics

As we have seen, advances in astronomy were aided by advances in mathematics. There were other needs for mathematics. Sailors needed better methods of navigation. In business and finance, interest rates had to be figured. Bookkeepers needed a way to show negative balances.

In the 1500s, mathematical symbols such as the signs for plus and minus, decimal points, multiplication brackets, and the radical sign (square root) came into use. Children were taught these symbols with the new mathematics textbooks that were then being printed.

Pure mathematics also advanced. In 1614, Scotsman John Napier published his work on *logarithms*. Logarithms, or exponents, are numbers that are used to

Torricelli and his barometer.

shorten complicated multiplication and division. Shortly afterward, René Descartes, a Frenchman, published the first work on analytic geometry. It combined algebra and geometry.

At around the same time as Sir Isaac Newton, Baron Gottfried von Leibniz (LIB nutz), a German, independently invented calculus. Calculus stimulated further development of mathematics. It was essential to the development of advanced physics and engineering.

Science also advanced through the use of better instruments. The Italian Evangelista Torricelli (TOR ree CHEL e) invented the *barometer*. This instrument measures air pressure and can be used to forecast the weather. Mercury thermometers were also improved.

Modern chemistry was born during the Age of Reason. Before, chemistry had been a mixture of magic, religion, and practical observations. Now, scientists questioned many ideas that had been accepted for centuries. They demolished the ancient theory that all *matter*, the physical substance of anything, was made up of four elements—earth, fire, water, and air. The new chemists searched for the basic elements of matter.

Robert Boyle (1627-1691), an Irishman, proved that air, earth, fire, and water were not basic elements. He conducted many careful experiments, especially with air pressure. Boyle formulated what is now called Boyle's Law, which concerns gases.

The person now considered the founder of modern chemistry is Antoine Lavoisier

Lavoisier and his wife experimenting with respiration and oxygen.

(LAH vwah zee A 1743-1794), a Frenchman. This brilliant chemist discovered twenty-three of the basic elements we know today. He also developed a theory on the conservation of matter. According to Lavoisier, matter cannot be either created or destroyed. It can only change its physical form, as when water boils and becomes steam, or enter into chemical compounds. Lavoisier also explained *combustion*, or fire, as a rapid form of oxidation. He showed how oxygen formed compounds.

In physics, the most important advances came in the area of electricity. William Gilbert, an English physician, discovered the characteristics of static electricity. In 1600, he wrote about the attraction of certain objects toward each other. Benjamin Franklin, the first important American scientist, flew a kite during an electric storm to show that lightning was a form of electricity. Charles Augustin de Coulomb (koo LOM), a Frenchman, formulated the laws of attraction and repulsion between electrically charged bodies.

Biology and Medicine Andreas Vesalius (vee SAY lih us 1514-1564) of the University of Padua in Italy began the practice of dissecting corpses. He used the bodies of dead criminals. Once, he even climbed the gallows to remove a corpse for study. His careful observations corrected many previous errors. However, his enemies bitterly attacked him. People did not like the practice of dissecting bodies. Disgusted, Vesalius left the University of Padua and became the personal physician of Philip II of Spain. Vesalius is often considered the founder of anatomy.

Ambroise Paré (pah RAY 1510-1590) helped raise the status of surgeons. Before him, physicians commonly believed that operations, being messy, were beneath them. The job of surgery was left to barbers. Paré questioned the practices that had been used for hundreds of years. He served as a

An illustration of the musculature of the body.

surgeon in the French Army and saw first-hand the results of warfare. He stopped treating gunshot wounds and surgical incisions with boiling oil. Instead, Paré began to rely on the power of nature and time to heal wounds. He sewed up arteries and experimented with many new surgical techniques. He later became a surgeon to Henry II of France and other French kings.

William Harvey (1578-1657), an English physician, discovered the circulation of blood through the arteries and veins. In 1628, he explained how the heart pumped

Did You Know?

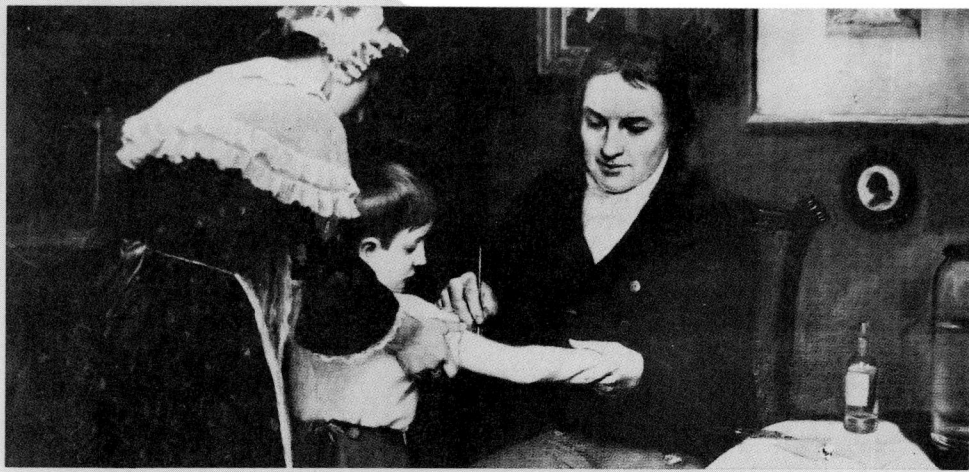

Dr. Jenner vaccinating a young patient.

Conquering Smallpox

Smallpox used to be one of life's terrors. It was one of the most contagious diseases among human beings. The victim first experienced high fever, headache, chills, and nausea. Then after three or four days, the first red spots erupted into little blisters filled with pus.

Smallpox spared no one. Rich and powerful rulers such as Elizabeth I of England and Louis XV of France had it as well as many poor peasants. The very young and the very old were especially likely to die from it. Those who survived were scarred.

Smallpox probably started in ancient times in India or tropical Africa. Europeans returning from the Crusades or Asia spread the disease into new places. It was recognized that the best way to control the disease was to *quarantine*, or isolate, the victims. However, people tried many methods. A popular practice was wrapping patients in red.

In 1520, Cortes and his army introduced the dreaded disease into the New World. The Aztecs had no immunity to the disease. The death rate in the New World ranged between 50 and 90 percent, compared to a normal rate of about 10 percent in Europe.

In 1717, Lady Mary Montague (MON tah gew) noted in Istanbul that a vaccination method kept people from getting smallpox. Lady Montague spread the practice of vaccination when she returned to England. Soon, wealthy people started to protect themselves against the disease.

Edward Jenner, an English physician, proved that using his vaccine based on cowpox, a mild form of smallpox, prevented the more serious disease. However, it was a long time before the general public accepted the practice of vaccination. After World War II, the World Health Organization (WHO) made the elimination of smallpox a priority. Millions of people, some unwilling, were vaccinated in all parts of the world. By 1980, WHO was able to announce that smallpox had been completely eradicated.

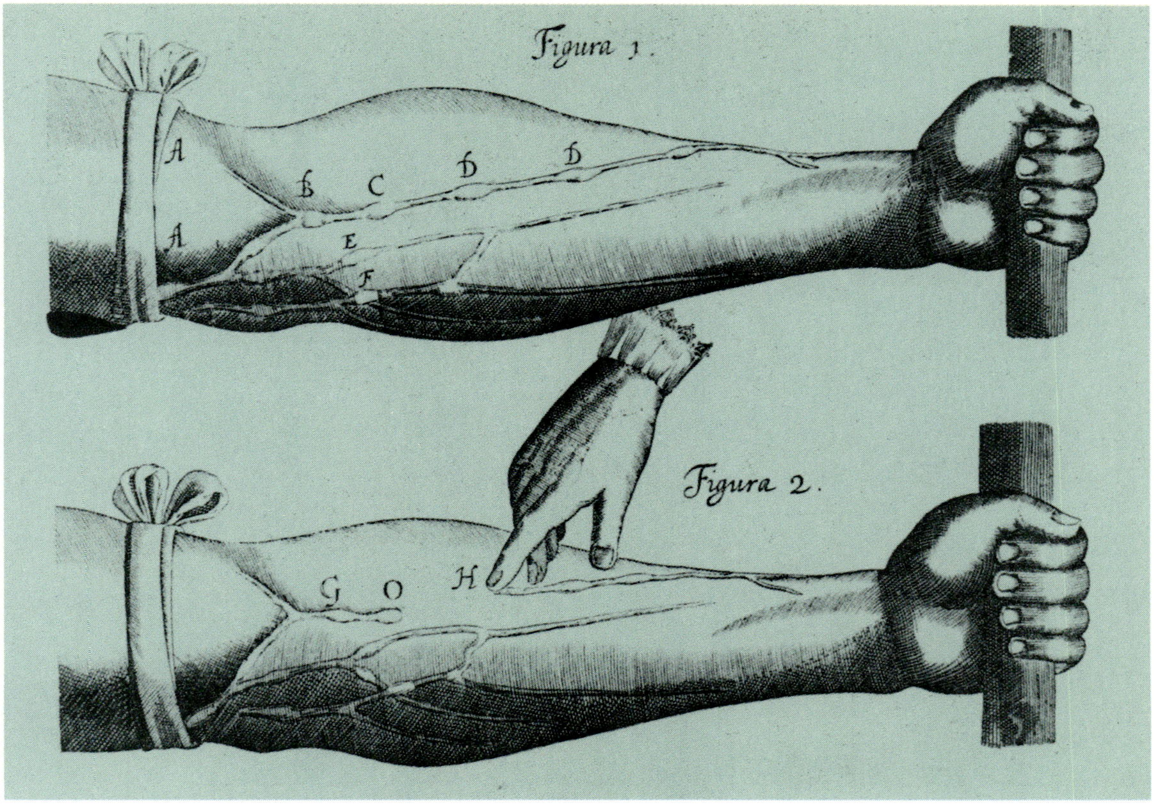

Dr. Harvey demonstrating the circulation of blood.

blood through the body. This was an important contribution to the study of medicine.

Harvey's work was based on careful direct observation of patients. In addition, he performed experiments on hundreds of small animals—frogs, fish, and so on. Harvey also served as a physician to James I and Charles I. His ideas were accepted even in his own lifetime. However, Harvey could not discover how the blood passes from the arteries to the veins. He could not see the capillaries.

Medicine and science were greatly aided when the first *microscope* was invented by the Dutch about 1590. A microscope magnifies objects by producing images larger than the original. Anton van Leeuwenhoek

Leeuwenhoek's microscope adapted for modern slides.

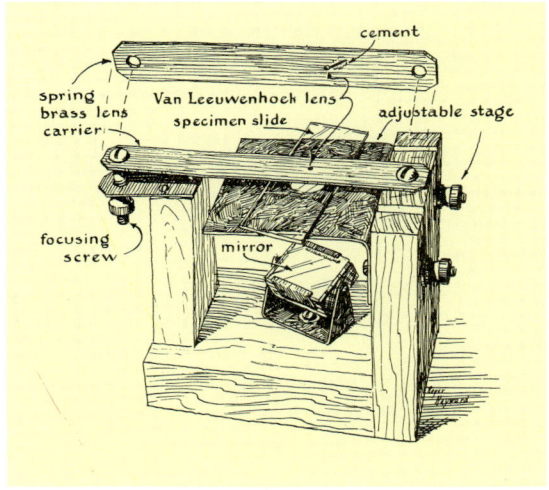

Leeuwenhoek in his laboratory.

(LAY ven hook 1632-1723) was a skilled Dutch craftsman. He built 200 microscopes, finally making one that enlarged over 100 times. This microscope was 50 millimeters (2 inches) high. Leeuwenhoek looked at many things under the microscope. He was the first to discover bacteria. He saw, for the first time in history, the structure of plant and animal tissues. His work revealed a whole new world of one-celled organisms that people had not known existed.

Science was now dealing with an expanding world. Newton explained how the universe operates. Leeuwenhoek introduced a new world of tiny organisms that are part of all living things. Results of scientific research were made public for others to duplicate and to check. With the use of this scientific method, knowledge about the world increased.

Section Questions

1. Why did people not want to accept Copernicus' ideas?
2. What kind of trouble did Galileo's ideas cause him?
3. Why was Newton's work important?
4. What advances did Lavoisier make in chemistry?
5. List some of the changes and advances in mathematics. How did these changes affect other areas of science or industry?
6. Why was the invention of the microscope important?

2. New Ideas About Society Became Popular

The Enlightenment or Age of Reason was an outgrowth of the advances in science. Galileo and other scientists had challenged the accepted ideas of the time. Using reason along with careful observation and experimentation, scientists were better able to explain the physical world.

The Philosophes A small group of intellectuals called *philosophes* (fihl us sofs) believed that by using reason in a similar way, human beings could improve society. This would include government, laws, education, and so on.

The philosophes were impressed by the theoretical achievements of science. The discoveries of Newton and other scientists made it appear that the universe and everything within it followed an orderly pattern. A natural law seemed to govern the universe and all living things. The task of scientists was to uncover the secrets of nature. They were to search for the natural order in what on the surface appeared to be disorder.

The philosophes were also impressed with the practical achievements of science. People were amazed at the flood of new inventions and techniques. For example, in agriculture, experiments were made on fertilizers, crop rotation, and new varieties of seeds. Breeds of animals were improved. In Britain, plows made entirely of metal speeded up plowing. All these improvements occurred in just one field, agriculture.

The achievements of science—both in theory and in practice—led the philosophes to believe in progress. They had faith in change. The philosophes believed that, armed with the power of reason, human beings could better themselves and society.

The philosophes lived in the major cities of western Europe, such as Paris, London, and Milan. Though small in number, they were an active group and published widely. The philosophes attacked the religious and political institutions of their time. This made their ideas popular with the middle class. Members of the middle class hoped to increase their power at the expense of such institutions. According to the intellectuals, people were fundamentally good and everywhere the same. Nature was also good. Given a chance, people would prove their goodness. They just needed the right environment. Bad institutions and bad leaders had to be discarded. Superstition and ignorance had to be eliminated. Reforms were needed in many areas—law, education, the arts, and even prisons.

The intellectuals, especially the French, were very critical of the Roman Catholic Church. They felt that it bound people to ignorance and superstition. The philosophes thus rejected traditional religions. *Deism* became popular among the intellectuals. Deism is the belief in a Divine Being who created the world and set it in motion. Like a skilled watchmaker, the Creator set up a perfectly running universe. But this Creator is an impersonal God. He cannot perform miracles. Therefore, according to the Deists, only foolish people hoped that God would intervene in human affairs. Deists also rejected the Bible and traditional religious practices. There were also a few *atheists*, people who denied the existence of God. The faithful Christians were stung by the attack of the intellectuals, and conflict arose.

The other major institution that the philosophes attacked was the state. The intellectuals believed strongly in natural rights. These included the right of free speech and the right to realize one's own talents. People were also said to have the right to knowledge and the right to happiness.

Not all of the intellectuals held all of these views. In general, though, they supported the main principles of the philosophes. The most important leaders of the Age of Reason came from England and France. The ideas of a few of the best known and most influential are discussed below.

John Locke John Locke (1632-1704), son of a Puritan lawyer, was a thinker and a writer. Locke plotted unsuccessfully against the Stuart kings and fled to the Netherlands. He returned to England when James II was deposed and William III and Mary II assumed the English throne. In 1690, Locke published a justification for the Glorious Revolution that had just occurred. His writings clearly outlined his views of government and society.

Locke believed that human beings in a state of nature are fundamentally good. Locke and many others at the time were impressed by the reports describing the American Indians. The Indians lived in a more primitive society than that which existed in Europe. Many believed that they had true dignity and lived good, simple lives. According to Locke, primitive people lived with freedom and equality. When people are hunters and gatherers, there is no need for private property because they constantly move from place to place. However, as society turns to farming, people stay on the land. They acquire property. This incites envy and conflict. Thus, the need for government arises.

In return for protection for their lives and property, people give up some power to a ruler. However, people reserve some rights, their natural rights, that cannot be taken away. For Locke, these natural rights were life, liberty, and property. The government must protect these natural rights. If the government does not do so, people have the right to rebel against it.

Thus, according to Locke, the power of the ruler is limited. The divine right of kings becomes an absurd idea, since power comes not from God but from the people. The English people were, therefore, justified

John Locke.

in ousting James II. According to Locke, James II had violated the natural rights of the English people.

Locke's ideas were popular in England. They amounted to a rationale for the revolution that had already taken place. Locke was also widely read in the American colonies and in western Europe. His books were translated into many languages. Just as Newton symbolized the new science, Locke was the guide to new ideas about the nature of government. Locke's writings influenced both the American and French revolutions.

Montesquieu The Baron de Montesquieu (MON tes KEW 1689-1755) was born in France to a noble family. He was taught Latin when he was two years old and was given an excellent education. Montesquieu became a lawyer and served in the local government. However, he became discouraged by the constant strife in French politics. He retreated to his estate, where he thought and wrote.

Montesquieu also traveled. He admired the British system of government. He particularly liked the British division of power into three branches of government. Parliament made the laws. The king, the executive, carried out the laws. The courts dispensed justice. Montesquieu believed that the British system was a great deal better than the government in France. There the king alone had power. Montesquieu believed that tyranny resulted when one person held all the power. With power divided, each branch checked, or curbed, each other. The law-making body, for example, made sure that the other branches of government did not get too powerful. Through this process a proper balance was achieved among the branches.

As a result of his travels, Montesquieu came to the conclusion that the British system was not suitable for all nations. Different countries needed different kinds of governments. The size of a nation, its geography, and its social conditions created different needs. Montesquieu's ideas influenced later writers of constitutions. They particularly affected the Americans who wrote a framework for their new national government in 1787.

Voltaire Voltaire (vol TAIR 1694-1778) was the chief intellectual leader of his time. His numerous writings helped pave the way for the French Revolution. Voltaire, whose father was a lawyer, found the law dull and boring. He had a knack for amusing people. His wit and clever writings earned

This popular engraving of the 1700s shows the "coronation" of Voltaire in a box at the theatre.

him financial support. However, they also got him into trouble with the nobility. Voltaire was twice sent to the Bastille, the prison where the royal government kept troublemakers. After his release, Voltaire was committed to fighting against the injustices in French society.

Voltaire went to England, where he became acquainted with the ideas of Newton and Locke. When he published writings praising English institutions, he caused an uproar in France. Voltaire translated Newton's *Principia* into French. He also popularized the ideas of Locke and others.

A constant critic of French society, Voltaire bitterly attacked the Roman Catholic Church. He publicized many cases of religious intolerance. Voltaire believed that people should be able to worship as they wanted and should have freedom of speech. He said: "I disapprove of what you say, but I will defend to the death your right to say it." By the end of his life, Voltaire had won the acclaim of the French people. Many of the French were becoming more and more discontent with their society.

Jean-Jacques Rousseau Rousseau (roo SO 1712-1778) was also influential in political thought. Rousseau was born of Huguenot parents in Geneva. His mother died at his birth. Eventually, Rousseau joined the intellectual circles and became a leading, controversial writer of the Age of Reason.

Rousseau's own childhood was very unhappy. Among other reforms, he called for the improvement of education. He felt that children and adults were naturally good. According to Rousseau, it was society's institutions that made people unhappy by corrupting the individual. Rousseau said: "Man is born free but everywhere he is in chains."

Rousseau outlined his ideas on education in a book titled *Emile*. Emile was not given a harsh, artificial education or forced to read. Instead, Emile lived in the country with his tutor. Nature was the child's first teacher. There he learned about trees, animals, and insects. The tutor was not there to compel Emile to learn. He simply answered questions and served as a resource for the child.

Both Locke and Montesquieu distrusted the rule of the masses. However, Rousseau was an advocate of democracy and equality. Rousseau also emphasized emotion rather than reason.

Rousseau believed that people had made a social contract with their rulers. He theorized that there was a general will— agreement about what was good for the people as a whole. For Rousseau, this general will was expressed when people voted for their rulers. Rousseau believed that the only good state was a democratic state.

Rousseau's ideas on the general will were not clear. They were later used by nondemocratic governments that claimed that a few should seize power and force everyone to follow the general will.

During the Age of Reason, much attention was given to the rights of people. However, little was written at that time about the rights of women. Mary Wollstonecraft (WOOL stun kraft), an English writer, was angered that Rousseau's recommendations covered the education of boys, but not of girls. Wollstonecraft believed that women, to be equal, must be trained for the professions and jobs that were at that time reserved only for men. In 1792, she published her views on the rights of women.

Wollstonecraft was just one person who criticized some of the ideas of the Enlightenment. Critics said that the philosophes had their own dogma. It was said that intellectuals like Voltaire could be just as fanatical as their opponents. It was charged that the philosophes were naive in their assumption that people were rational and reasonable. Nevertheless, the ideas of the Enlightenment spread. Peoples'

Did You Know?

An Early Feminist

A recent prize-winning Broadway musical, *Evita*, is based on the life of Eva Peron (pay RON), the wife of the president of Argentina from 1945 to 1955. Some Argentinians said she was unworthy of being the first lady of their country. Others, especially the urban poor, considered her a heroine who had overcome her humble origins in the slums and her life as a showgirl.

Eva Peron's life was remarkably like the life of Theodora, empress of Byzantium. In *The Secret History*, the historian Procopius (pru KO pee us) painted a seamy picture of the empress. Theodora was born about 500. Her father trained the bears that fought in the Hippodrome. After Theodora's father died, her mother led her and her two sisters into the arena. They sought help from the Blues and the Greens, groups that supported rival gladiators. The Greens rejected Theodora's mother. So the Blues, to show their hatred of the Greens, agreed to help the young family.

Theodora became an actress. Her reputation of beauty, intelligence, wit, and immorality made her an object of curiosity and scorn. Justinian, nephew and successor of the emperor, fell in love with Theodora. So his uncle repealed a law that forbade state officials from marrying actresses, servants, and other "unseemly" women. Theodora was cheered by the crowd in the Hippodrome on the day of her coronation. She may well have remembered when she appeared before the hostile Greens.

In 529, the empress decided to do something about the widespread prostitution in Constantinople. She turned one

Empress Theodora.

of the palaces into a convent. She tried to help her charges, some under ten years old, start a new life there.

On January 18, 532, a rioting mob stormed the Grand Palace. Theodora's decision to fight for her crown gave her husband the courage to protect the throne.

The Patriarch of Constantinople was charged with heresy, excommunicated, and exiled in 532. He disappeared from Constantinople. After Theodora died in 548, the Patriarch was found in one of her apartments.

Theodora had supported some of the practices of the heretics in the religious disputes that raged in the east. After her death, Justinian devoted most of his time to religious study. In time, he accepted the viewpoints that his wife had supported. Her critics, furious, charged that Theodora was continuing to influence the emperor from her grave.

Mary Wollstonecraft.

minds had changed. This was especially true in France. The members of the educated elite were transformed from loyal subjects to hostile critics of the regime. Soon, people would be ready to act upon the ideas of the Age of Reason.

Section Questions

1. What were the major ideas of the Enlightenment?
2. What improvements were being made in agriculture during the Age of Reason?
3. What was Deism?
4. Why did John Locke think people had a right to revolt against the established government?
5. What features of the British government did Montesquieu especially like?
6. In what major respect did the ideas of Rousseau differ from those of Locke and Montesquieu?

Chapter Summary

1. Scientists rejected the older traditional ideas and produced new knowledge by using the scientific method. Copernicus developed a new theory stating that the Earth revolved around the sun. Kepler's laws gave further proof of the validity of Copernicus' theory. Galileo used a telescope to look at the heavens. His data also supported the theory of Copernicus. Newton explained the movements of the sun and the planets. Great achievements were also made in mathematics, chemistry, and physics. Medicine advanced with Harvey's work on circulation and the discovery of the microscope.

2. The spirit of the Enlightenment was spread by intellectuals called philosophes. Rejecting traditional ideas about society and the teaching of religion, the philosophes had faith in reason above all. They believed that human beings were basically good and that, with the right environment, progress could be made in reforming humans and their institutions. Locke believed that people had natural rights that the government had to respect. Montesquieu admired the balance of power in the English system of government. Voltaire mocked all forms of what he considered to be injustice. Rousseau promoted the idea of democracy. Wollstonecraft wanted women to be better educated and to have more rights. The French philosophes in particular weakened people's loyalty to the established authorities.

Chapter 22 Review

Check Your Facts

1. Identify the following:
    a. Napier
    b. Montesquieu
    c. Newton
    d. Leeuwenhoek
    e. Voltaire
    f. Lavoisier
    g. Locke
    h. Wollstonecraft
2. What did people believe about the movements of the sun and the Earth before Copernicus?
3. What technical instruments helped the development of science?
4. Why did the middle class support many of the ideas of the philosophes?
5. Why were Locke's ideas popular in England?
6. What did Montesquieu think happened when one person held all power?
7. What rights did Voltaire think all people should have?
8. What were Rousseau's ideas about government?

Words to Know

Define the following words in one or two sentences. Then tell the significance of each during the Age of Reason.
    a. calculus
    b. logarithms
    c. atheists
    d. scientific method
    e. philosophes
    f. gravity
    g. microscope
    h. Deism

Developing Your Skills

1. List three discoveries or new ideas from each country:
    a. France   b. England   c. Italy
2. Place the following events in the proper chronological order.
    Newton publishes the *Principia*.
    Harvey explains the circulation of the blood.
    Locke publishes his defense of the Glorious Revolution.
    Galileo recants under pressure from the Inquisition.
    Rousseau publishes his *Social Contract*.

Thinking It Over

1. Do you agree with Montesquieu's idea that different nations should have different kinds of governments?
2. Why are scientists skeptical and always questioning of research and accepted ideas?
3. Rousseau believed in the value of feelings as opposed to reason and of impulse and spontaneity as opposed to self-discipline and restraint. Which qualities do you think should be encouraged in individuals?
4. Do you think scientists have helped people? In what areas?

Special Activities

1. During the Age of Reason, people started to think about better ways to treat criminals. In small groups, make up lists of what you think are the best ways in which to treat people who have broken the law.
2. Read about a recent scientific development that is of interest to you. You may wish to use *Science News, Scientific America*, or other science journals. Write down the ways in which the scientific method is used.

A public execution during the French Revolution.

Chapter 23 The French Revolution and Empire

Marie Antoinette (an twa NET) was Queen of France at the time of the French Revolution. She is reported to have said, "Let them eat cake" after being told that the French people had no bread. She did not really say this, but many of the French believed that she had. This helped weaken the loyalty that the French people had felt to the crown.

In 1789, France had about twenty-six million people. It was the most populous nation in Europe. People were divided into three social classes, or estates. The First Estate consisted of the clergy. It included the wealthy and powerful bishops and abbots as well

1789-1815

1789	Bastille falls
1791	Constitution of 1791
1793	King Louis XVI executed
1793-1794	Reign of Terror
1794	Robespierre executed
1799	Napoleon seizes power
1805	Napoleon defeats Russians and Austrians
1805	British win Battle of Trafalgar
1808	France invades Spain
1812	France invades Russia
1814	Napoleon resigns
1815	Battle of Waterloo

Marie Antoinette.

as the poorer and less powerful parish priests and monks.

The Second Estate was made up of the aristocrats, or nobles. As among the clergy, there were differences among the nobles. There were those who lived at the royal court in great luxury. There were also the country nobles—some prosperous and others almost impoverished. The clergy and nobles together made up about three percent of the total population. These two groups, despite their wealth, generally escaped paying taxes.

The rest of the French people were members of what was called the Third Estate. At the top of the middle class were the *grande bourgeoisie*, bankers and wealthy merchants. Below them in the middle class were the *petite bourgeoisie*, the skilled workers and shopkeepers. Both of these middle-class groups generally lived in the cities. Also in the cities were the unskilled laborers. These urban poor people had few resources. A small increase in the price of bread could be a disaster for them.

The largest group were the peasants—about twenty million people in all. Much of the burden of taxation fell on this group. About half of the peasants owned some land, though often only a small amount. The rest were very poor and worked as day laborers on other people's farms. In 1788, a year of bad crops made the poor urban workers and peasants desperate.

The government failed to respond to these economic problems. This failure plus the weakened loyalty to the crown, unfair taxation, and the new ideas of the Enlightenment triggered the French Revolution. The revolution transformed the lives of the French people and affected many other people throughout the world.

1. The French Revolution Began

In 1774, at the age of 19, Louis XVI became King of France. By 1788, the French government was almost bankrupt, even though France was actually a prosperous country. The basic problem was that the privileged classes did not pay taxes. Moreover, the costs of government were going up. Half of the government's budget went to pay interest on old war debts, including those from the War for American Independence.

In 1788, Louis XVI decided he needed new tax laws. He called for a meeting of the Estates General. This representative legislative body had not met since 1614. The Estates General consisted of elected members from all three estates. When they met in May 1789, the delegates argued about how the estates would vote. The clergy and nobles wanted the right of veto over laws recommended by the Third Estate. However, the members of the Third Estate refused to compromise on this issue. They were the majority of the delegates, and thus a system of one vote to a delegate was to their advantage. If the other estates had veto power, they could prevent a constitution from being adopted. The Third Estate wanted a constitution that would give them more power.

The National Assembly The king suspended the group and closed their meeting room. The members of the Third Estate walked out of the Palace of Versailles (vur SI) and reconvened at a nearby covered tennis court. There, they pledged that they would not disband until they had given France a new constitution. Some members of the clergy and nobility joined them.

Giving in, the king recognized the group, which was now called the National Assembly. However, it appeared that Louis XVI

The beautiful Palace of Versailles.

The storming of the Bastille.

did not really support the National Assembly and reform. He ordered paid troops to come to Versailles. His action caused great excitement in Paris.

On July 14, 1789, a mob of Parisians stormed the Bastille. This royal fortress was a prison for enemies of the state and a symbol of the king's power to oppress. The mob killed the soldiers guarding the fortress and seized the arms stored there.

Very few people had been jailed in recent years and the Bastille contained only seven prisoners when it was attacked. Even so, storming the Bastille was a truly revolutionary act. For the first time, the common people of Paris had taken direct political action. They had taken the law into their own hands. On hearing about the Bastille, the king announced that he had ordered the troops to leave Versailles. Louis XVI now was defended only by a small group of loyal Swiss guards.

The People Take Power At about the same time that the Bastille fell, violence broke out in the countryside. The peasants, badly hurt by the poor harvest 1788, refused to pay any feudal due rents. They burned the records obligations to their aristocratic l Some manor houses and ab burned. Other homes were people, including some g cials, were killed. Both i countryside, new grou from the old governm

On the night o tional meeting o the liberal nob titles, and

Assembly adopted the Declaration of the Rights of Man. This said that all French people had certain natural rights—the rights of liberty, property, security, and resistance to oppression.

The actions of the National Assembly and the riots throughout the country made many nobles fear for their safety. Some, including the king's two brothers, fled from France. Those who left were called *emigres*, and their property was seized.

However, the hungry working people of Paris were not satisfied. They felt that so far they had only gotten empty-sounding rights from the National Assembly. Bread prices were still high and there were food shortages. In October 1789, a group of women from Paris marched on Versailles demanding bread for their families. They were joined by the National Guard, the local soldiers, who now had arms. The angry mob forced the king and queen to move to Paris. A few days later, the National Assembly also left Versailles. In Paris, the Assembly was much more heavily influenced by the Parisians.

New Constitution Between 1789 and 1791, the members of the National Assembly wrote a constitution that limited the power of the king. Power was now given to the bourgeoisie. Only those who paid a certain amount of taxes could vote. The Assembly seized all the property of the Roman Catholic Church. They reorganized the government. The nobles lost their lands and titles; they were no longer lords. The cities took over elected few government officials. On August 4, 1789, the National Assembly, nobles gave up their rights. Later in the...

In October 1791, the National Assembly finished its work. It had produced a new constitution. The privileges and rights of the king, the clergy, and the nobles had been reduced. Equality was now guaranteed under the law. A powerful new society could now be built on the slogans of liberty and equality. It appeared that the revolution was over.

Problems of the Moderates Most of the members of the bourgeoisie were satisfied in October 1791. They now had more power. The new governing body was called the Legislative Assembly. Most of its members were in favor of the present form of government, a limited monarchy.

Most peasant families were also satisfied. Many could now become landowners. They did not have to pay cash for the land seized from the emigres and from the Roman Catholic Church. They could pay for it over a number of years.

However, the royal family and most of the nobles, upper clergy, and army officers were not pleased. Many wanted to return to the "good old days." Marie Antoinette urged her brother, the Holy Roman Emperor, to support her and her husband against the revolution. Many of the emigres had fled to Prussia, where they tried to persuade other nations to invade France.

Many of the working-class people of Paris were not satisfied. They felt that the revolution had not gone far enough. They wanted to be rid of the king. Inflation was hurting them badly. They blamed all problems on the enemies of the revolution.

The workers of Paris had the support of a few radical members of the Assembly. The radicals wanted to get rid of the king. The leaders of the radicals were Jean Paul Marat (mah RAW), a doctor and journalist, Georges Danton and Maximilian de Robespierre (ROBZ pih ur). Danton and Robespierre were both lawyers and effective speakers.

The Austro-Prussian invasion of France.

Steps to War Other European monarchs feared that the ideas of the French Revolution might affect their own people. Prussia and Austria proclaimed that other nations should step in and restore the king to his former power. However, it was France that took the initiative. On April 2, 1792, Louis XVI asked the Assembly to declare war. Almost all of the delegates voted for war.

About two-thirds of the officers had resigned from the army. Many had left the country. Thus, the army lacked experienced leadership. Louis, Marie Antoinette and the nobles expected and wanted the foreign enemies to win. Their powers could then be restored. On the other hand, the radicals felt that the war would expose the king and queen as traitors. They were optimistic that the French army could win. The moderates in the Assembly wanted to spread the benefits of the revolution beyond France.

The war began. At first, the Austrian and Prussian armies were successful. The ill-trained French troops fled at the sight of the enemy. The foreign troops moved toward Paris. The city was in panic.

Parisians believed that the king had plotted against the people for France to be defeated. On August 10, 1792, a huge mob broke into the royal palace in Paris. They massacred the king's Swiss guards. Frightened, the royal family turned to the Assembly for protection. Instead, they were imprisoned. The Assembly suspended all the powers of the king.

Louis XVI bidding farewell to his family.

Section Questions

1. Which groups were discontented in France about 1789? Why?
2. What factors contributed to the coming of the French Revolution?
3. What did the National Assembly achieve in 1789?
4. Why did the National Assembly seize the property of the Roman Catholic Church?
5. Why did the various groups in France want war in 1792?

2. The Radicals Gained Control of the Revolution

A new National Convention met in September 1792. It faced many problems. The first was what to do with the king. Then, a locksmith who had once worked for the king showed the authorities a secret iron safe. The safe was opened. It contained letters showing that Louis XVI was encouraging foreign intervention.

On December 11, 1792, the king was brought to trial on a charge of treason. Louis XVI denied the charge, but a majority of the Convention found him guilty. Fewer were in favor of a death sentence, but the king was condemned to death by a narrow margin.

In January 1793, Louis XVI was driven in a carriage to an open square, now the Place de la Concorde. The square was packed with troops to stop any attempt to save the king. Louis conducted himself with dignity and courage. At one point, as he climbed the steps of the scaffold, he told the drummers to be quiet. They were. The king was then executed by the *guillotine*, a machine for beheading. The guillotine was considered to be more humane than previous methods of execution. This form of execution was now used for all social classes.

The news of Louis XVI's death shocked the royal families in other nations. Now almost all of Europe united against France.

A few months earlier, in June, the royal family had tried to escape from Paris in disguise. However, their elaborate coach and the king himself were recognized. They were taken back to Paris in disgrace. Louis, a skilled rider, probably could have escaped by himself. However, he did not want to leave his family. As a result of this ill-planned affair, popular opinion turned against the king.

Order was partly restored in September 1792 after the French won a battle at Valmy in northeastern France. The defeat of the advancing Prussian army boosted morale. Meanwhile, however, the Assembly was now controlled by the radicals.

The execution of Louis XVI.

Great Britain, the Netherlands, Portugal, Sardinia, and Naples joined the fight. France was now faced with a serious threat.

In addition to the war, the Convention faced serious internal problems. The execution of the king contributed to these. Suddenly, open revolts broke out in the country and in some of the cities. Priests who had not taken the oath of loyalty incited rebellion. Many people also resented the drafting of men and the taxes that the war entailed.

The war and the riots allowed the extreme radicals to take control. The radicals imposed price controls to fight inflation and rationing to ensure adequate food for the cities. The Convention established the Committee of Public Safety. This group of twelve men had complete power over France. It was an oligarchy, a dictatorship controlled by a small group. They held secret meetings. There, the members of the committee listed their enemies and decided their fates. They could act before their opponents, the moderates, could defend themselves. The Committee of Public Safety had three main goals. The first was to win the war. The second was to put down the revolts within France. The third was to establish a Republic of Virtue in which the "general will" would allow natural rights to flourish.

The Reign of Terror To win the war, all males capable of fighting were drafted into the army in August 1793. This was the first time any European nation had drafted soldiers instead of hiring them. A propaganda campaign on the dangers of allowing foreigners or emigres to gain control of France greatly increased patriotic spirit. Morale was high among the troops. They felt that they were fighting for the French Revolution.

The war now went better for the French. New leaders had been found. The soldiers

"The Purifying Pot of the Jacobins." The Jacobins were a radical political society. Robespierre was the most influential leader of the Jacobins.

A bust of Danton.

fought well. The army pushed back the foreign invaders. By 1795, the armies were victorious everywhere.

To achieve their second goal, suppressing the revolts, the Committee of Public Safety began a Reign of Terror (1793-1794). Let "Terror be the order of the day," said Robespierre. Courts were set up to try people accused of being enemies of the revolution. Usually, a desire for vengeance overrode correct legal procedures. The newly won rights of the people were suspended. The government was given the right to arrest any person suspected of opposing the republic. Two main groups of people were executed. One group included prominent people who were active in politics. Among those condemned were Lavoisier, the founder of modern chemistry, and the Marquis de Condorcet, a famous mathematician. The most infamous execution, after that of Louis XVI, was that of Queen Marie Antoinette. She was executed nine months after her husband. Her children remained in prison. The heir to the throne, Louis XVII, became ill and died in June 1795.

The second group executed were mostly peasants and laborers. It is estimated that at least 20,000 people lost their lives in the Reign of Terror. Anyone who appeared to favor the old regime was found guilty.

The Reign of Terror worked. Within a few months, the rebellions stopped. The government regained control of the cities and towns. Opposition was also silenced. People did not dare to speak out against the government.

The third goal, the establishment of a Republic of Virtue, symbolized the hopes and dreams of the radicals. Robespierre and others believed in the need for public education. They also wanted to eliminate the power of the Roman Catholic Church. They felt that the church was a corrupting influence on the people. Thus, Robespierre promoted the worship of a Supreme Being to substitute for the teachings of the church. Special ceremonies were held for the new religion. The Roman Catholic churches were closed. Some were destroyed by mobs. The famous cathedral at Chartres, an architectural masterpiece, escaped destruction only because someone pointed out that the debris would block the streets. At the Cathedral of Notre Dame in Paris, ninety statues of the prophets were broken because the mob thought that they were statues of the French kings.

In 1793, the calendar was completely revised. The new calendar did not have Sundays and did not list the old holidays and feast days of the saints. It had three periods of ten days in each month. Now there was no longer a Sunday to remind people of church. The names of the days of the week and of the months were also changed.

For a few years after 1789, social life also changed. People tried to avoid appearing superior to others. Titles such as Monsieur (Mr.) and Madame (Mrs.) were no longer used. Instead, people were addressed as "Citizen." Simple clothing styles were now in fashion. Men wore long, plain trousers rather than knee breeches. Women wore simple gowns.

Both men and women stopped wearing wigs. Secular marriages were now possible. These marriages were not performed by a priest. For the first time, divorce was also made legal. Illegitimate children were given more rights, including the right to inherit property from the father. However, women did not gain real rights.

The Fall of Robespierre In early 1794, Danton, a hero of the revolution, decided that the Reign of Terror had gone far enough. He felt that enough blood had been shed. He was in favor of relaxing government control. However, Robespierre did not agree. He believed that there were still many enemies of the revolution to be eliminated.

This painting of the Reign of Terror is called "The Last Roll Call of the Condemned."

The execution of Robespierre and his fellow conspirators.

Robespierre felt strict control should still be maintained. Too many people, he was convinced, were not committed to the revolution. He believed that the working class was interested only in food and a higher standard of living. He was furious that a black market flourished and that some middle-class people made huge profits because of the shortages.

Robespierre was not ready to disband the Committee of Public Safety. He had Danton arrested on a charge of disloyalty. Some committee members feared that they would lose power if Danton's wishes were carried out. Thus, Danton was condemned to death in April 1794. He wisely predicted that Robespierre's turn would soon come.

The people of France were shocked when they heard of Danton's death. Rumors spread that Robespierre wanted to abolish private property. More importantly, many members of the Committee of Public Safety and the Convention did not feel safe with Robespierre around. On July 26, 1794, Robespierre gave a speech before the Convention. He hinted that there might soon be an end to the terror. However, he also threatened unnamed members. Robespierre said that he had a list containing the names of traitors to the cause. Some members, fearing for their safety, persuaded the Convention to arrest Robespierre. Robespierre then escaped but was recaptured. He was executed on July 28, 1794.

Robespierre's execution unexpectedly ended the Reign of Terror. People did not want to live in fear that some informer might accuse them of disloyalty. Gradually, the Convention stopped the executions. They removed the controls on food and wages.

The National Convention returned to its original mission, writing a constitution. In many respects, the document they drafted was similar to the Constitution of 1791. However, it did not provide for a king. Instead, executive power was placed in the hands of five directors, the *Directory*. There was a general return to normality. Most people were tired of revolutionary restraints and the Republic of Virtue. They quickly abandoned their high ideals. They became more concerned about protecting what they had gained from the revolution. They also sought the pleasures of the theater and other public amusements. Fashions changed.

However, the removal of price controls brought a sharp increase in food prices. In the spring of 1795, there were bread riots. This time, the Convention used the National Guard to break up the mob. In October, another group took to the streets. This time they were royalists loyal to the French crown. The Convention called upon a young general named Napoleon Bonaparte. He scattered the attackers with "a whiff of grapeshot," small cast-iron balls used in a cannon. The Convention then finished its session and dissolved itself to start the new government, the Directory.

Achievements Not all of the high ideals of the French Revolution were realized. Nevertheless, France in 1795 was much different from the France of 1789. Now the

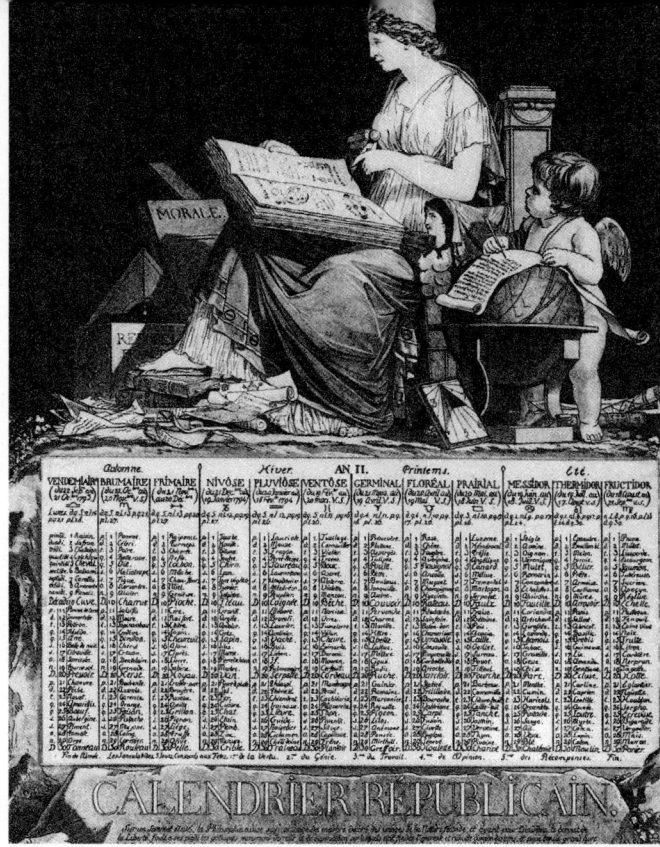

The Republican calendar.

bourgeoisie, instead of the king and nobles, had political power and was the most important social class in France. Important government positions were no longer reserved just for members of the nobility and the clergy.

The peasants also gained. Many obtained property. France became largely a nation of small farmers who owned their own land. In contrast to the bourgeoisie and the peasants, the Roman Catholic Church lost power.

The French people were now more patriotic and nationalistic. They were proud of their strong army. The soldiers had high morale. Most people were proud to be citizens of the French Republic. Tax laws were now fairer and more people could vote.

In many different ways, the revolution left its stamp on society. The metric system of measurement was adopted. Its units were based on multiples of ten. Thus, the new system was far more rational than the older traditional weights and measures. However, the new calendar did not take hold. The idea of providing public education for all citizens became more widely accepted. However, schools for the common people were not actually started until many years later. The revolution also encouraged the establishment of a more uniform system of law. The French Revolution prefigured much that would happen in the world in future years. The Reign of Terror showed what could happen when dictators or a few held all power, as Hitler and other leaders later would. The revolution also demonstrated that a government could control the economic life of its people by imposing price and wage controls.

Section Questions

1. Why were many European nations ready to fight against France?
2. Why were such extraordinary powers given to the Committee of Public Safety?
3. What was the Reign of Terror?
4. Why did members of the Convention vote to execute Robespierre?
5. What were some permanent effects of the French Revolution?

3. Napoleon Became a Dictator

The Directory—the new government of France—faced many grave problems. Foremost was the food shortage in the cities. Suicides and deaths from malnutrition were common. Food was rationed. Unemployment was high and inflation continued.

The directors were worried about possible riots among the people of the cities. They also feared revolts among the royalists. The direct heir to the throne, the young Louis XVII, had died. Louis XVI's brothers were in exile. The directors did not want one of them to take over. They would be likely to punish those who had killed the royal family and the aristocrats. The middle class and the peasants also feared that the royalists would try to have property returned to the original owners.

The various groups in France distrusted each other. They found it difficult to cooperate. During this period, bandits and royalists controlled some parts of the country. In addition to these internal difficulties, France was still fighting against Austria, Britain, and the states of southern Germany.

In 1796, the directors ordered two French armies to attack Germany and a third to invade Italy. The only real success came in the Italian campaign. There young General Napoleon Bonaparte (nuh PO lee un BO nuh part) led his army to impressive victories. Large sections of Italy came under French control. Napoleon became a national hero. He seemed to many the only bright light amid the difficulties that faced the nation.

While Napoleon's reputation was rising, the directors were becoming unpopular. It was charged that they were corrupt. Many people believed that the directors had assumed too much power and still were not giving France good government.

Napoleon Bonaparte Napoleon Bonaparte (1769-1821) was born in Corsica, an island in the Mediterranean. His parents were Italian. Corsica had been taken over by France in 1768, the year before Napoleon's birth. Thus, Napoleon was born a French subject. At the age of nine, Napoleon entered a military school in France under a scholarship. There he was teased by fellow students for his poor French and his small size. They called him a "foreigner." However, even at this early age, Napoleon had great confidence in his own ability. He had an excellent memory. He could master both large ideas and details.

Napoleon Bonaparte.

Napoleon had a great interest in history and mathematics.

During the French Revolution, Napoleon had opportunities for advancement. Many of the older and higher ranking officers had fled the country. Those who stayed and were successful were promoted rapidly.

As an officer, Napoleon showed good judgment. He was especially good at striking at the enemy's weakest point. This he did in 1795 when he dispersed the mob attacking the Convention. After this success, Napoleon was put in command of the French Army of Italy.

Napoleon triumphed in the Italian campaign. He promised his troops victories. They believed in the "little corporal," even when they were not paid regularly. The Italians soon found that the French looted and heavily taxed the areas they conquered.

Napoleon, not waiting for the diplomats, made the peace treaties. France took over part of northern Italy. Napoleon assumed powers far beyond those of a general. To strike at Britain, the last nation fighting against France, Napoleon invaded Egypt. Napoleon was successful on land. However, the British destroyed the French fleet and trapped Napoleon and his army. Napoleon escaped from Egypt and was greeted in Paris as a great hero. The French were not aware that the Egyptian campaign was really a disaster, not a victory.

In 1799, at the age of thirty, Napoleon seized power from the unpopular government of the Directory. He overthrew the constitution and assumed the executive power, taking the title "First Consul." To many, he seemed to be the "man of destiny" who would save France. Napoleon was expected to restore peace and stability at home and to defeat France's enemies abroad.

Achievements at Home Napoleon's first task was to restore order in France. He did this by centralizing the government. He replaced elected government officials with his own appointed officials. Men of ability were given the opportunity to rise in government service.

Napoleon appointed a group of lawyers to codify the many conflicting laws from the different regions of France. This group worked from 1804 to 1807. The Code Napoleon that it produced became the basis of French law. It was later used by many other countries.

In the Code Napoleon, the rights of citizens were defined. All males were considered legally equal regardless of their

Did You Know?

Madame de Staël

During Napoleon's time, women could not participate directly in political affairs by voting or holding office. A woman could influence political events only indirectly. One way was to be a prominent hostess and hold receptions to which important people would come. Of course, to do this, a hostess had to be intelligent and have a certain amount of wealth.

One such hostess was Madame de Staël (stawl). She was born Anne Louise Germaine Necker in 1766. Her father, a Swiss banker, was a finance minister for Louis XVI between 1776 and 1781 and again at the beginning of the French Revolution. Many important people visited their home and Germaine learned much about politics.

At the age of 19, Germaine married Baron Staël Holstein, the Swedish ambassador to France. Since people no longer used their titles in France, she was known as Madame de Staël. However, the arranged marriage was not a happy one and ended in divorce.

Madame de Staël supported the ideals of the early French Revolution. She knew the leading statesmen of the day and tried to influence the course of government. It was said of her that she welcomed "Jacobins (radicals) in the morning, emigres (royalists) at midday, and all the world at dinner." Madame de Staël felt that the best hope for France was a policy of toleration and compromise.

At first, Madame de Staël supported Napoleon. However, she soon decided that he was completely self-seeking. She became his constant critic. In 1802, in her novel *Delphine*, she wrote about prominent people. She disguised them

Madame de Staël.

so lightly that her readers could recognize them easily. Incensed by her criticisms, Napoleon ordered Madame de Staël not to reside within 40 leagues (110 miles) of Paris. Later, in 1810, he ordered her to leave France.

Madame de Staël was an outspoken writer and one of the most popular authors of her day. At a time when few dared to oppose Napoleon, she had the courage to do so.

birth. They were guaranteed equality before the law and the right to practice any religion. In addition, the legal power of the father was reinforced in the family. The husband had control of the family's property. He could obtain a divorce more easily than his wife. The Code Napoleon cancelled the revolutionary laws protecting equal division of property among heirs and the rights of illegitimate children.

Napoleon also settled the thorny problem of church-state relations. He and the pope agreed to a Concordat. This allowed the Roman Catholic Church to operate openly. However, the church did not regain the property that had been seized during the revolution. In addition, the church was under state control, since the government appointed all of the clergy and paid their salaries.

Napoleon also established a system of public higher education for France. He founded many technical and professional schools to train officials and officers to lead the country. These schools opened up opportunities for middle-class males. Napoleon had little interest in education for girls and women or in elementary education. The Roman Catholic Church lost its power over the education of French youth. Schools were now under the control of a board of education in Paris. Both public and private institutions had to meet certain standards.

Napoleon also sought to aid the French economy. He tried to promote industry and trade. He founded the Bank of France to help businesses obtain loans. However, people of business did not trust Napoleon fully. His aggressive military policy and the general uncertainty in foreign relations reduced business confidence and negatively affected the ability to plan ahead.

Napoleon brought internal peace and stability to France. His reforms in law and in education would remain as permanent contributions to the nation.

Section Questions

1. What were the weaknesses of the government of the Directory?
2. Why was Napoleon able to seize power?
3. Why was the Code Napoleon important?
4. Why was Napoleon interested in education?

4. Europe Fought Back

Britain and other nations were worried about the increased power of France, especially its large army. They had good reason to worry. There was thus no true peace after the French Revolution.

Napoleon's most determined enemy was Great Britain. Though Napoleon said that Britain was merely "a nation of shopkeepers," the British controlled the seas. To get money to fight his old enemy, Napoleon sold the Louisiana Territory to the United States. Napoleon also realized that he could not defend this distant territory from the British. The United States gained a huge territory as a result of Napoleon's difficulties.

In 1804, Napoleon crowned himself emperor of France and declared war against his enemies. He wanted to control all of Europe. In 1805, at the Battle of Austerlitz in Austria, his forces decisively defeated the Russians and the Austrians. However, in the same year, 1805, the British won a great sea battle off Cape Trafalgar on the coast of Spain. Napoleon's fleet lost over half its ships, while the British did not lose even one.

The great powers of France and Britain were now engaged in a bitter fight to determine who would be supreme in Europe. Britain had control of the seas. Napoleon was victorious on land.

Lacking sea power, Napoleon could not invade Britain. Therefore, he tried to choke off its trade. In 1806, Napoleon

Napoleon meeting Emperor Francis II after the Battle of Austerlitz.

prohibited British ships from docking in areas controlled by France.

In response, Britain tried to prevent both French and neutral ships from docking in French-controlled territory. Both Britain and France tried to set up a *blockade*—to prevent ships and supplies from reaching the other side. Each nation tried to capture any ship involved in trade with the other side.

The blockades caused problems in France, in the rest of Europe, and in the United States. Europe, including France, depended on Britain's manufactured goods. Europeans felt that France was trying to control the whole economy of Europe. The blockades also weakened Britain, but the British economy survived. Most affected were the working classes, who had to pay more for their food and goods. British industrialists made high profits supplying the needs of the army and navy. During the Napoleonic Wars, Great Britain increased its productivity and wealth. Napoleon's attempt to subdue Britain caused more of Europe to turn against the emperor. Nations that had been conquered regarded the French as foreigners. They resented the fact that the French imposed French laws and taxes on them.

Did You Know?

Preserved Food

How often in a given week do you open canned food or bottled drinks? Most of us, even in this day of frozen food, still use much preserved food.

Preserved food was invented in the time of Napoleon. Napoleon and other military leaders had to feed their armies. By 1800, armies were becoming larger, making it difficult for them to live off the land. They needed an adequate supply of safe food. Navies also needed a way to keep food for crews that were gone from port for a long period of time.

Napoleon encouraged inventors. Nicholas Appert (a PAIR), a former champagne bottler and cook, found a way to preserve food. He put food in glass bottles, sealed them tightly, and then boiled the bottles with the food inside. Among his successfully preserved foods were meat stew, soup, milk, vegetables, and fruit. For finding this simple way to preserve food, Appert was awarded a prize of 23,000 francs in 1810.

In Britain, Peter Durand worked with preserving food in metal containers called *cannisters*. This word was later shortened to can. At first canned goods were expensive and some canned goods spoiled. Nonetheless, people liked the idea of

Workers canning food.

eating foods such as cherries and peaches out of season. In the 1850s, Louis Pasteur (pas TOOR) discovered that the process of boiling food was successful because it killed the bacteria. Before that, people did not really know why food preservation worked.

Continuous improvements have made jars and containers easy to open and use. Soon, more and more preserved food appeared on the market. This process has greatly expanded the variety of available foods and has made cooking much more convenient.

Thinking Geographically: Use the scale on the map to determine about how far Napoleon's army traveled from Paris to Moscow.

Napoleon's Fall Napoleon continued to expand his possessions in Europe. His forces defeated the Prussians in 1806 and Russians in 1807. Napoleon completely reorganized the map of Europe. The small German states were joined together into the Confederation of the Rhine. The Grand Duchy of Warsaw was created out of Prussia's former province of Poland. Within a few years, France had acquired an extensive European empire.

Eventually, Napoleon began to make mistakes. One error was his decision to seize Spain in 1808. The proud Spanish people fought back, using guerrilla warfare. In addition, the British aided the Spanish. The war on the Spanish peninsula dragged on for five years, draining the French army. The rebellion in Spain inspired other people to revolt. The Austrians and the Prussians, who had lost territory, wanted revenge. Nonetheless, in 1810, Napoleon was at the height of his power.

Napoleon also used poor judgment in dealing with Russia. Napoleon had signed a peace treaty with Russia. However, the Russians soon began to trade with Britain again, contrary to the treaty. Napoleon was furious. In 1812, he invaded Russia with 600,000 troops—the largest army ever assembled. More than half were non-French recruits who had been drafted from European countries under French control.

In spite of their limited freedom, the Russian serfs remained loyal to Russia and fought against the French. The Rus-

Napoleon's army retreating from Russia.

sians retreated, burning all the available food and supplies. After the bloody Battle of Borodino (bah ruh DEE no) west of Moscow, Napoleon entered the capital. It was now September. After Moscow's fall, the city was constantly in flames. Three-fourths of the city was destroyed.

Despite the capture of Moscow, the Russian czar, Alexander I, refused to negotiate with the French. Napoleon was now in a very difficult situation. His troops did not have enough supplies or shelter. Discipline began to break down. In October, realizing that his troops could not survive a winter in Moscow, Napoleon ordered a retreat. However, the retreat was begun too late.

The weaknesses of the French army now became evident. The French troops were accustomed to living off the land. However, little food and few supplies were to be had. Moreover, winter was severe in Russia. Many of the men starved or were frozen as they tried to retreat. The Russian *cossacks*, armed horsemen, attacked the stragglers. About five-sixths of the troops were killed or captured.

Napoleon rushed back to Paris. There he tried to put together a fresh army. However, his reputation had suffered greatly as a result of the Russian campaign. Now all of Europe was united against him. The conquered people of Europe wanted to be rid of the French armies. They resented the taxation, the looting, and the drafting of soldiers. British, Austrian, Prussian, and Russian armies united to destroy Napoleon, their common enemy.

In 1814, Napoleon's generals asked for his resignation. By now many of the French people wanted the Bourbon monarchy restored. Napoleon was sent into exile on Elba, an island off the Italian coast.

Less than a year later, in 1815, Napoleon was again on the march. He landed secretly on the French coast. His troops welcomed him back and were willing to follow him again. The European powers then reunited and defeated Napoleon's army at the small Belgian village of Waterloo. This was Napoleon's final and complete defeat.

The British then sent him to Saint Helena, an island off the west coast of Africa. There he spent the last six years of his life. He explained his actions to his few companions. Napoleon presented himself as a person who believed in the principles of the French Revolution. He said that all his wars were in defense of France. He portrayed himself as both a national and world hero.

Critics looked at the heavy costs of Napoleon's wars. Many lives and resources had been lost. Some saw Napoleon as the first modern dictator. He alone made the major decisions for the whole nation.

Regardless of how Napoleon is evaluated, all agree that he was important in world history. He helped spread *nationalism*, the love of one's nation, throughout Europe. When the French conquered new lands, they ended the feudal privileges there. The French also weakened the power of the Roman Catholic Church throughout Europe. They imposed new ideas, such as the metric system, on the conquered peoples. The power of the nobility and the clergy was weakened, and the middle class grew stronger.

Section Questions

1. Why did Napoleon try to enforce a blockade against Britain?
2. What was the extent of Napoleon's empire in 1812?
3. Why was Napoleon's Russian campaign a disaster?
4. What caused the fall of Napoleon?

Chapter Summary

1. King Louis XVI of France faced a financial crisis and called together the Estates General. This group, afterwards called the National Assembly, became the lawmaking body of France. It reduced the power of the king and eliminated the old feudal privileges. The National Assembly also seized the property of the Roman Catholic Church. The moderates in the assembly faced two extremes. On the one hand, the royal family and the nobles wanted their power and prestige back. On the other, the more radical leaders, with the support of the Parisian working class, wanted a republic. In 1792, the French declared war against their foreign enemies, who seemed to threaten interference in France's government.

2. The radicals in the National Convention gained control by 1793. The king, the queen, and thousands of others were executed as enemies of the revolution. To fight the war, soldiers were drafted. Controls were placed on food and wages. By 1795, the foreign invaders had been ousted from French soil. Robespierre tried to launch a new society with his Republic of Virtue, a new "enlightened" order on Earth. Robespierre was executed in 1794, and the Reign of Terror gradually stopped. A new constitution was created that abolished the monarchy. A new government, the Directory, took office in 1795.

3. The Directory became unpopular because of economic problems and charges of corruption. Meanwhile, Napoleon Bonaparte became a military hero. In 1799, Napoleon seized power in France. Napoleon instituted governmental, legal, educational, and economic reforms.

4. Other European nations were afraid of the rising power of France. Britain had control of the seas. Napoleon, now an emperor, acquired a large land empire for France. Napoleon made mistakes with the blockade and by invading Spain in 1808 and Russia in 1812. In 1815, Napoleon was finally defeated. However, Napoleon's conquests had spread the ideas of the French Revolution throughout Europe.

Chapter 23 Review

Check Your Facts

1. Identify the following:
   a. Louis XVI
   b. Georges Danton
   c. Robespierre
   d. Madame de Staël
   e. Marie Antoinette
   f. Bastille
2. What was the importance of the fall of the Bastille?
3. Why did some nobles leave France in 1789?
4. Which groups were satisfied when the first stage of the revolution ended in 1791? Which were dissatisfied?
5. What were the goals of the Committee of Public Safety? Did the committee achieve its goals?
6. What changes took place in the social lives of citizens during the French Revolution?
7. Why did the conquered peoples unite against Napoleon?

Words to Know

Define the following words in one or two sentences. Then tell the significance of each.
   a. petite bourgeoisie
   b. estates
   c. grande bourgeoisie
   d. emigres
   e. guillotine
   f. oligarchy

Developing Your Skills

1. Identify the following places. Then find them on the map on page 458.
   a. Cape Trafalgar
   b. Austerlitz
   c. Grand Duchy of Warsaw
   d. Waterloo
   e. Elba
   f. Leipzig
2. Place the following events in the proper chronological order.

Napoleon invades Russia.
Louis XVI is executed.
The Bastille is captured.
Napoleon seizes power in France.
Robespierre is executed.

Thinking It Over

1. The National Assembly seized the property of the Roman Catholic Church. To pay the clergy, they offered a salary to the priests. The clergy were also to be elected. Thus, the office of bishop, as well as that of parish priest, would be voted on by all the people in the district. This included voters such as the few Jews and non-Catholics. What were the advantages of this plan? What were the disadvantages?
2. Robespierre is often blamed entirely for the Reign of Terror. Yet no one member of the Committee of Public Safety completely dominated the committee. Since their meetings were secret, it is not certain what actually went on in the meetings. What are the advantages of secret meetings? What are the disadvantages?

Special Activities

1. Marie Antoinette, the queen of Louis XVI, is a controversial figure. Find out why she became unpopular and how she influenced the French Revolution. Present your point of view on Marie Antoinette.
2. Napoleon has been one of the most controversial figures in history. Debate this topic: Did Napoleon Bonaparte carry out or destroy the ideals of the French Revolution?

Unit 6 Review

Words to Know

1. Explain the difference between an emigre and a colonist.
2. Give examples of the ways in which the French Republic became more secular.
3. Compare the creoles of Latin America with the Cavaliers of the English Civil War.
4. Contrast the idea of the divine right of kings with the idea of the natural rights of people.

Time and Place

1. In Latin America, many newly independent countries adopted constitutions based on the constitution of the United States. In France, the Code Napoleon defined the rights of citizens. Make a time line to show the approximate dates when citizens of these areas got written rights: England, France, the United States, Latin America.
2. Each statement below is true of only one of the revolutions you have studied in this unit. For each statement, answer North American, Latin American, or French.
   a. Allies (foreign powers) were important in achieving victory.
   b. Fighting against foreign nations added to the burden of the revolution.
   c. Guerrilla warfare was used effectively.
   d. Full-scale drafting of men was used.
   e. The rebels were able to get enough taxes from the townspeople to support the revolution.
   f. The revolution was *not* followed by a rule of a dictator.

Putting It Together

1. Copy the chart below. Then fill in the information.
2. Compare the causes of the American Revolution and Latin American revolutions in the economic, political, and religious areas.

	English Civil War	American Revolution	French Revolution
Major causes			
Immediate cause			
Leaders			
Type of government established after the war			
Results for people's rights			

Contemporary Parallel:
The Rights of Women

For hundreds of years, people struggled to achieve legal and political rights. However, people always spoke of the natural rights of man, not of woman.

A woman's legal rights were tied to those of her husband. In Europe and in America, a married woman could not control her property or her earnings. She could not make a will or get a divorce easily. She could not sign contracts. In most places, she could not vote or hold political office.

Some women gained power when they inherited property. Some religions supported the idea that a person should follow her or his individual conscience rather than tradition and authority. For example, the Quakers allowed women to preach at meetings.

In general, however, most people believed that men were responsible for the worlds of work and politics. The tasks of raising children and running the household were assigned to women.

A milestone in the modern women's rights movement was Mary Wollstonecraft's *A Vindication of the Rights of Women*, published in Britain in 1792. This book soon became popular and quite controversial.

Mary Wollstonecraft thought that education was the key to improving the position of women. She wanted women's education to develop strength of both mind and body. She felt that both sexes were being hurt by the old system. Wollstonecraft wanted women to be able to support themselves. Wollstonecraft, herself, had been forced to earn her living by teaching and writing. She fully realized the disadvantages of depending on a male as the sole source of income. Marriage, according to Wollstonecraft, could not reach its full potential until women became free to earn their own independent income.

Mary Wollstonecraft's *Vindication* became a bible for feminists. It set the tone for the demands for reform in women's education, for the right to vote, and for other legal rights, such as holding political office.

QUESTIONS

1. What legal rights have women gained since Wollstonecraft's time? What employment gains have been made? In what areas do women still lack equality with men?
2. Many gains in women's rights have been for employed women. Do housewives need increased rights, such as social security or pension benefits?

1760	1778	1814	1850	1900	1905	1914
Great Britain begins industrialization	European presence in Pacific begins	Congress of Vienna begins	British, French, Dutch, and Portuguese in Africa	Boxer Rebellion; Britain first urban nation	Japan wins Russo-Japanese War	Only two free nations in Africa

Unit 7
Industrialism and Imperialism

An early American railroad.

The term revolution means a great and sudden change in the lives of many people. Often the great change is fought out on the battlefield, but not always. Some people think that the Industrial Revolution produced more sweeping changes than the French Revolution.

The French Revolution produced tremendous changes in the lives of people. The Industrial Revolution was more gradual, but for many people it changed where they lived, what they did for a living, and how they saw themselves and their world.

The Industrial Revolution also made people throughout the world more dependent upon each other. For example, in the 1800s, the Civil War in the United States interrupted the flow of cotton to England. Many people lost their jobs in the English textile mills.

The Industrial Revolution also contributed to *imperialism*, or the control of one nation over another nation or area. As the Industrial Revolution spread, industrial nations needed raw materials such as oil, cotton, tin, and sugar. The industrialized nations wanted control of colonies so they could use the raw materials of the colonies and could sell the manufactured goods to the colonists. The industrialized nations also wanted to invest their profits in mines, railroads, and plantations in the colonies.

Industrialism and imperialism worked together to change the lives of people in many parts of the world.

Garibaldi landing at Marsala.

Chapter 24
Nationalism After Napoleon

Nationalism is the feeling of loyalty towards one's country. When people use the same language, and share experiences, they develop a sense of shared history. They feel different from other peoples. This makes for a common bond. They are willing to unite and to fight against their common enemies.

Nationalism is a recent development. At first, people gave their loyalty only to a small group—their own family or tribe. Later on, people expanded their support to a small geographic area. For example, Greek citizens were loyal to their own city-state such as Athens or Sparta.

1814-1890

1814-1815	Congress of Vienna
1830, 1848	Revolutions in Europe
1846-1848	War between Mexico, United States
1852	Napoleon III rules France
1854	Crimean War
1861	Russia abolishes serfdom
1866	Prussia defeats Austria
1867	Dual Monarchy, Dominion of Canada
1870	Italy unified
1870-1871	Franco-Prussian War
1871	Germany unified
1890	American frontier closed

Prince Klemons von Metternich.

Modern nationalism began during the French Revolution. During the Revolution, the French people feared an invasion. As they united to fight successfully for their homeland, French nationalism increased. Napoleon's military victories also stirred French pride and feelings of nationalism. The example of French nationalism spread throughout the world. Now more and more people wanted a new or enlarged nation of their own.

Nationalism can be a powerful force for evil or for good. It can further divide a country that is not unified. It can lead to rivalry and wars between nations. For good or bad, nationalism remains one of the strongest forces in the world today.

1. Metternich Tried to Hold Back Change

For about twenty-six years, from the French Revolution in 1789 until Napoleon was defeated in 1815, France strongly influenced Europe. One important result of this influence was the spread of nationalism.

During the Napoleonic empire, the Germans and Italians saw France as a nation that was strong and unified. They had failed to unite their countries at the end of the Middle Ages. They still lived in many separate states. Many Germans and Italians began to want national unity.

Nationalism also increased in Austria. Many groups in central Europe—Hungarians, Czechs, Slovaks—resented Austrian rule and wanted their own national identity. Feelings of nationalism increased among the conquered groups in Russia and the Ottoman Empire.

Another impact of the French Revolution was *liberalism*. Early ideas of liberalism included the right to rebel against unjust rulers and guarantees of freedom of speech, the press, and person. The French Declaration of Rights stated that people have certain rights. Under Napoleon, the French laws said that all citizens were equal before the law and that the previous privileges for the upper classes were wiped out.

The idea of democracy, the rule of the many, was also spreading. After 1815, nationalism, liberalism, and democracy were important ideas in Europe and the rest of the world. However, sometimes these ideas were in conflict with each other.

The Congress of Vienna After Napoleon was defeated, the leaders of the victorious powers—Great Britain, Prussia, Austria, and Russia—sat down to remake the map of Europe. They met in Vienna in 1814 and 1815. At the Congress of Vienna they tried to decide the future of Europe. They wanted a lasting peace. They were tired of war and weary of the disruptions caused by the French Revolution and Napoleon.

The most important person at the conference was the chief minister of the Austrian empire, Prince Klemons von Metternich (MET ur nick, 1773 to 1859). Metternich thought that monarchy was the best form of government. He was a *conservative*, a person who favored the traditions and values of the past. Metternich was horrified by the changes the French Revolution brought. He wanted to go back to the "good old days" and restore royal rulers to their thrones.

The Congress of Vienna.

Thinking Geographically: Compare this map with the map of Napoleon's empire on page 458. What territories did France have?

At the Congress of Vienna, the major powers built a ring of powerful states around France to keep France from becoming powerful again. Belgium was given to the Netherlands. Prussia was given extensive lands in the Rhineland. Russia was given Finland and part of Poland. Great Britain kept colonial possessions that it had seized during the Napoleonic Wars — Malta, Cape of Good Hope, Ceylon, the Ionian Islands near Greece.

Austria was now the strongest power in central Europe. It did not want a strong Prussia or a united Germany. Therefore the Congress divided Prussia into two parts and left Germany a group of powerless states without a unified armed force or a central treasury. There were now thirty-nine states in the German Confederation. The Confederation and Austria controlled eight separate Italian states.

In dividing up countries, the Congress of Vienna paid little attention to nationalism. Groups such as the Belgians, Poles, Finns, Italians, and Hungarians resented being ruled by others.

Metternich and others wanted to restore royal rulers to their thrones. Louis XVIII, a brother of the executed Louis XVI, was brought back to rule France. Louis XVIII, a moderate, acquired some degree of popularity and France regained some respect. France had been given generous peace terms. Its boundaries were the same as those in 1792. Within a few years, France was a major power again.

This cartoon shows European leaders observing American naval strength.

Revolts From 1814 to 1848 is sometimes called "The Age of Metternich." He wanted the great European powers to crush nationalism and liberalism. Metternich organized a way to handle international conflicts. The five powers—Great Britain, France, Austria, Prussia, and Russia—would have conferences to settle problems.

His ideas were soon put to the test, and in more than one spot. The king of Spain was trying to put down the rebellions in Latin America. However, Great Britain had a rich trade so it did not want Spain to regain control there. In 1823, the United States issued the Monroe Doctrine. The Monroe Doctrine warned foreign powers not to interfere in North and South America. The United States had the power of the British navy behind the declaration. The European powers decided not to test the United States and, indirectly, Great Britain.

Metternich next ran into trouble in Greece. Greece had been under the rule of the Ottoman Turks since 1453. The Greeks were allowed religious freedom and some local government under Turkish rule. However, they also had the memory of a great past. Nationalism stirred. The Greeks had built up a number of trading stations in the eastern Mediterranean. These stations were outside the confines of the Ottoman Empire. The stations became centers for plotting against the Turks.

In 1821, Greek rebels swept down from the mountains and captured many parts of Greece. At first, the Greeks were winning.

Turkish troops attacking the Greek rebels.

But in 1825, Egypt came to the aid of the Turks. The war began to go against the rebels. By 1827, the Greeks seemed close to defeat.

Metternich faced a problem. He did not want to encourage any revolts. However, the "courageous Christian" Greek rebels had won the sympathy of many Europeans and Americans. Greek revolt was a very popular cause. So in 1827, France, Great Britain, and Russia agreed to use force if necessary to end the fighting. The Turks refused to give up Greece, so Russia declared war in 1828. The Turks had to leave Greece to fight the Russians. By 1830, Greece was independent. The Serbs and Romanians were also given more local rule. The Greeks' independence was a victory for nationalism. It was a signal for other people in the Ottoman Empire to think of independence.

The Revolutions of 1830 In 1824, Louis XVIII of France died. His youngest brother, Charles X, was crowned. Charles soon aroused fear that he was taking the nation back to the old days of the nobility. He wanted to pay back the nobles who had lost their property during the Revolution. He pushed for more church control of education. He used censorship. In 1830, Charles suspended the constitution and tried to rule like a dictator.

Led by students and the urban working class, the French rebelled. Charles X was forced to flee. The rebels then faced a problem. What kind of government should they have? Some wanted to have no king at all. They wanted a republic. Others wanted a king with limited powers. As a compromise, the Duke of Orleans, Louis-Philippe (LOO e fee LEAP), a cousin of Charles, was made the ruler. Louis-Philippe was a moderate and a supporter of the constitution.

The 1830 revolution in France set off revolutions in Germany, Italy, Spain, Poland, Switzerland, and Belgium. Almost all of the rebellions were put down by force. The Belgians, however, won their independence from the Dutch in 1831. In Switzerland, the liberal forces also gained strength after a mild revolution.

The French revolution turned out to be a victory for the upper middle class, people such as bankers and businessmen. Louis-Philippe promoted the Industrial Revolution. With industrialization came growing slums, poor working conditions, and unemployment during recessions. Because of these problems, many workers began to support *socialism*. Socialism is an economic system in which factories and mines are owned by the people (the government), not by private individuals.

Meanwhile, Metternich continued to try to stop the ideas of liberalism and nationalism from spreading in the area of Austrian influence. He placed spies in the universities and schools. But people in Europe were still inspired by nationalism, liberalism, and now, socialism.

The French Revolution of 1848 In the spring of 1848, revolutions again broke out in Europe. Once more the first revolution started in France. The French upper middle class was gaining wealth and prestige. However, the intellectuals were dissatisfied and the workers were suffering. Wages were low. The workers could not vote or organize unions. Then the potato and grain crops failed in 1845 and 1846. With less food, prices shot up. The workers could barely buy enough to eat.

In February 1848, the workers rebelled. They set up barricades in the streets of Paris and gained control of the city. Louis-Philippe fled to England.

A new government was set up, but again the rebels were not united. Some middle-class people favored a republic but did not want the working people to vote. Some wanted votes for all. Some, such as Louis Blanc (BLAHNK), wanted a socialist government. It was agreed to hold an election to start a new government. All French male adults would be allowed to vote.

Meanwhile, Louis Blanc was allowed to start national workshops to put the unemployed workers to work. The workshops were not well organized. They attracted loafers. Yet the workshops were costly to the taxpayers. This frightened the middle class and the peasants. These two groups feared that the socialists might take away their property.

In the election of April 1848, the majority of votes went to conservative candidates. The new government abolished the workshops. The workers in Paris rebelled. The rebellion was put down by force. Over 1,500 workers were killed. The captured leaders were sent to overseas prisons.

The revolution of 1848 in France was the first class war. It was a split of the conservative rural and middle-class people against the radicals and urban workers. The only gain for the rebels was that all French males now had the right to vote.

In November, France voted in a new constitution. In December, Louis-Napoleon Bonaparte, Napoleon's nephew, was elected president of the Second Republic. In 1851, Louis-Napoleon seized power and set up a dictatorship he called the Second Empire. In 1852, the voters approved the restoration of an empire and Louis-Napoleon became Napoleon III.

The Other Revolutions of 1848 When German intellectuals heard the news of the French uprisings, they were thrilled. Could the thirty-nine states that made up the German Confederation be united? Could they, too, win free speech, a free press, and the right to vote? Riots broke out in many places. In most of the small and middle-sized states, the rulers quickly agreed to some reforms. Delegates met in Frankfort to form a united and liberal Germany. But the conference was a failure.

The German states could not agree. Some wanted a republic. Others wanted a monarchy. No one could agree on whether the German-speaking population of Austria should be included as part of Germany. The liberals wanted a more democratic society. The supporters of *autocratic* Prussia opposed

French women at the barricades during the revolution of 1848.

Paris mobs in the Throne Room.

this. (An autocratic ruler has great power.) The Prussian king refused to become emperor of Germany because he did not like the liberal constitution. The hope of a unified Germany—a Deutschland—failed.

The individual German states regained power. Some German liberals were forced to flee. They settled in America, Canada, Argentina, and Brazil. But the Germans who stayed believed that Germany could only be united under the direction of Prussia. Nationalism continued to grow in the German states.

In Vienna and other parts of the Austrian empire, students and intellectuals rioted in the streets when they heard the news of the 1848 revolution. Metternich fled for his life, and the "Age of Metternich" came to an end. Emperor Ferdinand abdicated in favor of his young eighteen-year-old nephew, Franz Joseph I. Under Franz Joseph, serfdom was eliminated and other reforms were made. He was to hold together the Austrian empire for his 68 years of rule.

People rebelled in other parts of the Austrian empire. Italians drove the hated Austrian troops from some cities. The people of Hungary won freedom for a short while. But the various ethnic groups in the Austrian empire were not united. The Russians intervened and defeated the Hungarian rebels. The Austrian armies put down the rebellions in Italy and other places.

The revolutions of 1848 seemed to be unsuccessful. Many Germans and Italians now were convinced that only strong leaders could bring about national unity. However, the ideas behind the revolutions of 1848 would not die.

Section Questions

1. How did Metternich think international problems could be solved?
2. What was the Monroe Doctrine?
3. Which revolutions in 1830 were successful?
4. Why did the French workers revolt in 1848?

Garibaldi is cheered on a visit to London.

2. Nationalism Began to Spread

The Italians, like the Greeks, had a long history. But for hundreds of years there was no Italy. Instead, there were states such as Sardinia, Naples, and the independent Papal States, where the pope ruled. In 1848, attempts to unify Italy had failed. Italy was still controlled by outsiders. But nationalism was growing among the middle class.

Italy Count Camillo di Cavour (kah VOOR) was one of the leaders for Italian independence. Cavour was the prime minister of the Italian state of Sardinia. Sardinia consisted of Piedmont (PEED mont), Sardinia, Savoy (suh VOY), and Nice (NEES). Cavour felt that the small Italian armies could not expel the Austrian troops. So in 1859 he made an agreement with Napoleon III of France. Cavour gave up the French-speaking territories of Nice and Savoy to France. In return, France agreed to help the Italians fight against the Austrians.

Thinking Geographically: Use the information on the map to make a time line. Use the dates on the map and list the areas that were added on each date.

UNIFICATION OF ITALY

Sardinia provoked a war with Austria. With the help of French troops, Sardinia gained control of most of northern Italy. Then Napoleon III withdrew his forces. Many Italians in the south wanted to join Sardinia to create a unified Italy. Revolutions broke out in all parts of Italy.

In 1860, Giuseppe Garibaldi (GAR uh BALL dee), a popular hero, sailed to Sicily with an army of 1,000 men. The soldiers were called the "red shirts" because of their uniforms. Garibaldi liberated Sicily from the king of Naples and then captured southern Italy. In 1861 Victor Emmanuel II, the king of Sardinia, became king of Italy.

In 1870 the pope lost control of the Papal States. All of Italy was now unified. Rome became the capital city in 1871.

Even with unification, Italy faced many problems. The different regions of Italy were jealous of each other. The south was poor, with few natural resources. It did not like being ruled by the industrial north. Taxes were heavy. The government was often corrupt. Workers were dissatisfied because they could not vote. The population grew quickly, forcing many poor Italians to emigrate.

Germany Many economic factors favored the unification of Germany. From the time of Napoleon's fall in 1814, the German states had realized that they needed some economic unity. Trade was difficult because the German states had different coinage systems and tariffs between states. Under Prussia, a uniform system of currency, weights, and measures was started.

In addition, the German population was growing. In 1850, there were more Germans than French people. With growing work forces and excellent natural resources such as coal, the German Confederation became industrialized and powerful.

In 1861, militarist William I became the king of Prussia. In 1862, he appointed energetic Otto von Bismarck (BIZ mark)

Otto von Bismarck.

as his prime minister. Bismarck wanted to unify Germany under Prussia and make the country a strong industrial giant.

William I and Bismarck agreed that Prussia first needed a stronger army. The Chamber of Deputies refused to vote for money for the military. Bismarck believed in an autocratic government. William I and Bismarck simply collected taxes without the consent of the Chamber. Soon Prussia had a large and efficient army. It used the latest technology in weapons. It incorporated the telegraph and train into its battle plans. The officers planned war strategy more carefully than had ever been done before.

Bismarck soon used his newly trained army. Prussia easily seized two provinces from Denmark. Then Bismarck provoked Austria to declare war on Prussia in 1866. Prussia defeated Austria within seven weeks. The king and the German military staff wanted to go farther into Austrian territory and to take Vienna. Clever Bismarck, however, was a realist who fought wars for

Thinking Geographically: Use this map and the map on page 469. How does the size of unified Germany compare with the size of the Austrian empire?

a limited purpose. He did not want Austria to become a permanent enemy. He feared that the Russians would then move into central Europe. Instead, Bismarck wanted an alliance with Austria.

The king of Prussia was now the leader of the German Confederation. With the exception of four large southern German states, all of Germany was now joined together.

Bismarck continued to maneuver. Napoleon III of France was worried about the increasing power of Germany. Bismarck manipulated France into feeling that it had been insulted. In 1870, the French, although unprepared, rashly declared war. The four southern German states then joined the rest of Germany to fight the French.

Within a few weeks, the Germans captured Napoleon III and his troops at Sedan. The Germans then moved quickly to Paris. For four months, Paris tried to hold out. The starving city finally surrendered in January 1871.

France was completely defeated. As part of the peace terms, Germany gained the French provinces of Alsace and the eastern part of Lorraine. The defeat left the French very bitter and humiliated, and eager to get revenge against Germany.

All of Germany was joined together under William of Prussia, the emperor of Germany. Germany was now the most powerful nation on the continent of Europe. Germany's industrial strength grew, especially in the steel and chemical industries. With industrialization, socialism became popular with the German workers. At first, Bismarck tried to wreck the workers' political parties. But this merely drove the socialists underground. So he tried his own "carrot stick." He started a state program to help workers. This included insurance against sickness and accidents, pensions, disability insurance, and regulations of hours worked and working conditions. By 1914 the Socialist Party was the largest political party in Germany. However, the socialists were concerned with practical issues such as working conditions. They did not preach violent revolution.

Austria and Eastern Europe As you read earlier, the Austrian empire lost two wars in less than ten years. It had to give up Italy to Sardinia in 1859. Then it lost to Prussia in 1866. The Austrian empire was getting weaker and weaker.

In 1867, Franz Joseph was forced to give Hungary more independence. A Dual Monarchy, the Austria-Hungary empire, was created. The two countries were united under one ruler, Franz Joseph. Franz Joseph directed foreign and military affairs, but there was a separate parliament for each nation.

The Austrian Germans were in control of Austria. The Hungarians were powerful in the kingdom of Hungary. However, millions of other minorities lived in each part of the Dual Monarchy. Slavs and other groups were discontented. They wanted the right to govern themselves.

Eastern Europe was poorer and less industrialized than western Europe. It held many different national groups, such as Serbs, Czechs, Croats, Poles, Bulgarians, and Romanians. These groups felt oppressed by the Austrian, Russian, and Ottoman empires. There were many struggles for independence in the Balkans. (The Balkans are a group of countries in southeast Europe including present-day Albania, Greece, Bulgaria, Rumania, and part of Turkey and Yugoslavia.) These uprisings were a source of severe disturbance to the rest of Europe.

Russia Compared with the rest of Europe, Russia had been little influenced by the French Revolution. During the war against Napoleon, patriotism increased. Only a few young officers were influenced by revolutionary ideas. Most of the Russian people were illiterate peasants, tied to the soil as serfs. The czars continued to rule as autocrats. The secret police rooted out all those who advocated reform or changes. But then came the Crimean War. The Euro-

The Light Brigade in battle during the Crimean War. For an account of the battle, read Tennyson's poem, "The Charge of the Light Brigade."

pean powers did not want Russia to gain control of the Turkish port city of Constantinople. With control of this city, Russia would have access to the Mediterranean and Middle East area. In 1854, Turkey, Great Britain, and France attacked Russia. By 1856, Russia was defeated.

The Russian people were deeply shocked by Russia's loss of the Crimean War. Alexander II (al eggs AN der) became czar in 1855. Alexander knew that he had to make Russia more modern. In 1861, he abolished serfdom for the peasants. Along with their freedom, the serfs were supposed to get land which they could pay for over a long period of time. In many cases, they got less land and poorer land than they had worked as serfs. They could not earn enough to pay for the land and for the taxes. Beyond all things, the peasants wanted land. They were not satisfied with the half-steps that the government made to provide them with land.

Did You Know?

Queen Victoria with sixteen of her children, grandchildren and great-grandchildren.

England's Royal Family

Queen Victoria and Prince Albert of England dreamed of uniting Europe. They planned to accomplish this through marriages of their nine children to members of European royalty.

Victoria's and Albert's dream of uniting Europe had a curious twist. Queen Victoria was a *hemophilia* carrier. Hemophilia is a hereditary disease in which blood does not clot normally. Any bleeding—large or small—is difficult to control. The disease strikes males but rarely strikes females. Today, hemophilia can be controlled. In Queen Victoria's time, males with hemophilia had a very shortened life span.

Prince Leopold, Victoria's youngest son, had hemophilia. Two of Victoria's daughters were carriers. As the royal families of Britain, Germany, and Russia were united by marriage, hemophilia appeared in these families.

The most famous case involved the young heir to the Russian throne. Nicholas II of Russia married Alexandra, one of Victoria's granddaughters. They were delighted at the birth of their son. But they soon found out that their young son, Alexis, had hemophilia. Religious Alexandra came under the influence of Rasputin (ra SPOOT un), a monk and a close adviser. She believed that he was saving their sick son's life. However, many other Russians hated Rasputin's influence on the Russian royal couple. This dissatisfaction contributed to the final downfall of the Russian royal family in 1917. Later, the whole family was murdered by the revolutionaries.

To fight the discontent of the people, Alexander II set up an even more powerful security police force. A huge network of spies reported on the activities of university students and other groups. Those suspected were arrested and sent to Siberia. A few were executed. Censorship was imposed to keep "dangerous" ideas from circulating.

The persecution caused many young intellectuals to decide that revolution was the only way to get a better government in Russia. These Russian revolutionaries were influenced by European ideas. In fact, many of them lived in exile in Europe or had studied there. Outside of Russia, they organized groups and newspapers. They tried to influence the peasants, and later, as the empire industrialized, the workers.

A few Russians became *anarchists*. An anarchist rebels against any authority, and often uses violent means to overthrow the government. These Russians saw their only hope in assassination of government officials. In 1881, they killed Czar Alexander II. He was succeeded by Czar Alexander III, who was opposed to reforms. During the 1890s, industrialization spread in Russia. As it had in other nations, the spread of industrialism caused many changes in Russian society. In foreign affairs, the Russians continued to try to move into the Balkans. They promoted the idea of *Pan-Slavism*, the emphasis of cultural ties among Slavic people. Their idea of course, was that all Slavs should be unified under Russian leadership. However, the great European powers continued to frustrate Russian attempts to gain land and influence in the Balkans.

Section Questions

1. How did Count Camillo di Cavour aid in uniting Italy?
2. What goals did Bismarck want for Germany?
3. What problems did the Russian czar face in the 1800s?

3. New Latin American Nations Faced Many Problems

The Latin American wars for independence helped unite many different groups within each area. The Latin American nations also cooperated in their fight against the common enemy, Spain. For example, the Argentine troops helped to liberate Chile. Then Chilean officers and soldiers fought to free Peru. However, the peoples of Haiti, Argentina, Mexico, and Brazil had achieved independence through their own efforts.

Types of Government One of the first issues to arise after independence was achieved was what kind of government to have. Some leaders doubted the ability of the common people to play an important

Thinking Geographically: Crimea is a part of Russia. Does the map suggest why the war was called the Crimean War rather than the Russian war?

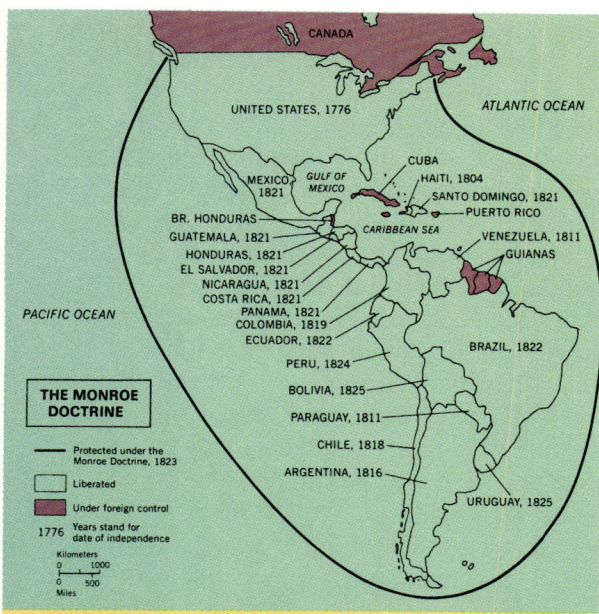

Thinking Geographically: Identify the original nations of Great Colombia and Central America.

Conservatives versus Liberals In addition to the conflict over central and local power, there was a split between the conservatives and the liberals. In general, the conservatives included the rich landowners. They wanted to leave the mass of the people without rights. The liberals drew their support from the professional middle classes, particularly lawyers. They wanted more changes in society.

A major issue that divided the conservatives and liberals was the role of the Roman Catholic Church. Many liberals wanted to restrict the church. The conservatives wanted the church to perform its traditional functions and provide stability.

The Rise of Military Leaders Most of the popular creole leaders of the wars for independence were soon replaced by military leaders. These military leaders typically took power by force. They were called *caudillos*, or military dictators.

Since power was based on force, there were frequent military *coups*, government takeovers by force. Mexico had 46 changes in government in the first 24 years of independence. Venezuela had about 50 civil wars between 1830 and 1902. For over 100 years, Bolivia averaged one civil war per year. Only Brazil, Chile, and Paraguay had some degree of stability.

Splits and Wars The process of nation building in Latin America was slow. In many areas there had been little development of nationalism before independence. In addition, many local areas resented the power of the central government. Some of the new countries fell apart. Bolívar's nation of Great Colombia broke up into Venezuela, Colombia, and Ecuador. Central America began in 1824 as a federal republic located between Mexico and Great Colombia. Within fifteen years, it had broken into smaller states, including Costa Rica, El Salvador, Guatemala, Honduras, and Nicaragua.

role in government. For example, Bolívar did not believe in establishing republics. Thus, in a few nations, such as Brazil, monarchy was retained as the basic form of government.

However, most of the Latin American nations established republics. Most of the constitutions were almost carbon copies of the constitution of the United States.

Political Inexperience Before independence, the creoles had held power at the local level. However, they had little practice running the central government of a nation.

Latin America also had lost all of the Spanish-born civil servants. There was thus no general administration left in many of the provinces. In those cases, power often reverted to the local level. A military group, bandits, or local creoles often took over.

In addition to the disunity within the Latin American nations, there were a few wars between nations. Uncertain boundaries were the sources of most of these quarrels. In 1825, war broke out between Brazil and Argentina over disputed territory. The peace treaty in 1828 established a new nation in Uruguay, in the disputed territory. Later, Paraguay fought against Uruguay, Argentina, and Brazil.

Economic Problems Before independence, most regions of Latin America had sent their products to Spain. They chiefly exported crops such as grain or sugar or minerals such as silver. They had purchased manufactured goods from the more industrialized nations. This colonial pattern continued after independence. However, Great Britain now assumed Spain's role as the chief trading partner. Britain remained the most important foreign trading nation in Latin America until about 1900.

The wars for independence disrupted trade and commerce. Many plantations were neglected or destroyed.

In the cities, the number of local industries and skilled workers declined. The artisans were now facing competition from cheap British goods. They were no longer protected by the Spanish trading laws. In addition, capital was in short supply. There was little money to invest in new techniques for increasing production.

Thus, along with political problems, economic difficulties contributed to the instability of the new Latin American nations. In many countries, it took years for trade and commerce to recover.

Foreign Affairs At first, the new nations of Latin America faced no serious foreign threats. Both Great Britain and the United States recognized their independence at once. Both nations were eager to trade with the Latin American countries. However, a conflict quickly arose between Mexico and the United States.

When Mexico first became independent, its relations with the United States were very friendly. In 1821, Mexican territory included what is now Texas, New Mexico,

A sugar mill in Cuba.

Indian silver miners at work.

Arizona, Utah, Nevada, and California. These areas had a few small, scattered Mexican settlements. Much of this vast region of northern Mexico was still occupied only by Indians. The Mexican territories of Texas, New Mexico, and California soon proved to be a source of conflict between Mexico and the United States.

At first, the Mexican government encouraged Americans to settle in Texas. They did this as a defense against the Indians. Then Mexico began to worry about the increasing numbers of American settlers. By 1830, there were about 20,000 Americans in Texas and only about 5,000 Mexicans. Most of the latter lived in the southern part of Texas. The Mexican government tried to stop further American immigration. It taxed goods imported from the United States. Each side began to fear and to mistrust the other. In 1836, the Texans refused to accept Mexican rule any longer. They declared their independence.

In 1836, an army under General Santa Anna, the dictator of Mexico, wiped out a force of Texans at the Alamo, a former mission in San Antonio. However, the loss at the Alamo united the Texans. Under General Sam Houston, they defeated the Mexican army at the Battle of San Jacinto and captured Santa Anna. Texas became the independent Republic of Texas. In 1845, the young Republic of Texas joined the United States. As a result of this action, the Mexican government broke off relations with the United States.

California also attracted American settlers. In 1845, President James K. Polk of the United States sent a representative to Mexico to try to buy California and New Mexico, as well as to settle the boundary of Texas. However, no members of the Mexican government would listen to any such American proposal.

The dispute over the boundary between Texas and Mexico led to war in 1846. The Americans at once seized California and New Mexico. By 1847, American troops

The Battle of the Alamo.

482

captured Mexico City, the capital. The Mexican troops had fought well, but they suffered from poor leadership and inadequate military supplies.

By the terms of the Treaty of Guadalupe Hidalgo in 1848, the United States, in return for $15 million, gained an enormous area, including present-day California, Nevada, Utah, and Arizona and parts of New Mexico, Colorado, and Wyoming. With this loss of territory, Mexico was reduced by about one-half in size. Only a few Mexicans had lived in the areas it lost. However, Mexico did lose territory rich in natural resources. The rest of Latin America began to worry about the United States, a giant that was growing in population, industry, and military strength.

Section Questions

1. In what ways did the Latin American nations help each other in winning the wars for independence?
2. What was the official form of government in most of the new Latin American nations?
3. What issue split the conservatives and liberals in Latin America?
4. How did trading patterns change in Latin America after independence?

4. Nationalism Grew in the United States and Canada

At the end of the American Revolution in 1783, the United States consisted of a few million people mostly clustered along the Atlantic coastal region. In the first decade after the revolution, settlers poured across the Appalachian Mountains into the Ohio and Tennessee valleys.

United States Growth In 1803 President Thomas Jefferson (1743-1826) negotiated the purchase of the Louisiana Territory from Napoleon Bonaparte. Suddenly the territory of the new nation was doubled. President Jefferson dispatched a survey expedition led by Meriwether Lewis and William Clark to explore this new territory. The Lewis and Clark expedition went all the way to Oregon on the Pacific Coast, thereby giving the country a claim to the Pacific Northwest region as well.

In 1819, Spain gave up Florida to the United States. In 1853, the United States purchased the Gila River valley from Mexico. This purchase established the southern boundaries of the present-day United States. In 1846, British and Ameri-

Daniel Boone escorting pioneers westward.

Lewis and Clark with their guide Sacajawea.

can diplomats negotiated a settlement in the northwest which gave the United States control of the Oregon Territory. The American Secretary of State, William Seward, negotiated the purchase of Alaska from Russia in 1867. American holdings on the North American continent were complete.

The phenomenal growth of America caused great changes among its people. As the nation expanded farther and farther west, the frontier moved with it. Life on this frontier was often harsh. In this daily struggle for existence, many American institutions were developed. The British legal tradition and the human rights ideas of the Enlightenment, still European in nature, became Americanized under the frontier experience. Those who moved west did not believe in restricting the right to vote to property owners. They did not like the idea of different social classes. They believed strongly in equality and democracy.

The constant American westward movement had another result, this one less noble. The original inhabitants, the Indians, were displaced. Under the *reservation* system, the Indians were forcibly moved to land that had been reserved, or set aside for them. This led to bitter wars from the 1850s through 1885. Meanwhile, whites had almost wiped out the buffalo herds, the primary source of food for the Plains Indians. Government policies after the wars almost destroyed the tribal cultures. These policies were not reversed until the 1930s.

The American Civil War The westward movement also intensified another problem. This was the issue of slavery. As the nation expanded, many of those who used

"The Battle of the Little Big Horn," as drawn by White Bird.

slaves to produce cotton and tobacco wanted to move west. They wanted to take their slaves with them. Northerners opposed to slavery, or at least to the spread of slavery, fought this. The issue reached a peak in the 1850s as northern and southern tempers flared. The population of the nation was growing faster in the North and West than in the South, so southerners saw the scales tipping away from them. In 1860, Abraham Lincoln (1809-1865) was elected President. Southerners believed that Lincoln opposed their way of life. Shunning compromise, they voted to secede from the Union.

The result was the American Civil War (1861-1865). Eleven southern states formed their own nation, the Confederate States of America, with Jefferson Davis as President. The North had many advantages. The population of the North was over twice the population of the South. The North possessed many economic resources. Most of the manufacturing, banking, gold reserves, and railroads of the nation were in the North, while the South was primarily an agricultural area. Despite the inequality, the conflict lasted four long, bloody years. The South, fighting a defensive war in its own backyard, had the superior military leadership. Southern generals, such as Robert E. Lee, working with meager resources, were able to best northern commanders for many years. In the end, the superior resources of the northern states made the difference. The war ended when Lee surrendered to Ulysses S. Grant in Virginia in 1865.

The campaigns of the American Civil War were studied carefully by European military experts. Many historians have called

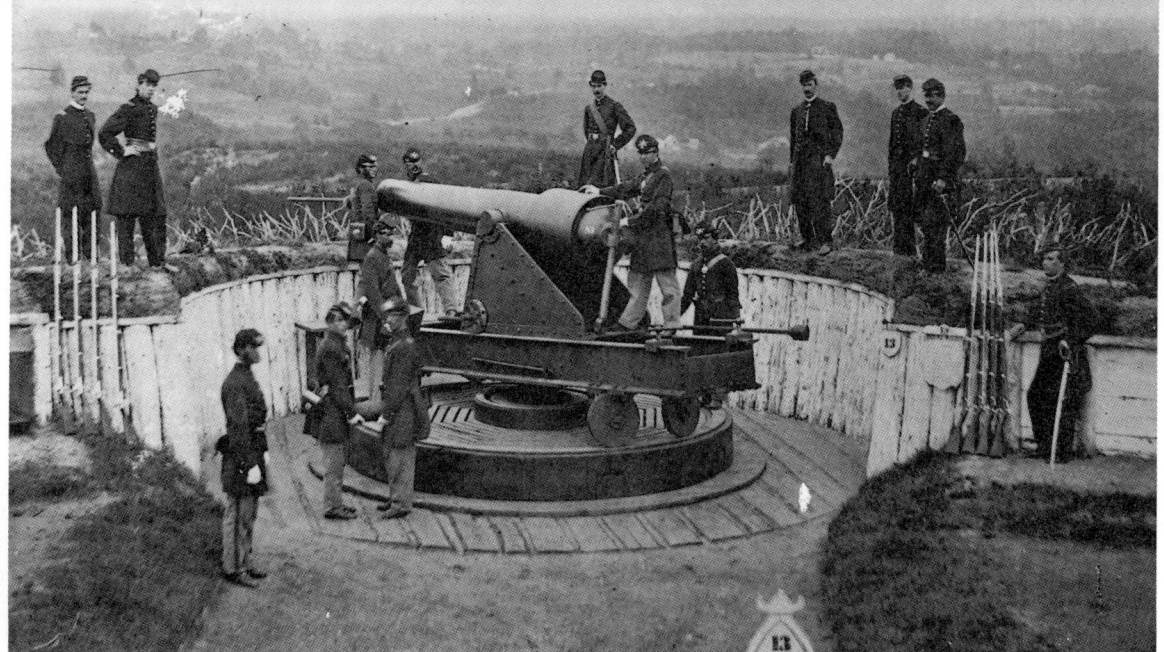

A photograph of a 100-pounder Parrot gun used in the American Civil War.

this war the first truly modern conflict. It was the first major conflict in which railroads were employed as a major means of moving troops and supplies. It marked the first extensive use of trench and field fortifications. For the first time, iron-clad naval ships were used in combat, manned balloons were used for military reconnaissance, and photographs were taken in combat. As a result, many European officers spent much time studying this conflict. One of their conclusions was that a heavy industrial base was indispensible in fighting a modern war.

The American Civil War ended the question of slavery in the republic. At the height of the war, President Lincoln abolished slavery in the southern states with his Emancipation Proclamation (1863). At the war's end, this was expanded to include all states. The United States was the last major western nation to end involuntary servitude. The war also strengthened the power of the American federal government by demonstrating that a state could not withdraw from the Union.

Western Expansion Continued After the American Civil War, industrialization skyrocketed. Westward expansion continued with the steady progress of railroad construction across the continent. In 1869, a transcontinental railroad linking the Atlantic and Pacific coasts was completed. In 1890, the Director of the Census reported that the frontier had closed.

In the northeast and midwest, the industrial age of Europe was duplicated in the United States. The nation had abundant human resources. European immigrants flocked to the rapidly growing cities of the North, assuring a seemingly endless supply of labor. There were also ample capital resources. New forms of business organization, such as corporations, allowed the financing of greater business ventures. In addition, the country had a seemingly inexhaustable supply of natural resources. Coal, iron, wood, oil, and other raw materials, it was felt, would last forever.

By 1890, the United States was truly a world power. Stretching from ocean to ocean, with a seemingly endless supply of natural resources, it had become an industrial giant. This strength would thrust the new nation onto the stage of world affairs in the twentieth century.

The Growth of Canada North of the growing United States was Canada. Originally colonized by the French, Canada passed under British control in 1763. After the American Revolution, many *loyalists*, those who remained loyal to Britain, fled the United States to Canada.

The French-speaking Canadians, mostly centered in Quebec, resented the influx of English-speaking immigrants from the former American colonies and from Britain. In 1791, the British government attempted to end these concerns by dividing Canada into two separate provinces, Upper Canada (predominantly English) and Lower Canada (predominantly French). However, this did not stop the quarreling. The British sent Lord Durham as special commissioner to investigate Canadian conditions and problems. In 1840, Durham recommended more self-government for the Canadians in domestic affairs. He recommended that Britain continue to control Canadian foreign relations.

Parliament passed the British North American Act of 1867. The Act formed a federal union called the Dominion of Canada. The Dominion originally consisted of the four provinces of Quebec, Ontario, Nova Scotia, and New Brunswick. By 1914, it had expanded to nine provinces.

This pattern of giving self-rule to the colonies was continued in other parts of the British Empire. Australia (in 1901) and New Zealand (in 1907) became independent. Yet they remained part of the empire.

Canada faced problems of transportation and communication. There were less than four million people in the huge country. There were barriers of mountains, water, and rocky forests. The climate was known for its brutal winters. Under Prime Minister Sir John A. MacDonald, transportation became a national priority. In 1885, a transcontinental railroad was completed. MacDonald and his successors encouraged the growth of industry and welcomed immigrants. By the turn of the century, Canada began a period of rapid industrialization similar to that experienced in the United States. This led to many of the social and economic problems that had faced Europe.

This painting is called "The Fathers of Confederation." They met in Quebec to plan the new form of government that led to the Dominion of Canada.

Section Questions

1. What territories did the United States gain after 1783? In what way was each territory acquired?
2. Name two results of the American Civil War.
3. What resources helped make the United States into an industrial giant?
4. What problems did Canada face after 1763?

Chapter Summary

1. The French Revolution and Napoleon's conquests spread nationalism, a feeling of love toward one's country. After Napoleon was defeated, the Congress of Vienna tried to maintain peace and to prevent the spread of revolutions and liberalism. At this time, Austria was the strongest power in central Europe. In 1830, revolts occurred in many parts of Europe. Fearing the power of the monarch, the French tried a new ruler. Belgium won its independence from the Dutch. The Greeks won their independence from the Turks in 1830 after the great powers helped the Greek rebels. Growing unrest led to many revolutions in 1848. In France, the socialists were crushed and a new government started under Louis-Napoleon Bonaparte III. The many other revolts in 1848 were unsuccessful.

2. After fighting the Austrians, Italy gained its independence in 1861. Under Bismarck, Germany became united and the most powerful nation on the continent. Germany defeated in quick succession Denmark, Austria, and France. The French were very bitter about the defeat at German hands and desired revenge. The czars in Russia tried to modernize the country, but the peasants and the intellectuals remained discontented. Russia and Austria tried to gain more land and influence in the Balkans. The people of the Balkans, made up of many different ethnic groups, felt intense nationalism. The United States expanded from the Atlantic to the Pacific.

3. In fighting against a common enemy, many Latin Americans cooperated. Leadership for the wars was generally supplied by the creole families. Most of the new Latin American nations became republics. However, the creoles did not have experience in running a central government. All the Spanish-born civil servants were gone. The issue of how much power the central or federal government should have over the local provinces became important. The central government usually assumed more power. Conservatives and liberals split over the role of the Roman Catholic Church in the new republics. Because of these many problems, military leaders often seized power. Great Colombia and Central America broke into smaller states. Boundary wars were also fought in Latin America. The wars for independence disrupted trade and commerce. Mexico lost about half of its territory to the United States in war.

4. The United States grew rapidly. Westward expansion was made possible by the Louisiana Purchase, the Mexican War, and negotiations with Spain, Britain, Russia, and Mexico. As Americans moved west, they developed a strong sense of democracy and equality. However, the Indian tribes were treated harshly. The American Civil War ended slavery in the United States and strengthened the power of the American federal government. Because of the technology and tactics, the Civil War has been called the first modern war. The United States became industrialized very rapidly after the Civil War because it was rich in human resources, capital resources, natural resources, and inventors. Canada moved from a colony to a dominion in 1867. With a huge country, few people, and two languages, Canada faced problems of transportation and communication. By 1900, Canada began a period of rapid industrialization.

Chapter 24 Review

Check Your Facts

1. Identify the following:
   a. Louis XVIII
   b. Charles X
   c. Alexander II
   d. Louis Blanc
   e. Victor Emmanuel II
   f. Lord Durham
   g. Count di Cavour
   h. Giuseppe Garibaldi
   i. William I
   j. Louis-Napoleon Bonaparte
2. Who was the most important person at the Congress of Vienna? What were his ideas?
3. What caused the war between Mexico and the United States?
4. What helped the Greek rebels gain independence?
5. Why did socialism seem attractive to many French factory workers?
6. Why was it difficult for Germany to unite in 1848?
7. Why did unified Italy and the new Latin American nations face many problems?

Words to Know

Define each of the following words in one or two sentences:
   a. nationalism
   b. socialism
   c. liberalism
   d. anarchist
   e. conservative
   f. caudillos

Developing Your Skills

1. Trace part of the world map in the Atlas. Mark three countries that Britain gave more independence.
2. Use the text and other sources. For each country below, tell what kind of government it had in 1815 and 1871.
   a. Greece
   b. Russia
   c. France
   d. Germany
3. Photography was first used in the 1800s. Look back through the chapter and list the pages in which it appears that a camera was used for the illustration.

Thinking It Over

1. Bismarck is said to have been a person who was a realist and not too greedy. Do you think Bismarck made a mistake by taking some French territory in 1871?
2. Although a royal person may sit on the throne, sometimes a close adviser—a prime minister—actually may have more power than the king or queen. Why may this happen? List such influential people mentioned in the chapter.
3. What helps to make a revolution successful? Discuss why the American revolutions were successful. Compare them with some of the unsuccessful revolutions in 1830 and 1848.

Special Activities

1. Many new nations were unified or became independent in the 1800s. Check the symbolism of the flags of one such nation.
2. Use the library to check on one of the following: How were Jews treated in Europe in the 1800s? What were the effects of the crop failures in the 1840s? How was the German army trained?

Women working in the cotton industry. They are carding, drawing, and roving.

Chapter 25
The Age of Industrialization

The Industrial Revolution was the shift from home manufacturing to large-scale factory production. It began in the English textile industry.

From 1760 and for over one hundred years, Great Britain led the world in almost every phase of industry and technology. By 1860, France and Germany were also becoming important industrial powers. From the 1860s to the 1900s, the United States moved to first place as an industrial power. It had more miles of railroad and produced more iron and steel than any other country in the world.

1760-1900

1760	Great Britain begins industrialization
1776	Adam Smith's *Wealth of Nations*
1799	Great Britain forbids unions
1807	First successful steamship
1830	First railroad
1834	Mechanical reaper
1837	First successful telegraph
1848	Marx's *Communist Manifesto*
1856	Steel making improved
1866	Transatlantic cable laid
1867	British males get the vote
1876	Telephone
1900	Great Britain is first urban nation

A woman working at a loom.

Industrialization is still going on. As developing nations change their ways of manufacturing products, industrialization spreads throughout the rest of the world.

Like all revolutions, the Industrial Revolution greatly changed the lives of many people. As late as 1850, the vast majority of people in the world lived in rural areas. No nation in the world was *urban*, consisting mainly of cities and their suburbs. Even by 1900, only Great Britain was urban. There, more than half of the population lived in cities. The development of *factories*, large buildings in which manufacturing is done by a large number of workers, changed the lives of workers. Workers moved to cities to work in the factories. The mushroom growth of the cities created problems of overcrowded and inadequate housing, poor sanitation, water and air pollution, and increased crime.

The Industrial Revolution also changed social relations. The middle class grew in size and power. Workers organized to get higher wages, better working conditions, and more political power. Women's roles changed as they began to work outside the home.

What were the advantages of industrialization? The disadvantages? This chapter will discuss the many changes started by the Industrial Revolution.

1. The Industrial Revolution Caused Many Changes

Before the Industrial Revolution, most products such as cloth were made in people's cottages or in small shops. Whole families worked together, using few machines. They sold most of their products locally. However, starting around 1760, a combination of causes led to the development of industrialization in Great Britain.

One factor was natural resources. For example, Great Britain had a good coal supply. Secondly, inventions such as the flying shuttle (a weaving machine, 1733) and the spinning jenny (a spinning machine, 1779) allowed workers to make more cloth at less expense and in less time. A third factor was workers. Many were needed to run the new machines. Great Britain had more than enough workers to supply this need. A fourth factor was capital. To set up factories, the owners needed money to buy expensive machinery. In England, money was available from the profits made in trade, including the slave trade. Fifth, the British government supported the efforts of the new industrialists. Sixth, Great Britain had a good merchant fleet to transport needed materials. Seventh, England had an empire. The colonies sent raw materials to England. Great Britain sold many manufactured goods back to the colonies.

All of the factors listed above contributed to make England the first industrialized nation in the world.

New Inventions and Technology The English made spectacular technological improvements in two key industries: mining and textiles. In mining, the British government gave property owners the right to develop mines. This provided one incentive. Another incentive was need. A fuel shortage was growing in England as wood became more scarce. New energy sources such as coal had to be used.

Great Britain also had the natural resources. Numerous coal fields were situated near waterways. Coal mining grew rapidly. In 1700, around three million tons of coal were produced in England. By 1800, production more than tripled.

A major invention provided yet another boost for mining. It was necessary to go deeper and deeper as mines were dug. Water collected in the deep mine shafts. The mine owners needed equipment to pump out the water. By 1769, James Watt, a Scottish engineer, improved on the work of others to produce the first successful steam engine. This engine could be used to drive other machinery. It was used to pump water from mines so more coal could be dug. It provided a cheap and convenient source of power. Often the steam engine is considered the most important invention of the Industrial Revolution.

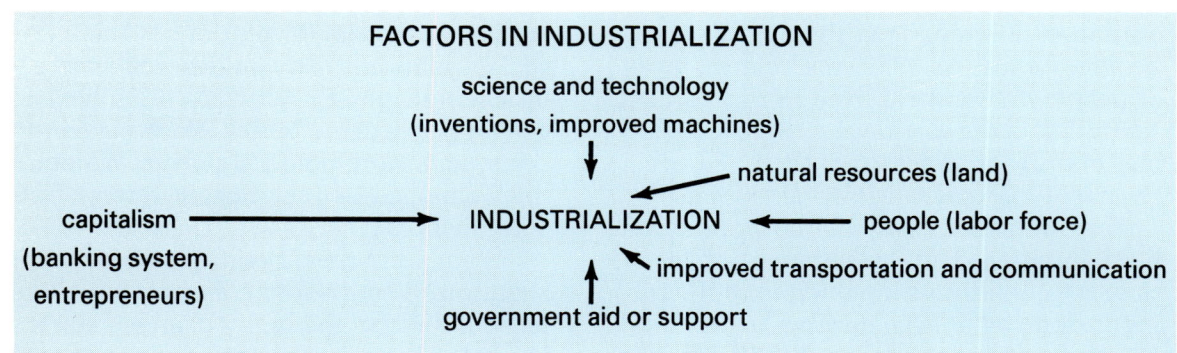

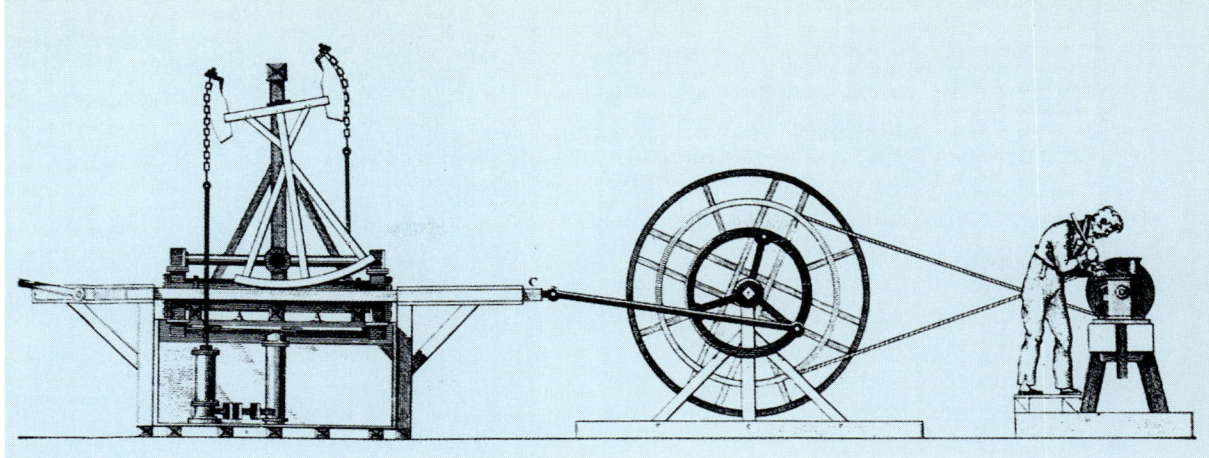

This patent drawing shows the earliest application of a steam engine for industrial use.

The textile industry became mechanized first because a series of inventions greatly increased production of cloth. The inventions included the flying shuttle, the spinning jenny, the spinning mule, and the power loom. Textile factories used two sources of power. Some used steam engines to drive the machinery. Others located near rivers and used falling water to run the machines.

People liked cotton cloth better than wool. Wool was hard to wash and was not as soft to the skin. However, cotton cloth was expensive because it was difficult to get the cotton seeds out of the fiber. In 1793, Eli Whitney, an American, invented the cotton gin. ("Gin" was short for "engine.") A cotton gin could remove seeds fifty times faster than workers using their hands. In the United States, the number of cotton plantations increased rapidly. They spread into new territory in the south. The American cotton provided the materials for the expanding cotton manufacturing industry in England.

Soon the English textile mills were producing more and more cotton cloth. Almost everyone can use cloth and there were more and more people to use it. Population

A woman at a New England spinning frame.

was increasing in Europe. The market for cloth was also increasing in other parts of the world—Asia, Africa, and the Americas. Cloth could be easily shipped throughout the world.

In 1835, England produced almost two-thirds of the world's cotton yarn and cloth. The English textile mills, with their new technology, could produce cotton cloth cheaper than cottage workers could. Textile workers, who had formerly worked in their own cottages in England or in other places such as India, were now displaced.

However, the textile industry needed more factory workers. The industry created jobs in other areas as well. More clerks were needed to keep track of the orders, materials, and goods. More salespeople were needed to sell the cheaper goods that more people wanted. Workers were needed to transport the cotton and the cloth.

Great Britain did not want other nations to start making cloth. However, a few skilled workmen emigrated to the United States and Europe. They knew how to build and repair the machines. The United States welcomed these workers. With them, America could also gain the profits of industrialization.

Mass production was now spreading throughout the world. Steam-powered machines made shoes, furniture, paper, and other machines. Improvements were made in the manufacturing processes for steel, rubber, oil, and gasoline. In 1856, Henry Bessemer, an Englishman, found a way to make steel from iron. Steel gradually replaced iron.

The Factory System To be effective, the factory system must work on a large scale. Huge new machines could produce large quantities of goods. The factories needed vast amounts of raw materials and many workers.

The workers were crowded into housing that was hastily built and cheaply made. Living quarters were built as close as possible to the factories, since people had to walk to work. Thus industrial cities such as Manchester grew up around the

Industrial workers often lived in slums such as this one in London.

factories. These cities were smoky, dirty, unhealthy places to live.

In Great Britain, the population had almost doubled between 1700 and 1800. From 1800 to 1900, the population tripled. Meanwhile, new methods of farming required fewer farm workers. Farm families were forced off the farms. They needed work. With so many unemployed, the factory owners in Great Britain did not have to pay their workers high wages.

The factories also employed many women and children. They paid the women and children even less than they paid the men. Women often were paid only half of the wages of men and children received even lower wages.

The average factory worker worked six

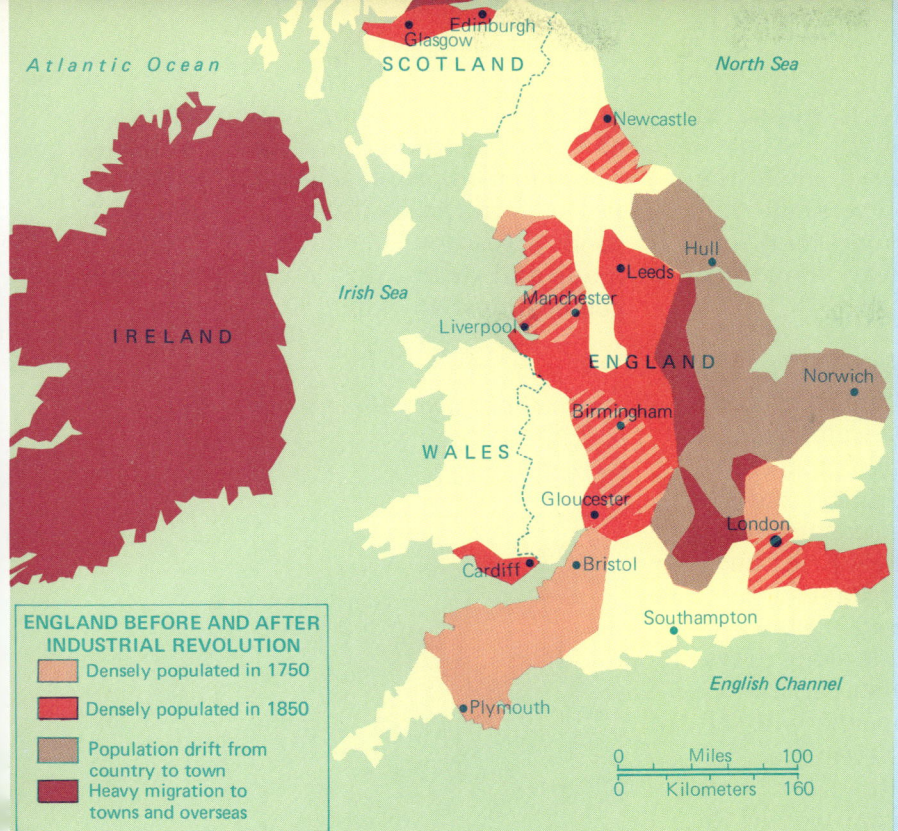

ENGLAND BEFORE AND AFTER INDUSTRIAL REVOLUTION
- Densely populated in 1750
- Densely populated in 1850
- Population drift from country to town
- Heavy migration to towns and overseas

Thinking Geographically: Name some of the cities that lost population between 1750 and 1850. Name some that gained population.

days a week, twelve hours a day, or from sunup to sundown. The factories were typically hot in the summer and cold in the winter. They were also unsafe, dark, and poorly ventilated.

Workers found it hard to concentrate on the monotonous tasks they performed all day. There were few safety precautions. Therefore, many accidents occurred. Workers had few rights to compensation for their injuries and most of them were too poor to sue the company. There were also less visible problems with factory work. In factories, workers had to keep up with the pace of the machine. There was no time for them to enjoy friendliness and warmth such as some had known working on the farm or in a small shop. It was hard for

Children working in an English spinning mill.

workers and their families to adjust to such changes in their lives.

At first, few people worried about the long hours of the workers. It was said that farm children also worked long hours and it was better for people to work than to be idle or to beg.

Improved Transportation Materials had to get to the factory. Finished goods had to get to the consumers. Industrialization could not happen without good transportation. Great Britain, France, and the United States built roads and canals to help move goods. New York State's Erie Canal, completed in 1825, was an instant success.

Steam power modernized transportation. Steamships moved goods along rivers, lakes, and oceans. They also carried the estimated 60 million Europeans who left Europe for North and South America.

In the 1830s, the railroad, or "iron horse," became the technical wonder of the day. A railroad could move tons of materials and passengers at the incredible speed of twenty miles an hour. At first there was almost no long-range planning in building railroads. There were many short lines, but track of different gauges (distances between the two rails) and different sizes of cars prevented early railroad lines from linking to one another. It took some time before standard gauges and cars were widely adopted.

Soon railroad tracks were being built in all parts of the world. By 1850, the United States had more railroad track than any European nation. Cities like Chicago grew rapidly as transportation centers for large regions. In 1903, the Russians completed the Trans-Siberian Railroad, a line of over 7,401 kilometers (4,600 miles) that ran from the Ural Mountains to the Pacific.

Vast amounts of money were required to construct railroad lines, so governments usually helped finance the railroads. It was a good investment, because railroads united a nation. They opened up new areas and lowered the cost of transportation. They enabled people to send large quantities of farm products and manufactured goods across long distances. By using railroads and steamships, people could send goods almost anywhere in the world.

An American locomotive of about 1880.

Communication During the 1800s, scientists made breakthroughs in understanding electricity. This started a wave of improvements in communication devices. The telegraph, telephone, trans-oceanic cable, typewriter, phonograph, and camera extended communication beyond the ordinary limits of sight and sound. Samuel F. B. Morse, an American, constructed a telegraph in 1837. An English team of physicists, working independently, also perfected a very similar type of telegraph. Within a few years, newspapers depended on telegraph lines for getting the news quickly.

In 1866, Cyrus Field succeeded in laying telegraph cables under the Atlantic Ocean. Ten years later, Alexander Graham Bell invented the telephone. Guglielmo Marconi (mar KO nee) developed the wireless telegraph between 1896 and 1901. J. A. Fleming's vacuum tube for the radio was invented in 1904.

Before the 1870s, most inventors worked alone or with a friend. Thomas A. Edison changed that. He was one of the first to establish a large laboratory. There he employed many people to work on inventions. The days of the individual inventor were being replaced by research and development centers. Edison patented almost a thousand inventions. His greatest invention was the electric light, but he also developed a successful motion-picture and improvements in the telephone.

Did You Know?

Travels and Holidays

The railroad greatly changed people's views. Before trains, most people did not travel far since it was expensive and uncomfortable. Many people lived and died in their own community without going more than thirty miles in any direction.

But the train made for cheaper transportation. Thomas Cook, an English minister, believed that the working classes needed some leisure and pleasure. In 1845, he conducted his first pleasure trip.

Cook traveled on the train and arranged hotel accommodations for the travelers. He also published a small guidebook of places of interest for his passengers. Cook's tours were an instant success. People felt protected on the organized tours. They could even travel in a foreign country, because the tour director would know the language. The tours encouraged people who had never traveled before to take long trips. Cook started the large travel industry of today.

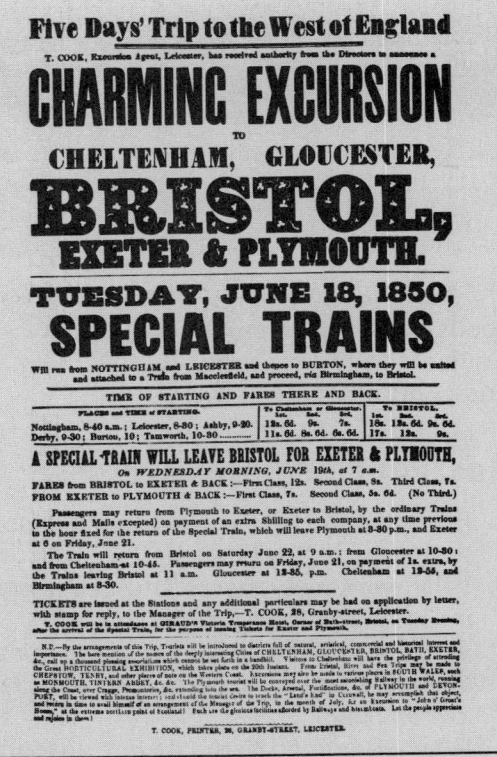

An advertisement for a Cook's Tour.

Thomas Edison in his laboratory.

2. People Responded to the Industrial Revolution

An industrial revolution changes a nation's economic system. But an industrial revolution also changes society.

The Industrial Revolution started at different time periods in different nations. Whenever it started, it was followed by labor unrest. In Great Britain, the Industrial Revolution started in the 1760s. It took place later in the United States, France, and Germany. The protests of the workers were greatest in the early 1800s. In Russia, factories were established in the 1890s. The workers were most discontented shortly before World War I (1914).

Factory workers had many reasons to complain. When recessions came, many workers lost their jobs. They had no unemployment or accident insurance, no retirement benefits, no hour limits, no minimum wage. They had shorter life-spans than other people in the same city.

In the factory system, workers did not work side by side with their employers. They could not talk informally with their boss about unfair treatment or poor working conditions. In fact, the workers seldom saw the owner or the manager.

The growing industrialization created more jobs and opportunities. But increasingly, each person did only a small part of a big job. Formerly, many factory workers had owned their own land or tools and made their own decisions about their work. Now they were told what to do and when to do it. Machines often dictated the pace of the work. Some workers felt that they were slaves to the machines.

Use of machines often cut off social contact. Workers could not talk to one another easily because of the noise or the distance that separated them and because of the need to concentrate on their work.

In certain industries, workers tried to start a *labor union,* an association that

The movement of raw materials, people, goods, and ideas greatly increased as a result of the improvements in transportation and communication.

Section Questions

1. In what nation did the Industrial Revolution begin? Why?
2. Why were new energy sources needed in Great Britain in 1700?
3. Why was the steam engine important?
4. Why did European factory workers receive low wages?
5. Why were improvements in transportation and communication important?

Workers in London marching to commemorate "Bloody Sunday." On Bloody Sunday, hundreds of unarmed Russian workers were killed while on strike.

In the 1820s, labor unions in England were allowed to organize and picket. Once unions were legal, their memberships grew. However, unions still were not allowed to strike, and a strike is labor's strongest weapon.

The Age of Reform The factory workers were not the only people who were concerned about the Industrial Revolution. Business people wanted more protection from *depressions*, periods of severe reduction in the demand for goods and services. Reformers charged that children were being harmed by the factory system. They were growing up ignorant because they did not attend school. Their health was endangered by working long hours.

At first, Parliament did not want to interfere between employer and employee. Members of Parliament were influenced by the ideas of Adam Smith, a Scottish economist. His book *Wealth of Nations* was published in 1776. In it, Smith argued that people put their time and money into activities that benefit them the most. These actions lead to a system in which consumers get what they want. Therefore, government should not interfere with business.

In 1819, however, the British government passed laws to protect workers. At first these laws applied only to women and children. Children under the age of nine were not allowed to work. Those between the ages of 9 to 18 were limited to 12 hours of work per day. Since there was no system of enforcement, these laws were not effective.

In 1833, Parliament passed a new law which provided for factory inspectors to report violations in the regulations. In 1847, Parliament passed a ten-hour law for women and children. This was a great advance. Men were also limited to ten hours of work per day since the factory worked on a shift. At first, these laws applied only to the textile industry. Later, they were extended to other industries.

would represent all the workers in dealing with employers. Unions were not supported by the public because people felt they would make prices higher.

In England, weavers at home could not compete with manufactured cloth. A few workers destroyed the machines in factories. The owners got the government to make the destruction of machines an offense punishable by death. A few workers were hanged. In 1799 and 1800, unions were declared illegal. Leaders who tried to organize the workers were sent to prison.

British voters using the secret ballot.

By 1900, Great Britain's government boards had established minimum wages for most industries. In a piecemeal fashion, without a violent revolution, the British government gradually restricted the power of employers and provided more protection for the workers.

There were also efforts to reform education, although a few people feared that educating workers would lead to unrest.

In 1832, a bill was passed that increased representation for the urban industrial areas. The urban leaders now had more power than the landed gentry and aristocrats. This was a significant change in the British government. The reform bill of 1832 also changed the voting requirements. In 1815, only about seven percent of adult males could vote. In 1832, the voting provisions allowed middle-class and professional men to vote. This doubled the number of voters. Most of the new voters were urban middle-class males.

In the reform bill of 1867, town householders (the great majority of urban workers) were permitted to vote. In 1872, the secret ballot was started. Individuals no longer had to state their voting choices aloud, perhaps before their landlord or employer. In 1884, farm workers won the vote. Now almost all males in England could vote. Aroused by the campaign to secure universal voting for all men, a few women also sought similar rights.

In 1918, partly as recognition of women's contributions to the war effort during World War I, the right to vote was granted to all women over 30 and to all men over 21. In 1928, the right to vote was given to all over the age of 21. Thus, in about 100 years, voting in Great Britain became truly democratic.

Political Responses to Industrialization Socialists want the government to own or control the major economic resources of a nation, such as land, factories, and mines. The ideas of socialism have been around for thousands of years. They became more important as the Industrial Revolution spread. The socialists wanted to redistribute wealth. They were in favor of taxing inheritances of private property and taxing incomes of the rich. They also believed that workers should work in *cooperatives*. The workers themselves would own and manage the cooperative and share the profits. A few socialists in the 1800s set up model communities based on economic cooperation. These usually failed because members could not agree on how things should be done.

Socialists also wanted each child to have a free public education and all working men to have the right to vote. Socialists

Did You Know?

Karl Marx

Karl Marx was a German journalist. He originally hoped to become a college professor. But his radical ideas forced him to flee to England. There he met the wealthy German reformer, Friedrich Engels. The two helped each other in their writing. In addition, Engels contributed to the financially pressed Marx family.

Marx believed that history is determined by the economic conditions of a society. At his time, he believed that power was in the hands of the bourgeois, the capitalists. The capitalists exploited the working class, the *proletariat*. Marx believed that the workers were getting poorer and poorer in the midst of plenty. He thought that the misery of the masses was increasing while the rich got even more prosperous and powerful. With the gap between the rich and the poor widening, Marx felt that the working class would then revolt.

Marx therefore advocated using violent means to overthrow the capitalistic governments of the industrialized nations. The last words of the Communist Manifesto say "The workers have nothing to lose in this (revolution) but their chains. Workers of the world, unite!"

A session of the Communist Women's Club.

were generally in favor of individual political rights such as freedom of speech, the press, and religion. The socialists believed that the capitalistic society had many faults, but that they could secure change by the democratic process.

However, not all socialists believed in peaceful, legal methods. The most influential of the radical socialists was Karl Marx (1818 to 1883). He was founder of an *ideology*, or belief system, now called communism. Marx and Friedrich Engels wrote the *Communist Manifesto* which was published in 1848. Later the volumes of *Das Kapital* (Capital), the most important books, appeared in 1867. In these books, Marx outlined the main ideas of communism.

Marx stressed the injustices found in capitalism, such as when thousands of workers lose their jobs. He thought the capitalistic system was not efficient. In addition, Marx denounced capitalism because of its emphasis on money and its bad influences on families.

Many workers in the industrial nations were attracted by the ideas of socialism. After 1864, socialists formed many political parties and unions. Socialism was especially popular in Europe. The popularity of socialism frightened many middle-class people. To prevent violence or mob action, they were willing to listen to some of the workers' demands. After the 1860s, most of the democratic nations—the United States, Great Britain, Belgium, France—allowed the unions enough power to balance the power of the large companies. In England and Germany, the conservative parties implemented popular socialistic ideas to please the workers.

Did the workers lose more than they gained with the Industrial Revolution? Conditions varied from nation to nation. The United States had an open frontier and a shortage of labor. American workers did not suffer as much as factory workers in Great Britain and Russia.

Skilled workers and white-collar workers made more gains than unskilled workers, and women's wage always lagged behind those of men. Yet even the unskilled workers could buy better and cheaper goods, such as ready-made clothing and canned goods. In 1900, most workers, while still dissatisfied with some aspects of their work, felt that they were making progress toward a better life. The major exception was among the workers in Russia.

Section Questions

1. Why did the workers want labor unions?
2. What reforms were made in Great Britain to protect the workers?
3. What do socialists believe in?

RURAL AND URBAN SOCIETIES

Pre-Industrial Rural Society	Industrial Urban Society
Home or small shops	Factory production
Little use of machines	Heavy use of machines
Little division of labor	Increased division of labor
Barter or simple money base	Extensive use of banks and credits
Local exchange of goods	National and international exchange of goods
Little interdependence	Extensive interdependence

3. Industrialism Soon Grew into Imperialism

The industrialization of Europe and the United States had a profound effect upon the way these nations viewed the nonindustrialized regions. Expansion during 1500 to 1700 was basically an attempt to extend national trade and power. Under this concept, colonies were branches of national commerce and traded only with the mother country.

After 1800, European interest in colonization began to decline. The successful revolutions in the United States and Latin America convinced many European statesmen that colonial costs greatly outweighed any projected benefits. As a result, European interference in Asia and Africa actually declined somewhat in the first half of the 1800s. Britain did expand into southern Africa and consolidated its hold on India. However, this was not done as part of a grand design. The expansion in southern Africa was primarily to check the power of the Boers. The unification of India was more by accident than design. The French movement into Algeria, too, was without specific goals. In both Britain and France, these colonial ventures were considered expensive luxuries. There were cries in the early part of the century that they should be dropped.

The New Colonialism By 1880, however, the Great Powers would be scrambling to seize as much of Africa and Asia as possible. Military and economic resources would be strained to the breaking point to gain possessions in these regions. Why would this be so? What caused Europeans to change their minds about expansion overseas?

One reason was the changing nature of patriotism and national pride. The rapid industrialization of Britain gave the British people a great deal of pride and satisfaction. The unification of Germany did the same for the Germans. As this pride grew, the desire to extend national influence followed. Putting the flag around the world gave one a greater feeling of nationalism. Thus, patriotic feelings would prove to be a strong motive for expansion abroad.

Closely allied with nationalism was the economic motive. Industrialization created a constant need for raw materials. The factories required a steady supply of raw products such as cotton, oil, rubber, coal, iron, wood, and other materials. European nations had imported most of these items from abroad. Industrialization also created a need for markets. Manufacturers needed to sell the items produced in the factories.

As international rivalries increased, nations began to put up trade barriers in the form of *tariffs*, or taxes on goods

The busy harbor of Calcutta, about 1880.

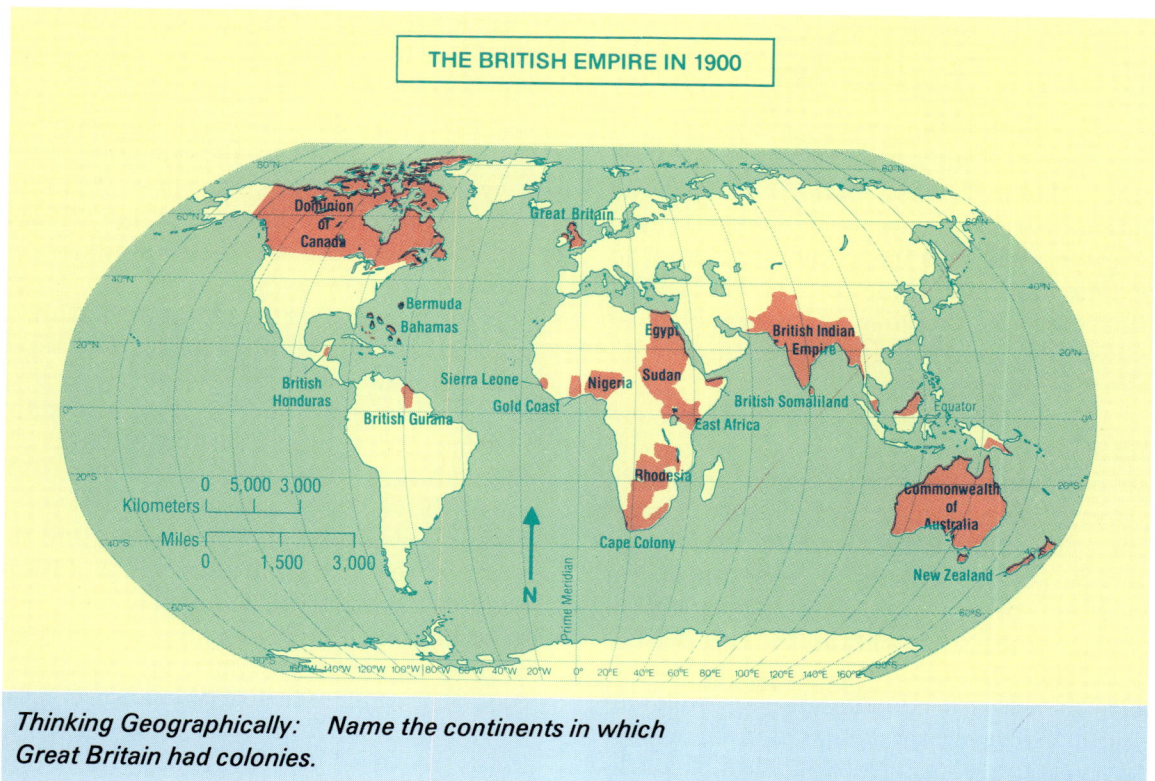

Thinking Geographically: Name the continents in which Great Britain had colonies.

imported into the country. Tariffs took much of the profit out of international trade, so the industrialists began to take a second look at colonial development. After all, the colonies traded exclusively with the mother country. Capitalists and merchants from the mother country would enjoy many privileges. Since the colonial areas were usually undeveloped, secure investments could be made and a high rate of return could be expected.

Another reason for increased colonization was the growth of Europe's population. Scientific and medical advancements in the nineteenth century increased the life expectancy and birth rate in Europe. The resulting increase in population created social and political unrest. It was felt that the acquisition of new lands overseas would give people someplace to settle, and relieve the mother country of the problems of overpopulation. The Great Powers forgot the lessons of the revolutions in the Western Hemisphere. They once again fooled themselves into believing that by settling their own nationals in these colonies they could guarantee political control of the area. This never really worked out when the scramble for colonies got underway. Nations with surplus populations, such as Britain and Germany, had to offer many inducements to get a few settlers to eventually make the trip.

Another reason for overseas expansion was the doctrine of racial superiority. The growth of European power and technology in the previous century convinced many people that there were superior races and inferior ones. This thinking, it was argued, agreed with Darwin's theory of evolution

The British poet and novelist Rudyard Kipling.

which appeared in 1859. Darwin's premise was that only the strong survive in nature and that it was only natural that the strong take from the weak. If one accepted the survival of the fittest as a matter of principle in the animal kingdom, then it was a simple matter to apply it to human beings.

Many people accepted the concept of racial superiority but could not accept the exploitation of those who lived in Asia and Africa. They viewed the superiority of the white race over the black and yellow races as incurring an obligation. They felt that whites should share their advantages with the weaker races and thereby uplift them, raising them up to their level in technology and culture. The main spokesman for this attitude was the British poet and novelist Rudyard Kipling (1865-1936). Kipling spent much of his life in British India. He was convinced the British presence in that area was a blessing to the natives. They could now experience the benefits of law and order, a higher standard of living, a longer life expectancy, and great expectations in the future. He believed that the great nations of the world were destined to share their superior culture and technology with the less fortunate, darker-skinned brothers and sisters. This he referred to as the white man's burden. Perhaps, among all the reasons for colonial development, this was the closest to being humanitarian.

Closely allied with the concept of the white man's burden were religious considerations. Missionary work had been a characteristic of Christianity since the travels of St. Paul. To many Christians, it appeared that the noblest expression of faith could be demonstrated by converting the heathens in the jungles of Africa and the deserts of Asia. Many times the missionaries preceded the flag. In some cases, the missionaries would enter an area where they faced stiff native resistance that created a danger to them. They would request military protection, thereby beginning a colonial occupation.

Another reason for the change of attitude toward colonial development was strategic or military considerations. An American naval officer, Alfred T. Mahan, wrote that the nation that controls the oceans can effectively control the world. However, a global navy needed bases and coaling stations around the world in order to be effective. Only then could shipments of raw materials to Europe and manufactured goods to the colonies be protected. An example of this policy was Britain's seizure of the Cape region during the Napoleonic wars in order to secure its trade route with India.

Dynamics of Imperialism As you read earlier, imperialism means that one nation dominates another. The domination exercised by the European powers in the late 1800s took three basic forms. Greatest control was achieved when an area was conquered by military force and settled by people from the mother country. In such areas, the government was directly under the control of the mother country. This area was called a colony. In some instances, an area might be controlled through a native chief. That ruler was often dependent on troops or weapons from the mother country to maintain power. This was called a *protectorate*. The last form of control was called a *sphere of influence*. In this case, two or more powerful nations agree to divide up a technologically backward area for the purpose of exploiting its natural resources. Often, other powers would recognize and respect a nation's sphere of influence and not interfere in such an operation. The areas involved in this age of imperialism were for the most part Africa, Asia, and the islands of the Pacific. South America, despite its lack of technology, was under the protection of the Monroe Doctrine and the British. The United States after 1880 was rapidly becoming an industrial giant and a world power, so few nations wished to challenge it.

Imperialism would have a tremendous effect on the 1900s. Even now, in the 1980s, we are still feeling the effects of the scramble for colonies in Africa and Asia a century ago. In the next two chapters, we shall see the extent of European imperialism in Africa and Asia.

Section Questions

1. What happened after 1800 to convince European leaders that colonial ventures would not be profitable?
2. Who promoted imperialism as a way of supposedly helping the darker-skinned peoples of the world?
3. Who promoted strong navies as a way of controlling other nations?
4. What do we call the exercise of control by one people or nation over another?
5. What areas of the world would be targets of European imperialism after 1850?

Chapter Summary

1. The Industrial Revolution started in Great Britain. It then spread to other nations. New and old industries expanded rapidly in growing cities. Using new machines and technology, workers now produced more goods faster and more cheaply. Men, women, and children worked long hours in poor working conditions. Improved transportation and communication brought about a rapid exchange of materials, goods, people, and ideas and made the growth of large businesses possible.
2. Workers had many problems under the factory system. To protect themselves, they joined unions. Laws were passed to improve the working conditions of the workers. Male workers got more political power by gaining the right to vote and to participate in the government. Some workers were attracted to socialism. People differ in their evaluations of the Industrial Revolution, but it appeared that many workers improved their standard of living.
3. After the New World revolutions, European interest in colonization declined. By 1880, that interest was renewed. Nationalism, industrialism, population growth, a feeling of racial superiority, religious and military considerations were the reasons for this renewed interest. Imperialism took three basic forms. In a colony, the mother country ruled directly. In a protectorate, a native ruler maintained power through the help of the mother country. In a sphere of influence case, two or more powerful nations divided up a weaker country for control of its raw materials.

Chapter 25 Review

Check Your Facts

1. Identify the following:
    a. Karl Marx
    b. James Watt
    c. Thomas Edison
    d. Eli Whitney
    e. Rudyard Kipling
    f. Samuel F.B. Morse
    g. Adam Smith
    h. Guglielmo Marconi
2. Why did the factory system replace the cottage or domestic system of production?
3. What inventions helped to increase the manufacture of cloth?
4. Which invention spurred the growing of cotton in the United States?
5. Why did the United States and other nations want to industrialize?
6. According to Marx, what were the major faults of the capitalistic system?
7. Why did Adam Smith recommend that the government not interfere with business?

Words to Know

1. Write a paragraph using the following words: *urban, factory, depression, proletariat.*
2. Explain the difference between a colony, a protectorate, and a sphere of influence.

Developing Your Skills

1. Use an encyclopedia. Find out why the following cities grew.
    a. Düsseldorf, Germany
    b. Pittsburgh, Pennsylvania
2. Place the following events in proper chronological order:
   Watt develops a successful steam engine.
   Eli Whitney invents the cotton gin.
   Alexander Graham Bell constructs a telephone.
   Adam Smith publishes *Wealth of Nations*.

Thinking It Over

1. Often it appears that inventors, working independently in different places, invent the same thing at the same time—such as the telephone. Why does this happen?
2. What is your definition of child labor? What reforms, if any, do you think are needed today?
3. Why wasn't France, the most populated nation in Europe at the time, the first nation to experience the Industrial Revolution?
4. Marx's ideas have been very influential. In what areas do you think Marx's predictions have come true? Which predictions have not come true?

Special Activities

1. What was the origin of your city or the city nearest you? How did it develop? What natural resources does the area have? What are its main advantages and problems today?
2. Check on labor union membership in the United States at the present time. What do you think is the future of unions?
3. Compare the speed of a person walking, riding a horse, a train, and a steamboat in the 1800s. How long would it take to go from London to Manchester by each way?
4. In small groups, discuss the advantages and disadvantages of a secret ballot.

This picture is from a souvenir album of the opening of the Suez Canal.

Chapter 26
The Exploitation of Africa

*I*n January of 1885, the fanatical dervishes stormed the walls of Khartoum (kar TOOM) in the Sudan. As they entered the city, they began a systematic slaughter of the Egyptian garrison. The governor of the Sudan, British General Charles Gordon, was killed. The Muslim dervishes presented his head to the religious leader of their sect, Muhammad Ahmed. For Gordon, his end was a fitting tribute to his colorful career. He had made his reputation twenty years earlier when he commanded a Chinese army against rebels fighting the Manchu dynasty. In 1882, the British took over Egypt. They were faced with the problem of what to do with the Sudan,

1811	Egypt declares independence
1822	Liberia founded
1830	French seize Algiers
1869	Suez Canal completed
1871	Stanley finds Livingstone
1884	German East Africa established
1885	Congo Free State established
1890	British arrive in Rhodesia
	French gain Madagascar
1894	French West Africa established
1895	Italians defeated by Ethiopia
1898	Fashoda incident
1899-1902	Boer War
1908	Belgian Congo established
1910	Union of South Africa

African explorer John H. Speke.

which had been occupied for a half century by Egyptian troops. It was decided that it would be better to evacuate the area rather than prop up the Egyptian army under an increasingly nationalistic leader. Charles "Chinese" Gordon was sent to Khartoum for the express purpose of overseeing the evacuation of the Egyptian troops. However, Gordon could not bear the thought of withdrawing. He announced his intention of remaining in the hopes of mustering support at home for a permanent British presence in that area. A tremendous debate took place over the desirability of moving into the Sudan. In the end, a relief expedition was sent out. It arrived at Khartoum less than three days after Gordon's death.

Gordon's death sent shock waves through Britain. Overnight, he became even more of a public hero. He was now a martyr. Patriotic artists painted glorified pictures of him standing before the motley Sudanese at the moment of his death. The nation cried to avenge his murder. In the end, Gordon received in death what he had failed to achieve in life—a permanent British presence in the Sudan. By 1900, that region was controlled by Britain as was almost forty percent of Africa. The imperialistic spirit of men such as Gordon expanded the European influence over the length and breadth of the continent.

A Dutch farmhouse in the Cape area.

1. Western Influence Expanded in Africa

During the first half of the nineteenth century, European influence began to be exerted in Africa. In this section, we shall see how this came about.

As you have read, the Portuguese began to trade with the Africans along the coast. As early as 1500, their trading posts dotted the west coast of Africa. However, the Portuguese did not establish colonies.

The Dutch in South Africa Not all Europeans came to Africa to trade and then leave the continent. Dutch settlers arrived at the southern tip of Africa in 1652 to make a permanent home in this region. They settled around what is now known as Cape Town, because the climate there was somewhat like the climate of Europe. The settlement was financed by the Dutch East India Company.

These Dutch settlers were a hearty Protestant people who followed the teachings of the Calvinist Dutch Reform Church. Fundamentalist in outlook, they had a strict moral code and believed in hard work. They felt that God had granted them this land to develop. They utilized all its resources, including the native Bantu, whom they often enslaved.

The fiercely independent settlers soon began to expand northward. By 1760, they had reached as far north as the Orange River. This northern movement led to wars with the Bantu who lived in the region. The difficulties were intensified because the Dutch felt that the Bantu were the Biblical "sons of Ham" and were thus appointed by God to be their slaves.

The Boers and the British Within several generations, the Dutch settlers no longer called themselves Dutch but Boer (BORE) or Afrikaner (af ri KAHN er). The latter name signified that while they remained culturally European, they considered their homeland to be in Africa. The Dutch East India Company rule ended in 1795. Two small Boer republics were then established in southern Africa.

During the Napoleonic Wars, the British seized the Cape area because of its strategic location. Control of the Cape was vital in maintaining contact with India. After the fall of Napoleon, the Cape area was recognized as a British possession at the Congress of Vienna in 1815.

The British and the Boers did not get along. The Boer policy of enslaving the Bantu conflicted with the gathering momentum in Britain to end the slave trade. Moreover, the British wanted peace in south-

Boers on the Great Trek.

ern Africa. They saw that peace was not possible so long as the Boers continued to take Bantu land. The Boers resented this British interference in their lives. They felt that they lived their lives according to the Bible. Therefore, compromise would be moral treason.

By 1830, the English language and judicial system had replaced Dutch in the running of the colony. When slavery was abolished throughout the British Empire in 1833, the Boers decided that they had to escape from this continuous interference. In 1835, they began migrating northward into the interior of the continent. The Great Trek, as it was called, included over ten thousand settlers over a two-year period. Traveling in their ox-drawn wagons, they moved boldly into lands that they really did not know. As they proceeded farther and farther north, they came in conflict with the Zulu (ZOO loo) tribes, the Bantu-speaking people of Natal (nu TAL). A fierce struggle ensued. The Zulu Wars lasted several years. At the decisive battle of the Blood River in 1838, Boer guns defeated Zulu spears. The Zulus continued to raid Boer settlements and threaten their security, but the Boers were there to stay. Eventually, the Boers established two small, independent states in the interior. The Transvaal (tranz VAWL) was established in 1852. The Orange Free State was established in 1854.

In 1843, the British had annexed Natal on the southeast coast of Africa. They hoped that this move would keep the Boer settlements isolated and land locked. The British recognized the independence of the Boer states in 1854, but they still tried to keep control over this area, especially in the field of foreign affairs. The British maintained that the right to such control was based on their authority as the trustee of South Africa. The Boers rejected this claim. The conflict and competition that followed intensified as the Boers held tightly to their independence.

The French taking Algiers.

The French in Algeria While the British and the Dutch were busy in the south, the French began to set up permanent settlements in North Africa. Muslim pirates operating out of Algeria (al JEER ee uh) and Tripoli (TRIP o lee) had been harassing European shipping since the Middle Ages. However, after 1800, strong reactions set in against this harassment. From 1804 to 1815, the young republic of the United States carried on a successful naval campaign against these pirates. This campaign eventually guaranteed the safe passage of American shipping in the Mediterranean.

In 1827, when the Algerian ruler insulted the French consul publicly, the French went to war. They invaded Algeria in 1830 with a large army. After a long and costly guerrilla war against the fierce Berber tribesmen in the interior, the French gained control of most of Algeria by 1847. French colonists were encouraged to immigrate to the Mediterranean coastal region. Most of these settlers were wine growers who planted vineyards along the Mediterranean. Others settled in Algerian cities. Despite the presence of a large French army, the Berbers still roamed at will in the interior.

Thus, in 1850, there were few European settlements in Africa. The settlements were restricted to the French colonists in Algeria to the north, British and Dutch settlers in Cape Colony, the Orange Free State and the Transvaal to the south, and a few Portuguese settlements along the eastern coast. For the most part, these settlements were not self-sufficient and did not generate any profit for the mother countries.

Section Questions

1. What were the Dutch settlers in South Africa called? What did the name signify?
2. List the areas of Africa settled by Europeans as of 1850. Identify the peoples who settled each area.

2. The British Took Over from the Cape to Cairo

Prior to 1850, the British in Africa were restricted to the Cape Colony in the south and Natal, Sierra Leone, and Gambia along the Gold Coast in the west. By 1900, British control would extend over almost forty percent of the continent and almost sixty percent of the population. They were able to expand so rapidly because they, alone among the Great Powers, had the resources to move rapidly overseas once the scramble began. They had the largest navy in the world, the financial means to invest in new ventures, and the most experience in dealing with non-western people.

British Exploration For Europeans, the big problem with Africa was that they knew nothing about it. By mid-century, a host of Europeans were moving into the hitherto unexplored interior. Probably the most famous explorer was Dr. David Livingstone (1813-1873).

Livingstone went to Africa in 1840 as a medical missionary to Cape Colony. After several years spent primarily as a missionary, he decided to explore the interior of the continent. His motives were purely Victorian, a mixture of scientific curiosity and a deep-seated desire to help the Africans. Despite the British ban on the slave trade, Arab traders from the East African coast continually made raids into the interior. He felt that these raids must be stopped. He reasoned that only a strong British presence coupled with a Christian missionary movement could achieve this.

Dr. David Livingstone freeing slaves from a yoke.

Livingstone made several trips into the interior of the continent. Wherever he went, he recorded what he saw. His reports had a romantic appeal. They became very popular in Britain and the United States. During 1851-1856, he crossed the continent from east to west, along the Zambezi (zam BEE zee) River. It was here that he witnessed the Arab slave trade. His vivid accounts of their atrocities shocked the British. They demanded that something be done. As a result, the British increased pressure on the Sultan of Zanzibar to abolish the slave trade. This began the British presence on the east coast of the continent.

The accounts written by Livingstone spurred other explorations. In 1858, John H. Speke and Sir Richard Burton discovered Lake Tanganyika. They were the first Europeans to reach the lake. Speke also sighted Lake Victoria, the main source of the Nile River.

In 1865, Dr. Livingstone set out to find the source of the Congo River. For the next

This drawing shows prospectors on the way to the Transvaal gold fields.

Southern Africa Britain's influence in southern Africa expanded rapidly. As you read earlier, Britain had gained Cape Colony and Natal. The Boer republics, the Orange Free State and the Transvaal, were north and west of Cape Colony and Natal. An uneasy truce existed between the British and the Boers.

In 1867, diamonds were discovered on the Orange River. When the word got out, the rush was on. By 1870, thousands of miners and prospectors from Britain, Australia, and the United States had moved in to seek their fortune. In 1871, the town of Kimberly was founded. It quickly became the second largest community in South Africa. Railway construction mushroomed. Telegraph lines, bridges, and roads followed. The mining area was claimed by both the Boers and the British. The British prevailed, and the area became a part of the Cape Colony.

Eventually, the easy diggings came to an end. Large mining companies then dominated the area around Kimberly. However, the rush was not over. In 1884, gold was discovered and the entire mad procedure began again. The center of the strike was around the town of Johannesburg (jo HAHN us burg), some 96 kilometers (60 miles) south of Pretoria. The gold was deep in the ground. Capital and a high degree of technical knowledge were needed to reach it. This did not deter the miners who flocked to Johannesburg. There were large amounts of cheap coal in the area to power mining machinery.

The Boers resented this migration of miners, whom they contemptuously called *uitlanders* or outsiders. There were soon more uitlanders than Boers in the South African Republic. The highly religious Boers resented what they saw as the uitlanders' greed and sinfulness. The great contrast between the two groups could be seen in the life-styles of the cities of Pretoria and Johannesburg. Pretoria was the capital of a sleepy rural republic. Its inhabitants spoke Afrikaans, the Dutch-Boer language, and tried to live according to God's law and the Bible. In marked contrast, Johannesburg, predominantly British, possessed all the trappings of a boomtown. Saloons, prostitution, gambling, and violence flourished.

The Boers were in the minority in their own country. However, they dominated the government by a law that required a fourteen year residence before one could vote. The miners were a highly transient lot, so very few of them would fulfill this residency requirement. It was almost impossible to rule Johannesburg from Pretoria, but the Boers kept trying. This angered the uitlanders. More and more they demanded a say in running the country.

Cecil Rhodes This aggravation between the British mining interests and the Boers was intensified by the presence of Cecil Rhodes (1853-1902). Rhodes arrived in Cape Colony during the diamond rush of 1870. He made a fortune by astute business deals. By 1890, he was one of the wealthiest persons in the area. He used his fortune to expand British influence. He had a consuming faith in the superiority of the British people. He envisioned a world united under the benevolent protection of the British crown. For Africa, he dreamed of a British corridor of influence 8,000 kilometers (5,000 miles) long. This corridor would extend from the Cape through Central Africa, Uganda, the Sudan, and all the way to Egypt. He wanted a British railway through it, the Cape to Cairo railroad. Rhodes realized that one obstacle to his dream was the Boer republics. Therefore, he sought to neutralize them.

In 1889, he gained a charter to open settlement in a huge tract of land north of

Cecil Rhodes.

the South African Republic and west of Portuguese East Africa. The purpose was to surround the Boers with British settlers. The Boers could then become a part of a Greater British South Africa. In 1890, Rhodes began to place miners and settlers in that region which came to be known as Rhodesia (row DEE zhuh). A capital was set up south of the Zambezi River. It was called Salisbury (SOLZ berry), after Robert Cecil Salisbury, the British Prime Minister who supported Rhodes's proposal.

In 1890, Rhodes became Prime Minister of the Cape Colony. He began to negotiate with the Boer president of the South African Republic, Paul Kruger (KROO ger). He tried to get Kruger to unite with the Cape Colony. He could not persuade Kruger to do so. He then tried to engineer a revolt of the uitlands living in the South African Republic. Once the revolt started, one of Rhodes's lieutenants, Dr. Leander Starr Jameson, was to lead an armed force into the republic to "restore order." However, the Boers had received advanced notice of this plan. They prevented the rebellion and captured Jameson. The political embarrassment of the Jameson Raid forced Rhodes to resign.

British infantry on the march in the Boer War.

The Boer War The uproar over the Jameson Raid was aggravated by the disclosure of the Kruger Telegram. The telegram was from Kaiser William II of Germany. The Kaiser congratulated President Kruger for successfully stopping the invasion. This greatly irritated the British. They saw a friendship beginning between the ambitious Germans and the Dutch-speaking Boers. Kruger sent his Foreign Minister to Berlin to confer with the Kaiser. The British feared the worst.

The British began to send troops into South Africa and to make stiff demands. In 1899, Kruger's South African Republic declared war on the British Empire. The Orange Free State soon followed. The result was the Boer War, which lasted from 1899 to 1902.

The war was an embarrassment to Britain. The greatly outnumbered and outgunned Boers actually took the offensive. In the opening months of the war, they nearly took Kimberly. Superior British forces finally drove them back. After many casualties, the British took Johannesburg and Pretoria in 1900. The Boers then reverted to a protracted guerrilla war against the British commander, Herbert Kitchener, the veteran of the Fashoda incident. Kitchener required over 300,000 troops and two years time to defeat the Boers. British use of concentration camps for Boer civilians gave the British a bad image. Their failure to secure a quick victory raised questions about their military effectiveness.

The peace terms gave the Boers money to rebuild, limited self-government, and the right to speak both English and Dutch in schools and courts. In 1908, the two Boer states, Cape Colony, and Natal were brought together under a single federation. The federation was approved by the British Parliament in 1910. The area was called the Union of South Africa. In the spirit of compromise, the legislative branch of the government was established in Capetown. The executive branch, the actual seat of government, was in Pretoria. The British and the Boers had taken their struggle over South Africa from the battlefield to the ballot box. During this time they were outnumbered by more than four to one by the native black Africans. No one had asked the native Africans what they wanted nor were their rights ever defined. The seeds of the current discontent in South Africa had been sown. By 1910, the British presence in Africa spread over more than 3,200,000 square kilometers (2,000,000 square miles). In many places they instituted a policy of *indirect rule*. That is, some attempt was made to preserve the traditional structure of African society. Basically, they used native auxiliary troops and native leaders to run the country. Of course, there was always an Englishman at the head of the colony. However, the use of African customs avoided much disruption and unrest. As a result, the British colonies in Africa remained remarkably stable until the mid-twentieth century.

Section Questions

1. How did David Livingstone encourage British interest in Africa?
2. Why was the Suez Canal vital to British national security?
3. Contrast the life-styles found in Johannesburg and Pretoria in the late 1800s.
4. What was the Union of South Africa?
5. What was the British policy of "indirect rule"?

3. The French and Belgians Occupied Much of Africa

The French presence in Africa began in 1830 when they seized Algiers. Revolts in the interior forced them to move deeper and deeper into the region. The French government did not want to use the French army in the frustrating and difficult rebel battles. Instead, in 1831, it organized a special mercenary army called the Foreign Legion.

The French in West Africa By 1870, the French had gained control over the central part of Algeria. Meanwhile, from 1854 to 1865, French interest on the west coast of Africa increased. Colonel Louis Faidherbe (fe DERB) was governor of Senegal. He hoped to link the upper Senegal with the upper Niger. From the Ivory Coast and Dahomey, the French expanded northward into the interior of the continent. The African peoples in the western Sudan were for the most part divided and fighting among themselves. Therefore, the French were able to move against them one at a time. After the disastrous Franco-Prussian War in 1870, these imperialistic ventures became more popular at home. They were seen as a means of spreading French culture and of building French power for the inevitable showdown with Germany.

During this time, the British expanded their holdings around the Niger River into the colony of Nigeria. However, with a few minor exceptions, most of West Africa was securely in French hands.

In 1881, the French seized Tunisia on the Mediterranean coast. The French claimed the Tunisians had failed to pay the interest on loans and Tunisian tribesmen were making raids in Algeria. From Tunisia, the French began to aspire to control the Anglo-Egyptian Sudan from the Atlantic Ocean to the Red Sea. This dream lasted until the withdrawal from Fashoda.

Did You Know?

The French Foreign Legion in Africa.

The French Foreign Legion

The French Foreign Legion is a mercenary military corps. It is manned primarily by non-French volunteers under the command of French officers. The mercenary aspect of the Legion gives it the romantic appeal it has known for years. The Legion promises an individual that it will keep his past a secret. Thus, for more than a century it has been a haven for criminals, men without countries, victims of broken love affairs, and people generally trying to forget the past. It does offer a new life because those Legionnaires who complete a satisfactory first enlistment will be granted French citizenship.

King Louis Philippe founded the French Foreign Legion in 1831 to man French ventures overseas. In the beginning, the Legion served in the long Algerian wars. However, as French imperialist ambitions expanded, so did the role of the Legion. The Legion served in most French territory in Africa, Mexico, and Indo-China.

Legion campaigns in North Africa spanned more than a century. Incredibly, during most of that time the uniform of the Legion was greatcoats. Not until the twentieth century were uniform requirements modified to fit the climate and terrain. The most striking characteristic of the Foreign Legion uniform is the white cap cover.

Despite the mercenary character of the Legion, it was a well-disciplined organization that amassed an outstanding combat record in the past century and a half. It served France's dreams of imperialism well. Because of it, native-born French citizens were not required to fight and die in far-off places.

Troops escorting the French consul home in Tananarive, Madagascar.

Other French Holdings During 1875 to 1878, Pierre de Brazza (BRAT za) led a French expedition into the Congo region of equatorial Africa. The French then claimed much of the area north of the Congo River. Brazza organized a protectorate called French Equatorial Africa. The French thus prevented the growth of the British colony of Nigeria and the German colony of the Cameroons (KAM uh roonz).

By 1894, the French had moved up from the Ivory Coast and Dahomey to join hands with their counterparts moving down from Algeria. They proclaimed the entire area to be French West Africa. The French empire in northwest Africa, French West Africa, and French Equatorial Africa was the largest single European block of territory on the continent. Starting on the Mediterranean coast to the north, it extended south through the Sahara Desert and the Sudan to the coast and around to the Congo River. As you read earlier, they also had a small holding along the Red Sea coast, French Somaliland.

Off the east coast of Africa was the large island of Madagascar (mad uh GAS ker). The French had maintained an interest in the island since the early 1800s. They began to get involved in its internal affairs around 1870. When the French government declared a protectorate over the island in 1883, war broke out with the native government. By the terms of the settlement in 1885, France ran the island. A violent revolution broke out when Madagascar was proclaimed a French colony in 1896, but it was put down by force.

German traders in German East Africa.

The Congo Free State The king of Belgium, Leopold II, also decided to become involved in empire building. Despite the small size and limited resources of his nation, he shrewdly managed to gain his ends. In 1876, Leopold organized the International Association for the Exploration and Civilization of Central Africa. On the surface, this was an international and humanitarian organization financed from the personal fortune of Leopold. Leopold, acting for the Association, commissioned Stanley to explore the Congo basin, starting at the mouth of the Congo River on the west coast. As Stanley traveled through the Congo, he persuaded the local rulers to sign treaties that, in effect, ceded their land to the Association. When Stanley finally returned, Leopold laid claim to the entire Congo basin in the name of the Association.

Many nations questioned the right of a private corporation to hold such a valuable piece of real estate. Since many other questions of legitimacy and boundaries had cropped up, the Great Powers met in the Berlin Conference in 1885. At the conference, Leopold skillfully played one statesman against another. He promised that all manner of humanitarian and progressive policies would be followed if his Association was allowed sovereignty in the Congo. The Great Powers saw Leopold as the least threatening to them. As a result, the Conference set up the Congo Free State under the nominal control of the Association. All of the Great Powers, including the United States, recognized the Congo Free State.

The recognition of the Congo Free State was a personal triumph for Leopold. Once he was in control, the humanitarian goals of the Association were quickly dropped. What many consider to be the worst exploitation of any African nation followed. Rubber and ivory were the desired products. The natives were quickly forced into labor camps to secure these items for their new masters. Under Leopold's direction, the Congo was ruled with an eye only toward business efficiency. Thus, the unfortunate inhabitants of this region suffered some of the worst abuses of imperialism. In 1908, by an act of the Belgian Parliament, the Congo Free States was annexed to Belgium and renamed the Belgian Congo. It was administered as a colony and many of the worst abuses suffered by the natives ended. However, during Leopold's twenty years of exploitation, he managed to increase his personal fortune several times over.

Government Policies The French and the Belgians instituted a policy of *direct rule*. This meant that French and Belgian colonial administrators usually governed directly, with few native leaders. Often, this meant overturning local language and customs and teaching the native population either French or Belgian. This method of colonial rule required a high ratio of colonial officials to the African population. With the British use of indirect rule, there was approximately one British administrator for every hundred thousand Africans in Nigeria. There was more than one French administrator for every five thousand Africans in French West Africa.

In comparing the policies of direct and indirect rule, it should not be assumed that the British indirect rule was always more humane. Often, the native rulers employed by the British ruled as harshly as any European overlord. The saving difference in the British system is that it allowed a native core to rule while learning western ways. Thus, when independence came to Africa in the twentieth century, these leaders were able to step in and run their country from experience.

Section Questions

1. How did the French defeat in the Franco-Prussian War encourage French imperialistic ventures in Africa?
2. What areas of Africa did the French seize in the late 1800s?
3. In what area of Africa did some of the worst European exploitation take place?
4. Who eventually took over the Congo Free State in 1908?
5. What was the policy of "direct rule"?

4. The Exploitation of Africa Was Completed

The lion's share of Africa went to the ambitious British and French. By 1900, these two powers had laid claim to 19,425,000 square kilometers (7,500,000 square miles) of the continent—from a total of little more than 28,490,000 square kilometers (11,000,000 square miles)—with a population of 60 million people. The rest of the continent was divided among other European powers. We have already seen how the Belgians managed to get their foot in the door. In this section, we shall see how the Germans, Portuguese, Italians, and Spanish secured parts of the continent for themselves.

The Germans in Africa German expansion in Africa began rather late. From 1850 to 1880, Germany's main concern was in creating a united Germany on the European continent. Bismarck was preoccupied with bringing the independent German states under his control and neutralizing France. Once this task was completed, he, too, became converted to the belief in overseas expansion and development. After all, if German rivals saw overseas expansion as a means of achieving greatness, how could Germany afford not to do the same?

German expansion in Africa began in 1882. A German merchant, Franz Luderitz (LOOD uh rutz), purchased large tracts of land on the west African coast between the Orange River and the Portuguese colony of Angola. The British saw this move as a threat to their Cape Colony. Bismarck formally declared a protectorate over this region in 1884, calling it German Southwest Africa. The British saw nothing but trouble in this move. The area was made up mostly of the Kalahari Desert and promised little economic return for the cost of occupation. Moreover, the British feared that the Germans would make direct contact with the Boer republics, thereby interfering with British expansion northward. These fears were not entirely groundless. The Dutch background of the Boers gave them an ethnic kindred with the Germans.

Southwest Africa was not the only place where the Germans were busy. In 1884, Gustav Nachtigal (nakh ti gall), a German explorer, proclaimed a protectorate over Togoland, adjacent to the British Gold Coast. He also proclaimed a protectorate over the Cameroons, located on the west coast north of the Congo River. However, German expansion from these points was restricted by French West Africa to the north and French Equatorial Africa to the east.

The greatest German successes in Africa came on the east coast. Much of this success can be attributed to the greatest of the German explorers, Karl Peters. In 1884, he signed a series of treaties with African rulers along the coast west of Zanzibar, between Mozambique and British East Africa. The following year, Kaiser William II set up the German East Africa Company. It went in to organize the territory. The Sultan of Zanzibar was quick to recognize German control over the area. When the German East Africa Company went bankrupt the following year, control passed directly to the German government. Peters was declared governor of German East Africa. The actual boundaries were negotiated in 1890.

German East Africa, later called Tanganyika, was the central jewel in the German African empire. However, discontent among the natives caused the Germans serious problems. Peters felt that the cheapest way to run the colony would be to employ the coastal Arabs as field agents. The Arabs felt little loyalty or obligation to the Germans and often misused their power. The Germans reserved themselves much of the better land. The native Bantu were displaced and often conscripted to work on public projects. German East Africa was ruled with brutality and an iron hand until a rebellion in 1905. This uprising led to a reform of some of the worst practices.

By 1900, Germany had over 2,590,000 square kilometers (a million square miles) of Africa. However, the territories were scattered. For the most part they cost more to maintain than they produced. They failed to attract significant numbers of German settlers. Only German East Africa, a fertile high plateau, attracted European settlement and showed profit. Even there, success was marred by Bantu uprisings.

The Portuguese The Portuguese did little to capitalize on their historic claims. Portuguese settlements were located on the west coast south of the Congo (Portuguese West Africa or Angola), on the east coast south of German East Africa (Portuguese East Africa or Mozambique), and on the Guinea coast in Portuguese Guinea. These settlements were four centuries old by 1850, but Portuguese authority was restricted to the coast. They had never seriously asserted control in the interior.

When the Great Powers began to make claims north of these Portuguese territories, the Portuguese claimed that the territories were theirs. However, they had no influence in these regions. Their claims were ignored by the Great Powers and eventually dropped by the Portuguese. The Portuguese dreamed briefly of expanding Angola and Mozambique into the interior until they met to create a Portuguese band across southern Africa. However, Cecil Rhodes effectively prevented this by creating the state of Rhodesia.

Angola and Mozambique had not changed much under Portuguese colonial rule. Both colonies had been founded to export slaves. They continued to do so until European outcries forced them to either shut down or become more secretive. Eventually, agricultural and forest products replaced slaves as the source of economic activity. Still, over the centuries, there was little increase in productivity in the colonies. Portuguese attempts to colonize the areas were dismal failures. With the exception of the colonial administrators and some social renegades, few Portuguese came. Exploitation of the natives was very harsh. It continued until the wars of liberation in the 1970s.

The Italians Italian gains in Africa were very modest. For years, they hoped to move into Tunisia. However, their failure to move quickly allowed the French to take over in 1881. They then turned to east Africa. In 1882, the Italians seized Assab on the Red Sea. This would later become the colony of Eritrea (er uh TREE uh). In 1889, they secured the strategic region called the Horn of Africa at the mouth of the Red Sea. This became known as the

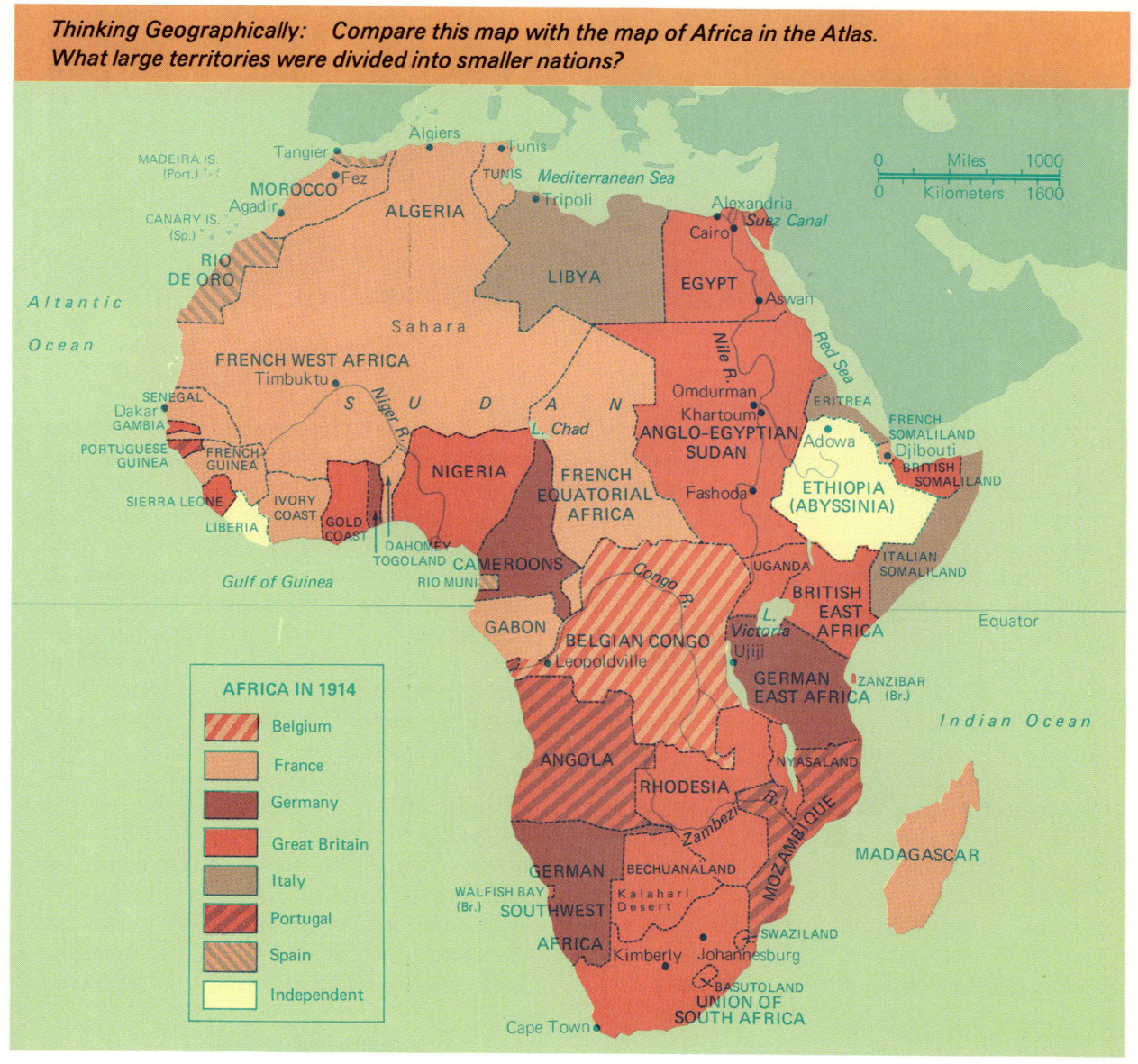

Thinking Geographically: Compare this map with the map of Africa in the Atlas. What large territories were divided into smaller nations?

Slave labor in Brazil.

Italian Somaliland. From these points, they proposed to move south and west into the interior. This pitted them against the independent kingdom of Ethiopia (ee thee O pee uh).

In 1891, the Italians secured recognition of their interests in Ethiopia from the British. This all but guaranteed the area as theirs for the taking. As Italian forces advanced in 1895, the Ethiopian ruler, Menelik (MEN e lik) II, declared war on Italy. The Ethiopians defeated an Italian army of more than 20,000 men at the Battle of Adua (AW doo wa) in 1896. This was one of the worst colonial defeats in modern history. The Italians negotiated a peace settlement that very year. They recognized Ethiopian independence and promised to restrict themselves to the coastal possessions they now occupied.

This Ethiopian victory against a European power astonished the world. More important, it assured the independence of Ethiopia. However, the Italians would long remember the humiliation they had suffered.

Italian expansion in Africa reached its height in 1911. The Italians took advantage of the weakness of the Ottoman Empire to move into Tripoli on the Mediterranean coast between Tunisia and Egypt. This would eventually become the Italian colony of Libya (LIB ee uh).

The Spanish Spain had control of Rio de Oro (REE o da O ro) on the northwest coast. It also had a burning desire to interfere in Morocco. However, France also wanted control of Morocco and was in an excellent position to get it because the French controlled Algeria. In 1912, Morocco was declared a French protectorate when the sultan agreed to a French military presence. The French Foreign Legion moved in. In the spirit of appeasement, a Spanish zone was set aside in Morocco.

The Independent States By 1914, almost all of Africa was under European domination. The only exceptions were the independent states of Ethiopia and Liberia.

Ethiopia is located in a mountainous region between the Nile River and the Horn area on the mouth of the Red Sea. The Ethiopians were primarily Christian. They had resisted invaders since the growth of Islam in the 600s. Their victory over the Italians in 1896 assured their independence from European domination.

Liberia (li BER i a), on the west coast, was founded as a refuge for freed American slaves in 1822. In 1847, it became the first independent African republic. Its constitution was remarkably similar to that of the United States. The United States helped Liberia retain its independence.

The European Influence Today, the European exploitation of Africa is generally viewed as a negative experience. There is much to support that view. The peoples of Africa were horribly abused during this period of European occupation. The excesses practiced in the Congo Free State can be pointed out as one of the worst examples of imperialist policies.

When carving out their colonies, the Great Powers often drew up artificial boundaries based on convenience and compromise. Not once was the ethnic composition of the people considered. This lack of consideration has caused much turmoil in modern Africa. The independent states that emerged from such colonies have many incompatible minorities, each seeking autonomy or independence. Therefore, we are still reaping the fruits of this nineteenth century exploitation.

President Roberts of the Republic of Liberia.

However, the Great Powers did end the slave trade which had drained the continent since the sixteenth century. They also created a measure of political stability by ending tribal wars. Roads, telegraph systems, and railroads were built. Industry was introduced. Many native Africans received a formal education, some in European universities. Western medicine was introduced and life spans were increased.

For better or worse, imperialism brought Africa into the highly technological twentieth century and made it a part of the world community.

Section Questions

1. What two European nations seized most of Africa in the late nineteenth century?
2. Why was Germany so late in getting started in the race for territories in Africa?
3. What areas of Africa did Germany take over?
4. Why did Spain fail to take control of Morocco in northwest Africa?
5. By 1914, what were the only two states in Africa free of European domination?

Chapter Summary

1. The first Europeans in Africa set up trading posts along the coasts. The slave trade was a major reason for such posts. In 1652, the Dutch came to the southern tip of Africa to establish homes. The Dutch farmers, called Boers, enslaved many of the Bantu people, causing wars. The British won the area in 1815. They disagreed with slave-holding and wanted peace in the area. To escape the British, the Boers moved north. After defeating the Zulu people, they established two Boer republics, Transvaal and the Orange Free State. The British recognized their independence but tried to maintain some control over the area.

The French gained control of most of Algeria by 1847. Thus by 1850, there were French settlements in North Africa, British and Dutch settlements to the south, and Portuguese settlements on each coast.

2. Dr. David Livingstone explored much of the interior of Africa from 1840 through 1873. His writings aroused the British against the slave trade and spurred further explorations. In equatorial Africa, the British established protectorates in Kenya, Uganda, and Nigeria. Meanwhile, Egypt had gotten deeply into debt and the British became the largest shareholders in the Suez Canal Company. By 1883, Britain had a large voice in Egyptian affairs. The French and British came close to war over Sudan, but the French withdrew, leaving Britain in control of much of northern Africa.

Diamonds and gold were discovered in southern Africa in 1867 and 1884. As outsiders flocked to the region, tension between the British and the Boers increased steadily until the Boer War broke out (1899-1902). After the British won the war, the Union of South Africa was established with limited self-government. The British used indirect rule for most of its African colonies.

3. The French presence in Africa began in 1830 when they moved into Algeria. They acquired Tunisia in 1881. The French moved into equatorial Africa in the 1870s. By 1894, they had moved up from the Ivory Coast and Dahomey to join Algeria, forming French West Africa. Thus by 1900, French West Africa and French Equatorial Africa made up the single largest European block of territory in Africa. They also held French Somaliland and the island of Madagascar.

King Leopold of Belgium maneuvered the Great Powers into putting the Congo Free State under his control in 1885. Because the natives were badly abused under Leopold's control, the Belgian government took over the Congo Free State in 1908, renaming it the Belgian Congo. Both France and Belgium ruled their colonies directly.

4. German expansion in Africa began in 1882, with the purchase of German Southwest Africa. In 1884, they established protectorates over Togoland and the Cameroons. In 1885, they established the German East Africa Company, which later became the German protectorate of Tanganyika. The Portuguese had 400-year-old settlements on the west coast, and the east coast, and Portuguese Guinea. However, they did nothing to expand these territories. The Italians won Eritrea and Italian Somaliland on the Red Sea. They tried to take Ethiopia, but were defeated in 1896. In 1911, they took Tripoli, which became the colony of Libya.

Spain controlled Rio de Oro and a Spanish zone in Morocco. Only two African countries were free of European domination by 1900. Liberia was founded as a refuge for freed American slaves. Ethiopia remained free by defeating Italy.

The European influence in Africa led to mistreatment of the native Africans and artificial boundaries which created tension among ethnic groups. It also led to reduced warfare, the introduction of industry, and longer life spans.

Chapter 26 Review

Check Your Facts
1. Identify each of the following:
   a. Fashoda incident
   b. Pretoria
   c. Jameson Raid
   d. Kruger telegram
   e. Foreign Legion
   f. Congo Free State
   g. Madhi
2. List three British explorers and the regions they discovered in Africa during 1840-1880.
3. List the events leading up to the British take-over of Egypt and the Suez Canal in 1882.
4. Why did Cecil Rhodes want the British to seize the Boer republics?
5. How did the Boer War prove to be an embarrassment to the British?
6. Why were Ethiopia and Liberia free of European domination in the nineteenth century?
7. List the positive and negative results of nineteenth century European imperialism in Africa.

Words To Know
Explain briefly the meaning of each word or phrase below.
   a. khedive
   b. uitlanders
   c. indirect rule
   d. direct rule

Developing Your Skills
1. Use the map in the Atlas. Identify the nation or territory in which each of the following is located.
   a. Lake Tanganyika
   b. Lake Victoria
   c. Khartoum
   d. Suez Canal
   e. Cape Town
   f. Johannesburg
   g. Tripoli
   h. Algiers
2. Pick three dates from the time line in this chapter. For each date, tell what was happening in Europe at about the same time. (See Chapters 24 and 25.)

Thinking It Over
1. The British were clear winners of European expansion in Africa in terms of land and valuable possessions. Why was this so? List reasons that would explain the British success in seizing African territory.
2. List the advantages or disadvantages of direct and indirect rule.

Special Activities
1. Write a report on the actual construction of the Suez Canal.
2. Read Rudyard Kipling's poem, "The White Man's Burden." State whether or not the poem would be considered racist today.

Admiral Tojo and his officers.

Chapter 27
The Exploitation of the East

It was the morning of 27 May 1905. Admiral Heihachiro Togo, commander of the Imperial Japanese fleet, was informed that the first Russian ships had been sighted. He immediately gave the call to general quarters. He watched confidently from the bridge of his flagship as the formation moved out to meet the invader. The Russian fleet had come halfway around the world, from the Baltic Sea via the Cape of Good Hope, to engage the upstart Japanese.

The Russians and Japanese had been at war for a year. The Japanese were winning. Both sides suspected that the battle with the Russian Baltic fleet would determine the final outcome of the war.

1728-1914

1728-1741	Bering explorations
1778	Cook reaches Hawaiian Islands
1788	First settlers in Australia
1839-1842	Opium War
1857-1858	Sepoy Mutiny
1894-1895	Sino-Japanese War
1895	French secure Indo-China
1898	Spanish-American War
1899-1901	Philippine Rebellion
1900	Boxer Rebellion
1901	Australia becomes a Commonwealth
1903	Trans-Siberian railroad completed
1904-1905	Russo-Japanese War
1912	China becomes a republic
1914	Panama Canal opened

Muslims at prayer in northern Caucasus.

The engagement between the two navies began in the afternoon off Tsushima (TSOO shi mah) Island. The Russian moves were just what Togo expected. His fleet had superior speed and firepower. It went to work with deadly accuracy. When dark came, the crippled Russian fleet tried to escape north of Vladivostok, but was harassed by Togo's torpedo boats and destroyers. The following morning, Togo closed in for the kill. He wiped out the remainder of the fleet.

The victory of Orientals over Europeans stunned the world. This was not a guerrilla operation but a highly technological naval engagement. How could such a thing happen? How could the Japanese become an imperialist nation? In this chapter, we shall look at the exploitation of Asia and the Pacific, including some dramatic twists and turns that shook the European world.

1. The Russians Moved into Siberia and Central Asia

In many ways, the story of European imperialism in Asia is remarkably similar to that of imperialism in Africa. However, there were also fundamental differences between the two. For one thing, the list of players changed. Britain, France, and Germany were involved as direct participants. However, Portugal and Belgium were not. And then, there were some new players, Russia and Japan.

Russian Expansion The history of the United States is one of westward movement. The history of Russia is one of eastern expansion and a search for an ice-free port. The Ural (YUR ul) Mountains are considered the division between Europe and Asia. The first Russian movement east of the Urals came in 1581, spurred by the fur trapping industry. Once across the Urals, the Russians were in the vast expanse of Siberia, which extended 3,200 kilometers (2,000 miles) to the Pacific. They moved rapidly across Siberia and founded the settlement of Okhotsk (o KAWTSK) on the Pacific coast in 1649.

In 1725, Czar Peter the Great had dispatched Vitus Bering, a Dane, to explore the coastal region of northeastern Siberia. Bering made a series of voyages lasting thirteen years, from 1728 to 1741. He discovered the Bering Strait, which separates Siberia from North America, and explored parts of the Alaskan coast. As a result of these voyages, the Russians laid claim to the Kamchatka (kam CHAT kuh) Peninsula in 1732 and to Alaska in 1741. In Alaska, the Russian-American Fur Company, chartered in 1799, had a virtual monopoly. By 1820, Russian claims on North America extended as far south as Oregon.

In this rapid expansion, the Russians clashed early with the Chinese empire. The first conflict occurred in 1689. China was under the control of the powerful Manchu dynasty. They forced the Russian settlers to withdraw from the Amur (ah MOOR) region.

By the 1800s, Russia had become one of the Great Powers. The Manchus had declined. Thus, the Russians felt confident in moving against their old adversary. Taking advantage of the confusion caused by the great Taiping Rebellion, the Russians annexed the Amur region during 1858 to 1860. They founded the port of Vladivostok (vlad uh vuh STAWK) on the Pacific. From here they were in an excellent position

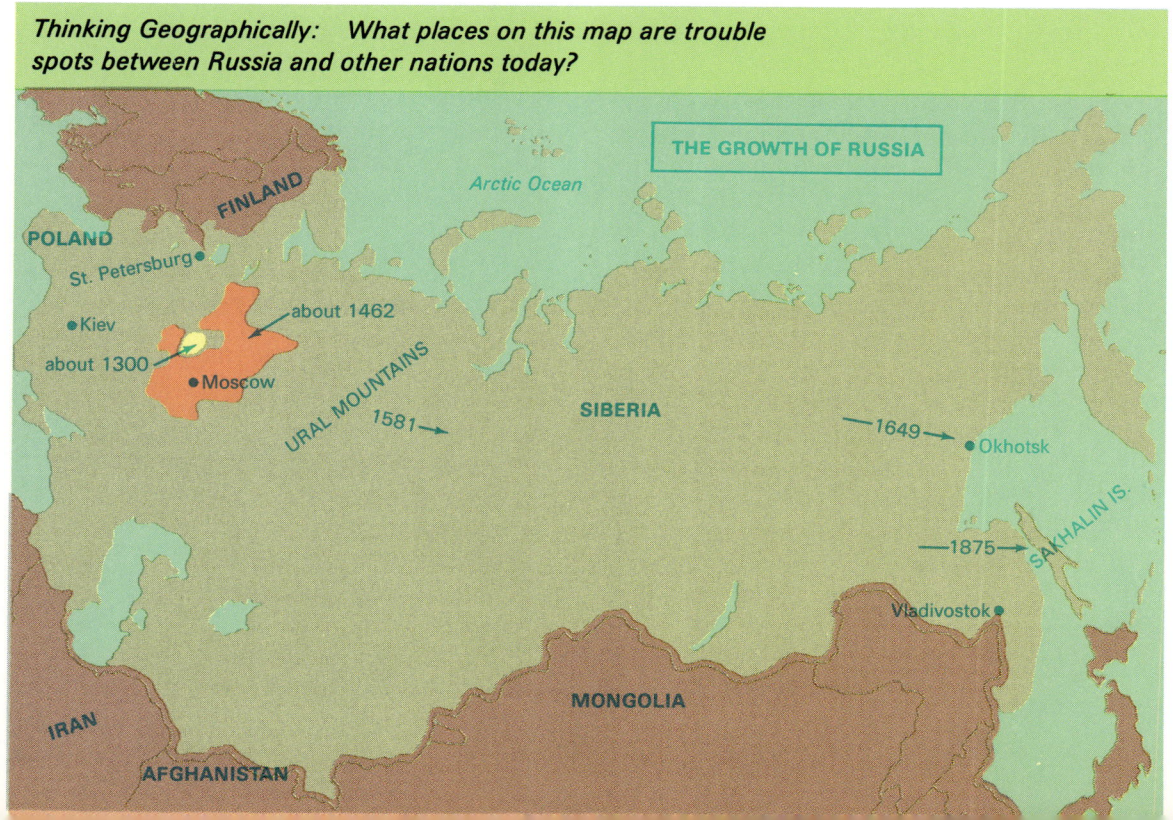

Thinking Geographically: What places on this map are trouble spots between Russia and other nations today?

THE GROWTH OF RUSSIA

A village council in Russia.

to interfere in Chinese affairs. They also began to create a Russian influence in Korea. By 1875, they had secured control of the Sakhalin (SACK uh leen) Island off the east coast of Siberia.

With this phenomenal growth in Russian territory, the czars worried about their ability to keep it. For one thing, the Siberian climate was extremely harsh. Russian attempts to attract settlers to the region were not successful. Moreover, they desperately needed a railroad to cover the great distances between settlements. They began the Trans-Siberian railroad in 1891. The Russians covered a distance of more than 6,400 kilometers (4,000 miles) through some of the most hostile terrain on this planet. When the railroad was completed in 1903, it gave the czar a direct rail line from Moscow to Vladivostok and made the region of Siberia more secure.

Central Asia In the meantime, Russian expansion was also aimed southward into Central Asia. By 1860, the Russians had secured the region between the Black and Caspian (KAS pee un) seas, south to the Caucasus (KAW kuh sus) Mountains. Further east, the Russians began to expand south into Turkestan (tur kuh STAN). By 1873, they had secured the region around the Aral Sea. By 1884, they had gained control of Merv on the border with Afghanistan. From Turkestan, the Russians were in a position to move into the Manchu province of Tibet or into Afghanistan or even Persia (present-day Iran). The prospect of any of these moves alarmed the British. They saw them as a threat to their control of India. Thus, when Russian troops attacked Afghan soldiers along the undefined Russian-Afghan border in 1885, the British prepared for possible war. Full scale fighting was averted when Anglo-Russian negotiations established a border. Despite the resolution of the issue, the fiercely independent Afghans kept a suspicious eye on their Russian neighbors.

The Russians were also active in Persia. Between 1820 and 1830, Russian forces seized small parts of Persia by force. However, when Mohammed became *shah*, or ruler, in 1835, the Russians changed from aggressor to friend. They set up an aid program for Persia. Within a half century, the Russians modernized the army, set up

Did You Know?

Russia's Search for an Outlet to the Sea

Russia is the largest nation in the world. It has the longest coastline of any nation. However, most of that coast lies above the Arctic Circle and is frozen for as much as nine months out of the year.

Russian foreign policy from the time of Peter the Great to the present has had one dominant theme. That is to gain a port that is ice-free and open. This amazing consistency in Russian foreign policy was first explained by Alfred T. Mahan. According to Mahan, the Russian empire typified the strength and weakness of a monumental landpower. Until the mid-twentieth century, Russia's size hindered communication and movement. This retarded industrial development and isolated Russia from other nations.

This isolation was compounded by the lack of ice-free and open ports. With the exception of the port of Murmansk, all Russian ports on the northern coast are frozen solid for more than six months out of the year. Russian ports in the Baltic are relatively ice-free. However, their accessibility in times of war is questionable. The entrance to the Baltic could be shut off at Denmark. In a war against Germany, this would be a very real threat. Russian ports on the Black Sea and the Sea of Azov are also ice-free. However, these seas could be shut off at the Dardanelles, south of Istanbul. On the Pacific there is the excellent ice-free port of Vladivostok. However, it is 6,400 kilometers (4,000 miles) from the Russian heartland and not feasible as an open route to Europe.

During czarist times, the Russian urge to expand to the sea led to thrusts against the Ottoman empire in the Crimean

Unloading a ship in a frozen Russian harbor.

War, toward the Indian Ocean through Afghanistan, and toward the Persian Gulf. A century later, Communist leaders have built up a strong Mediterranean fleet, acted as friend and benefactor to the Arab world, and invaded Afghanistan again.

As you can see, Russian foreign policy goals have remained remarkably consistent for the past three centuries.

a national telegraph system, and established a national bank. This assistance put the shah deeply in debt to his Russian benefactors. In 1900, Russia proposed that a railroad be built from the Russian border to the Persian Gulf. This would give them direct access to a warm-water port. The British saw a Russian naval presence as a threat to their sea route to India and protested strongly. In 1907, a compromise was reached. Northern Persia was declared a Russian sphere of influence and the Persian Gulf coastal region became a British sphere. In actuality, this settled nothing. However, both Britain and Russia were beginning to fear Germany. This fear made the compromise one of convenience. Russian troops occupied much of northern Persia while the British kept the coast. Afghanistan was a buffer state between Russian and British interests. In the end Russian imperialism would lead to war in Asia. But the war was not with Britain. The unlikely foe was Japan.

Section Questions

1. What European nations were involved in the exploitation of Asia in the 1800s? What non-European nation was involved?
2. Why did Russia interfere in the affairs of Persia and Afghanistan in the late nineteenth century?

2. Japan Became an Imperialistic Power

Western contact with Japan began sometime around 1550 when Portuguese traders visited the island and introduced firearms. Following this, Christian missionaries came and began converting the Japanese. This led to Japanese political unrest over the desirability of western ideas. After 1600, the shoguns began curtailing Christian missionary activity. By 1650, almost all western traders had been expelled from Japan and the nation lived in virtual isolation from the rest of the world.

The Opening of Japan By 1800, there were growing economic problems in Japan and a move to open the doors of trade. As early as 1820, American whaling vessels had been plying the northern Pacific. If any vessels were wrecked along the Japanese coast, their crews were imprisoned.

Beginning in 1837, the United States navy made several attempts to open up Japan. In 1854, Commodore Matthew Perry successfully led an American naval squadron into Tokyo Bay. He secured a treaty guaranteeing shipwrecked American sailors decent treatment. In addition, American merchants could trade in selected Japanese ports. By 1856, Britain, Russia, and the Netherlands secured similar treaties.

Changes in Japanese Life The introduction of western goods and ideas had a profound effect on Japan. The Japanese did not allow the miraculous technology of the West to overcome them. Instead, they learned quickly and adopted what they wanted.

One of the first changes was the decline in the power of the shogun. In 1867, the nobles restored the emperor, called the Mikado or Heavenly King, to the throne. A young emperor, Mutsuhito, was installed as Mikado. He changed his name to Meiji (MAY jee).

During the Meiji period from 1867 to 1912, the power of the feudal nobility was ended. A centralized bureaucratic government was set up along western lines. A national draft was put into effect. Under French and German advisers, a powerful military machine was started. Simultaneously, under British advisers, a large ship-building program was started, guaranteeing the Japanese a strong navy. In the meantime, the government instituted economic programs that encouraged the Japanese to open new banks, factories, and other business enterprises.

Thus, Japanese military and economic activities remained under Japanese control. They were not open to western manipulation. By 1900, the Japanese had undergone a startling transformation. On the surface, they appeared to be thoroughly westernized. They had begun to turn out industrial goods, especially textiles, that competed with those of the West. The Japanese had the most powerful non-western navy in the world. A constitution and parliamentary system of government had been put into effect around 1889. Compulsory education became law. Japan became the first non-western nation to achieve almost total literacy.

However, in many ways, the Japanese remained quite traditional. The emperor was still considered sacred. The schools built up a literate, skilled population. They also instilled in millions of children the belief in absolute obedience and loyalty to the state and emperor. Thus, the Japanese created a highly industrialized society while maintaining the strong group loyalties characteristic of medieval Japan.

Japanese Imperialism Japan's growing population and rising industry would make it one of the imperialistic powers of the world. In looking beyond their borders, the Japanese wanted to expand into Korea. Their reasons were both strategic and economic. The Japanese knew that the Russians were interested in Korea and would be able to move into that peninsula from Vladivostok. The occupation of Korea by an expanionist power like Russia was unthinkable to the Japanese. Further, Korean rice had proved vital to Japan's growing industrial population. Moreover, underdeveloped Korea would be a good market for Japanese industrial goods. However, Korea was a province of the Manchu emperors of China. Few people believed that the Japanese would chance a war with the Chinese.

In the summer of 1894, Japanese forces seized Seoul (SOLE), the provincial capital of Korea. This action led to the Sino-Japanese War in 1894. The outbreak of hostilities shocked the world. While conceding Japan's industrial advancements, most people felt that they could not stand up to the almost unlimited resources of China. However, within a year, Japanese forces crushed both the Chinese navy and army. In 1895, China ceded Formosa (for MO sah) to Japan, paid the Japanese government an indemnity, and declared the full independence of Korea. Korea soon became a Japanese sphere of influence.

The results of the Sino-Japanese War

This cartoon shows a Japanese asking an American for some of the "light" of western culture.

An engraving of the storming of Port Arthur.

were many. First, it gained Japan the respect of the western imperialistic nations. Second, it showed those nations the weakness of China. They wasted little time in attempting to "carve up the Chinese melon," as we shall see in the next section. Third, it signaled to the Russians that Japan would be their rival in the Orient.

The Russo-Japanese War When the British formally recognized Japanese interests in Korea in 1902, the Russians began to move into Chinese Manchuria. The Japanese did not like the idea of Russian expansion into this area. However, they offered to recognize Russian influence in Manchuria if the Russians would do the same for them in Korea. The Russians refused to discuss the matter. Diplomatic relations were severed in 1904. The Japanese responded by attacking, without warning, the Russian treaty port in China, Port Arthur. The attack was so successful that they were able to bottle up the Russian fleet there. In the meantime, the Japanese army invaded Manchuria. As with the Sino-Japanese War, the Russo-Japanese War caught the world by surprise. The Japanese had won grudging respect after their victory over China. However, most Europeans considered them no match for the Russians. After all, Asiatic people were engaging a European power.

However, the Japanese surprised the world. They not only drove the Russians out of Manchuria, they also took Port Arthur. In the meantime, as you read earlier, the Japanese navy annihilated the Russian fleet. Thus, within a year, the Japanese smashed the Russian navy and drove the army out of Manchuria. The stunned Russians felt obliged to end the war as soon as possible.

In fact, both sides were exhausted. The Japanese, too, wanted to end the conflict. Thus, both sides were ready to negotiate.

The Treaty In 1905, the President of the United States, Theodore Roosevelt, offered to mediate the dispute. Japanese and Russian delegates met at Portsmouth, New Hampshire to negotiate. The resulting Treaty of Portsmouth in 1905 ended the war with the following provisions. Japan received the southern half of Sakhalin Island and the Russian lease to Port Arthur. Russia promised to stay out of Manchuria and Korea. Japan promised to stay out of Manchuria also, thereby making it a buffer between the two powers. As for Korea, all doubt about it being a Japanese sphere of influence had been wiped away. In 1910, the Japanese annexed it outright. As a result of his mediation efforts, Theodore Roosevelt won the Nobel Peace Prize in 1906.

The Japanese victory in 1905 demonstrated to the world that Japan was truly the first non-white world power. Many of the exploited darker-skinned peoples of the world secretly enjoyed the Japanese victory. The spectacle of the hitherto invincible white men defeated by the Orientals was a boost to nationalism in Asia and Africa. They were quick to see the lesson that Japan had mastered. Western technology, weaponry, and business were the keys to power. These lessons were not lost on others, especially the Chinese. As we shall see in the next section, China was among the Asian nations most horribly exploited by the Great Powers.

Section Questions

1. How did increased Japanese contact with the west change Japanese life after 1850?
2. How did the results of the Russo-Japanese War shock the world?

3. The Great Powers Exploited Much of Asia

The Portuguese had developed trading posts in India modeled after their forts on the coast of Africa. In the 1600s and 1700s, they were quickly followed by the British, French, and Dutch. They all formed trading companies and attempted to monopolize certain areas.

British India In the 1700s, the British East India Company had become the largest trading company in India. By 1757, Robert Clive (KLIVE), an East Indian Company official, had made his company the dominant trading power in the area. India had never been politically united. The British were masters at taking advantage of internal quarrels between Indian princes. The British East India Company became master of the peninsula by 1818. This was not a simple trick. India was a complex area containing over three hundred million people of diverse religions, languages, and racial backgrounds.

However, the prize was a rich one. Many of the products from Britain's new industrial development were exported to India. India paid for these manufactured commodities with a seemingly endless supply of raw materials.

The westernization of India was resented by many Indians. They began to question the invincibility of the British army after hearing of the losses suffered in the Crimean War.

Finally, the Sepoy Mutiny brought about the end of the British East Indian Company rule in India.

The immediate cause of the rebellion was the introduction of a new type of rifle cartridge. The native troops employed by the British, called *sepoys*, made up over eighty percent of the British forces in India. Almost all sepoys were either Hindus or

Muslims. The Hindus considered the cow to be sacred and the Muslims considered the pig unfit for consumption. The new rifle cartridge was greased with the fat of pigs and cows. The sepoys refused to use the new cartridge. In the bloody uprising that followed, many British subjects were killed, including women and children as well as soldiers. Eventually, the British army restored order and the captured rebels were executed.

The British crown took more direct responsibility for running Indian affairs after the Sepoy Mutiny of 1857-1858. The area was divided into a number of provinces, each under the rule of a British governor. The actual administration of the province was handled by an efficient Indian civil service that was based on merit. This civil service gave the Indians some experience in government. British courts in India included Indian magistrates. Legislative councils were also set up.

As a result of this policy of indirect rule, India had a body of trained, experienced administrators who, for the most part, had some formal western education. For the average Indian, life continued as before. The village remained the center of Indian life. However, the western-educated Indian leaders resented the fact that the top positions in the government were reserved for the British. They noted that all commercial and industrial leaders were also British. They resented, too, the haughty attitude of the colonial officials. The British let the Indians know in no uncertain terms that they were in India to help the less fortunate Indians achieve a better life.

These Indian intellectuals formed the Indian National Congress to demand a system of home rule. The Congress began as a reform movement of the Indian colonial government. It soon became the nationalist voice of the Indian people. The communications systems established by the British (railroad, telegraph, postal services, and press) were employed to create a nation-wide network that pressed for independence. By the beginning of the twentieth century, the British began to grant more freedoms to the Indians. However, hard line nationalists began to demand more. The passage of the Indian Councils Act in 1909 gave Indians a greater voice in running their government. In spite of this, violence broke out against the colonial government after 1910.

A British family in India with their Indian servants.

A French mission in Indo-China.

French Indo-China The British were not the only Europeans who had an interest in Southeast Asia. In 1858, Napoleon III sent an expedition up the Mekong River. The expedition secured the strategic port of Saigon in Cochin, China (now Vietnam). From this point, the French moved up the coast and up the Mekong River into the heart of Southeast Asia. In 1863, the French established a protectorate over Cambodia. The French also occupied Annam in 1882, Tonkin in 1885, and Laos in 1893. For administrative purposes, they united these areas into what would be called French Indo-China.

French Indo-China proved to be the crown jewel of French possessions in Asia. The tropical, moist climate made possible the cultivation of rubber, hemp, quinine, tea, coffee, tobacco, and spices. Saigon was built up as the economic center of the area. It became known as the Paris of the Orient due to its heavy French influence.

Burma, Siam, and Malaya Between British India and French Indo-China were the independent states of Burma and Siam (si AM), now called Thailand (TI land). The British first began to move into Burma in 1824. By the 1860s, Burma was trading exclusively with British merchants. In 1886, the British annexed that area and declared it to be a part of India. This left Siam in the unenviable position of lying between British Burma and French Indo-China. However, the kings of Siam became masters at playing the British against the French. They signed many unfavorable commercial treaties and thus fell under western economic influence, but they managed to retain their political independence. By 1900, Siam existed as a buffer between the British and French in Southeast Asia.

The British and the Dutch were rivals for the Malay (MAY LAY) Peninsula and the outlying islands to the south and east: Malacca (mah LAK ah), Java, Borneo (BOR nee o), Sumatra (soo MAW truh), and a host of smaller ones. Through diplomatic manuevering, the British more or less gained possession of the peninsula, including the strategic port of Singapore. The Dutch retained control over most of the outlying islands.

Manchu China The richest prize in Asia in terms of wealth and resources was the Chinese empire. China was still ruled by the Manchu dynasty (1644 to 1912). As you read earlier, the Chinese greatly restricted the movement of Europeans in their country. The western traders had the unusual experience of being treated as inferiors. The Chinese were convinced of the superiority of their own culture.

All of this changed in the nineteenth century. After 1800, the Chinese empire began to suffer many economic problems as population outgrew the food supply. Another problem was the growth of the *opium* trade. Opium, a narcotic, was grown in British India. It was being sold on a larger and larger scale to the growing number of Chinese addicts. The addicts created social problems. The money spent on the drug caused a balance of payments deficit which threatened the Chinese economy. When the Manchus attempted to crack down on the opium traders, war broke out between Britain and China. The Opium War, or the Anglo-Chinese War, lasted from 1839 to 1842. The British fleet defeated the Chinese navy and seized several coastal ports. By the Treaty of Nanking in 1842, China ceded Hong Kong to Britain and opened up other ports to British trade. The rapid success of the British fleet and the commercial value of the treaties demonstrated China's weakness to the world.

Ships in Hong Kong Harbor.

Immediately the other Great Powers secured similar treaties with the Manchus. One common point in all the treaties was that foreign nations would not be subject to the criminal and civil jurisdiction of the Chinese courts. Instead, foreigners would be tried for crimes in the consular court of their own country. The Manchus felt that such favored status for the westerners was humiliating. Such a loss of face diminished their power in the eyes of the Chinese people.

The weakness of the Manchus could be seen during the Taiping Rebellion of 1850 to 1864. The government finally put down this rebellion, but it required the assistance of the West. Ending the rebellion took more than a decade and cost more than twenty million lives. It was during this rebellion that Charles "Chinese" Gordon, who would later be killed at Khartoum, became a British hero.

In the face of this Manchu decline, the Great Powers kept moving in. Western missionaries settled the length and breadth of China seeking converts to Christianity. In 1860, the Russians had seized the Amur region north of Manchuria. In that same year, Peking was occupied by 17,000 British and French troops. By 1885, France had seized most of Indo-China and in 1887 Macao was ceded to Portugal.

The Chinese Reaction The Chinese developed a deep-seated hatred toward the westerners. Many anti-western riots broke out. Western merchants, missionaries, and even diplomats were killed. The Chinese became more and more withdrawn. They shunned anything western as a threat to their ancient and sacred way of life. In this, they were supported by the Empress Dowager of China, Zi Xi (Tzu Hsi), a shrewd and remarkable woman who ruled China from 1862 to 1908. She put down the revolts against the Manchus and played the Great Powers against each other in a vain attempt to keep China's sovereignty.

Empress Zi Xi.

In a round of secret negotiations, the Great Powers divided China into spheres of influence. The Russians laid claim to Manchuria, the Germans to the Shantung Peninsula, the British to the Chang Jiang (Yangtze) Valley, and the French to the southern region bordering French Indo-China. The Japanese appeared content with their control over Formosa and attempts to secure Korea.

In the meantime, secret revolutionary societies sprang up throughout China. In 1898, Zi Xi, sensing the frustration in the air, allowed young Chinese intellectuals to institute reforms. In the Hundred Days of

Reform, they attempted to modernize China overnight, using Japan as a model. However, the reforms came too fast. Zi Xi, sensing an anti-Manchu overtone in all this, executed many of the reformers.

The United States was alarmed over the prospect of the spheres of influence. It feared that American businessmen might be excluded from the China trade. In 1899, Secretary of State John Hay requested that the major powers permit all nations to trade freely with China. He suggested an Open Door Policy. The policy was agreed to by many of the Great Powers in principle, but not much in practice.

The Boxer Rebellion The turmoil in China was too great to be stopped by vague attempts to promote free trade. The defeat in the Sino-Japanese War and the failure of the Hundred Days of Reform had shaken the authority of the Manchus. More patriotic societies were formed, dedicated to reviving the power of China. The largest of these was called the Society of Harmonious Fists. They practiced various martial arts (like kung-fu) and were called Boxers. At first, the Boxers were strongly anti-Manchu. However, they soon transferred their hatred to the foreigners who were humiliating China. In the spring of 1900, the Boxers set off a rebellion in northern China. Many foreigners were killed in the streets. The Boxers even killed Chinese Christians, whom they regarded as traitors for accepting foreign ideas. Foreign merchants and diplomats fled to the foreign settlement on the coast or to the foreign legation (the embassy quarters) in Peking. The situation in Peking soon became desperate. Refugees from all parts of China overflowed the legation area. It was defended only by several hundred embassy security guards and some marines who had been called in earlier from warships stationed off the coast.

Zi Xi claimed that she could not guar-

American troops in the Boxer Rebellion.

antee the safety of the embassy personnel or the refugees and that they should leave the Peking legation and head for the coast. As this issue was being debated, the German ambassador was murdered while on official business outside of the legation. As a result, those in the legation refused to leave what little security they had for the dangers of the open countryside. A seige of fifty-five days followed. The Manchu government did little or nothing to assist those foreigners under attack.

In the meantime, an international expedition made up of soldiers and marines from Germany, Britain, Russia, Japan, France, and the United States landed in

China. They took Tientsin on July 14, 1900. Moving inland, they reached Peking and relieved the legation on August 14.

The Boxer Rebellion gave the Great Powers an excuse to divide and dismember China further. Fortunately for China, several events kept the final settlement from being worse than it could have been. First, the American Secretary of State made a firm stand to preserve Chinese territory from further division. Second, the British were too engaged in the Boer War in South Africa to get seriously involved. Third, Japan and Russia were concerned with each other's intentions in Manchuria and Korea. In the final settlement, China had to pay for damages, apologize to the Great Powers, execute those involved in the uprising, and agree to a permanent western garrison to fortify the legation quarters in Peking. The one thing that the Boxer Rebellion proved was that the imperialist powers could work together against China. Before, they worked against each other. The Manchus had been able to exploit this rivalry for China's benefit.

Up to now, the Manchu and Chinese reaction to the rape of their country had been a greater rejection of western ideas and ways. However, during this period, Chinese students had gone abroad to study. When they returned home, they saw how their country was being ravaged by the foreigners. While abroad, they had seen the effects of nationalism as a moving force. They recognized the need for industrial expansion. More important, they too watched with great pleasure and glee as the Japanese defeated Russia. Thus, the time was ripe for a nationalist revolution.

The Chinese Republic The most effective of these nationalist leaders was Dr. Sun Yat-sen. As a student, he had studied in Hong Kong and Honolulu. He understood the lesson that Japan had mastered and felt that China must do the same. First, though, the Manchu dynasty must be overthrown. He organized a revolutionary society, the Young China movement. It consisted mostly of western-oriented students. He spread his doctrines throughout China and set up a truly national organization.

In 1908, Zi Xi died. A boy emperor was proclaimed and a regent set up to rule in his place. The turmoil continued. Taxes were increased to pay the Boxer indemnity. In 1910-1911, floods in central China brought famine and disease. All of these problems erupted into the Chinese revolution of 1911. Within several months, China was proclaimed a republic and Sun Yat-sen was declared the provisional president. In 1912, the last Manchu emperor abdicated.

The creation of the Republic of China did not end the problems brought about by imperialism. As we shall see later, Sun Yat-sen would install a representative government in a country that had no tradition of such a practice. He would try to maintain national unity and restore the power of the central government. He would also try to dislodge the Great Powers from their stranglehold on China. It would prove to be a monumental task.

Section Questions

1. What revolution in India resulted in the control of India passing directly under the British crown? What caused the revolution?
2. What type of rule did the British institute in India? What were the results?
3. What was the crown jewel of French possessions in Asia?
4. What territories did China lose as a result of the Sino-Japanese War of 1894-1895?
5. What policy did the United States propose to the Great Powers to permit free trade in China? Why?
6. Why did the Boxers attempt to force westerners out of China?

The official opening of the Australian Parliament House at Canberra.

4. Imperialism Extended Across the Pacific

Western imperialism in the nineteenth century also included the exploitation of the Pacific. Great Britain claimed much of the Pacific area because of the explorations of James Cook in three separate voyages spanning from 1768 to 1799. However, as in Africa and most of Asia, the British did little to follow up on these initial voyages.

Australia In 1788, the first shipload of British convicts landed at Botany Bay in Australia. Australia had been designated as a *penal*, or prison colony. However, free settlers followed in 1793. When the British feared possible French or Dutch settlement, they rapidly set up settlements along the coast. In 1803, a settlement was begun on the island of Tasmania (taz MAY nee uh). By 1829, Perth was founded on the west coast. In 1867, the last convicts were brought in. By that time, the free settlers outnumbered them by more than four to one.

Movement into the interior soon followed. As in western America and southern Africa, it was triggered by the discovery of gold. The original inhabitants in the interior, the Aborigines, employed a stone-age technology and were few in number. Therefore, they were almost no obstacle to the miners.

The coming of railroads and telegraph brought a sense of unity to the diverse settlements on the continent. Thus, by 1880, talk began in earnest for confederation. In 1897, a federal convention was held at Hobart. A constitution was drawn up similar to that of the United States. That constitution was approved by vote of the people in 1899 and by the British Parliament in 1900. Thus, on the first day of the new year 1901, the Commonwealth of Australia became an official state. The capital was set up in the city of Canberra (KAN ber uh) in 1909.

New Zealand British settlement in Australia was followed by the establishment of a colony in New Zealand in 1826. In 1840, the British proclaimed control over the island when they established a colony near what is now Wellington. The original inhabitants of the island were the Maori (MAWR ee), a Polynesian group. The Maori resisted the British and Australian settlers. Several wars broke out between the two groups from 1843 to 1870. The Maori, fighting a guerrilla campaign, were difficult to root out. In the end, the sheer number of settlers decided the issue as the natives were overwhelmed. By 1890, most of the good land on the island was settled and many outlying islands in the Pacific were annexed. In 1907, New Zealand became a Dominion, similar to Canada.

Throughout the nineteenth century, European powers annexed islands in the Pacific. The British annexed Pitcairn Island in 1838, and Fiji in 1874. The Dutch annexed western New Guinea in 1828. The French established a protectorate over Tahiti in 1842 and annexed New Caledonia in 1853. The Germans annexed the Marshall Islands in 1885. They established a protectorate over the Cook Islands in 1888.

The Americans The biggest expansionist power in Asia and the Pacific was the United States. In 1784, the first American cargo ship landed in China. This began a profitable trade relationship with that country. In the following decades, American whaling ships plied the Pacific. New England merchants sought trade wherever a profit could be made. By 1800, American ships were trading regularly with China, Java, Siam, British India, and the Philippines. Between 1840 and 1860, American clipper ships were the fastest items afloat. They could make the run between New York and Canton in as little as seventy-five days. This was a remarkable feat for a ship propelled by sail that had to travel around South America.

Perry's arrival in Tokyo Bay in 1854 showed the extent of American commitment in the Pacific. The commitment would rapidly grow in the second half of the nineteenth century.

As American interest in the Pacific increased, so did the American presence on the Hawaiian Islands. The islands were found by James Cook in 1778. The first

Harbor of Yokohama with locomotive and cargo ships.

Americans to arrive were missionaries in 1820. By the 1840s, most of the Great Powers recognized the independence of the islands. By 1850, five out of every six ships that called on the islands were American. A treaty was negotiated to annex the islands in 1854. However, it failed to win the ratification of the United States Congress. Despite this, interest in the islands remained high. In 1875, the United States obtained a lease on Pearl Harbor on the island of Oahu as a coaling and naval station.

After the American Civil War ended in 1865, the United States began to acquire Pacific territory outright. In 1867, the United States acquired the island of Midway, west of the Hawaiian Islands, as another coaling and naval station. The United States influence on Hawaii grew stronger and stronger. American sugar and pineapple planters engineered a revolt against the independent native government in 1890 and proclaimed the island to be a republic. In 1898, the United States annexed the islands.

The Splendid Little War The old American imperialism was called manifest destiny and it had consisted of expanding the new nation from ocean to ocean. This goal employed the energies of the nation for more than a century. In 1890, the Bureau of the Census announced that the frontier had closed. This fact had a heavy symbolic meaning. It appeared that the great land resources of the nation, long considered infinite, had now reached an end. Some feared that material shortages were imminent. Thus, the seeds were sown for a new look at overseas expansion. Perhaps the big impetus came from the economic sector. American exports were climbing to record figures. People feared that the nation was producing more than it could consume. They felt that overseas markets must be acquired if American industry was to expand. The successes of the imperialist powers in Asia and Africa were duly noted by Americans.

Coupled with this thinking was the emergence of Alfred T. Mahan. Mahan was the American naval officer who claimed that the growth of sea power was essential for a rising nation. As a result, by 1895, American interest in foreign expansion had grown dramatically.

The new American imperialism first manifested itself in Cuba, a Spanish possession south of Florida. In 1895, Cuban revolutionaries attempted to throw off Spanish control over the island. Most Americans were sympathetic to the Cuban cause.

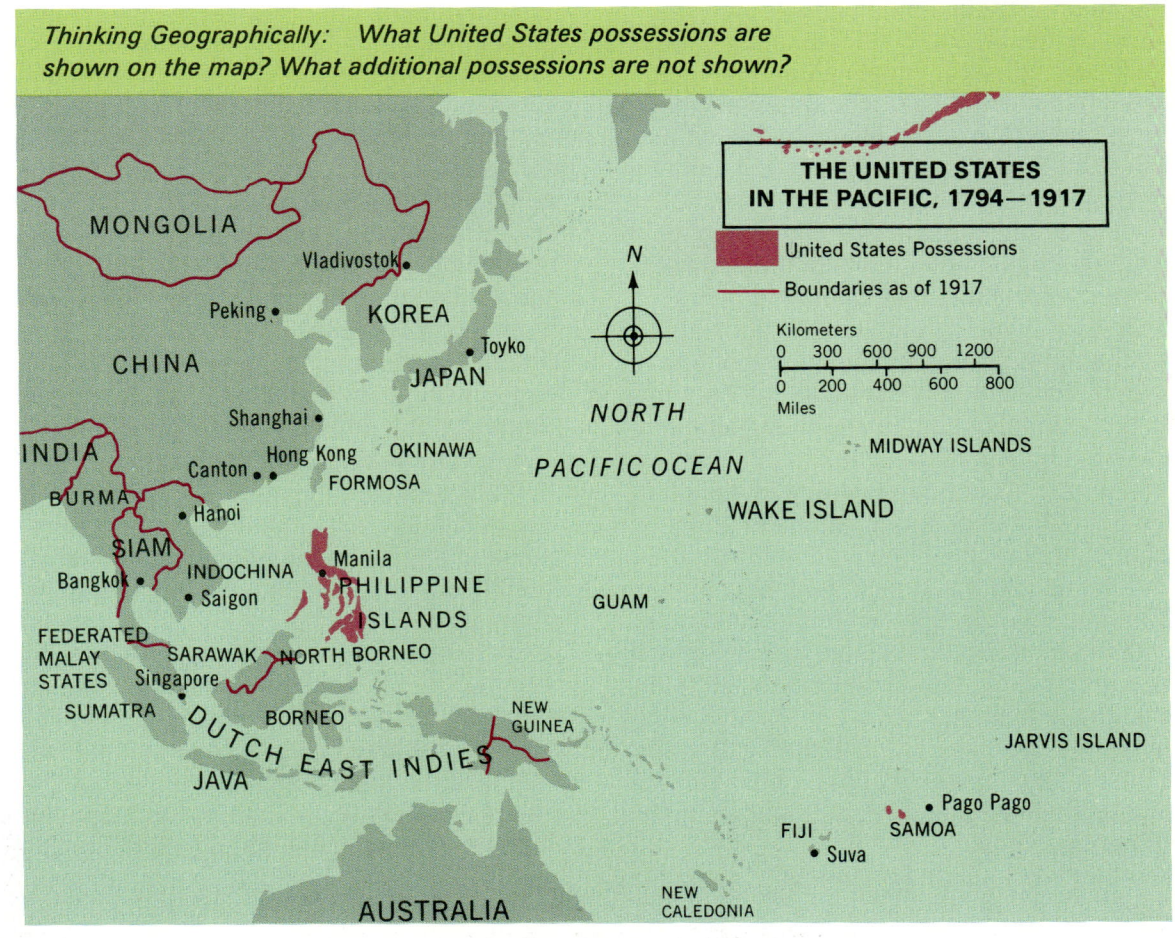

Thinking Geographically: What United States possessions are shown on the map? What additional possessions are not shown?

THE UNITED STATES IN THE PACIFIC, 1794–1917

The battle of Santiago.

President William McKinley sent the American battleship, the U.S.S. Maine, into Havana harbor to "protect American interests." In February 1898, the ship was blown up in the harbor. Over 260 sailors were lost. The nation called out for war. The American armed forces swung into operation.

The Spanish-American War lasted from April to August 1898. For the United States it was what John Hay called "a splendid little war." The United States Navy bottled up the Spanish fleet in the harbor of Santiago, Cuba. The army captured the port and drove the ships out to the destruction of the waiting American guns.

Another American fleet under the command of Commodore George Dewey attacked Manila, the seat of the Spanish administration of the Philippine Islands. By the summer, Manila was in American hands.

Reeling under these twin defeats, Spain sued for peace. Under the treaty of 1899, the United States acquired Puerto Rico in the Caribbean and Guam and the Philippines in the Pacific. The United States had joined the ranks of the great imperialist powers.

The Philippines America gained power, prestige, and territories from the Spanish-American War. However, the nation also acquired some headaches.

The acquisition of the Philippines in the western Pacific made the United States an Asiatic power. It greatly strengthened American interest in China. During the Boxer Rebellion in 1900, the United States had contributed some 2,500 troops to the rescue of the Peking legation. Thus, the United States had a hand in the peace terms at the end of the rebellion. It tried to persuade the other powers to maintain Chinese territorial integrity.

In the Philippines, the Filipino people were disillusioned. The coming of the Americans did not mean independence for them. Led by the guerrilla fighter, Emilio Aguinaldo, they rebelled. They fought the American army of occupation for two years, from 1899 to 1901. The United States lost twice as many troops fighting Aguinaldo as in the entire Spanish-American War. This cost in lives and money created the first hot debate in Washington over the wisdom of keeping so alien a territory.

Panama The climax of American imperialism came in Panama. Ferdinand de Lesseps had tried to construct a canal through the Isthmus several decades earlier but had failed. Americans were preoccupied with the defense of their new holdings in the Caribbean and in the maintenance of their new "two-ocean" navy. This revived interest in the project. Theodore Roosevelt was unable to come to terms with the government of Colombia, which owned Panama. He then supported a Panamanian revolution and recognized the new nation of Panama. The Panamanians granted the United States a lease on a zone of land 16 kilometers (10 miles) wide. Construction of the Panama Canal began.

The original Panama Canal project failed because of the many tropical diseases in the jungles of Panama. Here, the Americans were most fortunate. In 1900, an army surgeon, Dr. Walter Reed, learned that yellow fever was transmitted by mosquitoes. A wide-spread mosquito extermination program was launched. Not one case of this dreaded disease was reported during the canal construction. In 1914, the Panama Canal was officially opened under United States protection and control.

President Theodore Roosevelt, for many, personified the American imperialist. In 1905, he negotiated the Treaty of Portsmouth which ended the war between Japan and Russia. Two years later, he sent the Great White Fleet of sixteen battleships around the world to show off American power and strength. As the twentieth century dawned on the world, there was no doubt that the United States had become a Great Power.

An early photograph of tugs in the Panama Canal.

Section Questions

1. What type of British settler originally settled the colony of Australia?
2. Why were the Aborigines unable to stop the tide of British settlement in Australia?
3. What did the United States gain as a result of the Spanish-American War in 1898?
4. Who fought against the American occupation of the Philippines? Why?
5. Why was the Panama Canal important to the United States?

Chapter Summary

1. Beginning in 1581 when they crossed the Ural Mountains, Russians moved eastward steadily. They also sought constantly for an ice-free port. They claimed Siberia and Alaska as a result of explorations by Vitus Bering. The Russians clashed with the Chinese in 1689 and again in the 1850s. They annexed the Amur region and established the port of Vladivostok. They began to try to control Korea. They built the Trans-Siberian Railroad to unify their vast territory. They also tried to move into central Asia. They secured the region between the Black and Caspian seas. They reached an uneasy truce with the British over Afghanistan. They exerted influence in Persia.

2. Japan lived in isolation from the rest of the world from 1650 to 1854, when Commodore Matthew Perry led an American naval squadron into Tokyo. The Japanese quickly adopted western technology to their own culture. They moved into Korea in 1894. This led to war with China. Japan won, which earned Japan the respect of western nations and showed how weak China was. In 1904, Japan won a war with Russia over Manchuria and Korea. This demonstrated to the world that Japan was the first non-white world power.

3. In India, the Sepoy mutiny caused the British government to take over. Britain's policy of indirect rule led to a well-educated Indian civil service. These leaders began to resent British rule. Britain granted more self-rule to India. In spite of this, violence broke out against the colonial government after 1910.

The French established colonies in Cochin China (now Vietnam), Cambodia, Tonkin, and Laos. Britain annexed Burma in 1896. Siam remained independent as a buffer state between British and French possessions. The British gained the Malay Peninsula. The Dutch gained Borneo, Java, Sumatra, and smaller islands.

The Chinese kept westerners out until after 1800. The Opium War with Britain demonstrated how weak China was, so the other Great Powers rushed in to secure favorable trade treaties. Secret revolutionary societies sprang up in China. These societies hoped to reform China and restore its power. One such group, the Boxers, led a revolt against the foreigners. The foreigners fled to the legation area in Peking and were held in seige there until rescued by an international expedition. In 1911, Sun Yat-sen led a revolt against the Manchu dynasty and China became a republic.

4. In the Pacific, the British colonized Australia and New Zealand and annexed Pitcairn Island, Fiji, and the Cook Islands. The Dutch, French, and Germans also annexed Pacific islands. The United States purchased Midway Island in 1867 and took over the Hawaiian Islands in 1898. After the Spanish-American War of 1898, America took Puerto Rico, Guam, and the Philippines from Spain. Theodore Roosevelt encouraged Panama to rebel against Colombia. After Panama was established as a new nation, the United States leased land to construct the Panama Canal. The United States was now one of the Great Powers.

Chapter 27 Review

Check Your Facts

1. Identify each of the following:
   a. Paris of the Orient
   b. Indian National Congress
   c. Hundred Days of Reform
   d. Boxers
   e. Maori
   f. Splendid Little War
   g. Sepoy Mutiny
2. List those areas of the world controlled by Russia in 1820.
3. Why did Russia and Japan become rivals in Asia?
4. What were the results of the Russo-Japanese War?
5. Why was it difficult for India to become a unified country in the eighteenth century? How did the British manage to overcome these difficulties in the nineteenth century?
6. What was the purpose of the Open Door Policy? Why did the United States propose it?
7. How did Sun Yat-sen propose to make China great again?
8. What areas of the Pacific were under American control by 1900?
9. How did the Panama Canal help the United States in its imperialistic ventures in the Pacific?

Words to Know

Explain the meaning of each word below.
   a. shah
   b. Mikado
   c. opium
   d. penal

Developing Your Skills

1. Trace part of the map of North America in the Atlas. Mark the Russian claims that resulted from Bering's explorations.
2. Trace the map of the Pacific in the Atlas. Label the islands as to what nation claimed them in the 1800s.
3. Choose four dates from the list at the beginning of the chapter. Tell what was happening in Europe at about the same time. (See chapters 24-26.)

Thinking It Over

1. Why has a cornerstone of Russian foreign policy been the securing of a warm water port? Cite incidents from history and recent events to support your statements.
2. Through most of its history, was the United States more concerned with Latin America and the Pacific than with Europe? Explain.

Special Activity

Both China and Japan are great Asiatic civilizations. Yet the Chinese were dominated by the West in the nineteenth century while the Japanese became a great power on their own. Explain why Japan avoided the problems China faced with the West and became a world power.

Unit 7 Review

Words to Know

Answer questions a through d to compare the views of Smith and Marx.
1. capitalism as defined by Adam Smith
2. socialism as defined by Marx
    a. Who should own land, factories and mines?
    b. Who should decide what is produced?
    c. What is the role of government toward business?
    d. How will workers achieve higher living standards?

Time and Place

1. Tell when unity was achieved for each of the following nations.
    a. Greece
    b. Belgium
    c. Italy
    d. Germany
    e. Kingdom of Hungary
2. Compare pre-industrial England (1700) with industrialized England (1830) in each of the following categories.
    a. Use of machinery
    b. Hours worked
    c. Control of work schedule
    d. Health
    e. Work site
    f. Division of labor

Putting It Together

Copy the chart. Then fill in the information.

	Imperialism in Africa, Asia, and the Pacific	
	Africa 1850-1900	Asia and Pacific 1820-1915
France		
England		
Belgium		
Germany		
Portugal		
Italy		
Spain		
United States		
Russia		

Contemporary Parallel:
Industry and Interdependence

The Industrial Revolution created new forms of mutual dependence, or *interdependence*. The mill owners depended on their workers, the machinery builders, the cotton growers, the customers, and every line of transportation in between. Workers, too, found themselves locked in this interdependence. A dock strike in London or a poor harvest in India could mean the loss of wages.

After 150 years of growth, we now live with an industrial system that is even more complex and interdependent. Take a simple thing such as a chocolate bar. Look at the ingredients listed on the wrapper. Do you know where the major supplies of chocolate are grown? Where do we get our sugar? Where might the milk and vanilla come from? Just to make one simple product requires raw materials from many nations.

Hundreds of years ago there were not many chocolate candy bars available. In fact, until Mexico was conquered by the Spanish, most of the world did not even know that chocolate existed. Now, large factories produce enormous numbers of chocolate bars. They are shipped to many parts of the world. Some countries such as Switzerland have an international reputation for fine candy. But the introduction of chocolate may also have some undesirable effects. It might increase the number of dental problems.

Manufacturers are always looking for new markets for their products. If there is enough demand, a large company may establish a branch in a foreign country to sell a product. However, the introduction of new products into a country can also disrupt the economy. Local people selling food in the open market may now face the competition of fast-food chains.

The world has become a giant supermarket. We are all dependent on the products and services of many different people.

QUESTIONS

1. What are the advantages of global interdependence? What are the disadvantages?
2. What are some of the goods that we import from other countries? What are our major exports?
3. Some people claim that we should slow down the import of certain goods like cars and shoes. Others support free trade. What are some arguments for slowing imports? What are some arguments for free trade?

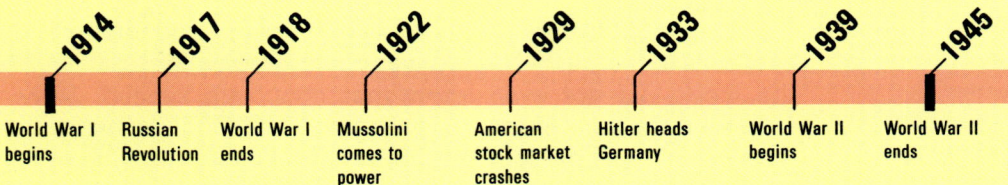

1914	1917	1918	1922	1929	1933	1939	1945
World War I begins	Russian Revolution	World War I ends	Mussolini comes to power	American stock market crashes	Hitler heads Germany	World War II begins	World War II ends

Unit 8
Global Conflict

*In the 1800s, modern technology increased the pace of change. Industry produced more goods in much less time. New developments in communication and transportation shrank time and space.

The industrial nations used their technological advantages to expand their power. They turned much of Africa, southern Asia, the Pacific, and parts of Latin America into colonies. China was independent in name only.

As a result, nationalism grew even stronger. Rivalries involving national pride continued into the 1900s. At times, some of the Great Powers came dangerously close to war, often over trivial matters. However, negotiation ended these disputes before serious fighting began.

Then came a conflict that did not die down. It began in 1914, triggered by the frustrated nationalism of Slavs who wanted freedom from Austria-Hungary. Within weeks, every major European power was caught up in the bloodiest war the world had ever seen. Before it ended, 30 nations from six continents were involved in the Great War, or World War I. Just 20 years after the "war to end all wars," the world was at war again. World War II was even more terrible than World War I.

In this unit, you will see how these two terrible global wars came about.

The mushroom cloud of an atomic bomb.

A caricature of the German army.

Chapter 28 The First World War

During the early weeks of summer in 1914, farmers concentrated on fields thick with grain. If the weather held, it would be an excellent harvest. City workers headed for their jobs in factories or shops, traveling by bicycle or bus or trolley car. The cities hummed with business activity. Those who were impatient for prosperity joined the crowds emigrating to America.

Exciting new things were happening everywhere. Automobiles had become popular, and more and more people could afford them. The airplane—an invention that had seemed impossible a few years earlier—was being improved constantly.

1914-1919

1914	The Great War begins
1915	Italy enters war
1915-1916	Invasion of Gallipoli fails
1916	Battle of Verdun
1917	The United States enters war
1917	Russian Revolution
1917	Austrians defeat Italians
1918	Treaty of Brest-Litovsk
1918	The Great War ends
1919	Treaty of Versailles

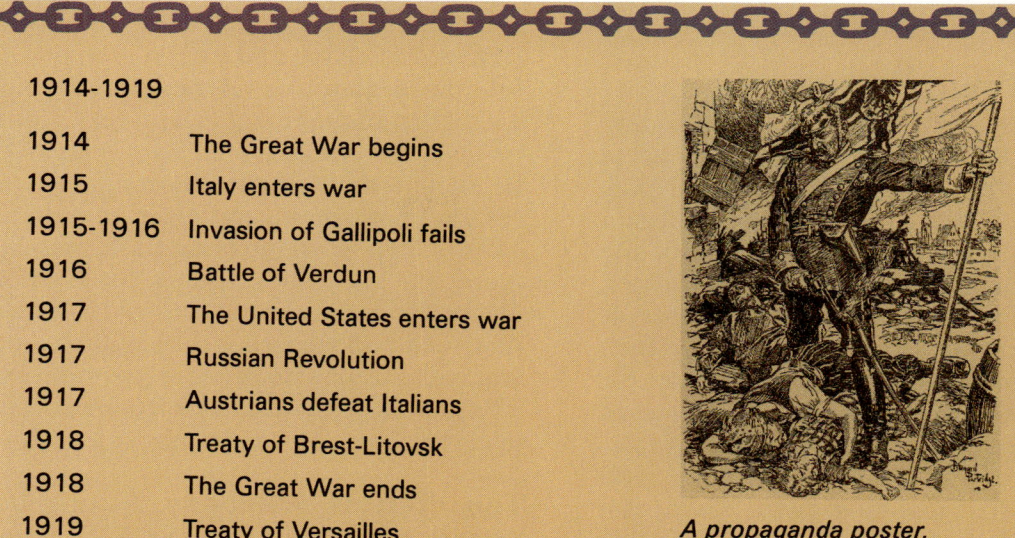

A propaganda poster.

People were finding new frontiers to explore. Marie Curie had made daring discoveries with radium. A Norwegian team had explored Antarctica, planting their flag at the South Pole. Motion pictures were bringing exciting events and faraway places close to everyone.

Few people noticed that war clouds were darkening the horizon. Trouble began in the Balkan Peninsula. This land had been a trouble spot for years, as many national groups struggled for independence. Some, such as the Slavic people of Serbia, had won their independence from the crumbling Ottoman empire. Others, such as the Slavic Croatians, were still under the rule of the Austro-Hungarian empire.

Within Serbia, bands of dedicated nationalists worked to free all the southern Slavs and unite them in a large state. In June 1914, they learned that the Archduke Franz Ferdinand, heir to the Austro-Hungarian throne, was making a tour of the Balkan area of the empire. This, they felt, was their chance to strike a blow for freedom for the Slavs.

On June 28, 1914, the archduke and his wife arrived in the mountain town of Sarajevo (SAW raw ye vo). As they rode through the streets in an open car, one of the Serbian plotters got within close range. He fired with deadly accuracy, killing the imperial couple.

This event was tragic, but it did not at first seem earth-shattering. Political assassinations were not unknown. For example, three American presidents and a Russian czar had been slain by assassins. However, this killing was the spark that set off an explosion that shook the world.

Why? What happened to cause this incident to spiral out of control? That is the major question we will explore in the first section. The rest of the chapter discusses what happened during the war and how this conflict changed the world.

1. Many Causes Led to the Great War

The mood in Europe had been building toward war for years. There were deep, long-lasting rivalries involving national pride or colonies. Many of the French people still hoped to revenge the humiliation of the Franco-Prussian War.

The nationalistic mood also led people to glorify the military. The people and their government leaders were thrilled by the sight of giant new battleships. They cheered as massive military units paraded in review. They were fascinated by ingenious new weapons like machine guns. *Militarism* was also promoted by the fact that there had not been a major war in Europe since the Franco-Prussian War of 1870-1871. People had simply forgotten how bloody and destructive wars can be. They remembered only the glory.

The manufacture of weapons and war materials became a vital part of the economies of the industrial nations. Armaments meant more mining for raw materials, more factories, more jobs, and greater prosperity. The race for colonies also involved wealth, since colonies could be sources of raw materials and new markets for factory goods.

The leaders and people of each country considered any threat to their military, economic, or colonial power serious. The British, for example, were troubled because their early lead in industrialization was eroding. In 1870, Britain had been the world's economic giant, turning out 31 percent of all industrial goods. By 1913, the United States had become the world leader. Germany had moved ahead of Britain into second place. As a result, the British did not want to end the arms race, they wanted to catch up. Germany was not interested in reducing arms either. The German military was growing steadily in power.

The fear of military attack grew greater in the years between 1900 and 1914. Armies were now so large and weapons so powerful that no nation could move quickly into war. Even in an emergency, weeks would be needed to *mobilize* military forces—to get them ready to fight. For military leaders, therefore, mobilization became a critical problem. The nation that could mobilize more quickly could strike a heavy blow before the enemy could gather its forces. As a result, in any crisis that might lead to war, all nations took steps to mobilize. This increased fear and made it more difficult to compromise on the issues.

The Web of Alliances Throughout modern times, the nations of Europe had made treaties of alliance with each other. Typically, two countries agreed to help each other if either was attacked by another nation or nations. The German Chancellor, Bismarck, had started a new system of alliances in the 1870s. His goal was to prevent France from starting a war of revenge for its loss in the Franco-Prussian War. Germany thus made alliances with Austria-Hungary, with Italy, and with Russia. Later, after Bismarck left office, the German kaiser changed this plan. He strengthened ties with Austria-Hungary, kept the treaty with Italy, but dropped the alliance with Russia. The French government was quick to take advantage of the change. France and Russia signed a treaty in 1894. Britain then signed a less binding friendship treaty with France in 1904 and with Russia in 1907.

By 1907, then, Europe was divided into two opposing groups of nations. The combination of Germany, Austria-Hungary, and Italy was known as the Triple Alliance. The other group—Britain, France, and Russia—was called the Triple Entente. This system of alliances turned the greater powers into two armed camps, with each nation tied to whatever happened to the others. Any time one country was in trouble, it would turn to its allies for help. This

Thinking Geographically: What governments gained from the division of lands at the Congress of Berlin? What government lost?

would, of course, set off a reaction in the other camp.

The two groups of European nations were rivals in many ways and in many parts of the world. It was particularly in the Balkans, however, that these conflicts came to a head. A large part of the Austro-Hungarian empire consisted of Slavic peoples, many living on the Balkan Peninsula. The nationalistic feelings of these Slavs were held in check by their Austrian and Hungarian rulers. The Austro-Hungarians were determined to hold on to their Slavic domains. Germany felt compelled to back its Austro-Hungarian ally. On the other hand, the Serbians dreamed of freeing their Slavic cousins from Austro-Hungarian rule and uniting all southern Slavs in one state. Russia considered itself the natural leader of all Slavs, those outside the Russian empire as well as those within. Thus, Russia acted as the protector of Serbia.

France and Britain were, of course, allied with Russia.

The murder of the Austrian archduke in 1914 set off a chain reaction within the European alliances. The rulers of Austria-Hungary were not satisfied that the conspirators had been caught. They wanted to deliver a crushing blow to Slavic nationalism. They asked Germany to support them in a war against Serbia. Germany agreed.

Austria then sent a harsh *ultimatum,* or list of demands, to Serbia. The Serbians seemed to try to avoid war by accepting all of the demands except one. At the same time, they appealed to Russia, the "protector" of the Slavs, for help.

War Begins Austria-Hungary's leaders were determined to have their war with Serbia. They announced that the Serbian reply was not acceptable. On July 28, 1914, they declared war. Three days later, Russia ordered a full mobilization. Now fear became important, especially in the mind of Germany's Kaiser William II. He felt betrayed by his cousin Nicholas II, the czar of Russia. Why would Russia mobilize except to attack him? Did France and then Britain (ruled by his cousin, George) plan to join this plot against him? He sent off frantic messages. The replies from Russia, France, and Britain did not ease his fears. Meanwhile, his generals were warning him that it would be fatal to allow Russia to mobilize.

Kaiser William decided to act, convinced that it was the only way to save Germany. Germany declared war on Russia on August 1, and, two days later, on France. Britain held back until the German armies invaded neutral Belgium. The independence of the Netherlands and Belgium had been the cornerstone of Britain's European policy for centuries. Thus, the Belgian invasion was enough to bring Britain into the war.

The system of alliances had now dragged all the great powers except Italy into war. The Italians hesitated, trying to decide which side was more likely to win. In 1915, Italy deserted the Triple Alliance and joined what became known as the Allied Powers—Britain, France, and Russia. The Ottoman Turks joined the cause of Germany and Austria-Hungary. These three empires were called the Central Powers.

The Failure of Peaceful Methods

There were, thus, many reasons why a single incident in the Balkans could set off a global war. The spirit of nationalism inspired the Slavic feelings of Serbia and Russia and the hunger of France for Alsace-Lorraine. Militarism, the arms race, and mobilization provided the means for war, the horrors of which had been largely forgotten. Rivalries over colonies and industrial output helped create an atmosphere of distrust and anger.

European leaders did have nonviolent methods for resolving conflicts. The most important method was the concept of the balance of power. Using alliances to maintain a power balance had seemed to work. There had been no general European war since the Napoleonic era a century earlier. In fact, some people were convinced that the balance of power made a full-scale war impossible.

Fear of losing that balance helped bring about World War I. Some leaders were convinced that Germany and Austria-Hungary were planning to take over the entire Balkan region. This might have swung the balance of power in their favor. This danger was a major reason for Russia's mobilization as soon as Serbia was attacked. At the same time, as we have seen, the German kaiser was convinced that everyone was conspiring to tip the power balance against Germany.

Diplomacy was one of the major ways of settling disputes. Ambassadors and other trained diplomats were sent by each nation to the capital of every other country. These people were experts at difficult negotiations.

The diplomatic system broke down in July 1914. One reason was that national leaders felt that national honor was at stake. As a result, they did not dare back down. Time was also a factor. Austria had allowed Serbia only 48 hours to answer the ultimatum. The whole crisis began to move too fast. There was no time for careful deliberation.

In addition to traditional diplomacy, there were new nonviolent ways to achieve international cooperation. Several international organizations had been set up to deal with common problems, such as postal rates, between nations. Two major peace conferences had also been held at The Hague, in the Netherlands, in 1899 and in 1907.

The Hague conference set up two ways for settling international disputes. One

The members of the Hague Conference of 1889.

system was *mediation*. In this case, two countries would ask a third to suggest a solution. The second method was *arbitration*. In this case, the conflict would be turned over to a permanent international court. The parties were to promise in advance to accept the decision of the court.

These new efforts were actively supported by many leaders and other people. There was considerable hope that they would work. When the crisis came in 1914, however, the passion of national pride proved far stronger than any desire to settle issues at the bargaining table.

Section Questions

1. Who was Archduke Franz Ferdinand? How did his death influence history?
2. Why were the British concerned about Germany's rapid economic growth?
3. Why was mobilization so important to military leaders?
4. What were the Triple Alliance and the Triple Entente?
5. What was Kaiser William of Germany afraid of?
6. What methods for settling disputes did the Hague conferences set up?

2. War Led to Stalemate and Then to Allied Victory

Throughout Europe, men and boys marched off to war. Bands were playing, and cheering crowds lined the streets waving flags. New uniforms and weapons shone. Newspapers stressed the belief that the war would be short—a few weeks of combat that would bring honor and glory to the nation.

This generation had had little experience with war. There had been no clash of arms among the great powers since the Franco-Prussian War, more than four decades earlier. Smaller conflicts against colonial peoples had simply made war look easy.

No one was really prepared for the kind of war that was to come. In the past, war had often had only limited effects on the civilian population away from the front. Weapons had relatively little destructive power. Armies were generally small. War had seemed to consist of gallant cavalry charges and of neat ranks of men in brightly colored uniforms exchanging volleys.

The Great War was very different. Whole societies were mobilized into the struggle. Larger guns, poison gas, submarines, air power, and so on made war more destructive. Millions of men went off to fight. The fighting itself degenerated into a bloody stalemate in the trenches.

Other, smaller nations joined the Great Powers in transforming the struggle into a global war. Eventually, thirty nations from six continents participated. President Woodrow Wilson was determined to keep America neutral. However, Americans watched the progress of the war closely. Some, especially those with family or friends in Germany, sided with the Central Powers. The majority of Americans, however, wanted an Allied victory. Britain and France were, after all, democracies. Americans also felt strong historical and cultural ties with both countries. In addition, American businesses and banks had invested millions of dollars in the Allied cause.

The key to who would win the war seemed to be the Western Front—the border between France and Germany. The French, with British help, would have to turn back the powerful German army.

Failure of the German Plan The German High Command had made plans for this attack years earlier. While the slower Russian forces struggled to mobilize, they would strike hard and fast at the French. France had established a mighty defense line, centered on the two great fortresses of Verdun and Sedan. Thus, the Germans would not attack head-on. Instead, they would go around the French lines. This meant they would have to go through Belgium, even though all powers had agreed to respect Belgian neutrality.

The plan called for the German armies to move through Belgium in six days. They would then race south, capture Paris, and

American troops wearing gas masks to protect against poison gas.

An American gun crew in battle. Notice that the tops of the trees have been blasted away.

Stalemate in the West

The trenches on the Western Front became more or less permanent. For three years, the opposing armies faced each other across the war-shattered stretch called "no-man's land." They lived in filth, hunger, and fear. Thousands suffered nervous breakdowns because of constant shelling and the danger of attack. Each side probed the other for weak spots. Airplanes proved their value as spotters over enemy territory. Machine guns and bombs were also mounted on planes. War was thus extended to the skies for the first time.

When either German or Allied generals felt the time was right, a major attack was launched. This usually began with a merciless bombardment of the enemy's trench system. The steady shelling by huge cannons might last for days. Then the infantry, later with tank support, went "over the top" and tried to cross no-man's land to the enemy lines. That is where an attack usually stalled. The machine-gun fire was deadly and the barbed wire was difficult to pene-

squeeze the French army between Paris and the German border. It almost worked. The Belgians, however, refused to cooperate. They put up a stiff resistance. They held back the German advance for eighteen days. This gave the French some time to regroup. In addition, the French were joined by the first divisions of the British army. The German attack was also weakened when some units were sent to the East Prussian front against Russia.

Still, the Germans almost broke through. The French and British finally held at the Marne River, about 65 kilometers (about 40 miles) from Paris. The Germans retreated a short distance. Both sides then began to "dig in." They dug deep trenches and tunnels. They built machine-gun posts. They strung endless rolls of barbed wire in front of their defenses. It was intended that these trenches would provide temporary shelter against the withering fire of the enemy. Everyone had been shocked by those opening battles and the deadly efficiency of modern weapons, especially the machine gun. Within a few weeks, the opposing lines of trenches stretched from the Swiss border to the sea, about 970 kilometers (about 600 miles) away.

German troops emerging from their sleeping quarters in the trenches.

563

trate. After every battle, bodies could be seen suspended in the wire for days.

On rare occasions, there would be a breakthrough. The enemy would then abandon its front lines of trenches and retreat to other lines of trenches dug in the rear. Thousands of lives would have been paid for a few acres of ground.

One of the costliest battles was the German effort to capture the fortress at Verdun (ver DUN) in 1916. The battle raged for 10 months. Despite almost constant bombardment, the French defenders held. The Germans finally gave up and withdrew. Their casualties had been 300,000 men. The French lost even more.

Ruins in the city of Verdun.

The War in Russia and Italy In other areas, the war tended to be more mobile than on the Western Front. In the east, the Russians began by advancing along a wide front into German and Austro-Hungarian territory. The Russian success was brief. Early in 1915, German and Austrian armies launched a counterattack. The Russians began to retreat.

In the months that followed, Russia's greatest struggle was to keep an army in the field. The men were disheartened by lack of ammunition, weapons, and food. Poor morale spread to the home front. Clothing, food, and fuel were in short supply. Rationing was severe. The weaknesses of the government were a major part of the problem. At the same time, the German navy controlled the Baltic Sea and the Ottoman Turks controlled the entrance to the Black Sea. This meant that no supply ships could get through to Russia from the Baltic or the Mediterranean. Only the distant and obscure ports of Murmansk (moor MANSK), Arkhangelsk (ur KAN gel y sk), and Vladivostock were open.

For several years, Czar Nicholas II managed to hold the Russian empire together and to keep the nation in the war. However, the battered Russian forces continued to retreat. The German-Austrian forces advanced into Russia itself. Then in March 1917, the Russian empire collapsed. The revolt that occurred is usually called the February Revolution because the Julian calendar was then in effect in Russia. The czar was overthrown, and a provisional government was formed. The new government, largely middle class and leaning toward democracy, promised to continue the war effort. However, Russia remained in a state of chaos. A second revolution in November, the so-called October Revolution, brought to power the Bolshevik wing of the Communist Party (see Chapter 29). Within a few weeks, the Bolsheviks asked the Central Powers for a cease-fire.

Thinking Geographically: In what country were the most battles fought?

After Italy declared war on Austria-Hungary in 1915, the Austrians and Italians became locked in a bitter struggle. The Italian front turned into much the same kind of trench warfare as in the west. In 1917, German troops combined with the Austrians to smash through the Italian lines at Caporetto (kaw po RAY to). This was one of the major battles of the war. However, the Central Powers were unable to follow through and drive Italy from the war.

Turkey The rulers of the Ottoman empire had joined the Central Powers as a means of clinging to their weakening empire. The

Turks had already been almost completely driven from Europe in earlier struggles against nationalist groups in the Balkans.

During World War I, the Turks tried to hold together their territory in the Middle East. They horrified the world by their actions against one minority group, the Armenians. More than a million of these stateless people were killed. Elsewhere, the British worked with nationalist groups against the Turks. However, the Turks managed to escape a major defeat. In 1915, a force of British, Australian, and New Zealand troops invaded Turkey at the Gallipoli (ga LIP o li) Peninsula. The aim was to open the Black Sea so Russia could be supplied. The Gallipoli attack was a great disaster for the Allies. They withdrew early in 1916 after suffering heavy losses.

There was also scattered fighting in other parts of the world. British, French, and South African forces seized German colonies on the west coast of Africa. In East Africa, the Germans eluded a larger British force throughout the war. In Asia, Japan captured German-held ports in China. The Japanese then joined with the Australians and New Zealanders in taking control of Germany's island colonies in the Pacific.

The Sea War The war at sea was critically important for two reasons: First, modern warfare placed a tremendous strain on the economies of all countries involved. Both sides needed food and other supplies. The United States, the world's leading economic power, was the most likely source for these goods. Second, the stalemate on the Western Front caused leaders to look for other ways to gain an advantage. The British navy blockaded the German coast to prevent food and supplies from getting through. The Germans counted on one of the most terrifying of war's new weapons, the submarine, to sink ships headed for Allied ports.

The importance of the sea war placed a strain on American neutrality. Each side desperately needed American supplies. Each was also determined to keep those supplies from the other. When the powerful British navy blockaded the German coast, explosive mines were spread throughout the North Sea. Then, to keep supplies from being shipped through neutral countries, the blockade was extended to the Netherlands, Denmark, Norway, and Sweden. The American government protested these acts as violations of neutral rights. Americans became even more angry when the British issued an order that all ships must stop at British ports.

Americans forgot much of their anti-British feeling when the Germans began their submarine campaign. This was an entirely new form of ocean war. Submarines lurked beneath the surface rather than giving a warning of attack. They disappeared after sinking a vessel instead of picking up survivors.

Early in 1915, after warning all neutral nations of the dangers, the Germans unleashed their submarines, called U-boats, in the Atlantic. The sinking of several British ships resulted in civilian deaths. Newspapers in the Allied countries and in the United States denounced the attacks as "barbarous" and "uncivilized." On May 7, 1915, the British ship Lusitania was torpedoed off the Irish coast. The death toll was 1,198 people, including 128 Americans. The Germans insisted that this was an act of war. They pointed out that the ship was also carrying war supplies. Nonetheless, the sinking of the Lusitania sharply increased American hostility against Germany.

For a time, the German government reduced its submarine attacks. Then, early in 1917, unrestricted submarine warfare was resumed. The members of the German High Command were now convinced that this would win the war. Even if the United

Did You Know?

These Armenian refugees fled to the United States to escape the Turks.

Ataturk, the Father Turk

Mustafa Kemal (ke MALL 1881-1938) is now called Ataturk (ah tah TURK), the Father Turk. He was given this title by the Turkish people for his work in making Turkey more modern.

During World War I, Turkey fought on the side of Germany. After the war ended, the victorious allies took non-Turkish provinces away from Turkey. To compound Turkey's defeat, a Greek army landed in Izmir in 1919. The sultan of Turkey felt powerless to do anything.

Ataturk and other Turks were outraged that Turkish land would be taken by Greece, their old enemy. Ataturk led a Turkish army against the Greeks. In 1922, he drove the Greeks out of Asia Minor. The allies then agreed to allow Turkey to keep its own borders.

In 1923, the hero Ataturk took over Turkey. He made the nation a republic and served as president until his death in 1938. Ataturk believed that Turkey's defeat in World War I was due to not being modern. He now set out to make Turkey modern by imposing western ideas.

His first step was to separate the Muslim church from the state. The state took over the educational system from the religious leaders. Ataturk pushed for the reform of the Turkish alphabet to make it easier for the Turkish people to learn to read. He forced the Turkish people to wear western dress and outlawed the wearing of the fez (a man's hat). Turkish women were given more rights. He ended the customs of men having more than one wife and of women wearing the veil. Ataturk also pushed for a new calendar and the metric system. He tried to encourage new industries.

Some reforms were just being implemented when Ataturk died.

The New York Times announcing the sinking of the Lusitania.

States did join the Allies, they believed, it could not help them in time to prevent a German victory.

One other incident helped to solidify American opinion. With British help, the government gained possession of a secret note sent by the German Foreign Office to its minister in Mexico. This "Zimmerman Note" suggested an alliance between Germany and Mexico. The Mexicans would then attack the United States and Germany would help them regain their "lost territory in New Mexico, Texas, and Arizona."

When the American government made the Zimmerman Note public, a wave of war feeling swept the country. On April 2, 1917, President Wilson asked Congress for a declaration of war. The United States must fight, he said, "for the ultimate peace of the world and for the liberation of all its peoples, the German peoples included....The world must be made safe for democracy."

The Allied Victory The United States fought in World War I as an "Associated Power" on the side of the Allied Powers. American entry into the war came at a time when the Allied cause looked bleak. The first Russian revolution had just taken place, deposing the czar. It was doubtful that Russia could stay in the war. Then, while American forces were mobilizing, Germany and Austria defeated Italy at Caporetto.

Early in 1918, Germany began its final major offensive. The German High Command hoped to force a breakthrough before American forces were at full strength. The "Yanks" were already arriving from the United States at the rate of 10,000 per day.

People dancing in the streets to celebrate the end of World War I.

However, the Germans had just signed a peace treaty with the new Bolshevik government in Russia. As a result, they could concentrate all their forces on the Western Front.

The Germans attacked the Allied lines at a number of points. By the end of May 1918, they were again at the Marne River. French, British, and Belgian troops, with help now from the inexperienced but fresh Americans, stopped the advance. On July 18, the Allied commander ordered a counterattack. With a million Americans now in France, the Allied forces began to move forward along the entire front. It was now clear that the Germans were beaten. The German people were ready to give up. The German empire began to collapse from within. On November 3, 1918, crews at a German naval base refused to head back into combat. Mutinies broke out in army barracks. Unrest spread to the cities, where there were street riots.

This sense of defeat and unrest extended throughout the Central Powers. The Turks gave up and asked for peace; so did Bulgaria. The Austrians signed a cease-fire with the Italians. Kaiser William II abdicated and left Germany. Power was assumed by a provisional government, which promised democracy. On November 11, 1918, the new German government signed an armistice with the Allied Powers and the United States.

Section Questions

1. What was the German plan of attack in 1914? Why did it fail?
2. What kind of fighting evolved in the Western Front?
3. What political upheavals occurred in Russia during the war?
4. Why was naval warfare so important?
5. How did the sea war lead to the entry of the United States into the war?

3. The Allies Imposed a Peace

Early in 1918, Russia's new Bolshevik government had signed a peace treaty with Germany—the Treaty of Brest-Litovsk. The Germans had made stern demand for large areas of Russia. The Bolshevik leaders had given in to those demands. Germany was to receive one-fourth of Russia's European territory, one-third of its population, more than one-half of its industry, and nine-tenths of its coal mines.

This harsh treaty would have been devastating for Russia. Its provisions were cancelled, however, when Germany lost the war. It was now the turn of the Allies and the United States to decide on peace terms with the defeated Central Powers. Many Allied leaders felt the Treaty of Brest-Litovsk showed the kind of peace the Germans would have imposed if they had won the war. To these leaders, it was the kind of treaty Germany itself deserved.

Woodrow Wilson, the American president, disagreed with this approach. A harsh peace, he warned, was no peace. He argued that imposing harsh demands would not settle the causes of conflict. Instead, such a treaty would make Germany seek revenge. The debate over the peace treaty centered around the contrast between Wilson's ideas and those of the Allied leaders.

Wilson's Idealism Wilson himself sailed for Europe to lead the American delegation at the peace talks. They were held at Versailles, a few miles outside Paris. He came prepared with a list of proposals that were already well known as the Fourteen Points. He was convinced that the Fourteen Points would not only lead to a fair treaty but would also resolve many of the conflicts that had led to war. The first five points were as follows:

1. Open covenants of peace, openly arrived at. The Bolsheviks had made public secret treaties Russia had signed with other Allies

President Woodrow Wilson.

during the war. These detailed how the Allies would divide up the spoils of victory. They seemed to prove Wilson's argument about the danger of such negotiations.

2. Absolute freedom of navigation upon the seas. This was the issue over which the United States had gone to war.

3. The removal...of all economic barriers and the establishment of an equality of trade conditions.

4. Adequate guarantees...that national armaments will be reduced. Wilson felt that disarmament was vital to the maintenance of peace. Small land armies would mean that no nation had to live in fear of attack. Freedom of seas would eliminate the need for large navies.

5. Absolutely impartial adjustment of all colonial claims. Wilson was advancing the new idea that the interests of colonial peoples should be considered along with those of the colonial powers.

Points six through thirteen dealt mostly with the evacuation and restoration of Russia, Belgium, and France (including the return of Alsace-Lorraine) and with the adjustment of borders along lines of nationality in Italy, Austria-Hungary, the

Balkans, the Ottoman Empire, and Poland. The fourteenth point was central to Wilson's plan. It proposed a general association of nations that would help keep the peace. This later led to the establishment of the League of Nations.

Behind the specific points lay several important principles. There was faith in democracy. Closely allied to this was a belief in national self-determination for all peoples—in Austria-Hungary, the Ottoman Empire, Poland, and even in the colonies. Wilson was also convinced that fair treatment of the defeated powers, free navigation and trade, disarmament, and international cooperation would make peace permanent. The president called for "a peace without victory." Wilson's Fourteen Points had been widely publicized during the war. They were translated into other languages and dropped from airplanes over enemy territory. These ideas gave hope to Slavic groups that were opposed to the rule of the Austrian emperor. As the war drew to a close, people in Germany who opposed the kaiser found new hope in Wilson's promise of fair treatment.

Before the meetings began at Versailles, the American president toured a number of European cities. Everywhere he was received as a great hero. This led him to believe that people not only understood his plan but believed in it.

German troops leaving Danzig, which was to become an "open city."

Revenge and Security To the Allied leaders, Wilson was a starry-eyed idealist rather than a hero. For four years, the French premier Georges Clemenceau (KLEM un so) had watched the French countryside laid waste by the heaviest fighting of the war. He had seen a generation of young Frenchmen almost wiped out by artillery shells, poison gas, and machine-gun bullets. Clemenceau felt that an American president could know nothing of these things. The French leader was convinced that Germany was responsible for this suffering and must pay for it. Steps would also have to be taken to see that such an attack never happened again. The British and Italian delegates agreed with Clemenceau.

The delegations of the Allies and the United States decided the terms of the Versailles Treaty. They reorganized Europe's political boundaries in ways that reduced the size of Germany. Alsace and Lorraine were returned to France. The nation of Poland was established. To give that new country an outlet to the sea, a "Polish Corridor" was carved through Germany.

571

German airplanes were destroyed to reduce Germany's ability to wage war.

This corridor separated East Prussia from the rest of Germany. Many Germans were thereby placed under Polish rule. The German port of Danzig was made an "open city" to be used by the Poles.

Strong measures were adopted to provide France with greater security. The region of the Rhine River in Germany was demilitarized. Never again would Germany be allowed to station troops in that area near France. The coal-mining region of the Saar Valley was turned over to France for fifteen years, in part as payment for the flooding of French mines. Germany's ability to wage war was sharply curtailed.

When the German delegation arrived at Versailles to sign the treaty, they were shocked. Two provisions were almost impossible to accept. According to one, Germany must accept full responsibility for bringing about the war. Tied to this "war guilt" clause was a second provision. This demanded that Germany pay reparations for the damage and suffering it had caused.

Perhaps if the German delegates had known how great these reparations would be, they would never have signed. The final bill, decided on in 1921, was $56 billion. This was a sum that the defeated nation simply could not afford to pay. However, the German delegates at Versailles knew they had no choice but to sign. With great reluctance, therefore, they signed the treaty. It brought humiliation to the new government that was struggling to create a democracy in Germany.

Self-Determination The Allied leaders more or less agreed with Wilson's idea of self-determination, at least in Europe. However, the mixing of nationalities made it impossible to draw boundaries that satisfied everyone. In addition, some lands had already been committed to the great powers in secret treaties.

Despite these problems, the leaders at Versailles did create a map of Europe that more nearly reflected national identities. Poland regained its independence for the first time in more than a century. Two groups, the Czechs and the Slovaks, were united to form the new nation of Czechoslovakia. Other Slavic areas were added to Serbia to create Yugoslavia. The remainder of the Austro-Hungarian empire became the two separate countries of Austria and Hungary. In northern Europe, the independent states of Finland, Lithuania (LITH uh WAY nee uh), Latvia, and Estonia (e STO ne uh) were carved out of the Russian empire. The new Communist government of Russia was not represented at Versailles.

Wilson had hoped that the Middle Eastern lands of the Turks would gain their independence. Instead, the area was divided

This cartoon showed how many people felt about the League of Nations.

into colonies. Britain and France were to rule these as mandates of the League of Nations. Britain took control of Palestine, Iraq, and Transjordan. France assumed power in Syria and Lebanon. In theory, Britain and France were answerable to the League for these areas. In practice, a mandate was not much different from a traditional colony. Germany's former colonies in Africa and the Pacific were disposed of in a similar way.

The League of Nations Wilson's one great triumph seemed to be the covenant, attached to the Versailles Treaty, that established the League of Nations. For the first time, the nations of the world had created a permanent institution for working out conflicts in nonviolent ways. The League of Nations consisted of (1) a Secretariat to handle administrative work, (2) an Assembly in which each nation would have one vote, and (3) a Council to serve as an executive.

The Council was the most important part of the League. It was to be made up of the five great powers — France, Great Britain, Italy, Japan, and the United States, with four others serving on a rotating basis. All League members agreed to try every possible peaceful solution before resorting to war. If the Council found that any nation was guilty of aggression, it could ask all members to impose *economic sanctions* — that is, to refuse to trade.

The League had many weaknesses. For example, Council decisions had to be unanimous. As a result, a single great power could block any action. Obviously, if one of the Great Powers committed an act of aggression, that country would not vote to punish itself. Nonetheless, the effort began with a good deal of hope. The headquarters of the League was established at Geneva, Switzerland. Within a short time, the feeling grew that the League represented a kind of moral authority.

The ability of the League of Nations to help prevent war was soon dealt a serious blow. President Wilson returned to the United States and tried to persuade the U.S. Senate to approve the Versailles Treaty and the League Covenant. The Senate refused to do so. There was a growing feeling among Americans that the nation should stay out of Europe's problems.

President Wilson tried to take his case directly to the American people. He collapsed from exhaustion during a long speech-making trip and soon had a stroke. The Senate never approved the treaty or the League. The peace, Wilson had warned his audiences, "cannot last more than a generation" without the support of the peoples and nations of the world. No one at the time could know just how right Woodrow Wilson was. The peace was to last only twenty years.

Section Questions

1. Who signed the Treaty of Brest-Litovsk?
2. What did the Fourteen Points say about Alsace and Lorraine?
3. What did the Versailles Treaty require Germany to pay?
4. What important country was not represented at Versailles?
5. What provision about its Council weakened the League of Nations?

Chapter Summary

1. The crisis that triggered World War I in 1914 was the assassination of the Archduke Franz Ferdinand, heir to the throne of Austria-Hungary. However, the real causes went much deeper. The Great Powers had been engaged in bitter rivalries for years. Disputes arose over national pride, colonial expansion, and trade. An arms race and the necessity to mobilize added to the atmosphere of suspicion and fear. People had forgotten the horrors of war.

The two systems of alliances that had arisen meant that any argument could involve all powers. Rivalries were particularly intense in the Balkans. Kaiser William II of Germany became convinced that there was some conspiracy against his country. Thus, Germany declared war on Russia and France. Britain, Italy, and the Ottoman Empire soon joined in. The concept of balance of power, which had long helped maintain peace, now helped bring on war. Diplomacy and other nonviolent means of avoiding war failed.

2. No one was prepared for the horrors of modern war. Mobilization, new weapons, mass armies, and trench warfare made fighting very different. The European conflict became a global war. The United States at first remained officially neutral.

The German plan to move through Belgium and capture Paris failed. The war soon became a stalemate in the trenches. In the east, after initial success, Russia began to collapse. Two revolutions took Russia out of the war in 1917. Also in 1917, the Italians suffered a disastrous defeat. Earlier, the Turks had stopped the Allies at Gallipoli. Both Germany and Great Britain counted on sea power to obtain much-needed supplies and deny them to each other. Britain blockaded Germany and neutral Europe; German submarines sank ships in Allied waters. Submarine warfare and the Zimmerman Note led to the entry of the United States into the war against Germany in 1917.

Russia had been driven from the war and Italy suffered a disaster. However, a German offense in 1918 failed and the Allies counterattacked. American troops and supplies allowed them to push back the Germans. By November 1919, the Central Powers collapsed. A revolution in Germany ended the empire and Kaiser William was replaced by a new government.

3. The peace negotiations at Versailles pitted the idealism of the American president, Woodrow Wilson, against the hard realism of the Allied leaders. Wilson hoped that his Fourteen Points would lead to a fair treaty and provide for a more peaceful world. The other Allies wanted revenge and security. Germany was reduced in size and its military forces restricted. The Germans were seemingly forced to accept blame for the war and were required to pay reparations. Wilson had some success with his idea of self-determination. A number of new nations were established. In addition, the League of Nations was established. It offered hope that ways could be found to settle disputes without war. The League's chances for success were lessened when the United States failed to join.

Chapter 28 Review

Check Your Facts

1. Identify the following:
   a. Sarajevo
   b. Nicholas II
   c. Woodrow Wilson
   d. Verdun
   e. Lusitania
   f. Zimmerman Note
   g. William II
   h. Brest-Litovsk
2. What happened to Great Britain's position as the world's leading economic power between 1870 and 1914?
3. What were the two major systems of alliances on the eve of World War I?
4. Why did Russia begin to mobilize when Austria attacked Serbia?
5. Why did the German High Command follow a policy of unrestricted submarine warfare?
6. How did President Wilson differ from the Allied leaders in his views on the peace treaty?
7. What was the key part of the new League of Nations?

Words to Know

Define the following words or terms in one or two sentences, then explain their historical importance.
   a. mobilize
   b. ultimatum
   c. mediation
   d. reparations
   e. arbitration
   f. economic sanctions

Developing Your Skills

1. Place these events in order:
   The assassination at Sarajevo
   The Triple Alliance
   Russian mobilization
   American troops in France
   German invasion of Belgium
   The first Russian revolution
2. Make two lists, one labeled *War* and the other *Peace Negotiations*. Place each of the following in the correct list:
   mobilization
   Fourteen Points
   mandate
   Versailles
   breakthrough
   Zimmerman Note
   reparations
   war guilt
   no-man's land
   Caporetto

Thinking It Over

1. How did the race for colonies contribute to a warlike atmosphere?
2. Germany was blamed by many for bringing about the war. How would you divide the responsibility for the war?
3. Why did people enter World War I in such a high-spirited mood?
4. Do you think the German High Command made a mistake in its use of submarine warfare? Why or why not?

Special Activities

1. Use newspaper sources to locate a contemporary conflict that is escalating or that has become violent. Trace the course of events through earlier reports. What similarities can you find between this situation and what happened in Europe in 1914?
2. Make a list of events involved in the escalation of conflict in June and July 1914. At what point(s) do you think action could have been taken to stop the escalation? What kind of action do you think might have worked?

Pierre Brissaud's "Learning to Dance the Shimmy."

Chapter 29 The Impact of War

The guns of war had finally fallen silent at 11:00 A.M. on November 11, 1918. This date became known as Armistice Day. Throughout the world, people shared a common hope—the hope that life would now return to normal. The successful Republican candidate for the U.S. presidency in 1920, Warren G. Harding, even based his campaign on the promise of "a return to normalcy."

In the industrial countries, the postwar period began in a spirit of optimism. Many shared Woodrow Wilson's belief that this had been "the war to end all wars." New democratic governments had

1903-1939

1903	Mensheviks and Bolsheviks split
1910	Mexican Revolution
1915	McMahon Letter
1917	Balfour Declaration
1917	Russian Revolutions
1920	Women gain vote in U.S.
1922	Japanese withdraw from Russia
1922	Union of Soviet Socialist Republics begins
1923	Ottoman empire overthrown
1924	Lenin dies
1924	German reparations reduced (Dawes Plan)
1928	Five-Year Plan in Soviet Union
1929	German reparations reduced (Young Plan)
1935-1939	Great Purge in Soviet Union

A parade in Moscow.

been formed. Soldiers were welcomed back home as national heroes. Factories began to pour out peacetime goods.

The years that followed did not, however, bring a return to "normal." The world of 1914 could not be restored. Peoples around the globe were going through an age of great social change.

At times during this postwar era, life seemed exciting and filled with progress and promise, much as it had in 1914. Technology seemed capable of creating a new era of permanent prosperity. For example, new devices and methods were rapidly transforming housework from the drudgery of past ages. These included electric sewing machines, refrigerators, prepared foods, and foods frozen by Clarence Birdseye's technique. Other things that had appeared earlier were now improved. Airplanes became mail carriers and then opened short passenger routes. Automobiles were now in mass production. Vast stretches of surfaced road were being built in the United States and western Europe. Radio launched a new age of home entertainment. Movies became "talkies." For some people, the 1920s brought excitement and newness and easy money. Many would look back with fondness on the "Golden Twenties."

The postwar years were, nevertheless, also troubled years. Thousands of veterans returned permanently disabled by wounds or the effects of poison gas. Others found that jobs were scarce. Unemployment remained high in every industrial country throughout the 1920s. At the same

An automobile assembly line.

time, thousands of farmers were driven to bankruptcy by impossibly low prices for their products. In 1930, for example, the price of bread was at its lowest point in 300 years.

Most people assumed that the war had settled the conflicts among nations. The Allies and the United States had won. Germany and the other Central Powers had lost. That should have settled matters. However, it did not. The French, for example, continued to hate and distrust the Germans. The Germans, on their part, would never forget what they considered the humiliating Treaty of Versailles. Other issues continued to cause unrest. Instead of resolving problems, the Great War had been merely one episode in a long series of conflicts. The major issues still had to be solved.

1. World War I Caused Major Changes in Most Lands

The old empires that had ruled much of Europe for so long were now gone. The Russian empire had been overwhelmed by two revolutions in 1917. The German and Austro-Hungarian empires had collapsed in the closing days of the war. The Ottoman empire was a mere shell. In 1923, a revolution transformed it into the Republic of Turkey.

The regal ceremonies and the extravagant courts were now only memories. Most imperial families moved to other countries, where they lived in quiet obscurity. Czar Nicholas II of Russia and his family were not that fortunate. Placed under arrest during the first revolution, they were later murdered by the Bolsheviks.

Shifts in Power As the old power centers disappeared, new ones emerged and others changed. Few people were aware of it at the time, but the age of great western European power was ending. Never again would these countries dominate the world as they had for centuries. On the surface, there were no clear signs of this waning power. Britain and France, for example, still possessed their colonial empires. In fact, new colonies had been added by the mandate system of the League of Nations.

The strongest evidence of shifting world power was economic. In the decades before the war, the western European countries had been the world's bankers. European investments in the United States, for example, had been a major reason for America's rapid industrial growth between 1865 and 1914.

Unemployment after World War I.

These positions were reversed by the war. At first, Europeans cashed in their notes in order to buy war materials. Then, they began borrowing from American sources to buy still more war items. When the war ended, Britain and France found that more loans were needed to begin rebuilding from the damage done during the war.

Both Britain and France were heavily in debt to the United States throughout the 1920s. There had been some hope that selling goods in the United States would create funds for repayment of these debts. However, the United States was pursuing a policy of *isolationism*, or separation from world affairs. Heavy tariffs were being placed on foreign goods. American business did not want competition from British or French products.

There was hope, too, that reparations from Germany would enable Britain and France to pay the United States what they owed. However, the reparations bill—$56 billion—was far too high for Germany, with its war-weakened economy. Agreements reached in 1924 (the Dawes Plan) and 1929 (the Young Plan) reduced Germany's bill, the latter lowering it to $8 billion. Even this proved too much, or at least the German government said so. The French angrily sent troops into German industrial areas to force an increase in production. The German workers reacted by going on strike.

By 1930, there were even hard feelings between the Allies and the United States. Both the British and the French felt that the United States should cancel part of their debts since they could not collect reparations from Germany. The American government refused, arguing that the debts had never been tied to reparations.

This matter was never settled. As we will see in the next chapter, new world crises made the collection of war debts or reparations impossible.

The economies of the European nations did recover from the war, at least during the 1920s. It was becoming clear, however, that they would never catch up to the output of American factories, farms, and mines. By 1929, the United States outproduced all the European countries combined. The war had demonstrated that, in the twentieth century, military strength depended on industrial power. That meant that the United States could become the superpower of the world.

Other New Power Centers In the east, a strange new power was rising from the ashes of the Russian empire. The Bolsheviks were creating a new kind of state, one that was dedicated to leading a worldwide Communist revolution. To the Bolsheviks, the capitalist nations of Europe, North America, and Japan were their enemies. Ever since Marx had issued the call for worldwide revolution in 1848, leaders of capitalist countries had hated and feared the dedicated socialist revolutionaries. In the past, such revolutionaries had been a nuisance. They had formed clandestine groups that caused labor unrest and street riots. Now they were in control of the world's largest country.

No one knew quite what to expect from this Bolshevik-led nation. In the postwar period, Russia seemed to be a helpless giant, ruined by war, revolution, and civil disorder. Even in 1914, Russia had been hopelessly behind the West in industrial development. Russia, then, was not an immediate threat. However, it did have the potential to become an economic and military power, with its wealth of natural resources. Against a disarmed Germany, this new power could be dangerous.

East of Russia, yet another new power was developing—Japan. For 50 years, the Japanese had been racing to catch up to the technology and ideas of the West. Now they were succeeding. In 1904-1905, they had shocked the world by easily defeating

Russia in the Russo-Japanese War. Japan then joined the Allies in World War I. It was recognized as one of the five great powers in the League of Nations. Japanese military leaders dreamed of expansion. Neither China nor any of the groups of Pacific islands would be able to match their growing strength. At the Versailles Peace Conference, one Allied leader had spoken of the need to "establish the old order." The old order no longer existed, but a new one had not yet emerged.

Aftermath of Total War World War I had been a total war. It had involved the civilian population as well as the military. This trend toward total war had begun during the era of the French Revolution and Napoleon. That was the first time nations had relied on massive "people's" armies rather than smaller forces of trained professionals. The American Civil War (1861-1865) had been another step toward total war. In it contending armies had depended upon civilians for vast amounts of food, clothing, shelter, weapons, and equipment.

Civilians were even more closely involved in the Great War. Those who lived near battle areas were frequently the victims of heavy artillery fire. About eight million civilians died in the war. This was nearly equal to the number of deaths among the armed forces. Civilians supplied food, clothing, tents, barracks, ships, airplanes, weapons, and medical supplies. Shortages of food or fuel for heating could sometimes cause greater hardship on the home front than on the battlefront. World War I was also total in that government became deeply involved in many areas of people's lives. The government controlled the economy and planned production. Workers were thought of as industrial soldiers fighting for the goal of full war production. As shortages of food and other goods appeared in every country, the government set up a system of rationing such products. In addition, every available method was used to encourage people to back the war effort. Newspapers and wall posters carried an unending flow of propaganda. The enemy was always pictured as a vicious menace to the very existence of civilization.

A World War I poster.

The experience of total war left millions of people in a state of shock. How could the "civilized" nations of the world have produced such senseless slaughter? Through many generations, a powerful faith in the idea of progress had grown in the West. Each stage of history seemed to show a steady forward march. The wonders of modern technology had appeared to speed up the pace of that progress.

Now, to many people, especially the young, the world seemed to be insane. They could find nothing to justify the horror

A young woman working as a welder during World War I.

they had experienced and helped create. A new generation of writers spoke for the disillusioned. The literary "Lost Generation" was centered in Paris. Writers like the American Hemingway and the French Celine expressed the frustration and bitterness felt by millions.

The war produced another kind of generation of misfits. There were men in almost every country who had grown too fond of war. The excitement and comradeship, the dangers, and even the uniforms gave these men a sense of belonging. Many stayed together, especially in areas of Germany and central Europe where fear of Bolshevism was strong. These "freebooters" were violent gangs in search of new leaders and new causes. You will read in the next chapter how a new ideology called fascism provided exactly what they wanted.

Women and Social Justice The war did contribute to positive social reforms. One of the most important was the improved status of women. During the war, the shortage of labor led to the employment of women in many traditionally male jobs. They performed heavy farmwork, ran machinery in factories, drove buses and mail trucks, took on more office duties, and worked in military hospitals.

These economic changes gave a powerful boost to women's demands for the vote. In 1920, an amendment to the Constitution of the United States granted that right after more than 70 years of struggle. British women had a tougher fight. They gained partial voting rights in 1923, and full rights in 1928. By the mid-1920s, women could also vote in Germany, the Soviet Union, and most of the new European nations. Gaining the vote did not, of course, end the struggles of women for greater equality. However, it was an important victory.

Other social reforms, many begun before the war, were also advanced. All restrictions on voting by males were removed. Laws were passed to protect women and children from unsafe work. Some countries began to provide relief for severe problems of unemployment.

Section Questions

1. How did economic changes show the decline of Europe's power?
2. Why were the Bolsheviks considered a threat to all western nations?
3. Why was there a "lost generation" after World War I? Why were there violent gangs of freebooters?
4. What were some of the positive social reforms caused by the war?
5. How did governments contribute to total war?

2. Many Nations Tried to Make Changes

National pride was as strong after the war as it had been in 1914. People in Allied countries felt very proud of their triumph over the Central Powers. Their fighting men had been given heroes' welcomes as they marched through the streets of New York, London, Paris, or Rome.

The peoples of central and eastern Europe had, for the most part, gained national independence. Some groups had not benefitted from Wilson's idea of self-determination—Austrians in Czechoslovakia, Hungarians in Romania and Yugoslavia, and Germans in Poland. In general, however, there was strong unity in the new countries created by the Versailles Treaty. Each of the new governments established a parliamentary democracy, modeling themselves after Britain and France. The new nations also began the process of creating industrial economies.

New Nationalism Self-determination had not been applied to the European colonies. The idea spread around the world, however, often carried by colonists who had served their European masters in the war. Many of these ex-soldiers returned home to create new nationalist movements or strengthen existing ones.

Throughout the 1920s and 1930s, the European powers had trouble over the issue of national independence for their colonies. The Europeans insisted that the colonies were not yet ready to govern themselves. Many of the colonial peoples had, of course, different ideas about this.

India In 1919, after World War I ended, the British allowed India more self-government in domestic affairs. But the British kept power in military and foreign affairs and the final authority to decide how fast India could gain self-rule. The British also retained a monopoly on domestic and foreign trade.

Mohandas Gandhi (GAHN dee) was a Hindu lawyer who had received his training in England. Gandhi engaged in a lifetime crusade against British rule in India. There were three major campaigns, in 1920-21, 1930, and 1942 to force the British out. Gandhi gave up his law career and all worldly possessions to lead a movement for national independence. He advocated nonviolent resistance to British rule. Thus, he encouraged the Indian people to boycott, or refuse to buy, British products. At the time, half of Britain's sales of cotton goods were to India. Now the British could only watch in embarrassment as many of the Indian people peacefully spun their own cloth. This movement reduced British sales by half. Gandhi also made use of hunger strikes and protest rallies. Although he was often imprisoned, he vowed not to give up until Indian was independent.

The Middle East Before 1914, Turkey's Ottoman empire officially controlled much of the Middle East. However, Turkey's power was weakening. The British, French, and Russians were gaining more power in the area. The Italians had taken over Libya and the area around Ethiopia.

Many Jews, especially in Russia, faced persecution. Some of these Jews yearned to return to Palestine, their promised land in the Bible, where the ancient Hebrew civilization had existed for several centuries. The movement for an independent Jewish state in Palestine was called Zionism. In the 1800s, a small number of Jews from eastern Europe emigrated to Palestine, or the Holy Land. The Arabs had conquered this area about 1300 years ago. They considered Palestine their own land.

During World War I, the British encouraged the Arabs in the Middle East to revolt against the Turks. They promised the Arabs independence. The McMahon

Letter of 1915 said that the British would support the independence of some Arab people.

At the same time, Zionists asked the British to recognize the Jewish claim for a homeland in Palestine. In 1917, the British government issued the Balfour Declaration which pledged support for a national homeland for the Jews in Palestine. Thus, the British made conflicting promises about Palestine.

In 1918, the British, with Arab help, drove the Turks out of Palestine. In the peace treaties following World War I, England and France gained control of the Middle East. The League of Nations gave them a mandate, an order to rule, for a limited time before complete independence was to be granted. In effect, they were to act to help the people living under the mandate.

France got Syria and Lebanon. The British were given Palestine, Iraq, and what is now known as Jordan. The two nations were allowed to station troops in Egypt, Palestine, Iraq, Syria, and Lebanon. The British wanted to protect the Suez Canal and the Persian Gulf. They also wanted to prevent any Soviet Union expansion into the Middle East. The British and the French were also interested in increasing their trade in the Middle East. In the 1930s, oil became another important resource that the industrialized nations wanted.

However, the Arab nationalists had not fought in World War I just to exchange one master for another. The Arabs were angry at the Western powers for not keeping their promise of independence. During the 1920s and the 1930s, nationalists in Middle Eastern areas staged demonstrations and strikes, and at times used force.

In response to the demands, the British gave partial independence to Egypt. However, they retained control of defense and foreign affairs. In 1932, Iraq gained partial independence.

Riots in Palestine.

Mexico City in the early 1900s.

Latin America In the 1870s, the larger and more stable nations of Latin America began to industrialize. They wanted improved transportation and communications systems. They wanted public services such as electricity. So these nations made agreements with foreign businesses to develop their resources and their economy.

In Mexico, modernization was encouraged by Porfirio Diaz (DEE aws), the dictator of Mexico from 1872 to 1911. A tremendous amount of foreign investment took place in Mexico during this time. Mexican public utilities were in the hands of the Americans and the British. Americans also invested in large ranches in the north and in the oil industry. The French were strong in banking. They also established some textile industries. The Germans were dominant in the drug business and hardware.

The Mexican Revolution Meanwhile, Diaz had deprived thousands of Indians of their communal lands and allowed the land to fall into the hands of the large landowners. The underfed peasants, in debt to their owners, were legally prevented from leaving the land. Millions were poorly housed and about 70 percent were illiterate.

The Mexican middle class felt that they were being denied opportunities that were granted to foreigners. They had little political power. Only four percent of the population could vote. The middle class wanted reforms.

Diaz was getting old, but he still wanted to run for another term as president. Discontent surfaced. The people were getting tired of the long one-man rule. Francisco Madero (ma DEH ro) dared to run as a candidate against the established ruler. Diaz put Madero in jail before the election. Diaz wanted no opposition in "his" elec-

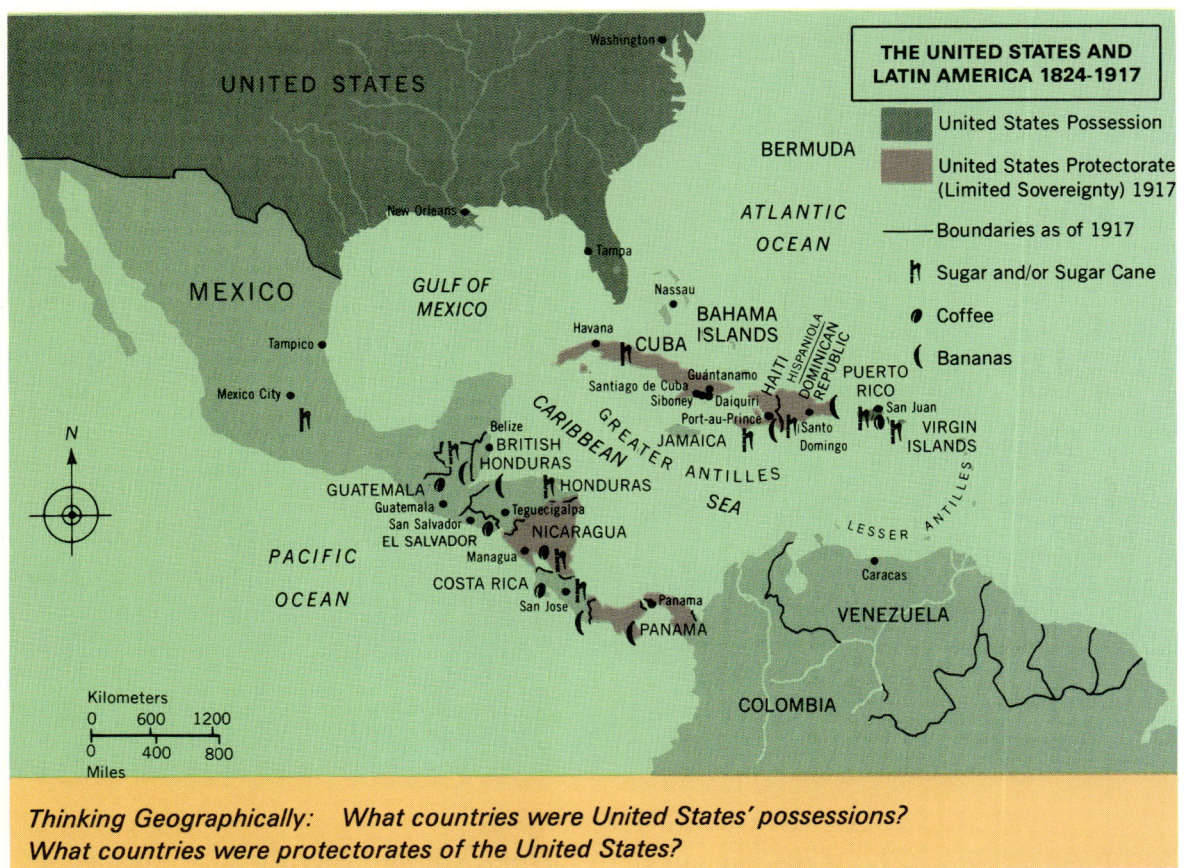

Thinking Geographically: What countries were United States' possessions? What countries were protectorates of the United States?

tion. When Madero was released from jail he fled to the United States. From there, he issued the call for revolution. The people in the north first rose up against the government. During the day, the peasants went about their usual tasks. But at night, they terrorized the haciendas, killing landowners and burning down estates.

In 1911, Diaz was forced into exile. But Madero could not control the situation. The country was in a state of anarchy, with little order and much violence.

In 1917, the major groups agreed to a new constitution for Mexico. For the good of the people, land could be taken from the large landowners and foreign businesses. The constitution also gave workers the right to form labor unions. Public educa-

tion was to be supported. The Roman Catholic Church's role in education was to be eliminated.

However, there was no haste in implementing the new reforms. Not until 1929 did the Mexicans evolve a stable one-party system of government. One person could hold the office of president for six years but could not be re-elected. This allowed the president power to do things without facing strong opposition.

In the 1930s, more social and economic reforms took place. In 1938, the Mexican government nationalized the oil industry. Land was redistributed to the peasants. More public education and health care were provided. The Mexican Revolution never really ended as the goals of the revolution were implemented.

The Mexican Revolution was the most significant social upheaval in Latin America since the independence movement. The conditions that caused the revolt in Mexico—land in the hands of a few, foreign dominance of the economy, middle class desire for power—were also found in many other Latin American nations. The Mexican Revolution was an inspiration to these nations.

Other Latin American Nations The investments made by the United States and other foreign nations in Mexico helped to flame the Mexican Revolution. The strong anti-foreign feelings that the Mexicans had were also shared by other Latin American nations. Latin American nations felt that the United States in particular was imperialistic. They blamed the United States for their poverty and felt that they were exploited by the United States. These ideas, of course, were similar to those held by Asians and Africans against their colonial rulers.

Latin Americans particularly resented the United States' military interventions. The United States victory in the Spanish-American War of 1898 ended with United States troops stationed in both Cuba and Puerto Rico.

Eventually the United States withdrew its troops from Cuba. But the United States retained the right to intervene there until 1934. Cuba became closely tied to the United States through business. Most of Cuba's sugar crop was sent to the United States.

The United States Marines landed in the Caribbean several times from 1905 to 1965. The Marines went into the Dominican Republic, Haiti, and Nicaragua to protect United States interests in those nations. The United States also wanted to make sure that European influence would not grow and to protect the Panama Canal. These actions by the United States caused great resentment in Latin America.

Diego Rivera's painting of the feast of Santa Anita.

The old order had changed with World War I. Nations in Latin America and around the world were determined to see that the old order would never rise again.

Section Questions

1. What kind of government was established in the new nations of central and eastern Europe?
2. What methods of conflict resolution did Gandhi try in India?
3. Why did the Jews regard Palestine as their homeland? Why did the Arabs regard Palestine as their homeland?
4. Why didn't the Mexican Revolution end?

Lenin addressing a crowd in 1917.

3. The Bolsheviks Created the Soviet State

The czars of Russia had faced unrest for many generations. Their autocratic rule was unpopular and led to occasional uprisings. The Russian economy was changing rapidly. The czarist political system could not adjust to these changes, and it began to break down. Like earlier czars, Nicholas II relied on his army and his secret police to maintain his power.

One of the staunchest opponents of czarist rule was Vladimir Ilyich Ulyanov, who became better known as V. I. Lenin (LEN in). He had given up a comfortable life and law career to become a revolutionary. In this, he was joined by his wife, Nadezhda Krupskaya (KROOP sku yu). The two firmly believed in the prediction of Karl Marx that someday the industrial workers of the world would revolt against the ruling class. Unlike Marx, however, Lenin did not feel the working class, or proletariat, could revolt unless it was properly led. He wanted to form a group that would become "the vanguard of the proletariat." This group would lead the workers on the path to revolution. In actuality, the vanguard was to substitute for the workers. Lenin's plan called for a small, tightly knit organization. Lenin had been in prison or in exile many times. However, he was still convinced that this small group could avoid being crushed by the czar's forces. The members would operate in secret and be highly disciplined.

Lenin's ideas led to a split in the Russian Social Democratic Workers' Party. One group wanted to form a regular political party and work for gradual reform until the working class was ready for revolution. This group was the majority in the party. However, they came to be called Mensheviks, which means "minority men" in Russian. They got this name because they were the minority at a party congress held in London in 1903. The Mensheviks split away. This allowed Lenin and his supporters to form their underground organization. They came to be known as Bolsheviks, which means "majority men." A minority in the Social Democratic Party, the Bolsheviks were the majority at the 1903 congress.

In spite of their belief in violent revolution, people like Lenin and Krupskaya were also idealistic. They were sincere in their belief that a better day was coming—an age of greater social justice and peace. After the revolution, the workers and peasants would establish state ownership of all business, industry, and agriculture. The upper- and middle-class owners would be dispossessed. This period would be the stage of socialism. Gradually, the workers would take over the operation of all productive activities and divide the products and proceeds in an equal way. There would no longer be a need for government. The state would "wither away." This would be the ultimate stage of communism. Under communism, private property would be abolished and all property would be held in common.

The First Revolution In 1905, after the disaster of the Russo-Japanese War, Czar Nicholas II made some concession to demands from the people for a voice in the government. A parliament, called the Duma, was formed although Nicholas later withdrew many of its powers. In 1906, an agrarian reform was instituted. This was an attempt to create a class of productive, property-owning peasants who would support the government.

While Russia moved sluggishly toward a slightly freer regime, the government drifted into World War I without adequate preparation. The czar had fallen under the spell of a strange monk named Rasputin.

People lining up for food in Petrograd.

Nicholas began to believe more in mysticism than in rational governing.

The unrest of the people increased as the war moved from one military disaster to another. In 1916, a group of prominent men who hoped to save the czar murdered Rasputin. However, it was too late. By 1917, even many of the military officers had lost their loyalty to Nicholas. In March, workers in St. Petersburg, called Petrograd by 1917, went on strike. Food riots broke out in the city's streets. The government ordered troops in to stop the unrest. However, the soldiers refused to fire on their fellow Russians. Some even joined the uprising. The czar was no longer in control and he abdicated.

The Provisional Government Between March and November 1917, Russia was ruled by a Provisional Government. It was made up of men who had served in the Duma. The key figure came to be Aleksandr Kerenski (ke REN ski). Many of the leaders of this government represented Russia's small middle class. This class included lawyers and businessmen who believed in the liberal democratic ideas of countries like Britain and France.

Kerenski planned to hold a constitutional convention that would establish a parliamentary democracy. He also declared that Russia would continue the war effort against Germany and Austria.

Throughout the period of the Provisional Government, Russia suffered from deep divisions. Millions of people remained loyal to the czar. Some of these "White" Russians formed military units that tried to bring down the Kerenski government. Others opposed the Provisional Government for the opposite reason. They felt that it was not undoing the czarist regime fast enough. These people wanted land to be taken from the wealthy and redistributed to the peasants. They demanded an end to the war. They asserted the right of minorities to form separate nations. Radical groups formed *soviets*, or special committees, governed by workers and war veterans. The soviets in Petrograd and Moscow were particularly strong. By the late summer of 1917, the great majority of Russians had given up on the Provisional Government or were actually fighting it. Kerenski and his ministers could not establish enough order to begin their reforms. In fact, the food scarcity and other shortages that had been so severe under the czar seemed to be getting worse. The German government began aiding the Bolsheviks. They hoped thereby to bring down the Kerenski government and knock Russia out of the war. Lenin was then in exile. The Germans wisely managed to get him back to Russia.

The Bolshevik Revolution Lenin brought a new leadership and a new slogan: "Peace, Bread, and Land." Those words won a loyalty that Kerenski could not command. They promised an end to the war, enough food, and land for the peasants. Lenin also demanded "all power to the soviets." He declared that every national group had a right to form its own nation. With loyal Bolsheviks involved with each of the soviets, Lenin felt ready to move. In late October 1917, the Bolsheviks decided to lead an armed uprising. Leon Trotsky (TROT ski) began organizing the Military Revolutionary Committee to take power in Petrograd. He won over the important garrison, the Peter-and-Paul Fortress, on November 5. Trotsky was given the order to start the revolution. It began on November 6. On November 7, Trotsky's forces seized the city easily. After some resistance, the Winter Palace was captured on November 8 and the Provisional Government was ousted.

The October Revolution gave the Bolsheviks control of Petrograd and also, on November 8, of Moscow. However, they did not control the country as a whole.

This painting by Soviet painter V. Serov is called "Working People Arise!"

Lenin's party, in fact, represented only a tiny fraction of the population. Many of their allies in the soviets were suspicious of them. They did not know what the Bolsheviks would do to create a government.

Panic spread throughout the country. Thousands fled the cities, only to find more chaos in the countryside. Most of the refugees were middle-class people who feared for their lives as well as for their property.

The disorder of the previous months became worse. There was no governmental machinery, no authority except the small band of Bolsheviks. Railroads, factories, stores, and offices stood idle. Food shortages turned to hunger and starvation. Disunity was increased by nation-wide fear. Russia could offer no opposition to the German armies. Most remaining military units preferred to join the "Whites" who were loyal to the czar rather than the "Red" army led by Trotsky. Lenin knew he had to make peace quickly before the nation was overrun by the German forces. That was why he was willing to sign the Treaty of Brest-Litovsk in March 1918. In that same month, the Bolshevik Party adopted the name Communist.

Once peace was established with Germany, Lenin could focus on gaining firm control of the country. That was not an easy task. There were two years of bloody civil war. Russia became one huge and highly confused battlefield. The White armies were divided and often quarreled. Other groups formed their own military units, such as a "Green" army fighting for the independence of the Ukraine. The Allies—Britain, France, and Japan—and the United States sent in troops. They did this in part to help crush the menace of Communism.

If the anti-Communist forces had been united, they might have ended Lenin's dream. However, their endless bickering was used by Trotsky to the advantage of the Red Army. The tide gradually turned in favor of the Communists. In 1920, the last of the Allied troops were withdrawn from western Russia. Japanese forces remained in the east until 1922. Only a few pockets of White resistance remained. Formation of a permanent new government, the Union of Soviet Socialist Republics, or more simply, the Soviet Union, was announced in 1922. A new constitution was ratified in 1924.

Soviet Government During the period of the civil war, Lenin and the other Communist leaders set about creating a socialist state. The state would take over ownership of all means of production—factories, banks, stores, transportation systems, and so on. The major take-overs were completed by 1920. In spite of tight controls, however, the economy remained stagnant. Food, fuel, and housing were all in short supply. The levels of malnutrition and starvation were higher than ever.

In 1921, Lenin softened his approach by announcing a New Economic Policy (NEP). The peasants were to be allowed to own their own land and profit from it. The government would still control most of industry, but some smaller businesses would be privately owned. This "retreat from socialism" created some incentive to increase production. The new government also began a series of social reforms. Women were to have the same rights as men. They were encouraged to apply for traditionally male jobs in industry. They were also urged to seek the training needed to enter the professions—medicine, law, engineering.

The many minorities that had made up the old Russian empire were encouraged to keep alive their languages and cultures. Major national groups were formed into separate republics within the Soviet Union. This was the reason for the name Union of Soviet Socialist Republics.

Productive work of all kinds was glorified. There were to be no special rewards or status for skilled work. In practice, however, it soon became clear that members of the Communist Party (about 500,000 people) did form a new kind of elite. The capital of the Soviet Union was moved from Petrograd to Moscow, the ancient capital of Russia. Petrograd (then St. Petersburg, now Leningrad) had been made the capital by Peter the Great. He thought of it as Russia's "window on Europe." Lenin wanted to move away from European influence. In addition, he sought to stress the unity of the Soviet people. Lenin also believed in modernization. Only through industrial growth, he argued, would the Soviet Union become strong enough to defend itself against the capitalist nations.

Unity was also achieved in the Soviet Union by allowing only one political party—the Communist Party—to exist. In fact, it was the party that ruled the country. Its major organization was the Politburo, or Political Bureau, made up of leading party members. Decisions reached by the Politburo became the official policy of the national government. Through all the lower levels of the government and the economy, party members made sure that directives of the Politburo were carried out.

The Communist Party became, therefore, like a government within a government. Members of the government itself were chosen almost solely from the party. The All-Union Congress of Soviets (later called the Supreme Soviet) was the major legislative body. It was run by various committees, councils, and presidia. The

A Russian peasant promoting Communism among his fellow workers.

executive was the All-Union Council of People's Commissars, theoretically responsible to the Congress. Since the party leaders also served on the Council, there was no possibility of conflict between party and government.

The party also became important as a means of ensuring loyalty both to Communism and to the Soviet Union. For example, the party was in charge of a variety of organizations, such as youth and professional groups. Since Karl Marx had taught that religion was a tool of the capitalists, the party tried to suppress all forms of religion. Religion, especially the Russian Orthdox Church, was seen as a dangerous competitor for people's loyalties. Finally, the party leadership could preserve unity by crushing opposition, especially by using the secret police.

During the 1920s, with the help of Lenin's NEP, the Soviet economy began to improve. In 1927, the production of goods finally caught up to the 1914 level. Lenin did not live to see this improvement or to see socialism fully realized. He suffered a series of strokes and in January 1924 he died.

Lenin had achieved unity of the nation and had taken steps to build up heavy industry. His successor as Soviet leader, Joseph Stalin, was determined to make the Soviet Union and Communism powerful forces in the world.

Section Questions

1. Why did the Russian Social Democrats split into the Bolsheviks and Mensheviks?
2. Why was the czar unable to stop the March Revolution in Petrograd?
3. What kind of government did Aleksandr Kerenski favor?
4. Who were the "Whites" and "Reds"?
5. What was Lenin's policy toward national minorities?

Leon Trotsky.

4. The Threat of Communism Grew

Lenin's death led to a struggle for power—both in the Communist Party and in the Soviet Union as a whole. The logical person to replace him was Trotsky, the brilliant military organizer. Joseph Stalin (STA lin) was Trotsky's major rival. Stalin did not have the intellectual sparkle of either Lenin or Trotsky. However, he did have a genius for organization and knew how to make the most of it. In 1922, he had been named General Secretary of the Communist Party. He used this position to build a party structure of people loyal to him. Gradually, Trotsky was ousted from positions of authority. He was finally deported in 1929. Stalin became the real ruler of the Soviet Union.

Lenin's rule had been dictatorial, but it was mild compared to the regime that Stalin now developed. Stalin instituted *totalitarianism*, total state control over people's lives. As we will see in the next chapter, totalitarianism was now emerging as the modern extension of traditional dictatorship. Mass society and massive government bureaucracy combined with modern technology—such as radio—to give men like Stalin control over people's lives and even their thoughts.

Stalin ruled the Soviet Union for nearly three decades until his death in 1954. During that time, he used his power to force the nation to become a modern industrial society. At the same time, Communism came to be feared throughout the world.

International Communism From the beginning of the revolutionary socialist movement, it was seen as a worldwide force. Karl Marx had said that an international uprising of workers was inevitable. Between 1870 and 1917, socialists from different nations frequently met together. They often shared exile in cities like Paris. They also shared the belief that their movement had little to do with national boundaries.

This international dimension was a major reason for anxiety over the Bolshevik revolution in Russia. To both supporters and enemies of Communism, it seemed possible that the revolution would spread through war-torn Europe. In the aftermath of the war, in fact, Communist uprisings broke out in Germany and other places in central Europe.

Lenin applauded these rebellions and hoped that the international uprising was beginning. He also believed that the revolt could spread to the colonial peoples of the world. Colonialism, the Communists believed, was the last stage of capitalism. It was, they felt, the capitalists' final effort to spread their system of exploitation.

Even though Communist uprisings were

crushed throughout Europe, Lenin encouraged the international movement. In 1919, Communists from all over the world were invited to the Soviet Union for the Third International, also called the Communist International or Comintern. This meeting also caused concern among government leaders in other countries. A second meeting held in 1920 issued a call to the workers of the world. "Working men and women!" the International proclaimed, "There is only one banner which is worth fighting and dying for. It is the banner of the Communist International." Over the next few years, authorities throughout Europe and North America suppressed Communist activities. The idea of an international uprising seemed remote.

When Stalin came to power, he changed the Soviet approach. If, he said, the Soviet Union was not strong enough to stand up to Germany or any other capitalist power, then Communism would not survive. The movement thus depended on the success and power of the Soviet Union. Consequently for the time being at least, there must be an emphasis on "socialism in one country."

Stalin's Methods To achieve "socialism in one country," Stalin's first goal was rapid industrialization. As long as the Soviet Union lagged behind the West, he felt, it was in danger of being destroyed. A strong nation would need a powerful military force and this could only be created by a healthy economy.

A series of Five Year Plans was begun. These still form the basis for directing the Soviet economy today. The first plan, which went into effect in 1928, provided detailed goals for what was to be produced in each segment of the economy and each region of the country. All the privately owned businesses allowed under Lenin's NEP were done away with. The state would now control and plan the entire system.

The early Five Year Plans gave highest

Joseph Stalin.

priority to laying an industrial foundation. The Soviet Union needed railroads and trains; roads and trucks; ships, docks, and warehouses; factories and machines; and power plants. These are considered the building blocks, or *infrastructure*, on which a modern economy is built.

Goods for the consumer were lowest on the list of priorities. In plan after plan, it never seemed possible to provide people with coats and shoes, simple household items, or even a few luxury items. The Soviet people became used to waiting in long lines to pay high prices for often shoddy goods.

Workers found during those early plans that their conditions did not improve. Long hours were expected of them and their pay was low. Housing shortages were so severe that many lived in barracks. Propaganda constantly urged the workers to do more. Those who set production records—named Stakhanovites after a famous coal miner—became "heroes of the people." Later, these "activists" would receive free vacations and other benefits.

Brutality and Terror Another of Stalin's major goals was to establish firm control over farmland. The well-to-do peasant farmers, the *kulaks*, had been granted freedom by the czar years earlier. They had continued to own and farm their own land. This had been permitted under Lenin's NEP. In 1929, Stalin wanted to end this private ownership and increase production by creating a series of collectives, small farms joined together and worked in common. Being larger units, the collectives would be better able to make use of heavy machinery and new large-scale agricultural techniques. The grain produced by the collectives was to be purchased by the government at low prices. By then reselling it at higher prices, the government would earn profits that could finance industrialization. A "turnover tax," introduced in 1930, enabled the government to control prices in agriculture and the rest of the economy.

The kulaks and other peasants resisted. They did not care that collectives were supposed to improve productivity. Nor did they care to hear arguments about the advantages of using machinery or working common fields. The kulaks were doing well and felt no need to change. Moreover, they did not intend to give up all they had without a fight. As Soviet authorities moved into each region, farm families were told to turn over their land, tools, crops, and farm animals. Thousands slaughtered their cattle, goats, and sheep rather than turn them in. It would take many years for the country to recover from this loss of livestock. There would be less food for years to come, as well as less leather and fertilizer and fewer work animals. Stalin responded with a heartless campaign against the kulaks and other dissidents. Thousands were shot on the spot. Thousands more were sent to forced-labor camps in remote frontier areas. Persecution and famine cost millions of lives. By 1930, the once energetic kulaks no longer existed as a class.

The collectivization of the farms was completed by the late 1930s. Each collective was allotted certain production goals in the Five Year Plans, much like a factory. "Machine-Tractor Stations" were set up regionally to make equipment and expert help available. These also permitted tighter control of the collectives. In addition, experiments were begun with larger state farms. On these, the laborers worked as employees rather than sharing in a collective.

Stalin made one important retreat from the collectivization of farms. Each family was allowed a small plot of land for its own use. That did not seem important at the time. However, it soon became clear that farm workers were much more careful with this land than with that of the collective. Today, the small, privately owned gardens still produce a high percentage of the nation's food.

A collective farm.

A purge trial.

The Great Purge Stalin was as brutal with those who opposed him politically as he was with the peasants. His policy against the kulaks had aroused strong opposition. He decided to destroy that opposition before it could mobilize against him.

Between 1935 and 1939, Stalin put the country through a horrifying bloodbath known as the Great Purge. Anyone even mildly suspected of harboring anti-Stalinist feelings was arrested. Millions were executed or sent to slave-labor camps without a trial.

Others were saved for the special purge trials. Their minds numbed by the tortures of secret police, these people confessed to a long list of crimes of which they were probably innocent. Then came the executions and trips to Siberia. Most of the victims of the purge trials were party or government leaders, including 50 out of 71 members of the Central Committee.

In this fashion, Stalin purged the Soviet Union of most of the "old Bolshevik" leaders—those who had helped make the revolution. Even Trotsky, living in exile in Mexico, was killed by an assassin. Stalin also persuaded many that he had saved the nation from a counter-revolution. All the vacant positions were filled by younger people who owed their careers to Stalin. The Great Purge created the kind of unity Lenin had wanted. There was no longer any open opposition to Stalin or to Communism.

An assembly plant in Moscow.

At the same time, forced industrialization was beginning to work. By 1940, Soviet factories were producing trucks, tanks, warplanes, and ships. Hunger and poverty seem to have decreased but Stalin insisted that people must wait still longer for an easier life. By 1940, the Soviet Union had the world's second-largest economy but was still far behind the United States.

The Spread of Communist Influence

Outside the Soviet Union, reactions to Stalin's dictatorship were strangely mixed. Most people were shocked by the purge trials and by the stories of mass executions and slave-labor camps. It seemed likely that a Communist revolution anywhere else would also lead to terror and bloodshed. In dozens of countries, therefore, governments tried to suppress Communist movements and political parties.

In nearly every country, however, other people continued to believe in or sympathize with Communism. They felt that the Soviet Union represented a great experiment, an effort to create a better and more equitable world. They seemed to close their eyes to Stalin's blood-stained rule. After all, they said, every revolution led to some excesses.

During the 1920s and 1930s, therefore, Communist movements continued to grow in many countries. Serious economic problems usually favored the spread of Communism. The Great Depression of the 1930s (see Chapter 30) convinced many people in the United States and Europe that capitalism had failed. This led many to become Communist "sympathizers," if not members of the party.

The appeal of Communism also spread to colonies and other countries under European domination. China had never been an actual colony. However, many of the Chinese people felt that their country had been exploited by the industrial powers.

In the 1920s, many young Chinese students like Mao Zedong (Mao Tse Tung) were impressed by the successful Communist revolution in Russia in 1917. They wanted a new program that would regain China's national strength and unity. Mao and other students formed the Chinese Communist Party (CCP).

In 1927, General Chiang Kai-shek, the most powerful leader in China, tried to curb the power of the Chinese Communists. But the communists retreated to the countryside and gained control over more and more land. They won the land-hungry peasants to their side.

In 1937, Japan attacked China. Patriotic Chinese formed a united front against the Japanese, with both Chiang Kai-shek and the Chinese Communist Party fighting against the Japanese. However, they still distrusted each other. No real unity existed between the two groups even during the war against Japan from 1937 to 1945.

Did You Know?

Mao Zedong on the Long March.

The Long March

In 1927, Chiang Kai-shek set out to eliminate the Chinese Communists. Mao and other Communists moved away from the cities and founded guerrilla bases in a rural province in southern China. In 1934, the Chinese Communists were trapped there. The Red forces broke the encirclement and headed west with 100,000 people. Thus, on October 16, 1934, the Red Army started on the famous "Long March." This march would take them over 9,656 kilometers (6,000 miles) to a dry mountainous province in northwest China.

Mao had originally planned only to march to the next province. However, attacks forced the Red Army to seek refuge in the remote hinterland. After more than a year, 30,000 tired and ragged troops completed the long journey. It is estimated that only 10 to 20 percent of those who set out from the various Red bases survived.

During the Long March, Mao emerged as the supreme leader of the Communist Party in China. Completing the difficult Long March renewed Mao's confidence that he and his party would succeed despite the odds against them. It was the beginning of the Communist road to victory.

Section Questions

1. How did Stalin gain control of the Soviet Union?
2. What was the Third International?
3. Who were the kulaks? What happened to them?
4. How did Stalin eliminate opposition to his dictatorship?
5. How successful was Stalin's effort to industrialize the Soviet Union?
6. What conditions favored the spread of Communism around the world?

Chapter Summary

1. World War I was actually one episode in a long period of conflict and upheaval. The war led to major changes in the world's power system. The once-mighty empires that had controlled much of Europe—Russia, Germany, Austria-Hungary, and the Ottoman empire—were gone. The power of Europe was declining. The United States soon had the world's major economy, outproducing all of Europe combined. Russia and Japan were also new centers of power.

The war changed the world in other ways. Civilians had been involved in the war as much as the fighting men. Some young people became discouraged and disillusioned by the horrors of total war—a Lost Generation. The war also had some positive results, such as greater equality for women.

2. Nationalism remained strong in the post-war years. The new nations carved out of the old empires began to build parliamentary democracies and industrial economies. The idea of self-determination spread throughout Europe's colonies. India's great leader Gandhi emerged as the creator of a nonviolent struggle for national independence. Nationalism also arose in China.

3. In the Middle East, the Jews and Arabs clashed over Palestine. The Arabs resented the fact that the Allies did not keep their promise of independence for Arab nations. In Latin America, resentment of foreign dominance in economic affairs was one cause of the Mexican Revolution. Other Latin American nations also resented foreign powers, particularly the United States.

The triumph of Communism in Russia marked one of the most far-reaching changes in this century. Led by V. I. Lenin, the Bolshevik wing of the Social Democratic Party formed an underground revolutionary group. The unrest of the people and the misrule of the czar played into Lenin's hands. In March 1917, Czar Nicholas II was removed from power and replaced by a Provisional Government, later led by Aleksandr Kerenski.

Kerenski hoped to create a parliamentary democracy. However, the Provisional Government was attacked by the "Whites" loyal to the czar and by the Bolsheviks and other leftist groups. In November 1917, the Bolsheviks seized power and began building a socialist state. Gradually, Lenin's government gained control of the country and took control of most of the economy. The New Economic Policy, social reform, modernization, and unity through the party were promoted by the Communists.

4. After Lenin's death, Joseph Stalin, the party leader, gained control. He established a form of modern dictatorship called totalitarianism. He wanted the Soviet Union powerful enough to withstand attack by capitalist nations. Stalin's methods were ruthless. He promoted forced industrialization. To collectivize farms, he destroyed the kulaks. He eliminated all opposition to his rule by the Great Purge. The Soviet Union began to develop a powerful economy. Despite Stalin's dictatorship, Communist movements spread to other parts of the world, both industrial nations and colonial countries. In China, Mao Zedong's Communist Party challenged Chiang Kai-shek's rule.

Chapter 29 Review

Check Your Facts

1. Identify the following:
   a. Mohandas Gandhi
   b. Nadezha Krupskaya
   c. Mensheviks
   d. Duma
2. Which empires came to an end during the era of World War I?
3. Why were Britain and France in debt to the United States after the war?
4. On which side did the Japanese fight in World War I?
5. How did the idea of self-determination often spread to colonial peoples?
6. What did World War I have to do with voting rights for women?

Words to Know

Define each word or phrase in one or two sentences; then explain its historical importance.
   a. isolationism
   b. nonviolent resistance
   c. totalitarianism
   d. kulaks
   e. Bolshevik
   f. Communism

Developing Your Skills

1. Indicate whether each of the following is more closely associated with V. I. Lenin or with Aleksandr Kerenski:
   a. New Economic Policy
   b. Provisional Government
   c. Red Army
   d. parliamentary democracy
   e. staying in the war
   f. "Peace, Bread, and Land"
2. Place the following events in the proper chronological order:

   Great Purge begun by Stalin.
   Ottoman empire overthrown.
   United States women win the vote.
   World War I ends.
   Bolsheviks and Mensheviks split.
   February Revolution takes place.

Thinking It Over

1. Why do you think European powers did not want self-rule in the colonies? How would you have felt if you lived in one of these colonies?
2. Powerful feelings of nationalism had contributed to World War I. What evidence do you find that nationalism remained a cause of conflict through the 1920s and 1930s?
3. How did Lenin and Stalin differ in their use of power? How were they similar?
4. Why is it significant that private farm gardens produce much of the Soviet Union's crops?

Special Activities

1. Read passages from one of the Lost Generation writers (for example, Hemingway's *A Farewell to Arms* or Celine's *Journey to the Edge of Night*). For the rest of the class, select paragraphs that show their feelings of being lost.
2. Find out more about the life of Gandhi and his approaches to conflict. Discuss the extent to which these methods seem more or less successful than "standard" ways of dealing with disputes. For a comparison to Black Americans' peaceful protest, survey the writings of Martin Luther King, Jr., or of Bayard Rustin.

A concerned crowd gathered outside the New York Stock Exchange Building during the 1929 stock-market crash.

Chapter 30
Dictators and the Great Depression

*I*n October 1929, the American stock market crashed. Within hours, there was a wave of panic selling. Everyone wanted to sell stocks but no one was buying.

No one knew quite what was happening. The stock-market crisis deepened into an economic depression—the Great Depression of the 1930s. While desperate depositors clamored for their money, many banks closed their doors forever. Many factories cut back production and laid off workers. Others shut down completely.

People in Europe did not understand how the American stock market could affect them, but it did. Within months, the Depression

1918-1939

1918	Republic of Germany established
1922	Mussolini comes to power
1923	Nazis fail to seize Bavaria
1929	American stock market crashes
1931	Japanese attack Manchuria
1932	Roosevelt elected U.S. president
1933	Adolf Hitler heads Germany
1934	Soviet Union joins The League of Nations
1935	Italy invades Ethiopia
1936-1939	Spanish Civil War
1938	Hitler unites Germany and Austria
1938	Germans invade Czechoslovakia
1939	World War II begins

Adolf Hitler.

had become worldwide. In every city, men and women without hope walked the streets and slept in parks. The entire industrial world seemed to be breaking down.

Government leaders did not know what to do about such massive problems. Nothing like this had ever happened before. The Republican President of the United States, Herbert Hoover, did little. He insisted that government should not interfere with business. Besides, he said repeatedly, "Prosperity is just around the corner."

Well before the Depression hit, there were those who said the democratic system was the reason for people's troubles. Many thought it was too weak and indecisive to take action. The Communists believed that the solution was a revolution. They would follow the lead of the Soviet Union and completely destroy the present system.

Other groups, bitter enemies of the Communists, called for a powerful dictator. They believed one man, one special leader, could restore national strength and pride. The more powerful of these groups became known as Fascists. As the uncertainty of the 1920s became the gloom of the Depression years of the 1930s, many lost faith in democracy. They became more willing to believe in the simple solutions offered by the Communists or Fascists.

In this chapter, you will read how this mood of desperation led to a new age of dictators. In addition, you will see how the actions of these dictators led the world toward another global war.

A Communist protest strike in Paris.

1. A New Age of Dictators Began

The period between the two world wars—from 1918 to 1939—was a time of great uncertainty in the Western world. The owners of businesses and land who led the industrialized societies remained shocked by the triumph of Bolshevism in Russia. Above all else, they wanted protection from a Communist revolution.

Many factory workers and farmers, on the other hand, wanted reforms. The present system seemed to them to favor the rich at the expense of the lower classes. The workers wanted better wages, shorter hours, and protection against economic uncertainties like unemployment. Farmers wanted decent prices for their crops. In some countries, they wanted to end the control of wealthy landowners.

The divisions within each society began to deepen. The frightened property owners began to see every movement for reform as another step toward Bolshevism. Many workers and farmers began to feel that the government was failing them. Some were ready to accept more radical ideas like Communism.

The economic situation and the conflicts it created made possible a new kind of dictatorship that became known as Fascism. In many ways, the new dictators followed the tradition of powerful one-man rule. However, important new elements were added. During the war, for example, governments found they had to assume sweeping powers over social and political conditions. The new dictators would have that massive government machinery under their control.

The first of the Fascist dictators—who served as a model for others—was Benito Mussolini (MOOS so LEE nee) of Italy.

Mussolini In the years after the war, Italy seemed more like one of the losing powers than a victor. The economy remained in a depressed state. Unemployment was rising steadily. Strikes became frequent as workers struggled for decent wages. In the south, peasant farmers lived in poverty.

Italian leaders felt cheated by the Treaty of Versailles. They had agreed to join the Allies in 1915 on the secret promise of large amounts of Austrian land. Wilson's idealism had ruined that plan.

There was another reason for the growing desire for a new direction. Business leaders and landowners were afraid that the strikes and uprisings could lead to a Communist revolution. They wanted a government that would restore order and respect for the law.

The man who promised to solve these problems was Benito Mussolini. Born in 1883 in a small town, Mussolini began his career as a socialist and a journalist. On the eve of the war, he was the editor of one of the leading socialist publications.

The socialist parties voted against entry into the war. Mussolini then immediately broke with them and enlisted in the Italian army. He later told of his great exploits as Corporal Mussolini. In actuality, he went out of his way to avoid danger.

Mussolini was one of those men who loved the war experience. This led him to model the new movement he founded on military lines. He called his group the Fascio di Combattimento, or "battle band." The party became known as the Fascists.

Thousands of former soldiers flocked to Mussolini's banner. He put them in uniforms, so that they became known as the "Black Shirts." He organized them into vigilante groups called *squadristi*. These groups began to break up strikes. They burst in on Communist, Socialist, or labor union meetings and beat people viciously. These violent acts terrorized the workers. They also convinced many industrialists that Mussolini could keep order. Financial contributions to his movement poured in.

The Seizure of Power No one was yet sure what Mussolini stood for. Mostly, he talked about the need for action and the weakness of democracy. Only one person could lead the nation in the kind of action needed, he declared. That man was, of course, Mussolini himself. His followers already called him Il Duce, "the Leader."

In 1922, Mussolini announced that he wanted control of the government. "Either they will give us the government, or we

Young Black Shirts on maneuvers.

Mussolini leading a parade.

will march on Rome." Startled government leaders did not know what to do. They had not taken Mussolini that seriously. To many, he seemed like a comic figure, always strutting and shouting. Now his gangster Black Shirts were marching on Rome from all directions.

The king, Victor Emmanuel III, refused to call out the army. Some of his advisers, who included friends of Mussolini, had persuaded him that the Fascists had overwhelming power. As a result, the king gave in. Mussolini thus became the head of the government in a fairly legal way.

Fascist Theory and Government

There was no real philosophy of Fascism as there was for democracy, Marxism, or capitalism. In a very real way, Mussolini invented the theory as he went along. "Il Duce" himself said: "Fascism was not... a doctrine worked out beforehand with detailed elaboration; it was born of the need for action." Mussolini carried nationalism to a fever pitch and united it with the "cult of the leader." The nation—or state—was supreme. "Everything for the state, nothing outside the state, nothing against the state."

The supremacy of the state was Mussolini's excuse for removing all opposition—much as Stalin did in the Soviet Union. All political parties except the Fascists were outlawed. This kept them from threatening national unity. Trade unions were suppressed. Workers were forbidden to strike. The "purity" of the nation was to be guaranteed by forcing undesirable minority groups to leave.

Mussolini and his Fascists used all available means to control public opinion. He knew that a modern dictator needed strong public support. A single person could no longer rely on keeping power solely through military means. Secret police were used. Newspapers and the newer media, radio and film, were controlled. Moreover, they were used to deluge the public with a constant flood of propaganda. By the late 1920s, the people of Italy heard or saw very little except what the Fascists wanted them to.

Fascism thus meant total control of the life of the nation. The national will was to be expressed through a supreme leader and one party. This force was to control the government and politics of the state. The party was also to penetrate all other aspects of national life, including the economy and the communications media. These were the elements of totalitarianism—total state control. One force in particular, the Roman Catholic Church, could have challenged the power of the Fascists. However, in 1929, Pope Pius XI and Mussolini signed the Lateran Agreements. These provided for the creation of an independent state, Vatican City. This was to be the headquarters of the pope and the church. However, the agreements also placed the church in Italy under the effective control of the Fascist state.

The Great Depression Many factors were involved in the development of Fascism in Italy. Deep class divisions, frustrated nationalism, reaction to the war, economic problems, and the powerful organizing ability of the Fascists all contributed to it. In the years following Mussolini's rise to power in 1922, other countries also turned to Fascism. The Great Depression was often the main cause for this.

As we have seen, the Depression began in the United States and then spread around the world. In October 1929, when stock prices suddenly dropped, millions of people lost confidence. They tried to sell in a panic. Banks, which were also involved

Mussolini replaced the Boy Scout movement with a cadet system designed to build loyalty to the state.

with stocks, began calling in customers' loans. People rushed to get whatever cash they could. When a bank ran out of money, it simply went out of business. By 1933, one-third of the nation's banks had closed. With money disappearing and demand falling, other businesses cut back or closed.

American investors then began to draw on their holdings in Europe. This set off the same kind of chain reaction. Banks closed, factories laid off workers, businesses failed. Unemployment in most areas reached 25 percent.

Franklin D. Roosevelt.

The more stable democracies began to experiment with new solutions. In the United States, Democrat Franklin D. Roosevelt was elected president in 1932. He promised a New Deal—ambitious reforms designed to strengthen the economy. In Great Britain, the reforms were similar to those of Roosevelt, but not as ambitious. Still, few British joined the ranks of the extremist groups—the Communists or the Fascists.

The other major democracy, France, faced serious internal problems. Many of the French people had never had strong faith in the republic. Some still believed in monarchy. Others preferred a military dictator. As the Depression deepened, growing numbers joined socialist, Communist, or Fascist organizations. A left-wing coalition managed to win control of the government for a year. Throughout the 1930s, the French economy continued to sputter. The nation remained deeply divided.

In other parts of Europe, Fascist-style dictators used the troubled economic times to gain power. In most of these countries, democratic government did not have a long history. As you have read, it was easy to blame these new governments for economic and social upheavals. At the same time, the dictators appealed to the wealthier classes because they promised protection from Communism.

Many of these new dictators lacked the totalitarian control achieved by Mussolini. Marshal Pilsudski (pel SOOT skee), for example, established a traditional military dictatorship in Poland. The military also gained control in Greece. Dictatorships in Yugoslavia, Bulgaria, and Rumania were built around traditional monarchies. The dictatorships of Salazar in Portugal and Franco in Spain most closely resembled the model created by Mussolini. Hungary also had a Fascist dictatorship. By the late 1930s, fewer than half of Europe's nations were still democratic. By far the most important of the modern dictatorships was Nazi Germany under Adolf Hitler.

Section Questions

1. In any society, what groups would be most troubled by Communism?
2. Why did many people in Italy want a new government?
3. In what ways was Mussolini's movement militaristic?
4. What was the Fascist idea of the state?
5. How did the Great Depression contribute to the rise of dictatorship?

2. Hitler Gained Control of Germany

The end of the German empire in 1918 marked the beginning of a brave experiment in democracy. This was the Weimar (VI mar) Republic, named after the German city in which it was formally established. The republic had been formed in the closing days of the war. Its representatives had signed the Armistice with the Allies. The Weimar Republic lasted only 14 years. In 1933, Hitler came to power. Within a few months, the democratic experiment ended.

Germany's Special Problems Germany did not have a long tradition of democracy. Indeed, Germany had been a unified nation only since the early 1870s. This lack of democratic and political experience is considered one reason for the failure of the Weimar Republic. However, during the Weimar period, Germany faced several special problems. These would have severely strained any government.

The first problem was the war and the treaty. The German generals asserted—falsely—that the army had not been defeated by the enemy but had been "stabbed in the back" by fellow Germans. The republicans and socialists, who led Weimar, were supposed to have done this. Moreover, it was the Weimar government that had been forced to sign the Treaty of Versailles. Most Germans felt that the war-guilt clause was a great disgrace to their country. Many said that the Weimar representatives should have refused to sign. Blame for the treaty was, therefore, a serious handicap for the government from the start.

The second problem was fear of Communism. With its army reduced to 100,000

Poor people in Berlin rummaging through trash heaps.

men by the treaty, Germany seemed vulnerable to the spread of Communism. Communist uprisings troubled the new government in 1918 and 1919. The Weimar authorities managed to restore order. However, many people wondered how long the government could withstand Communist pressure.

The third problem was nationalism. Many industrial leaders and former military officers regarded the Weimar government as hopelessly weak. They felt that Germany needed a government with the will to act. They wanted it to tear up the Treaty of Versailles and restore Germany's position in the world.

A fourth problem was economic crises. The post-war economic upheaval was worse in Germany than in other countries. The war was followed by a devastating inflation. Prices rose so fast the new values were simply stamped on old currency. Anyone with savings or a fixed income found themselves penniless. Suitcases filled with the savings of a lifetime were used to pay for a sack of coal. The economy recovered between 1924 and 1929, but more trouble lay ahead.

Under these difficult conditions, the Weimar Republic struggled for survival. The government did make improvements in benefits to workers. Through negotiations, the reparations bill was lowered. An agreement was signed with the Allies in 1926 that allowed Germany to join the League of Nations. In addition, the government signed a nonaggression treaty with the Soviet Union.

Despite these achievements, the uncertainties of the period provided a breeding ground for discontent. Especially during times of economic trouble, the extremist groups gained in strength. People were fed up, angry, or without hope. The promise of action began to sound more appealing. It was this atmosphere that made Adolf Hitler's rise to power possible.

Hitler making a speech.

Hitler and the Nazi Party Hitler, born in 1899, was a few years younger than Mussolini. In many ways, Hitler's rise to power followed the pattern Mussolini had set. In the years before World War I, Hitler seemed a loner who never would fit in. He had hoped to become an artist. However, the Vienna Academy of Fine Arts in his native Austria turned down his application for admission. He moved to Munich in Germany and managed to sell a few watercolors. Then the war broke out.

The war gave Hitler something he needed—a sense of belonging. He fought well, was decorated twice, and was temporarily blinded by poison gas. Later, like other veterans who could not adjust to civilian life, he longed for the excitement and power of war.

He joined one of the many groups of former military men. This small band took the name National Socialist Workers' Party, and later came to be known as the Nazis. Hitler turned out to be a powerful and persuasive public speaker. He quickly rose to the party leadership.

In 1923, the Nazis tried to follow Mussolini's example and seize control of the government. Their effort to take over the German state of Bavaria was a complete failure. Hitler was arrested, convicted, and served nine months of a five-year prison sentence. While he was in prison, Hitler put together a book called *Mein Kampf*, meaning "my struggle." This was to become the Nazi bible. With confused and angry ranting, he set forth his ideas of the struggle that he must lead. All life, he said, was a "continuous struggle between strength and weakness, an eternal victory of the strong over the weak." This struggle involved nations as well as people. The strong must inevitably "rise above the weak."

Hitler's Racism *Mein Kampf* also presented Hitler's distorted view of race. He decided that most Germans were part of an ancient "master race" of the Aryans. "All human culture," he insisted, "all the results of art, science, and technology that we see before us today are almost exclusively the creative products of the Aryans." He warned that the "purity" of this race was in danger. "Inferior races," among which he numbered Slavs, Gypsies, and Jews, had become far too common, he said. These groups, he asserted, were useful for nothing but forced labor. He threatened that they would have to be separated from the Aryans.

Once Hitler was out of prison, he found that his speeches on race could fire up an audience. The Jews became his special target. The Jews, he would shout, had lost the war for Germany. "Jewish liberalism" in the western democracies was, he warned, a menace to civilization. He claimed that

A German Jewish family fleeing their home. Note the stars they were forced to wear for identification.

international conspiracies of Jewish bankers and industrialists were trying to control the world. Even the Soviet Union, he argued, was now in the grip of "Jewish Marxism." In normal times, Hitler's prejudiced ravings would have seemed absurd. However, at that time, things were not normal in Germany. People were confused, frightened, and angry. They needed a *scapegoat*—someone to blame—for the bewildering problems they faced.

Jews had been persecuted in Europe for centuries. In many places, they had been forced to live in segregated areas. This, plus their non-Christian religion, had made them more visible than other minority groups.

In Germany, Jews made up only a small fraction of the population, about 600,000 in all. They were, in fact, loyal Germans. Indeed, a disproportionately large number had fought for Germany in the war. Many had worked hard and had become prominent in education, law, business, and other professions. Now a growing number of non-Jewish Germans began to resent that success. Hitler provided the scapegoat many people were looking for.

The Nazi Rise to Power Like Mussolini, Hitler put his party followers in uniform. These "Brown Shirts" also broke up labor rallies and Communist meetings. They marched into Jewish neighborhoods. There they wrecked businesses and dragged Jews into the street for public beatings. As in Italy, business leaders provided aid. They thought of the Nazis as gangsters, but were pleased that they terrorized the Communists. Hitler recognized the need for popular support. Impressive rallies and hysterical speeches drew larger and larger crowds.

During the period of solid economic recovery in Germany, from 1924 to 1929, the Nazis made little headway. They seemed to have little chance of gaining control of the Reichstag, or parliament. In 1928, the Nazi Party held only 12 seats out of 472 in the Reichstag.

Then came the Depression, which greatly weakened people's confidence. About six million German workers were unemployed. The Weimar government had few ways of dealing with such a crisis. Corrective measures we take for granted today, such as food stamps or unemployment benefits, were unknown at the time. Thousands turned to Communism in desperation. Thousands more responded to Hitler's promise of action. By 1932, the Nazi Party had become the largest single political group in Germany. It was, however, still a minority. The party then had 107 seats in the Reichstag. Hitler demanded to be named chancellor, or prime minister. Industrial and military leaders persuaded President Paul von Hindenburg to name Hitler. These leaders were convinced that they could control Hitler and the Nazis. Adolf Hitler became leader of the German government through democratic means. He then began to move swiftly to end democracy in Germany.

Totalitarian Rule Within months of becoming chancellor, Hitler began the ruthless Nazification of Germany. He established a totalitarian government through methods similar to those of Fascist Italy and the Communist Soviet Union.

When a fire broke out in the Reichstag building, probably set on Hitler's order, he blamed the Communists. This gave him an excuse for outlawing the Communist Party and then all other parties except the National Socialists. Real and imagined enemies were rounded up by his efficient secret police. These "enemies of the state" were then either killed or shipped to concentration camps.

The campaign of hatred against the Jews was intensified. All Jews had to register with the authorities. They were excluded from many careers, such as law, medicine, education, and government service. Towns and neighborhoods put up signs warning that Jews were not welcome.

Soon Jews began to disappear from their homes. Usually, they were seized quietly at night and taken to the growing concentration camps. This was the first step in Hitler's determination to destroy all Jews.

The German people said little against the brutal methods of the Nazis. Most of those who opposed them were simply too afraid to speak out. Others found it possible to ignore these episodes. They were more concerned with jobs, wages, security, and a growing national pride.

Hitler launched an ambitious program of public works—roads, highways, railroads, sports arenas, and other public buildings. Suddenly there was a demand for workers. To many, it did not appear to matter that unions and strikes were illegal. Money to pay bills and buy food seemed much more important. Factories producing weapons and war materials began to operate at full capacity. This of course created still more jobs.

The key Nazi leaders were masters of the art of propaganda. Their use of all

This German assembly line produced tanks at a "prodigious" speed.

forms of communication to control opinion was more ambitious and effective than in any other totalitarian state. The Nazis controlled movies, newspapers, books, art, radio, and the schools. All Germans, including young children, were taught to believe in the greatness of Germany and in the supreme leadership of Hitler, who was called Der Fuhrer, or "the leader." Huge public rallies were carefully staged. They presented a spectacle of color, music, and military might. They symbolized the unity of the German people, with workers marching side by side with members of the Nazi Party and regular military units.

Each of these public events reached its peak with one of Hitler's passionate and strangely hypnotic orations. He lashed out at the Jews, at the supposed conspiracy of the Versailles Treaty, and at the allegedly weak and fragmented democratic powers. He spoke of creating a Third Reich, or empire, that would last a thousand years. He also told his audiences to believe in their own greatness, in their destiny to rule others.

Germany was rebuilding with remarkable speed. Hitler began talking of undoing the hated Treaty of Versailles. The army leaders warned him of the risk of war. France, they said, still had the world's largest and most powerful army. Hitler scoffed. Britain and France would not dare to go to war again, he claimed. After all, he argued, they would see that a strong Germany was the best defense against Communism.

Section Questions

1. What special problems did the Weimar Republic face?
2. How did Hitler's hatred of the Jews actually help the Nazi cause?
3. What happened to the popularity of the Nazi Party during the Great Depression?
4. How did the Nazis use the Reichstag fire to their advantage?

3. The Dictators Turned to Aggression

Normally, a peace treaty marks the end of a conflict. That is what most people thought about the Treaty of Versailles after World War I. A number of nations, however, were deeply dissatisfied with the Treaty.

As we have seen, many Germans were angry over the treaty's provisions. Italians, too, felt they had been cheated of the gains they had hoped for. The Soviet Union also regarded the settlement as unsatisfactory. The Soviet leaders felt that the Allies had deliberately erected a buffer zone of anti-Communist countries between themselves and the Soviet Union. All three of these powers wanted to see the settlement revised. Germany and Italy, in fact, were willing to wage war to undo the treaty. Another major revisionist nation was Japan.

Japanese Aggression Japan continued to grow as an economic and military power during and after World War I. Within Japan, power was concentrated in a few hands. In form, Japan had a parliamentary government. In fact, however, this structure came to be controlled by the industrial leaders and military officers.

These leaders were convinced that Japan must expand. The nation's population was growing fast. Already, food supplies were strained. Raw materials and new markets were needed for the continued growth of industry. In addition, the Japanese economy was suffering from the Great Depression.

The Japanese leaders came to the conclusion that Asia should be their sphere of influence and provide the food, raw materials, and markets that Japan needed. China was for the Japanese, as for the western powers before them, an important outlet for expansionist energies. In particular, the Chinese province of Manchuria, with its rich natural resources, was a tempting prize. Moreover, Japan was fearful that the Soviet Union too had designs on Manchuria.

In September 1931, the Japanese

Japanese troops in Manchuria.

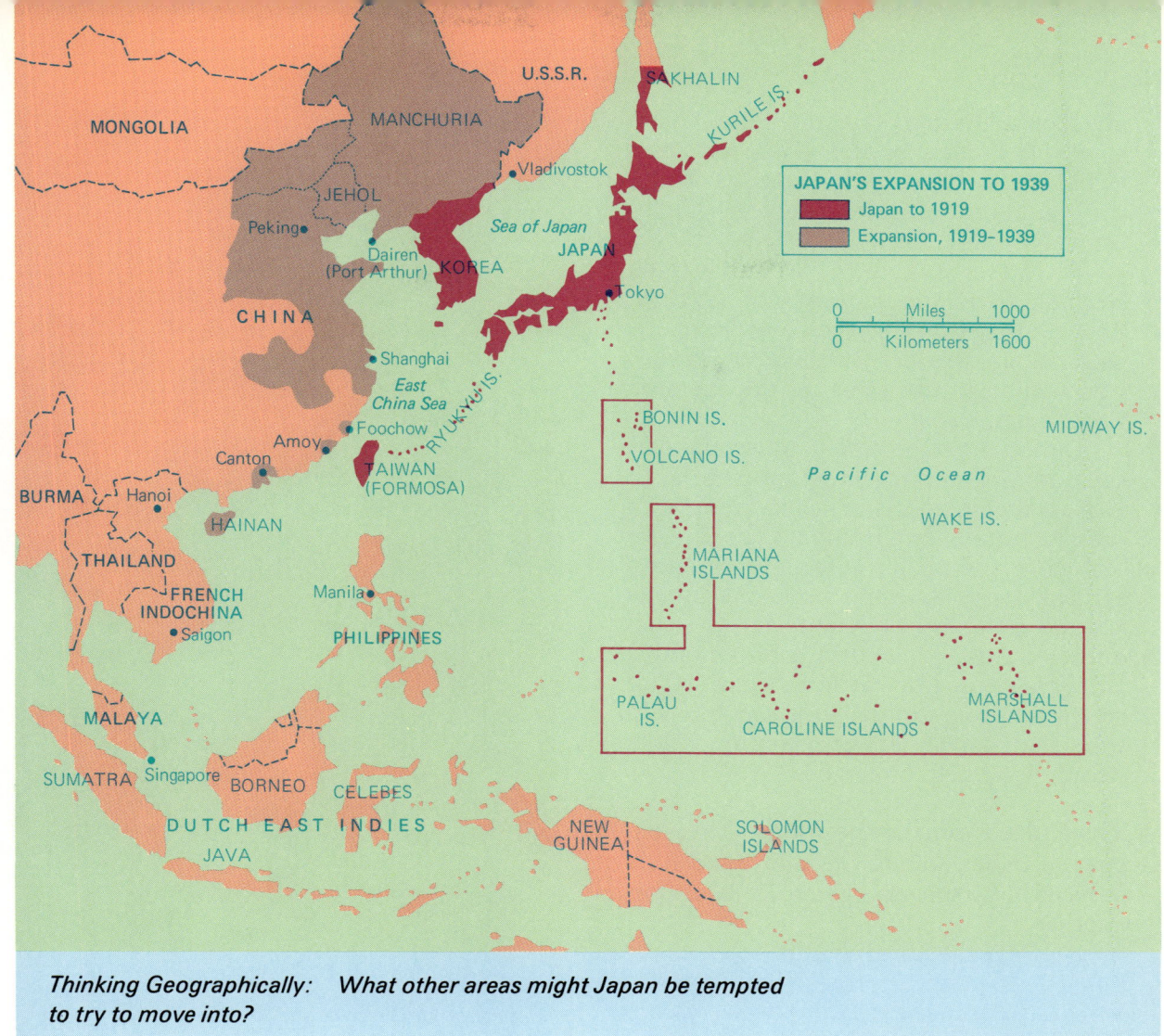

Thinking Geographically: What other areas might Japan be tempted to try to move into?

launched a full-scale attack against Manchuria. The Japanese easily defeated Chiang Kai-shek's poorly equipped armies. Over the next three years, more Chinese provinces were seized.

The governments of the United States and Europe voiced strong objections to this aggression. A commission of the League of Nations found Japan guilty of disturbing the peace. Japan responded by withdrawing from the League. No action was taken against Japan.

Nazi and Fascist Aggression Once Hitler was firmly in control of Germany, he began planning his great "Third Reich." In 1935, he announced that Germany was engaged in full-scale rearmament. This was a violation of the Treaty of Versailles. That agreement had limited Germany's army to 100,000 men. Hitler now dared the Allies to go to war again to maintain that provision of the treaty. The Allied powers objected, but took no action to stop Hitler.

On March 7, 1936, German troops

marched boldly into Germany's Rhine Valley, near the French border. This was also forbidden by the treaty. However, Hitler was sure that France would not fight. He was right.

Then, two years later, in March 1938, German divisions moved into Austria. That country was absorbed into Germany. Once again, neither Britain nor France was willing to use force in order to stop Hitler's aggression.

During the same period, Mussolini pursued his dream of creating an empire. In 1935, Italian planes and troops launched a massive attack on Ethiopia. The League of Nations called for economic sanctions against Italy. Scarcely bothered by the League actions, Italy completed the conquest of Ethiopia within a few months. Ethiopia's emperor, Haile Selassie (HI lee se LA see), continued to plead for help from the League. However, nothing more was done to help him.

The Reluctance of the Allies Throughout the 1930s, Japan, Germany, and Italy succeeded with one aggressive act after another.

People in the Allied countries were reluctant to risk war to protect the Treaty of Versailles. Some, for example, were convinced that the treaty had been too harsh on Germany. Also, the memories of World War I were still vivid, especially for the French. Half the young Frenchmen of 1914, those between the ages of 20 and 32, had been killed in the war. To avoid another such horror, the French had built powerful fortifications along their entire border with Germany. These were known as the Maginot Line. If another war should come, France would count on these defenses for protection.

The British, too, were anxious to avoid war. Neville Chamberlain, who became prime minister in 1937, developed a policy called *appeasement*. His idea was that

Italian troops in gas masks marching in celebration of the conquest of Ethiopia.

giving into some of the dictators' demands might appease, or satisfy, them.

In the United States, President Franklin D. Roosevelt had come to feel that war was almost certain. However, many members of the U.S. Congress, as well as many other Americans, were determined to keep their country isolated from outside conflicts. Special neutrality laws were passed.

In a reversal of their position, the leaders of the Soviet Union now called for united action against aggression. Stalin did not like the Versailles settlement. He had not forgotten Allied interference in the Russian Civil War. However, he feared Germany's military power and Hitler's boast that he would destroy Communism.

To show its good intentions, the Soviet Union joined the League of Nations in 1934. Through the Communist International, all Communist parties were ordered to cooperate with other groups in their own countries against Fascism. In addition, Stalin signed defense treaties with France and Czechoslovakia. The great powers were not yet ready, however, to cooperate to stop the dictators. Hitler was keenly aware of this, and made use of this knowledge.

Spain Events in Spain during this period showed how deeply the world was divided between Fascist and anti-Fascist forces. These events also proved to be a rehearsal for the world war that was to come soon.

In 1931, the Spanish king had been forced to flee his country and a republic was formed. The Spanish republicans, many of them socialists, started an ambitious campaign of reform. The largest land-holdings were seized and divided among the peasants. The Roman Catholic Church lost much of its traditional authority. Catholic schools were abolished and the Jesuit order was banned.

These sweeping changes caused a sharp reaction from the army, the church, and property owners. To rally support, the socialists now united with the Communists and other radical groups to form what became known as the Popular Front. The Popular Front scored major victories in the election of 1936 and announced more reforms.

This time, the reaction of the army and its supporters was more decisive. They gathered forces in Spanish Morocco and began a civil war for control of the country. This Spanish Civil War dragged on from 1936 to 1939. It was the bloodiest war in Spain's history. About 600,000 people were killed. Many were victims of a new approach to war—the large-scale bombing of cities.

Outsiders became involved in the Spanish Civil War. As a result, Spain became a symbol for the larger conflict in the world. General Francisco Franco, leader of the

French barricades along the Maginot Line.

Did You Know?

The Outcast Nations

Adolf Hitler used the Spanish Civil War in 1936 as a setting to display and to test Germany's latest weapons. Observers from other countries were amazed by what they saw: dive bombers screaming out of the sky in steep, swift dives; tanks with armor that defied anti-tank guns; artillery more accurate and powerful than anything seen before.

How could Germany develop this ultra-modern war machine without the world knowing? The Treaty of Versailles had severely limited Germany's military forces and armaments. Hitler openly defied the Treaty, but he had been in power only 3 years, not enough time for such changes.

One answer to the puzzle was in secret arrangements made by the German government and military leaders 10 years before Hitler came to power. After the war, Germany was an outcast. The same was true of Lenin's Soviet Union. The major powers wanted nothing to do with either country.

In 1923 the two outcasts came together and signed a treaty of friendship. A second treaty was signed in 1928. Both treaties contained secret military agreements: the German General Staff would train Bolshevik officers in the techniques of modern warfare. In return, the Russians provided the Germans with factories, workers, and testing grounds in remote areas of the Soviet Union. The Western world heard rumors of these agreements but no one paid much attention. Not until 1936 did Hitler give the world a glimpse of what had been accomplished.

A woman who was left homeless by the Spanish Civil War.

military, received help from both Hitler and Mussolini. They sent tanks, armored cars, and aircraft. Italy supplied 100,000 soldiers. For Hitler and Mussolini, the Spanish Civil War provided an excellent chance to test the latest advances in weapons. The Popular Front received smaller amounts of supplies and weapons from the Soviet Union.

Neither Britain nor France offered to help the republican government. Leaders in both nations feared that a general European war would result. However, thousands of volunteers from the United States and the Allied countries joined the Popular Front forces. Their cause was hopeless. Franco's superior weaponry gave him a great advantage. In 1939, Madrid fell and Franco became the dictator of Spain.

The Road to War Hitler's excuse for annexing Austria had been that the Austrians were actually Germans. In addition, Nazis in Austria had demanded union with the German Reich. These facts had made it appear that Hitler was following the principle of self-determination. About three million German-speaking people also lived in Czechoslovakia. In 1938, Hitler declared that this minority must also be incorporated into Germany. Czechoslovakia was in a good position to resist Hitler. The democratic government there seemed to work well. Its well-trained, modern army had good natural borders to defend. Czechoslovakia had made defensive alliances with France, the Soviet Union, Yugoslavia, and Rumania.

As Nazis in the Sudeten part of Czechoslovakia began to start street riots, the Czech government ordered mobilization. By August 1938, Europe tottered on the brink of war. Then British Prime Minister Chamberlain made three trips to confer with Hitler. At the third meeting, in Munich, Mussolini and the French premier were also present. The British and French gave in to all of Hitler's demands. This really meant that they were giving him Czechoslovakia without a fight. Without the Sudeten section, Czechoslovakia would not have good lines of defense. In addition, its major arms industry would be in German hands.

The French and British leaders seemed to believe sincerely that this appeasement would end the threat of war. Chamberlain flew back to London and announced that he brought with him "peace in our time." The Czechs could do nothing but accept Hitler's terms.

Only a few months later, in March 1939, the world learned that Hitler was not satisfied with having united all Germans into one nation. It became evident that Hitler had wider aggressive aims when German troops moved into the main part of Czechoslovakia. It was also now clear to everyone that nothing would stop Hitler's aggression except force. At the same time, Italy, now allied with Germany as the Axis Powers, seized Albania.

Britain and France at last began to prepare for war. They expected help from the Soviet Union. However, in a surprise move, Hitler and Stalin approved a nonaggression pact in August 1939. Thus, the powers representing the two conflicting ideologies, Fascism and Communism, agreed not to fight. This gave Hitler a free hand against either Poland or the West.

On September 1, 1939, German dive-bombers appeared over Poland's cities. Swift armored units crossed the border into Poland. On September 3, 1939, both Great Britain and France declared war against Germany. World War II had now officially begun.

Section Questions

1. What were the revisionist nations?
2. Why did Japan attack China?
3. What were the first aggressive acts by Hitler and Mussolini?

4. Why did the Allies not try to stop the first acts of aggression?
5. Why did the Spanish Civil War have broad significance?
6. What did the Allies learn about Hitler after the Munich agreement on Czechoslovakia?

Chapter Summary

1. The period 1918 to 1939 was not a peaceful era throughout the world. Economic and social upheaval, much of it begun during the Great War, made people feel uncertain, angry, or afraid. The owners of businesses and land feared they would lose everything in a Communist uprising. Workers were troubled by high unemployment and low wages. As the uncertainty continued, people became more willing to listen to simple solutions. Communists wanted to destroy the system by revolution. A new group, the Fascists, promised action to make the system work.

Benito Mussolini became the first of the Fascist dictators. His major interest was power rather than a new theory of government. He developed the theory of fascism as he went along. He seized control of the Italian government in 1922 and established a totalitarian dictatorship. The nation or state was supreme. Individual liberties meant nothing.

Worldwide depression, beginning with the crash of the American stock market in 1929, made matters worse. The democratic countries wrestled with massive economic problems. Other countries fell under the spell of dictators. By 1939, fewer than half of Europe's nations remained democratic.

2. The sense of hopelessness was greater in Germany than in other nations. The Weimar Republic faced several special problems, including blame for the war and the Treaty of Versailles, fear of Communism, extreme nationalism, and economic crises.

Adolf Hitler, the leader of the National Socialist Workers' Party, or Nazis, copied many of Mussolini's ideas and tactics. Hitler blamed the Jews for all of Germany's problems. This provided many people with a scapegoat for their troubles. Hitler's informal army of Brown Shirts was modeled after Mussolini's Black Shirts. He used them as a weapon against Communists and other workers' groups and against Jews.

As the Depression developed, the Nazi Party gained strength and Hitler became chancellor. He ended Germany's democracy and became an absolute dictator. The Nazi leaders were masters in totalitarian control, including the control and use of all forms of communication.

3. Like Italy and Germany, Japan did not accept the peace settlement at Versailles. All three countries wanted to create a new world order. Gradually, military and industrial leaders gained control of Japan's government. They wanted to conquer territory to provide more food, raw materials, and markets to aid Japan's rapid growth. In 1931, they took the first step by conquering the Chinese province of Manchuria.

In the mid-1930s, Hitler and Mussolini also took aggressive steps. Italy invaded Ethiopia. Hitler defied the Versailles Treaty by rearming Germany and sending troops into the Rhine region. In 1938, Hitler completed a union of Austria and Germany.

The Allies did little to stop this aggression. They wanted to avoid another destructive war at all costs. The British Prime Minister, Neville Chamberlain, thought the policy of appeasement would work. Giving the dictators something might satisfy them, he felt. However, the Spanish Civil War provided an ominous warning of what was to come. Appeasement was tried when Hitler threatened Czechoslovakia. The eventual cost was the loss of Czech independence. However, appeasement did not work. When Germany attacked Poland, Britain and France declared war.

Chapter 30 Review

Check Your Facts

1. Identify the following:
   a. Lateran Agreements
   b. Mein Kampf
   c. Paul von Hindenburg
   d. Haile Selassie
2. What methods did the Fascists use to control people's opinions?
3. Why did depression in the United States spread throughout the world?
4. In what ways did Hitler use people's prejudices against the Jews?
5. How was the strength of the Nazi Party changed by the Depression?
6. Who were the real rulers of Japan?
7. How did Hitler violate the Treaty of Versailles?
8. How was the Spanish Civil War like a "rehearsal" for a larger war?

Words to Know

Explain how each word or term on the left is associated with one of the persons named on the right.

Der Fuhrer	Chamberlain
Reichstag	Hitler
squadristi	Mussolini
appeasement	Roosevelt
Il Duce	
New Deal	

Developing Your Skills

1. On a map of Europe, indicate each of the areas mentioned below:
   a. Stalin believed the Allies had created a buffer zone of anti-Communist countries to isolate the Soviet Union. Which countries made up this zone?
   b. Italy had hoped to gain land from the Austro-Hungarian empire. What area would they have been likely to claim?
   c. France built a powerful defensive line—the Maginot Line—to protect against German invasion. Where would the Maginot Line have been?
2. Arrange the following events in Germany in the proper chronological order:
   The Weimar Republic begins.
   The Nazis attempt to seize Bavaria.
   The Great Depression begins.
   German troops enter the Rhineland.
   Hitler is appointed chancellor.

Thinking It Over

1. In what ways do you think the Great War made Fascism an appealing idea to many people?
2. Try listing some of the ways in which modern dictatorships are different from dictatorships in the past.
3. Suppose you lived in Nazi Germany in the 1930s. What would you say or do if you saw German Jews being taken to concentration camps?
4. How was the Fascist idea of the state different from traditional nationalism?

Special Activities

1. Read and report on Ernest Hemingway's novel *For Whom the Bell Tolls*, which deals with the Spanish Civil War. In what ways does he portray the supporters of the Popular Front as heroes? What does he say about the newer horrors of war, such as killing civilians?
2. Use library sources to trace the history of Communist and Fascist movements in the United States during the 1920s and 1930s.

World War II caused even greater destruction than World War I.

Chapter 31 The Second World War

The German army that invaded Poland in September 1939 moved with amazing speed. Hitler's attack was launched by the air force, the Luftwaffe. Its dive bombers plunged in close to their targets. The army advanced in motorized columns, with tanks, troop-carrying trucks, and even motorcycles. No one had thought it possible that an army could move so swiftly. This method of warfare became known as blitzkrieg, or "lightning war." The Germans swept through Poland in less than a month.

Military leaders could not think of a way to stop such a fast armored assault. Most were still thinking in terms of war as it had

1936-1945

1936	Anti-Comintern Pact
1939	World War II begins
1940	Battle of Britain
1940	Japan joins the Axis
1941	Germany invades Soviet Union
1941	Japanese attack Pearl Harbor
1942	Battle of Midway
1942	Allies defeat Germans in North Africa
1943	Battle of Stalingrad
1943	Allies invade Italy
1944	Allies invade France
1945	World War II ends

Winston Churchill.

been fought in 1914-1918. The Poles even sent traditional cavalry units mounted on horseback in suicide attacks on German tanks.

The more powerful nations of the West also had outmoded ideas of warfare. The French, for example, relied on their large land army and on massive fortifications. They saw little need for developing air power. In the United States, an army general had been court-martialed for arguing too long and too loudly for air power.

German scientists were at work on even more devastating tools of war. Their experiments with jet engines might lead to much faster aircraft. Rockets were being developed that could strike distant enemy cities. More frightening was the knowledge that Germany was working to create the ultimate weapon—an atomic bomb.

German forces had a commanding lead over others in key areas of military technology. Hitler intended to use it.

1. The Dictators Tried to Conquer the World

Hitler absorbed part of Poland into a larger Germany. Some Polish territory also went to the Soviet Union. In addition, the Soviets occupied the Baltic countries, Estonia, Latvia, and Lithuania, in 1939 and annexed them in 1940. Stalin also wanted land from Finland. The Red Army invaded Finland in 1939. However, the Finns fought well. They held onto their independence, though they did lose some territory. Thus, Stalin had regained much of the land the Russians had lost in World War 1.

During the brief "Winter War" between the Soviet Union and Finland in 1939-1940, the Western Front remained strangely quiet. People began to hope that somehow all-out war could be avoided.

German troops in Norway.

"Lightning War" in the West In April 1940, Hitler struck again. His first target was Norway, where the first invaders were landed by parachute.

As Norway fell, Denmark was overrun. On May 10, a full-scale attack was launched against the Netherlands, Belgium, Luxembourg, and France. The defenders, mostly French and British, reeled back from the shock of the blitzkrieg. German dive bombers controlled the skies. German tanks rumbled through the supposedly impassable Ardennes region and around the northern end of the Maginot Line.

The German forces now drove a wedge across northern France. This divided the Allies, trapping thousands in Belgium. The Netherlands and Belgium surrendered. Large segments of the French army also gave up. The British and a few French were trapped against the Belgian seacoast at Dunkirk. British ships and even fishing and pleasure boats managed to evacuate 338,000 of these men.

Hitler's armies turned south and easily captured Paris. On June 22, France asked for peace. Within six weeks, Hitler had conquered an empire equal to that of Napoleon. The world was stunned by Germany's easy victory over France.

The Battle of Britain In 1940, the future of the world seemed to depend on Great Britain. Only Britain remained active in the war against the Nazis. If the island kingdom fell, it would be impossible to

Nazi troops questioning civilians in Paris.

dislodge Hitler from Europe.

After France fell, the British began to prepare for a German invasion. Winston Churchill, the new prime minister, vowed that the British would never surrender. To Britain's friends in the United States he promised: "Give us the tools, and we will finish the job."

The United States gradually did away with its neutrality laws. Weapons and supplies began to flow to England in a program called Lend-Lease. The U. S. Government also started to prepare for war. In 1940, it began a military draft.

Hitler held back from invading Britain. The speed and easiness of the victory in France had surprised the German leaders. Germany was not ready to launch a large-scale invasion. Instead, Hitler became convinced that bombing by the Luftwaffe would quickly force the British to surrender. The bombing raids began in the summer of 1940 and reached their peak in the fall. Never had the world witnessed such mass destruction in civilian areas.

A handful of battered British planes kept the Luftwaffe from complete control of the air. In fact, the British defense effort began to take a heavy toll of German planes. In the fall of 1940, Hitler suddenly changed his strategy. He gave up his plans for invading Britain for the time being and turned his attention to the East.

The Russian Front Hitler was worried about the possibility of the Soviet Union

Did You Know?

Winston Churchill: Democracy's Soldier

Through the mid-1930's, Winston Churchill had repeatedly spoken out in Parliament against the policy of appeasement. Hitler would not be appeased, he warned again and again, until he had conquered Europe. He could be stopped only by force.

As Hitler's blitzkrieg stormed across Europe in the spring of 1940, the British people realized how right Churchill had been. They cheered when the king named him to replace Chamberlain as prime minister.

It was nearly too late. Germany controlled most of the continent and the Russians seemed about to collapse. England itself appeared on the brink of defeat in the closing months of 1940. People waited grimly for the Nazi invasion.

In those darkest of days, Winston Churchill was at his best. He proved to be a tower of strength and inspiration. In stirring speeches he touched deep chords of national pride and confidence. Like a pugnacious English bulldog—and some people said he looked like one—he refused to give an inch in his determination to beat Hitler. People believed him when he solemnly declared, "We shall never surrender."

For the next 5 years he worked tirelessly, often 16 or 18 hours a day. He seemed to be everywhere at once—chatting with wardens during air raids, visiting factories, air raid shelters, neighborhoods and training areas. He was always sporting a cigar, a jaunty hat, and holding his fingers in the famous "V for Victory" sign. He often terrified his security officers by insisting on "having a look" at the battle fronts in North Africa, the Mediterranean and then the coast of France.

He worked closely with America's President Roosevelt. They shared a common

A victim of the London blitz.

love of ships and each had been a naval administrator. Churchill signed his messages to FDR "Naval Person." In one of those cables, as the tide of the war began to turn, Churchill said, "It's fun to be in the same decade with you."

In recognition of his leadership, Churchill received the Nobel Prize for Peace. He also found time to write a brilliant history of the war. The book helped him earn a second Nobel Prize, this time for literature. In summing up his role in World War II, one historian has written that his appointment as prime minister was for Hitler "the single greatest disaster he would experience." Another wrote simply: "Remember him, for he saved all of you."

pushing westward. To counter this, he began to move east. First, Rumania, Hungary, and Bulgaria were persuaded to join the Axis Powers. German troops were stationed in all three to make sure of their loyalty. Next, he ordered an invasion of Yugoslavia. Germans occupied that country. However, guerrillas led by Josip Broz, known as Tito (TEE to), fought them throughout the war. Greece was also added to Hitler's conquests.

On June 22, 1941, Hitler ordered Operation Barbarossa, the invasion of the Soviet Union, to begin. The Communists were among his most-hated enemies. He had long planned this attack. The treaty he had signed with Stalin in 1939 meant nothing. He hoped that, by invading in the summer, Germany could complete the conquest by fall. This would give the Germans the huge Soviet grain harvest. They could then move toward the vital oil fields to the south.

About three million German soldiers stormed across the Soviet border, along a front 3,200 kilometers (2,000 miles) long. The now familiar air power, heavy artillery, and tanks pushed back the Soviet armies. By fall, the Germans had gained most of the European part of the Soviet Union. They were within 40 kilometers (25 miles) of Moscow.

Entire Soviet armies had been captured and the rest had retreated. However, the Soviet leaders and people were determined not to give up. Army divisions regrouped behind the front. Factories were rebuilt east of the Ural Mountains. Huge amounts of aid began to arrive from the United States—food, clothing, trucks, weapons, and ammunition.

Just as the cold Russian winter set in, the Soviets began a counterattack. The German troops were prepared neither for the attack nor for the winter. Their advance stalled within sight of Moscow.

Hitler was furious. It was clear that Moscow could not be captured by direct attack. He now took personal control of military operations and turned the main thrust of the invasion southward. His plan was to take the key city of Stalingrad and then move into the oil regions. He was sure that it was only a matter of time before the Soviet defenses would collapse. Around the world, many people felt that the Soviet Union was doomed.

Japan and the United States Throughout the 1930s, Japan had directed its aggression toward China. However, toward the end of the decade, the situation began to change. Japan desperately wanted the oil and other raw materials of Southeast Asia. It became clear that the United States would not allow Japan to fulfill its aim of dominating Asia. The United States had steadfastly opposed the Japanese moves against China. There was a sign of what was to come in 1936, when Japan joined Germany and Italy in the Anti-Comintern Pact, an alliance against Communism. In September 1940, Japan became a member of the Axis. Shortly thereafter, an American embargo on exports of iron and steel scrap, aimed at Japan, became effective.

The United States was becoming the only possible barrier to Japanese expansionism. Japan and the Soviet Union signed a nonaggression pact in April 1941. France, Britain, and the Netherlands were involved in the war in Europe. Their power in Asia was greatly reduced. Japan moved quickly to fill this vacuum. In July 1941, Japanese forces occupied French Indochina. The American government immediately froze Japanese credits. This brought trade between the two countries to a halt.

In October 1941, General Hideki Tojo (to jo) became prime minister of Japan. His government opened negotiations with the United States, presenting a list of demands to Washington on November 20. The American government offered counterproposals on November 26. Two days later,

Japanese officials going to the State Department for a conference on December 5, 1941.

Japan publicly rejected the American proposals. The official Japanese reply arrived in Washington on the morning of December 7. Before it could be given to the American government, Japanese forces launched an attack on the American naval base at Pearl Harbor in the Hawaiian Islands.

The Japanese light bombers, launched from aircraft carriers, caught the American forces completely by surprise. More than 2,000 lives were lost and the Pacific fleet was crippled. However, the American aircraft carriers survived because they were at sea. Americans were shocked and outraged by this "sneak attack." The U.S. Congress passed a declaration of war the next day.

The Darkest Hour The United States was not completely prepared for war. After war had broken out in Europe, military expenditures had been increased and in 1940 a military draft had been instituted. Nonetheless, time would be needed to train and equip a fighting force large enough for a major war. American industry had to be converted to war production. American industry did manage to turn to all-out war production with remarkable speed. By 1943, the United States was outproducing all the Axis powers combined.

However, during 1942, the issue was in doubt. In Asia and the Pacific, neither the British nor the Americans could immediately stop the Japanese. During the early months of 1942, the Japanese conquered the Philippines, the oil-rich Dutch East Indies, and other islands. With an airstrip on New Guinea, they were in a position to strike at Australia. Japanese forces advanced on the mainland of Asia as well. Establishing control in most of Southeast Asia, they then took Burma. It seemed that India would be next. Japanese forces would be close to meeting up with the Germans. The two Axis powers could then complete the conquest of all of Europe and Asia.

Even the United States no longer seemed safe from attack. In June 1942, the Japanese landed in the Aleutian (ah LOO shun) Islands, a string of American islands leading to Alaska. All along the West Coast, Americans expected Japanese attacks.

While the Soviets were counterattacking the Germans with some success, other German units were on the move in North Africa. Mussolini's forces had started the North African campaign in 1940. From Libya they had invaded Egypt. They wanted to gain control of the Suez Canal, which was essential to Allied shipping. Mussolini hoped that this would lead to Italian control of the entire Mediterranean Sea.

Although badly outnumbered, the British began pushing the Italians back. At the same time, they ended Mussolini's brief empire in Ethiopia.

Then German troops and tanks arrived in North Africa. They were commanded by one of Germany's most brilliant generals, Erwin Rommel. In tank battles that stretched for miles across the desert, Rommel forced the British into retreat. By mid-1942, the British prepared for a last stand at El Alamein (el al a MAIN).

In 1942, the Allied cause also appeared in doubt on the seas. Japanese battleships and aircraft carriers were in control of the western Pacific. The German submarines were a deadly menace in the Atlantic. The survival of both Great Britain and the Soviet Union depended on a steady supply of aid from the United States. The American economy, in turn, depended in large part on raw materials from the Americas and elsewhere. During 1942, the German submarines took a heavy toll of the shipping that carried these goods. Indeed, ships were being lost faster than they could be replaced.

There seemed to be a real possibility that the Axis would conquer the whole world. However, even in the darkest days of 1942, there were signs of hope. British air defenses, for example, aided by the development of radar, reduced German air raids. The people of the Soviet Union were putting up a heroic defense. In the Pacific, the American navy turned back the Japanese at the Battle of the Coral Sea in May 1942. A few weeks later, at the Battle of Midway, American planes sank four of Japan's essential aircraft carriers. The wave of Japanese conquests was now beginning to recede.

Section Questions

1. What was new about the German method of waging war?
2. Why did France fall to Hitler so quickly?
3. Why did everything depend on Britain in 1940?
4. Why did Germany attack the Soviet Union?
5. What led the Japanese to attack Pearl Harbor?
6. Why did the Allied cause look so bleak in 1942?

The British at El Alamein.

The Allied forces worked together. General Eisenhower is in the center of this photograph.

2. The Allies Turned the Tide

The Axis Powers—Germany, Italy, and Japan—did not work together closely in waging war. Each nation followed its own policy independently of the others.

The Allied Powers depended on close cooperation, especially between Britain and the United States. It often proved difficult to extend that coooperative spirit to the Soviet Union. Churchill bitterly hated Stalin and Communist rule. Stalin was just as distrustful of his capitalist Allies. Roosevelt tried to smooth over the differences.

Allied Cooperation Britain's Winston Churchill and America's Franklin Roosevelt had held meetings even before the United States entered the war. In 1941, they issued the Atlantic Charter. This document pledged their countries to protect basic freedoms against the threat of totalitarianism. Shortly after the Japanese attack on Pearl Harbor, they invited all the world's nations to sign a Declaration of the United Nations. The two leaders urged all countries to join in the struggle against "the savage and brutal forces" seeking to conquer the world.

The declaration did not yet create the organization of the United Nations. However, it did advance the idea of the world's nations working together for their collective security.

Great Britain and the United States developed a new kind of wartime cooperation. Top-ranking military officers formed a "Combined Chiefs of Staff." This group planned a joint war strategy for the two nations. It was agreed that Germany must be defeated first since it represented the greater danger to the world. They would do what they could against Japan until the

630

European war was won. The close coordination between the two countries was an important factor in the outcome of the war.

Stalin was later invited to join Churchill and Roosevelt in broad planning meetings. Stalin agreed to do so, but he remained distrustful. Beginning in early 1942, he insisted that the Allies must open a "second front." That is, he wanted them to invade the continent of Europe from the west. This would force Hitler to shift troops west. It would thus ease the pressure on the Soviet army and people. Stalin could see no reason for delaying such an invasion.

Churchill and Roosevelt had planned on a second front from the beginning. However, they knew their countries were not prepared to launch an invasion in 1942.

Resistance to Hitler While his empire expanded, Hitler set about creating a "New Order" in Europe. It was to be an armed continent—a "European Fortress." The rulers would be the German people. They, in turn, would follow the lead of Der Fuhrer and the Nazi Party.

Familiar totalitarian methods were used to crush any opposition. Those caught in acts of spying or sabotage were tortured and then killed. An unsolved crime often led to the execution of ten or more citizens chosen at random.

Despite the risks involved, resistance movements were active in every country. Men and women radioed military information to Allied listening posts in Britain. They helped Jews and downed bomber crews to escape. They blew up troop trains and committed other acts of sabotage. In Yugoslavia, they formed an independent army in the hills, led by the Communist Tito.

A key element in Hitler's New Order was his wild plan for "racial purity." Those who seemed most like "Aryans" were to be treated well. This was to include groups like the Scandinavians and the Dutch. Through education, these people would be made ready to join a "Greater Germany."

Inferior groups, like the Slavic peoples, were to be used only as a source of hard labor. In parts of Poland, the Slavs were ordered to leave. The land was incorporated into Germany and opened to German "settlers." An estimated seven million Slavs were sent to work on special slave-labor projects.

In one of the most vicious acts in history, Hitler now proceeded with his plan for *genocide*, or murder of the entire Jewish population. Different methods were used. In the occupied areas of the Soviet Union, special execution squads rounded up people known to be Jews and killed them. Elsewhere, they were herded into airless cattle cars and taken to concentration camps. Some of the victims were used as subjects in gruesome medical experiments. Others died slowly from starvation or disease. Thousands more were sent to their deaths in the gas chambers. The full horror of this Holocaust was not known until the camps were liberated near the end of the war.

In Germany itself, there was no regular resistance movement against Hitler. However, there was opposition, especially among the army and navy officers.

Marshall Tito of Yugoslavia.

This war poster was called "This Is the Enemy."

In 1944, the military officers created an elaborate plan to assassinate Hitler and seize control from the Nazis. Some of Germany's key leaders, including General Rommel, took part in the plot. A bomb was planted in Hitler's secret *bunker* (an underground bomb shelter). However, when it exploded he was not seriously injured.

Hitler's response was to have the Gestapo arrest 5,000 officers who might have been involved. Rommel was allowed to commit suicide. Others were tortured and then executed. This eliminated many of the men who might have led any anti-Hitler movement.

The First Allied Victories In the closing months of 1942, the war began to change. American industry became what President Roosevelt called "the arsenal for democracy." The United States did not just make enough war materials to meet its own needs. It also produced enough to send millions of tons of weapons, food, and supplies to its Allies, especially to Britain and the Soviet Union.

The American naval victory at Midway in June 1942, shocked the Japanese. Instead of organizing an invasion of Australia, they now had to pull back. In August, Americans landed at Guadalcanal (gwad al can AL) in the Solomon Islands. This was the first step in a long drive to take the Japanese held islands in the Pacific.

In Egypt, the British under General Bernard L. Montgomery scored a major victory at El Alamein early in November 1942. Rommel's German forces began to retreat. Meanwhile, American and British troops commanded by General Dwight D. Eisenhower were landing in the western part of North Africa. Caught between these two forces, the Germans were eventually forced to surrender. By May 1943, all of North Africa was in Allied hands.

At the same time, one of the most amazing battles in history was taking place at Stalingrad in the Soviet Union. The Germans had fought their way into the city in September 1942. However, the Soviets would not give up. Soldiers and citizens fought for every bombed-out building and street.

Once again, the bitter Russian winter struck at the German army. When the Soviets began a counterattack in November, the Germans could fight no more. Against Hitler's orders, 330,000 of Germany's once invincible army surrendered at Stalingrad in February 1943.

In July 1943, the western Allies invaded Sicily and then, in September, the mainland of Italy. Mussolini was immediately driven from power and a new government asked for peace. However, Hitler ordered army divisions into Italy and continued the war. In fact, aided by the mountainous terrain, the Germans needed few troops to pin down the Allies. Consequently, the fighting in Italy did not in itself relieve the German pressure on the Soviet Union. The Italian campaign became a grim struggle for every foot of land. The Allies did not gain complete control of the peninsula until the end of the war.

The Invasion of Europe During 1943 and early 1944, German military leaders tried to turn Europe into a true fortress. Beaches and harbors were covered with explosive mines. They knew the Allied invasion would come, but they did not know when or where.

D-Day, the invasion day, came on June 6, 1944. It was the largest sea-land invasion in history. The supreme Allied commander was General Eisenhower. The target was the coast of Normandy in France.

In spite of heavy bombing from the air and shelling from ships, the Germans in Europe put up a stiff defense. However, the Allies kept coming in greater and greater numbers, and they forced their way inland. In less than a month, about a million soldiers had been shipped across the English Channel to France.

For a brief time in late 1944, Germany made one last counterattack. In the famous Battle of the Bulge in December, the Germans managed to cut off thousands of Allied troops. However, they could not press the advantage. Hitler also hoped that new weapons could still salvage his ambitions. Jet aircraft, far faster than propeller-driven planes, had been successfully tested. However, they could not be mass-produced in time to make a difference. Other advances were the V-1 and V-2 rockets. The V-1 was a jet-propelled drone containing a bomb. The V-2 was a long-range rocket. Once again, people in Britain listened in dread for the air-raid sirens. However, these weapons came too late to make a significant difference.

By early 1945, the Allies regained the offensive in the west and swept into Germany. The Soviet forces were also moving in from the east. In addition, in 1944 and 1945, the Soviets were taking over other German-controlled lands—Rumania, Bulgaria, Yugoslavia, Hungary, Poland, and parts of Austria. When the fighting reached the streets of Berlin, Hitler committed suicide. A few Nazi leaders escaped. Many were caught and held for trial as war criminals. On May 8, 1945, the war in Europe ended.

The End of the War The war in the Pacific had already been a long, bloody struggle. Fighting in the dense jungles of Pacific islands became a nightmare for American and British marines and soldiers. The Japanese defenders fought tenaciously.

As soon as one island was taken, the military leaders planned the next invasion. Ships' artillery and airplanes "softened up" the Japanese defenses. Then the troops landed. Their enemies included the climate and disease as well as the Japanese.

In October 1944, the Philippines were invaded by American forces under General Douglas MacArthur. There, in the naval Battle of Leyte (LAY te) Gulf, much of the Japanese fleet was destroyed. When the island of Okinawa (O ki NAH wah) was taken in 1945, the Americans were within 575 kilometers (360 miles) of Japan.

Some Japanese leaders were now ready to surrender. However, the military leaders refused to do so. It seemed as if an invasion of Japan itself would be needed. This judgment led to one of the most momentous decisions in history—the first use of the atomic bomb in warfare.

Harry S. Truman was now president of the United States. He came to office after Roosevelt died suddenly in April 1945. Truman's advisers said that an invasion of Japan might cost a million American lives—nearly three times the nation's dead for the whole war. To avoid this suffering, the president decided to use the atomic bomb. This new weapon had been tested for the first time at Alamogordo (al a ma GOR do), New Mexico, in July. A single atomic bomb was dropped on the city of Hiroshima (he ro SHE ma) on August 6, 1945 (August 7 in Japan). Much of the city was destroyed in the most awesome explosion in history. Two days later, the Soviet Union declared war on Japan. When the Japanese still would not surrender, a second bomb was dropped on Nagasaki (nag a SAK e) on August 9 (August 10 in Japan). The Japanese government then asked for peace on August 14. American troops began

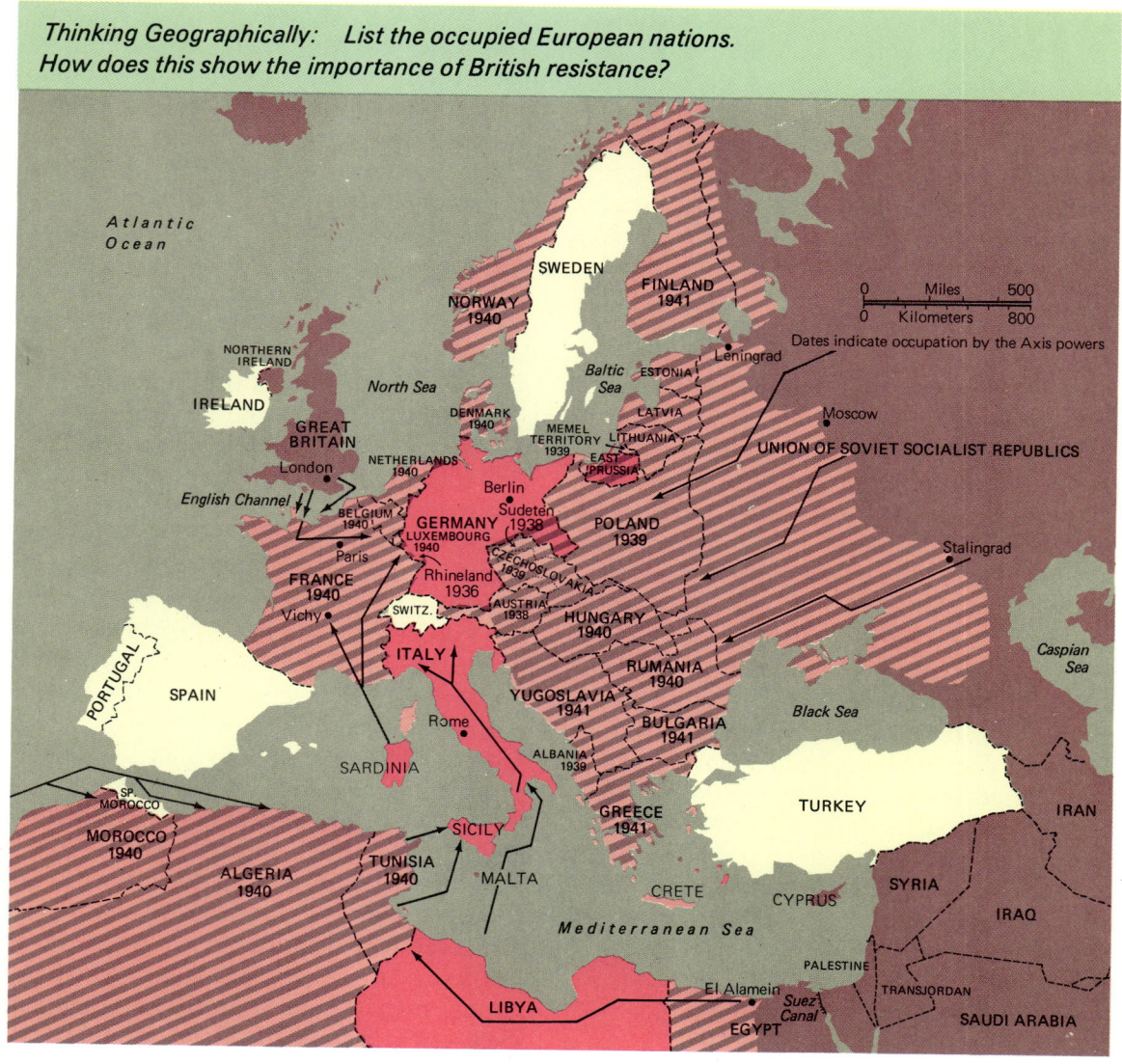

Thinking Geographically: List the occupied European nations. How does this show the importance of British resistance?

moving in to occupy Japan on August 27. The formal Japanese surrender came on September 2.

Section Questions

1. What was the "second front"? Why did Stalin insist on it?
2. What were Hitler's intentions concerning the different groups in his empire?
3. Why was the Battle of Stalingrad so important?
4. What "secret weapons" did Germany have?
5. Why was the decision made to use the atomic bomb?

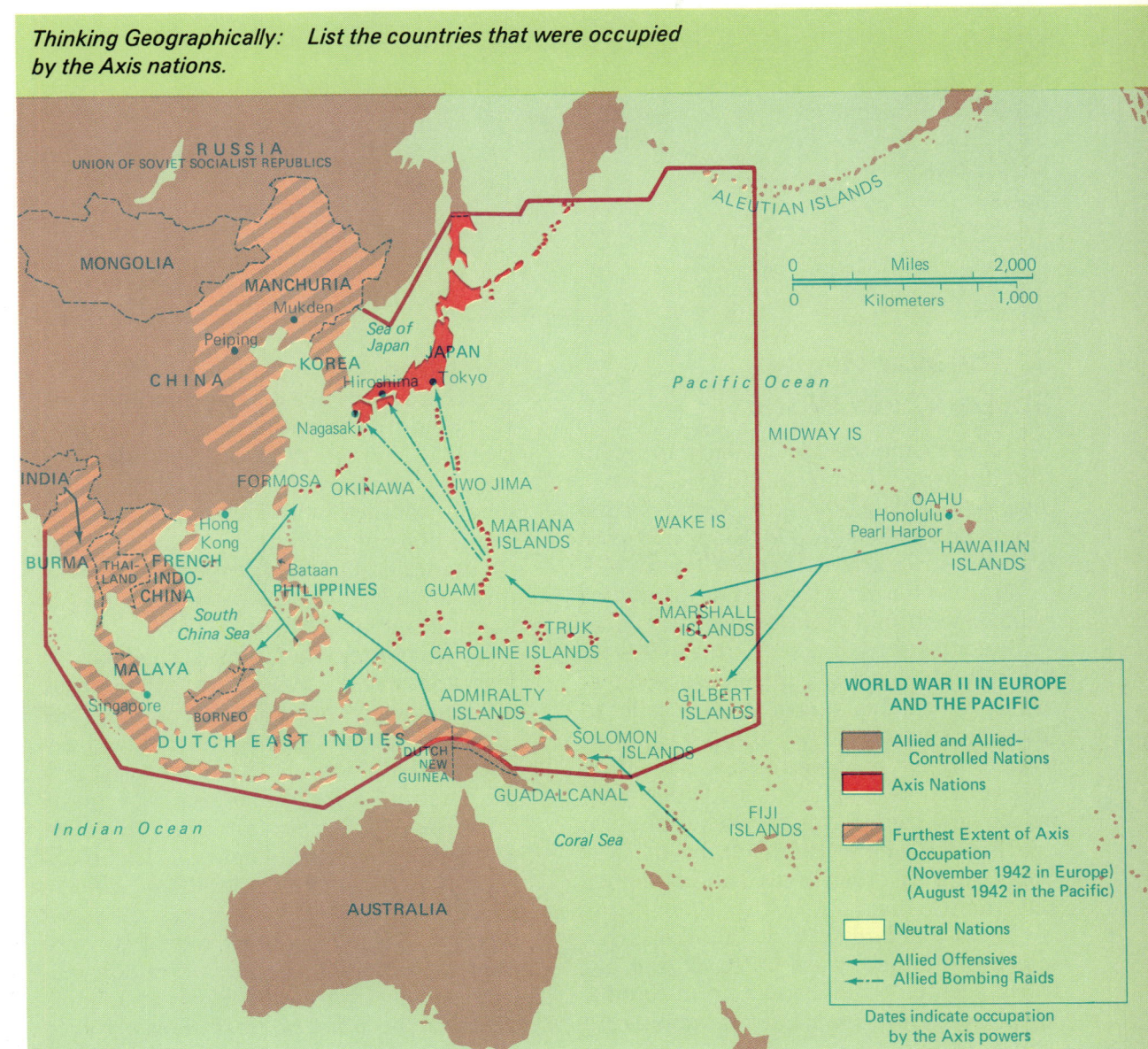

Thinking Geographically: List the countries that were occupied by the Axis nations.

Berlin in 1945.

3. The War Helped Shape a New World

In 1945 the world was very different from the way it had been in 1939. The two most powerful dictatorships, Germany and Japan, lay in ruins. Allied troops occupied both countries and governed them.

Much of the industrialized world seemed reduced to rubble by the endless bombing. Entire cities were in ashes. Harbors were blocked by sunken ships. Hundreds of bridges and thousands of miles of railroad track had been destroyed. Millions of people were *refugees*, men, women, and children with no homes, no place to go. Quick work by the new United Nations Rehabilitation and Relief Agency (UNRRA), by the Red Cross, and by other organizations helped save many lives.

The world had survived another experience with total war. Much of the old world seemed to have gone up in flames. People were unsure what the new world would be like.

Total War The statistics of World War II are too large to have much meaning. About 15 million military personnel died. Estimates of civilian deaths are even higher, perhaps as many as 30 million. So many died uncounted in bombing raids and concentration camps that there are no really accurate figures. The number of Jews who died in the Holocaust is usually put at about 6 million.

The country that suffered the heaviest losses was the Soviet Union. About seven million Soviets were killed in combat. Total Soviet deaths are estimated to have been about 20 million. Suffering, death, and destruction were widespread in many countries. In Berlin, for example, after more than two years of heavy Allied bombing, 75 percent of the buildings were in ruins. The eastern European cities of Warsaw, Kiev, and Minsk were destroyed even more by the Germans. London suffered heavily from German bombing. Some cities had been fire-bombed. This involved using incendiary bombs that could create a "fire storm." Thousands in Hamburg, Germany and in Tokyo, Japan were killed in such fire storms. In some ways, Japanese cities suffered more damage because so many buildings there were made of wood.

Japan had also suffered from the atomic bombs dropped on Hiroshima and Nagasaki. In Hiroshima, a circle 13 kilometers (8 miles) across showed where the bomb had hit. No buildings were left standing within that area. Somewhere between 80,000 and 100,000 people died in the blast. Thousands more faced certain death from radiation sickness, cancer, and other bomb-related diseases.

Even where civilians were not direct victims of war, the total population was involved in other ways. The United States, for example, did not suffer direct damage. Factories and cities were not bombed or attacked. Nonetheless, all elements of the American economy and society were caught up in the war.

The production of peacetime goods was greatly reduced. People who had worked on automobile assembly lines began making tanks. Watchmakers built bombsights. Clothing manufacturers produced uniforms. Cosmetics companies turned out medical supplies. Practically all ordinary goods were rationed, including food. Government regulations seemed to touch every corner of life. There was even a long set of directions for grocers on how to price cabbage.

Many Americans, like many people in other countries, went out of their way to do still more. They bought War Bonds, collected scrap materials, and grew their own food in Victory gardens. In some way, then, war touched the lives of all Americans,

Women factory workers during World War II.

not just the 15 million who served in uniform.

The horror of total war did not seem to affect people as deeply as in 1914-1918. Endless pictures in magazines and newsreels began to dull people's minds. There was just too much suffering for one person to grasp. Psychiatrists call this the *megadeath syndrome*. The number of deaths was so great that no emotional response to them was possible.

Power Changes The war led to major shifts in world power. Often, these were changes that had begun during World War I. For example, the decline of Europe as a power center continued. All the once-great European countries suffered tremendous wartime damage, especially Germany. Germany was now an occupied nation, with control divided among the Soviet Union, the United States, Great Britain, and France.

The economic recovery of Europe would require years of hard work. Outside help was also needed. The United States was the only possible source for that assistance.

At the same time, all European countries faced the loss of their colonial empires. After World War I, the colonial peoples had hoped that the idea of self-determination would be applied to them. It was not. The Treaty of Versailles had even led to the establishment of new colonies under the mandate system of the League of Nations.

Now, after World War II, colonial peoples not only hoped for independence, they demanded it. Nationalist movements grew stronger in every colony. One by one, these movements succeeded. Within two years of the war's end, Syria, Lebanon, Jordan, the Philippines, India, and Pakistan became independent nations. Over the next 18 years, 50 more nations gained independence from Western control.

At the same time, another important power change was taking place. The United States and the Soviet Union were emerging as the world's great superpowers.

The Superpowers By 1918, it had been clear that the United States was the world's major economic power. As you read earlier, American factories were producing more than 40 percent of the world's goods in the years between the world wars. The second global conflict had also made it clear that economic strength was essential to military power. Germany had managed to conquer much of Europe with ease. The reason for this was that the German economy had been geared to war production during the 1930s.

During the war, while Europe's industry was being devastated by bombing, American industry grew as never before. The use of machinery in agriculture also provided huge food surpluses from fewer farms.

The economy of the Soviet Union had also been growing in the years between the wars. By the late 1930s, it was second to the United States. Much was lost when Hitler's troops overran the western part of the country. The Soviets removed whatever machinery and equipment they could. They destroyed the rest so that it could not be used by the Germans. The Soviet people then rebuilt much of their industry east of the Ural Mountains. There it was safe from German planes and artillery. They also received a great deal of material from the United States.

When the war ended, therefore, the Soviet Union still had a strong economy. It was far behind the United States, but it was well ahead of any European nation. Both of the superpowers had the combination of elements needed for world power: large populations, strong industries, good supplies of raw materials, and modern technology.

The emergence of these two countries as the superpowers tended to divide the world in two. The Soviet Union was a Communist nation. Stalin had never lost sight of his goal of expanding Communist power. The United States led the nations

Churchill, Roosevelt, and Stalin at Yalta.

that were regarded as "free," or capitalist, or democratic. That meant that the United States would now have to lead the struggle to keep Communism from expanding. The war led to a great increase in Communist-held territory.

As early as 1940, the Soviet Union had absorbed the Baltic states and parts of Finland, Poland, and Rumania. These areas, plus some others, were regained by the Soviets with the defeat of Germany. As the countries of eastern and central Europe were freed from German control by Soviet troops, Communist-led governments dominated by the Soviet Union usually came to power. This occurred in spite of the fact that Stalin had promised Churchill and Roosevelt at the Yalta Conference in February 1945 that free elections would be held there. Roosevelt hoped that Soviet power would be contained and peace ensured by the threat of the American atomic bomb and the promise of the United Nations. A charter for the new international organization was approved by fifty nations in San Francisco in June 1945. However, the hopes for the postwar world symbolized by Roosevelt expired not long after the great American leader himself died. The "hot war" between the Allies and the Axis was then followed by a "cold war" between the superpowers.

Section Questions

1. In what ways was World War II a "total war"?
2. What happened to European power during the war?
3. Why is a strong economy needed for military power in the modern world?
4. How did the power of the Soviet Union expand as a result of the war?

Chapter Summary

1. Hitler's invasion of Poland gave the world a preview of blitzkrieg, or lightning war. Moving with surprising speed, his armored divisions simply overpowered the Poles. April 1940 marked the beginning of Hitler's all-out assault on Europe. Within two months, much of western Europe—Norway, Denmark, the Netherlands, Belgium, and France—had been crushed by German power. The Battle of Britain, Germany's effort to bomb the British into surrender, began in the summer.

Hitler did not invade Britain. Instead, in 1941, he turned east and launched a surprise invasion of the Soviet Union. He hoped to defeat the Soviets within weeks, take advantage of their large grain harvest, and then push south toward the oil fields.

The Soviet resistance and the harsh Russian winter pinned down the German armies. Hitler gave up on taking Moscow and aimed his forces southward.

Late in 1941, Japan made a surprise attack on Pearl Harbor, the American naval base in the Hawaiian Islands. This brought the United States into the war. For months in 1941, the Axis powers continued to expand.
2. The Allies fought as the defenders of freedom against totalitarian control. The United States and Great Britain worked in close harmony, planning strategy jointly. While the Allies prepared to invade Europe, Hitler tried to turn it into a fortress. However, in every country, resistance movements developed to fight Nazi rule. Even in Germany, there was an unsuccessful plot to assassinate Hitler. Among the many brutal actions of the Nazis, the worst was their attempt to exterminate the Jews and others whom they considered inferior or undesirable. Millions of people were put to death in the gas chambers of the concentration camps.

The war began to change in late 1942. Allied forces began to move against Japanese-held islands. The British stopped Rommel in North Africa. A brave stand by the Soviets at Stalingrad dealt a heavy blow to the German war machine.

The Allies invaded France in June 1944. With the Soviets pushing in from the east and the other Allies from the west, the German empire gradually shrank. In 1945, Hitler committed suicide and Germany surrendered.

In the war with Japan, the decision was made to use the world's newest and most terrifying weapon—the atomic bomb. After such bombs were dropped on Hiroshima and Nagasaki in 1945, the Japanese surrendered.
3. The war caused great death and destruction and speeded up changes that had begun earlier in the century. With its industries badly damaged, the economic power of Europe declined. The nations of Europe also faced the loss of their colonies. Colonial peoples began to demand and gain national independence.

At the same time, the Soviet Union and the United States emerged as the world's two great superpowers, each far stronger than any other nation. Soviet ambitions to expand Communism made conflict inevitable. The United States was now looked on as the leader of the "Free World" against Communism. Soviet power expanded as a result of the war. American atomic weapons and the new United Nations failed to contain Soviet power or ensure genuine peace.

Chapter 31 Review

Check Your Facts

1. Identify the following:
   a. Winter War
   b. Dunkirk
   c. Lend-Lease
   d. Operation Barbarossa
   e. Stalingrad
   f. Hideki Tojo
   g. Erwin Rommel
   h. Guadalcanal
   i. Harry S. Truman
2. What was the Battle of Britain?
3. Why did the German attack in the Soviet Union slow down near Moscow?
4. What made the Battle of Midway important?
5. Why did Stalin insist on a "second front"?
6. What were resistance movements?
7. Why was the Allied invasion of Italy less significant than the Normandy invasion?
8. What was the importance of the Battle of Leyte Gulf?

Words to Know

Explain the meaning and historical importance of each word or term:
   a. blitzkrieg
   b. V-1
   c. genocide
   d. Holocaust
   e. bunker
   f. refugees
   g. megadeath syndrome

Developing Your Skills

1. On a map of Europe, indicate the following:
   a. areas that the Soviet Union absorbed during and after World War II.
   b. how Hitler hoped to defeat the Soviet Union.
2. Place the following events in the proper chronological order:

   Battle of Midway
   Battle of Britain
   D-Day
   Japanese surrender
   Battle of Stalingrad
   Battle of the Bulge

Thinking It Over

1. Why do you think leaders in many countries were unprepared for Hitler's blitzkrieg warfare?
2. Suppose Hitler's New Order in Europe had lasted 10 years more. What do you think it would have been like?
3. It had always been thought that bombing an enemy's cities would lead to surrender. However, bombing did not make the British and Germans give up. Can you think of reasons why?
4. Why does modern military power depend on such factors as a large population, strong industry, raw materials, and technology?
5. The idea of self-determination developed during World War I. How did it become important after World War II?

Special Activities

1. Read Hersey's *Hiroshima* or Bradley's *No Place to Hide*. Discuss with the class the authors' reactions to the arrival of the nuclear age. To what extent do you as a group feel there is a nuclear danger?
2. Find out more about the Holocaust. Try to analyze how it could happen and whether it could happen in another place or time.

Unit 8 Review

Words to Know

1. Each term below has been paired with a single country. Explain the significance of that word or term for that nation in the period between the wars.

   isolationism (U.S.)   *Mein Kampf*
   purge trials (USSR)   (Germany)
   Il Duce (Italy)   appeasement
                             (England)

2. Explain how each word in column 1 was of special importance to a nation or group in column 2.

   Lend-Lease   Jews
   V-2 rocket   Germany
   atomic bomb   United States
   Stalingrad   Soviet Union
   blitzkrieg   Japan
   Holocaust
   Hiroshima

Time and Place

1. Compare political maps of Europe before and after World War I. Identify the three great empires that disappeared and explain what happened to the lands they occupied.
2. In terms of geography, explain the following:
   a. why Germany's failure to capture Moscow before winter was such a disaster.
   b. why the war for North Africa was so important.
   c. what made the North Atlantic a key war zone.

Putting it Together

1. What political, economic and social factors made possible the rise of dictators in the 1920s and 1930s?
2. In what ways do you think that Stalin's dictatorship was like that of Hitler? In what ways was it different?
3. Some historians believe that World War I was a much greater shock to modern humanity than was World War II. Review the text sections on the impact of each war and draw your own conclusion.
4. How did Hitler make use of prejudice against Jews in his drive for power?
5. What did the Japanese hope to achieve by the attack on Pearl Harbor? Did the plan work?
6. In your own words, explain how the United States and the Soviet Union emerged from the ashes of war as the world's only super powers.

Contemporary Parallel:
The Sparks of War

In 1914, an archduke was killed. This event "did not at first seem earth-shattering." However, this killing was the spark that led to World War I.

In contrast, Japan, Germany, and Italy succeeded with one aggressive act after another throughout the 1930s. Not until Germany invaded Poland did World War II begin.

Since the end of World War II, there have been many "small" wars. These wars involve only two or three nations, or do not engage the warring nations' total capacity. Yet, there is always the danger that a small war can grow into a global conflict.

Another possible spark of war is *terrorism.* Terrorism, the use of force or an act of violence for political reasons, is often in today's news. Usually the terrorists want publicity to make the whole world aware of their cause. Sometimes they want to secure the release of their members who are prisoners. In some cases, acts of terrorism are motivated by revenge.

Some terrorists operate within their own nation, as in Ireland and in Spain's Basque county. In other cases, terrorists such as those associated with the Palestine Liberation Organization (PLO) have cooperated with each other across national borders. The world was shocked in 1972 when Palestinian terrorists murdered Israeli athletes at the Munich Olympic Games.

Some people fear that as nuclear power becomes more widespread, a group may take over an atomic plant or capture some barrels of atomic waste as an act of terror. It is possible that such an act could be the spark that sets off World War III.

QUESTIONS

1. Nuclear weapons have not been used since World War II. Do you think it is possible that a global war might be fought without the use of nuclear weapons?
2. What are some of the acts of terrorism, civil wars, or wars between nations that have occurred recently? Which of these acts or wars would be most likely to lead to global war? Why?
3. What can citizens do to help prevent war?

1945	1947	1950	1954	1960	1965	1979	1982
World War II ends	Independence for India, Pakistan; Marshall Plan	Korean War begins	Independence for Laos, Cambodia	Independence for 17 African nations	United States sends troops to Vietnam	USSR invades Afghanistan	Martial law in Poland

Unit 9

The Postwar World

The space shuttle Columbia.

*P*rotesters march in the streets of Quebec, demanding that their province become independent of Canada. In New Mexico, a Navaho youth decides he will live on the reservation rather than move to the city. In the Pyrenees Mountains, the Basque people insist that they are not part of Spain. In Africa, the Eritreans fight to gain their freedom from Ethiopia.

Throughout the world, small groups are insisting on the right to their own identity. They don't want to be swallowed up by a larger unit—the nation. They want to live and preserve their own culture and heritage. They do not want to be absorbed by the majority culture.

As the 1900s draw to a close, nationalism seems powerful. People now live in 160 or so different nation-states. Nationalism has been a unifier by drawing people together under a common government and common culture.

But in many nations there are those who resist. Some, like the Navaho youth, accept being part of a nation. Their concern is for keeping alive a way of life in which they believe. Others go further. They are called *separatists* and they seek a separate political unit of their own.

How can each nation create a balance that satisfies its minority groups while maintaining central control? That is a question that many nations and people are trying to decide.

The United Nations.

Chapter 32
Postwar Europe and the Americas

There they sat, the surviving top twenty-two leaders of the Nazi world. They were on trial for crimes against humanity—murder, atrocities, persecuting Jews and other groups—and for starting World War II. Among those on trial were Air Marshall Hermann Goering (GUR ing) and Rudolf Hess, former Deputy to the Fuhrer.

The judges were from the four victorious Allied powers. During the trial, witnesses, films, photographs, orders, and so on were brought forth to show the guilt of the defendants. The evidence was shocking. But almost all of the Nazi leaders pleaded not guilty. Only Albert Speer, who organized German industries during the later part of the war, admitted some guilt. The court convicted nineteen defendants and freed three. Of those convicted, twelve, including Goering, were sentenced to be hanged. Goering, however, escaped the hangman's noose by committing suicide in his cell. The others were executed on October 16, 1946.

Other trials were held at Nuremberg and in other occupied zones.

1945-1981

1945	United Nations created
1947	Marshall Plan
1948	Berlin Blockade
1949	NATO starts
1953	Stalin dies
1956	Revolts in Eastern Europe
1957	Common Market begins
1959	Castro takes over in Cuba
1962	Cuban missile crisis
1970	Allende government overthrown in Chile
1972	Nixon visits China and USSR
1978	Panama Canal Treaty
1979	USSR invades Afghanistan
1981	Martial law imposed in Poland

Harry S. Truman.

The Nuremberg Trials.

Those tried included military leaders and special officers of Hitler's special army. Civilians included industrialists charged with operating forced labor camps, doctors charged with conducting experiments on people in concentration camps, Nazi judges, and other government officials. Most were found guilty and sentenced to prison.

The trials for the Nazi leaders and a few Japanese leaders were regarded as a first step in punishing crimes against humanity. But critics said that the trials were just a way for the winners to get revenge on the losers. Some believed that Germany and Japan were not wholly responsible for starting World War II. Some defendants said "they were just following orders." Regardless of the value of the trials, most people hoped that such trials would never again be needed.

1. The Cold War Began

In 1945, World War II finally was over. Europe's wreckage was immense. The USSR, Poland, eastern Germany, Yugoslavia, Normandy (northern France), the Netherlands, and parts of Italy were devastated. Millions of people were without food and shelter. Between 1945 and 1947, the United States gave $11 billion to United Nations relief agencies.

Even the victors were in poor financial condition. Great Britain and other nations were near bankruptcy. They were losing their trade and former colonies. The whole economy of Europe was disorganized.

The balance of power also had been broken. Two great powers—the United States and the Soviet Union—towered over the rest of the world. The United States was now the most powerful nation in the West. In 1945, it was the only nation with atomic weapons. It had suffered little physical damage from the war. It was the world's leading industrial power.

The other superpower of the world was the Union of Soviet Socialist Republics, also called USSR or the Soviet Union. The Soviet Union was even more damaged from the war than Germany. At least seven million Soviet troops were killed and an estimated fourteen million civilians died. But although the Soviet Union had suffered, the Soviet armies were powerful. Stalin, the Soviet leader, was determined to protect the borders of the Soviet Union from any future attack.

The Yalta Agreements The Big Three—U. S. President Franklin Roosevelt, Soviet Premier Joseph Stalin, and British Prime Minister Winston Churchill—had met several times during World War II. They made plans both for winning the war and for peace. The most important conference was held in February 1945, at Yalta in the Soviet Union. The Big Three agreed on the structure of the United Nations Charter, including the veto power of the Security Council. They also agreed on a policy toward Germany. Germany was to be divided into four occupation zones. Each zone was to be run by one of the allies—France, England, the United States, or the Soviets. Other details about Germany were to be worked out in later conferences. The Big Three agreed that there should be free elections in the eastern European nations. They also made provisions for the Far East.

President Roosevelt died in April 1945, before World War II ended. The three major powers were already disagreeing about the Yalta agreements. In particular, there were disputes with Stalin over the eastern European nations.

The Soviets began to put eastern European nations under strict communist control. In Albania, Yugoslavia, and Poland, the process began before the war ended. Bulgaria's government fell under communist control in September 1946. Communist rule began in Hungary in May 1947. In Rumania, all power was in communist hands by the end of 1947. In February 1948, the communists took over Czechoslovakia in a bloodless coup.

Harry S. Truman had become president of the United States after Roosevelt died. Truman favored a tough policy toward the Soviet Union. In March 1947, President Truman announced his plans to curb the Soviet Union. The United States sent military and economic aid to Turkey, Greece, and Iran to resist communism. President Truman did not want any more nations to be under the control of the Soviet Union. The western European nations were still very weak because of wartime devastation. In 1947, the Marshall Plan offered economic aid to all European nations except Fascist Spain. The European nations were to cooperate with each other, improve their economic systems, and help rebuild themselves. The United States gave about $13

Truman signing a bill authorizing more funds for the Marshall Plan.

billion for the Marshall Plan.

All the western European nations accepted the offer of aid. But the Soviet Union felt that the Marshall Plan was a hostile capitalistic plot to lure away their eastern European nations. They did not allow their satellite nations to participate in the Marshall Plan.

Instead, the Soviets started their own economic plan for the eastern European nations. In addition, Stalin made sure that all leaders in the eastern European nations were completely loyal to him. Many patriotic and moderate leaders were purged from the communist parties in eastern Europe. Only in Yugoslavia, led by Marshall Josip Tito, did resistance to the Soviets develop. In 1948, Yugoslavia broke with the Soviet Union.

Both camps also developed military alliances. Western Europe and its allies formed an alliance called the North Atlantic Treaty Organization (NATO) which was started in 1949. American troops were stationed at many military installations in Europe as well as other parts of the world. In turn, the Soviet Union designed a military pact with the eastern European nations called the Warsaw Pact Agreement (1955).

Both NATO and the Warsaw Pact pro-

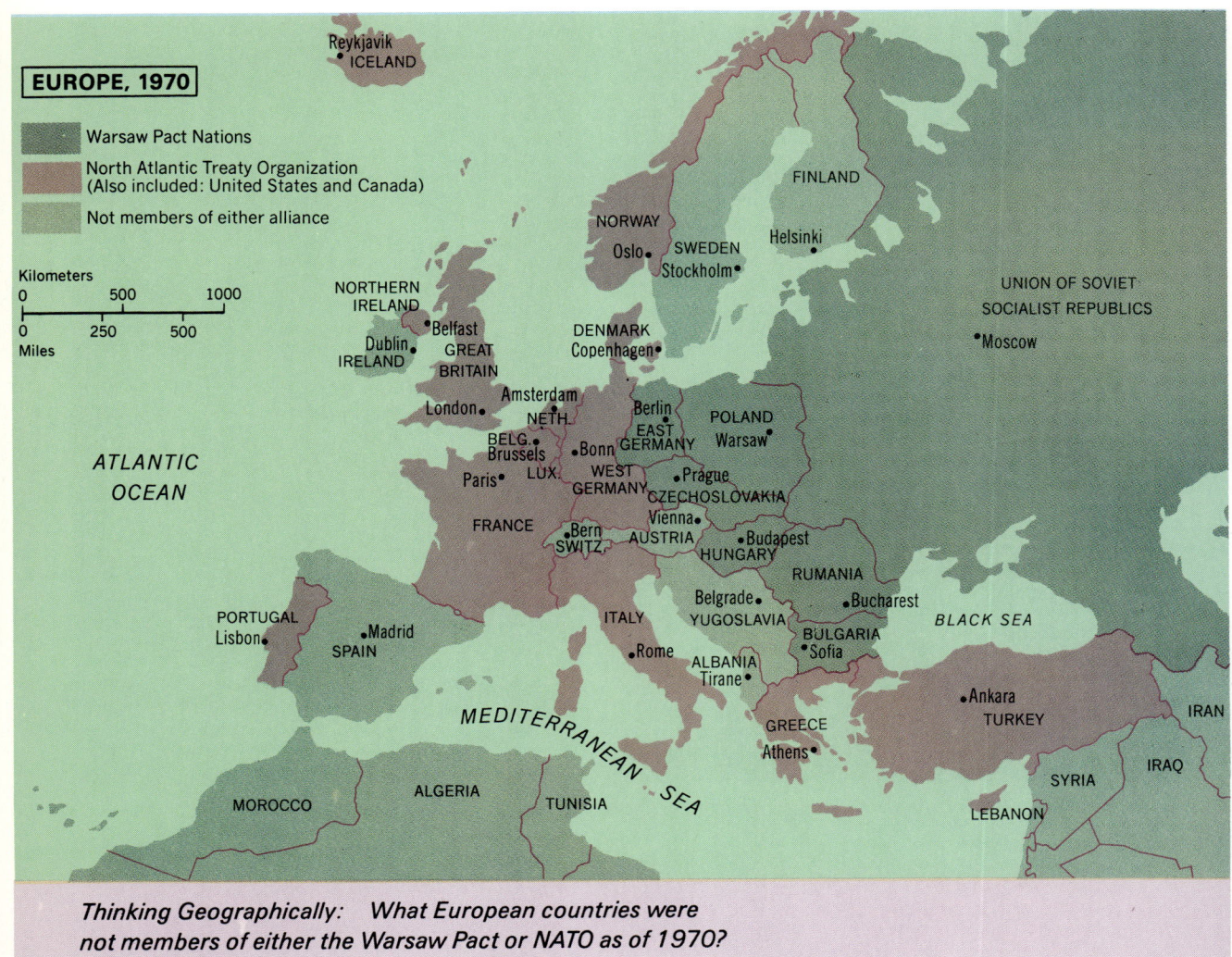

Thinking Geographically: What European countries were not members of either the Warsaw Pact or NATO as of 1970?

vided that an attack against any nation in the alliance would bring support from the rest of the alliance. There came to be two worlds. The West was made up of the Atlantic community, consisting of western Europe and the United States. The communist bloc, the Soviet Union, and eastern European nations made up the East. The two sides became increasingly separate and opposed. Each wanted to halt the expansion of the other.

Section Questions

1. What problems did Europeans face at the end of the war?
2. Who were the two superpowers? Why were they the most powerful nations?
3. What were the main provisions of the Yalta Agreements?
4. What was the Marshall Plan? NATO? The Warsaw Pact? How did these organizations contribute to international tension?

2. The Cold War Thawed

Soviet expansion in eastern Europe worried the United States and Britain. They looked to Germany as a possible ally against the Soviet Union. On the other hand, the Soviets wanted Germany to be kept weak. In the Potsdam Agreements of July 1945, the allies agreed that certain nations should receive money and labor, or reparations, from Germany to repair the damages of the war. The Soviet Union stripped their German zone of much machinery. They refused to release German war prisoners. The prisoners were used as forced laborers for a number of years.

The United States wanted Germany to be able to support its own people. Germany's low production of coal and steel was delaying the recovery of other European nations. The United States also encouraged Germany's industrial growth. The United States, Great Britain, and France unified their three zones in West Germany. Berlin was in the Soviet zone, but it was run by all four powers. Berlin was like an island in the Soviet-controlled territory.

In response to these attempts to unify West Germany and after a quarrel over the administration of Germany, the Soviets in 1948 blocked all land routes to Berlin. The Soviets hoped to starve out the western allies. The United States and Great Britain then set up the Berlin airlift. They sent huge amounts of food, coal, and other supplies to their section by planes. There were more than 270,000 supply flights. After about a year, the Soviets lifted the blockade and the Berlin crisis cooled down. But many people had feared that a world war might start over Berlin.

A Slight Thaw: Coexistence Stalin died in 1953. After a three-year power struggle among Soviet leaders, Nikita S. Khrushchev (kroos CHEF) emerged as premier. He appeared to be more peaceful. He seemed willing to relax Soviet control over the satellite nations in eastern Europe. He invited Marshall Tito of Yugoslavia to Moscow. In 1956, Khrushchev shocked the communist world when he spoke out about the crimes that Stalin had committed against the Soviet people. Khrushchev also allowed more freedom in the Soviet Union and had many people released from labor camps.

Khrushchev's words had some effect in eastern European nations. In 1956, the Poles rebelled. Russian tanks rolled toward Warsaw. But Khrushchev flew to Warsaw to meet the new Polish leaders. In a compromise, the Soviet troops were called back. However, in the same year, 1956, a revolt broke out in Hungary. This rebellion was put down bloodily by the Soviet troops. Thousands of Hungarians were killed and about 200,000 fled to non-communist nations. Khrushchev was not ready to release much power to the eastern European nations. In 1968, Czechoslovakia's attempt for more freedom was crushed.

A statue of Stalin was pulled down during the Hungarian revolt.

The Berlin Wall.

However, the eastern European nations now had more freedom to develop their own economies.

In 1949, West Germany, or the German Federal Republic, came into existence as a separate nation. It was closely tied to the United States and the West. The Soviets also set up their own satellite nation, East Germany, or the German Democratic Republic. The USSR was fearful of the threat of a rising powerful West Germany and concerned with the growing split with the Chinese communists. Khrushchev began to talk more about friendly relationships with the United States and the West. He said that war was not necessary between communist and capitalist nations. Instead, Khrushchev stated that the communist and capitalist nations could *coexist*, or live peacefully without harming each other. He asked for *coexistence* between East and West.

In 1959, Khrushchev became the first high-ranking Soviet leader to visit the United States. The United States and the Soviet Union were now friendlier than at any time since 1945. Both nations feared a nuclear war. A small issue might get magnified into a global conflict. Yet both sides continued to produce nuclear weapons and guided missiles.

The attempts at increased friendship were strained by the Berlin Wall Crisis. From 1949 to 1961, about three million East Germans escaped into West Germany. In 1961, the Soviets put up a wall to stop the flow of people and to isolate West Berlin. But President Kennedy of the United States said that he would defend West Berlin. He sent more American troops to West Germany. Again the crisis cooled down.

In 1962, the Soviets tried to install missile-launching pads in Cuba. Many Americans regarded the Soviet action as an expansion of communist influence in their own continent. In October 1962, President Kennedy ordered a naval blockade to halt the twenty-five Soviet ships that were carrying the missiles to Cuba. Premier Khrushchev said that if the United States tried to stop the Soviet ships, World War III would start. Both sides threatened each other with missile attacks.

At once, the United Nations and other leaders pleaded with Kennedy and Khrushchev to settle the dispute for the sake of world peace. At this point, Premier Khrushchev backed down and promised not to place the missiles in Cuba. The Soviet ships returned home. As a result of the Cuban crisis, a "hot line" was set up in 1963 between Washington, D.C. and Moscow. Leaders of the United States and the Soviet Union could communicate with each other directly and immediately by telephone. The Soviet Union and the United States also agreed to broader programs for cultural and scientific exchanges.

Khrushchev and Kennedy.

Soviet troops in Afghanistan.

Detente In 1964, Khruschev lost power. Leonid Brezhnev (BREZH nef) became the leader of the Soviet Union. Worried about the growing strength of China, Brezhnev wanted to improve relations with the United States.

President Nixon and his foreign advisor Henry Kissinger wanted to improve relations with both the Soviet Union and China. Nixon and Kissinger felt that traditional diplomacy could work. They sought *detente*, a relaxing of strain and hostility among nations. It was felt that both sides could compromise to lessen tension.

President Nixon visited the Soviet Union in 1972 and again in 1974. In return, Brezhnev visited the United States in 1973. One result of these discussions was the signing of SALT I (Strategic Arms Limitation Treaty) that limited the arms production in both nations. This treaty showed the interest of both sides in avoiding a major war.

In the 1970s, there were further ties. A trade pact was signed. It reduced the tariff on imported Soviet goods and allowed the sale of more American goods to the Soviet Union, especially grain. Both nations also agreed to exchange more scientific information. The Soviets gained better access to western technology.

However, the Soviets continued to try to expand their influence in the Middle East, the Indian Ocean, Asia, and Africa. They supplied the Arabs with arms to fight against Israel and threatened to enter the Israel-Arab war in 1973. They transported Cuban troops into troubled areas such as Angola, Ethiopia, and Southern Yemen.

President Carter's stress on human rights also disturbed the Soviets. Prospects dimmed for the second Strategic Arms Limitation Treaty (SALT II). Then in 1979, the Soviets moved their troops into Afghanistan. This created a major crisis between the United States and the Soviet Union. President Carter reduced the trade between the two nations. President Reagan increased the budget for American arms and defense.

In 1981, the United States and the Soviet Union began talks to explore ways to decrease their nuclear weapons in Europe. Many people in Europe and the rest of the world were protesting the buildup of nuclear arms.

Section Questions

1. Why did the United States want to rebuild West Germany? Why did the Soviet Union oppose this policy?
2. What was the Berlin blockade in 1948? What did the United States and Britain do in this crisis?
3. What were Khrushchev's ideas about coexistence?
4. How did the Soviets and Americans cooperate more in the 1970s? What evidence was there of renewed hostility?

Did You Know?

The Space Age

On October 4, 1957, the world was awed when the Soviets launched the first artificial Earth satellite, Sputnik I, into space. By 1958, the United States placed Explorer I in orbit. In 1961, the Soviets sent up the first astronaut, Yuri Gagarin, on the spaceship Vostok. The first American space voyager was Alan Shepard. In 1962, John Glenn became the first American to orbit Earth, in the spaceship Mercury. The crowning achievement for the United States was on July 20, 1969, when Neil Armstrong and Edwin "Buzz" Aldrin became the first astronauts to walk on the moon.

Both the United States and the Soviets are experimenting with space stations, space shuttles, and reusable spaceships capable of carrying larger cargos of satellites and laboratories into the Earth's orbit. In 1981, the United States successfully reused the spaceship Columbia. Columbia was launched twice. An added first was that Columbia was launched as a rocket yet landed as an airplane.

Further planetary explorations of Mars, Venus, Mercury, Saturn, and of Jupiter and its moons are giving a more accurate view of our solar system.

Space achievements by both the Americans and the Soviets show the great technological and scientific developments of two highly industrialized societies. It also shows their concern with the most advanced forms of defense.

Neil Armstrong called his first step on the moon, "One small step for a man, one giant leap for mankind."

3. Latin America Faced Economic and Political Problems

Latin America usually refers to all of the nations from south of the United States to the tip of South America. This huge stretch of land is called Latin America because the basic languages there—Spanish, Portuguese, and French—are derived from the Latin language.

Sometimes the term Latin America is applied to former British possessions such as Guyana and Jamaica, or to Surinam, the former Dutch colony. In this case, we speak of Latin America as including all nations in Central America, the Caribbean, and South America. Wide differences exist among the nations of Latin America. Brazil, Argentina, Mexico, and Venezuela are developing into industrial nations. Mexico and Venezuela now have oil money. Brazil has the potential of the development of the Amazon. However, most Latin American nations are poor or developing nations. Because of poverty, illiteracy, and unstable governments, much of Latin America is similar to parts of Asia and Africa.

The Latin American countries have different ethnic groups. In some nations, such as Guatemala, Ecuador, Bolivia, Peru, and Paraguay, Indians are the majority population. In Argentina and Uruguay, the majority of people are descendants of Europeans. Mestizos, people of mixed races, are the majority in Mexico, Colombia, Chile, and Venezuela. Blacks are the majority in Brazil, Guyana, Haiti, Jamaica, and other places.

Yet to some degree all Latin American nations face two major problems. The first is to improve the economic system to help millions of poor people have a better life. The second is to develop a stable form of government. Many Latin American nations claim to be republics and to support basic

A South American Indian woman.

freedoms and rights. In most cases this claim is not true. This goal has not been reached. Rule by the few, often the military, is the most common pattern in Latin America. Many changes in government occur by force. In general, power is concentrated in the hands of the military, the wealthy, and the large landowners. These two problems—economic and political—have made it difficult to achieve progress in Latin America.

Latin America and the United States

In 1948, the United States agreed to respect the rights of Latin America. The United States said that it would not use force in any Latin American nation.

But American aid to Latin America after World War II helped the dictators and the upper classes maintain power. Meanwhile, the mass of poor people were becoming more restless. Many were attracted to communism. The growing resentment against the United States was shown in 1958 when Vice-President Richard Nixon and his wife visited Latin America. There Mr. and Mrs. Nixon were greeted with insults and stones.

Several Latin American countries *nationalized* certain industries. That is, the government took over the industry from a private company. Often the company was owned by United States' citizens. Chile, Venezuela, Peru, and Bolivia took over North American companies in the 1960s and 1970s.

However, in the 1960s, the United States began helping Latin American countries economically. In 1978, the United States signed a treaty that gave control of the Panama Canal to Panama.

Cuba Compared to the rest of Latin America, Cuba was fairly prosperous. It had the third highest standard of living in Latin America. Along with money from sugar, people were employed in mining, light industry, and tourism. Cuba also had good standards of health.

But perhaps three fourths of the land was held by absentee owners, Cuban or foreign. Americans owned about one fourth of the sugar plantations. The workers on the plantations were underpaid. There were few public schools. Seeing American tourists made the Cubans feel poor. They blamed the United States for Cuba's distress.

Sabotage and bombings took place

Fidel Castro in the mountains, before the Cuban revolution.

in different parts of Cuba. Into this volatile situation came Dr. Fidel Castro, a Cuban revolutionary who was born into a wealthy family.

After an unsuccessful attack on a military barracks in 1953, Castro and others were taken prisoner. Castro was sentenced to fifteen years in jail. Later, Castro was pardoned. He went to Mexico with his friends to plan to take over Cuba. He met there the Argentinian revolutionary Ernesto "Che" Guevara (gay VAR rah).

In 1956, Castro and his supporters landed in Cuba. He and his armed guerrillas went into hiding in the Sierra Mestra Mountains. Castro gained the support of most of the poor Cuban peasants and urban workers. Castro said that the corrupt Cuban dictator, Fulgencio Batista (bah TEES ta), must go and that the Cuban society would be remade. In 1959, Fidel Castro, at the age of 32, gained complete control of Cuba. His victory was hailed even in the American media as a victory over tyranny and oppression.

Castro did not like the fact that Cuba's main crop, sugar, depended on the prices received from the United States. He moved toward closer ties with the Soviet Union and China. As he moved openly toward communist ideas, about 10 percent of the population fled Cuba. The refugees were mostly professional people—doctors, lawyers, scientists, and engineers.

Some of the Cuban refugees came to the United States. Backed by the American Central Intelligence Agency (CIA), a force of refugees landed in Cuba in 1961 to fight against Castro. They were completely crushed. Castro gained even more support from the Cuban people. He boasted of having a socialist reign "under the nose" of the United States.

Castro's prestige in Latin America rose even higher. He was a hero, the leader of a small nation that had defied the great United States. The Latin Americans also admired a "strong man" who with a small guerrilla band had broken the power of the old corrupt regime.

Castro became the dictator of Cuba. He got rid of his enemies by shooting hundreds and imprisoning others. Opposition was suppressed. Castro now had a one-party system, the Cuban Communist Party. He

A sugar plantation in Cuba.

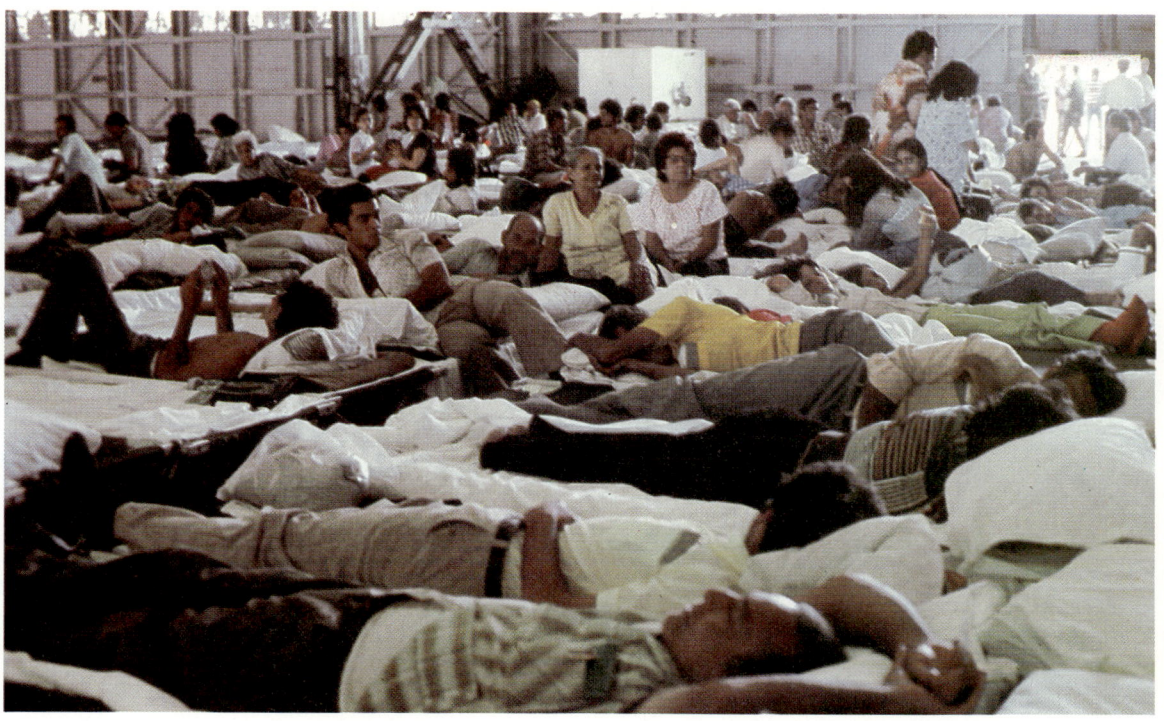
Cuban refugees.

took over all property, including that owned by Americans. By 1968, Cuba had little trace of private economic activity.

In foreign affairs, Castro made a complete break with the United States. Now the sugar crop was sent to the Soviet Union. In effect, Cuba moved from a dependency upon the United States to a dependency upon the Soviet Union.

Cuba did not make great economic progress. Twenty years later, the standard of living was lower than that under Batista. But most people were pleased by the social gains. A great push was made to improve education. All Cubans were to get six years of education. About 85 percent of the school-age children were in school. In addition, discrimination against the blacks was reduced.

However, the society was still unequal. College graduates, technicians, military officers, and the bureaucracy gained in power and salaries. The party elite became the new ruling class.

In 1980, Castro admitted that Cuba had economic problems. Efforts were made to increase productivity. Farmers could now sell their surplus on the open market for higher prices. Castro also allowed discontented Cubans to leave. Over 125,000 Cubans made their way to the United States. Meanwhile, Castro continued to fight against what he considered to be imperialism. In the 1970s and 1980s, Cuban troops, helped by the Soviets, were sent to Africa as military advisers and fighters. Castro wanted to export his revolution to the rest of the world.

Unrest in Latin America Castro's revolution in Cuba had an enormous impact on all of Latin America and the United States. Castro's support of the Soviet Union meant that a Marxist-Leninist government was firmly anchored in the Western Hemisphere.

Castro sent his military agents to help rebels in other Latin American nations. Castro's ideas about a small guerrilla force assuming power had great appeal to some students, middle-class intellectuals, and the poor. The Cuban revolution inspired these groups to set up guerrilla forces to bring down the government. Che Guevara was killed in an unsuccessful Bolivian guerrilla raid in 1967.

Violence exploded in many Latin American nations. The labor unions held strikes in support of the left-wing groups. Compromise was difficult. The Roman Catholic Church, for example, was torn between support for the rebels and its concern for order. Army officers were often split between those who favored some degree of reform and those who feared any reform as being communistic.

In Chile, a socialist leader, Salvador Allende (aw YANE day), was elected president in 1970. He launched his presidency by stating that he would not be "the President of all the Chileans." Instead there would be a class conflict in which he could not be neutral and would not compromise. Following his ideas, he nationalized much of the industry, including that owned by American businesses. The CIA and private United States interests spent money to stir up the Chileans, who were already greatly upset with Allende. Fearing that the economy was breaking down, a right-wing military government took over in 1973. They executed Allende and thousands of his followers.

In 1979, after years of fighting, with 30,000 lives lost, a leftist government took over in Nicaragua. In 1979, El Salvador's government was overthrown in a bloodless

Poverty and wealth in Brazil.

military coup. The new government took over all large farms and attempted a land redistribution. Meanwhile, the right and left were fighting violently. The bloody battle continued. An election was held in 1982 but no party won a clear victory.

In the 1980s, Latin America faced serious social problems. The population grew from 284 million in 1970 to 373 million in 1980, a huge increase. The mushrooming cities were filled with unemployed migrants from the country. In some nations, 50 percent of the labor force was unemployed or underemployed.

The governments were often in debt due to the high price of oil and imported manufactured goods. Even nations like Mexico faced problems. The Mexican oil boom was increasing the gulf between the rich and the poor. Furthermore, inflation and low productivity led to slow growth. Cooperative efforts among Latin American nations improved regional trade. But the growth in trade frequently helped the wealthy instead of the poor. The poor and the middle class, who wanted more power, kept pressure on the government to improve the lives of the people.

Section Questions

1. Why were there strains between the United States and the Latin American countries after World War II?
2. Why did the Cubans rally around Castro?
3. Why did Latin Americans admire Castro?
4. What problems did Latin America face in the 1980s?

4. Europe Became Powerful and Independent

In 1945, the European economies were seriously weakened. In many nations, people were discouraged from the war and morale was low. There was resentment toward their own people who had collaborated with the enemy.

The Marshall Plan, the most successful of the various aid programs of the United States, helped western Europe's recovery. Finally, in 1951, western Europe's industrial output rose above the pre-war level. The rebuilding of West Germany helped the economic well-being of all of western Europe. By the 1960s, there was full employment in the industrialized northern European nations. However, southern Europe, which had been less industrialized, had more problems and made less progress.

The Europeans realized that they could not improve their standard of living if each nation looked out for only its own interests. So the European nations helped themselves by forming economic associations.

In 1958, building on previous efforts since 1946, six European nations—France, West Germany, Italy, Belgium, Netherlands, and Luxembourg—formed the European Common Market. It made for a vast market of capital, workers, and goods. This organization promoted trade among its members by reducing tariffs and allowing movement of people and materials to where they were needed. Later, four more nations joined the Common Market and other nations were allowed certain privileges. Western Europe under the Common Market became the largest trading area, second only to the United States.

This economic unity was a great step forward in cooperation. Distrust and conflict declined as barriers were reduced. Europe now had more vitality and power. With more economic stability, Europe had fewer strikes and less social unrest. The workers' standard of living went up. They had higher wages, shorter hours, and more paid vacation. The workers in western European nations also gained benefits such as health and unemployment insurance and retirement plans.

Many nations in western Europe now had socialistic governments. More economic planning was worked out by government officials than by the leaders of industry. In addition, farming changed as it became more mechanized.

By the 1960s, western Europe was exporting large amounts of potatoes, vegetables, and milk products. Factories were modernized, with new machinery and more mass production. Europe was becoming a superpower. While the United States and the Soviet Union were still strong, both the alliance systems in the East and West became looser. Both western European and eastern European nations wanted a more equal partnership. They were not as docile as they had been just after the war.

Western European Nations General Charles de Gaulle (de GALL), the leader of France, became the spokesperson for more European power. De Gaulle believed that the United States could not be trusted for western Europe's security. He did not want France or other western European nations to be totally dependent upon the United States for military aid. He felt that France and the other western nations were losing their independence by being tied to the

Charles de Gaulle returned to lead France in peacetime.

United States. In addition, de Gaulle felt that the quarrels of the two superpowers created international tension. He wanted Europe to be a third force against both the United States and the Soviet Union. So France developed its own atomic power and stopped allowing American troops to be stationed in France.

France's economy improved. Yet the success of the economy was partly drained off by wars. France tried to hold on to its old empire, especially in Vietnam and Algeria. De Gaulle paid little attention to social reform. This created discontent among students and the unions. In 1969, de Gaulle was forced to resign. Moderate governments held power in France until 1981, when François Mitterand (ME tur ran), a socialist, was elected president. His election caused some people in France and other NATO countries to fear that the French government might move away from moderate policies.

After the war, Great Britain did not have serious political problems. It was a stable nation with high morale. But low productivity and the loss of its overseas empire caused economic problems. The Labor Party took power in 1945. They nationalized the nation's basic industries and set up an extensive social welfare program. Inflation and labor problems plagued the government. In 1979, the Conservative Party won a landslide victory. Conservative Margaret Thatcher became Britain's first woman prime minister. She energetically set about trying to change Britain back to a capitalistic economy. Inflation and unemployment got worse.

Great Britain had a sizable economic boost from the discovery of oil in the North Sea. In spite of that, its economy remained sorely troubled.

West Germany was the success story, the "German miracle." It was the most prosperous of all the European nations. Industrialists, the government, and unions cooperated and worked hard. The Germans concentrated on rebuilding their nation and improving their standard of living. The economy has had one of the lowest levels of inflation. West Germany, because of its growing economic power, is expected to play a more important role in the world economy in the 1980s.

Southern Europe never had been as industrialized as northern Europe. Economic progress there was slower. There were not enough jobs for the millions of people, especially the people coming from the rural areas with little in the way of skills. In the 1950s and early 1960s, many Italians and workers from other southern European nations moved to the more industrialized European nations such as West Germany to work.

Italy had severe problems in achieving a stable government. Even in the 1980s, there were frequent political kidnappings and shootings. Spain and Portugal replaced their dictators with more democratic governments and moved toward industrialization.

Eastern Europe With the exception of Yugoslavia, eastern European nations followed the Soviet model for economic planning and development. Previously much of the land had been in the hands of a few landowners. Now the land was collectivized. Agricultural workers worked on the large state-run farms. However, in some eastern European nations the family might have a parcel of land for its own use. Private trade was greatly reduced as the state took over most of the large industries such as banks, mines, and industrial firms. In addition, the government played an important role in planning the whole economy. Trade unions had a subordinate role compared to the power of the state.

The Soviets also gave technical assistance to help start industrialization in eastern European nations. The eastern European nations were linked with each other and also tied into the economy of the Soviet Union. Later, the eastern European nations were allowed to trade more with the nations in western Europe. In 1981, Poland's

Lech Walesa leads the Polish workers on a strike.

debt to the West reached $25 billion.

In the summer of 1980, the Polish workers went on strike. They were angered by food shortages and food price increases. The workers blamed the Polish Communist Party for the economic problems. The workers gained generous wage increases and union independence from the Communist Party. The workers wanted to liberalize the whole society.

The actions of the Polish workers aroused western fears that the Soviets would invade Poland. The Soviets feared that the Polish unrest would spread to other eastern European nations. In December 1981, the Polish government imposed martial law and arrested many dissidents, including the leader of the Solidarity Union Lech Walesa (vah WEN sah). The economic and political crisis deepened.

The economic problems of Poland showed the growing economic difficulties of eastern European nations. Slower growth was partly the result of increased oil prices (see Chapter 34). However, the effects of the oil price increases were not just confined to eastern European nations. The whole world faced multiple economic problems in the 1980s. The oil price increases intensified inflation, already a severe problem in many nations. Economic growth for most European nations, the Soviet Union, and the United States appeared likely to be slower in the 1980s than in the 1960s and 1970s.

Section Questions

1. What helped in western Europe's economic recovery?
2. What is the Common Market? Why is it important?
3. Why was de Gaulle critical of the United States? What did he do?
4. What changes were made in the economic systems of eastern European nations?

Chapter Summary

1. In 1945, Europe was in ruins from World War II. There were millions of refugees. There were two superpowers, the United States and the Soviet Union. The Yalta Agreements did not settle the problem of eastern Europe. Gradually the Soviets established satellite governments in the eastern European nations. A cold war developed between the West, the democratic nations, and the East, the communist nations. The United States sent economic and military aid to western Europe. Defensive alliances were formed. The West formed NATO. The Soviets formed the Warsaw Pact Agreement.
2. Berlin was a trouble spot in the cold war. The Berlin Crisis developed when the Soviets blocked all land routes in 1948 and later when they set up the Berlin wall. Khrushchev announced a policy of coexistence but the Soviets were not willing to allow too much freedom in their satellite nations. Revolts were crushed in Hungary in 1956 and Czechoslovakia in 1968. A crisis developed over the missiles that the Soviets were planning to send to Cuba, but this dispute was settled peacefully. Renewed interest in improving relations between the superpowers was shown by both President Nixon and Premier Brezhnev. Relations improved in 1972 when both leaders signed SALT I. After the Soviets invaded Afghanistan in 1979, relations cooled.
3. The American foreign policy toward Latin America caused resentment in Latin America. Fidel Castro, a Cuban revolutionary, was successful in gaining control of Cuba. With his communist government, he broke with the United States. Castro exported his brand of anti-imperialism by trying to stir up revolutions in Latin America and Africa. Castro's success inspired left-wing groups in Latin America. Chile was briefly socialist. In 1979, a leftist government assumed control in Nicaragua. El Salvador was torn with conflict.
4. Gradually economic and political stability improved in western Europe. The Marshall Plan aided nations in western Europe. The Common Market also promoted trade. Europe became more prosperous and more modern. General de Gaulle wanted the western European nations to become more independent of the United States. Britain faced economic difficulties in the post-war years. West Germany achieved a high level of productivity and stable government. Southern European nations also made some progress toward industrialization. Most eastern European nations collectivized farms and reduced private trade. The Polish workers went on strike in 1980, demanding unions separate from the Communist Party. The world, including Europe, faced the prospect of slower growth in the 1980s.

Chapter 32 Review

Check Your Facts

1. Identify the following:
   a. General de Gaulle
   b. Premier Khrushchev
   c. President Kennedy
   d. President Truman
   e. Henry Kissinger
   f. Common Market
   g. President Nixon
   h. Hermann Goering
   i. U. N. Charter
   j. Security Council
   k. SALT I
   l. Marshall Tito
2. Why were many people displaced after World War II?
3. Why did the Soviets want control of eastern European nations?
4. Why didn't the eastern European nations participate in the Marshall Plan?
5. Why didn't the United States favor reparations for the Soviets after 1946?
6. What did the Hungarian Revolt in 1956 show about the intentions of the Soviet Union?
7. Why did Nixon believe that the policy of detente might work with the Soviets?
8. Why did the Polish workers strike in 1980?
9. Why was economic growth more likely to slow down in the 1980s?

Words to Know

Define these words in one or two sentences. Then tell the significance of each in the postwar history of Europe.
   a. cold war
   b. reparations
   c. coexistence
   d. detente

Developing Your Skills

1. Trace a map of Central America. Indicate the areas of unrest.
2. Trace a map of Europe. Indicate all countries that have been invaded by the Soviets since World War II.

Thinking It Over

1. In what ways were Tito and de Gaulle similar?
2. Do you think international trials for war crimes are a good idea?
3. Why was West Germany, a defeated country, able to make a stronger recovery than Great Britain or France?
4. Who or what nations caused the cold war?
5. What are the advantages of having two superpowers in the world? Disadvantages?
6. Do you think that the United Nations has been successful? Do you think it will become more powerful?

Special Activities

1. Look in your library for cartoons on the early postwar period. How is the Soviet Union portrayed in the cartoons?
2. Do some background reading on the Berlin Crisis. Then pretend that you are living in West Berlin at the time. Write a letter describing the situation.
3. Do a survey in your class to see if anyone had a relative who was a refugee or displaced person after 1945. Where did that person settle?
4. Do a survey to find if any relatives served in the armed forces in World War II. What work did your adult relatives do during the war?
5. Secure a speaker from your community who has visited Europe recently. Ask the speaker to describe the economic picture.

A scene in busy, prosperous Tokyo.

Chapter 33 Postwar Asia

In 1945, Japan was completely defeated. Most of her major cities had been severely bombed. Hiroshima and Nagasaki had been atomic bombed.

When the American military occupation ended in 1952, Japan's total production was about one-third that of Britain or France. Since that time, Japan's power has steadily grown. Japan now has a population of about 115 million, about half that of the United States. This population is densely concentrated. Japan's land area is about the size of California. The islands of Japan have little in the way of petroleum, coal, iron ore, or other mineral resources. Yet by the 1980s, Japan was second only to the United States in industrial production.

1945-1979

1945	World War II ends
1947	India and Pakistan become independent
1949	Communists gain control of China
1950-1953	The Korean War
1954	Laos and Cambodia become independent
1958	Civil War starts in Vietnam
1965-1975	U.S. becomes involved in Vietnam
1971	Bangladesh becomes independent
1976	Mao Zedong dies
1979	Vietnam takes over Cambodia

Indira Gandhi.

1. China and Japan Became Powerful

At the present time, Japan cannot feed itself and must import about 30 percent of its food. To pay for its food and energy needs, Japan exports a wide variety of manufactured goods such as cars, steel, television sets, tape recorders, and microwave ovens. Japan's industrial resources pay for the highest standard of living in Japanese history. Its gross national product is as large as that of Britain and France combined and more than half that of the United States. Japan has surpassed West Germany, itself a success story.

Japan's success has been helped by the close cooperation of industry, the government, schools, and many community organizations. In addition, the skilled work force has quickly adopted the most modern and scientific ways to manufacture goods. Japan also pays little for its national defense which is largely provided by the United States.

China At the end of World War II in 1945, Chiang Kai-shek's power diminished. The Red Army took control of more and more provinces, pushing Chiang's armies to the sea. On October 1, 1949, Mao Zedong achieved control over the whole of mainland China. Chiang Kai-shek fled to Taiwan, an island off China which was protected by the United States. In 1950, China signed an alliance with the Soviet Union and began to receive Soviet aid.

The Korean War In August 1945, American troops occupied South Korea while Soviet troops controlled the North. The United States and the Soviet Union could not agree on a united government for Korea, so Korea was divided into two nations, North and South Korea. The boundary line was the thirty-eighth parallel. In 1948 and 1949, both the Soviet and American troops left Korea. However, minor border clashes continued.

In June 1950, North Korean forces were believed to have invaded South Korea. Prob-

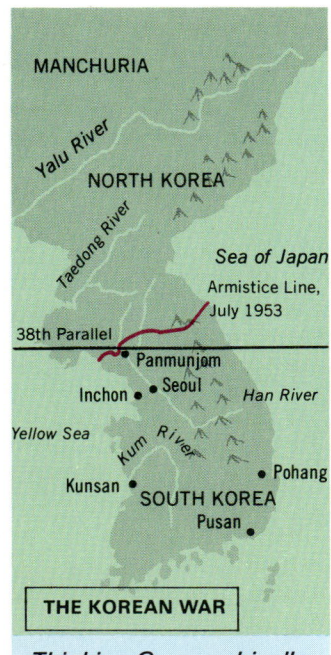

THE KOREAN WAR

Thinking Geographically: What part of the United States does the 38th parallel cross?

American prisoners of war released from North Korea.

ably North Korea did not expect the United States to defend South Korea. However, President Truman sent American troops to support the South Korean government. In addition, the United Nations Security Council, taking advantage of the Soviet's absence, condemned North Korea as an aggressor and sent assistance to South Korea. The United States supplied most of the men, money, and equipment to fight the war. The Chinese and the Soviets in turn supplied aid to North Korea.

In 1950, General Douglas MacArthur, the American commander of the UN forces, drove back the North Koreans and moved across the thirty-eighth parallel. Then over 200,000 Chinese, backed by Soviet support, entered the war. The Chinese forces were successful in driving back the UN forces. Bitter fighting in below-zero weather followed. Finally, in 1951, peace talks started.

But the war and the talks dragged on for almost two years. In 1953, after three years of fighting, both sides agreed to a fragile peace. The boundaries between North and South Korea were the same as before. Meanwhile, a great deal of death and destruction had occurred. China and the United States were very hostile to each other.

China's Forward Leap The Chinese troops had held back the American troops in the Korean War. China had recovered its self-respect and national pride even though there had been about a million Chinese casualties. In 1953, Mao and his party began the enormous task of changing China into a modern industrial and international power.

The first priority was land reform. Land was taken from the landowners and redistributed to the peasants. Later, *communes*, or large shared farms worked by 10,000 to 15,000 peasants, were established. Most peasants also were allowed to have small plots of their own. The Chinese started many soil reclamation projects. These depended heavily upon human strength plus limited technological help from the Soviet Union. Irrigation, erosion control, drainage, and other reclamation projects have now changed the physical landscape of China.

In 1958, the Chinese began the "Great Leap Forward." Under this plan, China was to produce twice as much as before in both agriculture and industry. Since little machinery was available, much work was done by hard manual labor. The Great Leap Forward had many failures from poor planning and poor harvests.

However, the standard of living improved. Life has become better for the vast majority of the Chinese even though daily life is still simple and frugal.

Mao decided that the Chinese were losing some of their revolutionary spirit. In the "Cultural Revolution" of 1966 to 1969, Mao took up a personal campaign against some of his old friends. Mao believed that many party members were out of touch with the common people. He thought that the Chinese Communist Party was an elite group. Mao felt that the bureaucrats were promoting capitalistic tactics of money incentives and encouraging western ideas. He thought he had to seize power from the party to reverse the trends.

Mao sent the youth of the nation, called the Red Guards, to purge society. The Cultural Revolution unleashed power struggles between the different provinces and between the young and the old. There was turmoil and disorder in some areas of China. The economy was disrupted and the schools were closed. With the Red Guard's support, Mao was successful. The moderate elements in the Chinese Communist Party lost power.

Now Mao had to worry about foreign affairs. China and the Soviet Union had become bitter enemies. They openly disagreed about the proper way to achieve a communistic society. China feared that the Soviets would expand into their land. In 1968, sharp conflicts broke out over border violations. To protect China, Mao reached out toward the United States. In 1972, President Nixon visited China. The visit was a symbol that relations between China and the United States had improved.

Women farming rice in China.

669

Nixon and Mao in China.

After Mao's death in 1976, China gradually moved away from his ideas. Moderate Chinese Communists gained control. The Chinese, with a billion people to feed, turned toward western technology. China decided to become fully industrialized by 2000. In order to achieve this goal, China sought technology and capital from foreign sources. In 1979, the United States and China established normal diplomatic relations.

Other changes were made, such as economic incentives to motivate people to produce more. Brighter students were taught the skills of modern science. People were encouraged to marry later and to have fewer children in order to keep down population growth. With these changes, China seemed to be on a new road.

Section Questions

1. What has contributed to Japan's economic success?
2. Why did Chairman Mao start the Cultural Revolution?
3. What was the result of the Cultural Revolution?
4. In what ways did China change in the 1970s?

2. The Indian Subcontinent Achieved Independence

Opposition to British rule in India continued to grow. However, at first it was difficult for the Indians to form a united political movement. There were differences between the two major religions, Hinduism and Islam. The many different languages spoken throughout India made communication difficult. Differences also existed between castes and regions.

India During World War II, in 1942, the Japanese advanced toward India. The Indian Congress refused to declare war against Japan or to support the British war effort because the British plan for independence would allow the Muslim states to be separate from India. The Muslim League, under Mohammed Ali Jinnah (JIN ah), remained loyal to the British government.

After World War II, the British agreed to give India complete independence. But Jinnah and the Muslims insisted on a separate state. In Calcutta this problem caused a riot that killed over 5,000 people. The *partition*, or separation, of India into two nations appeared to be the only solution. In 1947, two new nations, India and Pakistan, came into being. The Dominion of India had some 350 million people, with the majority being Hindu. Pakistan's population of around 70 million was mostly Muslim. Gandhi's dream of a united India had vanished.

Some people were afraid to stay in a region in which they would be a religious minority. Approximately 10 million refugees moved to new homes as the Muslims left India and the Hindus left Pakistan. Massacres broke out. Perhaps 300,000 or more people were killed and many more wounded. The exact number is uncertain. In 1948, trying to stop the riots, Gandhi was assassinated by a Hindu who feared

Muslim refugees bound for Pakistan.

Muslims as fellow citizens. Thus, a nonviolent man met a violent death. The riots stopped in India as the grief-stricken nation mourned its great leader.

Under Prime Minister Jawaharlal Nehru (NAY roo), India tried to unite its people and to solve major social problems. In 1951, the government started its first five year plan. Unlike the Soviet model, the factories remained in the hands of private individuals. Laws were passed to end discrimination against the untouchables. Women gained more rights. People voted in the general elections.

Foreign affairs presented problems for the Indian government. In 1948, open war erupted between India and Pakistan. A cease-fire was arranged by the United Nations. Then in 1962, the Indians and the Chinese fought in a remote, sparsely populated mountainous region of their border. India was defeated but the Chinese withdrew their troops and did not go any farther into India. In 1965, India fought another brief war with Pakistan. A cease-fire was arranged in January 1966. These wars forced the Indian government to spend more money on defense.

In 1966, Mrs. Indira Gandhi, Nehru's daughter, became the prime minister. Mrs. Gandhi faced severe domestic problems, including rapid population growth. India today is estimated to have around 635 million people, one-fifth of the world's population, in a land one-third the size of the United States. India had difficulty improving the standard of living for such a large population, especially for the farm families. The government pushed ahead with industrialization and agricultural improvements. India now ranks as the eighth largest economy in the world. It produces steel, textiles, and other manufactured products. One-fourth of the agricultural land is now irrigated. Grain production has increased and India is now

Did You Know?

Farming with ox-drawn plows in India.

Rich vs. Poor Nations

Of the over four billion people on Earth, the United Nations classifies about two thirds of them as poor.

Formerly these nations were often called the "Third World." The poorest thirty nations were called the "Fourth World." These nations had the lowest per capita income, little manufacturing, and a high rate of illiteracy. The "First World" was made up of nations such as western Europe, the United States, and Japan. The "Second World" was the communist bloc dominated by the Soviet Union. The "Third and Fourth Worlds" were defined as the underprivileged nations in Asia, Africa, and Latin America. However, many poor nations prefer to be called "developing nations."

The poor nations have demanded that the rich nations give them economic assistance to help them to achieve a better life. The poor nations have been hurt by the high oil prices imposed by OPEC. The OPEC nations now give about 3 percent of their income to help the poorer nations but many believe that the aid is not enough.

Some poor nations resent multinational corporations which have set up branches in the poor nations. They think that these companies are gaining at their expense.

The poor nations also want to stabilize the prices that they get for their products. The United Nations is working to fix prices on such items as coffee and cocoa. Many problems remain for the developing nations in a time of worldwide inflation and high oil prices. But developing nations do not want to stay poor. They want to improve their own future.

Farming in the Punjab region of India.

able to feed all of its people.

India's progress was uneven. Mrs. Gandhi was blamed for failing to eliminate the chronic poverty in which millions live. In 1975, she declared a state of emergency. She then reduced civil rights and jailed thousands of her political opponents.

Mrs. Gandhi was accused of eliminating democracy. Her party lost control in the elections in 1977. However, her opponents made little progress with achieving unity or controlling inflation and population growth, so Mrs. Gandhi made a comeback in 1980. India is making progress in economic development and education. The rate of population growth is declining.

Pakistan The nation of Pakistan was created in 1947. The new nation had a strange geography. It was divided into two parts which were more than 1,440 kilometers (900 miles) apart. In 1948, leader Ali Jinnah died. After Jinnah's death, Pakistan could not achieve a stable democratic government. By 1958, it was ruled by a military dictatorship.

West Pakistan had a higher standard of living than East Pakistan. At first it also had political control of East Pakistan. However, East Pakistan had the larger population. In 1970, East Pakistan gained control of the legislative body. The military dictator of West Pakistan refused to accept the election results and massacred thousands of people in East Pakistan. This civil war sent over eight million refugees pouring into India from East Pakistan.

India, eager to keep Pakistan weakened, helped East Pakistan achieve independence by giving aid and troops. After a brief war, West Pakistan surrendered and East Pakistan then became an independent nation, Bangladesh. Bangladesh is now one of the poorest nations in the world.

The Indian subcontinent is now divided into three major nations: India, Pakistan, and Bangladesh. The Soviet invasion of Afghanistan in December 1979 worried both India and Pakistan. Mrs. Gandhi urged the Soviets to remove their troops from Afghanistan. But she was polite about it because India is buying modern weapons from the Soviet Union at a very low rate of interest. Pakistan, under a military dictatorship which follows traditional Muslim laws, did not like communist influence in nearby Afghanistan. Over 700,000 refugees fled from their homes in Afghanistan to Pakistan. The Soviet-backed leaders of Afghanistan accused Pakistan of supplying arms to the Afghanistanian rebels. Thus, foreign affairs remain unsettled on the Indian subcontinent.

Section Questions

1. Why did a partition occur in India in 1947?
2. What are India's greatest problems?
3. Why did India support East Pakistan's bid for independence?
4. What problems in foreign affairs has India faced since achieving independence?

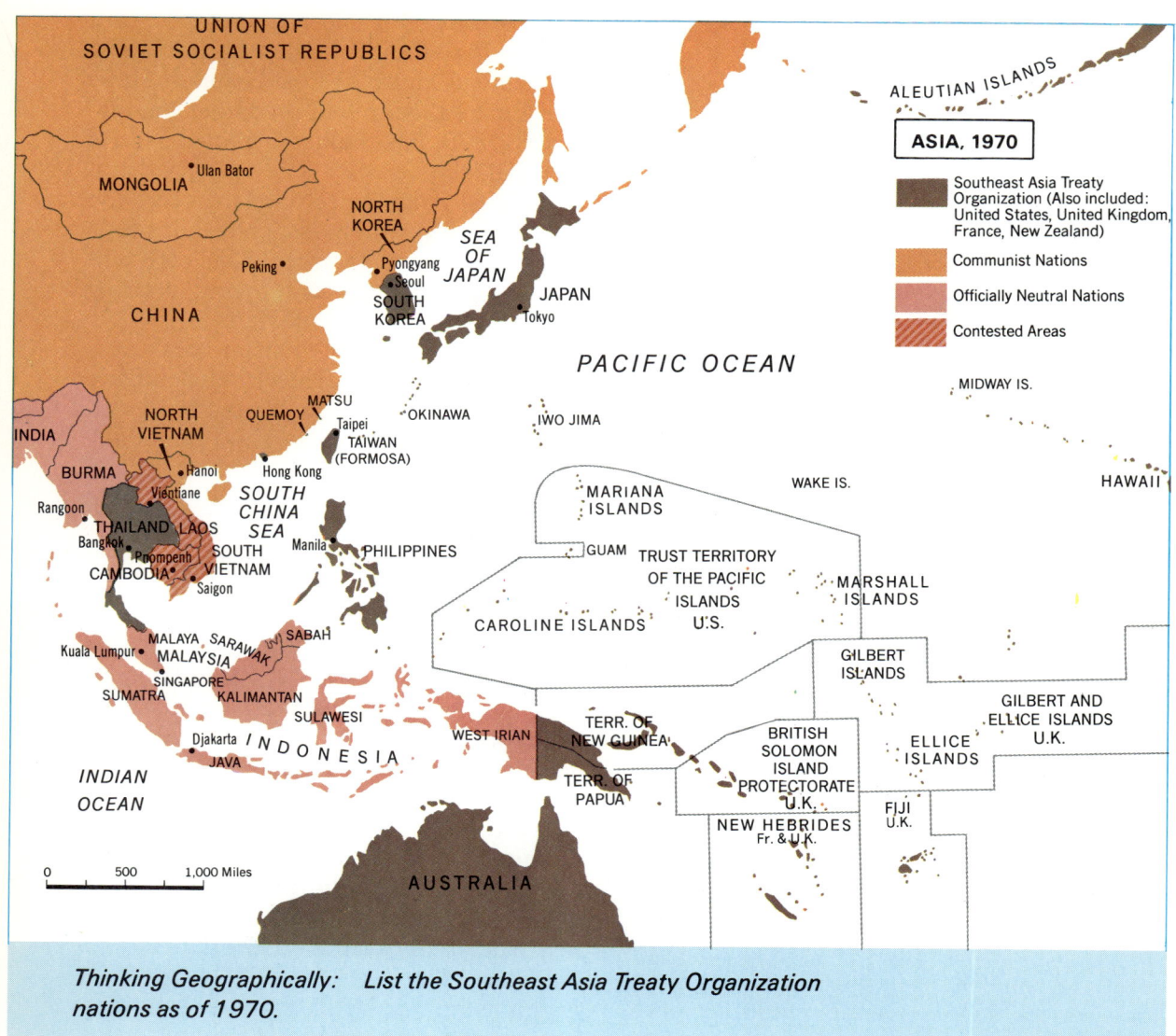

Thinking Geographically: List the Southeast Asia Treaty Organization nations as of 1970.

3. Southeast Asians Revolted

Southeast Asia is populated by a diversity of people living on the mainland and on a large number of islands. The area has been a cultural crossroads with many ideas and customs moving back and forth. The influence from India has been great.

The steamboat and the Suez Canal changed Southeast Asia. Now tin, rubber, rice, oil, and sugar from Southeast Asia could be shipped everywhere. As you read earlier, Europeans began to exploit the area.

As the Europeans opened up new mines and plantations, they needed a cheap labor supply. But the natives often did not choose to do this type of work. So foreign workers were imported. Chinese workers spread all over Southeast Asia. Indians moved into

Burma and Malaya. Vietnamese moved into Cambodia. This meant that many areas now had a minority population living in their midst. Often resentment arose against the minority groups.

Urban areas grew rapidly under colonialism. Singapore, Rangoon, and Manila became great cities with huge populations. In such cities, a new middle class arose. This class had different values from the poor peasants in the countryside. The middle class was usually the group most dissatisfied with colonial rule. Therefore, most of the leaders for the independence movement in Southeast Asia came from the middle class.

Growing Nationalism During World War II, the Japanese conquered and occupied most of Southeast Asia. Most of the conquered people did not resist Japanese rule. Only in the Philippines, Malaya, and Vietnam was there active resistance.

The Japanese established some independent nations, freed from European rule. After Japan collapsed in 1945 and before the former colonial powers could take over again, many nationalists proclaimed their independence. In Indonesia, Sukarno directed his people not to accept Dutch rule. Ho Chi Minh (ho che min), a Vietnamese Communist, told his people to resist French rule.

In 1950, Indonesia celebrated the fifth anniversary of its declaration of independence.

The Philippines celebrating independence.

Indo-China The longest and most bitter war for independence occurred in Indo-China—Vietnam, Cambodia, and Laos. The French refused to recognize the government of Ho Chi Minh. War started in 1946. By 1954, the French were completely defeated. France agreed to end the colonial relationship in Vietnam, Cambodia, and Laos.

The 1954 peace agreement divided Vietnam into two parts: North and South Vietnam. Elections were to be held in July, 1956. In this election the people of Vietnam would choose to be united with Ho Chi Minh's Communist government in the north or to remain under noncommunist rule in the south. The rulers of South Vietnam did not hold the elections because they were afraid that Ho Chi Minh would win. The country remained split into two nations. The north continued guerrilla attacks in the south.

Except for the United States with the Philippines, the colonial powers thought they could again control Southeast Asia. Events proved otherwise. The Philippines gained independence by mutual agreement on July 4, 1946. In 1947, Burma achieved independence from Great Britain. Malaysia received final independence in 1957 after an unsuccessful Communist uprising.

The Dutch wanted to keep Indonesia because the country provided a chief source of income for large numbers of Dutch people. After 1945, about 150,000 Dutch troops were sent to regain control of Indonesia. However, the Dutch gave up in 1949. After about 350 years of Dutch rule, Indonesia gained its independence.

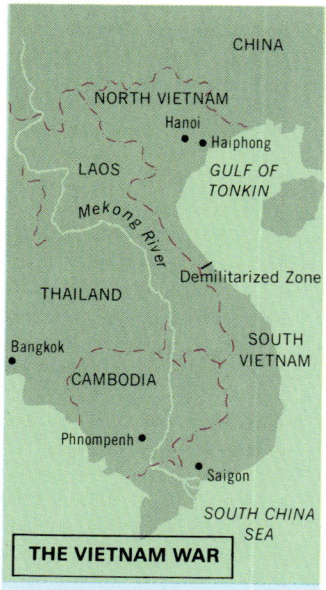

THE VIETNAM WAR

Thinking Geographically: Why would China be concerned about Vietnam?

Thousands gathered in Washington, D.C. to protest the Vietnam War.

The South Vietnamese leaders found the war going from bad to worse, partly because they lacked popular support. But gradually America increased military aid to South Vietnam. In 1963, President Kennedy sent 16,000 American troops as "military advisers." However, more of the country fell into the hands of the North Vietnamese.

President Johnson felt that if the communists gained control of Vietnam, the whole of Southeast Asia would fall. By 1967, over a half million American troops were fighting in Vietnam. The war was ruthless, filled with incidents of terrorism, chemical warfare, and atrocities. The countryside of Vietnam was being destroyed. The war also involved neighboring landlocked Laos and Cambodia, since both nations were used by North Vietnam for moving supplies.

As the war escalated in Vietnam, it became more unpopular in the United States and the rest of the world. In 1968, Richard Nixon was elected president, partly because he promised to stop the fighting in Vietnam. In 1973, a cease-fire agreement was signed. The United States gradually moved its troops out. Without the support of the

South Vietnamese refugees fleeing from the North Vietnamese troops.

American troops, the South Vietnamese army was completely overrun by the North Vietnamese. In 1975, the South Vietnamese nation was completely crushed. The Vietnamese communists, aided by the Soviet Union, were now in control of the whole of Vietnam.

In 1975, there were also new communist governments in Laos and Cambodia. But the people in this area were ancient ethnic enemies. In 1979, Vietnam gobbled up Cambodia and Laos, the buffers between the communist world and the pro-western nations in the region. Vietnam became more supportive of the Soviet Union. This offended China. Thailand and other nations worried about possible Vietnamese expansion. The United States, China, and the Soviet Union were greatly concerned about events in Southeast Asia.

Section Questions

1. What was the effect of the colonial experience in Southeast Asia?
2. How did the Japanese occupation in World War II promote nationalism in Southeast Asia?
3. Why did the Dutch want to regain control of Indonesia?
4. What happened in Vietnam between 1945 and 1954? Between 1954 and 1975?

Chapter Summary

1. By 1949, the Communist Party gained control of mainland China. In the Korean War, Chinese troops held back the United Nations forces. After the Korean War, China tried to move ahead economically. But the Chinese leaders differed on how to achieve economic progress. In the Cultural Revolution, Mao was able to oust his opponents. After his death, moderate leaders tried to modernize China by using more outside foreign help.

2. After World War II, the British agreed to give India complete independence. However, the Muslims and Hindus could not agree to remain together as one nation. Two independent nations, India and Pakistan, were created in 1947. India fought brief wars with both Pakistan and China. India supported the separation of East Pakistan (Bangladesh) from West Pakistan. India's growing population made it difficult to raise the standard of living although India made progress in industry and agriculture.

3. Nationalism increased in Southeast Asia during the Japanese occupation. After World War II ended, many groups demanded complete independence from colonial powers. Indonesia gained independence in 1949. The most prolonged struggle was in Vietnam. After the French were defeated, the nation was divided into North Vietnam and South Vietnam. The United States sent troops and aid to South Vietnam, but after the American troops left, South Vietnam was defeated by North Vietnam. Vietnam, aided by the Soviet Union, gained control of Laos and Cambodia.

Chapter 33 Review

Check Your Facts

1. Identify the following:
   a. Mao Zedong
   b. Lyndon Johnson
   c. Indira Gandhi
   d. Jawaharlal Nehru
   e. Douglas MacArthur
   f. Ho Chi Minh
2. In foreign affairs, what nations worried India?
3. How do the Japanese maintain a high standard of living?
4. What were the consequences of the Chinese entering the Korean War?
5. Why were elections not held in 1956 in Vietnam?
6. Why did President Johnson send large numbers of American troops to Vietnam?

Words To Know

Define these words in one or two sentences. Then tell the significance of each in the history of postwar Asia.
   a. Cultural Revolution
   b. Great Leap Forward
   c. communes
   d. partition

Developing Your Skills

1. Look at maps in the Atlas. About how far would the Chinese troops have to travel to reach Korea? How far would United States troops travel?
2. Use the Time Line from Chapter 32. Tell what happened in Europe or the Americas in the year each event below happened.
   Vietnam takes over Cambodia.
   India and Pakistan become independent.
   Communists gain control of China.

Thinking It Over

1. Why was Chairman Mao concerned about the younger generation? Are concerns about the younger generation justified?
2. One of the most famous of the slogans of the Cultural Revolution was "to rebel is justified." What are the risks of rebellion? The advantages?
3. What reactions do Americans presently have to the American participation in Vietnam? Ask members of the family and older people.
4. Both China and Cambodia have at times sent urban people to the country. What are the advantages of this policy? The disadvantages?
5. Some have argued that Gandhi's nonviolent methods only work in nations where there is freedom of speech and press. Do you think that nonviolent methods could work in a totalitarian society?

Special Activities

1. Check on what is happening in Cambodia and Laos today.
2. Gather information on the progress China and India are making on reducing the birth rate.
3. Dramatize a debate between the leaders of the Hindus and Muslims in 1946 on what should be done in India.
4. Because of the unstable situation in Southeast Asia, groups of refugees have fled from Vietnam, Cambodia, and other places. Check where the refugees have settled.

Sadat, Carter, and Begin.

Chapter 34
The Middle East and Africa

Where is the Middle East? The most common definition includes all the land from Afghanistan to Egypt. But Morocco, Algeria, and Libya may also be included in the Middle East. These three nations, all in North Africa, are predominantly Arab and much of the Middle East is Arab. The term Arab refers to people whose ancestors were a specific Semitic people inhabiting Arabia and parts of northern Africa.

But not all people of the Middle East are Arabs. The ancestors of the people of Iran and Turkey are non-Arab. Turks were Ural Altaic and Iranians were Indo-Europeans. People in these two nations do

1945-1981

1945	World War II ends
1946	Syria, Jordan, Lebanon become independent
1948	Israel established
1954	Algerian revolt begins
1957	Ghana becomes independent
1960	Independence for 17 African nations
1961	South Africa leaves British Commonwealth
1967-1970	Nigerian Civil War
1967	Arab-Israeli War (Six-Day War)
1973	Arab-Israeli War (Yom Kippur War)
1975	Angolan independence
1979	Iranian revolution
1979	Egypt-Israel Peace Treaty
1980	Iran and Iraq at war
1981	Sadat assassinated

An off-shore oil rig.

not speak Arabic. However, Iran and Turkey, like all of the Middle East, have been heavily influenced by the Muslim culture which began in Arabia.

An older term sometimes used for this area is the Near East. Europeans usually thought of Asia as the Far East and the area around the Red Sea and the Mediterranean Sea as the Near East or Middle East.

The Middle East is one of the most important areas of the world. It is the crossroads of three continents: Europe, Asia, and Africa. In addition, the area includes over half of the world's known oil resources. Large productive oil fields are found in Saudi Arabia, Union of Arab Emirates, Kuwait, Qatar, Iran, Algeria, and Libya.

1. Israel and the Arab World Clashed in the Middle East

In the 1930s, Hitler began persecuting the Jews in Germany. Thousands of Jews escaped Germany and settled in Palestine. They started to buy up land from the Arabs. The British limited the amount purchased but the displaced Arabs became more hostile to the Jews. From 1936 to 1939, the Arabs waged guerrilla warfare against the Jews living in Palestine. They tried to get the British to stop the Jewish immigration. In 1939, in an attempt to stop the fighting and to gain Arab support, the British limited Jewish immigration into Palestine to 75,000 for the next five years.

At the end of World War II in 1945, some of the few survivors of the Nazi

Jews arriving in Israel.

Israel's Wars In May 1948, the Jews living in Palestine proclaimed the new republic of Israel. But five Arab nations—Egypt, Iraq, Lebanon, Syria, and Jordan—attacked Israel almost immediately. Israel, although tiny, had more modern weapons and financial support than the Arabs. After a year of fighting, Israel won. It expanded its borders by taking about half of the land that the United Nations had said belonged to the Arabs. The remaining half was taken

Thinking Geographically: How does the size of the Sinai Peninsula compare with the original state of Israel?

holocaust wanted to settle in Palestine. The western nations, including the United States, wanted to allow this. But the newly independent Arab nations—Syria, Jordan, and others—wanted the British to stop the Jewish immigration. They regarded the Jews as imperialists taking over their land. Meanwhile, tens of thousands of Jews were smuggled illegally into Palestine. In 1946, one third of Palestine's population was Jewish.

Terrorist acts by both Arabs and Jews increased in Palestine. The British then gave Palestine to the United Nations to manage. In 1947, the United Nations divided Palestine into a Jewish state and an Arab area. Jerusalem, the holy city, was to be under international control.

by Jordan. The United Nations arranged a series of truces. However, no final peace agreements were signed by the Arab nations.

The Israeli-Arab War created many refugees. Hundreds of thousands of Arabs left Palestine, some voluntarily and some not. They moved to other Arab nations. In a similar manner, Oriental Jews from the Middle East and North African nations came to Israel for safety.

Egypt became the leader of the Arab bloc which was trying to eliminate Israel. In 1956, Egypt seized the Suez Canal. Great Britain, France, and Israel attacked Egypt to regain control of the canal. The short war was settled by pressure from the United States and the Soviet Union. Israel was forced to move out of Egypt. Egypt lost the fighting, but won the final battle in diplomacy.

In 1967, Egypt blocked Israel's only port on the Gulf of Aqaba (UH koh bah). The Israelis suddenly attacked their enemies. They knocked out the Soviet-supplied air forces of Egypt, Jordan, and Syria, and won the war in six days.

Through this victory, Israel expanded its original size by about three times. To the west, Israel's borders expanded into Egypt's territory. On the east, they included Syria's Golan Heights and land in Jordan. East Jerusalem was also annexed.

The Arab world was humiliated by this third defeat. They again built up their forces with the Soviet's help. In October, 1973, the people of Israel were observing Yom Kippur, one of the most important Jewish religious holidays. Egypt and Syria suddenly attacked. Israel suffered a setback at first. Then, aided by fresh United States arms, Israel defeated its enemies, crossing into Egyptian territory. At this point, the Soviet Union threatened to come directly to the aid of Egypt. Both the United States and the Soviets supplied economic and military aid to the Middle East, but they wanted to avoid a major conflict. A settlement was arranged. The Israelis were forced to give up the land acquired in 1973 as well as some land acquired from Egypt in 1967.

Egypt, although defeated, felt better about the Arab-Israeli War of 1973. Initially they had driven back the Israeli forces and they had regained some of their territory. In contrast, the Israelis suffered a loss of morale compared to their former high confidence.

A Peace Treaty Worldwide support for Israel gradually decreased as Israel took more land. Furthermore, in 1973 and 1974, the Arab nations started the oil embargo. They stopped oil supplies to the United States and the Netherlands, the two nations that had supported Israel in the war. The embargo later ended. However, the Organization of Petroleum Exporting Countries (OPEC), a group that sets oil prices, raised oil prices by about 70 percent.

Nations that depended on OPEC oil worried about these huge price increases and about getting adequate supplies of oil. Some nations now moved toward support for the Arab nations in their demand that Israel return the conquered territory. Israel, however, maintained that it must have buffer zones because Israel would not be safe until the Arab nations recognized its right to exist. Israelis continued to develop communities in the disputed occupied territories.

The Israeli-Arab conflict had been going on for about thirty years. The United States put more pressure on Israel to agree to some of the Arab demands.

Egypt had a fast-growing population and not enough cash for development. It was now more willing to discuss peace, and more friendly toward the United States.

In 1979, with President Carter's support, President Sadat (sah DOT) of Egypt and Premier Begin of Israel signed the

Sadat visiting Jerusalem in 1978.

Egyptian-Israeli Peace Treaty. Israel was to withdraw from the Sinai Desert. "Administrative autonomy" would be given to the West Bank and the Gaza Strip where the Palestinians lived. The details for these plans were to be worked out later.

The Arab world did not like Egypt's peace treaty with Israel. Trouble spots were the West Bank, the Gaza Strip, and Arab Jerusalem. The Palestinians wanted their own state. They also wanted half of the city of Jerusalem. Meanwhile, Israeli forces continued to remain in the area.

On October 6, 1981, President Sadat was assassinated by anti-Israeli army officers. Many people of the western world mourned the death of a peace-maker. Some Arabs felt that a traitor had been eliminated. How Sadat's death would affect the Middle East was a frightening question.

Section Questions

1. Why did the Jews regard Palestine as their homeland? Why did the Arabs regard Palestine as their homeland?
2. Why did the United Nations agree to divide Palestine into two areas in 1947?
3. What were the results of the Arab-Israeli War in 1967?
4. What were the results of the Arab-Israeli War in 1973?

2. Political Changes Came to the Middle East

In 1952, not all of the Arab nations were ready to follow Egypt's directions. President Nasser's socialism and his friendship with the Soviet Union scared the more conservative Arab governments. The oil-rich nations of the Middle East, especially Saudi Arabia and Iran, became more powerful as nations began to use oil as a political and economic weapon.

Saudi Arabia Saudi Arabia is the largest kingdom on the Arabian Peninsula. It is about one-fourth of the size of the United States. This nation is also the birthplace of Islam. Within its borders are the holy cities of Mecca and Medina. About 750,000 pilgrims come to these cities every year.

Saudi Arabia, like the other nations in the Middle East, had been conquered by the Turks. Turkey's declining power allowed Abdul Aziz Ibn Saud (ab DOOL a ZEEZ IBN suh OOD), a strong leader, to unite the various warlike tribes of the Arabian Peninsula. After Ibn Saud conquered a large part of Saudi Arabia in 1926, he proclaimed himself the king of what is now Saudi Arabia. In the 1930s, great quantities of oil were discovered there. Saudi Arabia presently has more known oil resources than any other nation in the world.

In the 1930s, Saudi Arabia did not have the technology or skilled people needed to extract the oil. So the king allowed a combination of American oil companies, called the Arabian American Oil Company or Aramco, to extract the oil. Later, the Saudis nationalized the oil industry. With money coming in year after year, Saudi Arabia moved from a more or less isolated society into a participant in world affairs.

In 1973, with the huge OPEC increases in the price of oil, the Saudis had more money than ever before. Their income leaped from $1.2 billion in 1970 to about $70 billion in 1979. These revenues were used for massive industrialization.

Because Saudi Arabia was strongly anti-communist, the United States regarded it as a friendly nation. Yet anti-American feelings surfaced in Saudi Arabia when the ideas of Ayatullah Khomeini (ho MAY ne) of Iran spread. The conservative Saudis also worried because there were over two million foreign workers among some five million Saudis. They feared that these foreign workers might be subversive to their society.

Iran Iran, with 36 million people, is the third most populated nation in the Middle East. Iran has a long history of unity in its cultural traditions. Formerly it was called Persia. As you read earlier, the early Persian empire was strong. Between 1200 and 1900, Iran lost much of its wealth and power.

Iran developed into a modern nation under Riza Shah Pahlevi (ri ZAW SHA PAH lah vee), an army officer who became shah in 1925. He tried to use Iran's oil revenues to modernize the nation. But during World War II (1939-1945), the British and Russians, fearing German control of the Middle East, took over oil-rich Iran. They

The Saudi Arabia Institute for Petroleum.

forced Riza Pahlevi to abdicate in favor of his young son, Mohammed Riza Pahlevi, who became the new shah.

After World War II, Iran became strongly nationalistic. The Iranians were angry at the British, who controlled the oil industry in Iran. Iran found it difficult to run the oil fields, so in 1954 it made agreements with the western nations to develop the oil. Now, however, half the profits went to Iran.

The shah pushed to make Iran a modern nation. He gave women greater freedom, including the right to education and to vote. Over 100,000 students were sent to Europe and the United States for college training. Vast areas of land that formerly belonged both to the crown and the clergy were given to the peasants. The income of the *ayatullahs*, or religious leaders, was reduced. The clergy and other believers also feared that traditional values were being eroded. They were shocked at the sight of bars, casinos, and women without the traditional veils.

The shah moved too quickly in trying to impose western technologies and lifestyles on the Iranians. The bazaar merchants worried over competition from foreign imports. As workers moved from the villages to the cities, they saw unfair economic practices first-hand. The royal family's plunder of the national treasury was criticized. Worse, the shah's secret police used brutal methods, including torture, to suppress political opposition.

All of these hostile groups, led by religious leaders, brought Iran to a crippling halt by rioting, strikes and demonstrations. In 1979, the shah and his family were forced to leave Iran. Ayatullah Ruhollah Khomeini became the power behind the new government.

The rise of Khomeini, an ayatullah, showed a resurgence of Muslim influence. The religious wanted to make the Islamic religion the center of all areas of life. They wanted a path that was different from that

Ayatullah Khomeini.

of the United States, the European nations, or the Soviet Union. They did not reject modernization. They rejected the shah's way of achieving it.

The United States had supported the shah because it felt he was a strong force against Soviet expansion. When the United States allowed the shah to enter the United States for medical treatment, 52 American hostages at the American Embassy at Tehran were seized by militant students in November 1979. The American hostages were released in January 1981 after almost 15 months of imprisonment.

The Iranian revolution in 1979 left Iran in an unsettled condition. Iran's oil production dropped as its economy was disrupted by the revolution. The ethnic minority groups within Iran—Kurds, Baluchis, and others—became more restless in their quest for independence. Iraq and Iran had disputed previously over borders, water rights, and the treatment of ethnic groups. In 1980, Iraq attacked Iran. Iraq initially took some territory, but the Iranians refused to give in. The war dragged on with no victory in sight for either side.

Afghanistan Afghanistan is one of the poorest nations in the world. It never has been a unified nation, but a group of warring tribes. The mountainous area of Afghanistan is a strategic spot between the Middle East and India/Southeast Asia. Because it has always been a gateway, Afghanistan has been conquered many times—by the Persians, Alexander the Great, the Indians, the Arabs, and the Mongols.

In more recent times, the British and the Russians have competed for control of Afghanistan. After 1878, the British took control of Afghanistan's foreign affairs. They kept that power for about fifty years. The British created Afghanistan's artificial borders. The only common unity among the different tribes was their common Islamic heritage.

After Afghanistan won independence in 1919, its government was unstable. In 1947, Afghanistan and Pakistan got into a boundary dispute. Afghanistan wanted the Pushtan tribe of Pakistan to have its own nation. Pakistan wanted to keep control of the region.

Afghanistan took aid from both the

Resistance fighters in Afghanistan.

Did You Know?

The "Magic Carpet" airlift of refugees to Israel.

Refugees

At the end of World War II, there were about thirty million refugees—people without a home. These included prisoners of war from all nations, survivors of concentration camps. But some people could not go home because of political changes. Millions of Germans fled from the Soviet advance. About six million Germans had to leave Poland, Czechoslovakia, Rumania, and other nations. Two million Poles moved into the new territory that they had taken from Germany. In what is now West Germany, about ten million new people were received.

Many of the surviving Jews did not want to return to their old homes. They emigrated to new homes in Israel or South America. Relief organizations and the allies had a big job in helping people find new homes.

War, oppression, and poverty continued to make new refugees. The United Nations estimated that there were ten million refugees in 1980. The problem of finding new homes continues.

Soviet Union and the United States. Yet it remained very unstable. Three governments were overthrown in the 1970s.

For years the Soviet Union had military advisers in Afghanistan to help the weak Afghanistan army try to put down the Afghan Muslim rebels. Muslim rebellion against the pro-Soviet government was growing. The Soviets felt that they could not allow such a strategic nation as Afghanistan to slip out of their hands. In December 1979, the Soviet Union marched troops into Afghanistan.

Sending Soviet troops into Afghanistan was regarded as a brutal act of aggression against a small Muslim neighbor. In 1980, the United Nations Assembly condemned the Soviets and called for a pullout of the Soviet troops.

The United States now had more worries about the possible expansion of Soviet power. The presence of the Soviets in Afghanistan might affect the Persian Gulf. The eleven Muslim nations in the Persian Gulf control about 40 percent of the world's exportable oil. The Soviets appeared willing to encourage revolts in the area. Presidents Carter and Reagan moved to build up the area against any possible control by the Soviets. However, many nations in the Persian Gulf were concerned about United States interference in their area. Thus, the Middle East remained a vital, volatile area in a very unsettled condition.

Section Questions

1. What nation was the Arab leader in the 1950s and 1960s? What two Arab nations became important in the 1970s and 1980s?
2. Why did Saudi Arabia become more important in world affairs?
3. Why did Shah Mohammed Riza Pahlevi become unpopular?
4. Why did the Muslim religious leaders not like Shah Pahlevi?

3. African Nations Gained Independence

Even though fighting took place in North Africa, Africa became more prosperous during World War II. Its raw materials such as minerals, palm oil, coffee, sugar, and cocoa were needed by the Allies. Jobs opened up to African people who migrated to the cities. Furthermore, about 200,000 African soldiers fought in the war. They came back with new skills, such as the ability to drive a truck. Africans from different tribes learned to work together during their military service.

In 1954, only four independent nations existed in the whole of Africa. These were Egypt, Ethiopia, Liberia, and the Union of South Africa. The European colonial powers wanted to keep their colonies in Africa and other parts of the world.

But nationalism was building in Africa. Africans greatly resented the Europeans, who often presumed that they were better than the blacks. Africans also had pride in their own traditions and culture and did not want outsiders to make their laws. Africans hated the special privileges the whites had, privileges that blocked Africans from moving ahead economically and politically.

Africans who had been educated in the missionary schools or abroad formed a variety of organizations: political parties, trade unions, and professional associations. All of these groups demanded complete independence.

The French France was not willing to give independence to its African colonies after World War II. Instead, it wanted its colonies to have close economic ties with France. This was especially true of the large French colony of Algeria. This colony, close to France, had about one million French settlers and about eight million Arabs. The French had held Algeria since

Algerians celebrate the end of the rebellion.

1830. They thought of Algeria as part of their own land. They also had made heavy economic investments in Algeria.

When World War II ended, Algerians hoped for freedom. But France regained control after the fighting stopped. The resentful Arab Algerians revolted in 1954. In this savage war, Algerian urban terrorists and rural guerrillas fought against a French army of 500,000. The French army had some control in the cities but could not put down the guerrillas in the country. Both sides practiced torture and other crimes against human rights.

In 1956, France gave Morocco and Tunisia their independence. The French army officers in Algeria were afraid that the French government, weary of war, also would grant Algeria its independence. In 1958, they mutinied. General de Gaulle, the hero of the French in World War II, was called back from retirement to solve the Algerian problem. He agreed to give independence to Algeria. In July 1962, Algeria won its independence from France.

In 1958, General de Gaulle also offered independence to all of the French colonies throughout the world. The French colonies had two choices. One was complete independence with no financial or cultural ties to France. This meant no economic aid. The second choice was to join a voluntary partnership with France and continue to receive French aid.

Only French Guinea refused to join the partnership with France. The French withdrew from French Guinea. Ghana, a former British colony, gave a loan of two million dollars to help Guinea. Later, China and communist nations in Europe also furnished aid to Guinea.

Seeing that Guinea had survived, the rest of the French African colonies reconsidered. Two years later, in 1960 the fourteen remaining French colonies in Africa asked for complete independence from France. In all, seventeen nations in Africa secured independence in 1960. Thus, the 1960s were the time of independence for much of Africa.

The British and the Belgians The independence of India and Pakistan encouraged the British colonies in Africa to demand independence. Sudan had been ruled jointly by Great Britain and Egypt. In 1953, steps were taken to create Sudanese independence, and in 1956, Sudan became an independent country.

In sub-Saharan Africa, the pacesetter for independence was Ghana, formerly the Gold Coast. There was a relatively high number of native college graduates in Ghana, about 5,000 in 1957. Ghana thus became the leader in the black African liberation movement. In 1957 Ghana was the first black nation south of the Sahara to gain independence.

One by one, other African British colonies became independent. Most of the independence movements were peaceful. However, there was trouble in larger colonies that had significant white populations.

In Kenya, a secret movement called the Mau Mau formed in order to force independence. The Mau Mau began raiding. They killed a few white settlers and blacks loyal to the British. British troops were called in to control Kenya. After nine years, the Mau Mau rebels were defeated, but Kenya won independence in 1963.

In 1953, Britain set up the Federation of Rhodesia and Nyasaland. The Federa-

Did You Know?

Different Paths: Kenya and Tanzania

Kenya and Tanzania are neighbors, but they are taking different paths in economic development. Tanzania wants to achieve a more equal society by emphasizing farming. Almost all of its available capital is devoted to education and cooperative efforts in the rural areas. The government wants to halt the gap in the standard of living between the country and the city.

Tanzania does not want to depend on foreign aid so foreign investment is restricted. Tanzania has some of the best wild animal parks. However, it does not encourage tourism because it wants to be free from outside influence. It has nationalized its banks, insurance companies, and many other businesses.

In contrast, Kenya is a more capitalistic nation. It wants foreign investment. The capital city, Nairobi, has become the headquarters of many foreign businesses in Africa. However, the government of Kenya wants the skilled white workers to be replaced by Kenyans within a few years.

Using modern farming methods in Kenya.

Jomo Kenyatta, first president of Kenya.

Robert Mugabe.

tion included Southern Rhodesia, Northern Rhodesia (now Zambia), and Nyasaland (now Malawi). Malawi and Zambia became independent in 1964. Rhodesia demanded independence, but Britain balked at the proposal Rhodesia presented. The whites, less than five percent of the population, offered the blacks almost no voice in the government. Only Rhodesia was left as a British colony. Fearful of allowing the blacks power, the whites declared themselves independent of Great Britain in 1965. Rhodesia's "independence" was not recognized by any nation in the world. Great Britain then tried various methods that would ensure power to the seven million black people of Rhodesia. Black guerrillas rebelled against the existing government. In 1976, white Rhodesian leaders agreed to the transition to a black-majority government. In 1980, Rhodesia (now called Zimbabwe) had an election. Robert Mugabe (mu GAH be), a Marxist guerrilla leader, was elected Prime Minister.

Belgium made little preparation for giving the Congo independence. But Belgium finally bowed to pressure. In 1960 Belgian Congo (now Zaire) was created as an independent nation. Within a few days, a mutiny and civil war tore the country. One area, Katanga (now called Shaba), a rich mineral area, proclaimed its independence from the rest of Zaire. Conflict lasted from 1960 to 1965. The United Nations forces had to restore some unity and order to Zaire.

Other European Powers By the 1960s, only a few places in Africa remained under European control. Spain and Portugal still had colonies in Africa. Portugal regarded its colonies as overseas extensions of its own land. By the 1960s, the Portuguese army was fighting guerrilla wars in all three of its African colonies of Guinea, Mozambique, and Angola. Military expenditures took one half of the national budget. The drafting of soldiers also made the war unpopular.

In 1974, the Portuguese government

was overthrown by a revolution. In 1975 the new government granted independence to its three African colonies. Two guerrilla forces then fought a civil war against each other for control of Angola. The winner was a group that had been armed and trained by the Soviet Union and Cuba. Cuban troops were also stationed in Guinea, Mozambique, and Ethiopia.

Spain still had Spanish Sahara, Equatorial Guinea, and Ifni. Equatorial Guinea became independent in 1968. In 1969 Ifni was incorporated by Morocco. In 1975, unarmed civilians from Morocco demonstrated against Spanish rule. They moved into Spanish Sahara waving copies of the Koran. Spain's new king, Juan Carlos I, then gave up control of the Spanish colonies in Africa. Spanish Sahara was divided between Morocco and Mauritania. Morocco gained control of the area in which the Shawawi nationalists lived. They wanted their own independence and fought against Morocco. These rebels were supported by Algeria.

By 1980, all of Africa had won independence from the colonial powers. The continent with the oldest evidence of human beings was now the area of the newest nations. But independence had not brought solutions to the many critical problems that Africa faced.

Section Questions

1. In 1950 what African nations were independent?
2. What were the roots of African nationalism?
3. Why did France want to keep Algeria? How successful was the French army in the Algerian War?
4. What choices were given to the African colonies by General de Gaulle? What choice did Guinea make?
5. What nation was the leader for independence in South Saharan Africa?

4. New African Nations Faced Many Problems

During the political campaigns for independence, the African people had been told that the alien rulers were the reason they had not made progress. Nkrumah, the leader of Ghana's independence movement, said, "If we get self-government, we'll transfer the Gold Coast into a paradise in ten years." Other leaders said much the same thing.

But the hope that independence would open a better world immediately was soon dashed. Most new African nations faced two major interwoven problems. One was nation building, or development of a stable government. The other was creating an economy that offered a better life for the African people. Let us look at these two important areas.

Nation Building The colonial experience created several artificial boundary lines. Often, different ethnic groups or tribes were put together into one nation although they did not share a common heritage. Northern light-skinned Muslim farmers and herders were grouped with southern coastal blacks who had different religious beliefs and lived in a rain-forest environment. In other cases, the colonial powers divided a tribe between two nations. Thus, those living in the west belonged to one nation and those in the east to another nation. The frontiers of Ghana cut through seventeen major tribes.

Furthermore, the colonial powers often had allowed various tribes some degree of independence or autonomy. There had been no attempt to integrate the various tribes into one nation. So in many African nations there was little in the way of shared experiences. When independence came, the new central government commanded little loyalty. Africans often had no experience in placing the interests of the nation over

Biafran children in food lines during the Nigerian civil war.

those of the local unit.

In addition, different languages were spoken within one nation. Zaire officially had four languages. In some African nations such as Tanzania, the government, trying to foster unity, introduced one common language—Swahili—for the whole nation. Other nations retained French or English for use in government, business, and education.

Civil wars broke out when a religious or ethnic group wanted independence or semi-independence. A civil war occurred in Nigeria in 1967 when the people of the eastern province of Nigeria, the Ibo, proclaimed themselves the nation of Biafra. The Ibo were more highly trained and assertive in business than the other Nigerian groups. They had acquired government jobs and businesses throughout Nigeria. The other tribal groups resented the power of the Ibos and conflict broke out. Many Ibos were killed.

Biafra contained the oil-producing region and its loss would have crippled the rest of Nigeria. So the Nigerian army blocked the food and supplies coming into the Biafra area. In 1970, the Biafra movement was defeated when the Ibo were starved out.

Sudan also encountered difficulties. The southern blacks resented the rule of the Nubians and the Muslims in the north. Problems of different ethnic groups also existed in Zaire, Chad, and Burundi.

Sometimes the conflict within a nation was aggravated when a neighboring nation helped the rebels. In a disputed area of Morocco, the rebels were aided by Algeria. In 1978 and 1979, rebels in Zaire attacked from bases in Angola. Tension was diminished only when Angola agreed not to harbor the rebels.

However, civil wars were much more common than wars between nations. The Organization of African Unity was founded in 1963. The members agreed that all African nations should accept the boundaries in Africa as drawn by the colonial powers. There would be too many disputes if changes were made on the basis of cultural ties or historical unity. The African nations also reaffirmed that one nation should not attack another. Only in a few cases, such as Uganda and Tanzania, has this rule been violated.

Political Leaders The new African leaders faced many challenges. Often, they felt they needed complete authority, without opposing political parties. In the vast majority of nations, a new leader took over through a coup, a change in government by force. Ghana had three coups in less than ten years: 1972, 1978, and 1979.

Instability in the governments forced the leaders to be very concerned with security. The leader built up an army and police force that were loyal to him. Sometimes these forces were also used to curb violence.

An important issue for the leader was whether to accept economic assistance from the former ruling power or other outside nations. Here the Soviets and the Chinese had an advantage. Neither of these nations had ever exploited Africa. Thus they were free to identify themselves with the liberation movements. The Chinese stressed their identification with problems in the rural areas. France still maintained close economic arrangements with the former French African colonies.

In time, most of the African nations developed more unity among their people. Unity was helped through better communication, shared experiences, the establishment of schools, and other social welfare programs. But unity also depended on solving economic problems.

Economic Problems Contrary to the hopes of the people, freedom from colonialism did not bring relief from poverty. Africa was primarily an agricultural continent. The African nations sold cash crops such as cotton, nuts, coffee, tea, and sugar to the rest of the world. Twenty products

Cutting sisal fiber in the Sudan.

The ancient and the modern meet near an airport in Ibadan, Nigeria.

accounted for about three-fourths of the exports. The prices that the Africans received for their crops were not directly under their control. Yet Africa had potential. About one third of the world's potential hydroelectric power was located in Africa.

With independence, many African nations took over the major institutions such as banking and transportation. Africans did not want these important assets in the hands of foreigners. The African nations also developed new economic institutions such as trade unions and farmers' associations. Stores and shops started to replace the open markets which had served as the basic way of exchanging goods in the past.

But growth was slow. The African nations supplied raw materials, then had to buy higher priced manufactured goods. Therefore, investment funds for new projects were short. Some African nations were reluctant to accept foreign investment because they feared that they would lose control of their economy. In turn, foreign investors were reluctant to send capital into areas of political instability. However, mining expanded. Oil, iron ore, diamonds, uranium, bauxite, phosphates, chrome, and asbestos became important sources of income. But both mining and industrialization required a skilled labor force. Many African nations did not have enough trained and educated people for these skilled jobs. Therefore, all African nations pushed education, especially at the primary level. Almost all of the African nations also established universities.

Agriculture remained a difficult problem. A typical African nation had a few large commercial farms. These farms exported a large percentage of the crops. The vast majority of people lived by *subsistence* farming, farming which supplied food only for their own needs. By the simple farming methods they used, these farmers could not easily raise their output.

Economic growth usually has been concentrated in nations with valuable mineral resources. It appears that some African nations will have a hard time just to maintain their existing standard of living.

South Africa Great hostility exists between other African nations and the Republic of South Africa. By the 1980s, South Africa was the only African nation south of the Sahara that was still controlled by whites. Black Africa was committed to freeing the entire continent from white rule. They were angered by South Africa's racist policies.

South Africa is a modern industrialized nation. It is the richest nation in Sub-Sahara Africa. But South Africa follows the policy of *apartheid*, or white supremacy based on separation of the races. In South Africa, blacks number about twenty million. There are three million mixed races or Asians. It is ruled by the white minority of 4.5 million. Blacks are not allowed to vote or to be in the national lawmaking body. All blacks must always carry an identification pass. They must have this pass to work or to live in certain places. Blacks are restricted as to where they can live. About 13 percent of the land, much of it poor, is reserved for the Africans. The education system is also segregated. There are vast inequalities for black students in terms of the money spent, ratio of teachers, and school buildings.

The British Commonwealth criticized South Africa for its racist practices, so in 1961 South Africa withdrew from the Commonwealth. South Africa was censured by the United Nations in 1961 for its racial policies and economic sanctions were imposed. Critics of South Africa particularly wanted to stop investment funds from flowing into South Africa. Previously foreign investors had found good profits in South Africa since labor was cheap.

South Africa became more isolated after Rhodesia came under black control. In addition, the fast-growing black population was putting more pressure on the job market and there was rising unemployment. Riots worsened. So in the 1980s, South Africa took some small steps to

A "blacks only" bus in Johannesburg, South Africa.

improve the racial situation. New job opportunities and wage increases were given by industry as the government tried to buy racial peace.

697

Section Questions

1. Why did African nations expect dramatic changes to occur after independence was achieved?
2. Why were some African nations not unified at the time of their independence?
3. Why did a civil war break out in Nigeria?
4. Why was economic growth slow for many African nations after independence?
5. What problems does South Africa face?

Chapter Summary

1. During the 1930s, many Jews who were able to flee from Germany settled in Palestine. The increased Jewish immigration led to conflict. In 1947, the United Nations divided Palestine into a Jewish area and an Arab area. The Arabs refused to recognize Israel. Israel fought many wars during the next thirty years. Victories in these wars expanded Israel's original size. After the oil crisis of 1973, more nations favored the Arab view that Israel should return the conquered territory to the Arabs. In 1979, Egypt and Israel signed a peace treaty in which Israel promised to give back the Sinai Desert to Egypt and to work for "administrative autonomy" for the West Bank and the Gaza Strip. How to settle the Palestinians remained a problem.

2. After 1952, Egypt was the leader of the Arab world. But Saudi Arabia became more important as its oil revenues increased. The Saudi Arabian rulers were conservative in their practice of Islamic principles and were anti-communist. Iran also became more powerful from oil money. In 1963, Shah Mohammed Riza Pahlevi tried to make Iran a modern nation. The clergy became his enemy. The shah also won enemies because of his repression of enemies, the dissatisfaction of the workers, and the corruption of the royal family. The shah and his family were forced to leave Iran in 1979. A new government then took over Iran. Khomeini's power showed the resurgence of Muslim influence. The Soviets invaded Afghanistan. The United Nations protested this act of aggression. There were fears that the Soviets might expand into the Persian Gulf.

3. At the end of World War II, only a few nations in Africa were independent. The French tried to keep their colonies in Africa but revolt broke out in Algeria in 1954. France gave independence to its North African colonies and offered independence to its other colonies. By 1960, all of the French African colonies were independent. Gradually the British gave independence to their colonies. Belgian Congo was ill prepared for independence and a civil war broke out just after independence was achieved. In the 1970s, Portugal and Spain gave up their colonies in Africa. With the help of Cuban troops, Marxist governments gained control of the former Portuguese colonies.

4. African nations faced the problems of trying to secure stable governments and offering their people a better way of life. Artificial boundary lines caused problems in developing unity. Different languages were also a barrier. Civil wars broke out in Nigeria and Zaire after independence but the government was successful in putting down the secessionist movements. One-party governments were most typical in African nations. Coups were frequent. African nations had to decide whether to accept aid from foreign nations. New economic institutions were started in many African nations. Agriculture remains a problem since large numbers of Africans are subsistence farmers. Overpopulation has caused many Africans to move to the growing cities, but very often these migrants cannot find jobs. African nations are hostile toward white-ruled South Africa, which practices racism.

Chapter 34 Review

Check Your Facts

1. Identify the following:
   a. Mau Mau movement
   b. Ibo
   c. Khomeini
   d. Robert Mugabe
   e. Anwar Sadat
   f. Nkrumah
   g. Organization of African Unity
   h. OPEC
2. What were the provisions of the Egyptian-Israeli Peace Treaty? What provision is most difficult to implement?
3. Why did the Soviets invade Afghanistan? How did the Muslim world react to the invasion?
4. What were the causes of the war between Iran and Iraq in 1980?
5. In what ways did Africa make progress during World War II?
6. What problems did Rhodesia pose for Great Britain?
7. What type of government evolved in most African nations?
8. Why were coups common in some African nations?

Words to Know

Define the words in one or two sentences. Then tell the significance of each in the recent history of Africa and the Middle East.
   a. apartheid   b. ayatullah

Developing Your Skills

1. Trace the map of Africa in the Atlas. Then write the date that each country achieved independence.
2. Compare Israel's size with the size of your state and county.

Thinking It Over

1. Argue for and against the proposition that the shah's rule was no more despotic than that of other Middle East nations.
2. Israel has a censorship law to protect its military. What are the advantages and disadvantages of such a policy?
3. In what ways was the Soviet involvement in Afghanistan like that of the United States in Vietnam? In what ways was it different?
4. Nigeria, sometimes called Africa's future giant, has large revenues from oil. Assume that you are one of the government planners. How would you use the money? Would you give more help to the urban areas? To the rural area? A combination of the two? Why?
5. Should African nations promote tourism? What are the advantages and disadvantages of tourism?
6. Do developing nations have a right to part of the resources of rich nations? Why or why not?

Special Activities

1. Find out more about the roles of women in Arab nations such as Iran, Egypt, and Saudi Arabia.
2. Check the financial section of your newspaper for the commodity prices of cash crops that come from Africa—gold, coffee, sugar, etc. Compare the prices to the previous year.
3. Check the most recent state of racial relations in South Africa. Has there been an improvement?

Unit 9 Review

Words to Know

1. What is the difference between a coup and a revolution?
2. Discuss the effect of reparations after World War I (Chapters 28 and 29) and after World War II (Chapter 32).
3. Compare the idea of coexistence (Chapter 32) with the idea of spheres of influence (Chapter 25).

Time and Place

1. Tell what form of transportation people would be most likely to use for each trip below.
    a. around the world in 1982
    b. across a country in 1905
    c. around the world in 1894
    d. across a country in 1820
2. For each time period below, what method would an American use to send an urgent message over a long distance?
    a. 1820   b. 1900   c. 1980

---

1. Classify each of the governments below in terms of how much power they have.

    Government
    a. United States
    b. Soviet Union
    c. Japan
    d. Iran
    e. Cuba
    f. India
    g. Great Britain
    h. West Germany
    i. Nigeria

Putting It Together

Level of Power
Very Low: unstable government; unstable economy; severe domestic problems
Low: government fairly stable but periodic coups and political terrorism; economy subject to political shocks
Moderate: stable government and usually stable economy
High: very stable government with strong economy; industrialized; strong alliances

Contemporary Parallel:

The Dilemma of Disarmament

In the fall of 1981, Soviet and American delegates faced each other across a long table in Geneva, Switzerland. The purpose of the meeting was to explore ways of reducing nuclear weapons, especially those aimed at targets in Europe.

In the years before 1914, some people watched the arms race with alarm, convinced that weapons once built would be used. But others argued that the enormous destructive power of those weapons was a guarantee of peace. No national leader would dare use them, knowing what the results would be for his own people.

A number of historians agree that the arms race helped bring about war in 1914. The German kaiser feared that others planned to attack Germany, so he decided to strike first.

Today, the same two arguments are still heard. Many believe that the nuclear arms race between the Soviet Union and the United States makes war almost inevitable. But others refer to what Winston Churchill called the nuclear "Balance of Terror." Since both sides would lose, neither side would dare to use the weapons.

Most people agree that steps toward disarmament are desirable. However, they also agree that any arms reduction is foolish if it endangers national security. That is the dilemma of disarmament.

The people of Europe feel caught in the middle. In mid-1981, millions of people in Europe took part in huge demonstrations against the arms race. They want both sides to pull back and to give Europe a chance for lasting peace. The pressure of their protests helped to bring about the meeting in Geneva. For the Soviet and American delegates, the dilemma of disarmament remains: will either side dare take the risk of giving the other an advantage?

QUESTIONS

1. If you were a leader of a European country, would you support the demonstrations? What would you say to the United States and the Soviet Union?
2. If you were the leader of either the United States or the Soviet Union, would you take the risk of cutting back on arms if the other side did not?
3. Do you think war is inevitable, or that the "Balance of Terror" will prevent war?

Planet Earth as photographed by the Apollo 16 astronauts.

Epilogue: What Kind of Future for Planet Earth?

*I*n what occupations will there be plenty of jobs? How much money will I make in ten years? What type of housing will be available?

People have always thought about the future. Generally they have hoped that the future would be better for themselves and for their children. But now people realize that their own decisions determine the future. In effect, we ourselves create our future. Thus, there are many possible futures—some good and some horrible. Presently, experts in future studies usually can be divided into the three following groups.

Continuation of Major Trends This group sees the future as a continuation of present trends. In other words, the world population will grow but there will be no major world famines. Local wars and revolutions will continue with increased acts of terrorism. However, there will be no major international wars between the superpowers. In addition, technology will continue its rapid advancement in all fields—space, biology, and communications, to name just a few. In developed nations there will be more time and money spent on leisure—games, sports, entertainment, travel, dance, theater, and video. In addition, there will be more options available in careers for both men and women. However, the price of natural resources, especially oil and natural gas, will continue to rise. This will make it more difficult for people, especially those in developing nations, to make a real improvement in their standard of living.

Pessimistic Approach In contrast to the continuation of major trends approach, pessimists see the worst things happening in the future. Pessimists predict that developing nations will not be able to feed their growing population. The population explosion will lead to malnutrition, widespread unemployment, growing urban slums, increased pollution, and widespread social unrest that could lead to civil wars and revolutions. Because of the huge problems that the developing nations face, poor nations will feel even more resentment against the rich industrialized nations. According to the pessimists, tensions between the rich and poor nations and between the United States and the Soviet Union are likely to lead to major international wars, possibly a catastrophic nuclear war. There also may be costly local wars as nations fight for resources.

Even if major wars are avoided, pessimists see serious problems with increased air and water pollution, acid rain, high inflation, and slow economic growth and progress during the coming years.

The Optimistic Approach Optimists are those who see a positive future. In general, optimists believe that technology, as in the past, will continue to solve the multiple problems facing the world. According to this view, 200 years ago almost all the people in the world were poor and at the mercy of nature. Now, in the 1980s, more people are rich. We have a superior technology to use. Thus, continuing this trend, in the future the rich will get richer. More poor people will rise out of poverty. Higher yields from crops and multiple plantings per year should allow the many people in the world to be fed. In addition, population growth can be controlled with better birth control methods.

For the optimists, the world will not run out of energy or any other critical resources. Instead, new breakthroughs in energy will allow us to use different sources of energy. Even with a growing population of billions of people, there still can be a high standard of living. People will have a variety of choices: from the type of home that they wish to live in to more opportunities for women and men in their occupations and in their leisure activities. Workers will have more decision making in setting up their job tasks. Citizens will become more involved in political decisions.

Variations Variations exist within these three main opinions on what the future holds. For example, some people are qualified optimists. They are hopeful for the future. However, they think that a major war or poor management could cause serious difficulties. They feel that there may be negative consequences from "good" scientific advances. For example, what will be the impact if vast numbers of people live ten years longer? In a similar manner, some pessimists think that conservation of energy resources and more help for developing nations could move us away from disaster.

There are important issues that humans throughout the world, including you, have to consider. The future will be what people make it. Looking at both the good and the bad can contribute to better decision making. Four areas to consider are population, food, health, and energy.

Population According to United Nations predictions, the world population should increase in twenty years from 4.4 billion to 6.2 billion. The greatest increases have been occurring among poorer nations. Such population increases place a heavy burden upon the economies of poor nations. Advances made in agriculture, industry, or business go to support the added population. This makes it hard to improve the standard of living for already poor people. Also, social unrest increases if people's basic needs are not met.

Developing nations can reduce their population. As late as 1949, the Chinese government did not try to reduce the population. The Chinese population increased by 600 million. Now the Chinese government is very concerned about the population growth. Rewards are given to couples who have only one child while penalties are given to those with larger families. The legal age for marriage in China has been raised to 22 for males and 20 for females. China hopes for a zero population growth in the year 2000. At that time it will have a total population of 1.2 billion, about one-fifth of the world's population.

Questions for the Future Should efforts to reduce the population be intensified? Should families have a basic right to decide on the number of children they want? Should the United States and other nations raise the legal age for marriage?

Food With world population growing, more food is needed. We are not adequately feeding our present world population. The United Nations estimates that about 23 percent of the total population, about 1.1 billion people, have an inadequate diet. These people eat less than 1,600 calories a day. In such developed nations as the United States and Canada, people average about 3,100 calories per day.

Developing nations can probably improve their food production. New technology, increased used of fertilizers, and better food processing and conservation can improve food yields. For example, due to rodents, molds, and insects, about 20 percent of the food produced in developing nations spoils or rots. This food could be saved.

Yet major problems exist in food production and distribution. To help increase food production, governments often give farmers a higher price (a farm subsidy) for their products. But these prices help the larger producers who have a surplus. They do little for the poorer farmers who only feed themselves and their families. Small farmers also need support to be able to use new seeds, irrigation, and technology to increase the yield of their crops. Food shortages may increase due to the increase in the price of oil and other energy supplies. Water supplies are critical in some areas. In other places, forests are being cut down without reforestation.

Questions for the Future What should the government of a developing nation do to increase food production? What do you think are the best ways to feed the urban poor?

Health The best measure of the health of a nation is the life expectancy at birth. In developed nations, people on the average live over seventy years. In poorer nations the life expectancy can be less than forty-five years, as in Afghanistan, Angola, Ethiopia and other nations. In Africa the life expectancy is forty-nine years.

The reduced life expectancy in poorer nations is due mainly to infant mortality. Many infants die the first year of life. Those fortunate enough to survive childhood usually live six to eight years less than people in rich nations. The life span in poorer nations is reduced by inadequate diet, unsafe water, and little or no health services. The vast majority of the medical resources of the world go to people in developed nations or the wealthier class in developing nations. Yet the rich societies are filled with people who overeat, overuse drugs, and drive recklessly.

Questions for the Future Should we intensify our efforts to discourage people from smoking and overusing drugs? Should more attention be given to home care and self-help rather than expensive hospital care? Should we push research that will help more people live to be ninety or one hundred?

Energy Since 1973, when OPEC sharply increased the price of oil, nations have faced an energy crisis. Formerly cheap oil has become an expensive fuel. It appears that there may not be enough traditional energy resources to serve the world's population. The supply of energy resources is expected to become even tighter in the 1990s as competition for existing energy resources rises. Thus, there probably may have to be a transition from fossil fuels such as oil and gas to a mixture of other energy sources—synfuels, solar, nuclear, wind, and ocean power. How soon this transition can be made is uncertain.

Questions for the Future Should cars be the major means of transportation? Do you think people are willing to conserve energy resources? What are the best ways to make people conserve energy?

Science and Technology Science has become increasingly important in our lives. Advances in medicine have improved people's lives in many ways. Advances in electronics have made possible the widespread use of computers, radio, television, and many other products. The use of computers is rapidly changing the way people work, and may soon affect education and home life as profoundly.

Nuclear energy has offered new possibilities for both good and bad. Some feel that nuclear energy could solve all our energy problems. Others feel that nuclear energy plants are too dangerous to use. They worry because the problem of disposing of nuclear wastes remains unsolved.

Many people are worried about the increasing destructiveness of atomic weapons. They fear that some nation will launch a nuclear war. This would increase the risk of radiation exposure for the whole world. Increasing concern about atomic weapons has led to more thinking about the control of advanced weapons. However, people also worry about whether or not disarmament agreements can be enforced.

Questions for the Future Will the production of new atomic weapons bring us closer to war? Closer to peace? Will nations agree to disarm?

You have examined some of the possible futures. What do you think the future should be?

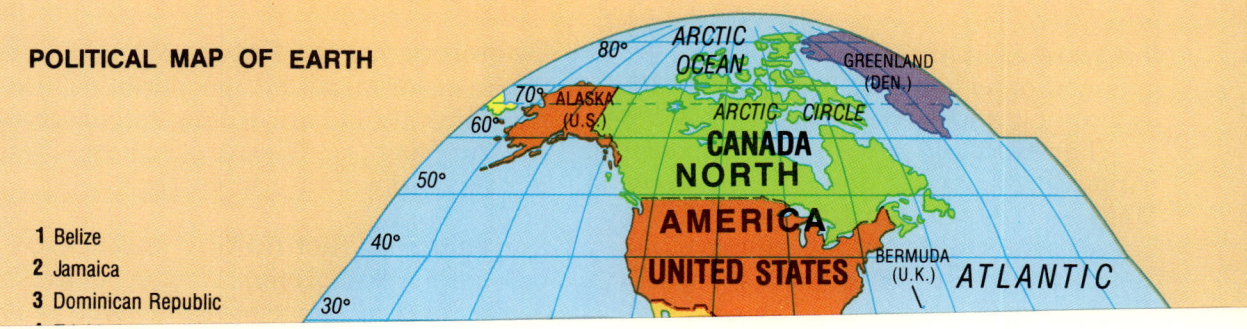

POLITICAL MAP OF EARTH

1 Belize
2 Jamaica
3 Dominican Republic

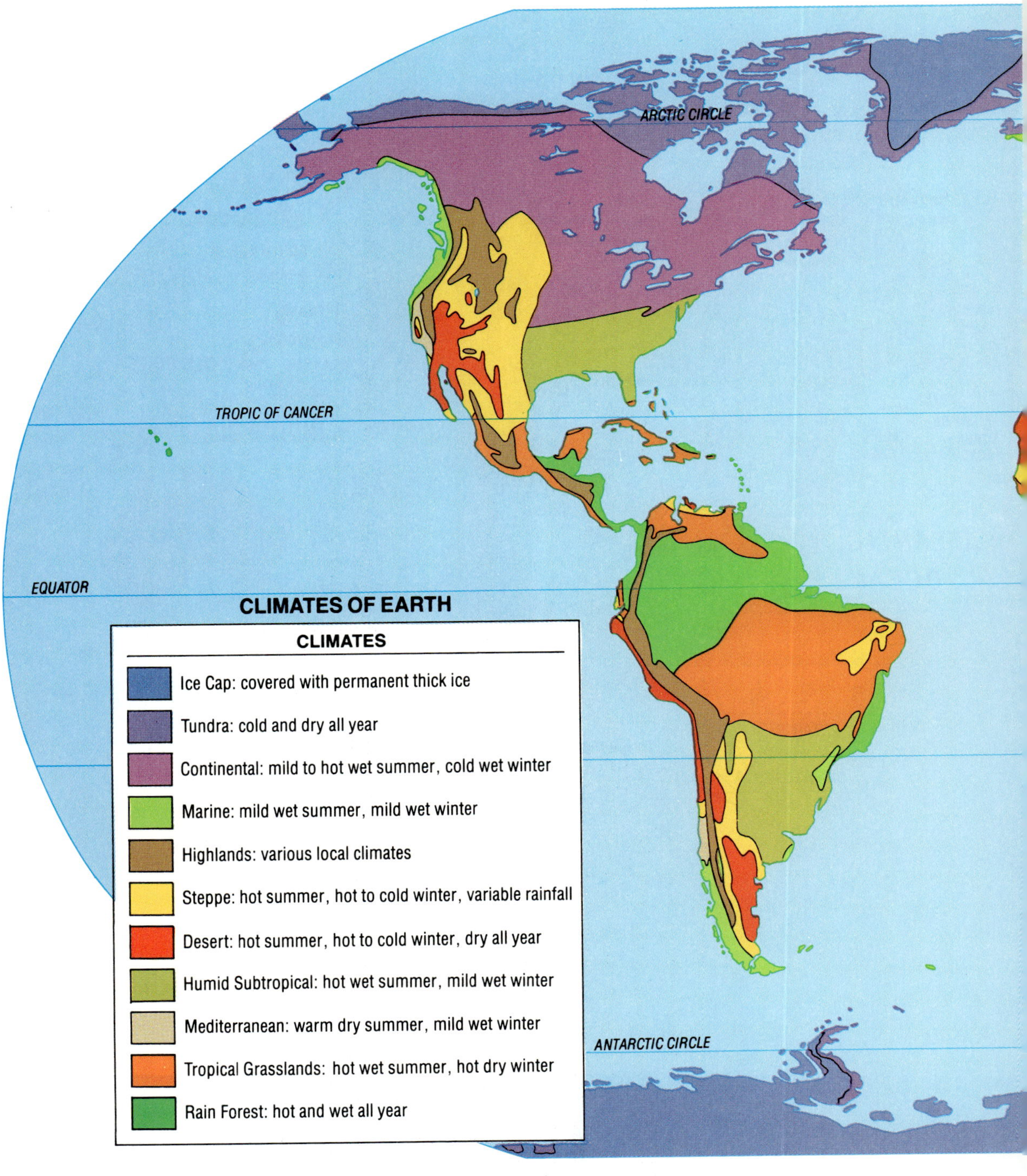

ARCTIC OCEAN
80°
70°
60°
50°
40°
30°
ALASKA (U.S.)
GREENLAND (DEN.)
ARCTIC CIRCLE
CANADA
NORTH AMERICA
UNITED STATES
BERMUDA (U.K.)
ATLANTIC

ARCTIC CIRCLE
TROPIC OF CANCER
EQUATOR
ANTARCTIC CIRCLE
CLIMATES OF EARTH
CLIMATES
Ice Cap: covered with permanent thick ice
Tundra: cold and dry all year
Continental: mild to hot wet summer, cold wet winter
Marine: mild wet summer, mild wet winter
Highlands: various local climates
Steppe: hot summer, hot to cold winter, variable rainfall
Desert: hot summer, hot to cold winter, dry all year
Humid Subtropical: hot wet summer, mild wet winter
Mediterranean: warm dry summer, mild wet winter
Tropical Grasslands: hot wet summer, hot dry winter
Rain Forest: hot and wet all year

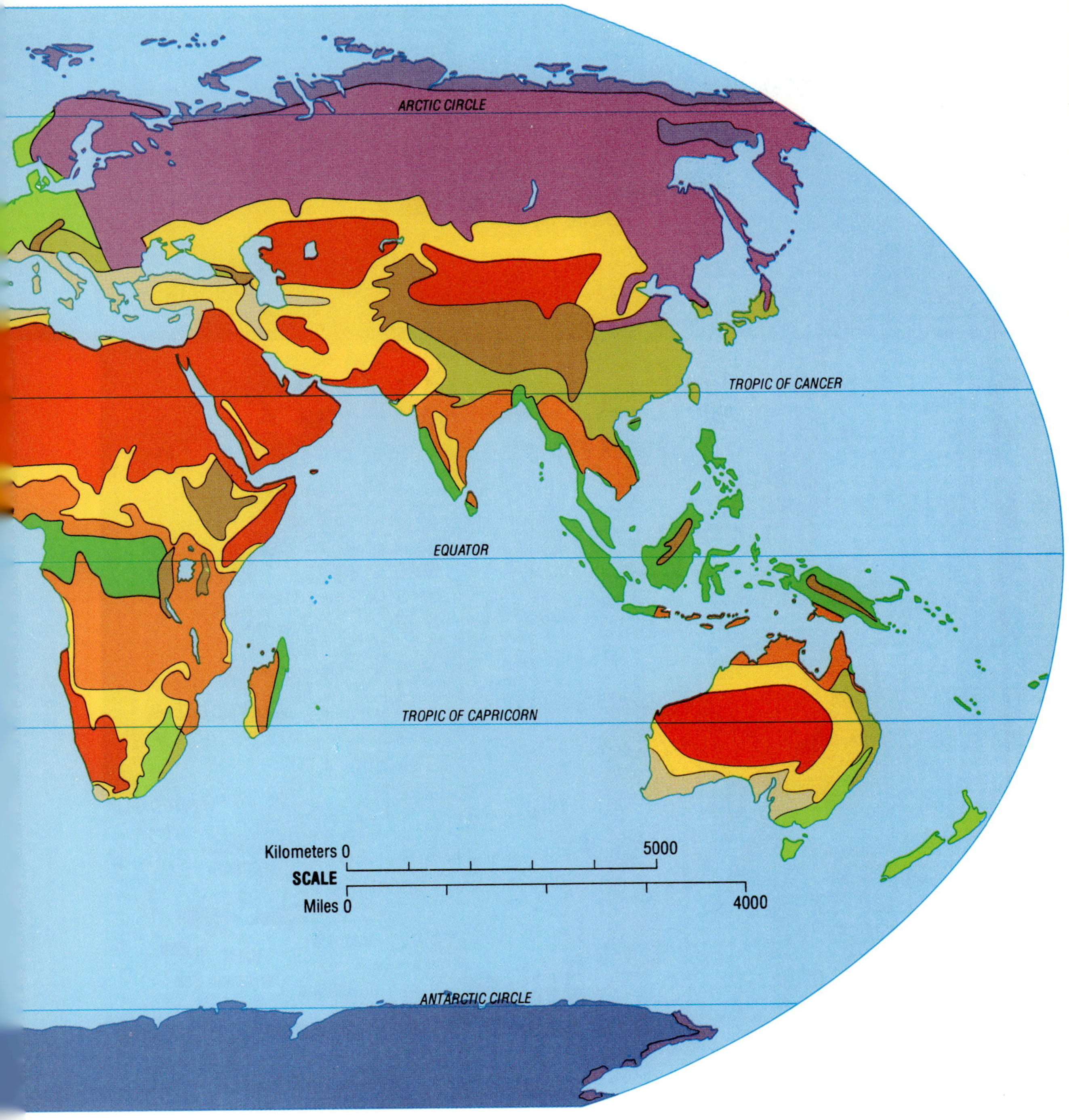

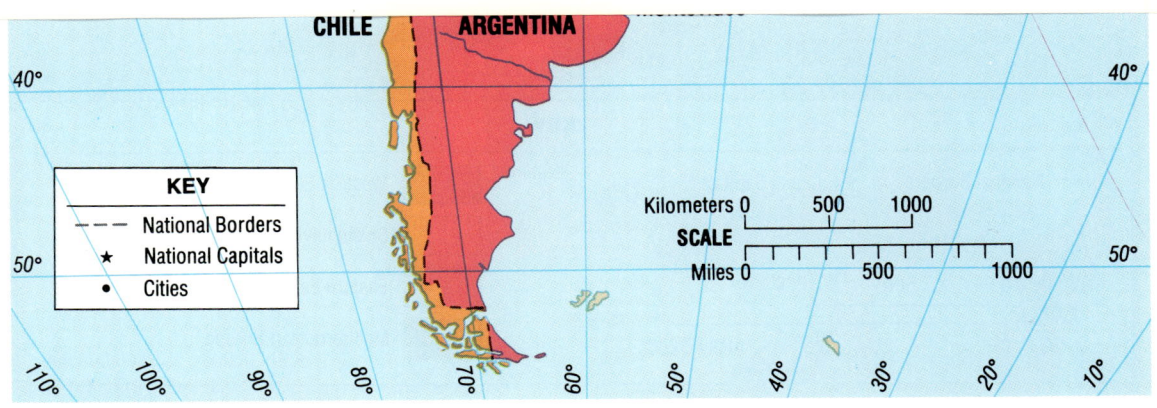

709

711

713

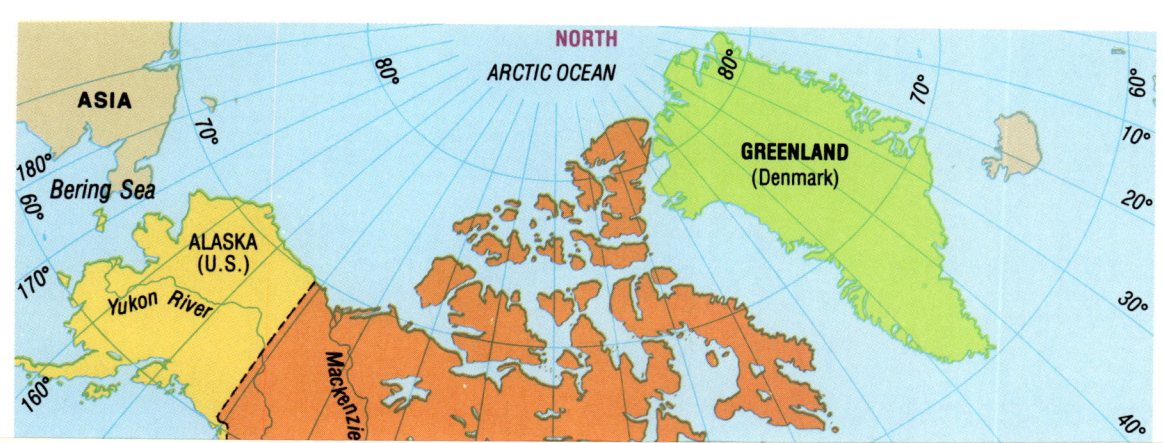

PHYSICAL MAP OF ASIA

ELEVATION

Meters	Feet
over 4,000	over 13,100
2,000 to 4,000	6,600 to 13,100
1,000 to 2,000	3,300 to 6,600
200 to 1,000	660 to 3,300
sea level to 200	sea level to 660
below sea level	below sea level

KEY

— — — National Borders   • Cities

Glossary

absolute monarch (AB suh loot MON ark) A ruler with no limits to his or her power.
acropolis (uh KROP uh lis) High city.
acupuncture (AK yoo PUNGK cher) A technique in which hot or cold needles are inserted into the body along the pulse routes to bring relief.
adobe (uh DO bee) Sun-dried brick.
Afrikaners (AF ruh KAH nerz) Dutch settlers who considered Africa their homeland but remained culturally European.
agora (AG er uh) Marketplace.
agriculture (AG ruh KUL cher) A systematic way of producing crops and raising animals.
Allah (AH luh) In the Islamic religion the one god who knows all, sees all, and guides all.
Allied Powers (Al lied) World War I, Britain, France, and Russia. World War II, Britain, United States and the Soviet Union.
augustus (aw GUS tus) Emperor.
ally (ah LY) To fight together.
ally (al LY) A state which has agreed to help another state.
anarchists (AN ark ists) Those who rebel against any authority and often use violent means to overthrow the government.
annul (uh NUL) Set aside.
anthropology (AN thruh PAHL uh jee) The scientific study of the origins and cultural development of human beings.
apartheid (uh PART hayd) White supremacy based on separation of the races.
appeasement (uh PEEZ muhnt) Satisfying by giving in to some demands.
aqueducts (AK wuh dukts) Roman structures that carried drinking water across rivers and valleys.
arbitration (AR buh TRAY shun) Turning a conflict over to a permanent international court.
aristocracy (AIR uh STOCK ruh see) Ruling class.
Arabic numerals (AIR uh bik) Components of a number system developed by the Hindus that uses the numerical symbols 1, 2, 3, 4, 5, 6, 7, 8, 9, and 0.
arcades (ar KAYDZ) Arched, covered passageways.
archaeologists (AR kee AHL uh jists) Scientists who study how people lived long ago.
artifacts (AR tuh fakts) Objects made by people.
artisans (AR tuh zunz) Skilled workers.
atheism (AY thee iz um) Belief in no gods.

atheists (AY thee ists) People who do not believe in God.
ayatullah (eye YEH tuh luh or eye yeh TUH lah) Religious leader.

baptism (BAP tiz um) The act of submerging the body in water that symbolized the washing away of sins.
barbarians (bar BAIR ee uhnz) Inferior foreigners.
barometer (buh ROM uh ter) An instrument that measures air pressure and can be used to forecast the weather.
barter (BAR ter) Trade of one good for another.
bias (BY uhs) Distorted or personal judgement.
bilateral (by LAT er uhl) Societies that trace descent from both parents.
Black Shirts Groups of former soldiers who actively supported Mussolini.
blasphemy (BLASS fuh mee) An insult to God.
blitzkrieg (BLITS kreeg) Method of warfare in which an army moves with amazing speed.
blockade (blah KAYD) To prevent ships and supplies from reaching the enemy.
Boer (BOR) Dutch settlers in Africa.
Bolsheviks (BOHL shuh viks) "Majority men," those favoring a small underground organization to lead the workers to revolt. Also, participants in the Russian Revolution who belonged to the Communist Party of the Soviet Union.
bourgeoisie (BOOR zhwah ZEE) A middle class that included merchants and skilled craftworkers and their families.
Boxers Patriotic society whose members practiced the various martial arts and were dedicated to reviving the power of China.
boyars (boh YARZ) Russia nobles.
boycott (BOY cot) To refuse to buy.
brahman (BRAH muhn) A universal spirit.
bridewealth (BRYD welth) Payment of cattle, weapons, pieces of iron, or other goods by the husband's family to the family of his new wife.
Brown Shirts Followers of Hitler.
bunker (BUNG ker) An underground bomb shelter.
bureaucrats (BYUR uh krats) Government workers.

cabinet (KAB uh nuht) A small group of leaders in Parliament.

caesar (SEE zuhr) Assistant and eventual successor to the emperor.
calculus (KAL cyuh lus) A branch of mathematics dealing with changing quantities.
caliph (KAY luhf) Successor of Muhammad.
calligraphy (kuh LIG ruh fee) Beautiful handwriting.
cannisters (KAN uh sterz) Metal food containers.
canon law (KAN un) Church law.
capital (KAP uh tuhl) Money.
capitalism (KAP uh tuh LIZ um) An economic system in which money and resources are put into business and industry to make more money.
caste system (KAST) People's inherited class positions.
castles (KAS uhlz) Structures with heavy walls and high lookout towers built as forts for security and protection.
catapults (KAT uh pults) Ancient military machines for hurling large stones.
cataract (KAT uh RAKT) Rapids on a river.
catechisms (KAT uh KIZ umz) Books that summarized the teachings of the church.
cathedral (kuh THEE drul) The main church of a bishop.
caudillos (kaw DEE lyohz) Military dictators.
Cavaliers (kav uh LEERZ) Royalists, people who supported the king.
cavalry (KAV uhl ree) Soldiers mounted on horses.
censors (SEN serz) Roman officials elected to draw up the list of citizens on the tax rolls and to oversee work on public buildings and roads.
census (SEN sus) A counting of all the people and a recording of every piece of land, its size, and taxes paid.
Central Powers During World War I, Ottoman Turks, Austria-Hungary, and Germany.
charter (CHAR ter) A written document giving the town or city the right to make its own laws and have its own courts.
chastity (CHAS tuh tee) Virginity.
chiaroscuro (kee AR uh SKYUR oh) Variations in the shades of light and dark.
chivalry (SHIV uhl ree) A code of honor or proper conduct.
Christian doctrine (KRIS tyun DOK trun) A system of beliefs and principles based on the teachings of Jesus.
citadel (SIT uh duhl) A fort.
city-state The city and its surrounding lands.
civil service (SIV uhl) System by which government officials were chosen through written tests.

clans (KLANZ) Communities of people related to each other.
classifying (KLASS uh fy ing) Ordering information in a useful way.
clergy (KLUR jee) Individuals ordained for religious service.
Code Napoleon (KOHD nuh POHL ee uhn) A code defining the rights of citizens that became the basis of French law.
codification (KOD uh fuh KAY shun) Organization in systematic form.
coexist (KOH ig ZIST) To live peacefully without harming each other.
coexistence (KOH ig ZIS tuns) Living together in peace.
cold war A state of tension between nations, stopping short of actual, full-scale war.
collectives (kuh LEK tivz) Small farms joined together and worked in common.
colony (KOL uh nee) Area in which the government was directly under the control of the mother country.
combustion (kum BUS chun) Fire.
Common Market An economic association that promotes trade among its members by reducing tariffs and allowing movement of people and materials to where they were needed.
communes (KOM yoonz) Large shared farms worked by 10,000 to 15,000 peasants.
communism (KOM yuh niz um) The abolishment of private property with all property held in common.
Communist (KOM yuh nist) Name adopted by the Bolshevik Party.
compound (KOM pownd) A fenced-in group of dwellings.
conservative (kun SER vuh tiv) A person who favored the traditions and values of the past.
consul (KON sul) Office of chief executive of the Roman Republic.
cooperative (koh OP uhr uh tiv) An enterprise owned and managed by the workers themselves for a share in the profits.
cossacks (KOS aks) Russian armed horsemen.
council of elders (EL derz) A law-making body of twenty-eight Spartan men over the age of sixty who had retired from the army.
coup (KOO) A change in government by force.
cremation (kree MAY shun) Burning of bodies.
creoles (criollos) (KREE ohlz) People of Spanish ancestry born in Latin America.
crop rotation (roh TAY shun) Growing different

crops at different times of the year so that the same minerals are not taken from the soil.

Crusades (kroo SAYDZ) Wars against the Muslims to regain control of the Holy Land.

cultural anthropologists (KUL cher uhl AN thruh pahl uh jists) Scientists who study present-day cultures.

Cultural Revolution (KUL cher uhl rev uh LOO shun) A personal campaign by Mao to restore the revolutionary spirit to the Chinese Communist Party.

culture (KUL chur) The traditional body of acceptable customs that a group has.

cuneiform (kyoo NEE uh form) Sumerian system of writing.

czar (ZAR) Supreme ruler.

daimyo (DI mee o) Local leaders of Japan who controlled small areas.

Dark Ages Early part of the Middle Ages in which little advancement was made in knowledge and in the arts in Europe.

deductive reasoning (dee DUCK tiv) Arriving at a conclusion through the use of reason.

Deism (DEE iz um) The belief in a Divine Being who created the world and set it in motion.

delta (DEL tuh) Fertile triangular area at the mouth of a river.

demilitarized (dee MIL uh tuh ryzd) Prohibited from having troops stationed in that area.

democracy (duh MOK ruh see) Rule by the people.

depressions (di PRESH unz) Periods of severe reduction in the demand for goods and services.

Der Fuhrer (der FYUR er) "The leader," a name given Hitler.

detente (day TAHNT) A relaxing of strain and hostility among nations.

dharma (DAR muh) The laws of one's caste and society.

diadem (DY uh dem) Crown.

Diaspora (di AS puh ruh) The scattering of the Jews throughout the world.

dictator (DIK tay ter) Officer of the Roman Republic exercising absolute power in wartime.

dikes (DYKS) Banks of built-up soil.

Directory (duh REK tuh ree) The government of France after the French Revolution. Five men held executive power.

direct rule Colonial administrators governing directly, with few native leaders.

divination ceremonies (DIV uh NAY shun SAIR uh MOH neez) Ceremonies using oracle bones to interpret answers to written questions.

division of labor The occupational structure in which workers become specialists.

doctrine (DOK trun) Set of principles underlying government policy.

domestication (duh MESS ti KAY shun) Taming and control of animals and plants.

dowry (DOW ree) A gift of currency or goods given by the bride's father to her husband's family.

druids (DROO idz) Celtic leaders or sages.

duchies (DUTCH eez) Kingdoms ruled by dukes.

Duma (DOO mah) A parliament formed by Nicholas II as a concession to the demands of the people.

dynasty (DY nuh stee) Ruling family that maintains its position for a considerable time.

economic sanctions (EE kuh NOM ik SANGK shunz) A measure to prohibit the sale of raw materials or weapons to an aggressor.

edicts (EE dikts) Orders with the force of law.

ellipse (ih LIPS) Oval-shaped path.

emigres (EM uh grayz) Nobles who fled from France.

emmer (EM er) A coarse wheat.

empire (EM pyr) A large area ruled by one leader or government.

ephors (EF erz) Overseers.

Epicureanism (EP uh kyu REE uh niz um) Philosophy teaching that pleasure is the goal of society.

estates (eh stayts) Social classes in France.

Estates General French legislative body consisting of elected members from all three estates.

evidence (EV uh dens) Anything that offers proof.

excavate (EK skuh vayt) To dig up.

excommunication (EK skuh MYOO nuh KAY shun) Power of banishing sinners from the community of the faithful.

exiled (EG zyld) Sent away.

facts Any pieces of information.

factories (FAK tuh reez) Large buildings in which manufacturing is done by a large number of workers.

fallow (FAL loh) Plowed but not seeded.

fascism (FASH iz um) A dictatorship in which the state was supreme and controlled the life of the nation.

Fascism (FASH iz um) The government system of Italy under Mussolini.

feudalism (FYOO duhl iz um) A political system lacking a strong central government.

fiefs (FEEFS) Feudal states.

figureheads (FIG yer HEDZ) Rulers in name only.

filial piety (FILL ee ul PY uh tee) The loyalty and respect of children toward their parents.

Foreign Legion (FOR uhn LEE jun) A French mercenary army.

fossils (FOSS ulz) The remains of plants and animals that are buried in rock.

freebooters (FREE boo terz) Violent gangs in search of new leaders and new causes.

frescoes (FRESS kohz) Paintings made on wet plaster walls.

garrisons (GAIR uh sunz) Fortified towns.

genealogy (JEE nee AL uh jee) Record of the descent of a family or group.

genius (JEE nyus) In ancient Rome, the spirit who guarded the family and represented the fertility of the father.

genocide (JEN uh syd) Planned murder of the entire Jewish (or other) population.

gens (JENZ) In Etruscan society, the large family.

gentiles (JEN tylz) Non-Jews.

gentry (JEN tree) In Russia, a new group of nobles who served the state as military officers or government officials.

geologist (jee AHL uh jist) Scientist who studies the Earth.

ghee (GEE) Clarified butter used in India for rituals and sacrifices.

glaciers (GLAY sherz) Large ice sheets.

go mata (GO MAH tuh) Cow mother.

Gothic (GOTH ik) Architectural style that was light and airy and featured arches and flying buttresses.

grand bourgeoisie (GRAND BOOR zhwah ZEE) Bankers and wealthy merchants.

gravity (GRAV uh tee) A force that pulls objects together.

Great Leap Forward Mao Zedong's plan to double China's production in agriculture and industry.

Great Purge (PURJ) A four-year period during which anyone suspected of harboring anti-Stalinist feelings was eliminated.

guerrilla warfare (guh RILL uh WAR fair) Fighting in which small armed forces make surprise raids and then flee before the enemy can capture them.

guilds (GILDZ) Organizations to protect the common interests of various trades or occupations.

guillotine (GILL uh teen) A machine for beheading.

haciendas (hah see EN duz) Estates in Latin America.

harquebus (HAR kwuh bus) An early type of portable gun.

Hegira (hih JY ruh) Migration of Muhammed from Mecca to Medina.

Hellenic (heh LEN ik) Ancient Greek culture that was a mixture of Aegean, Mycenaean, Minoan, and Dorian influences.

Hellenistic (HEL uh NIS tik) A blend of Greek and Oriental culture.

helots (HEL uts) Enslaved farm laborers thought to be descendents of Aegeans.

hemophilia (HEE muh FILL ee uh) A hereditary disease in which blood does not clot normally.

heraldry (HAIR ul dree) Coats of arms and other symbols.

heresy (HAIR uh see) A religious opinion contrary to church doctrine.

hermits (HER mits) Small groups of Christians living simple lives of prayer and fasting.

hierarchy (HY uh rar kee) Levels of power.

hieroglyphics (HY er uh GLIF iks) Egyptian writing using pictures and symbols for words, ideas, and sounds.

Holocaust (HAHL uh kost) Widespread attempt by Hitler to exterminate the Jews.

holy of holies The innermost sanctuary of the Jewish temple where only the high priest was allowed to enter.

Homo erectus (HO mo ee REK tus) Prehistoric people with an erect stance.

Homo habilis (HO mo huh BIH lis) "Able Human beings." Scavengers and gatherers who roamed the Earth over one million years ago.

Homo sapiens (HO mo SAY pee enz) "Modern man," or "wise, or thinking, human being."

Huguenots (HYOO guh nahts) French Calvinists.

ideographs (ID ee uh grafs) Symbols combined to produce ideas, as in ancient Chinese writing.

idols (IY duhlz) Statues of the gods used as objects of worship.

ideology (IY dee AHL uh jee) Belief system.

Il Duce (ill DOO chay) A name given Mussolini meaning "the Leader."

imperialism (im PIR ee uh LIZ um) Domination of one nation over another.

incisions (in SIZH unz) Impressions marked on clay tablets.

indigo (IN dih goh) Raw material from which blue dye is made.
indirect rule A ruling policy under which some attempt was made to preserve the traditional structure of African (or other colonial) society.
individualism (in duh VIJ oo uh LIZ um) Discovery of the self.
indulgences (in DULL jun suz) Remission of temporal punishment for sins.
inflation (in FLAY shun) A sharp increase in the prices of goods and services.
infrastructure (IN fruh STRUK cher) The building blocks on which a modern economy is built.
Inquisition (in kwuh ZISH un) A court established to find and root out heresy.
insignia (in SIG nee uh) An emblem.
institutions (IN sti too shunz) The long-lasting customs or rules in society.
isolationism (IY suh LAY shuh niz um) Separation from world affairs.

jen Humanity, an ideal of Confucianism.
jihad (juh HAHD) Holy war, the struggle against the enemies of Islam, or against evil in one's own life.
jizya (jeez YAH) A special tax on non-Muslims.

Kaaba (KAH buh) A small black stone set in the side of the Great Mosque at Mecca.
kamikaze (KAH mee KAH zee) "Divine wind" that destroyed Mongol ships on their way to attack Japan. (In World War II, Japanese pilots who were sent on suicide missions.)
khedive (kuh DEEV) The title of rulers of Egypt in the late 1800s.
Koran (ku RAN) A sacred book recording the revelations Muhammad received from Allah.
kulaks (koo LAHKS) Well-to-do peasant farmers.

labor-intensive Economy favoring human labor.
labor union An association that would represent all the workers in dealing with employers.
Lateran Agreements (LAT er un) An agreement creating an independent state, Vatican City, to be the headquarters of the pope and church.
latifundia (LAHT uh FUN dee uh) Large estates used mainly for cattle grazing.
latitude (LAT uh tood) The distance north or south of the equator.
legation (li GAY shun) Embassy quarters.
legion (LEE jun) An organization of soldiers positioned about 2½ meters from each other.

Lend-Lease (LEND LEES) Program in which weapons and supplies were sent to England from the United States during World War II.
levy (LEV ee) Law that allowed the Roman Republic to draft citizens into the army.
li (LEE) Solemn rites and music for people to follow in ancient China.
liberalism (LIB er uh LIZ um) In the late 1700s and early 1800s, the idea that people had the right to rebel against unjust rulers and were guaranteed freedom of speech, the press, and person.
lineage (LIN ee ij) All people who can trace their descent to a common ancestor.
linguists (LING gwists) Scientists who study language.
loess (LES) Yellow silt.
logarithms (LAW guh RITH umz) Exponents used to shorten complicated multiplication and division.
lost-wax method Method of sculpting bronze heads by first sculpting a wax figure, covering it with clay, heating it and draining out the melted wax through straws, and then pouring molten bronze to replace the wax.
loyalists (LOY uh lists) Those who remained loyal to Britain during the American Revolution.
Luftwaffe (LUFT vah fuh) German air force.

Maginot line (MAZH uh noh) Powerful French fortifications along their border with Germany.
mandates (MAN dayts) Regions administered by nations authorized by the League of Nations.
manors (MAN erz) Farming units during feudalism.
manorial agriculture (muh NOR ee uh) Economic system of feudalism.
maritime (MAIR uh tym) Overseas.
Marshall Plan (MAR shul) A plan offering economic aid to all European nations except Fascist Spain after World War II.
martial (MAR shul) Military.
matrilineal (MAT ruh LIN ee ul) Societies that trace descent through the mother's side.
matter (MAT er) The physical substance of anything.
Mau Mau movement (MOW MOW) Secret movement formed in Kenya to force independence.
mayor of the palace In Frankland in the 600s, one who ran the royal home and estates of the king.
mediation (MEE dee AY shun) Two countries asking a third to suggest a solution to an international dispute.

megadeath syndrome (MEG uh deth SIN drohm) A lack of emotional response when the suffering is too great for a person to grasp.

Mein Kampf (MYN KAHMF) A book written by Hitler that became the Nazi bible and set forth his ideas of all life being a continuous struggle.

Mensheviks (MEN shuh viks) "Minority men," a Russian group wanting to form a regular political party and work for gradual reform until the working class was ready for revolution.

mercantilism (MUR kun ti liz um) The idea that a nation's wealth was determined by the amount of gold and silver in the country.

merit (MAIR it) To prove capable. In government, workers selected by ability rather than through political influence.

Messiah (muh SY ah) A person inspired by God to deliver the Jewish people from oppression.

mestizos (meh STEE zohz) (usually Spanish) People of mixed white and Indian backgrounds.

microscope (MY kruh skohp) An instrument that magnifies objects by producing images larger than the original.

migrated (MY grayt ud) Moved.

mikado (muh KAH doh) Heavenly King, or emperor.

militarism (MIL uh tuh RIZ um) The glorification of the military.

minarets (min uh RETS) Slender towers used in Muslim architecture.

minutemen (MIN it MEN) Armed colonists in the North American colonies.

missionary (MISH uh nair ee) One who went to another country to teach a faith to the natives.

mobilize (MOH buh lyz) To get military forces ready to fight.

moksha (MOK sha) In the Hindu religion, freedom from rebirth.

monarchy (MON er kee) Rule by a king.

monasteries (MON uh STAIR eez) Simple religious communities.

monopoly (muh NAHP uh lee) Control of the source of a product, how much should be traded, the price it should bring, and who could buy and sell it.

monotheism (MON uh THEE iz um) A belief in one god.

monsoons (mon SOONZ) Winds that blow outward, sweeping across India and other countries, and toward the Indian Ocean.

mosaics (moh ZAY iks) Pictures or patterns made with bits of colored glass, stone, or enamel.

mosque (MOSK) A place of worship for Muslims.

mulattos (muh LAT ohz) People of mixed African and European background.

mummified (MUM uh fyd) Preserved or embalmed the body of a dead person.

mystics (MIS tiks) People who believed they could know God directly, without the aid of the church.

National Guard Local soldiers.

nationalism (NASH uh nuh LIZ um) The love of one's nation.

nationalize (NASH uh nuh lyz) The government takes over privately owned industry.

NATO (NA toh) North Atlantic Treaty Organization, a military alliance among western Europe and its allies.

New Deal Ambitious reforms designed to strengthen the economy during Franklin Roosevelt's presidency.

nirvana (neer VA nuh) In Hinduism, liberation from the chain of rebirths.

nobles (NOH bulz) Ruling class in Egyptian society (and later societies).

nomads (NOH madz) People who moved about from place to place.

nonviolent resistance (non VY uh lunt ri ZIS tuns) Use of peaceful means such as boycotts, hunger strikes, and protest rallies to gain independence.

oasis (oh AY sis) Water hole in the desert.

obelisks (OB uh lisks) Tall, pointed stone columns.

oligarchy (AHL uh GAR kee) A government ruled by a small group.

omens (OH munz) Events that Sumerian priests know how to interpret.

OPEC (OH pek) The Organization of Petroleum Exporting Countries, a group that sets oil prices.

Operation Barbarossa (BAR buh RO suh) The German invasion of the Soviet Union in World War II.

opium (OH pee um) A narcotic.

oracles (OR uh kulz) In religions such as the Sumerian, people whose voices gods use to speak.

ordination (ORD in AY shun) Ceremony in which bishops appointed the priests.

page (PAYJ) The first step, at age seven, in a boy's training for knighthood.

paleontologists (PAY lee un TOL uh jists) Geologists who study fossils.

Pan-Slavism (PAN SLAH viz um) The emphasis of cultural ties among Slavic people.

parables (PAIR ub bulz) Simple stories that taught moral lessons.
parliament (PAR luh munt) Council of state.
partition (par TISH un) Separation of India into two nations, India and Pakistan.
paterfamilias (PAY ter fuh MIL ee us) Father of the family.
patres (PAH trayz) Fathers, heads of the gens.
patriarch (PAY tree ark) Eldest male member and ruler of the family.
Patriarch (PAY tree ark) Highest church official in the Byzantine Empire.
patricians (puh TRISH unz) Nobles who served as the king's advisers in Rome.
patrilineal (PAT ruh LIN ee ul) Descent traced from the father.
Pax Romana (PAKS roh MAHN uh) Period of Roman peace, 27 B.C. to A.D. 180.
Pax Sinica (paks SIN ih kuh) Period of Chinese peace, 206 B.C. to A.D. 220.
peasants (PEZ ents) Farmers.
peers Equals or fellow vassals.
penal (PEE nul) Prison colony, or having to do with prison.
peninsulares (pen IN suh LAR ayz) People from the Spanish peninsula who ran the governments in Latin America until the Latin American revolutions.
peons (PEE onz) Peasants in Latin America.
perioeci (per ee EE si) "Dwellers around," the status given to people subjected to Spartan rule.
perspective (pur SPEK tiv) A technique that gives an appearance of depth in a two-dimensional medium such as painting.
petite bourgeoisie (pi TEET BOOR zhwah ZEE) Skilled workers and shop keepers.
pharaoh (FAIR oh) Ruler of ancient Egypt.
philosophes (fihl us SOFS) A small group of intellectuals who believed that by using reason along with careful observation and experimentation, human beings could improve society.
philosophy (fih LOS uh fee) A science that examines the basic questions about human values and the nature of reality.
physical environment (FIZ uh kul en VY run ment) The air, land formations, water, climate, and natural resources.
pictograph (PIK tuh graf) In writing, a character representing an object or idea, roughly the equivalent of an English word.
pilgrimage (PILL gruh mij) A trip to a holy place for religious reasons.

pillaged (PILL ijd) Looted and destroyed.
plague (PLAYG) A very serious epidemic disease.
plateau (pla TOH) High, relatively flat land that rises sharply from the land around it.
plebians (pli BE unz) Middle and lower class Romans.
poaching (POHCH ing) Hunting or fishing on the lord's land.
polis (PAHL us) City-state.
Politburo (puh LIT BYUR oh) Major organization of the Communist Party.
polyarchy (POL ee AR kee) Many states.
polygyny (puh LIJ uh nee) Practice by which a man can have more than one wife.
polytheism (POL ee THEE iz um) A belief in many gods.
pontiff (PON tif) Office of the Roman Republic that interpreted the law.
Popular Front A union in Spain of the socialists, Communists, and other radical groups to rally support during the Spanish Civil War.
porcelain (POR suh lin) Fine pottery made from white clay mixed with powdered rock and sand.
praetorian guard (pree TOR ee un) An elite corps of Roman troops trained to act as bodyguards.
praetors (PREE terz) Office of the Roman Republic created to administer justice and govern the city in the absence of the consuls.
prehistory (pree HIS ter ee) The time before writing.
premises (PREM is ez) Assumptions.
presbyters (PRES buh terz) Board of elders in a church.
primary sources Sources of evidence used by historians that include written records, oral tradition, and artifacts.
prime minister First minister.
private property Legal ownership of land and possessions.
proletariat (PROH luh TAIR ee ut) Working class.
propaganda (PROP uh GAN duh) The use of all forms of communication to control opinion.
prophet (PROF it) Person who feels compelled to speak for God, telling people of God's plan for them.
protectorate (pruh TEK ter it) An area controlled by a native ruler dependent on help from the mother country to maintain power.
Protestants (PROT uh stunts) Those who protested against the teachings and practices of the Roman Catholic Church.
pylons (PY lonz) Ceremonial walls of the Egyptian temple courtyards.

pyramid (PEER uh mid) Triangular burial place of the Egyptian pharoahs.
Pyrrhic victory (PEER ik) A victory at too great a cost.

quadrant (KWOD runt) Instrument to determine latitude.
quarantine (KWOR un TEEN) To isolate.
queue (KYOO) A braided pigtail.

race (RAYS) A group of people belonging to the same stock, or ancestory.
racism (RAY siz um) The belief that one race of people is superior to another.
Ramadan (ram uh DAHN) The ninth month of the Muslim calendar, the month when Muhammad had his first revelation.
realism (REE uh LIZ um) In painting, portraying things in a lifelike way.
redeemed (ri DEEMD) Atoned for.
Red Guards Chinese youth sent by Mao to purge society.
Reds Those loyal to Trotsky during the time of the Russian Revolution.
Reformation (REF er MAY shun) A religious movement to reform the Roman Catholic Church.
refugees (REF yuh jeez) Men, women and children with no homes, no place to go.
regent (REE junt) Acting ruler.
Reichstag (RYKS tahk) German parliament.
reincarnation (REE in kar NAY shun) In Hinduism, the position of the soul after rebirth.
Renaissance (REN uh SAHNS) A rebirth of the ideas of the ancient Greeks and Romans in Europe toward the end of the Middle Ages.
reparations (REP uh RAY shunz) Payment from a defeated nation for damage caused.
republic (ri PUB lik) Government in which power is divided among various offices and institutions, with the officers elected by the people.
reservation (REZ er VAY shun) Land set aside for a group of people, e.g., the Aborigines in Australia or the Indian tribes in the United States.
reservoirs (REZ er VWARZ) Large brick-lined tanks that caught and stored excess rains.
rhetoric (RET er ik) The art of persuasion.
Romanesque (ROH muh NESK) Architectural style using Roman features such as rounded arches and heavy walls.
Roundheads In the English Civil War, those supporting Parliament, so-called because of their short hair.

sacraments (SAK ruh munts) Rites believed necessary to achieve salvation.
sahel In Africa, marginal land between the savanna and desert regions.
SALT I Strategic Arms Limitation Treaty that limited the arms production in the United States and Soviet Union.
samurai (SAHM uh ry) Provincial warrior class of Japan.
Sanskrit (SAHN skrit) The language and system of writing of the Hindus that is used in the Vedas.
satrapies (SAY truh peez) Large districts of the Persian empire.
savanna (suh VAN uh) Tropical grasslands.
scapegoat (SKAYP GOHT) Someone to blame.
scholar-officials Men trained in the principles of Chinese government.
scientific method Searching for data and their meaning by careful observation and objective collection of data and verification of the accuracy of a finding or assertion.
scribes People whose job was to read and write.
secondary sources An account of an event or period that was written at a later time.
secular (SEK yuh ler) Everyday matters, as distinct from religious matters.
seismograph (SYZ muh graf) Device used to record the direction of earthquakes.
self-determination (SELF di ter muh NAY shun) Freedom of a people or area to decide its own political status.
seminary (SEM uh NAIR ee) A school for training priests.
sepoys (SEE poyz) Native troops employed by the British in colonial India.
serfs (SURFS) Slaves or near-slaves who lived and worked on the land owned by their masters.
shah (SHAH) A ruler in Iran (Persia).
sheriffs (SHAIR ifs) Local nobles who collected taxes and maintained the peace in feudal England.
Shi'ites (SHEE ites) In the Islamic religion, supporters of the house of Ali.
shoal (SHOHL) Sandbar.
shogun (SHOH gun) "Supreme military commander" in Japan.
silt Rich soil deposited by rivers.
slash-and-burn Cutting the trees and then burning the area to ensure the fertility of the land.
socialism (SOH shuh LIZ um) An economic system in which factories and mines are owned by the

people (the government), not by private individuals.
Socratic method (soh KRAT ik) A method of posing a series of related questions.
solar year The number of days it takes Earth to revolve around the sun.
soviets (SOH vee ets) Special committees formed by radical groups of workers and war veterans in Russia following World War I.
sphere of influence A technologically backward area which two or more nations agree to divide up for control of its raw materials.
spiritual (SPIR uh choo ul) Religious.
spyglass Telescope.
squadristi (sqod REES ti) Vigilanti groups organized by Mussolini.
squire A personal servant to the knight who was his master.
Stakhanovites (stuh KAHN uh VYTS) Those who set production records in the Soviet Union.
stelae (plural of stele) (STEE lee) Monuments on which dates are recorded.
steppe (STEP) Grassy plain.
stylus (STY lus) Stick used for writing on moist clay tablets.
subsistence farming Farming which supplied food only for one's own needs.
sudan (soo DAHN) The savanna in northern Africa.
sultan (SULT an) King.
Sunnites (SUN nyts) Those who believed the caliph could be appointed by the consent of the Islamic community.
surplus (SUR plus) More than what is needed or required.
syllogism (SIL uh jiz um) An argument based on deductive reasoning.
synagogue (SIN uh gog) Meeting house that was the center of Jewish life.

tanka (TAHNG kuh) Short poems with thirty-one syllables.
tariffs (TAIR ifs) Taxes on goods imported into the country.
technology (tek NOL uh jee) The use of complex tools and ideas.
tells (TELZ) Mounds.
theocracy (thee OK ruh see) Kind of government where the ruler is considered a god or a representative of a god.
theses (THEE seez) Statements.
toga (TOH guh) A cloak that was draped around the body in folds.

totalitarianism (toh TAL uh TAIR ee uh iz um) Total state control over people's lives.
totem (TOH tum) Clan symbol.
tribune (TRIB yoon) Roman office headed by two officers called tribunes who were to act as protectors of the plebians.
tribute (TRIB yoot) A form of tax.
Triple Alliance (al LY ens) The combination of Germany, Austria-Hungary, and Italy before and during World War I.
Triple Entente (ahn TAHNT) Before World War I, the group of Britain, France, and Russia.
triumvirate (try UM ver it) Rule by three.
tunic (TOO nik) A woolen or a linen garment sewed at the sides and held at the shoulders by clasps.

uji (oo gee) Family groups living in Japan 20,000 years ago.
uitlanders (Ayt lan derz) A boer term meaning "outsider" that referred to the miners who migrated to South Africa.
ulama (oo luh MAH) Islamic scholars.
ultimatum (UL tuh MAY tum) List of demands.
urban (UR bun) Consisting mainly of cities and their suburbs.

vandalism (VAN dul iz um) Willful or mindless destruction.
vassals (VAS ulz) In feudalism, servants who owe their allegiance to the noble.
Vedas (VAY duhz) A collection of thousands of sacred Hindu hymns.
veld (VELT) The savanna in southern Africa.
vizier (VIH zee ur) Second in command to the Egyptian pharaoh.

Warsaw Pact Agreement (WOR saw) A military alliance among the eastern European nations.
White Russians Those loyal to the czar during the Russian Revolution.
writs of assistance Broad search warrants.

yoga (YOH guh) Art of self-discipline.
yurts Felt tents used by Mongolian nomads.

ziggurat (ZIG u rat) In Sumer, a large temple built in the central part of the city.
Zionism (ZY uh niz um) The movement for an independent Jewish state in Palestine.
zodiac (ZOH dee ak) Map of the heavens used by astrologers to predict the future.

Index

A

Abbas, uncle of Muhammad, 198
Abbasid Caliphate. *See* Abbasid Dynasty.
Abbasid Dynasty, 189, 198-204, 288, 290
Abder-Rahman III, 189, 201
Aborigines, Australian, 2, 545
Abraham, as Muslim prophet, 194
Absolute monarch, *def.*, 251
Abu-Bakr, 194
Abu-Hamid al-Ghazali, 201
Abu-Nuwas, 199
Abu-Tammam, 199
Achaian, tribe of early Greeks, 86-88
Acropolis, *def.*, 88
Acupuncture, *def.*, 142
Adams, Sam, 408
Adena People, 310
Adobe, *def.*, 309
Adrianople, 171
Adriatic Sea, 106
Adua, battle at, 526
Aegean Sea, 88
Aeneid, 127
Aeolian tribe of early Greeks, 86
Aeolis, 86
Aeschylus, 99
Aetius, 172
Afghanistan, 143, 284, 290, 367, 533, 535-537, 550, 647, 654, 673, 680, 687-689, 698
Africa, agriculture, 14; and trade with Arabs, 200;
   history and development of, 260-280;
   kingdoms of, by 1400, 386-387;
   and slave trade, 375, 386, 387-389; 390;
   imperialism in, 384, 386, 387 506, 508-527; 528, 654;
   and First World War, 566; after Second World War, 689-698
Africaner, 510
Afrikaans, Dutch-Boer language, 517
Age of Industrialization, 490-506
Age of Justinian, 169, 176-177
Age of Metternich, 470, 473
Age of Reason, 422-438
Agora, *def.*, 89
Agriculture, *def.*, 14, ancient, 9, 11, 13-17, 18, 21, 34, 38, 50, 55-56, 64, 67, 68, 69, 70, 76, 77, 89-90, 106, 107, 115, 116, 132-133, 136, 139, 140, 156, 174, 175, 176; in middle ages, 190, 201, 204, 212-214, 220, 222-223, 236, 240, 262, 297;
   in the Americas, 307, 308-309, 313-314, 320, 322, 324;
   and early Slavic people, 359;
   in Ming dynasty, 369-370, 372;
   in Age of Reason, 433;
   during and after Industrial Revolution, 494, 596, 600, 638, 661, 663, 664, 668-669, 671, 696
Aguinaldo, Emilio, 548
Ahriman, 49
Ahura Mazda, Persian god, 49
Airplane, 563, 577, 623, 624, 625, 627, 629, 633, 651;
Aix-la-Chapelle, 183
Ajanta, 138
Akbar, Mogul emperor, 366-368, 372
Akkad, 41
Alamo, battle at, 482
Alamogordo, New Mexico, 634
Alaric, leader of Visigoths, 171-172
Alaska, 307, 308, 484, 532
Ala-ud-din Khilji, sultan, 285

Albania, 618, 648
Albert, English Prince, 478
Aldrin, Edwin "Buzz," 655
Aleutian Islands, 628
Aleuts, 308, 309. *See also* Eskimos, Innuits.
Alexander the Great, 48, 85, 96-97, 102, 131, 150, 687
Alexander I, czar of Russia, 459
Alexander II, czar of Russia, 477-479
Alexander III, czar of Russia, 479
Alexandra, wife of Nicholas II of Russia, 478
Alexandria, 97, 98, 135, 175, 181, 515
Alexis, Russian Prince, 478
Alfonso, king of the Kongo, 274-275, 280
Algeria, 195, 203, 503, 512, 528 662, 680, 681, 689-690, 693, 695, 698
Algiers, 509
Ali, cousin of Muhammad, 197
Allah, 49, 191, 204
Allende, Salvador, 647, 660
Allia River, 112
Allied Powers
   and First World War, 560, 562, 568, 570-573, 574
   and Second World War, 623, 632-633, 640, 646
All-Union Congress of Soviets, 592-593. *See also* Supreme Soviet.
Ally, *def.*, 93
Almohads, 203
Almoravids, 203
Alphabet, 37, 45, 50, 178
Alsace, 358, 476, 570, 571
Amazon River, 656
Amenhotep IV, 29. *See also* Ikhnaton.
American Civil War. *See* Civil War, in United States.

725

American Revolution, 407-411, 417
Amir Khusrau, Persian writer, 287
Amon-Re, 20, 29, 31
Amorites, 42-43, 50
Amur region, 532, 550
Anabaptists, 345
Analects, 72
Anarchist, *def.*, 479
Anastasia, wife of Ivan IV, 363
Andes Mountains, 320
Andhra empire, 133, 134, 135
Angles, 173, 174
Anglican Church, 331, 347, 348, 352, 399, 400, 401, 420
Anglo-Chinese War, 541, 550. *See also* Opium War.
Anglo-Egyptian Sudan, 519
Anglo-Saxons, 175, 186
Angola, 523, 524, 528, 654, 681, 692, 693, 695
Animals, domestication of, 14, 15-16
Annam, 540
Anne, queen of England, 405, 420
Annul, *def.*, 347
Antarctica, 557
Anthony, Mark, 120, 151
Anthropologists, 1, 381
Anti-Comintern Pact, 623, 627
Antigonus, founder of kingdom of Macedonia, 98
Antioch, 175
Antoninus, Antonio, Roman emperor, 124-125
Antwerp, 381
Anyang, 69
Apartheid, *def.*, 697
Apennine Mountains, 106
Aphrodite, Greek goddess, 98
Appalachian Mountains, 310
Appeasement, *def.*, 616; 618, 620, 626
Appert, Nicholas, 457
Aqaba, Gulf of, 683
Arabian American Oil Company, 685
Arabia, 189, 204, 680
Arab-Israel Wars, 681. *See also* Yom Kippur War.

Arabs, *def.*, 680; 181, 185, 186, 189, 190, 191, 261, 524, 583, 584, 600, 654, 682-683, 690, 698
Aramco. *See* Arabian American Oil Company.
Aragon, Spanish state, 227
Aral Sea, 533
Arbitration, *def.*, 561
Arcade, *def.*, 126
Archaeologists, *def.*, 2; 107, 265-266, 306-307, 313, 321
Archimedes, 101
Architecture, 29, 30-31, 34, 39, 47, 87, 99, 108, 117, 125-126, 137, 151, 159, 180, 184, 186, 197, 225, 229, 233, 239-240, 261, 268, 287, 290, 309, 313, 318, 337, 367
Ardennes, 624
Arequipa, 412
Argentina, 419, 437, 481, 656
Arianism, 178
Aristocracy, *def.*, 322
Aristophanes, 99
Aristotle, 85, 95, 100
Arkhangelsk, 564
Armada, Spanish, 355, 357, 372
Armenians, 566
Armistice, 569
Armistice Day, 576
Armstrong, Neil, 655
Arno River, 106
Art. *See* sculpture, architecture, painting, theater, music, dancing, literature.
Artemis, Greek goddess, 88
Artisan, *def.*, 26
Aryabhata, 137
Aryans, in India. *See* Indo-Aryans.
Aryans, Persian people, 47
Aryans, in Hitler's view of race, 611, 631
Asabaje, Juana Inés de, 380 *See also* Sister Juana.
Ashanti, 386, 387
Ashikaga, period of Japanese history, 303
Asia Minor, 92, 93, 97-98, 116, 118, 128, 157, 361, 506

Asoka, Indian king, 133, 140, 146
Assab, 525. *See also* Eritrea.
Assyrians, 21, 36, 37, 41, 45-47, 50
Astrolabe, *def.*, 376; 199
Astronomy, 284, 315, 341, 423-426
Atahualpa, Incan ruler, 378-379
Aten, Sun God, 29
Atheism, *def.*, 160
Atheist, *def.*, 433
Athene, Greek goddess, 88, 98
Athens, 85, 88, 89-90, 94-95, 99, 102, 157
Atlantic Charter, 630
Atlantic Ocean, 566, 629
Atomic bomb, 633-634, 637, 639, 640, 666
Attica, 86, 89
Attila, leader of huns, 169, 172
Augsburg, Peace of, 343
Augustine, Benedictine missionary, 175
Augustine, Saint, in North Africa, 171
Augustus Caesar, 105, 121, 122-124, 127, 135, 151, 152 *See also* Octavian.
Augustus, Roman title, 158
Aurangzeb, Mogul emperor, 368-369
Aurelius, Marcus, Roman emperor, 125, 156
Austerlitz, battle at, 455
Australia, 2, 487, 531, 545, 550, 566
Austria, 182, 226, 356, 441, 445, 452, 455, 458, 459, 467, 468-469, 473, 475, 488, 557, 572, 603, 616, 618, 620
Austria-Hungary Empire, 477, 557, 558, 559, 560, 564-565, 568, 570, 571, 572, 578, 600
Austrian Empire, 469, 477
Austrian Hapsburg Empire, 356
Automobiles, 577
Avars, 181
Averroes, 201-202
Avignon, 239, 249, 253, 254
Axis Powers, 618, 623, 627, 630

Ayacucho, Peru, battle at, 419
Ayatullah Khomeini. *See* Khomeini, Ayatullah Ruhollah.
Ayatullah, *def.*, 686
al-Azhar Mosque, 203
Azores, 376
Aztecs, 307, 308. 316-320

B

Baber, Mogul emperor, 286, 366, 372
Babylon, capital city of Sumer, 42, 43-44
Babylonia, 41, 42-43, 44, 45, 47, 266, 280
Babylonian Captivity, popes in France, 249
Babylonian Empire, 37, 50
Bacteria, 423, 432
Bactria, 143
Bactrians, 133-134, 146
Baghdad, 189, 198-200, 204
Bailiff. *See* steward.
Balance of power, 560, 574, 648
Balboa, Vasco Nunez de, 378
Balfour Declaration, 577, 584
Balkans, 178, 477, 479, 488, 557, 559-561, 571, 574
Baltic States, and Soviet control, 639
Baluchis, 687
Bangladesh, 667, 673, 678
Banking, 233, 579-580, 607
Bannockburn, battle at, 247, 398
Bantu, African people, 261, 270, 271, 273, 274, 280, 510, 511, 524, 528
Bantu, language, 270-371, 273, 274
Baptism, *def.*, 155
Baptism, adult, 345
Barometer, 423
Barter, *def.*, 184
Baruch, Hebrew prophet, 49
Basil III, Russian ruler, 362
Bastille, 436, 441, 443
Batista, Fulgencio, 658, 659
Battle of Britain, 623, 624-625, 629, 640

Battle of the Bulge, 633
Bavaria, failure of Nazis in, 603
Begin, Menachem, 683
Belgian Congo, 509, 522-523, 528, 692, 698. *See also* Congo Free State, Zaire.
Belgium, 182, 223, 469, 471, 488, 522-523, 528, 560, 562-563, 569, 570, 574, 624, 640, 661, 692
Belisarius, Roman general, 177
Belize country on Yucatan Peninsula, 312
Belize, stage of pre-Mayan culture, 307
Bell, Alexander Graham, 497
Benedict, Christian monk, 175-176
Benedictine Rule, 175, 176
Bengal, Bay of, 54
Benin, 279, 386-387, 390
Berber tribes, 195, 266, 512
Bering Strait, 11, 307, 308, 324, 532
Bering, Vitus, 531, 532, 550
Berlin, 522, 636, 647, 651, 652, 664
Bernard, Saint, 254
Bessemer, Henry, 494
Biafra, 694
Bias, *def.*, 102
Bible, 152, 160, 175, 178, 343, 433
Big Three, 648
Bilateral societies, *def.*, 276
Bill of Rights:
   English, 397, 404;
   in American Constitution, 412, 420
Bini, African people, 279
Biology, 423, 429-432
Birdseye, Clarence, 577
Bismarck, Otto von, 475-476, 488, 523, 558
Black Death. *See* plague.
Black Shirts, and Mussolini, 605, 606, 620
Black Plague. *See* plague.
Black Sea, 533, 550, 564, 566
Blanc, Louis, 471-472
Blasphemy, *def.*, 154

Blitzkrieg, *def.*, 622; 624, 626, 640
Blockade, *def.*, 456; 566
Blood River, battle at, 511
Bloody Mary. *See* Mary I, queen of England.
Boak, A.E.R., historian, 176
Boccacio, Italian writer, 334, 335
Boer War, 509, 518-519, 528
Boers, 510-511, 516-519, 528
Boeotia, 86
Bohemia, 226, 356, 358
Boleyn, Anne, 347-348
Bolívar, Simón, 418, 480
Bolivia, 480, 656
Bolshevik Party, 589, 591, 600
   See also Communist Party.
Bolshevik Revolution, 590-592, 594
Bolsheviks, *def.*, 589; 564, 568, 570, 577, 578, 580, 588-593, 600
Bombay, 138
Bonaparte, Joseph, king of Spain, 417
Boniface, Apostle of the Germans, 175
Boniface VIII, pope, 249
Book of Common Prayer, 400
Bookkeeping, 233
Book of Marco Polo, 283
Borneo, 540-541, 550
Borodino, battle at, 459
Boston Tea Party, 408
Botany Bay, 545
Bourbons, 358
Bourgeois, 501
Bourgeoisie, *def.*, 233
Bouvines, battle at, 249
Boxer, *def.*, 543
Boxer Rebellion, 531, 543-544, 548, 550
Boyars, *def.*, 362
Boycott, *def.*, 407; 583
Boyle, Robert, 428
Boyle's Law, 428
Brahe, Tycho, 424-425
Brahman, as soul, *def.*, 62
Brahmans, *def.*, 58, 133, 139
Brazil, 275, 376, 389, 414, 419, 420, 480, 481, 656

Brazza, Pierre de, 521
Brest-Litovsk, treaty of, 557, 570, 591
Breughel, Peter, painter, 339
Brezhnev, Leonid, 654, 664
Bridewealth, *def.*, 276
Britain, 124, 173-174, 175, 186, 224. *See also* England, Great Britain.
British East Africa, 524
British East India Company, 542
British North American Act, 487
Britons, 173
Brittany, 115, 173
Bronze, 18, 69, 77
Bronze Age, 9, 18, 38
Brown Shirts, 612, 620
Bronz, Joseph. *See* Tito.
Bruce, Robert, 398
Brutus, Marcus, 119
Bubonic plague. *See* plague.
Buddha, 53, 63. *See also* Gautama, Siddhartha.
Buddhism, 61, 62-64, 83, 133-134, 137, 139-140, 146, 288, 295, 300, 304
Bulgaria, 569, 627, 633, 648
Bunker, *def.*, 632
Bureaucrat, *def.*, 132
Burgundians, 173
Burma, 540, 550, 628, 676
Burton, Sir Richard, 513
Burundi, 273, 695
Bushmen, 12, 262, 270, 280
Byzantine Empire, 178-181, 186, 194, 196, 227, 229, 231, 359
Byzantium, 159, 160, 162, 178
See also Constantinople

C

Cabinet, *def.*, 405
Cabot, John, 383
Caerularius, Michael, Byzantine patriarch, 178
Caesar, Gaius Julius, 105, 118-119, 128, 150
Caesar, title, 158
Caesarea, 160
Cairo, 203, 515

Calculus, 426, 428
Calcutta, 670
Calendar, 32, 110, 119, 300, 306, 315, 319, 324, 449
California, 482
Caligula, Roman emperor, 124
Caliph, *def.*, 194, 204
Calligraphy, *def.*, 183. *See also* writing.
Calvin, John, 331, 344-346, 352
Calvinism, 344-346, 352, 358
Cambodia, 540, 550, 667, 676 677, 678
Cameroons, 271, 521, 524, 528
Campania, 106, 107
Canaan, 46
Canada, 308, 383, 385, 408, 467, 487, 488. *See also* Dominion of Canada.
Canary Islands, 376
Canberra, capital of Australia, 545
Cannae, 114
Cannister, *def.*, 457
Canon law, *def.*, 175
Canton. *See* Guangzhou.
Canute the Great, 224
Cape Colony, 511, 513, 516, 517, 519, 523
Cape of Good Hope, 262, 469
Cape Town, 510, 519
Capital, *def.*, 382
Capitalism, *def.*, 346, 382; and the Protestant Reformation, 346; and investment in trade, 382
Capitoline, Roman hill, 108
Caporetto, battle at, 565, 568
Caribbean area:
  pre-Mayan cultures of, 307; U.S. marines in, 587
Caribbean Sea, 378
Carolingian Empire, 169, 182-185
Carolus Magnus, Latin name for Charlemagne, 182
Carter, Howard, discoverer of Tutankhamen's tomb, 32
Carter, Jimmy, 654, 683-684, 689
Carthage, 106, 112-116, 128, 172, 181

Carthaginians, 105
Cartier, Jacques, 375, 383
Caspian Sea, 40, 171, 533, 550
Cassius, Gaius, 119
Caste System, 58-59, 63, 64, 133, 158, 286-287, 671
Cataract, *def.*, 22
Castile, Spanish state, 227
Castle, *def.*, 211
Castro, Fidel, 647, 657-659, 664
Catapult, *def.*, 289
Catechism, *def.*, 351
Cathedral, *def.*, 225
Catherine of Aragon, 347
Catherine, Saint, 254
Catholic Church. *See* Roman Catholic Church.
Cato, Roman senator, 116
Caucasia, 178
Caucasus Mountains, 290, 533
Caudillos, *def.*, 480
Cavaliers, *def.*, 400
Cavalry, *def.*, 47
Cavour, Count Camillo di, 474
Celts, 115, 175, 186
Censors, in Roman Republic, 111
Central America, 308-309, 379, 390, 480. *See also* names of individual countries.
Central Asia, Russian expansion in, 533-535, 550
Central Intelligence Agency (CIA), 658, 660
Central Powers, in First World War, 560, 562, 564, 565, 569
Cervantes, Miguel de, Spanish writer, 331, 340
Ceylon, 200, 469. *See also* Sri Lanka.
Chac, Mayan god, 313
Chad, 695
Chad, Lake, 262
Chaldeans, 47
Chaleur Bay, 383
Chalons, battle of, 172
Chamberlain, Nevile, 616, 618, 620
Champagne Fairs, 231, 232
Chan Chan, Peruvian city, 321
Chandragupta Maurya, 131-133, 146

Chandragupta II, 136-137
Chang Jiang River, 68
Chang Jiang Valley, 542
Changan, Chinese capital, 294, 302, 304
Charlemagne, 169, 178, 182-184, 186, 208, 220
Charles I, king of England, 396-397, 399-402, 403, 420
Charles II, king of England, 403, 420
Charles V, Holy Roman Emperor, 342, 343, 347, 355, 356-357, 372
Charles VII, king of France, 250
Charles IX, king of France, 358
Charles X, king of France, 471
Charles the Bald, king of the Franks, 184
Charter, *def.*, 233
Chartres, cathedral at, 449
Chastity, *def.*, 175
Chemistry, 428-429, 438
Chiang Kai-shek, 598-599, 600, 667
Chiaroscuro, *def.*, 337
Chicago, 469
Chichen Itza, Mayan ceremonial center, 316
Chiefdoms, African political structures, 277-278, 280
Child labor, 494, 499, 500
Chile, 321, 419, 647, 656, 660
China:
    ancient, 14, 19, 40, 66-71, 74-76
    classical age, 83, 131, 139, 141-145, 146;
    middle ages, 200, 209, 223, 229, 238, 283, 288, 289, 290-291, 293-302, 303, 304;
    Manchu dynasty, 371, 372, 377, 541-542, 544, 550
    and imperialism, 531, 536-537, 541-544, 550
    and First World War, 566;
    and Communism, 598-599, 600, 667, 668;
    war with Japan, 599, 614-615, 620;
    after Second World War, 667, 668-670, 671, 678, 690, 695
China's Sorrow, Huang He River, 68
Ching dynasty. *See* Manchu dynasty.
Chivalry, 210
Christian Church. *See* Church, Christian.
Christianity, 45, 148-162, 186, 219, 223, 226-227, 274-275, 295, 359
Christians, 149, 290
Church, Christian, 115, 155-156, 175, 178, 182, 183, 186
Christian doctrine, *def.*, 154
Church of England. *See* Anglican Church.
Churchill, Winston, 624-625, 626, 639, 648
Cicero, Marcus, 120
Cincinnatus, Roman hero, 109
Citadel, *def.*, 56
Cities, 9, 18, 30-31, 37, 38, 41, 43-44, 50, 64, 107, 138, 143, 196-197, 199, 213, 290, 296-297, 313, 314, 316-317, 318, 322, 324, 338, 491, 494, 496, 636-637, 660, 675
City of God, The, 171
City-State, 37-41, 50, 85-91, 93-98, 100, 102, 106-107, 108, 314, 332, 387
Civilization, origins, 19
Civil Service, *def.*, 142
Civil War, in United States, 485-486, 488, 581
Civil war, in England, 397, 400-402, 403, 420
Civilians, role of in total war, 581
Clan, *def.*, 273
Clare of Assisi, 219
Clark, William, 483
Classifying, *def.*, 100
Claudius, Roman emperor, 124
Cleisthenes, 89
Clemenceau, Georges, 571
Clement V, pope, 249
Clement VII, pope, 253
Cleopatra, 119, 120
Clergy, *def.*, 159
Clive, Robert, 542
Clock, mechanical, 241
Clothing, 56, 107, 168-169, 252, 287, 314, 449
Clotilda, queen of the Franks, 181
Clovis, king of the Franks, 169, 181, 186
Cluny, 207, 218
Coal mining, 492
Cochin, China, 540, 550
Code Napoleon, 453-455
Coexistence, *def.*, 652
Cold War, 648-650, 651-654, 664
Colombia, 470, 656
Colonies, 375-386, 405-409, 414, 415, 487-488, 492, 503-506, 508-528, 579, 583, 594, 638, 675-676, 678, 689-693
Colony, *def.*, 506
Colosseum, 126
Columbia, spaceship, 655
Columbus, Christopher, 308, 375, 378, 390
Combined Chiefs of Staff, 630
Combustion, *def.*, 429
Committee of Public Safety, rulers of France during revolution, 447, 448, 450
Commodus, Roman emperor, 156
Common law, 245
Common Market. *See* European Common Market.
Common Sense, 415
Commons, House of, 399
Commonwealth, British, 681, 697
Commune, *def.*, 668
Communication:
    improvements in, during Industrial Revolution, 491, 497;
    Soviet-American "hot line," 653;
Communism, *def.*, 589; 580, 592-595, 598-599, 600, 603, 608, 609-610, 612, 617, 638-640, 648, 649, 657-660, 664, 667, 669, 675, 676, 678
Communist Manifesto, 491, 501, 502

Communist Party, 564, 591-593, 600, 669, 678
Compass, 199, 376
Compound, *def.*, 276
Concentration camps, 518, 631, 640
Concerning the Revolutions of Celestial Spheres, 424
Condorcet, Marquis de, 448
Confederate States of America, 485
Confederation of the Rhine, 458
Confucianism, 70, 72, 73, 78, 141-142, 146, 295, 300
Confucius, 67, 72
Congo Free State, 509, 522-523, 528
Congo River, 265, 271, 274, 280, 513, 514, 521, 522, 523
Congress of Vienna, 467, 468-469, 488, 510
Cooperative, system of working, *def.*, 501
Conservative, *def.*, 468
Constantine, Roman emperor, 149, 159-161, 162
Constantinople, 159, 174, 175, 176, 181, 183, 186, 229, 355, 361. *See also* Byzantium, Istanbul.
Constantius, Roman official, 159
Constitution, French, in early revolution, 444
Constitution, United States, 411-412, 420, 480
Consul, *def.*, 109
Continental Congress
 first, 408
 second, 408-409
Cook Islands, 546, 550
Cook, James, 531, 545, 546
Cook, Thomas, 497
Copán, Mayan ceremonial center, 313, 315, 316, 324
Copernicus, Nicholaus, 331, 341, 423-424, 425, 426, 438
Coral Sea, battle of, 629
Cordoba, 201, 204
Cornwallis, Lord, 411
Corpus Juris Civilis, 169, 177
Corsica, 113, 226, 452

Cortés, Hernando, 307, 320, 375, 378, 430
Cossack, *def.*, 459
Costa Rica, 481
Cotton gin, invention of, 493
Coulomb, Charles Augustin de, 429
Council of Constance, 253
Council of elders, *def.*, 278
Council of Nicaea, 149, 160
Council of Trent, 331, 350
Counter-Reformation. *See* Reformation, Catholic.
Coup, *def.*, 480, 695
Court of Star Chamber, 400
Court Systems, beginnings of, in Britain, 211
Cow, as sacred animal, 61
Crafts, 87, 279, 309. *See also* pottery, weaving, metalworking.
Crassus, Marcus, 105, 118-119
Crecy, battle at, 250
Credit, letters of, 233
Cremation, *def.*, 62
Creoles, *def.*, 414, 414-417, 418, 420, 480, 488
Crete, 86, 87
Crimean War, 467, 477
Criollos. *See* Creoles.
Croatians, 557
Cro-Magnon people, 9, 10
Cromer, Lord, 515
Cromwell, Oliver, 401-403, 420
Crop rotation, *def.*, 17
Crusades, *def.*, 181, 209, 223, 227-229
Cuba, 378, 419, 531, 547-548, 587, 647, 652-653, 657-659, 660, 664, 693
Cultural anthropologists, 1
Cultural diffusion, *def.*, 83
Culture, *def.*, 4
Cuneiform writing, *def.*, 41
Curie, Marie, 557
Cush, kingdom of, 261, 266, 280
Cuzco, Incan capital, 307, 320-321, 324
Cyprus, 195
Cyrillic alphabet, 178
Cyrus the Great, 93

Czar, *def.*, 362-363
Czechoslovakia, 182, 226, 345, 468, 572, 603, 617, 618, 648, 651
Czechs, 572

D

da Gama, Vasco, 375, 376-377, 390
Dahomey, 386, 387, 519, 528
Daimyo, Japanese leaders, 303-304
Damascus, 197, 204
Dante, Italian writer, 331, 334-335
Danton, Georges, 445, 449-450
Danube River, 156, 176, 231
Danzig, 572
Darius, king of Persia, 93, 96, 97, 131
Dark Ages, 207. *See also* Middle Ages.
Darwin, 505
Das Kapital, 502
Dasas, 58, 64
David, Hebrew king, 46
da Vinci, Leonardo, 330, 331, 335-337
Davis, Jefferson, 485
Dawes Plan, 577, 580
D-Day, 633
Deccan, 54, 133, 368
de Gaulle, Charles, 661, 664, 690
Declaration of the Rights of Man, 444, 468
Declaration of Independence, 397, 409, 411, 415, 420
Declaration of the United Nations, 630
Deductive, *def.*, 101
Deism, *def.*, 433
de Lesseps, Ferdinand, 514, 549
Delian league, 94
Delhi, 202, 286, 368
Delhi, sultanate of, 283, 284-287, 304
Delos, 94
Delphine, novel by Madame de Staël, 454

730

Democracy, 85, 88-89, 102, 109
Denmark, 224, 343, 358, 475, 566, 624, 640
Depression, *def.,* 499; 603
Der Fuhrer, 613. See also Adolf Hitler.
Dervishes, Muslim sect, 508
Descartes, René, 428
Detente, *def.,* 654
de Vega, Lope, Spanish writer, 340-341
Developing nations, 672
Dewey, George, 548
Dharma, *def.,* 62
Diadem, *def.,* 107
Diamonds, discovery of, in Southern Africa, 516, 528
Dias, Bartholomeu, 376
Diaspora, *def.,* 151
Diaz, Porfirio, 585-586
Dictator, *def.,* 109
Dictatorship, 594-598, 600, 604-607, 612-613, 620, 623-629, 657, 658, 663, 673. See also Totalitarianism.
Dike, *def.,* 23
Diocletian, Roman emperor, 149, 158, 159, 161, 162
Dionysian cults, 117
Dionysus, 117
Diplomacy, 560, 574
Direct rule, European, in Africa, 523, 528
Directory, French revolutionary government, 451, 452, 453, 460
Disarmament, 570
Disraeli, Benjamin, 515
Divination ceremonies in Shang dynasty, 69
Divine Comedy, 331, 335
Division of labor, *def.,* 18
Doctrine, *def.,* 141
Dnieper River, 171, 359
Dolores, Mexican town, 418
Domestication, *def.,* 14; 9, 12, 15-16, 18
Dominicans, 219
Dominion of Canada, 487, 488
Dominion of India. See India.
Domitian, Roman emperor, 124
Donation of Pepin, 182

Don Quixote, 331, 340
Dorians, 85, 87, 88
Dowry, *def.,* 59, 276
Draft, military:
  and people's armies in French Revolution, 581;
  in United States, 625, 628
Drama. See Theater.
Dravidian speaking peoples, 133
Druids, *def.,* 115
Du Fu, Chinese poet, 295, 296
Dual Monarchy, 467, 477
Duchy, *def.,* 208
Duma, Russian Parliament, 589
Dunkers, German religious group, 405
Dunkirk, 624
Durand, Peter, 457
Durham, Lord, 487
Dutch East India Company, 510
Dutch East Indies, 628
Dutch West India Company, 384
Dynasty, *def.,* 28

E

East Franks, 208. See also Germans.
East Germany, 652
East India Company, 384
East Pakistan, 673, 678. See also Bangladesh.
Eastern Orthodox Church, 178
Economic sanctions, *def.,* 573
Ecuador, 321, 480, 656
Edict, *def.,* 158
Edict of Milan, 149, 159, 162
Edict of Nantes, 355, 358
Edison, Thomas A., 497-498
Education, 89-90, 141, 183, 199, 201-202, 207, 210, 220, 224, 276, 333, 338, 351, 436, 452 455, 500, 536, 586, 659, 670, 696, 697
Edward III, king of England, 250
Edward VI, king of England, 348-349
Egypt, 14, 16, 19, 20-35, 45, 46, 47, 92, 97, 98, 119-120,
122, 123, 133, 135, 175, 194, 203, 204, 266, 280, 453, 508, 509, 514, 515, 528, 584, 628, 632, 680, 681, 683-684, 685, 698
Egyptian Desert, 23-24
Egyptian-Israeli Peace Treaty, 681, 683-684, 698
Eight Fold Path, 63
Einstein, Albert, 427
Eisenhower, Dwight D., 632, 633
El Alamein, 629, 632
Elba, 459
Elbe River, 123
Electricity, 429, 497
Elite, *def.,* 412
Elizabeth I, queen of England, 339, 349, 352, 398, 430
Ellipse, *def.,* 425
El Salvador, 481, 660
Emancipation Proclamation, 486
Emigres, *def.,* 444
Emile, 436
Emmer, *def.,* 22
Empire, *def.,* 42
Engels, Friedrich, 502
Engineering, 38, 56, 67, 71, 77, 113, 117, 125-126, 132-133, 136, 180, 201, 204, 223, 288, 289, 306, 309, 315, 322, 324, 369, 384, 496, 509, 514, 515, 516, 531, 549, 550, 669
England:
  middle ages, 209, 223, 240-243, 245-247;
  modern, 339, 346, 347-349, 352, 357, 375, 383, 384, 388, 390, 397, 398, 400-405.
  See also Britain, Great Britain.
English Channel, 633
Enlightenment, 414, 420, 484. See also Age of Reason.
Ephor, *def.,* 91
Epic Age, in India, 53, 57, 58, 61
Epicureanism, 117
Epoch of a Warring Country, period of Japanese history, 303
Epirus, 113
Equatorial Guinea, 693

Eratosthenes, 101
Ericson, Leif, 224, 374, 390
Eritrea, 525
Eskimos, 308, 309. *See also* Aleuts, Innuit.
Estate, *def.,* 251, 440
Estates General, 251, 442, 460
Estonia, 572, 623
Ethiopia, 509, 526, 527, 603, 616, 620, 629, 654, 693
Etruria, 106
Etruscans, 106-108, 128
Euphrates River, 37-38
Europe. *See* names of individual countries.
European Common Market, 647, 661, 664
European Fortress, under Hitler, 631
Eusebius, bishop, 160
Euclid, 101
Evidence, *def.,* 4
Environment, physical, *def.,* 4
Evita, 437
Evolution, Darwin's theory of, 505
Excommunicate, *def.,* 156, 220
Exile, *def.,* 267
Exploration:
 early European voyages of, 270;
 Age of, 374-390
Explorer I, satellite, 655
Ezekiel, Hebrew prophet, 49

F

Fact, *def.,* 4
Factory, *def.,* 491, 494-496, 498-500, 502, 506
Faidherbe, Colonel Louis, 519
Fallow, *def.,* 214
Family life, 34, 59-60, 64, 76-77, 78, 117, 120, 124, 275-278, 280, 288, 455, 670
al-Farabi, 200
Fascio di Combattimento. *See* Fascism.
Fascism, 582, 603, 604-607, 608, 617-619, 620

Fashoda, 509, 515, 518, 521
Fatima, daughter of Muhammad, 197
Fatamids, rulers of North Africa, 203, 204
Federation of Rhodesia and Nyasaland, 691-692
Ferdinand I, ruler of Austrian-Hapsburg empire, 356, 372, 473
Ferdinand, king of Spain, 347, 378
Feudalism:
 in China, 67, 69, 70, 74, 78, 209;
 in Europe, 207, 208-216, 217, 220, 231, 238-254
 in Japan, 283, 302-303
Fief, *def.,* 70, 209
Field, Cyrus, 497
Fiji, 546, 550
Filial piety, *def.,* 76
Filipino people, 548
Finland, 469, 572, 623, 639
Finns, 226
Firdausi, 200
First estate, French social class, 440-441
First World Nations, 672
First World War, 556-574, 576-582
Five Pillars of Islam, 192
Five Year Plan, 577, 595, 671
Flanders, 231, 239, 242-243
Fleming, J. A., 497
Florence, Italy, 332, 334
Florida, 484
Flying shuttle, invention of, 492
Formosa, 536, 542
Fossils, *def.,* 2
Fourteen Points, 570-571, 574
Fourth World Nations, 672
France:
 early, 92;
 in middle ages, 182, 197, 209, 220, 224, 240-243, 247-251, 346, 356, 357-358;
 and exploration, 375, 383-384, 385-386, 388, 390;
 and French Revolution, 440-452;
 and Napoleon, 452-460;

 and nationalism, 467, 469, 471, 472, 477, 488;
 and Industrial Revolution, 471, 490, 498;
 and imperialism, 503, 509, 512, 515, 519-521, 523, 526-527, 528, 531, 540, 542, 546, 550, 676, 678;
 and First World War, 560, 562-563, 564, 569, 570, 572-573, 574;
 after First World War, 578, 579, 580, 583, 584, 608, 616, 618, 620;
 and Second World War, 616, 617, 620, 623, 624, 633, 640;
 after Second World War, 648, 651, 661-662, 664, 683, 689-690, 695, 698
Francis of Assisi, 207, 218-219, 254
Franciscans, 219
Franco, Francisco, 608, 617, 618
Franco-Prussian War, 467, 519
Frankland, 181, 184, 186
Franklin, Benjamin, 429
Franks, 173, 174, 175, 176, 181-185, 186, 208
Franz Ferdinand, archduke of Austria, 557, 574
Franz Joseph I, emperor of Austria, 473, 477
Frederick I, Holy Roman Emperor, 244-245
Frederick Barbarossa, 244-245
Frederick, ruler of Saxony, 343
French Equatorial Africa, 521, 524, 528
French Foreign Legion, 520, 527
French Indo-China. *See* Indo-China.
French Revolution, 415, 416, 417, 420, 440-452, 460, 466-467, 488, 581
French Somaliland, 515, 521, 528
French West Africa, 509, 521, 524, 528
Frescoes, *def.,* 87
Fujiwara, Japanese family, 302
Fujiwara, Yoshifusa, Japanese emperor, 302

G

Gagarin, Yuri, 655
Galen, Claudius, Greek physician, 125
Galilee, 150
Galileo, Galileo, 331, 341, 423, 425, 438
Galla Placidia, basilica, 180
Gallipoli Peninsula, 557, 566, 574
Gambia, 513
Gandhi, Indira, 671, 673
Gandhi, Mohandas, 583, 600, 670-671
Ganges River, 53, 54, 57-58, 62, 133, 136
Gao, 261, 268
Garibaldi, Giuseppe, 475
Gaspée Bay, 383
Gaul, 105, 112, 113, 128, 169, 172-174, 181
Gauls, 105, 115
Gautama, Siddhartha, 63-64
Gaza Strip, 684, 698
Genealogy, *def.*, 3
Geneva, Switzerland, 346, 573
Genghis Khan, 283, 285, 288-289, 290, 297, 304
Genius, Roman spirit, 111
Genoa, 229, 231
Genocide, *def.*, 631
Gens, *def.*, 108
Gentiles, *def.*, 154
Gentry, *def.*, 364
Geologists, *def.*, 2
Geometry. *See* mathematics.
George I, king of England, 405
George II, king of England, 405
George III, king of England, 406, 408
German Confederation, 469, 475
German Democratic Republic. *See* East Germany.
German East Africa, 509, 524 *See also* Tanganyika.
German East Africa Company, 524, 528
German Federal Republic. *See* West Germany.
German language, 184
German Southwest Africa, 523, 528
Germany, 83, 156-157, 162, 168-170, 175, 176, 186, 208, 209, 212, 220, 244-245, 254, 343, 345, 346, 356, 358, 372, 383, 452, 458, 476;
  unified, 467, 472-473, 475-476, 488
  and the Industrial Revolution, 490, 498;
  and imperialism, 521, 523-524, 528, 542, 546, 550;
  and First World War, 558, 559-560, 562-563, 564-565, 566-569, 570, 571-572, 573, 574;
  after First World War, 577, 578, 580, 590-591, 594, 603, 609-613, 615-616, 618, 619, 620, 622-623, 640
  in Second World War, 623-629, 631-633, 640;
  after Second World War, 636, 638, 648, 651
Gestapo, 632
Ghaghatay, Mongol ruler, 290
Ghana, 261, 266-267, 280, 386, 681, 690, 691, 695
Ghee, *def.*, 61
Ghor, Turkish kingdom, 284
Gibbon, Edward, historian, 176
Gila River valley, 484
Gilbert, William, 429
Giza, 30-31, 32
Glenn, John, 655
Glorious Revolution, in England, 397, 404-405
Gobi Desert, 67, 144, 288
Goering, Hermann, 646
Golan Heights, 683
Gold, 266-267, 376, 379, 381, 382-383, 516, 528, 545
Gold Coast, 513, 524. *See also* Ghana.
Golden Horde, 290
Go mata, Indian term for cow, 61
Gordon, Charles, British general, 508, 509, 515, 542
Gospels, Christian, 152
Gothic, architectural style, 225
Goths, 157
Government:
  ancient, 25-26, 38-39, 48, 56-57, 69, 70, 74;
  in classical age, 89, 109-110, 118, 122-125, 142, 158, 160, 176;
  in middle ages, 184, 193, 196-198, 209, 211-212, 234-235, 244-251, 254, 267, 271-273, 277-278, 285, 286, 290, 300-304, 321-322, 323;
  modern, 354, 356, 367, 397-401, 404, 405, 412, 435, 436, 438, 442-446, 448, 451, 452, 453, 479-480, 487, 500, 523, 535, 536, 539, 544, 564, 590, 592-593, 600, 604-613, 614, 619, 620, 631, 659, 660, 661
Gracchus, Tiberius, 117–118
Granada, 202, 378
Grand bourgeoisie, *def.*, 441
Grand Duchy of Warsaw, 458
Grant, Ulysses S., 486
Gravitation, 426
Gravity, *def.*, 427
Great Britain, 405, 441, 447, 452, 453, 455-456, 459-466, 468-469, 477, 510
  and the Industrial Revolution, 490, 491, 492-496, 498
  and imperialism, 503, 508-509, 510-511, 513-519, 523-524, 528, 533, 538-539, 540-542, 545-546;
  and First World War, 558, 560, 562, 563, 566-569, 571, 572-573, 574;
  after First World War, 579, 580, 583, 584, 592, 608, 616, 618, 620;
  in Second World War, 623, 624-625, 630-631, 628, 629, 632, 633, 640;
  after Second World War, 648, 651, 662, 670, 678, 681, 682, 683, 685-686, 687, 690-692, 698

733

Great Colombia, 480
Great Depression, 598, 602-603, 607-608, 612, 614, 620
Greater British South Africa, 517
Great Leap Forward, 668, 669
Great Purge, 577, 597, 600
Great Schism, 253, 254
Great Trek Dutch migration in Africa, 511
Great Wall of China, 67, 71, 78
Greece, 21, 85-91, 93-94, 95-96, 98, 99, 102, 105, 116, 122, 157, 470-471, 627, 648
Greek language, 98, 122, 150
Greek Orthodox Church, 207, 218, 226, 359, 362
Greeks, 45, 83, 86, 98, 99, 100-102
Greenland, 224
Gregory I, pope, 175, 176
Gregory VII, pope, 218
Gregory XI, pope, 253
Guadalahara, 412
Guadalcanal, 632
Guadalupe Hidalgo, Treaty of, 483
Guam, 548, 550
Guang Wu Di, 144
Guangzhou, 68, 71, 297
Guatemala, 312, 481, 656
Guerilla warfare, *def.*, 410
Guevara, Ernesto "Che," 657, 660
Guilds, 223, 234-235
Guillotine, *def.*, 446
Guinea, 690, 692, 693
Guinea, Gulf of, 386, 387, 390
Gunpowder, 223, 297
Gupta empire, 131, 133, 135, 136-138, 146
Guru Nanak. *See* Nanak, guru.
Gutenberg, Johann, 338
Guyana, 656
Gypsies, 611

H

Hacienda, *def.*, 413
Hadrian, Roman emperor, 124, 152

Hagia Sophia, 180, 184
Hague, The, 560
Haile Selassie, 616
Haiti, 416, 417, 420, 656
Haley, Alex, 327
Halley, Edmund, 427
Hamburg, Germany, 637
Hamilcar Barca, 113
Hammurabi, Babylonian leader, 37, 42-43, 50
Hancock, John, 408
Han dynasty, 67, 71, 73, 131, 141-145, 146
Hangzhou, capital of Song dynasty, 296
Hannibal, 105, 113-114
Hanover, House of, 405, 420
Hapsburg family, 245. *See also* Hapsburg Empire.
Hapsburg Empire, 356-358, 372
Harappa, 52-53, 55-56
Harding, Warren G., 576
Harquebus, 269
Harun al-Rashid, 198
Harvey, William, 423, 429-431, 438
Hasan, Islamic caliph, 197
Hastings, battle of, 226
Hatshepsut, 28-29, 34
Havana, 548
Hawaiian Islands, 531, 546, 550, 628, 640
Hay, John, 543, 548
Hebrews. *See* Jews.
Hegira, *def.*, 197
Hellas, 88
Hellenes, 88
Hellenic culture. *See* Hellenistic culture.
Hellenistic culture, 88, 97-98, 101, 102, 121-122, 150, 151
Helots, *def.*, 90
Hemophilia, *def.*, 478
Henry IV, Bourbon king of France, 358, 372
Henry IV, emperor, 218
Henry V, king of England, 250
Henry VII, king of England, 247, 383
Henry VIII, king of England, 331, 347-348, 352

Henry, Portuguese prince, 376
Heva, Greek goddess, 88
Heresy, *def.*, 178, 220, 253-254
Heretic, 351
Herod Antipater, king of Judea, 151
Herodotus, 101
Hess, Rudolf, 646
Hidalgo, Miguel, 418, 420
Hierarchy, *def.*, 76
Hieroglyphics, *def.*, 31; Mayan, 306, 315, 324
High Middle Ages, 207
Himalayas, 53-54, 67
Hindenburg, Paul von, 612
Hindi language, 60, 287
Hindu Kush Mountains, 131
Hinduism, 60-62, 64, 131, 137, 139-140, 146
Hindus, 284, 286-287, 367, 368, 670, 678
Hippocrates, 101
Hippodrome, 176-177
Hiroshima, 634, 637, 640, 666
Hispaniola, 416
History, 4, 101
Hitler, Adolf, 603, 610-613, 615-616, 618, 620, 631, 632, 633, 640
Hittites, 21, 37, 45, 50
Hobart, Australia, 545
Ho Chi Minh, 675, 676
Hohenstaufen family, 239, 244
Holland. *See* Netherlands.
Holocaust, genocide under Hitler, 631, 636
Holy Land, 227, 240. *See also* Palestine.
Holy of Holies, in Judea, 150
Holy Roman Empire, 217, 239, 244-245, 254, 335, 343, 356
Homo erectus, 9-11, 69
Homo habilis, 8, 9
Homo sapiens, 9, 10
Honduras, 481
Hong Kong, 541
Hoover, Herbert, 603
Hopewell people, 310
Horace, 127
Horn of Africa, 526. *See also* Italian Somaliland.

Horus, Egyptian God, 30
Hot line, Soviet American communication system, 653
Hottentots, 270. *See also* Bushmen and Khoisan.
House of Commons, 247
House of Lords, 247
Houston, Sam, general, 482
Hsiung-nu. *See* Huns.
Huang He River, 68
Huang He Valley, 19, 66, 69
Huang, pictograph for, 75
Hudson Bay, 384
Huitzilopochtli, Aztec god, 316, 318
Hundred Days of Reform, 542-543
Hudson, Henry, 384
Hudson River, 384
Huguenots, French Calvinists, 346, 358, 405
Hundred Years' War, 239, 240, 247, 250, 254
Hungary, 226, 245, 346, 356, 467-468, 473, 572, 627, 633, 648, 651
Hungarian, origin of term, 172
Hungarians, 207, 208
Huns, 83, 138, 142-143, 144, 170-171, 176
Huss, John, 239, 254
Hyksos, tribe, 21, 28, 34
Hypotenuse, *def.*, 101

I

Ibn-Batuta, 202
Ibn-Khaldun, 202
Ibn-Saud, Abdul Aziz, 685
Ibo, 694
Ice Age, 9, 11, 14, 18, 308
Iceland, 224
Ideograph, *def.*, 75
Ideology, *def.*, 502
Idols, *def.*, 20
Ife, African people, 279, 280
Ifni, 693
Ignatius, 351
Ikhnaton, 29. *See also* Amenhotep IV.

Il Duce, 605, 606. *See also* Mussolini.
Imperialism, *def.*, 506; 374-386, 387, 503-506, 508-527, 528, 530-549, 550, 654, 659, 664
Incas, 307, 320-324, 378-379
India:
  ancient, 19, 43, 52-57, 58, 64
  classical age, 131-138, 145, 146;
  and Muslims, 189, 195, 197, 200, 201, 283, 284-287, 304, 306;
  and exploration, 366, 375, 376, 377, 538;
  and Mogul Empire, 366-369, 372;
  and British imperialism, 406, 538-539, 550;
  and independence, 583, 600, 623, 638, 667, 670-673, 678;
  after Second World War, 670, 671, 673, 678
Indian Councils Act, 539
Indian National Congress, 539
Indian Ocean, 654
Indians of the Americas, 308-310, 379-381, 385-386, 390, 415, 485-486. *See also* Pueblo Indians, Woodland Indians, Hopewell people, Aleuts, Innuit, and Adena people.
Indigo, *def.*, 407
Indirect rule, *def.*, 519; 523, 528
Individualism, *def.*, 333
Indo-Aryans, 53, 57-60, 64, 85, 86. *See also* Indo-European languages.
Indo-China, 531, 540, 542, 550, 627, 676, 678. *See also* Vietnam, Cambodia, and Laos.
Indonesia, 135, 384, 675, 676, 678. *See also* Dutch East Indies.
Indo-European languages, 57
Indulgence, *def.*, 342
Indus River, 19, 54, 57-63, 97, 131
Industrialization, 479, 486-487, 488, 491, 558, 580, 592, 595, 598, 600, 638, 661, 662-663,
664, 666, 668, 669, 670, 671, 685. *See also* Industrial Revolution.
Industrial Revolution, *def.*, 490; 471, 490-506
Inflation, *def.*, 381, 664
Infrastructure, *def.*, 595
Innocent III, pope, 207, 218, 253
Innuit, 308, 309. *See also* Aleuts, Eskimos.
Inquisition, 207, 219, 220, 351, 426
Insignia, *def.*, 183
Institutes of the Christian Religion, 344
Institutions, *def.*, 4
International Association for the Exploration and Civilization of Central Africa, 522
Intolerable Acts, 408
Inventions:
  ancient, 17, 18, 50, 58, 69;
  classical ages, 101;
  middle ages, 207, 209, 212, 213, 220, 222-223, 241;
  modern, 250, 272, 297, 331, 338-339, 352, 376, 423, 428, 431, 457, 491, 492, 493, 494, 497-498, 563, 577, 619, 623, 629, 633
Ionian Islands, 469
Ionian Greeks, 86
Iran, 133, 198, 648, 681, 685-686, 687, 698
Iraq, 37, 194, 198, 284, 573, 584, 681, 682, 687
Ireland, 175, 186, 402, 404-405
Iron, 77, 266, 271, 274, 280
Isabella, queen of Spain, 347, 378
Islam, 45, 188-204, 284, 288, 290, 295, 685, 687. *See also* Muslims.
Island-hopping, military strategy, 633
Ismail, Egyptian ruler, 514, 515
Isolationism, *def.*, 580
Israel, 46, 47, 681, 682-684, 698
Issus, 97
Istanbul, 361
Italian Somaliland, 526, 528

735

Italy:
  ancient, 92, 104-120, 157, 174, 176;
  middle ages, 174, 176, 177, 182, 185, 209, 226, 231, 240-243, 245, 254;
  modern, 351, 383, 452, 467, 473, 474-475;
  imperialism in Africa, 525-526, 528, 603, 616, 620
  and First World War, 557, 560, 564-565, 568, 570, 571, 573, 574;
  fascism and Mussolini, 604-607, 618, 620, 627;
  in Second World War, 628-629, 632-633;
  after Second World War, 648, 661, 663
Ivan III (the Great), Russian ruler, 355, 362, 372
Ivan IV (the Terrible), Russian czar, 362-364, 372
Ivory Coast, 519, 528

J

Jahan, Shah, 367
Jain, religion, 63
Jalal-ad-Din, 290
Jamaica, 656
James I, king of England, 397, 398-399, 420. See also James VI, king of Scotland.
James II, king of England, 403, 420
James VI, king of Scotland, 398. See also James I, king of England.
Jameson, Dr. Leander Starr, 517
Jameson Raid, 518
Jamestown, Virginia, 375, 384
Japan:
  and feudalism, 283, 302-303, 304;
  invasions of China in Ming dynasty, 370;
  and Portuguese exploration, 377;
  Meiji period, 535-536;
  and imperialism, 536-538, 542, 550
  Russo-Japanese War, 531, 537, 538, 549
  and First World War, 566, 573;
  after First World War, 580-581, 592, 614, 627;
  war with China, 599, 614-615, 620;
  in Second World War, 623, 627, 628, 632, 633-635, 640
  in Southeast Asia, 627, 675, 678
Java, 384, 540, 550
Jefferson, Thomas, 409, 483
Jen, *def.*, 72
Jenner, Edward, 430
Jerusalem, 118, 175, 194, 197, 209, 228, 682
Jesuits, 350-351, 352, 370, 617
Jesus, 124, 148, 149, 152-154, 162, 194
Jews, 45, 46, 50, 162, 233, 290, 583-584, 600, 611, 612, 613, 620, 631, 636, 640, 681, 682, 698
Jihad, *def.*, 192-193
Jinnah, Mohammed Ali, 670, 673
Jizya, *def.*, 369
Joan of Arc, 239, 250
Jochi, Mongol ruler, 290
Johannesburg, 516-517, 518
John, king of England, 218, 246, 249
John, king of France, 250
John VI, king of Portugal, 419
John, Prester, 374
Johnson, Lyndon, 677
Jonson, Ben, English writer, 339
Joint Family, in Indo-Aryan society, 59-60
Jones, H.M., historian, 176
Jordan, 638, 681, 682, 683
Jordan River, 150
Juana, Sister, 380
Juan Carlos I, king of Spain, 693
Judaism, 45
Judas Maccabaeus, Jewish leader, 150
Judea, 46, 150-154, 162
Judeans, 46
Julian, Roman emperor, 161
Jupiter, planet, 425
Jury, 246
Justin, Christian leader, 148
Justinian, Roman emperor, 169, 176-177, 180, 186
Justinian's Code, 177
Jutes, 173, 174

K

Kaaba, sacred stone, 190, 191, 192
Kalahari Desert, 12, 262, 523
Kalidasa, 137
Kalinga, 133, 140
Kamakura, period of Japanese history, 283, 303
Kamchatka peninsula, 532
Kamikaze, *def.*, 303
Karnak, 31, 32
Katanga, 692
Kennedy, John F., 652-653, 677
Kenya, 514, 515, 528, 691
Kepler, Johannes, 341, 425, 438
Kerenski, Aleksandr, 590, 600
Khadija, wife of Muhammad, 191
Khafre, Pyramid of, 30
Khartoum, 40, 508, 509, 514, 515
Khedive, *def.*, 514
Khoisan people, 270. See also Bushmen and Hottentots.
Khomeini, Ayatullah Ruhollah, 685, 686, 698
Khruschchev, Nikita S., 651, 652, 653, 654, 664
Khufu, Pyramid of, 30
Kiev, 359, 360, 372, 636
Kimberly, 516, 518
Kingdom, group of African chiefdoms, 278, 280
Kipling, Rudyard, 505
Kish, Sumerian city, 37
Kissinger, Henry, 654
Kitchener, Herbert, 515, 518
Knights, 209-211, 220
Knossos, 87
Knox, John, 346

Kocabas River, battle of, 97
Kongo, African people, 261, 274-275, 278, 280
Koran, *def.*, 193; 196, 204
Korea, 142, 283, 298, 371, 533, 536-537, 538, 542, 550
Korean War, 667-668, 678
Krishna, deity in Epic Age, 61
Kruger Telegram, 518
Kruger, Paul, 517, 518
Krupskaya, Nadezhda, 588, 589
Kshatriya princes, 63
Kshatriyas, *def.*, 58
Kublai Khan, 290-291, 297-298, 304
Kulak, *def.*, 596, 600
Kumbi-Soleh, capital of Ancient Ghana, 267
K'ung Fu Tzu, Chinese name for confucius, 72
Kurds, 687
Kushans, 83, 131, 134-135, 145, 146
Kuwait, 681
Kyoto, Japanese capital, 302, 303

L

Labor-intensive, *def.*, 78
Labor union, *def.*, 499; 491, 499, 502, 506, 586, 606, 660, 663, 664, 696
Lagash, Sumerian city, 37
Lancaster, house of, 247
Land bridge, between Asia and Alaska, 307, 308, 324
Land reform, in Tang dynasty, 293
Language:
  of early Semitic people, 41;
  Indo-European, 57;
  Sanskrit, 64;
  Dravidian, 133;
  German, in Frankland, 184;
  Arabic, spread of, 261;
  in ancient Egypt, 266;
  click sounds in African, 270, 280;
  Bantu, 270-271, 273-274;
  Nilotic, 273, 280;
  Swahili, 273-274;
  written, and Cushites, 280;
  Hindi, 287;
  Urdu, social role of, 287;
  Persian, and Delhi sultanate, 287;
  various, among Mongols, 288;
  of Aztecs, 319;
  growth of nativae, in Renaissance, 339
  spoken, of Incas, 322;
  Italian, in Renaissance, 334;
  German, written standard for, 343
  French, at Russian court, 365;
  English in the Cape colony, 511, 519;
  Afrikaans, Dutch-Boer language, 517;
  English and Dutch, after the Boer War, 519;
  of Latin America, 656;
  on Indian Subcontinent, 670;
  diversity of, and new African nations, 694, 698
Laos, 540, 550, 667, 676, 677, 678
Lar, Roman household god, 111
Lateran Agreements, 607
Latifundia, *def.*, 116, 157
Latin America, 412-419, 520, 470, 479-480, 481, 585, 587, 656-657, 660, 664
Latin Kingdom of Jerusalem, 228
Latin language, 122, 128, 183, 184
Latin League, 112
Latins, 113, 128
Latitude, *def.*, 376
Latium, 106, 106, 112
Latvia, 572, 623
  and Versailles Treaty, 572
Laud, William, archbishop of Canterbury, 400
Lavoisier, Antoine, 428-429, 448
Law:
  Hammurabi's laws, 37, 42-43;
  Roman, 125, 128, 177, 186;
  early British court system, 211;
  and Roman Catholic Church, 219-220;
  in Medieval Europe, 224, 245-247, 249, 250, 254, 356;
  Genghis Khan's code, 290;
  the Taika reforms in Japan, 300-302;
  English, 397, 400, 404, 405, 407-408, 484, 499-500, 506, 511;
  French, 452, 453-455;
  after First World War, 577, 582
League of Nations, 571, 573-574, 579, 603, 610, 614, 616, 617, 638
Lebanon, 573, 584, 638, 682, 681
Lee, Richard, and Bushmen, 12
Lee, Robert E., 486
Leeuwenhoek, Anton van, 431-432
Legalism, 70, 72-73, 78
Legislative Assembly, 444, 445
Leibniz, Baron Gottfried von, 428
Lend-Lease program, 625
Lenin, V. I., 577, 588, 589, 590-593, 595, 600
Leo I, pope, 172
Leo III, pope, 182
Leo IX, pope, 178
Leon, Spanish state, 227
Leonidas, 93-94
Leopold, English prince, 478
Leopold II, king of Belgium, 522, 528
Lepanto, battle at, 355, 357, 361
Lepidus, Marcus, 120
Letters of credit, 233
Leveling system, 143
Levy, *def.*, 109-111
Lewis and Clark expedition, 484
Lewis, Merriwether, 483
Lexington, 408, 420
Leyte Gulf, battle at, 633
Li, *def.*, 72
Li Bai, Chinese poet, 295
Liberalism, *def.*, 468
Liberia, 509, 527, 528
Libya, 175, 189, 526, 628, 680, 681

Licinius, Roman emperor, 159
Life expectancy, *def.*, 81
Lima, Peru, 412
Lincoln, Abraham, 485, 486
Lineage, *def.*, 275, 280
Linguists, *def.*, 57
Li Qingzhao, Chinese poet, 297
Literacy rate, *def.*, 81
Literature:
    ancient Egyptian, 32;
    Indo-Aryan Vedas, 57, 62;
    of Greeks, 99;
    in late Roman republic, 117;
    in later Roman empire, 127–128
    Tamil, in India's classical age, 136;
    of Hindo poet-saints, 139;
    Confucian, in Han dynasty, 142;
    preservation of classical, by church, 174, 175;
    spread of early Greek and Roman, 178;
    in Carolingian empire, 183;
    Arab, in Abbasid caliphate, 199–200;
    in Persian language, 287;
    in Song dynasty, 297;
    Japanese, 301, 302;
    in Tang dynasty, 295, 304;
    Aztec legends, 320;
    Incan legends, 320–321;
    of the Renaissance, 334–335;
    "Lost Generation," 582, 600
Lithuania, 245, 572, 623
Liu Bang, 71, 141
Lives of the Twelve Caesars, 128
Livingstone, Dr. David, 509, 513–514, 528
Livy, 127
Locke, John, 423, 434, 436, 438
Loess, *def.*, 68
Logarithms, *def.*, 427–428
Lombards, 176, 177, 182
London, 636
Long March, 599
Long Parliament, 400
Lords, House of, 399, 401
Lorraine, 358, 476, 570, 571
Lost Generation, writers, 582

Lost-wax method, *def.*, 279
Lothair, king of the Franks, 184
Louis XIV, king of France, 406
Louis XV, king of France, 430
Louis XVI, king of France, 441, 442–443, 445, 446, 460
Louis XVII, French prince, 448, 452
Louis XVIII, king of France, 469, 471
Louis-Napoleon. *See* Napoleon III.
Louis Philippe, king of France, 471, 520
Louis the German, ruler of the Franks, 184
Louis the Pious, king of the Franks, 184
Louisiana Territory, 455
Low Countries. *See* Netherlands.
Lowe-ha, pre-Mayan culture, 307
Loyalist, *def.*, 487
Lueritz, Franz, 523
Luftwaffe, 622, 625
Lusitania, 566
Luther, Martin, 331, 342–343, 352
Lutheranism, 343, 346, 347, 352
Luxembourg, 624, 661
Luxor, Egypt, 29, 31, 32

M

Macao, 377, 542
MacArthur, Douglas, 633, 668
MacDonald, Sir John A., 487
Macedonia, 48, 85, 95–97, 98, 116, 122, 133, 157
Machiavelli, Niccolo, Italian writer, 335
Machu Picchu, Incan city, 322
MacNeish, Richard S., archaeologist, 307
Macon, Georgia, and early Indians, 309
Madagascar, 509, 521, 528
Madeiras, 376
Madero, Francisco, 585–586
Magadha, region of India, 131, 136

Magellan, Ferdinand, 375, 378
Maginot Line, 616, 624
Magna Charta, 239, 246–247, 254
Magyars, invaders of Europe, 185, 186
Mahan, Alfred T., 505, 534, 547
Mahmud, sultan, 284
Maimonides, 202
Malacca, 540
Malaria, 514
Malawi, 692
Malay Peninsula, 540–541, 550
Malaya, 200, 675
Malaysia, 271, 676
Mali, 261, 267–268, 280, 376, 386
Malta, 469
Mama Huaco, 320
Mama Occlo, 320, 321
Mamluk, 203, 204
Manchu, Manchurian nomads, 371
Manchu dynasty, 371, 372, 532, 541–542, 544, 550
Manchuria, 142, 371, 503, 537–538, 542, 550, 614–615, 620
Manco Capac, 320, 321
Mandingos, 267
Manifest destiny, 546
Manila, 548, 675
Manor, 212, 213–216, 240
Manorial agriculture, 212–214, 220
Mansa Musa, king of Mali, 260–261, 268, 280
al-Mansur, caliph, 198
Manufacturing, 230, 231. *See also* Industrialization.
Man'yoshu, or *Collection of Ten Thousand Leaves*, 301
Mao Zedong, 598, 600, 667, 668–670, 678
Maori, 545–546
Marat, Jean Paul, 445
Maratha confederacy, 368
Marathon, 93
Marcellinus, 176
Marconi, Guglielmo, 497
Marie Antoinette, queen of France, 440, 445, 448

Marion, Francis, 410
Maritime, *def.*, 133
Marius, Gaius, 118
Marlowe, Christopher, English writer, 339
Marne River, 563, 568
Marshall Islands, 546, 550
Marshall Plan, 647, 648-649, 661, 664
Martel, *def.*, 181
Martel, Charles, ruler of the Franks, 181, 186, 195
Martin V, pope, 253
Marx, Karl, 491, 501, 502, 588, 593, 594
Mary I, queen of England, 349
Mary II, queen of England, 404-405, 420
Maryland, English colony, 384
Masada, 151
Masai, African warrior tribe, 273
Mathematics, 32, 37, 101, 137, 199, 284, 306, 315, 324, 427-428, 438
Matope, Bantu king, 274
Matrilineal society, *def.*, 276, 277
Matter, *def.*, 428
Mau Mau, 691
Mauritania, 693
Mauryan empire, 131-133, 146
Maximian, Roman emperor, 158, 159
Maya, 40, 306, 307, 312-316, 324
Mayor of the Palace, *def.*, 181
McKinley, William, 548
McMahon Letter, 577, 583-584
Mecca, 188, 189, 190, 192, 197, 204, 260
Medians, 47
Mediation, *def.*, 560-561
Medici family, 332
Medicine, 32, 101, 125, 142, 199, 423, 429-432, 438
Medina, 191-192, 204, 685
Mediterranean Sea, 24, 45, 86, 564, 628, 681
Megadeath syndrome, *def.*, 638
Meiji, period in Japan, 535-536
Mein Kampf, 611

Mekong River, 135, 540
Melinda, pre-Mayan culture, 307
Memphis, Egypt, 28, 30-31
Menander, Bactrian king, 133-134
Menelik II, ruler of Ethiopia, 526
Menes, pharaoh of Egypt, 28, 30
Menkaure, Pyramid of, 30
Mennonites, 405
Menshevik, *def.*, 589, 577
Mercantilism, *def.*, 382, 390
Mercury, spaceship, 655
Merit, *def.*, 142
Meroe, Cushite capital, 266, 271, 280
Merv, 533
Mesopotamia, 19, 36, 37, 41-42, 49-50, 56
Messiah, *def.*, 151
Messina, city of, 113
Mestizos, *def.*, 414; 418, 655
Metalworking, 56, 69, 77, 107, 323
Metamorphoses, 127
Metternich, Prince Klemons von, 467, 468-471, 473
Mexico, 307, 308-309, 312, 316, 319, 324, 375, 378, 417-418, 420, 467, 480, 481-483, 488, 568, 577, 585-587, 656, 660
Mexico City, 316, 412, 483
Michelangelo, 331, 335, 336
Microscope, 423, 431-432
Middle Ages, 207, 208-220, 222-226, 230-236, 238-254, 354-366
Middle colonies, 406-407
Middle East, 14, 18, 37, 40-41, 45-47, 50, 583-584, 600, 654, 680-689
Middle Kingdom, in Egypt, 21, 28, 34
Middle Kingdom, name for early China, 74-76, 299
Middle Kingdom, area of Frankland, 184
Midway Island, 546, 623, 629, 632
Migrate, *def.*, 49
Mikado, *def.*, 535
Milan, 158

Militarism, *def.*, 558, 560
Minamoto, Japanese family, 303
Minamoto, Yoritomo, Japanese ruler, 303
Minaret, *def.*, 367
Ming dynasty, 283, 291, 298, 304, 369-370, 372
Minoan people, 87
Minsk, 636
Minutemen, *def.*, 408
Missionaries, 149, 224-226, 381, 505, 535, 542
Mitterand, François, 662
Mobilize, *def.*, 558, 560, 574
Mogul Empire, 286, 355, 366-369, 372
Mohenjo-Daro, 52-53, 55-56, 132
Moloch, 113
Moksha, *def.*, 62
Monasteries, 184, 207, 218, 227, 241, 253, 295, 302, 346, 350, 359
Money, 235-236
Mongol Empire, 283, 288-291, 304
Mongolia, 144, 171, 290, 371
Mongol language, 288
Mongols, 189, 204, 285, 288-291, 297-298, 303, 369
Monopoly, *def.*, 267
Monophysite beliefs, 178
Monotheism, *def.*, 29
Monroe Doctrine, 470, 506
Monsoons, *def.*, 55
Mosaics, *def.*, 180
Mosque, *def.*, 191
Montague, Lady Mary, 430
Montaigne, Michel de, French writer, 340
Monte Cassino, monastery, 175
Montesquieu, Baron de, 176, 423, 434-435, 436, 438
Montezuma II, Aztec emperor, 320, 378
Montgomery, Bernard L., 632
Montreal, 383
Moors, 208, 226-227
More, Sir Thomas, 348
Morocco, 195, 203, 269-270, 526-527, 680, 690, 693

Morse, Samuel F. B., 497
Moscow, 360-362, 372, 459, 590, 592
Moses, as Muslim prophet, 194
Mozambique, 524, 528, 692, 693
Mugabe, Robert, 692
Muhammad, 189, 190-192, 204
Muhammad Ahmed, 508, 515
Muhammad Ali, governor of Egypt, 514
Muhammad Askia, king of Gao, 268-269, 280
Muhammad ibn-Qasim, 284
Muhammad of Ghor, 284-285
Mohammed Riza Pahlevi, 686, 698
Muhammad Said, 514
Mulatto, *def.*, 417
Mummify, *def.*, 21
Murasaki, Lady, Japanese poet, 301
Murmansk, 534, 564
Music, 137, 183, 278-279
Muslim League, 670
Muslims, *def.*, 192; 49, 226-227, 260, 266-270, 280, 283, 284, 285, 286-287, 304, 367, 376, 670, 671, 678, 681, 686, 689, 694
Mussolini, Benito, 603, 604-607, 612, 618, 620, 632
al-Mutanabbi, 200
Mutota, Bantu king, 273, 274
Mutsuhito. *See* Meiji.
Mycenae, 85, 86
Myceneans, 86-88
Mystic, *def.*, 253
Mysticism, 253-254

N

Nachtigal, Gustav, 524
Nagasaki, 634, 637, 640, 666
Nahuatl, Aztec language, 319
Namib Desert, 262
Nanak, guru, 287
Naniwa, early Japanese capital, 302
Nanking, Treaty of, 541

Napier, John, 427
Naples, 447, 474
Napoleon Bonaparte, 416, 417, 441, 451, 452-460, 483
Napoleon III, 467, 472, 474, 476, 488, 540
Napoleonic Wars, 456
Nara, early Japanese capital, 302
Naseby, battle at, 401
Nasser, Gamal Abdel, 685
Natal, 511, 513, 516, 519
National Assembly, in France, 442-444, 460
National Convention, in French Revolution, 416, 446, 447, 448, 460
National Guard, French soldiers, 444, 451
Nationalism, *def.*, 460; 466-473, 474-479, 488, 538, 539, 544, 558, 560, 574, 584, 606, 612, 620, 638, 675, 678, 686, 689
Nationalization, 657, 662, 685
Nationalize, *def.*, 657
National Socialist Workers Party. *See* Nazis.
Navarre, Spanish state, 227
Navigation Acts, 403
Nazareth, 152
Nazis, 603, 611, 612, 618, 620, 646-647
Neanderthal people, 9, 10
Near East. *See* Middle East.
Necker, Anne Louise Germaine, 454. *See also* Madame de Staël.
Nefertiti, queen of Egypt, 29
Nehru, Jawaharlal, 671
NEP. *See* New Economic Policy.
Nepal, 64
Nero, Roman emperor, 124, 149, 156
Nerva, Roman emperor, 124, 128
Nestorianism, 178
Netherlands, 182, 223, 345, 358, 383, 384, 385, 388, 390, 403, 411, 447, 469, 510-511, 512, 528, 540-541, 546, 550, 560, 566, 624, 640, 648, 661, 675, 676, 683
New Caledonia, 546
New Deal, 608

New Economic Policy (NEP), in Soviet Union, 592, 593, 595, 596, 600
New England, English colonies, 375, 384, 406-407
Newfoundland, 224, 383
New Guinea, 546, 628
New Kingdom, in Egypt, 21, 28-29, 34
New Mexico, 482
New Netherland, 384. *See also* New York.
New Order, of Hitler, 631
New Stone Age, 9, 11
New Testament. *See* Bible.
Newton, Sir Isaac, 423, 426-427, 432, 434, 438
New York, 384
New Zealand, 487, 545-546, 550, 566
Nicaragua, 481, 660
Nice, 474
Nicholas, pope, 178
Nicholas II, czar of Russia, 478, 460, 564, 578, 588, 589, 600
Niger River, 202, 265, 514, 519
Nigeria, 271, 514, 519, 521, 528, 681, 694, 698
Nile Delta, *def.*, 22
Nile River, 19, 21-23, 24, 34, 265, 513, 515
Nilotes, African people, 273
Nimrod, Hebrew prophet, 49
Ninevah, 47
Nippur, Sumerian city, 37
Nirvana, *def.*, 63
Nixon, Richard M., 647, 654, 657, 669, 677
Nkrumah, Kwame, 693
Nomads, *def.*, 9; 41-42; 262
Nonaggression pact: Germany and the Soviet Union, 618; Japan and Soviet Union, 627
Normandy, 209
Normandy Coast, and D-Day, 633
Normans, 209, 223, 226
Norse, tribes of, 224
North Africa:
 early, 122, 172, 174, 177, 181, 195, 203;

modern, 361, 623, 628-629, 632, 640, 681
North America, 308, 309-310, 324, 374, 379, 390, 405-406, 532.
See also names of individual countries.
North Atlantic Treaty Organization (NATO), 647, 649, 664
Northern Rhodesia, 691
North Korea, 667-668
Northmen. See Vikings.
North Sea, 566, 662
North Vietnam, 676, 678
Norway, 224, 343, 557, 566, 624, 640
Northwest Passage, 383, 384
Notre Dame, cathedral of, 449
Novgorod, 362
Nova Scotia, 383
Nubian Desert, 262
Nubians, 694
Numerals, Arabic, 199
Nuremberg trials, 46
Nyasaland, 691

O

Oahu, Island of, 546
Oasis, *def.*, 23
Obelisk, *def.*, 29
Ocmulgee, early name for Macon, Georgia, 309
Octavia, wife of Mark Anthony, 120
Octavian, Gaius, 120, 121, 128
See also Augustus Caesar.
October Revolution. See Bolshevik Revolution.
Odoacer, 173, 186
Oedipus, Greek hero, 99
Oedipus Rex, 99
Ogadai, Mongol ruler, 290
Oil, 672, 681, 683, 685, 687, 698
Okhotsk, 531
Okinawa, battle at, 633
Olaf, king of Norway, 224

Old Kingdom, in Egypt, 21, 28, 34
Old Stone Age, 9, 10, 11, 18
Old Testament. See Bible.
Oligarchy, *def.*, 100, 447
Olmec, early Mexican culture, 312-313
Olympic games, 85, 92
Olympus, Mount, 98
OPEC. See Organization of Petroleum Exporting Countries.
Open Door Policy, 543
Operation Barbarossa, 627
Opium, *def.*, 541
Opium War, 531, 541, 550. See also Anglo-Chinese War.
Orange Free State, 511, 512, 516, 518, 528
Orange River, 510, 516
Ordination, *def.*, 156
Organization of African Unity, 695
Organization of Petroleum Exporting Countries, 672, 683, 685
Orkhon inscriptions, 288
Orleans, Duke of. See Louis-Philippe, king of France.
Osiris, 21
Ostrogoths, 171, 174, 176, 177
Otto I, Holy Roman Emperor, 217
Ottoman Empire, 204, 240, 361, 468, 514, 526, 557, 565-566, 571, 574, 577, 578, 600
Ottoman Turks, 203, 355, 356, 361, 365, 372, 470-471, 572-573

P

Pacific Ocean, 545-549, 628, 629, 632, 633
Page, in chivalry, 210
Paine, Thomas, 415
Painting, 10, 87, 99, 107, 137, 178-180, 297, 331, 333, 335-337, 339
Pakistan, 198, 623, 638, 670, 671, 673, 678, 687

Palaeologus, Sophia, wife of Ivan III, 362
Palatine, Roman hill, 108
Palenque, palace of, 313
Paleontologists, *def.*, 2
Palestine, 181, 573, 583-584, 681-682, 698. See also Israel.
Panama, 549; 550, 647, 657
Panama Canal, 531, 549, 550, 657
Panama Canal Treaty, 647
Panama, Isthmus of, 549
Papal States, 182, 253, 474-475
Pan-Slavism, 479
Paper, 142
Parable, *def.*, 152
Paraguay, 481, 656
Paré, Ambroise, 429
Pariah, *def.*, 619
Paris, 247-249, 443, 445, 624
Parliament, *def.*, 247, 254, 397-401, 420
Parsis, 49
Parthenon, 99
Parthia, 157
Parthians, 135, 157
Partition, *def.*, 670
Pasteur, Louis, 457
Pataliputra, 132
Pater familias, *def.*, 111
Patres, *def.*, 108
Patriarch, *def.*, 59
Patricians, *def.*, 108
Patrick, Christian missionary, 175
Patrilineal, *def.*, 111
Patrilineal society, *def.*, 275; 277
Paul, Christian missionary, 149, 154-155, 162
Pax Romana, 105, 121-128, 145, 149, 155, 156, 162
Pax Sinica, 130, 131, 141. See also Han dynasty.
Pearl Harbor, 546, 623, 628, 640
Peasants, *def.*, 24
Peasants' War, in Germany, 343
Pedro I, emperor of Brazil, 419, 420
Peer, *def.*, 211
Peking, 290-291, 542, 543
Peking man, 69

741

Peloponnesian War, 85, 95, 102
Peloponnesian War, history by Thucydides, 102
Peloponnesus, 86, 90
Penal colony, *def.*, 545
Penates, Roman household god, 111
Peninsulares, *def.*, 414
Pennsylvania, Anabaptists in, 345
Peon, *def.*, 414
People's Republic of China. *See* China.
Pepin the Short, ruler of the Franks, 169, 178, 181, 182, 186
Pericles, 90, 94
Period of Warring States, 70-71, 72
Perioeci, *def.*, 90
Peron, Eva, 437
Perry, Matthew, 535, 546, 550
Persia, 47-49, 85, 96, 131, 189, 194, 196, 203, 290, 291, 304, 368, 533-535, 550. *See also* Iran.
Persian Empire, 37, 47-49, 50, 93-94, 685
Persian Gulf, 37, 42, 139, 535, 584, 689
Persian Wars, 85, 93-94
Persian Wars, The, history by Herodotus, 101
Persians, 4, 21, 47, 157
Perspective, *def.*, 337
Perth, Australia, 545
Peru, 320, 321, 419, 656
Peter, disciple of Jesus, 154
Peter I (the Great), czar of Russia, 355, 364-366, 372, 532
Peters, Karl, 524
Petite bourgeoisie, *def.*, 441
Petition of Right, 399
Petrarch, Italian writer, 334, 335
Petrograd, 590, 592. *See also* St. Petersburg.
Pharaoh, 25-26, 34
Philadelphia, 407
Philip Augustus, king of France, 248-249
Philip II, Hapsburg emperor, 356-357, 372

Philip II, king of Macedonia, 95-96, 102
Philip II, king of Spain, 349, 355, 356-357
Philip IV, king of France, 249
Philip V, king of Macedonia, 114, 116
Philippines, 378, 548, 550, 628, 633, 638, 675, 676
Philosophes, *def.*, 433
Philosophy, *def.*, 72-74, 100-101, 117, 125
Phoenicians, 37, 45, 50
Photius, Byzantine patriarch, 178
Physics, 429, 438
Pi, *def.*, 101
Picasso, 279
Pictograph, *def.*, 75
Piedmont, 474
Pilgrimage, *def.*, 188, 188-189, 192
Pillage, *def.*, 142
Pilsudski, Marshal, 608
Pitcairn Island, 546, 550
Piux XI, pope, 607
Pizarro, Francisco, 307, 323, 378-379
Place de la Concorde, 446
Plague, *def.*, 238; 239, 240-243, 254
Planets, 423-425. *See also* names of individual planets.
Plateau, *def.*, 265
Plato, 85, 100
Plebians, *def.*, 108
Poaching, *def.*, 215
Poitiers, battle at, 250
Poland, 224, 226, 245, 345, 346, 458, 469, 571, 608, 618, 620, 622-623, 633, 639, 640, 648, 651, 663, 664
Polis, *def.*, 89
Polish Corridor, 571-572
Politburo, 592
Polo, Marco, 290
Polyarchy, *def.*, 160
Polygyny, *def.*, 60
Polytheism, *def.*, 39; 160
Pompey, Gnaeus, 105, 118-119, 150-151
Pontiff, *def.*, 109

Pontius Pilate, governor of Judea, 154
Pope, 156, 182, 217-218, 253, 254, 475
Popular Front, 617, 618
Population, 666, 670, 671, 673, 675, 703
Porcelain, *def.*, 142
Porcelain making, 297
Po River, 106, 107
Port Arthur, 537, 538
Portugal, 227, 261, 273, 274-275, 280, 357, 366, 370, 376-377, 384, 387-388, 390, 414, 419, 447, 524, 528, 608, 663, 692-693, 698
Portuguese East Africa, 517, 524, 528. *See also* Mozambique.
Portuguese Guinea, 524, 528
Portuguese West Africa, 524, 528. *See also* Angola.
Poseidon, Greek god, 98
Potsdam Agreements, 651
Potter's wheel, invention of, 38, 50
Pottery, 17, 55, 56, 66, 67, 87, 99, 115, 142, 309, 312, 323
Po Valley, 172
Power loom, invention of, 493
Praetor, *def.*, 111
Praetorian guard, 123, 124
Pre-Mayan culture, 307
Premise, *def.*, 101
Presbyter, *def.*, 346
Presbyterians, 346, 399, 400-401, 420
Preserved food, 457
Pretoria, 516, 517, 518, 519
Primary sources, *def.*, 3-4
Prime minister, *def.*, 405
Prince Edward Island, 383
Prince, The, 335
Principia, 423, 427
Printing, 295, 338, 352
Printing press, invention of, 331, 338, 352
Private property, beginnings of, 18
Procopius, 437
Progresso, pre-Mayan culture, 307

Proletariat, *def.,* 588
Propaganda, 607, 612-613
Prophet, *def.,* 49
Protectorate, *def.,* 506
Protestant Reformation. *See* Reformation.
Protestantism, 207, 219, 254, 358. *See also* Reformation.
Protestants, *def.,* 331. *See also* names of individual denominations.
Provisional Government, Russian, 590
Prussia, 226, 372, 445, 458, 459, 467, 468-469, 475
Ptolemy of Alexandria, astronomer, 128, 423-424
Ptolemy, ruler of Egypt, 98, 119
Pueblo Indians, 309, 324
Puerto Rico, 419, 548, 550, 587
Punic Wars, 113-116
Puritan Revolution. *See* civil war in England.
Puritans, 346, 349, 399, 400-401, 402-403, 405, 420
Punjab, 54, 131, 284
Pygmies, 274
Pylon, *def.,* 31
Pyramid Age, 28
Pyramid of the Sun, 318
Pyramids, *def.,* 25; 21, 27, 28, 30, 313, 316, 318
Pyrrhic victory, *def.,* 113, 172
Pyrrhus, Greek King, 113
Pythagoras, 101

Q

Qatar, 681
Qin, 296
Qin dynasty, 67, 70, 71, 74, 77, 78
Qin Shi Huang, 66-67, 71, 73, 75, 78, 141
Quadrant, *def.,* 376
Quakers, 405
Quarantine, *def.,* 430
Quebec, 375, 487
Quebec Act, 408

Quebec City, 383
Quechua, Incan language, 322
Quetzalcoatl, Aztec god, 318, 320
Queue, *def.,* 371
Quito, 323, 412

R

Rabelais, François, French writer, 340
Race, *def.,* 389
Racism, *def.,* 389; and Hitler, 611, 620; and Hitler's New Order, 631; apartheid, 697, 698
Radar, 629
Radio, 577
Railroads, 491, 496, 497, 514, 531, 533, 550
Rain forest, 262, 265
Rajputs, Hindu warriors, 367
Ramadan, *def.,* 192
Rangoon, 675
Raphael, Italian painter, 335
Rasputin, 478, 589-590
al-Razi. *See* Rhazes.
Raziya, woman sultan of India, 285
Reagan, Ronald, 647, 654, 689
Realism, *def.,* in painting, 337
Red Army, 591, 592
Red Cross, 636
Redeem, *def.,* 155
Red Guards, 669
Red Sea, 139, 681
Reed, Walter, 549
Reformation, *def.,* 331
Reformation, Catholic, 350, 352
Reformation, Protestant, 219, 342-351, 352, 372
Religion, 29, 34, 39-40, 48-49, 56-57, 60-64, 69-70, 78, 98, 115, 117, 133, 140, 148-162, 175, 188-204, 278, 280, 284, 286-287, 294, 299-300, 304, 313, 316, 317-318, 323, 331, 332, 333-334, 342-351, 352, 359, 367, 399, 404
See also Buddhism, Christianity, Hinduism, Taoism, Zoroastrianism, Shinto, Judaism.
Religious orders, in Roman Catholic Church, 219
Renaissance, *def.,* 330, 331, 332-351, 352
Refugee, *def.,* 636, 688
Regent, *def.,* 348
Regulus, Roman dictator, 113
Reichstag, 612
Reign of Terror, 441, 447-449, 451, 460
Reincarnation, *def.,* 62, 63
Reparations, 580
Repatriations, *def.,* 651
Republic, The, 100
Republic, *def.,* 109
Republic, French, 451
Republic of Great Colombia, 418
Republic of South Africa. *See* South Africa, Republic of.
Republic of Texas, 482
Republic of Virtue, 447, 448, 451, 460
Reservation, *def.,* 484
Reservoir, *def.,* 139;
Restoration, in England, 403
Revolutionary War, American, 408-411, 420
Revolutions, Latin American. *See* Latin America, and independence.
Revolutions of 1830, in Europe, 471
Revolutions of 1848, in Europe, 472-473, 488
Rhazes, 199
Rhetoric, *def.,* 333
Rhine River, 176, 184, 231, 572
Rhodes, Cecil, 517, 524
Rhodesia, 509, 517, 524, 691-692, 697. *See also* Zimbabwe.
Rhone Valley, 173
Ricci, Father Matteo, Jesuit in China, 370
Rift Valley, eastern Africa, 265-266
Rig Veda, 57-58, 62
Rio de Oro, 526
Robert the Bruce, 247

Robespierre, Maximilian de, 441, 445, 448, 449-451, 460
Robin Hood, 242
Rockets, 633
Roman Catholic Church, 178, 207, 210, 217-220, 224-226, 233, 239, 240, 246-247, 249, 253-254, 331, 333-334, 342-343, 347-351, 352, 358, 381, 400, 403, 404-405, 415, 420, 424, 425-426, 433, 436, 444, 445, 449, 451, 455, 460, 480, 488, 586, 607, 617, 660
  See also Christian Church.
Roman Empire, 121-138, 156-157, 159, 161-162, 168-174, 176, 186, 206
Roman Republic, 104-105, 106, 108-111, 112-120. See also Roman Empire.
Romanesque, *def.*, 225
Romanians, 471
Romanov, Michael, Russian czar, 355, 364
Romanovs, 364, 372
Rome, 21, 83, 105, 107, 113, 124, 128, 148-152, 154, 156-162, 169, 171, 172, 176, 475. See also Roman Empire, Roman Republic.
Rommel, Erwin, 629, 632, 640
Roosevelt, Franklin D., 603, 608, 626, 633, 639, 648
Roosevelt, Theodore, 538, 549
Roots, 327
Roundheads, *def.*, 401
Rousseau, Jean-Jacques, 423, 436, 438
Rowzi, African people, 274
Rumania, 627, 633, 639, 648
Rump Parliament, 401
Rus, Vikings, 359
Russia, 224, 290, 304, 345, 355, 359-366, 372, 467, 468, 471, 477, 479;
  and Napoleonic Wars, 441, 455, 458-459, 460, 477
  and Congress of Vienna, 468-469;
  and the Industrial Revolution, 498;
  eastward expansion, 531-535, 537-538, 542, 550;
  and First World War, 559-560, 562-563, 564-565, 569, 570, 572, 574;
  and Revolutions of 1917, 557, 564, 568, 574, 577, 578, 589-592, 600
  after First World War, 580, 583, 588-593
Russian-American Fur Company, 532
Russian Orthodox Church, 362, 363, 593
Russian Revolution (1917), 557, 564, 568, 574, 577, 578, 589-592, 600
Russo-Japanese War, 531, 537-538, 549
Rusticus, Roman prefect, 148-149
Rwanda, 273

S

Saar Valley, 572
Sacraments, *def.*, 219
Sadat, Anwar, 681, 683, 684
Sahara Desert, 201, 262, 264, 265, 387
Sahel, *def.*, 262
Saigon, 540
Sakhalin Island, 533, 538
Salamis, battle of, 94
Salazar, Portuguese dictator, 608
Salisbury, 517
Salisbury, Robert Cecil, 517
Samudragupta, 136
Samurai, *def.*, 302, 303, 614
San Jacinto, battle at, 482
San Martín, José de, 418-419, 420
San Salvador, 306, 308
Sand Hill, pre-Mayan culture, 307
Sanskrit, 60, 62, 140
Santa Anna, dictator of Mexico, 482
Santo Domingo, 416
Sarai, Tatar capital, 360, 362
Sarajevo, 557
Saratoga, battle at, 411
Sardinia, 113, 226, 447, 474-475
Sargon I, 37, 41-42
Sassanian empire, 149, 157, 158, 177, 194, 196
Sassanid family, 157
Sassanids, 162, 181
Satrapy, *def.*, 48
Satelite nations, 649
Saturn, 425
Saudi Arabia, 681, 685, 698
Saul of Tarsus. *See* Paul.
Saul, Hebrew King, 46
Savanna, *def.*, 262
Savoy, 474
Saxons, 173, 174, 182
Scandinavia, 224, 229. *See also* names of individual countries.
Scapegoat, 611
Scholar-officials, in china, 74
School at Athens, Italian painting, 335
Science, 32-33, 100, 101, 125-126, 137, 142, 199, 341, 422-432, 438. *See also* medicine, mathematics, engineering.
Scientific method, *def.*, 423, 438
Scipio, Publius Cornelius, 114
Scotland, 115, 209, 247, 346, 398, 400, 402, 405
Scribe, *def.*, 27
Sculpture, 99, 137, 279, 280, 335
Second estate, French social class, 441
Second front, 631
Second World Nations, 672
Second World War, 603, 619, 623, 624-639, 640, 667, 681
Secondary sources, *def.*, 4
Secret History, 437
Secular, *def.*, 218
Security Council of the United Nations, 668, 648
Sedan, 476, 562
Seismograph, *def.*, 142
Seleucid Kingdom, of Syria, 116, 133
Seleucus, ruler of the kingdom of Syria, 97-98, 132

Seljuk Turks, 189, 227, 203-204
Seminary, *def.*, 350
Semitic people, 189, 190. *See also* Arabs.
Senegal, 519
Seoul, 536
Sepoy, *def.*, 542
Sepoy Mutiny, 531, 542, 550
Septimus Severus, Roman emperor, 156
Serbia, 557, 559, 560, 572
Serbs, 471
Serf, *def.*, 44; 214-216, 220, 235, 236, 319, 364, 467, 477
Sermon on the Mount, 153
Seth, Hebrew prophet, 49
Seven Years' War, 397, 406. *See also* French and Indian War.
Seward, William, 484
Seymour, Jane, 348
Shaba, 692
Shah, *def.*, 533
Shakespeare, William, 331, 339-340
Shang dynasty, 69-70; 77, 78, 209
Shankara, 139
Shantung Peninsula, 542
Shawawi, African nationalist rebels, 693
Shepard, Alan, 655
Sheriffs, medieval, *def.*, 245
Shi'ites, 197-198, 204, 290
Shinto, Japanese religion, 300, 614
Shoal, *def.*, 282
Shogun, *def.*, 303
Shona, African people, 273, 280
Shotoku, Japanese prince, 283, 300, 304
Siam, 540. *See also* Thailand.
Siberia, 308, 363, 364, 531, 533, 550, 597
Sicily, 113, 226, 475, 632
Siemens, Wilhelm, 272
Sierra Leone, 513
Sierra Mestra Mountains, 657
Sikh, religion, 287
Silkmaking, 78
Silk Road, 83, 144-145
Silt, *def.*, 22

Silver, and Spanish conquests, 379, 381, 382-383
Sinai, 150
Sinai Desert, and Egyptian-Israeli Peace Treaty, 684, 698
Sind, 54, 284, 304
Sindbad the Sailor, 200
Singapore, 541, 675
Sinkiang, 371
Sino-Japanese War, 531, 536-537, 543
Slavery, 27, 34, 42, 43, 44, 48, 58, 89, 90, 109, 116-117, 118, 125, 128, 132-133, 135, 151, 160, 171, 184, 266, 275, 280, 290, 315, 319, 375, 379-381, 386, 387-389, 390, 405, 407, 416, 485, 510, 511, 513, 514, 522, 525, 527, 528, 631, 651
Slovaks, 572
Smallpox, 430
Smith, Adam, 491, 499
Socialism, *def.*, 471; 476, 501-502, 506, 589, 592, 594, 605, 608, 617, 661, 662, 685
Society of Harmonious Fists, 543
Society of Jesus. *See* Jesuits.
Socrates, 85, 100
Socratic method, *def.*, 100
Soga, Japanese clan, 300
Solidarity Union, 663
Solomon, Hebrew king, 46
Solomon Islands, 632
Solon, 89
Song dynasty, 283, 291, 296-297, 304
Songhai, 268-270, 280, 386, 387
Sosso, African kingdom, 267
South Africa, Republic of, 516, 517, 518, 681, 697, 698
South Africa, Union of, 509, 519
South America, 307, 308, 379, 390. *See also* names of individual countries.
South Korea, 667-668
South Pole, 557
South Vietnam, 676, 677, 678
Southeast Asia, 14, 64, 133, 139-140, 142, 283, 371, 540, 628, 674, 675, 678
Southern Rhodesia, 691

Southern Yemen, 654
Soviet, *def.*, 590
Soviet Union. *See* Union of Soviet Socialist Republics.
Space age, 655
Spain, 113-116, 122, 157, 172, 174, 177, 182, 189, 195, 201-202, 203, 204, 226-227, 229, 351, 355, 357, 372, 378-381, 390, 411, 414-415, 417, 444, 447, 458, 460, 470, 526-527, 528, 603, 608, 617-619, 620, 648, 663, 693, 698
Spanish-American War, 531, 548, 587
Spanish Hapsburg Empire, 356
Spanish Sahara, 693
Sparta, 85, 90-91, 95, 102
Spartacus, 118
Spartans, origins of, 90
Speer, Albert, 646
Speke, John H., 513
Sphere of influence, *def.*, 506
Spinning jenny, invention of, 492
Spinning mule, invention of, 493
Spiritual, *def.*, 218
Sputnik I, 655
Sphinx, at Giza, 30-31
Spyglass, *def.*, 425
Squadristi, *def.*, 605
Squire, in chivalry, 210
Sri Lanka, 64, 133, 200. *See also* Ceylon.
Staël, Madame de, 454
Stakhanovites, 596
Stalin, Joseph, 594-598, 600, 617, 639, 647, 648, 649, 651
Stalingrad, battle at, 623, 632
St. Helena, island, 460
St. Lawrence River, 375, 383
St. Petersburg, 365, 372, 592
St. Peter's Basilica, 337
Stamp Act, 397, 407, 408
Stanley, Henry M., 509, 514, 522
Statira, wife of Alexander the Great, 97
Steam engine, 101, 492, 496
Steamship, first successful, 491, 496
Steel, 261, 272, 491, 494
Stelae, Mayan monuments, 315

Steppe, *def.*, 288
Stetl, *def.*, 611
Steward, role of, in English manorial society, 215
Stilicho, general, 171
Stock company, *def.*, 382, 390
Stoicism, 155
Stone Age, in China, 67
Strategic Arms Limitation Treaties, SALT I and SALT II, 654, 664
Stuart family, 398, 405
Stylus, *def.*, 41
Su Dungbo, Chinese poet, 297
Submarines, 566-568, 574
Subsistence farming, *def.*, 696
Sudan, *def.*, 262
Sudan, 203, 508-509, 514, 515, 690, 694. *See also* Anglo-Egyptian Sudan.
Sudeten, area of Czechoslovakia, 618, 620
Sudras, *def.*, 59
Svetonius, 128
Suez Canal, 509, 514, 515, 584, 629, 674, 683
Suez Canal Company, 515, 528
Suez, Isthmus of, 514
Sui dynasty, 145, 293, 304
Sukarno, Indonesian ruler, 675
Sulla, General Lucius Cornelius, 118
Sultan, *def.*, 203
Sumatra, 541, 550
Sumer, 37, 38, 40-42, 50
Sundiata, African king, 261, 267-268, 280
Sunni Ali, king of Gao, 261, 268
Sunnites, division of Islam, 197-198
Sun Yat-sen, 544, 550
Superpowers, 638-639, 640, 661
Supreme Soviet, 593
Surinam, 384, 656
Surplus, *def.*, 18
Susa, site of marriage of Alexander the Great, 97
Swahili, African culture, 261
Swahili, African language, 273-274, 694
Swamp Fox. *See* Francis Marion.

Sweden, 224, 343, 358, 365, 566
Swiss guards, 443
Switzerland, 345, 346, 358, 471
Syllogism, *def.*, 101
Synagogue, *def.*, 46
Syracuse, Greek colony in Sicily, 92
Syria, 47, 97-98, 116, 118, 133, 150, 151, 177, 181, 197, 573, 584, 638, 681, 682, 683

T

Tacitus, 127-128
Tahiti, 546
Taika reforms, 300-302
Taiping Rebellion, 532, 542
Taira, Japanese family, 303
Taiwan, 667
Tai Zong, Chinese emperor, 293
Taj Mahal, 367
Tale of Genji, 301
Tamerlane, Mongol leader, 286, 290
Tamil, Dravidian language, 133
Tamil kingdoms, 133, 134, 135
Tamil people, 83
Tanganyika, 524, 528
Tanganyika, Lake, 513
Tang dynasty, 238, 283, 288, 293-296, 304
Tanka, *def.*, 301
Tannenberg, battle at, 245
Tanzania, 694, 695
Taoism, 67, 70
Tao, *def.*, 73
    development of, 73-74, 78
    in Tang dynasty, 295
Tarentum, 113
Tariff, *def.*, 504
Tarim Desert, 143
Tariq, 195
Tasaday, discovery of, 81
Tasmania, 545
Tatars, 355, 360-362, 372
Taxes, 25, 116, 158, 297, 298, 300-302, 359, 360, 361, 362, 365, 367, 369, 397, 398, 399, 401, 403, 406-408, 415, 420, 441, 442, 444, 447, 504, 544, 596
Tea Act, 397, 420
Technology, *def.*, 4
Tehran, 686
Telegraph, invention of, 491, 497
Telephone, invention of, 491, 497
Tells, *def.*, 36
Telugu, Dravidian language, 133
Temujin, 288-289. *See also* Genghis Khan.
Tenchi, Japanese emperor, 300, 304
Tenochtitlan, Aztec city, 316-317, 318, 324, 378
Teotihuacan, Aztec city, 318
Texas, 482
Texcoco, Lake, 316
Textile industry, 492-494
Thailand, 540
Thatcher, Margaret, 662
Theater, 99, 278, 339-340
Theban princes, 28
Thebes, Egypt, 28, 29, 31, 32
Thebes, Greece, 95, 96
Theocracy, *def.*, 39, 266
Theodora, Roman empress, 177, 437
Theodosius the Great, Roman emperor, 161, 162, 171
Thermopylae, 93
Theses, Martin Luther's statements, 342
Thessaly, 86
Third estate, French social class, 441, 442. *See also* National Assembly.
Third Reich, 613, 615
Third World Nations, 672
Thirty Years' War, 355, 358, 372, 398
Thomas à Kempis, 254
Thrace, 124, 171, 172
Thracian, ancestry of Spartacus, 118
Thousand and One Arabian Nights, 200
Thucydides, 102
Thutmose II, 28
Thutmose III, 29

Tiberius, Roman emperor, 124
Tiber River, 106
Tibet, 67, 371
Tientsin, 544
Tigris River, 37-38
Tigris-Euphrates Valley, 37-38
Tikal, Mayan ceremonial center, 313, 316, 324
Timbuktu, 202, 261, 268, 269
Titian, Italian painter, 335
Titicaca, Lake, 320
Tito, 627, 631, 649
Toga, *def.*, 169
Togo, Heihachiro, Admiral, 530
Togoland, 524, 528
Tojo, Hideki, prime minister of Japan, 627
Tokyo, 637
Toleration Act, 404
Toltecs, 307, 316, 324
Tonkin, 540, 550
Torah, 45, 46
Torricelli, Evangelista, 523, 428
Total war, 581, 600, 636-638
Totalitarianism, *def.*, 594, 600, 606-607, 612-613, 620, 637
Totem, *def.*, 276
Tours, 169, 181, 189
Toussaint L'Ouverture, 416
Towns, 230, 231-236, 239. See *also* cities.
Trade:
  ancient, 43-44, 45, 54, 58, 83, 87, 107;
  Roman, 108, 116, 121, 157, 176
  early Indian, 133, 134-135, 136, 138, 139, 146;
  during Han dynasty, 144-145, 146;
  in Middle Ages, 176, 180, 184, 190, 197, 198, 200, 201, 203, 224-226, 228, 229, 230-231, 239, 240, 247-248, 250;
  and Africa, 261, 262, 265-267, 268, 273, 280, 376
  and Asia, 284, 288, 290, 294, 296-297, 304, 359, 361, 366, 370;
  and Hopewell people, 310;
  and exploration, 377, 381, 384, 385, 386, 387-389, 390, 407-408, 415;
  and nationalism, 470, 475, 481;
  and the Industrial Revolution, 492, 493, 503, 504, 506
  and imperialism, 535, 538, 541-542, 543, 546, 583, 584, 627;
  after Second World War, 654, 660, 661, 663, 664, 667, 674, 695-696
Trade unions. See Labor unions.
Trafalgar, Cape, battle at, 441, 455
Trajan, Roman emperor, 124
Transjordan, 573
Transportation, 496
Trans-Siberian Railroad, 496, 531, 533, 550
Transvaal, 511, 512, 516, 528
Treaty of Portsmouth, 538, 549
Treaty of Versailles, 557, 578, 604, 609, 610, 613, 614, 615, 619, 620, 638
Treaty of Westphalia, 358, 372
Tribute, *def.*, 42, 359
Triple Alliance, 558, 560
Triple Entente, 558
Tripoli, 512, 526, 528
Triumvirate, *def.*, 118;
  first Roman, 105;
  second Roman, 120
Trotsky, Leon, 590, 592, 594, 597
Truman, Harry S., 633, 648, 668
Tsushima Island, battle of, 531
Tudor, house of, 247, 398
Tula, Toltec city, 316
Tungus language, 288
Tunic, *def.*, 169
Tunisia, 195, 203, 519, 525, 690
Turkestan, 143, 288, 533
Turkestan, battle of, 197
Turkey, 477, 565-566, 574, 578, 583, 584, 648, 681. See *also* Ottoman Empire.
Turkic empire, 283, 288
Turkish language, 288
Turks, 181, 240, 685
Tuscany, and Italian language, 334
Tutankhamen, pharaoh of Egypt, 32

U

Uganda, 273, 514, 515, 528, 695
Uitlanders, *def.*, 516
Uji, early Japanese family groups, 299-300
Ulama, 199
Ulyanov, Vladimir Ilyich, 588. See *also* Lenin, V.I.
Umma, Sumerian city, 37
Umayyad, 189, 197-198, 201-202, 204. See *also* Sunnites.
Unemployment, 577
Union of Arab Emirates, 681
Union of South Africa. See South Africa, Union of.
Union of Soviet Socialist Republics:
  establishment of, 577, 592, 593, 594, 598-600, 617, 618 619, 623;
  and Second World War, 623, 625-627, 630, 634, 636, 640;
  after Second World War, 638-639, 647, 648-654, 655, 659, 660, 667-670, 673, 678, 683, 685-686, 687, 689, 693, 698. See *also* Russia.
Unions. See Labor unions.
United Nations, 631, 639, 647, 648, 653, 668, 671, 672, 682, 683, 689, 692, 697, 698
United States:
  early cultures in, 15, 308, 309-310;
  and African slaves, 389;
  independence, 397, 411-412
  growth, 455, 467, 470, 481-485, 488
  American Civil War, 485-486, 488
  industrialization in, 486-487, 488, 490, 494, 496, 498
  imperialism in Asia and the Pacific, 531, 546, 550;

and First World War, 557, 562, 566-569, 571, 573, 574, 577, 580
after First World War, 580, 587, 592, 602-603, 607-608, 620;
and Second World War, 623, 625, 628, 629, 630-631, 632, 633, 637;
after Second World War, 637, 638-639, 640, 648, 655, 657-659, 660, 664;
and Korean War, 667-668;
relations with China, 669;
and Vietnam War, 677, 678;
and Middle East, 682, 683, 685, 686, 687, 689
Ur, Sumerian city, 37
Ural Altaic people, 680
Ural Mountains, 185, 532
Urban, *def.*, 491
Urban II, pope, 227
Urban VI, pope, 253
Urdu language, 287
Uruguay, 481
Uruk, Sumerian city, 37

V

Vaccination, for smallpox, 430
Vacuumtube, invention of, 497
Vaishyas, *def.*, 58-59
Valens, Roman emperor, 171
Valentinian III, Roman emperor, 172
Valmy, battle at, 446
Vandalism, *def.*, 172
Vandals, 169, 172, 174, 176
Van Eyck, Jan, painter, 339
Van Leeuwenhoek, Anton, 423, 431-432
Vassals, *def.*, 69, 209, 211-212, 220
Vatican City, creation of, 607
Vedas, 53, 57-58, 60-62, 63, 64
Vedic Age, 53, 57-58, 60-64
Veld, *def.*, 262
Venezuela, 480, 656
Venice, 229, 231
Vera Cruz, 378

Verdun, 557, 562, 564
Verdun, Treaty of, 184
Vergil, 127
Verrazano, Giovanni da, 383
Versailles, palace of, 442, 443
Versailles, town of, 570, 571
Versailles, Treaty of, 571-573
Vesalius, Andreas, 429
Vesta, Roman household god, 111
Viceroy, 414
Victor Emmanuel II, king of Sardinia and Italy, 475
Victoria, queen of England, 478, 515
Victoria Falls, 265
Victoria, Lake, 513, 514
Vietnam, 143, 662, 667, 675, 676-678
Vikings, 185, 186, 207, 208, 224, 359
Villages, 9, 17, 18, 156, 276-278, 286-287, 307, 308-309
Vindhya Mountains, 54
Vinland, 224
Visigoths, 117, 169, 171, 174, 176, 181
Vizier, *def.*, 25
Vladivostok, 532, 550, 564
Volga River, 171, 390
Voltaire, 435-436, 438
Vostok, spaceship, 655

W

Watt, James, 492
Wales, 405
Walesa, Lech, 663
Wang, *def.*, 75
Wang Anshi, Chinese reformer, 283, 297
Wang Mang, Chinese emperor, 144
War of the Roses, 239, 247, 254
Warsaw, 636
Warsaw, Grand Duchy of, 458
Warsaw Pact, 649, 664
Washington, George, 408-409, 411
Waterloo, battle at, 441, 460

Water Screw, 101
Wealth of Nations, 491, 499
Weapons, 18, 45, 47, 105, 562 563, 566-568, 574, 619, 623, 633-636, 640, 652
Weaving, 323
Weimar Republic, 609-610, 612, 620
Wellington, New Zealand, 545
Welsh, descendants of Britons, 173
Wessex, 175
West Bank, in Middle East, 684, 698
Western Sudanic states, 386, 390
West Germany, 652, 661, 662-663, 664
West Indies, 378, 379, 384, 389, 414
West Pakistan. *See* Pakistan.
Westphalia, 358
White Russians, 590, 591, 600
Whitney, Eli, 493
William I, king of Prussia, 475
William II, German Kaiser, 518, 524, 560, 569, 574
William III, king of England, 404-405, 420
William of Prussia, German emperor, 476
William, Norman conqueror of England, 209, 226, 245
Williamsburg, 413
Wilson, Woodrow, 562, 568, 570-574, 576
Winter War, 623
Wollstonecroft, Mary, 436, 438
Women:
in ancient civilizations, 12, 17, 27, 28, 34, 43, 59-60, 62, 75, 76-77, 78;
in classical age, 89, 90, 91, 107, 110, 115, 124-125, 169;
in Middle Ages, 193, 216, 220, 235, 252;
in Africa, 276, 277;
in Asia, 285, 287, 289, 295, 302;
in Incan society, 323;
in modern society, 333, 405, 436, 444, 449, 454, 455, 491,

748

494, 499, 500, 502, 542, 577, 582, 592, 662, 671, 673, 686
Woodcarving, 309
Woodland Indians, 309, 324
World Health Organization, 430
Worms, Germany, 342
Writing:
  in ancient Egypt, 30, 31;
  in China, 40, 69;
  in Sumer, 40-41, 50;
  Harappan, 56;
  sanskrit, 62;
  and Indo-Aryans, 64;
  Chinese, 74, 75, 78, 81;
  calligraphy defined, 183;
  Caroline miniscule, 184;
  Mayan, 306, 312, 315, 324;
  and Russians, 359
Writs of Assistance, 407
Wu Di, emperor in Han dynasty, 141, 142-143
Wu, empress of China, 295
Wycliffe, John, 239, 254

X

Xavier, Francis, 351
Xerxes, 93
Xia dynasty, 67, 69

Y

Yalta Conference, 639, 648, 664
Yamato, Japanese clan, 300
Yang Qian, founder of Sui dynasty, 293
Yasa, legal code of Genghis Khan, 290
Yangtze River. *See* Chang Jiang River.
Yathrib, 191. *See also* Medina.
Yen Zai Commune, archaeological discoveries in, 66
Yin and Yang, in Taoism, 73-74, 142
Yoga, *def.*, 62
Yom Kippur War, 681, 683
York, House of, 247
Yorktown, battle at, 411
Young China movement, 545
Young Plan, 577, 580
Yu, founder of Xia dynasty, 69
Yuan dynasty, 283, 290, 297-298, 303, 304
Yucatan Peninsula, 312, 324
Yuezhi people, 143
Yugoslavia, 572, 627, 631, 633, 648, 649
Yurt, *def.*, 288

Z

Zaire, 692, 694, 695, 698
Zambezi River, 265, 513
Zambia, 691, 692
Zanj, land of, 387
Zanzibar, 514, 524
Zanzibar, Sultan of, 513, 514
Zealots, in Judea, 151
Zeus, Greek god, 98
Zhang Heng, 142
Zhangdu, 289
Zhang Qian, 143
Zhongguo, 74-76
Zhou dynasty, 67, 70, 77, 78
Zhoukoudian, 69
Zi Ki, Chinese emperor, 296
Zi Zhang, 72
Ziggurat, *def.*, 39
Zi Xi, Empress Dowager of China, 542-543, 544
Zimbabwe, 273, 280, 692
Zodiac, *def.*, 39
Zimmerman note, 568, 574
Zionism, *def.*, 583
Zoroaster, 48-49, 50
Zoroastrianism, 295, 304
Zulu tribes, 511, 528
Zulu Wars, 511

Acknowledgments

Quoted Material

72 William Theodore de Bary, editor, *Sources of Chinese Tradition*. (New York: Columbia University Press, 1960) p. 26; Burton Watson, *Early Chinese Literature*. (New York: Columbia University Press, 1962) p. 176. **73** *Sources of Chinese Tradition*, p. 52. **110** Quoted in Julia O'Faolain and Lauro Martines, editors, *Not in God's Image: Women in History from the Greeks to the Victorians*. (New York: Harper Torchbooks, 1973) pp. 35, 57-58. **160** Ernest Barker, Translation and Introduction, *From Alexander to Constantine: Passages and Documents Illustrating the History of Political and Social Ideas 336 B.C.-A.D. 337*. (London: Oxford University Press, 1956) pp. 477-479. **282-283** Edwin O. Reischauer, *Ennin's Diary: The Record of a Pilgrimage to China in Search of the Law*. (New York: The Ronald Press Co., 1955) p. 6 **301** Column 1, Edwin O. Reischauer and Albert M. Craig, *Japan Tradition and Transformation*. (New York: Houghton Mifflin Co., 1978) p. 27; Column 2, Donald Keene, *Anthology of Japanese Literature*. (New York: Grove Press, 1955) pp. 106-107. **396** Ramsey Muir,

A Short History of the British Commonwealth, 7th ed., Vol. I, *The Islands and the First Empire (to 1763)*. (London: Geo. Philip & Son, Ltd., 1961) p. 456

Illustrations

Cover Photo Editorial Photocolor Archives
ii-iii Editorial Photocolor Archives **v** EPA/Scala **vi** Nigel Cameron/Photo Researchers **vii** Culver Pictures **viii** George Holton/Photo Researchers **ix** National Maritime Museum **x** Yale University Art Gallery **xi** New York Public Library/Picture Collection **xii** The Bettmann Archive, Inc. **xiii** NASA **1** Frank Siteman/Stock, Boston **2** Left, Ken Heyman; right, American Museum of Natural History **3** Marc and Evelyne Bernheim/Woodfin Camp **4** Tass from Sovfoto **5** Victor Englebert **6** George Holton/ Photo Researchers **8** John Launois/Black Star **9** American Museum of Natural History **12** Brian Seed/Black Star **15** Borromeo/EPA **16** Peter Arnold, Inc. **17** The Metropolitan Museum of Art, Rogers Fund, 1947 **20** Borromeo/EPA **21** Metropolitan Museum of Art, Museum Excavations, 1913-1914, Rogers Fund, 1928 **23** George Holton/Photo Researchers **24** Borromeo/Scala/EPA **25** Editorial Photocolor Archives **26** Mary M. Thatcher/Photo Researchers **27** Editorial Photocolor Archives **29** Metropolitan Museum of Art **30** George Holton/Photo Researchers **31** George Holton/Photo Researchers **32** Metropolitan Museum of Art **33** The Bettman Archive, Inc. **36** Editorial Photocolor Archives **37** Editorial Photocolor Archives **39** Georg Gerster/Photo Researchers **40** The Bettmann Archive, Inc. **42** The Bettmann Archive, Inc. **44** EPA/Scala **45** EPA/Alinari **46** Editorial Photocolor Archives **49** EPA/Scala **52** Paolo Koch/Photo Researchers **53** Frances Mortimer/Photo Researchers **55** Brian Blake/Photo Researchers **56** Frances Mortimer/Photo Researchers **58** Eunice Harris/ Photo Researchers **60** New York Public Library/Picture Collection **61** Doranne Jacobson **62** Bernard Wolff/Photo Researchers **63** Doranne Jacobson **66** Audrey Topping/Photo Researchers **67** Smithsonian Institute, Freer Gallery **69** New York Public Library/ Picture Collection **70** Sotheby Park-Bernet/EPA **71** Georg Gerster/Photo Researchers **73** From *Foundations of Chinese Art*, by William Willetts, McGraw-Hill, Inc. **74** Virginia Copeland **76** Seth Joel/Metropolitan Museum of Art and People's Republic of China **82** EPA/Scala **84** Turner/Image Bank **85** David Follansbee/Photo Researchers **86** Farrell Grehan/Photo Researchers **87** Nigel Cameron/Photo Researchers **88** Luis Villota/The Image Bank **90** EPA/Alinari Scala **91** The Bettmann Archive, Inc. **93** The Bettmann Archive, Inc. **94** Brooklyn Museum, Gift of R.B. Woodward **95** EPA/Scala **97** The Bettmann Archive, Inc. **99** EPA/Scala **100** EPA/Scala **104** Robert Rattner **105** EPA/Alinari-Scala **107** EPA/Scala **108** EPA/Scala **110** John Verde/Photo Researchers **112** Robert Rattner **114** The Bettmann Archive, Inc. **115** EPA/Scala **117** Editorial Photocolor Archives **119** Upper, The Bettmann Archive, Inc.,; lower, EPA/Scala **120** The Bettmann Archive, Inc. **122** EPA/Scala **123** Peter Silver/Image Bank **124** EPA/ Alinari Scala **126** EPA/Scala **130** Doranne Jacobson **131** Brooklyn Museum **132** Doranne Jacobson **135** Doranne Jacobson **137** EPA/SEF **138** Matthias Oppersdorf/Photo Researchers **140** Doranne Jacobson **141** From *Foundations of Chinese Art*, by William Willetts, McGraw-Hill, Inc. **144** The St. Louis Art Museum, gift of the heirs of Berenice Ballard **145** George Holton/Photo Researchers **148** EPA/Scala **149** Margot Granitsas/Photo Researchers **150** Robert Rattner **151** Bullaty Lomeo/Image Bank **152** EPA/Scala **153** Dan Porges/Peter Arnold **154** Buchenholz/Photo Researchers **157** EPA/Alinari-Scala **160** EPA/Alinari-Scala **161** Jim Hubbard/Photo Researchers **166** Scala **168** EPA/Scala **169** Culver Pictures **170** New York Public Library/Picture Collection **171** New York Public Library/Picture Collection **172** The Bettmann Archive, Inc. **173** The Bettmann Archive, Inc. **175** EPA/Scala **176** Culver Pictures **178** EPA/SEF **181** The Bettmann Archive, Inc. **183** Upper, The Bettmann Archive, Inc.; lower, EPA/Scala **184** The Bettmann Archive, Inc. **188** Abu Hander/Woodfin Camp **189** The Bettmann Archive, Inc. **190** The Bettmann Archive, Inc. **192** Gerhardt Liebmann/Photo Researchers **193** Tony Howarth/Woodfin Camp **194** The Bettmann Archive, Inc. **195** The Bettmann Archive, Inc. **198** New York Public Library/Picture Collection **199** The Bettmann Archive, Inc. **200** New York Public Library/Picture Collection **201** A. Kalnik/Photo Researchers **202** Luis Villota/Image Bank **203** EPA/SEF **206** The Bettmann Archive, Inc. **207** The Metropolitan Museum of Art, the Cloisters Collection, Munsey Fund, 1932 **208** Editorial Photocolor Archives **211** EPA/SEF **212** The Bettmann Archive, Inc. **213** EPA/Scala **214** The Bettmann Archive, Inc. **215** EPA/Scala **216** EPA/Scala **217** Editorial Photocolor Archives **218** The Bettmann Archive, Inc. **219**

Editorial Photocolor Archives **222** EPA/Scala **223** Culver Pictures **224** EPA/SEF **225** Adam Woolfitt/Woodfin Camp **226** Porterfield-Chickering/Photo Researchers **227** The Bettmann Archive, Inc. **232** The Bettmann Archive, Inc. **233** The Bettmann Archive, Inc. **234** The Bettmann Archive, Inc. **235** EPA/Scala **238** EPA/Scala **239** Culver Pictures **241** EPA/Scala **242** New York Public Library/Picture Collection **243** New York Public Library/Picture Collection **244** Culver Pictures **245** The Bettmann Archive, Inc. **246** Culver Pictures **247** Culver Pictures **248** EPA/Scala **249** Culver Pictures **250** Culver Pictures **251** Culver Pictures **252** New York Public Library/Picture Collection **258** Georg Gerster/Photo Researchers **260** New York Public Library/Picture Collection **261** The Metropolitan Museum of Art, the Michael G. Rockefeller Memorial Collection of Primitive Art, Gift of Nelson A. Rockefeller, 1964 **264** Victor Englebert/Photo Researchers **265** Don Carl Steffen/Photo Researchers **268** Georg Gerster/Photo Researchers **272** New York Public Library/Picture Collection **274** Don Carl Steffen/Photo Researchers **275** Trustees of the British Museum **277** Thomas D.W. Friedmann/Photo Researchers **278** Pamela Johnson Meyer/Photo Researchers **279** George Holton/Photo Researchers **282** Paolo Koch/Photo Researchers **283** The Bettmann Archive, Inc. **285** Fritz Henle/Photo Researchers **286** Culver Pictures **289** George Holton/Photo Researchers **291** George Holton/Photo Researchers **293** Metropolitan Museum of Art, Rogers Fund, 1923 **296** Paolo Koch/Photo Researchers **298** Metropolitan Museum of Art, Fletcher Fund, 1947 **299** Paolo Koch/Photo Researchers **300** Lawrence L. Smith/Photo Researchers **301** Sekai Bunka **302** Culver Pictures **306** George Holton/Photo Researchers **307** The Bettmann Archive, Inc. **309** Georg Gerster/Photo Researchers **310** Georg Gerster/Photo Researchers **312** Porterfield-Chickering/Photo Researchers **314** Georg Gerster/Photo Researchers **317** New York Public Library/Picture Collection **318** Hamilton Wright/Photo Researchers **321** Christa Armstrong/Photo Researchers **323** Carl Frank/Photo Researchers **328** EPA/Scala **330** EPA/Scala **331** The Bettmann Archive, Inc. **332** The Bettmann Archive, Inc. **334** EPA/Scala **335** New York Public Library/Picture Collection **336** EPA/Scala **337** Georg Gerster/Photo Researchers **338** The Bettmann Archive, Inc. **339** EPA/Scala **340** New York Public Library/Picture Collection **341** The Bettmann Archive, Inc. **342** EPA/Scala **345** The Bettmann Archive, Inc. **347** EPA/Scala **348** Top, New York Public Library/Picture Collection; bottom, The Bettmann Archive, Inc. **349** New York Public Library/Picture Collection **350** The Bettmann Archive, Inc. **351** The Bettmann Archive, Inc. **354** Georg Gerster/Photo Researchers **355** The Bettmann Archive, Inc. **357** National Maritime Museum **359** New York Public Library/ Picture Collection **360** Both, Tass/Sovfoto **361** The Bettmann Archive, Inc. **362** Tass/ Sovfoto **363** Both, Sovfoto **366** Sovfoto **367** New York Public Library/Picture Collection **368** EPA/Scala **369** The Bettmann Archive, Inc. **370** Metropolitan Museum of Art, Gift of Robert E. Tod, 1937 **371** Metropolitan Museum of Art, Bequest of John D. Rockefeller, Jr., 1960 **374** New York Public Library/Picture Collection **375** The Bettmann Archive, Inc. **377** New York Public Library/Picture Collection **379** Culver Pictures **380** Museo Nacional de Historica, Mexico **382** The Bettmann Archive, Inc. **383** Culver Pictures **388** Culver Pictures **394** The Bettmann Archive, Inc. **396** Delaware Art Museum **397** The Bettmann Archive, Inc. **398** The Bettmann Archive, Inc. **399** Culver Pictures **401** Culver Pictures **402** British Department of the Environment **403** The Bettmann Archive, Inc. **404** The Bettmann Archive, Inc. **406** Culver Pictures **407** The Bettmann Archive, Inc. **409-410** The Bettmann Archive, Inc. **411** The Bettmann Archive, Inc. **411** Yale University Art Gallery **412** Photo European/FPG **413** Bernardo Magalhaes **414** Culver Pictures **415** Sotheby Parke-Bernet/EPA **416** The Bettmann Archive, Inc. **417** The Bettmann Archive, Inc. **418** Culver Pictures **419** The Bettmann Archive, Inc. **422** The Bettmann Archive, Inc. **423** The Bettmann Archive, Inc. **424** The Bettmann Archive, Inc. **425** The Bettmann Archive, Inc. **426** Both, The Bettmann Archive, Inc. **427** Culver Pictures **428** The Bettmann Archive, Inc. **429** The Bettmann Archive, Inc. **430** Culver Pictures **431** Top, The Bettmann Archive, Inc.; bottom, New York Public Library/Picture Collection **432** The Bettmann Archive, Inc. **434** The Bettmann Archive, Inc. **435** The Bettmann Archive, Inc. **437** EPA/Scala **438** New York Public Library/Picture Collection **440** The Bettmann Archive, Inc. **441** The Bettmann Archive, Inc. **442** Nicholas Foster/ Image Bank **443** French Cultural Services **445** The Bettmann Archive, Inc. **446** The Bettmann Archive, Inc. **447** French Cultural Services **448** Left, The Bettmann Archive, Inc.; right, French Cultural Services **449** New York Public Library/Picture Collection **450** The Bettmann Archive, Inc. **451** The Bettmann Archive, Inc. **453** French Cultural Services **454** The Bettmann

Archive, Inc. **456** The Bettmann Archive, Inc. **457** Culver Pictures **459** The Bettmann Archive, Inc. **464** New York Public Library/ Picture Collection **466** The Bettmann Archive, Inc. **467** The Bettmann Archive, Inc. **468** New York Public Library/Picture Collection **470** Both, The Bettmann Archive, Inc. **472** Culver Pictures **473** The Bettmann Archive, Inc. **474** EPA/SEF **475** New York Public Library/ Picture Collection **477** The Bettmann Archive, Inc. **478** New York Public Library/ Picture Collection **481** Culver Pictures **482** Top, Culver Pictures; bottom, The Bettmann Archive, Inc. **483** Washington University, St. Louis **484** The Bettmann Archive, Inc. **485** The Bettmann Archive, Inc. **486** The Bettmann Archive, Inc. **487** The Bettmann Archive, Inc. **490** The Bettmann Archive, Inc. **491** The Bettmann Archive, Inc. **493** Both, The Bettmann Archive, Inc. **494** BBC Hulton Picture Library **495** BBC Hulton Picture Library **496** The Bettmann Archive, Inc. **497** Thomas Cook, Inc. **498** United States Department of the Interior, National Park Service, Edison National Historic Site **499** The Bettmann Archive, Inc. **500** BBC Hulton Picture Library **501** The Bettmann Archive, Inc. **503** BBC Hulton Picture Library **505** The Bettmann Archive, Inc. **508** The Bettmann Archive, Inc. **509** The Bettmann Archive, Inc. **510** Culver Pictures **511** Brown Brothers **512** The Bettmann Archive, Inc. **513** The Bettmann Archive, Inc. **515** The Bettmann Archive, Inc. **516** The Bettmann Archive, Inc. **518** South African Consulate **520** Photoworld/FPG **521** Culver Pictures **522** The Bettmann Archive, Inc. **526** The Bettmann Archive, Inc. **527** New York Public Library/Picture Collection **530** Sekai Bunka **531** Sovfoto **533** Sovfoto **534** Tass/Sovfoto **536** The Bettmann Archive, Inc. **537** The Bettmann Archive, Inc. **539** BBC Hulton Picture Library **540** Culver Pictures **541** BBC Hulton Picture Library **542** Smithsonian Institute, Freer Gallery of Art **543** The Bettmann Archive, Inc. **545** Australian News and Information Bureau **546** The Bettmann Archive, Inc. **548** EPA/Scala **549** The Bettmann Archive, Inc. **554** United States Department of Energy **556** The Bettmann Archive, Inc. **557** The Bettmann Archive, Inc. **561** The Bettmann Archive, Inc. **562** The Bettmann Archive, Inc. **563** Both, The Bettmann Archive, Inc. **564** Wide World Photos **567** The Bettmann Archive, Inc. **568** Wide World Photos **569** The Bettmann Archive, Inc. **570** The Bettmann Archive, Inc. **571** The Bettmann Archive, Inc. **572** The Bettmann Archive, Inc. **573** The Bettmann Archive, Inc. **576** The Bettmann Archive, Inc. **577** Sovfoto **578** Ford Archives/Henry Ford Museum, Dearborn, Michigan **579** The Bettmann Archive, Inc. **581** The Bettmann Archive, Inc. **582** The Bettmann Archive, Inc. **584** The Bettmann Archive, Inc. **585** The Bettmann Archive, Inc. **587** Collection, Museum of Modern Art, Gift of Abby Aldrich Rockefeller **588** The Bettmann Archive, Inc. **589** Sovfoto **591** New York Public Library/Picture Collection **593** The Bettmann Archive, Inc. **594** Culver Pictures **595** Brown Brothers **596** Tass from Sovfoto **597** Sovfoto **598** The Bettmann Archive, Inc. **599** Rene Burri/Magnum **602** The Bettmann Archive, Inc. **603** The Bettmann Archive, Inc. **604** Wide World Photos **605** Wide World Photos **606** The Bettmann Archive, Inc. **607** Wide World Photos **608** The Bettmann Archive, Inc. **609** The Bettmann Archive, Inc. **610** The Bettmann Archive, Inc. **611** The Bettmann Archive, Inc. **613** The Bettmann Archive, Inc. **614** Sekai Bunka **616** Wide World Photos **617** Wide World Photos **618** Wide World Photos **622** Department of the Army, Office of the Chief of Military History **623** The Bettmann Archive, Inc. **624** The Bettmann Archive, Inc. **625** The Bettmann Archive, Inc. **626** The Bettmann Archive, Inc. **628** Wide World Photos **629** Wide World Photos **630** BBC Hulton Picture Library **631** The Bettmann Archive, Inc. **632** The Bettmann Archive, Inc. **636** The Bettmann Archive, Inc. **637** The Bettmann Archive, Inc. **639** The Bettmann Archive, Inc. **644** NASA **646** United Nations **647** Elliott Erwitt/ Magnum **649** The Bettmann Archive, Inc. **651** United Press International **652** Roger Malloch/ Magnum **653** C. Capa/Magnum **654** SIPA Press/Black Star **655** NASA **656** Lisa Limer **657** The Bettmann Archive, Inc. **658** Fred Ward/Black Star **659** Olivier Rebbot/Black Star **660** Geoffrey Hiller **662** Bruno Barbey/Magnum **663** Peter Marlow/ Magnum **666** Bruno J. Jehnder **667** Scheler, Stern/Black Star **668** Wide World Photos **669** Audrey Topping/Photo Researchers **670** C. W. Owen/Black Star **671** Wide World Photos **672** United Nations **673** United Nations **675** Wide World Photos **676** Wide World Photos **677** Magnum **678** Wide World Photos **680** C. W. Owen/ Black Star **681** Exxon **682** Israel Office of Information **684** Jean Gaumy/Magnum **685** Rene Burri/Magnum **686** Marc Riboud/Magnum **687** Raymond Depardon/ Magnum **688** Consultant General of Israel **690** Nicholas Tikomiroff/Magnum **691** United Nations **692** Left, Ian Berry/Magnum; right, United Press International **694** Dourdin/ Photo Researchers **695** United Nations **696** United Nations **697** Jane Latta/ Photo Researchers **702** NASA